God and the Between

Illuminations: Theory and Religion

Series editors: Catherine Pickstock, John Milbank, and Graham Ward

Religion has a growing visibility in the world at large. Throughout the humanities there is a mounting realization that religion and culture lie so closely together that religion is an unavoidable and fundamental human reality. Consequently, the examination of religion and theology now stands at the center of any questioning of our western identity, including the question of whether there is such a thing as "truth."

ILLUMINATIONS aims both to reflect the diverse elements of these developments and, from them, to produce creative new syntheses. It is unique in exploring the new interaction between theology, philosophy, religious studies, political theory, and cultural studies. Despite the theoretical convergence of certain trends they often in practice do not come together. The aim of ILLUMINATIONS is to make this happen, and advance contemporary theoretical discussion.

Published:
Sacrifice and Community: Jewish Offering and Christian Eucharist
Matthew Levering

The Other Calling: Theology, Intellectual Vocation and Truth
Andrew Shanks

The State of the University: Academic Knowledges and the Knowledge of God
Stanley Hauerwas

Theology and Work: Theological Critiques of Capitalism
John Hughes

God and the Between
William Desmond

Forthcoming:
After Enlightenment: Hamann as Post-Secular Visionary
John Betz

God and the Between

William Desmond

Blackwell
Publishing

BLACKWELL PUBLISHING
350 Main Street, Malden, MA 02148–5020, USA
9600 Garsington Road, Oxford OX4 2DQ, UK
550 Swanston Street, Carlton, Victoria 3053, Australia

First published 2008 by Blackwell Publishing Ltd

1 2008

Library of Congress Cataloging-in-Publication Data
Desmond, William, 1951–
  God and the between / by William Desmond.
    p. cm.—(Illuminations: theory and religion)
  Includes bibliographical references and index.
  ISBN 978-1-4051-6232-6 (hardcover : alk. paper)
  ISBN 978-1-4051-6233-3 (pbk.: alk. paper) 1. God. I. Title.

BL473.D47 2007
211—dc22

                                        2007013122

A catalogue record for this title is available from the British Library.

Set in 9.5/11 pt Sabon
by Newgen Imaging Systems (P) Ltd, Chennai, India
Printed and bound in Singapore
by C.O.S. Printers Pte Ltd

The publisher's policy is to use permanent paper from mills that operate a sustainable forestry policy, and which has been manufactured from pulp processed using acid-free and elementary chlorine-free practices. Furthermore, the publisher ensures that the text paper and cover board used have met acceptable environmental accreditation standards.

For further information on
Blackwell Publishing, visit our website at
www.blackwellpublishing.com

Sacrificem tibi famulatum cogitationis et linguae meae, et da quod offeram tibi

St Augustine, *Confessions*, XI, 2

For Maria, William óg, Hugh, and Oisín

Contents

Preface

God and the Between has been long in the making, and brings a trilogy of works to a completion of sorts. It can be read on its own terms, but it also belongs with its companion volumes *Being and the Between* and *Ethics and the Between*. *God and the Between* is a venture in the philosophy of God, offering also something of a philosophical theology, but I have long been assailed by worries about the resources one would need to undertake any such a venture. To say nothing of what almost impossibilities it would ask in terms of religious porosity to the divine – purity of heart, for instance – it would require of the philosopher, at a minimum, something of finesse for both metaphysical and ethical perplexities. In the previous two works, I have tried to face up to these perplexities, as best as I could. Against some currently fashionable views, I see metaphysics as a living option, and have tried to articulate a viable metaphysics in *Being and the Between*. I also hold to the inseparability of ethics and metaphysics, and something of the result is to be found in *Ethics and the Between*. As the metaxological metaphysics I have developed opens us to transcendence as other, so a metaxological ethics culminates in the community of agapeic service, on the border between the ethical and the religious. Both ask for openness to the question of the divine. *Being and the Between* asks: What does it mean to be? *Ethics and the Between* asks: What does it mean to be good? *God and the Between* asks: What does it mean to be divine or God? As the metaphysics of the first work points further to the ethical philosophy of the second, *God and the Between* represents the philosophy of God continuous with both the metaphysics of the first work and ethics of the second.

Some of my recent work helps fill out a number of considerations that I cannot fully treat of here. Specifically, *Hegel's God – A Counterfeit Double?* tries to take the fuller measure of Hegel's dialectical-speculative reconfiguration of God, beyond what I could say in the present work about the dialectical way in more general terms. *Is there a Sabbath for Thought? – Between Religion and Philosophy* offers more extended reflections on notions like postulatory finitism, religion as the intimate universal, the poverty of philosophy, the counterfeit doubles of God, reverence, and so on. There is also an engagement with an array of thinkers such as Kant, Hegel again, Nietzsche, Pascal, Shestov, Solov'ëv, to name but some. I have been meditating of the many sides of the metaxological from the days of my doctoral studies, and not least with reference to the irreducibility of the divine to the terms of speculative dialectic, and in the context of post-Hegelian and post-Nietzschean atheism. The present work comes out of those long years of thinking about the between and God.

In relation to God, we all run the risk of being frauds. Knowing one does not know absolutely, one does know one must necessarily fall short. I do not lack in estimation for the atheist. To be a philosopher at all is to invite the atheist to take up lodging in one's soul. One wants to understand – understand even what one's understanding does not endorse. I do not doubt but that the dialogue with this lodger has no univocal, incontrovertible end. I do not doubt but that this guest can dislodge much of superstition and obfuscation. I do not also doubt but that, alas, much of true reverence can also be unhoused. This lodger of the soul can lay a clutch of cuckoo's eggs. Something like this, I believe, has happened in the souls of not a few intellectuals, and indeed in a more widespread cultural regard, in the last couple of centuries. These eggs hatch and evict the less robust religious fledglings. Are there more robust fledglings?

I believe there are. One finds witness to this in the ability of religion recurrently to resurrect itself, even in the direst of circumstances. One witnesses it at the heart of mindfulness itself, in its quarrel with its own atheist possibilities, and its intimate dialogue with the promise of the divine. One witnesses even the paradoxical resurrection of the religious at the heart of atheist philosophy itself. There are secular intellectuals who are engaged in a kind of colonization of religious notions, like grace, for instance. This might seem benign, but one worries that, in the end, this is an evacuation of the more properly religious significance of these notions. Pascal suggests that atheism displays a certain vigor of soul, but also that there is a religious faith whose vigor exceeds even this atheistic vigor. The dialogue of the soul with itself is the dialogue of the soul with what is other to it, with what exceeds it. Our dialogue with what transcends us will never cease, even when we say there is nothing there. The conversation, holy and unholy, is resurrected in the emptiness. We find vigor for it because we are first invigorated. The promise of being religious is recurrently resurrected because it is constitutive of what we are, what we are given to be, and what we are to be.

God and the Between may seem to the philosophical too religious, to the religious too philosophical. It speaks from a space between religion and philosophy and perhaps I will call down curses from the two sides. But stressed as it is, I think this is a good between in which to be. As a religious person, I cannot escape philosophical perplexity. As a philosopher of religion, I must necessarily be between philosophy and religion. Moreover, this between is not just dictated by religion having to prove its credentials to rational philosophy. It is also a matter of philosophy wondering if perhaps religion is the more original and ultimate partner in dialogue, such that the very identity of philosophy is itself called into question – an identity to be reformulated in terms of a porosity of thinking to what exceeds its determination purely through thought's own immanent resources.

There is a porosity between religion and philosophy, not a rigid separation, and communications can carry or be received from both sides. A new poverty of philosophy is needed, one all but the opposite of Hegel's absolute knowing whose attainment he describes as the point when knowing no longer needs to go beyond itself. Rather we begin to "know" the absolute, in a knowing that does not know, just when we understand that there is nothing more necessary for philosophy than that it should just so go beyond itself, without immanent reserve, without reserving the divine for its own immanence – in an agapeic exceeding of mindfulness beyond thought thinking itself. Without the proper friendship of the religious, it is hard to see how this would be possible for philosophy.

In keeping *God and the Between* within acceptable limits of length, I have had to exclude more detailed discussion of certain issues and thinkers. I have also tried to keep footnotes in hand, again for reasons of compactness, but also lest a clutter of erudition distract from the record of the journey undertaken. For *God and the Between* records a journeying – a crossing and criss-crossing in and of the between, and a venturing beyond the between. I think of the book as like a kind of passport, and I had toyed with the idea of having the whole text crossed out. No publisher would stand for that of course, and there is the fact that the gesture would appear tedious, if carried beyond a certain limit. One thinks of Heidegger's gesture of crossing (out) being – at first provocative, but the point once made tends to redundancy. My thought of crossing out the text was this rather. One recalls how old passports used to be crossed in red, when they had served their purpose, and a new one needed to be issued. But under the crossing out, stamps of the stations of a journey are still to be beheld. There is no substitute for the journey itself. But a passport that has served for passage is at least a witness that a journey, or journeys have been undertaken.

Abbreviations

AOO: *Art, Origins, Otherness: Between Art and Philosophy*, State University of New York Press, 2003

BB: *Being and the Between*, State University of New York Press, 1995

BHD: *Beyond Hegel and Dialectic: Speculation, Cult and Comedy*, State University of New York Press, 1992

DDO: *Desire, Dialectic and Otherness: An Essay on Origins*, Yale University Press, 1987

EB: *Ethics and the Between*, State University of New York Press, 2001

HG: *Hegel and God: A Counterfeit Double?* Ashgate Press, 2003

IST?: *Is There a Sabbath for Thought?: Between Religion and Philosophy*, Fordham University Press, 2005

PO: *Philosophy and its Others: Ways of Being and Mind*, State University of New York Press, 1990

PU: *Perplexity and Ultimacy: Metaphysical Thoughts from the Middle*, State University of New York Press, 1995

Introduction

Between You and all of us   The first word comes   Wooed into words
We do not have the   In the cooing of the mother   We come too early
First word   & we are wooed into words   To presumption
We are spoken to first   Coming into conversations   And complaint
     Long under way
     Without us

BREAKING SILENCE ABOUT GOD

There is a natural hesitation in speaking about God. One fears presumption. God exceeds if not our reach certainly our grasp. We overextend our powers and wound ourselves. There is also something intimate in so speaking. God is not to be bandied about in the highways and byways of facile discourse. One wonders if, rather, one should speak to God, and not with human witnesses to overhear. There seems to be an intimacy about being religious to which philosophical thought will never quite be true. Yet there comes a time when one must break silence, and break a silence that has been philosophically chosen or enforced in recent centuries. If one dares to speak, whether in interrupting that philosophical silence, or in venturing to say anything at all, one had better have something considered to offer.

Through much of the history of philosophy, to be a philosopher at all seemed to carry with it, as an inner part of the philosopher's vocation, concern with the question of God. In recent centuries, perhaps dating from around the time of Kant, it has not been possible to take that concern for granted, and, in our time, it seems rather that silence about God is the norm. That this silence seems to be so self-evident and self-evidently justified to many philosophers strikes me as perplexing. Relative to the longer history of the human family, and indeed most human beings today, such a silence is the anomaly rather than the rule. True, there is a certain analytic tradition that keeps alive the issues of natural theology, and, since the early 1990s, there has been a so-called phenomenological turn to religion. Nevertheless, the more general rule is an atheism that has been common among intellectuals since the Enlightenment, an atheism now in a phase of seeming to be entirely undisturbed about itself. I find this disturbing. For there are silences and silences. There is a silence of reserve and respect. There is a silence of reverence. There is a silence of disinterest. There is a silence of indifference. There are philosophers who affect this latter silence. Not for them the passionate repudiation of the monotheistic God of some earlier atheists, like Nietzsche. The matter is no longer an issue.

One can discover that once one scratches the surface of indifference, flashes of an old hostility flare up. It may take the form, for instance, of an irritation that anyone should invest this issue with seriousness at all. Nevertheless, it still is perplexing that there should be indifference at all, since surely it is the most natural thing that such a question should strike one as of the most ultimate seriousness. I began to wonder if the hostility might be like the irritation of someone who, sleeping or half-sleeping, wants to be left alone and not bothered. I began to wonder if our being asleep to the question betokened a kind of bewitchment. Is it possible that an age could fall under a bewitchment? Could it be that especially since the early nineteenth century many of the major intellectuals of the era live under the bewitchment of godlessness? For the question of God is no longer a matter of reason or argument. Nietzsche, as usual, hits the nail on the head: God, he says, is not now to *our taste*. But who are we, and what is our taste? Why have we no taste for God? I have come to think that a postulatory finitism (*IST?*, especially Chapter 1) polices the kinds of questions allowed to arise as significant, and God is not among those questions. But what if one were to hold that this question not only should but does arise? Arguments alone will not wake people who are under the spell of an enchantment. More is needed.

The arising or not of the question of God has much to do with our understanding of the ethos of being wherein we dwell. If this ethos is dominated by, for instance, a devaluation of nature as other-being and an apotheosis of human autonomy, the issue of God as a superior transcendence other to our own immanent self-transcendence will not easily arise. We inhabit the ethos of being, but we also reconfigure the given ethos in terms of what we consider to be most important and ultimate. It is within this reconfigured ethos that questions proximately arise. Nevertheless, the proximate questions allowed to arise are dependent on a whole set of background assumptions and presuppositions that themselves never or rarely enter the foreground picture. These presuppositions take on a life of their own, and function as enablers and censors in terms of the questions that emerge in the foreground of the reconfigured ethos. They may block the arising of the question of God, or dull our taste for it. They may cast a spell in which atheism seems self-evident.

What then would it be to address a bewitchment? Among other things, it would mean trying to understand the recessed as well as the expressed, the backgrounding presuppositions as well as the foregrounded claims and articulations. We live and think *in* the foregrounded articulations, but we live and think *out* of these backgrounding presuppositions and sources. To see again if the question of God can arise, and how properly it must arise, would mean investigating not only the reconfigured ethos in the foreground but also its background sources and presuppositions. It would mean asking whether there is any sense of a primal ethos of being within which all our reconfigured ethē participate. For there are different reconfigured ethē, and differences might be noted between the premodern, the modern, and now the postmodern, and yet what each configures is the ethos as the given milieu of being. This ethos I also call the between. If the ultimate question is to be addressed, we must ask about God and the between.

GOD AND THE ETHOS OF BEING

I offer, in the two opening chapters of Part I, an account of why in the reconfigured ethos of modernity the question of God tends not now to arise for many, as well as suggestions for a renewed passageway beyond Godlessness. A reader might prefer to go immediately to that discussion, but I want to say something about the overall orientation of this book which, in the nature of the case, makes better sense after the fact. Nevertheless, it may be helpful for those who are worried about making a beginning at all. Something must be ventured about the ethos of being, since what is at stake is a complex interplay of ethos and ways to God or from God, including along those ways various silences and express arguments.[1]

There is first the ontological ethos of what I call the between. We are in this intermedium of being and our participation in it contributes to shaping the form it takes for us. Our participation contributes to a *second* ethos which is the *reconfigured* ethos – reconfigured

---

[1] See "God, Ethos, Ways," in *International Journal of the Philosophy of Religion*, 45 (1999), pp. 13–30, where I say something about the ethos and the proofs of God. Here my remit is broader than the proofs.

in light of our fundamental orientations to what is, both actual and possible, our basic senses of good and evil, and so on. Consider a few instances with subtly different attunements to the ethos: the Greeks and their putative dread of the unlimited; Bruno and the infinite spaces as full, filling the soul with enthusiasm and furor; Pascal and the infinite spaces empty, stripped of univocal signs of the divine, fearful to the soul; Nietzsche and the immanent infinite as the open sea, limitlessness bringing on a dizzying creativity; beyond Nietzsche the fullness of the immanent ethos as a between, wooing us beyond the between with its hyperbolic tokens of the divine. These subtle differences of attunement engender variations in how we inhabit the second reconfigured ethos, and with repercussions for the quest(ion) of God.

The ethos of the between, the given milieu of being is the more primordial. The ways we construct formulate more definite passages of existing and thinking in and out of this first ethos. The ethos seems to be indefinite, since it is not this determinate thing or happening or that, and so cannot be definitively pinned down. It is the enabling milieu without which there would not be this or that determinate process or thing. When we find or construct a way, it helps to make determinate for us what otherwise seems to be indefinite in the ethos. But what seems indefinite for us is not necessarily indefinite in itself. We may have not yet understood what is at play in the ethos and so we think of it as something indefinite. In fact, it may be in excess of our determinations and hence not indefinite at all but overdetermined – not lacking in determination but more than any finite determination, and our self-determination. The given ethos of the between is overdetermined.[2]

We always live in a second ethos, since we find ourselves in the midst of things, as having already taken on a particular complex order of determinate happenings, relations, and so on. Waking up into that order, we tend to be taken up with what is before us – the network of determinate happenings, relations, and so forth. We are dull to the possibility that this configured ethos is in fact *second*, and possibilized by the ontological resources and reserves given with the first ethos. Now and then, in moments of astonishment and perplexity, an intimation of this first ethos may break through, and the second ethos takes on a new light of strangeness. Briefly, it seems other, and seems to show something other. Too briefly, for soon the more familiar second ethos reassumes its more domestic sway over us, and our readiness for mystery and strangeness falls asleep again. It seems to me that if we are to find true ways to God anew, we must be awoken from this sleep of the second reconfigured ethos, even while granting that it is there, in the midst of things, that we find ourselves. A fresh rethinking of God would have to do justice to where we find ourselves in a particular second ethos, but also undertake the venture of finding some ways to open again, or be opened again to, what is communicated of the primal ethos of being.

This is not simply a matter of reasserting old "proofs" of God or devising new. It calls for an exploration of what is prior to determinate "proof." This is not to deny that in trying to situate "proofs" in light of the primal ethos, it might well happen that something of their slumbering promise is refreshed. It is not a matter of slighting them, but of stepping back, so to say, from the foreground of certain arguments, to try to discern some of the enabling metaphysical conditions that fund their intelligibility and potential persuasiveness. Of course, reference even to these "proofs" helps one make the present point about the importance of the ethos. Thus different arguments for God, even their repudiation, will reflect certain features of a second ethos. At the same time, if they have any truth, they tend to give expression to something of the primal ethos. It may be that not all of them put their roots deep enough down into the primal ethos. If they do not, they will tend to reflect, shall we say, the passing preoccupations of the *Zeitgeist*, perhaps its idolatries and bewitchments. Gods can be affirmed on the basis of these bewitchments, but they are gods destined to ephemeral existence. The best ways not only reflect

---

2   On "overdetermination," see, for instance, "Being, Dialectic and Determination: On the Sources of Metaphysical Thinking," *The Review of Metaphysics*, 48 (June, 1995), pp. 731–69; also *BB*, pp. 13ff.

the second ethos, they also break through its idolatries into the first ethos of elemental ontological resource, and hence have a perduring character that can survive the passing or alteration of the second ethos or its dominant configuration.

Ways to God are not identical with proofs about God. It may well be the case that many of the traditional proofs were too tied to determinate aspects of a reconfigured, second ethos, aspects that had their day, and that now no longer serve as signs to communicate the divine. This need not be always so, for even in the second configurations something can be shown of the first ethos, as the following consideration indicates. In Paley's argument from design, the image of the watch and its maker has communicative power in an era (say, modernity) when mechanical design serves as a paradigm of intelligible order. In an age not bewitched by mechanical design this sign has a weaker communicative power. And yet something about this argument continues to exert an attraction, because mechanical design is one rendition of intelligible order, which might equally be rendered by another sign, for instance, an organic whole. Nature conceived as an organic whole can also serve as a sign of intelligible order, and for pan(en)theistically inclined thinkers the organic whole is more beloved, and carries more communicative power, than the mechanistic sign. My point: intelligible order, whether mechanically or organically figured, exceeds these two ways of configuring it, but both qua intelligible order can put us in mind of an origin that, while not just an intelligible order, communicates the sign of intelligible order. It would seem that every age exhibits some attraction to this basic ontological possibility in the ethos as a *precipitating occasion* for thought on the divine. In that occasion is communicated, even if sometimes obscurely, something exceeding the particular configuration of being that we determine.

If there is an interplay of primal ethos and ways that we configure in the second ethos, there is no absolutely univocal way to God, for any such a way is itself a derivative from the interplay of ethos and ways. It seems to me that the search for God has to be approached in terms of that interplay and not just in terms of the produced configurations of the interplay, even granting that these might be powerful and suggestive as "proofs" that *probe*. Instance: the ontological "proof" can be interpreted as a deep probe. Probing of the thought of God in inwardness can loosen in us the bewitching effect of a finite configuration of the ethos, and open us, through the passageways of inwardness, to the thought of God as overdetermined, a thought that, in its excess to us, is a sign communicating of God. In the determinations, indeed self-determinations that we meet in the second reconfigured ethos we are shown something concerning the overdeterminacy of the primal ethos of the between, and its reserved promise.

These overdetermined signs I will later explore in terms of what I call the *hyperboles of being*. There is something ambiguous, in a saturated sense, about the hyperboles. They are overdeterminate signs in immanence communicating of what exceeds exhaustive immanent determination or self-determination. They do not announce themselves with literal univocity; but there is something importantly positive in this. They ask for mindful attention and for discernment. They ask of us, in Pascal's terms, *l'esprit de finesse* rather than just *l'esprit de géométrie*. There are ways to God that seek to univocalize the passage in terms of "geometrical" configurations in the second ethos. Think of how the concept of a triangle is used, for instance, by Descartes to offer a variation on the ontological argument. If what I am saying is correct, any such "geometrical" strategy risks being misleading, for it is tempted to reconfigure the ethos as a totality of determinations or self-determinations, and hence within the second ethos there can be no way to God as communicated to us through such overdetermined signs. "Proofs" will be a matter of passing from determination to determination, with at most the heuristic anticipation of the totality of all determinations, in Kant's terms the unconditioned as a regulative ideal.

If we are approaching God in terms of accession to the primal ethos, via the second ethos, God is not, cannot be such an unconditioned totality of determinations. God is in an other dimension. As the astonishment that breaks through the second ethos to the first finds itself released into a space of mystery, so God as origin of the primal ethos is in a space of mystery redoubled yet again. Does this other dimension entail such an utter transcendence that we end up with a dualism of immanence and transcendence? I do not think so. If the ethos of finitude is shaped by signs or communications that are themselves overdeterminate, then even the "geometrical" ways cannot do justice to the fullness of what is at play *within* the ethos, much less to the origin communicating in those signs. If we think purely in terms of univocal determination, there can be no such signs, and hence it is not surprising that we end up with the putative destruction of the proofs of God's existence. This outcome is already an outcome dictated by a certain configuration of the ethos, rather reconfiguration of it in light of the univocal *mathēsis* of nature in modernity.

If there is a diversity of interplays of ethos and ways, and we have to do justice to this diversity, we need not succumb to a "relativism" which weakens any claim to binding truth. This would be to surrender to an equivocalism which backs off mediating the ambiguity of the signs. If we do this we then give up on a univocal way, and think we have no way at all. But there is *another* relativism in which the notion of *being in relation* is crucial. The ways are ways of relating to our being in the between and our attempts to comprehend what the signs communicate. This does not imply the relativism that, for instance, claims that faith is fine for the faithful but indifferent for others, that unbelief is suitable for secularists but neutral as to others. There can be a self-serving apartheid through which the religious, the non-religious, and anti-religious protect themselves, immunized from questions they cannot always handle, a live and let live attitude that amounts to a collusion in evasion. The diverse interplays of ethos and ways means that ways must be returned to the ethos and understood as relative to that intermedium. Philosophy is indispensable here, since there is always something about the ethos that is not comprehended entirely, and that shapes or influences basic attitudes to life. The "too muchness" of the ethos presents the occasion out of which the most pressing perplexities emerge. Philosophy can be a participation in articulating our finding of a way within the ethos – not only in ruminating on the ways already available for passage, and in keeping them open, but in the probe for new ways that reflect current configurations of the ethos.

Our being formed by the reconfigured ethos influences, in an often implicit and subtle manner, the forms of life we take to be acceptable, as well as the categories and patterns of argumentation we deem persuasive. The traditional "proofs" of God often mirror an implicit sense of the first ontological ethos, and should not be taken as "results" that can be detached from the context out of which they are constructed. Rather than just being jettisoned as "outmoded," they might offer us yet some essential guidance into how we might diversely conceive the ethos, primal, and reconfigured. Deracinated from their ethos they wither. In some instances, the reconfigured ethos that lent them life might now be gone, but if there is a primal ethos there may be another promise of their life in a root not dead at all. To cultivate such a "root" would not be just to tell a historical, hermeneutical tale relative to the presuppositions of a particular era that we have now outgrown. It is not merely a question of historical relativism, applicable to a particular reconfiguration of the ethos but not to the primal ethos. It is a question of a systematic exploration of the fundamental ontological presupposition at stake in the primal ethos, refracted through the reconfigured. The question of truth is not done away with in favor of meaning. For the meaning of our configurations will be a function of their fidelity to the truth of the primal ethos.

Sometimes the diversity of basic contexts between the believer and non-believer is granted, with insulating tolerance as its justification: They just live in different worlds, that's that, we say. This insulation is not my point. Each lives a configuration of the ethos of being and hence each enacts a shaping of the primal ethos, to which they may or may not be truthful. Being truthful is not a univocal affair, and hence each, believer and non-believer, is in question. It is not a case of the first having to offer the convincing argument, while all that remains for the second is to evaluate it critically. The fundamental sense of being of the latter is also in question. The ethos wherein "critique" seems self-evidently the task of the intellectual is in question as equally as an ethos wherein atheism appears as the anomaly. As already indicated, we secularized Westerners are the freaks, considering the long history of humankind, when we take our secular ethos as the self-evident truth of the matter. That ethos, when blithely taken for granted, is in question *vis-à-vis* the perplexing truth of the between. Seen in a certain light, traditional ways can sometimes exemplify in concentrated manner what is fundamentally at issue in our religious being, and our perplexity about the ultimate. This is again not univocal, since they too can be severed from their enabling ethos – sometimes with disastrous results. Religion thus severed can become a matrix of atheism.

PASSING IN THE ETHOS: BETWEEN THE GIVEN AND THE GOOD

How to say anything at all about the primal ethos? It seems to retreat into elusiveness, beyond the determinacies and self-determinations within the reconfigured ethos. In due course I will be concerned with how the fourfold sense of being, as well as the hyperboles of being, orient us to some sense of it, and further again to some sense of the God of the between. I offer an anticipatory pass between the boundaries of the ontological and the ethical, the given and the good.

The primal ethos is more mindfully approached if we think less of determinate entities within the between than of the between in its primordial *ontological givenness*. It is always already given to be, before we understand it and reconfigure it through our determinate relations to it. Its being given to be is never identical with any of the determinate beings that are given to be within it. Moreover, we generally reconfigure the primal ethos in terms of figurations that reflect our own determinate concerns, our preponderant engagement with determinate beings, as well as our own desire to be self-determining. Thus ways can also be figured in terms of determinate forms of being or beings. And so, relative to the latter, and traditionally, we come across proofs of God as the highest being, or we anthropomorphically think of God in terms of magnified human qualities, and so on. The deeper way tries to be mindful of the primal ethos as given to be. We dwell in mindfulness of the "that it is at all" – given to be and not nothing. Struck by this, our thinking need not be dominated by any particular determinate thing or happening in the between – not the figure of the machine or the organism, nor indeed the human being.

Such mindful dwelling might be said to resource, say, the Third Way of Aquinas, or more generally the argument from contingency. The fullness of this argument means appreciating it at the level of the primal and not the reconfigured ethos. If we remain at this reconfigured level, it will be hard to avoid conceiving divine being in terms of infinitude construed as magnified finitude, and not in terms of the giving origin of finitude. Our ontological perplexity concerning primal givenness concerns our appreciation of finitude not first as becoming, but as *coming to be*: not becoming this or that, but finitude's coming to be at all. This is extremely difficult to approach, for it lies at the boundary of determinate knowing, even though everything determinate, as already given to be, presupposes not just its becoming this or that, but its already having come to be.

The "that it is at all" is not the only access in which our ways open to something of the primal ethos. Something of our ethical being, our *being ethical at all* can be of immense moment. Kant, for instance, suffered ontological cramp relative to creation in its being given to be (surprising in that Leibniz influenced him). Nevertheless, Kant's resort to the human being as a moral being seems to compensate for what he lacks in the way of ontological astonishment. Something about our moral being, in the unconditional demand immanently made on us, brings us into the nearness of the primal ethos – ethos here as the promise of the ethical. We are dealing with what at all is worthy to be affirmed as unconditional in an immanent world seemingly fully determined by conditional occurrences. This ethical way, in fact, cannot be separated from ontological presuppositions and consequences. The call of the good is such that we can never be its master but are always solicited to an often obscure obedience to what is unconditional. How make sense of this obedience? If nothing else, we must consider the hospitality of the ethos of being to unconditional ethical worth. Through the unconditional ethical charge on us, we are opened to the ethos of being as a milieu of hospitality to the good, and made to ponder if something of a more ultimate original good is communicated in the signs of immanent good.

The turn to the ethical self opens a kind of pathway of "inwardness," and a way to God as the good, and there is something very traditional about it. But the interplay of primal ethos, reconfigured ethos, and our way needs to be kept in mind, since the last two can be excessively determined in terms of our human-all-too-human sense of the good. Since human ethics, as Nietzsche reminded us with relish, can be human-all-too-human, this ethical way can become a consecration of idols rather than a faithful opening to transcendence as other. The possibility of generating idols is perennial in all ways, given the fragile complexity of the dynamical interplay of ethos and ways.

Unconditional good: there is something of an absolute charge laid on us coming from the difference between good and evil, and it is not something we produce, for we are always already what we are (to be) within this charging difference. We can configure the meaning of this difference in a variety of ways. However, it is our being within the charge of this difference which defines our situation in the ontological ethos. We become this or that moral character within this more original givenness. Reflecting on this, or finding our way back to this, is not simply finding the ethical charge within us; it is more *our finding within ourselves that we are "within" it*. Within the immanent exigence of the ethical, we find ourselves exceeded by the call of a good we do not produce ourselves. To come to some mindfulness of this excess is to approach something of the overdeterminacy of the primal ethos as communicative of a goodness that surpasses our measure. Ethos, thus minded, can become the deepest (re)source out of which our approach to the divine takes place. We are always "within" what makes that approach possible, though we may mistakenly think of our approach as one thing this side, and the thing approached as another thing on the other side. This last view makes no sense, and is rather due to a determination of the ethos, which misleadingly thinks of the ground of the ethos as another thing within it, or even as a determinate thing outside it.

GOD, ETHOS, AND THE FOURFOLD SENSE OF BEING

What metaphysics is and means is not a simple matter, and is much contested today. Since metaphysics itself and the philosophical quest for God are often criticized, if not dismissed, as "onto-theology," I want to say something about it with relation to God.

Metaphysics, as I understand it, is not just the philosophical discipline that examines and evaluates categories and arguments for their rational cogency; not just the philosophical interpretation of the ethos as reconfigured in lights of the fundamental presuppositions and enabling (re)sources of intelligibility and value of a particular era, or people, or particular way of life; deeper than these, it seeks to open a pathway of philosophical mindfulness concerning the primal ethos of being. It is in virtue of such a mindfulness that light can be thrown on the particular configurations that shape ways of life, as well as determinate categories and arguments that claim rational cogency.

Metaphysical mindfulness of the primal ethos, thus understood, is to a degree reminiscent of the ancient understanding of the philosopher as seeking to understand the "whole." I would rather speak of the between than the whole – this reflects our situation in the ethos, which, if it is a whole at all, is an "open whole" (see *BB*, 288), since it cannot be exhaustively defined in terms of a totality of determinations or self-determinations. There is no totalization of the overdetermined excess of being as given to be. There is a constitutive openness to the between which is not to be described in terms of either a totality of finite determinations or a self-determining totality. This openness makes it porous to what, as other to it, exceeds it. We find a double call on our mindfulness: both an ontological exploration of what is given in immanence and a metaphysical transcending in immanence to what exceeds any totalized immanence. This second call, moving mindfully beyond determinate and self-determining totality, though guided by what an exploration of immanence shows, is crucial in the philosophical search for God.

I do not subscribe to the view that Heidegger has a corner on being, and that to think God we must do so without being (Marion), as if Heidegger had a lock on being. Nor, for that matter, does Levinas have a lock on ethics. To have being without God seems as unsatisfactory as to have God without being. Likewise to have the good without out being or God seems as unsatisfactory as to have being and God without the good. I understand the rationale of wresting God or the good free of (Heideggerian) being, if by this we intend to confine thought to immanent finitude. A different approach to being, to metaphysics, a different metaphysics and ethics informs my essay. I speak of God beyond the whole – the "totality" of immanent being – but speak from the between as the rich milieu of finite being, as given to be. At the same time, I dissent from the God of the whole of Hegel, as well as the deconstructive philosophies of immanence that are reactive to Hegelian holism. Despite major differences as to whether we affirm the whole, or deconstruct all wholes, both philosophies share this: they are philosophies of finally unremitting immanence. The issue here is not just a local one for late modernity, but a deeper one that is elemental and constitutive of our ontological endowment. There is the immanent between. Then there is the issue of what is between this immanent between and what is other to it. This is particularly urgent with respect to that between defining our relation to the origin, and our relation to the "beyond," and how both these enter our passing sojourn in the middle of a given life.

This is not to deny the necessary exploration of immanence. Quite to the contrary, a philosophy of the between always thinks from the midst. Nevertheless, it is open to the possibility that in its exploration of immanence, it may come across what exceeds immanence. It is not a philosophy of sublationary infinitism such as we find in Hegel: the finitude is sublated in the infinite. Neither is it a philosophy of postulatory finitude, such as we find in Nietzsche and his heirs: finitude is postulated as the horizon of thought, greater than which none can be, none is to be, conceived. A philosophy of the between is not only in the between, but is of the between, that is, on the borderline between finitude and infinitude. It is on this borderline in a manner wherein the difference of the two is neither relativized as parts of an inclusive whole (as with sublationary infinitism), nor waved away or collapsed such that there is no other to finitude (as with postulatory finitism). On the border between, there is an opening of the finite between to what exceeds it: the God of the between is also the God beyond the between.

There are signs in immanence of what transcends immanence and cannot be fully determined in immanent terms. Among these signs are what I term the hyperboles of being. Being between is a communication of the beyond of the between. This beyond is not a dualistic opposite, the inversion of which, or its collapse, or its speculative sublation, is taken to institute the reign of unsurpassable immanence. Our thinking of God relates to, while not being reducible to, the meaning of being, as understood by us, here and now. Taking our bearings from the being of the between, on the basis of the richest understanding and forms of being there, we venture thought about God. This venture is not one of compensation for some perceived lack in immanence, but rather proceeds from excess: what is too much for immanence in immanence itself points to what is more than immanence. Our best thinking about the richest and most ultimate senses of being offers us guidance in thinking about God.

One might object that this is still too immanent, too philosophical, too mum about claims of revelation. One might even accuse such a metaphysics of the between of making an idol of the God of the philosophers. I demur. A true philosophy of the between cannot a priori close off porosity to the divine and its communication. I accept that philosophers can put conceptual idols in the place of God; I cannot accept this as justifying the jettisoning of metaphysics. If there is revelation, or a communication addressed to our ultimate porosity, we still have to ponder its meaning, with a heart tempered by fear and trembling but with a head schooled in the best of human wisdom we have available. One might claim that Jerusalem and Athens have nothing to do with one another, and there is something very important to their difference, but I protest if we fixate on the difference as an unsurpassable dualism. Metaphysicians think in the between, and this may also mean *between* Jerusalem and Athens. We must listen to the voices of Jerusalem, but we must listen mindfully. These voices may shock and shatter some of the inherited ways of philosophy and some ways of doing metaphysics. But while they provoke metaphysical thinking to a perhaps new self-understanding, they do not make it redundant. A metaxological metaphysician – or metaphysician of the middle way – listens to the voices of important others, such as religion and art, and is willing to grant that his or her own voice must re-voice itself to do justice to those others that have spoken, and, one hopes, been heard. It may indeed entail a new poverty of philosophy in which it is not simply religion that has to justify itself before the tribunal of philosophical reason, but philosophy itself may have to divest itself of its own conceptual hubris, and part ways with the rational idols that tempt it to adore its own counterfeit doubles of God.[3]

There are some who have nothing to do with Jerusalem but who also seem to want to have nothing to do with Athens, certainly not with the "onto-theological" philosophers. When it is said that we must think beyond or without metaphysics, one fears this "other" thinking is secretly captive to presuppositions that shape an inarticulate metaphysics. In claiming to be beyond metaphysics, we become unknowing metaphysicians – an inarticulate sense of the meaning of being informs our post-metaphysical, or non-metaphysical thinking. There seems no escape from metaphysics. Every escape is itself informed by a secret sense of the ethos of being, as well as a host of unexamined presuppositions, and so is no escape. One can fall into a self-congratulation ignorant of itself, for one's repudiation of metaphysics is marked by neglected relations to being – an implicit metaphysics. One congratulates oneself that there is no shadow of metaphysics, but the shadow is not seen because one looks away, or in the wrong way, and does not turn and see what one cannot jump over. In the end there is only good and bad thinking – good and bad thinking about the senses of being already at work in all our efforts to make intelligible sense of our being in the midst of things. Genuine metaphysics is just the effort to think well, with reflective understanding of the work of those fundamental senses. We must also come to know our shadows.

As mindful of the ethos, metaphysics, I hold, must be metaxological, that is, attempting a *logos* of the *metaxu*, an articulated account of the between – and this with respect to the ultimate power(s) of being that make it possible to be, not only as thus and thus, but to be at all. As suggested, to speak of the primal ethos is to speak of the between: the milieu of immanent being which enables all beings to be, in their rich singularity, intricate communications, and complex intermediations. To speak more articulately of its overdeterminacy, and not mere indeterminacy, we resort to the fourfold sense of being: the univocal, equivocal, dialectical, and metaxological. There is a given metaxological community of being, though we do not know this in the beginning. Always participating in it, we can come to mindfulness of it through the immanent articulations it already communicates. We, as philosophers, must remain true to these articulations, thereby trying to construct a metaxological philosophy. With the aid of the univocal, equivocal, dialectical, and metaxological senses, we need to work through these different articulations to be brought mindfully into some knowing of this community.

Very crudely, the univocal sense stresses sameness to the diminution or underplaying of differences. The equivocal sense reaffirms the importance of difference(s), indeed a more dynamic sense of differing and differentiation, but sometimes to the neglect or shortchanging of more lasting constancies also emerging in the universal impermanence. The dialectical way is a mediation of the univocal and equivocal, and tries to do justice to the dynamic interplay of sameness and otherness, and while it can remain open, one finds a

---

[3] See "Religion and the Poverty of Philosophy," in *IST?* Chapter 3. I have an educated person's sense of Buddhism, Hinduism, Confucianism, Taoism, and I would feel I were faking it were I to speak as if with any authority. The silence is a reflection of this, not any slight. In my own conversations with scholars and my own students from Asia I have found an immediate recognition that the between requires modes of thought that are not objectifying or merely subjectifying.

tendency to privilege a more ultimate identity as inclusive of identity and difference. This is especially so in the modern form of dialectic: the forms of mediation tend all to lead to the supreme form of an encompassing self-mediation of the whole that includes all differences within itself. The danger is a higher speculative univocity, and an underplaying of robust otherness and indeed enigmas and recesses of being not amenable to articulation or communication in the form of self-mediation. This self-mediating dialectic moves from the indeterminate (indefinite) to the determinate (definite) to the self-determining – but this can lead to the occlusion of the overdeterminacy.

The metaxological, as a philosophical logos, stands in openness to the overdeterminacy, even as it recurs to the interplay of sameness and difference. It reengages with the pluralism of intermediations, finding the "inter" itself to be irreducible. The participants in the intermediations are themselves not reducible to one all-inclusive self-mediation. There is no whole of wholes that includes everything in the majestic solitude of the immanent one. The all inclusive self-mediation of dialectical-speculative totality is not true enough to this "inter" and its participants. The immanent between is multiply stressed by differings and mediations, is witness to stirring constancies that give space for life in the universal impermanence but that are in passing. This passing is one that is also passing beyond, and hence is not just passage as from immanence to immanence but passage as fundamental porosity to what eludes determination or self-determination in the terms of immanence itself. This is the between as a porous passing, in community, in the universal impermanence, that is given to be by an enigmatic origin that is not itself the between, nor self-produced by the between, and that can never be closed into itself in terms of any totality of holistic immanence. Within the between there are hyperboles of being which communicate more than the terms of immanence can circumscribe: pointers to ultimate transcendence as other to the immanent between.

The struggle for mindfulness of the primal ethos is inseparable from appreciation of the importance of these hyperboles in the between. It is on the basis of the fullest senses of being thus given in the between, and our best efforts to articulate what this fullness communicates, that I think a philosophical renewal of the question of God is best approached.

GOD, PHILOSOPHICAL SYSTEMATICS, RELIGIOUS POETICS

The reconstruction of thinking about God here attempted has systematic aspects, but it also has existential, aesthetic, ethical, and religious, perhaps even mystical dimensions. We need a plurivocal practice of philosophy, one which while being systematic is mindful of what exceeds system. For one can reflect systematically without necessarily claiming possession of *the* system in a closed and totalizing sense. We might here speak of a metaxological "systematics," by contrast with "the system." We need systematics in the sense of a disciplined understanding of enabling connections; connections stabilized but not frozen by samenesses; connections defined and developed by dynamic differences; connections not enclosed in one immanent whole; and all in all, connections enabling complex interplays between samenesses and differences, interplays exceeding the closure of every whole on itself.

By the very nature of such systematics, we are awakened to mindfulness of what exceeds system. So also we need what we might call a *religious poetics*: mindful attentiveness to coming to be. We are marked by an original porosity which opens us to all that is other and that marks us with the passion of being, the *passio essendi*. One might say: Without religious poetics, no systematics. And: Without a more original porosity of being, and our given *passio essendi*, no religious poetics either, and hence also no systematics. This means there is a more original sense of being religious prior to being artistic and being philosophical. Poetics and systematics are ultimately less original than the porosity of being that opens us up as a being between, or as being a between. A human being is a medium of passage – a middle capable of becoming mindful of what has passed, what is passing, and what is coming to pass. There is an original sense of being religious which is granted in the poetics of the given porosity of our being. There is the later being religious which is a way of life that lives this porosity, and that at certain extremes might find itself called to the impossible finesse of prophetic mindfulness or mystical love. Ultimately these are gifted and perhaps are some of the ultimate gifts.

Without the poetics of coming to be, for us there is no systematics of being at all. Poetics deals with a bringing or coming to be; systematics finds interconnections in what has come to be. Poetics deals with creative overdetermination; systematics tends to deal with created determinations and self-determinations. Poetics reveals the more original coming to be; systematics articulates forms of interconnection that issue from the more original forming. Poetics concerns the forming power(s), prior to and in excess of determinate form, and intimate with the overdetermination of the original source(s). In truth, systematics makes no intelligible sense without presupposing the poetics, poetics often forgotten when more formed intelligibilities have arrived and when what they bring has come to occupy us.[4]

Modernity after Descartes has often been infatuated with the systematics to the neglect of the poetics, especially in its religious significance. We might think of Hegel as the tutelary divinity of the system, of Nietzsche as the Orpheus of immanent poetics. By contrast, our metaxological approach to God and the between is neither the sublationary infinitism of the first nor the postulatory finitism of the second. It is systematic in following the lines of articulation of an interconnected web of thoughts, or happenings, each related to others. It also gives heed to a religious poetics which asks that we bring the mind of finesse to bear on the hyperboles of being and what they communicate concerning the immanent between – namely, that it is porous to something other to it. When the system overreaches the poetics and the systematics (as it does with Hegel), the overdetermination of poetics is turned into an indeterminacy lacking intelligibility until it is given determinacy and form by the systematics; systematics itself is overtaken by the absoluteness of the system as the apotheosis of self-determining thinking; immanent absolute self-determination claims to come to itself absolutely through its own otherness. Thus system, in its self-sublationary infinitism, overtakes religious poetics, and closes down the porosity of systematics to what is beyond system. This also has the effect of closing down our religious porosity to the transcendence of God. And a philosophy that *only* deconstructs such a system, even in the name of an immanent poetics, does not *per se* unclog our porosity to the divine, especially if the deconstruction of system is exactly like the system in being determined by entirely immanent considerations, though now dictated by postulatory finitism rather than sublationary infinitism. We need more than both of these.

EXCEEDING SYSTEM, HYPERBOLES, UNCLOGGING WAYS

Metaxological systematics requires both immanent openness to otherness and metaphysical hospitality to transcendence. It requires attentiveness to the hyperboles of being. The reader may find helpful a brief first description of four especially significant hyperboles.

The idiocy of being: the sheer "that it is" of given finite being. This can stun us into astonishment and rouse thought that is hyperbolic to finite determinacy or our own self-determination. In the stunning of mindfulness, our thinking can become porous to what exceeds finite determination rather than insisting that immanent finitude is the horizon greater than which none is to be thought.

The aesthetics of happening: the incarnate glory of aesthetic happening as given also rouses astonishment and appreciation before finite being yet it seems to exceed finitization. The aesthetic glory of finitude is impossible to characterize exhaustively in finite terms.

---

[4]On this more fully, see my "Between System and Poetics: On the Practices of Philosophy," in *Between System and Poetics: William Desmond and Philosophy after Dialectic*, edited by Thomas A. Kelly (Aldershot: Ashgate, 2007), pp. 15–36 .

Something more tremendous is incarnated in the beauty and sublimity of finitude that communicates an otherness exceeding all finitization.

The erotics of selving: finite though we are, we are also infinitely self-surpassing. We might claim to be the measure of finite being, yet we are not the measure of ourselves. Our being the measure exceeds itself as its own measure. As beyond measure in terms of ourselves as measure, we point and are pointed to a measure exceeding finite measure. The erotics of selving is more than a self-overcoming driven to its own most complete self-determination in immanence. It incarnates a primal porosity to what exceeds its own determination and self-transcending. In the fecund poverty of its given porosity, it is an opening to transcendence as other beyond self-transcendence.

The agapeics of community: in our relation to others, our being is in receiving and in giving. In the finiteness of our lives, there is the promise of a generosity beyond finite reckoning. We are given to be before we can give ourselves to be. Nothing is alone, hence the idea of finitude as for itself alone, and nothing other, cannot be taken as the last word, or the first. The agapeics of community intimates a surplus generosity that makes itself available in an absolved porosity of the *passio essendi* that ethically lives itself as a *compassio essendi*. This is a sign of something more than the ethical, since it incarnates the holy.

These hyperboles dovetail with what I see to be the existential, aesthetic, ethical, and religious unclogging of ways to God.

The existential unclogging: once again, system is not enough, if we think of system as a totality of abstract universals whose relation to concrete being is problematic. I am called to ponder the issue. No one else can do it for me, though every other person is called to do it. There is an intensive passion here, and an intimacy that strains to give birth to the right words. This is not a matter of the merely private, for there is a questionable privatization of the religious. Being religious has to do with the intimate universal. If one has not being there on the edge, on the extreme that juts into emptiness, or there where consent or sorrow or mercy breaks through, the philosophical categories will remain the mere letter of the abstract. We will be strangers on whom a foreign tongue falls incomprehensibly. If the tongue has fallen into disuse on a wide scale, one may find oneself an almost autistic member of an elusive remnant, stammering a strange language to strangers in one's time or place, no longer now one's own time or place.

The aesthetic unclogging: we need a continually refreshed attentiveness to the material marvel of sensuous givenness. This appreciative attendance is also at the edge of system, and cannot be produced or guaranteed by any system. There is no method or technique to bring it into being. There is an ineluctable singularity about our fostering of its power, or our being gifted with it. This is not something just subjectivistic. Marveling turns us to the manifestness of being as sensuous showing. We live in this manifestation and take it for granted, but then we take for granted the fact that it is granted, and that it is also a granting of itself. The giving of itself of sensuous being ceases to arouse our admiration. There is a poetics but no science of admiration. It is the happening of an opening in our self-transcending in a communicating with, or a going towards, the beauty or good of other-being.

The ethical unclogging: a certain integrity of mindful selving is asked; we are asked to embody a certain "being true." We make difficulties for ourselves the more we make ourselves into selves lacking this integrity. But there is no way a release beyond our shabby selves can be guaranteed by any system. At most, a system will offer a kind of abstract map where important pitfalls and encouragements will be marked. Of course, even to read the marks, one must *already* be the kind of person who has something of the discernment necessary to see their point or purpose. One must actually traverse the equivocal, and attempt to mediate it in life. The act of writing philosophically about God may be the end product of this traversal, but only a fraction of what emerges on the traversing appears in the surface of the categorial, or even extra-categorial account. If a philosophy is a kind of face, it is also a kind of mask. Faces can come to enflesh the becoming of a soul. Philosophies come to wear the physiognomy of souls, even as they mask intimacies of soul, be these intimacies divine or gargoyle. Perhaps the question of God requires of us a kind of catharsis. In the initiation rites of contemporary professional philosophy, no academic credits are given for catharsis. One cannot even audit a course, or attend a workshop on it. The brilliance of cleverness is not enough. One must quietly close one's door and undergo in solitude the bitter purge.

The religious unclogging: the more one struggles, even as called to ethical integrity and solidarity, the more there crystallizes an estimation of the religious as not fully determined by the moral. The more one struggles the more one grows cognizant, not only of one's own equivocity, but of being much more deeply enchained than one thought to counterfeit doubles of God. There is a freeing not from equivocity but of knowing how much one is enthralled by, in thrall to, false doubles of God, conjured in the equivocity, especially of one's own being. One cannot free oneself from the equivocal magic of these false doubles completely. Even when one is rationally self-determining and thus "free," one is not free. Our autonomous freedom does not free us, for we are tempted to make ourselves the double of the divine and so to counterfeit God. Our being in thrall to this counterfeiting equivocity seems to be intractable. Brought to some realization of this, at a certain limit beyond all system one lays oneself open in an ultimate abandon to the mystery of all that passes beyond one's ken. This abandon, out of the intractable (en)thralldom, is companioned by an overdeterminate trust that comes to grace our suffering of coming to nothing. There is the willingness to assume the undergoing of what comes to one. Our abandon is a religious consent to ultimate community and our participation in the intimate universal. There are many sides to this, though one of them is consent to the excess of our own equivocal being as beyond complete sifting by ourselves alone. One whose being is equivocal cannot completely sift its own equivocal being. We have to be changed utterly, and not changed at all, changed into what we are, re-created into what we are to be. There is entry into a night, not simply of the equivocal, but of divine mystery.

STRUCTURE OF THE WORK

Here is a down-to-earth statement of the overall structure of the book. Part I addresses hard perplexities about Godlessness, as well as offering a reflection upon passage beyond Godlessness.

Part II is an exploration of ways to God, guided by the fourfold sense of being. First, the univocal way stresses sameness. We seek God as a One to be determinately fixed, but we end up with an unfixing of God. Second, the equivocal way accentuates difference beyond univocal fixation. Enabling a renewal of a sense of the mystery of the divine, it can also seed a post-univocal atheism, since there seems to be nothing there answering to the univocalized God. Third, the dialectical way mediates something of this difference in the direction of the togetherness of opposites. The modern form of dialectic, influenced by the ethos of autonomy and the perceived eclipse of divine transcendence as other, tends to stress the mediation which is self-determining. But there is more to the otherness of the divine than the speculative dialectic of the same. Fourth, the metaxological way renews fidelity to intermediated community, not in terms of the self-mediation of the same, but as hospitable to the communication of transcendence as other, out of its own otherness. It keeps open the spaces of otherness in the between. It helps unclog our porosity to the God beyond the whole, as well as the God intimate to the idiocy of our own being. At the culmination of Part II, we venture to speak not only of God and the between, but of God beyond the between.

Part III addresses the fact that we encounter a plurality of conceptions of the divine, such as the monotheistic, polytheistic, personalistic, Gnostic, pan(en)theistic, theistic, and mystic. We need to understand these differences with discrimination. We need to make sense of this plurality, without making it a mere diversity without relation. The fourfold sense of being and the hyperboles allow us to make sense of these different conceptions, as following from definite emphases placed upon different dimensions of our being in the between.

In Part IV we venture to say something about God. Beginning with Godlessness and passing beyond it, we pass through different ways to God, we pass through different understandings of God, and finally we venture thought on the names of the agapeic God. The fourfold sense of being and the hyperboles offer us the means to give a plurivocal account of these "attributes," moving towards speculative metaxology as the least untrue. That speculative metaxology is expressed in ten metaphysical cantos, ranging from God Being Over-Being to God Being (Too) Good.

Part I

Godlessness

Chapter 1

Godlessness and the Ethos of Being

They overlay the land
The locusts of development
Lay their eggs of promise
& hatch the larvae
Of meaninglessness

We have wiped out the line
& the horizon now is
Between us and nothing
Nothing
Except ourselves
We think

The light in between
We do not see it
We look on what is below
The sun is always above
It casts no shadow
We never see it
We face only forward
Nothing but ourselves
Before us
Our faces flat
Towards the future

GODLESSNESS

There is no question more ultimate than the question of the ultimate. This is the question of God. Non-philosophers may well be willing to grant this claim. They may even expect philosophers to come to their assistance. But we philosophers have long listened to the voices of suspicion, voices that when they do not make us hostile to the question, paralyze our thinking on the ultimate. We have become embarrassed by the question.

This is something astonishing. The most important question, the most fascinating question, the most enigmatic question, makes us squirm – squirm though we wear the unmoved mask of agnostic indifference. How make sense of this shame? Can we mark some of the way stations on this path of shame? And when we have passed along it, can we then ask: What then?

We in the West are heirs of a number of religious traditions, but as descendants we have turned our inheritance into hostility to itself. We emerge from religious traditions, notably the Jewish and Christian, but certain developments of just those traditions have made trouble for any untroubled living of those traditions. I mean that certain forms of theism are not to be absolved from atheisms that seem to be their opposite. Godlessness emerges from our being in relation to God. We think of ourselves as at the end of a "good" progress, even when we debunk progress. We are enlightened even when we pour scorn on Enlightenment. We see our scorn as our light – but suppose we are freaks. How freaks? Freaks because the natural condition is to be religious: it is unnatural to be atheist. This crime against nature arises from nature as we interpret it.

We open our eyes, we smell, we breathe, we touch, we are touched, by rock, by the satin of a flower petal, by skin. We are amazed, even delighted, we attend on a certain music of things. When much seems rough and repulsive our horror is the shadow of our astonishment. What is strangely there is strange because it intimates an other – in and through its very own otherness. There is no shadow of a question, yet: the divine is there, though there as also not there, for there is nothing to which one could point univocally and say: That is God. But what that means one does not know.

Or say, one hears one's breath, in the quiet of sitting still, or in trepidation as if trailed, and one hears oneself in an intimacy idiotic to every conceptual objectification, and one does not know what the soul is, beyond knowing that one does not know. There is hinted a depth to selving beyond self, and the haunting of self by an other that slows one into uncertain expectancy. Is this then our being, this uncertain expectancy? But we do not yet know what this means.

Or again, another stirs delight and disquiet in us. We behold a beautiful boy or girl, woman or man, and the beauty can lift one up unbidden and yet also be unbearable, almost. It flows over one, and away from one, though one reaches to it, but it is always in excess, and gone. It comes forward to meet one, and yet is fugitive in its forwardness. A gift has been offered; it seems everywhere and nowhere; and one might be surprised into asking: Is this gift a sacramental sign? But what this all means, one does not know, and perhaps may never know.

But – knowing or not-knowing – there is *nothing contrived* about the question of God. It is elemental and enigmatic – elemental because of the givenness of self, other, nature; enigmatic because one is struck into an as-yet-uncomprehended astonishment by the givenness. The astonishing gift perplexes us about what offers it, or who. And our question is not something to which history determines us, even when it is histori-cally mediated. It is not something grammar imposes on us, even when our speaking is grammatically conditioned. It is not the sly unconscious that presses it on us, though its roots go down deeper than the conscious or unconscious. It is not something to which our social status condemns us. It is not something insidious metaphysics imposes on us, though we cannot escape metaphysics, twist and turn as we will. The question is elemental and inescapable. But we have to be with the elemental, and face what cannot be evaded, to know what this means. Nor will we "overcome" the question, when we have baptized our chains as historicist chains, grammatological, psychoanalytical, socio-political, philosophical chains. There are other fetters, harder to unbind, for instance, the lie in the soul, not to mention vices not always dignified with names in philosophy.

Why has the face of being come for many to seem void of communication of God, when everything within and without seems to press on us the question? The changed attitude to being marking modernity has much to do with the matter. This has been recognized by many, and with many different emphases.[1] My emphasis falls on our reconfiguration of the primal ethos along a particular line of response to the equivocity of givenness. This produces a certain devaluation of being stripped of signs suggestive of divine transcend-ence. This is coupled with a culture of autonomy which, tempted to absolutize itself, eclipses transcendence as other, though behind the mask of autonomy is a will to power usurping absoluteness in a world said to be void of absolutes. The specter of nihilism, now expressed, now recessed, in which all other-being is instrumentalized haunts our claim to mastery, finally inverting into an outcome in which it all seems to come to nothing.

Suppose one holds to a God the creator of all, a God other than creation. Suppose, further, that the creation is given its own being for itself – given to be, it yet has its own otherness. Suppose God is other yet intimate, and other with an unsurpassable transcend-ence that nothing finite in creation can match. Suppose we seek to relate genuinely to this transcendence. If the transcendence is absolute, the search seems futile. If the search augurs of success, the transcendence seems not absolute. What then are the options? If we say the transcendence is absolute, we drive God away from us into a beyond, and our futility is just our search itself: the search drives away from itself what it seems to be driving towards, and hence lacks the basis to yield even a half success. Better then to search by not searching at all? If to seek God is to drive God away, cease to search, and

---

[1] For example, the progress of the more exact sciences, the increase in technological control over the conditions of life, the secularization of everyday life, the alleged maturing of rational humanity, human self-responsibility, or perhaps the refusal of given nature, or self-intoxicated will to power, and so on. All these have their truth, but we must still pitch the question at the level of what it means to be.

let God come towards one. But if no God seems to come? Let us wait. How long must we wait? Since we wait for eternity, must we wait for an eternity? But we grow restless and impatient. We have waited and nothing seems to come. Or perhaps it came but we did not see it pass? And perhaps it is there, and there is no wait, only the call of transformation? We have waited, and still wait, and no God seems to come. What then? Why then transcendence seems to turn over into immanence: first, immanence grieving over its own failure of self-surpassing; then immanence hostile over its previous desire for God; then immanence hostile to God as depriving its own self-surpassing of its own esteem in itself; finally, immanence as willing the immanent esteem of its own worldly self-transcendence. And then there is no more waiting and expectancy. We have arrived – God has arrived. Transcendence overturned. We–God–Ourselves.

If thought is too condensed in these statements, I will thin things in the sequel. To round off this opening sortie: We search other-being as *outer* – nature's astonishing thereness. We search other-being as *inner* – the enigmatic abyss of our own selving. Each of these teases us into thought of God. (Kant: the starry sky above, the moral law within.) And yet God is other to both. But what if we conceive of divine transcendence in *dualistic terms*, as can easily happen? Then no community seems possible between God and creation. Not only does it seem that God withdraws into self-sufficient independence; world and we can seem to do so too. Or it might seem as if the flood tide of the divine ebbs, and world and we find ourselves beached on the solitude of a Godless shore. Something like this ebb of the great tide seems to occur in modernity.

What causes the ebb is very perplexing. Is it the self-withdrawal of God, as some have thought? Or was that space of transcendence always empty? Or have we, in a series of slight shifts – slight as singular, but momentous as a continuing series – blinded ourselves, deafened ourselves, numbed ourselves, though we call our sightlessness, our silence, our anesthesia enlightened? Something of the latter, I think, though I think so as one hard of hearing and as squinting. Yet, given the mystery of God, and the potential for equivocity in our openness to communication, there is some truth to the first suggestion. Our reconfiguration of the primal ethos produces a second ethos, and this makes more difficult our attunement to the signs of the divine. We can see this relative to the ebb: First relative to other-being as outer; then relative to other-being as inner. I mean, first, the desacralizing effects of the devaluation of being in modernity; I mean, second, the atheistic consequences of the self-assertion of human self-transcendence and its idolization of autonomy. In turning now to these points, our concern is the muffling of the signs communicating the divine in the ethos of being, a muffling our reconfiguration effects. At the ultimate, all this comes to nothing. In the chapter to follow, a reborn mindfulness of those signs, a mindfulness born out of the return to zero, will be at issue.

DEVALUED BEING: THE STRIPPING OF THE SIGNS

The sources of the question of God are many, but major sources occur in astonishment and perplexity: astonishment before the sheer givenness of being; perplexity about the intelligibility, the meaning, indeed goodness of that given being. The astonishment is a beginning that is overdetermined, in excess of all determinacy. The perplexity follows the beginning in being a troubled thought about intelligibility, meaning, worth; it begins a move from the overdetermined givenness to a more determinate articulation for us. This perplexity, in turn, begets definite curiosity about the processes at work in the givenness. Out of curiosity the determinate cognitions of science emerge, and with a definite drift towards the utmost possible univocity in our articulation of intelligibility. (I say nothing yet about the urge to use the givenness, to exploit it for our own desires.) This movement from astonishment to perplexity to definite curiosity shows the transcending power of our mindfulness, but it can be fatal with equivocation relative to God. For the question of God does not arise in the determinate cognition of a definite matter of fact about which we are curious. It concerns more our metaphysical astonishment before the givenness of the being-there of being, also our perplexity as to what it might all mean, in relation to origin and end, what the point of it all is in relation to its worthiness to be affirmed as good. The beginning, as indeed the end, is in excess of every curiosity and every determinate cognition.

The question of God precedes science, outlives it, but also always shadows it. It exceeds the will to complete determination that marks the move of curiosity to definite answers. Its excess is not that of an emotional murk that surrounds, like a penumbra, the clear light of our cognition. It bears on a mindfulness impossible to capture completely in the determinate categories of a definite cognition. This mode of mindfulness has not been well respected in modernity, and now is less and less spontaneously understood. Why? Because the momentum of modernity dominantly conceives our development as away from astonishment and perplexity towards as definite a determinate cognition as possible. Even if wonder, astonishment, perplexity are granted in the beginning, these are to be dispelled once the proper unfolding of mind is effected. The former are merely indefinite, and our task is to make things as definite as possible, that is, to conquer completely the putative indefiniteness of the beginning. We may even erect this into a historical destiny: religion for the primitives or children; metaphysics for the rationalistic adolescents; science for the adults come of age. And, of course, *we* are the grown-ups – enlightened, post-Comtean adults. For us, no more religion or metaphysics.

This claim to maturity, one suspects, is rife with misunderstanding, and misunderstanding derived, ironically, from a surfeit of cleverness. For this surfeit of cleverness is accompanied by an enfeebling of astonishment and an irritability with perplexity, especially metaphysical perplexity. The latter resists encapsulation in definite conceptualizations and hence chastens our intellectual self-esteem. Impatience with this resistance, irritation with intractable perplexity, these issue in an unprecedented will to univocalize being, a will that also makes being God-forsaken. But this is not evident at first.

The will to univocalize being is manifest in the project to mathematicize nature such as we find in Galileo, Descartes, and others. My interest is the changed attitude to being in this reconfiguration of the primal ethos. Most important is the loss of intimacy between being and the good, an intimacy witnessed to in a variety of ways in the premodern ethos. In the modern reconfiguration there comes to be a separation of being and the good. For the good is enigmatic and resistant to complete objectification and determination; it poses challenges to the univocalizing mind that this mind cannot fully meet. The premodern sense of the good was often identified with the end, in Aristotle and others, but the end is not univocally determinable. Even less is it possible to subject it to mathematical measure. To the univocalizing mind this is not satisfactory, and so this good is called into question, indeed put out of question, by being denied any place in explanatory schemes of intelligibility.

Excise thus the good and what results? We find ourselves in the between, which is now the ongoingness of process without end: a purposeless between, unless perhaps we reconstruct *ourselves as purposing in the face of the purposelessness of other-being*. The beginning is not good either; it is efficient cause reduced to the mechanism of effecting a happening. The mechanical effecting happens; it has no purpose; it has no good; it is valueless happening. And our condition? Between a worthless beginning and a purposeless end, without end; in a middle that in itself has no worth or inherent end. Upshot: the devaluation of being. Being is in itself worthless. It is there, yes; it is a happening, yes. Does it have value in itself, is its being a good in itself? Such questions should arise but do not properly. Univocalizing mind issues in the devaluation of being.

Can one find signs of God in being thus devalued? Very hard. It is not that efforts were not made; by Pascal, for instance, by Descartes, by many others. The efforts often have a taint of artificiality and strain; they lack the tang of the elemental. It is as if the devalued milieu forces us to more and more twisted ways of finding a way back into the proximity of the divine, and none quite works. Then there comes a point when the atheism of devalued being comes to seem elementally *self-evident*. The twisting and turning is given up; but so also is the mystery of God. Our question then: Are we true to being in devaluing it? Is being as devalued true to being? If not, do we not have to find a different way? Of what is devalued being itself a sign? Nothing, it seems. The outcome seems nihilism. Does the issue, then, become, at least in part, one of a "revaluation" of being, at least in the sense of some restoration of other-being as other, and its inherent worthiness to be affirmed as, in some enigmatic sense, good? If so, would perplexity about God again flare up with passion?

IDOLIZED AUTONOMY: ECLIPSE OF TRANSCENDENCE AS OTHER

Devalued being is not the end of the matter. When we take into account our *own* being, the changed attitude also affects *us*. Just as the givenness of other-being in nature is stripped of the signs of qualitative worth, so also we assume an analogous relation to our own being given to be. For we are given to be before we give ourselves to be. There is a *passio essendi*, a patience of being, more primordial than our *conatus essendi*, our endeavor to be. This patience is intimately connected with our porosity to the divine, for we are first as having received our being rather than as having determined it for ourselves, through ourselves. The *passio essendi* is closer to the more ultimate energizing source of our *conatus essendi* but it also defines the vulnerability of our finitude. This vulnerability may seem exacerbated, if the ethos of other-being is valueless in itself; in fact, our *conatus essendi* seems rather spurred into an activism, a self-activation that can lead even to an extreme of hyper-activism. Then the *passio essendi* is forced into recess as the *conatus essendi*, expressing itself without hindrance, goes into overdrive. The patience of being is overridden in this overdrive of the endeavor to be, so overridden that the porosity to the divine constituting our being religious falls out of focus.

In the reconfigured ethos of devalued being, *we* find *ourselves* between a worthless beginning and a valueless, endless end. Nevertheless, in the middle *we* determine a relation to things. *Our* relativity is not neutral but charged with value. Even if other-being is valueless, *we* cannot be but as valuing being, again even if the value thus unavoidable is value *for us*. There's the rub. If we value other-being as *for us*, can we finally avoid a slide from valueless being into being as instrumentalized? Being is a means to an end; and what is the end? We are the end. Why? Because one necessity we cannot negate is that we are oriented to an end, some end, any end. Nietzsche hits the bull (albeit for different purposes than ours): man would rather will nothingness than not will.

We cannot be but valuing being; we cannot will not to be willing beings; for not willing or willing nothing is still willing. The question is what to will; and indeed how to will. What is the implicit sense of being that determines our relation to other-being, and the sense of our own being as willing? In the context of valueless being, being as a whole cannot escape its demotion to being instrumentalized. But is this not finally true of us also? We may assert ourselves as the power wielding the instrument, but the other we instrumentalize will finally be not only nature but human being itself. The end: *ontological tyranny on ourselves*. I will come to this, for at first the exact opposite seems the truth: namely, that now we are truly released into our own original freedom. As it turns out, the freedom is at best equivocal, at worst delusionary and megalomaniac.

How dare one say this? Do we not live in the epoch of freedom? And was not Hegel at least right about this, though his critics will begrudge him? Let freedom ring! Unhesitatingly, we fall prostrate before this god. But is the prostration not in collusion with the devaluation? For the univocalizing of other-being wills to make being completely determinate, with the loss of inherent value, and so it prepares an empty space *for us* as its proper users. It makes straight the way for *our determining power* as the sole source of value. And so we are a determining origin that passes into and through other-being as a means to itself as the true end. Other-being becomes the medium of our own self-determination. This tends to be the dominant logic of modern freedom, and not in any merely negative sense of freedom from external restraint. There is that, but there is more, namely our freedom to become the power of being we are already in promise. It may take centuries to unfold the implications of these views.

My point is not to deny freedom, but to question any absolutizing of autonomy as the fullest truth of freedom. Modernity exhibits the self-assertion of autonomy: determination comes to mean our power to determine other-being, so that in the medium of other-being, *determination is self-determination.* What is the problem then? The recession of the patience of being, and the reconfiguration, to the point of distortion, of the essential relation to other-being. Other-being serves as the medium of our self-determining: we mediate with other-being because we finally want to mediate with ourselves. We also do not do justice to the intimate otherness of our own *passio essendi.* Self-determination can become a kind of idol, so enchanting to our self-understanding we do not see the equivocal relation to the other it generates. The other may be a means to further freedom or a possible threat, but if the primary stress is on autonomy, the other will always be secondary, serving for the self. The idol: autonomy as a *nomos* of *to auto* subjecting *to heteros* to its law. Not only nature, but God and other humans carry the insinuations of threats to the *auto,* and so their otherness as other has to be "overcome." Of course, if my autonomy must coexist with the justified autonomy of the other, then autonomy cannot be absolutized. We have to rethink freedom outside of the hegemony of autonomy (see *EB, passim* on this). This also means revisiting both our own intimate otherness and God's.

The ontological danger here is that we idolize ourselves and think it our destiny to create the world anew in our image. This project of the will to power is the open secret of modernity. It is an *ontological necessity* that human beings be will to power if being as such is valueless. It has no good, it is no good, it is worthless; we cannot live with this; we must hence *make it worthy.* Worthy of what? Worthy of itself, worthy of God? Rather, worthy of ourselves. We are original, we are the power. And the goal? What could be the point of it all? We are not given the point; we make the point; we will the point to be ourselves. So we say. And the other? The point of the other must be the self. But what is the point of the self when the self is just for itself, and the other is for the self? Finally, no point at all, and the outcome is nihilism. We will come again to this.

TRANSCENDENCES

We can better find our bearings if we distinguish the following senses of transcendence. In broad strokes, they correspond to the other-being of nature, of the self-being of the human, and the difference of the divine. It is not only their character but their interrelations that are important. How we understand them is rooted in our attunement to the primal ethos, and reflected in the reconfigured ethos.

First transcendence (T^1): The transcendence of beings as other in exteriority. The transcendence of such beings consists in their not being the product of our process of thinking; their otherness to us resists complete reduction to our categories, especially in so far as they simply are at all. Their otherness as being at all gives rise to the question: What makes possible both their possibility, as well as their actuality? What makes possible the possibility of their being at all? This is a metaphysical question not about the "what" of their being but the "that" of their being there at all: Why beings and not nothing? The possibility of a further transcendence as other to their transcendence is opened by such questions.

Second transcendence (T^2): The transcendence of *self-being,* self-transcendence. The meaning of possibility is here realized in interiority rather than determined externally. Human self-transcendence is of special moment here. There is possibility as freedom, as the promise of self-determination. We are impelled to the further question: Is this self-transcendence, in relation to the first transcendence (T^1), an anomalous overreaching into emptiness, or a genuine self-surpassing towards an even further transcendence as other? Is our self-surpassing driven by a lack to fulfill only itself, or to seeking fulfillment in what is other to itself? Is it more than lacking and seeking what is infinitely more than itself, whether lacking or not? An important question here: Does our understanding of our own self-transcending rely too much on the *conatus essendi* and not enough on the *passio essendi*?

Third Transcendence (T^3): original transcendence as still *other – transcendence itself,* not as the exterior, not as the interior, but as the superior. This would be a *hyperbolic* sense of transcendence, bringing to mind the question of God beyond the immanence of transcendence in nature and human being. If we were to call this third hyperbolic form "Transcendence itself," it would be in excess of determinate beings, as their original ground; it would be beyond human self-transcendence, as its most ultimate possibilizing source. It would also be beyond the ordinary doublet of possibility/reality, as their most ultimate possibilizing source. It would not be just a possibility, nor indeed a determinate realization of possibility. It would have to be "real" possibilizing power, in a manner more original and other than immanent possibility and realization. It would have to be original, creative possibilizing beyond determinate possibility, and "real" beyond all determinate realization, beyond all self-determining self-realization.

If such third transcendence were in excess of determinacy and our self-determining, would it be but a merely *indefinite beyond* to finite being? If so, would not its participation in the happening of the between be feeble? Is there rather a third transcendence that is not such an empty indefinite but excessive: overdetermined in a surplus sense, hyperbolic, not indefinite? If so, it would not be comprehended under any finite category of the possible or real. It would be above, *huper, über* them, and yet most intimate to finite being as enabling it to be at all, and to be free. What must this possibilizing power be, such as to give rise to finite being as *other* to itself, and hence as possibilizing the finite space, or middle, for first and second transcendence? Such a third transcendence could not be identified with any projection onto some ultimate other of the first two senses. There could be no objectification (T^1) or subjectification (T^2) of third transcendence (T^3). Rather it would seem that second transcendence (T^2), in its ineradicable recalcitrance to complete objectification, is pointed beyond both objectness and subjectness to transobjective and transsubjective transcendence (T^3). And perhaps first transcendence (T^1) is not also devoid of its own ambiguous signs of this hyperbolic transcendence.

Much more must be said, but for now this is the relevant point.[2] Third transcendence (T^3) has been made problematic in modernity, both by a univocalizing objectification of first transcendence (T^1), and by developments of second transcendence (T^2), especially when this last defines itself hugely in terms of its own autonomy. Then a logic of *self-determination* stands guard over all our thinking, and the thinking of what is other to our self-determination. Inevitably, third transcendence (T^3) becomes endowed with an equivocal position. There is a tension, indeed an antinomy, between autonomy and transcendence. This is not just a mere contradiction, but a tension wherein different possibilities for human thought and life take shape. In this equivocal space the traditional respect accorded to third transcendence (T^3) from an essentially religious point of view comes under onslaught. Into that space of equivocality, our "creativity," our "poetry," so to speak, inserts itself, as somehow answering the tension of autonomy and transcendence. Human "art" comes to assume roles previously accorded to religion. Is the antinomy resolved? Or does third transcendence still remain mockingly "beyond" – or welcoming?[3]

THE ANTINOMY OF AUTONOMY AND TRANSCENDENCE

What might be said here of this antinomy of autonomy and transcendence? The ideal of autonomy accents our determining power; it may indeed grant our relatedness to others, yet the primary stress is on self-determining, the *nomos* of the *auto*. By contrast, transcendence must put the stress on the importance of otherness; for the *trans* is a going beyond or across towards what is not now oneself. If God is third transcendence, there is an otherness not reducible to our self-determining. Third transcendence cannot univocally coexist with an absolutized autonomy which is absolutely for itself. Alternatives: if autonomy is primary, third transcendence has to be subordinated; if third transcendence is primary, autonomy cannot be absolute. Western modernity generally has opted for some version of the first alternative, with incalculable consequences for the second.

---

2 We will come to explore the connections between these different senses of transcendences and the hyperboles of being: T^1 is perhaps more intimately tied to the idiotic and aesthetic, T^2 and T^3 (especially with respect to the porosity and passage between them) are more bound up with the erotic and the agapeic.

3 See *AOO*, Chapter 8 "Art and the Impossible Burden of Transcendence," where I also remark on the postmodern response to the antinomy, which tends to equivocate between the aesthetic and the religious.

The choice is more complicated in that the need of transcendence does not die, cannot die. Indeed autonomy is a formation of self itself derived from an energy of transcendence of which we are first beneficiaries rather than possessors. Something of this may even be granted when we acknowledge that the human being is an immanent transcending power. This power is *self-transcendence* (T^2). And so we are tempted to say that in self-transcendence we have *both* autonomy and immanent transcendence; we have no need for an other transcendence.

Can we sustain this reassurance? Suppose we find ourselves, so to speak, slipping below the surface of our own self-transcendence? Open the door into this dark, and what then? What answers this opening is itself a new darkness. The more our self-transcending delves into its own immanent power, the more enigmatic that power comes to seem, and the less we are assured of our autonomy. Our self-transcendence goes beyond itself to what as outer is other, but it also goes beyond itself into its immanent resources, into depths bottomless, depths murky, depths terrifying. The infinite restlessness of human selving in its outward throw shows to us the external side of an infinitely enigmatic abyss in inwardness itself. Step into that abyss and the warm self-esteem of autonomy will soon shiver in strange icy blasts that blow from undiscovered bourns. There is an inward otherness whence energies erupt or surface, and the sure "self" is no master but a derivative therefrom. In a sense, these depths are more intimate with the mystery of the givenness of being in the primal ethos. Perhaps, then, autonomy is less the sovereign it takes itself to be as the dark issue of an origin more enigmatic than its own self-determining powers. Autonomy as self-transcendence opens into transcendence beyond autonomy – opens into, because it opens up out of this more mysterious other transcendence.

There is a dialectical lesson here, rather a double dialectical lesson. First autonomy as self-transcendence only *seems* to solve the antinomy and dialectically overcome the tension of autonomy and transcendence, and indeed surmount every need for reference to a "beyond." This is the first dialectic. But there is a kind of doppelgänger dialectic behind or beyond this. There is an *other otherness* beyond the seemingly dialectically overcome otherness. Immanent exploration of autonomy as self-transcendence shows the self to be the issue of a transcending source not itself self-transcendence. Our self-transcending is first energized by the given endowment of the *passio essendi*, and only then by the endeavor of the *conatus essendi*. Self-transcendence is not made possible by an autonomous self, but the transcendence of the autonomous self is made possible by transcendence as other to self-transcendence. This other transcendence brings us back into the neighborhood of perplexity about God.

This last point is not often granted. If the *other* origin is granted at all, and if there is any breakthrough into the energies of the primal ethos, it tends to be in terms of the occlusion already pervasively at work in the reconfigured ethos. I mean that the devaluation of being produces further results here, both in thinking of human self-transcendence and thinking of the origin as other. The latter is seen in terms of what I will call the *dark origin*; the former is often understood as some variation of *will to power*.[4] To these two points in turn.

DARK ORIGINS AND TRANSCENDENCE AS OTHER

What I mean by "the dark origin" concerns, first, the continued exigence for transcendence as other, even in devalued being, and second, a view of this transcendence that, nevertheless, perpetuates a reflection of the reconfigured ethos of worthless being – "worthless" sometimes in the sense of being merely neutral, other times in the presentiment of its being

---

[4] My points of reference here include Schopenhauer and Nietzsche, as well as Hegel, Kant, and others, and you might say "Surely these thinkers are behind us?" Yet Nietzsche brings something to a head that has not yet had its adequate response. What he uttered was in formation through those who came before him. We still live in the shadow of these thinkers, and how they found themselves in the antinomy of autonomy and transcendence.

hostile to us, perhaps even evil. Still we cannot but ask about the ground or origin of that valueless middle: What is ultimate, what is being ultimately, at bottom, or in origin? Above the reply was heard: there is no ultimate good in the end. Now we hear: there is no good at all in the beginning.

Undoubtedly, we are always tempted to define the ultimate relative to our being in the middle: we reconfigure the primal ethos in terms of ourselves. If we see the middle as worthless, it is hard not to think of the origin/ultimate as also worthless. You interject, benignly, "the middle as valueless is there, indifferently there, neutral: neither good nor evil." I hear you. But can we maintain this stance, finally? For in the middle we twist in the tension of plurality, racked by strains between us and ourselves, between humans, between humans and other beings of nature, between beings in nature other than us. "Nature red in tooth and claw" is hard to blink away, despite all precautions of agnostic indifferentism. *Homo homini lupus*, no honest person can deny, despite all quarantines of studied neutralism. In truth, *no immunization from value is effective finally.* Any agnostic indifferentism seems only a way station along a slippery path from the worthless middle to the worthless origin. More, any suggestion that the origin might be good becomes incredible to those gliding along the frictionless pathway of ontological neutralization. And it is not that *we fail,* that *we* cannot live the truth of a "neutral" world. That is true but not the main point. We cannot live it, because to live always shows the truth of the value of life. Valueless neutrality is impossible because there lives no such thing. Its truth is death. And perhaps not even death, since there is nothing neutral about death.

The point could be elaborated relative to the longer arc of modernity, for the turning of this arc from its upward motion to its downward spiral can be shown *in nuce* in the transition from Hegel to Schopenhauer. It is not incidental that Hegel's *Science of Logic* (1812–16) was written at almost exactly the same time as Schopenhauer's *World as Will and Representation* (Vol. I, 1818). We fail to take much notice of this, perhaps because Schopenhauer only exerted influence well after Hegel's death. And yet the Hegelian hymn to ascendant reason is contemporaneous with the Schopenhauerian descent into a more ultimate darkness prior to reason. Can the ascent of one be divorced from the descent of the other? Do we not still live out of the consequences of that ascent and descent?

Hegel might be seen as the epitome, the consummation of the upward movement of modern self-determination from its first primitive expression to an extraordinarily complex dialectical determination. To be absolute is to be self-determining. I have given many essential qualifications elsewhere (e.g., *Hegel's God*), but Hegel's absolute is identified with the free self-realization of reason itself: the origin becomes itself fully by overcoming the indefiniteness of the beginning, becomes thus completely self-mediating and self-fulfilled. Hegel is one of the major philosophers in modernity who struggled against devalued being (he might not put it thus); but equivocities in his dialectic, with respect to self-determining being and relative to otherness, issue in *both* a claim to the completion of self-determining being, and the dialectical reversal of that completion.

The following is *one way* I would put it (there are others): thought thinking itself is reversed into thought thinking what is *other* to thought. The difficult question is: What is this other? There have been different responses, and the matter is still deeply in question. Schopenhauer reveals something about the reversal, though, oddly enough, it is already prepared in Kant, unbeknown to Kant himself. Reason becomes the bright side of a more basic energy of being other to reason; indeed, in the present instance, other in a way that turns reason into an instrument or means. Reason becomes the slave of will – not sovereign master but a tool. It can be both a *weapon* of the will identified with the dark origin, and a *protection* for humans against this very darkness. Schopenhauer's will is a blind, insatiable striving, a dark version of an erotic absolute; Hegel's *Geist,* or Idea, is a bright rational version of the erotic absolute (see *BB,* pp. 242–51, 260–1; *PU,* pp. 238–51). Could one venture that, after Hegel, the erotics of being present themselves more and more in the form of *eros turranos?*[5]

---

[5] Whitehead speaks of the "eros of the universe" – *Adventure of Ideas* [1933] (New York: The Free Press, 1967), p. 253; also pp. 68, 251, 268; *Process and Reality: An Essay in Cosmology* [1929],

Schopenhauer explicitly stylizes himself as an "atheist," contemptuous of the moral God (Hegel and Nietzsche share something of this contempt). Nevertheless, Schopenhauer has his "god," though this god looks more like Descartes' evil genius than any benevolent Providence. Hegel too has his "atheist" side, detected by Kierkegaard, enacted by Feuerbach and Marx, and other left-Hegelian spawn. A lesson I take from this: the question of God and atheism is not amenable to simple oppositional categories, despite the polemical crudities of some of Hegel's successors. This is the main point here: there is something ironical, in an entirely *just* respect, in the emergence of the dark origin against the horizon of the consummate self-determining rational origin in Hegel. The dream of this idealistic origin begins to bring forth monsters. The human being also becomes hard to see as more than a puppet of this dark origin. We witness the beginnings of the decomposition of the "god" autonomy. More, we see the eruption of dark transcendence *in* human self-transcendence, and yet this darkness tells of a deeper, unfathomable darkness that is other to human self-transcendence.

Here begins the *downward* movement of the arc of self-determining being. It is foolish to think the question of God is finished because of the rash of "announcements" in recent centuries of humankind being beyond religion or God. The downward movement brings us to this point about will to power. We come to think of ourselves in the image of the origin, as well as the origin in our own image. For we are originals, are we not? What does this mean? It means we are sources of origination that instantiate the original power of the ultimate source. If the latter is will, other to thought thinking itself, we too are will, or more affirmatively, will to power. This resort to will to power unfolds rather than transforms the basic ontological attitude governing the situation. And so to the second point.

WILL TO POWER AND THE COUNTERFEIT DOUBLE OF "YES"

In Schopenhauer, art and religion are releases from the *eros turranos* of the dark origin, art episodically, ascetic religion more completely. It is by a radical "no" (a "no" at the roots) to the erotic origin that, pace Schopenhauer, ascetic religions release us. Religion is thus reconfigured in the image of the dark origin as itself the great "no" to life and the evil of the "to be." There is here a certain reversal of "yes" and "no," by contrast with the "yes" to life and the good of the "to be" that we find, for instance, in the great monotheistic religions deriving from biblical inspiration. This reversal is more reminiscent of a Gnostic revulsion to creation as given: "It is not good." At one level Nietzsche inherits this reversal from Schopenhauer, but he also wants to say "yes" against Schopenhauer's "no," and so in a way reverse that reversal. Yet Nietzsche also revolts against the counterfeit double of "yes" he claims to find in the alleged religious "no." But has the deeper truth of the primal religious "yes" to the good of the "to be" already been inverted and corrupted here? A more ultimate "yes" to the God of amen? A God and an amen impossible to grant, finally, outside of some agapeic sense of the origin, and not just an erotic sense? Yes, I think, though the equivocations at play in our intermediate condition are subtle.

Turn again to the downward movement. Kant's affirmation of the autonomy of the moral subject, Hegel's absolute as self-determining spirit, are high points in the upward curve of autonomy. But in the recesses of this development all is not quiet. Both Kant and Hegel contribute to a peculiar *chastening* of reason, the first by the putative *delimitation* of reason's legitimate exercise, the second by its putative *release* from all such delimitation. The other of thought thinking itself shadows the ideal of autonomous being. For our reconfiguration of the primal ethos is always (under)grounded by those ontological reserves of

---

edited by David Griffin and Donald Sherburne. Corrected edition (New York: The Free Press, 1985), pp. 244, 346; *Religion in the Making* [1926] (New York: Macmillan, 1960), pp. 68, 73). Other process thinkers, as well as evolutionary thinkers like Teilhard de Chardin, tend to agree. This eros tends to have resonances of a benign ontological desire, but what of the *tyrannical* form of eros? Mention of this can quickly dissipate the magic charms of eros – unless, of course, one is under the enchantment of a blacker magic.

the ethos that our reconfiguration consigns to recess. Thus our reconfiguration always has its reserved side, and what is recessed is not thereby put out of play. When we begin to suspect this, we will never cease to look over our shoulders at the source of the shadow we cannot see. Our reconfiguring reason will become unsettled and uncertain about itself. Not incidentally, Kant's idealism can be seen as the *self*-critique of reason. Hegel's idealism can also be seen as such – only the self-critique here claims to *overcome* its own critical nature in a speculative affirmation of thought thinking itself; it claims to consume its own shadow. Yet if the other to thought thinking itself gains a hearing, the self-critique opens into an abyss beyond reason; or at the least, reason's pretension to sovereignty is countered. The shadow we flee grows larger as we flee it. The dark on the other side of reason has no sufficient reason, at least in the classical sense: human reason emerges out of this other, and hence is derivative. Schopenhauer calls this other "will," claiming that it is really Kant's thing in itself. Nietzsche calls it will to power. I prefer to resort to the terms of the agapeic origin, for reasons that will emerge.

Will to power seems intelligible enough (paradoxically) if the world is not intelligible in itself. Moreover, if intelligibility is the product of will, we too must "create" the intelligibility, as well as the good of being. Of course, will to power can be given different renditions: the more common acceptation as power *over* the other, through superior dominance and so on; alternatively, as self-affirming power that affirms itself in its own self-increase. In either case, be it the cruder form or the more refined, will to power is finally for its own sake. Nietzsche mixes these senses, though the second is for him the most creative and ultimate source of value. Nevertheless, there is no inherent hospitality of being to value: there is a *disjunction* of being and good, a discordance. Nietzsche sees what is at stake: we cannot finally live with this discordance. Either we have to protect ourselves from the *horror of the truth of being*, be it through Apollonian illusion, Dionysian intoxication, or Socratic–Alexandrian dialectic, or, we can transvalue all value: sing the world beyond good and evil, in all its joy and monstrousness, its rapture and suffering. Nietzschean will to power seeks to overcome the discordance of being and good by affirming all being as "good": highest will to power is the will that in affirming itself affirms all being as it is. Something of all this is to be gleaned from Nietzsche's ultimate love: *amor fati*.

There is much more that could be said here (see *IST?*, Chapter 6). For myself I would ask: What love is this *amor*? Is it eros, or self-affirming love, or philia, or agape? What fate is this? Eternal necessity? *Moira*? The eternal return of the same? But why *love* that? You say it is consent to the happening of becoming? But does "It is so" now become "It must be so"? What kind of amen is this "must"? What kind of "So be it"? For there are counterfeit doubles of "yes." These are not entirely false, but something false in them makes what is true in them false, finally. Then they are false doubles of "yes." What is true in the "yes" to fate? The ultimate love of will to power seems altogether too close to an *eros turranos*. Is there not too much of a hypertrophied *conatus essendi* in this, to the atrophy of the religious porosity of the *passio essendi*? And what then of the bloody crushing of innocence: are we also to sing our "yes" to an evil fate? What kind of "yes" is this? Nietzsche has no satisfactory response to monstrous evil. And he joyfully tells of the world as a *monster* of energy, will to power, and nothing else besides.[6] Who would dream of bowing to this monster? Who would dream of loving it?

You remind me: Nietzsche would not speak of being and good. I grant that, but that is not my problem. Nietzsche, properly interpreted, and this means sometimes interpreted against himself, is on the right track in asking about the ultimate amen; but he is betrayed by the whole horizon of his thinking. What is this horizon? I note four major aspects: First, it is defined by the view of valueless being, worse, by being as pain, even horror, at bottom. Second, by a view of the protective, recuperative power of creative will to power as affirming, *despite* worthlessness and horror. I call this whistling in the dark.

---

6 *Der Wille zur Macht. Versuch einer Umwertung aller Werte* (Leipzig: Kröner, 1930), pp. 696–97 and *The Will To Power*, trans. W. Kaufmann and R. J. Hollingdale (New York: Random House, 1967), pp. 549–50; see *AOO*, pp. 205–6.

Third, by a totalizing claim with respect to will to power (*all being* is will to power, and in either of the above two senses). But this totalized claim cannot sustain in full the sought affirmation. A different consent to otherness is needed – beyond the will to power that either dominates the other or wills its own will. We need an agapeic origination and self-transcendence. Fourth, by the fact that our affirming will to power collapses in view of the totalized will to power: if all being is valueless, we too are valueless finally, in the valueless whole, and all our brave, heroic valuing is swallowed by the valueless whole. Inference: for the Nietzschean affirmation to make any sense at all, there must be some *inherent hospitality* of being to good,

Nietzsche never provides us with the proper ground of this ontological hospitality. Quite the contrary. Despite the self-authorized official profile, he never really escaped from Schopenhauer's pessimism, and the bitter wisdom of the Silenus, companion of Dionysus, expressed in words Nietzsche, as Schopenhauer well before him, liked: "Best of all, not to be; and second best, to die quickly."[7] There are no ontological resources in the later Nietzsche, which allow us unashamedly to say "It is good to be"; though this is just what Nietzsche in practice wants to sing. The song of affirmation of will to power is a song masking its own metaphysical despair, even as it overtly seeks metaphysical consent beyond despair.

What do we learn from this? Taking into account the reconfigured ethos of modernity, and against Nietzsche's own self-interpretation and self-advertisement, the metaphysics of will to power is a *reactive* response to the sickness of devalued being. Try as hard to hide it as he did, it seeks to affirm *despite*. Its sense of human will to power mirrors the sense of the origin as valueless. Is Nietzsche willing to say the origin is good? No. Why? Were he to do so, we would need some straighter talk about God, drawn otherwise than in the crude lines of polemical cartoons. If there is a worthlessness about the origin, there must be a futility about its consummation: there can be no end, only futile striving in the end; and our middle condition is an evasive alternation between a dishonest "creativity" that prides itself on being the original of the value of being and a half honest confession about the ultimate horror of being at all. Schopenhauer had already taken us closer to this point, with less baroque subterfuge. Perhaps Nietzsche never knew that he too arrived there, namely, back at his beginning, circling around a never dispelled despair. And even if active, really reactive, will to power acts, reacts once more, and once more again, there is no really *honest* way finally to avoid the futility of it all.

Valueless being leads to nihilism, it does not matter whether by a scientific, political, or aesthetic route. Let will to power sing its songs, hurl its curses, it still sings and howls within this horizon. It only produces the *posture* of affirmation. And where it seems to allow an other, it is still enthralled by its song of itself. Despite its posture of release to all being other than itself, it is a prisoner of the idol of autonomy. If the origin comes to nothing, the world comes to nothing, our will to power comes to nothing, our affirmation comes to nothing. The rest is rhetoric and pretense. We need an other thinking of origin, world, ourselves and others, an other affirmation. With a singular confusion of vision and blindness, Nietzsche felt the snap of chains, but he leaves us still in chains, even as he exhorts us to lift our legs in dance. We lift our legs, but it is despite the weight of chains. And in the soaring song, ecstatic in its strained and fevered beauty, we cannot quite deafen ourselves to the grim clink of iron. This song, too, is a counterfeit double of the ultimate amen.

RETURN TO ZERO: COMING TO NOTHING

Suppose though there is *some* truth to nihilism. Suppose the origin is worthless, the world void of inherent value, our energy of being either reactive to or transformative of

[7] See especially, Die Geburt der Tragödie (The Birth of Tragedy, 1872), sect. 3: Das Allerbeste ist für dich gänzlich unerreichbar: nicht geboren zu sein, nicht zu *sein*, *nichts* zu sein. Das Zweitbeste aber ist für dich—bald zu sterben." Also AOO, Chapter 6 "Eros Frenzied and the Redemption of Art: Nietzsche and the Dionysian Origin." See AOO, Chapter 5 on Schopenhauer's dark origin.

this worthlessness. What then? No transformation we can effect will change the basic truth of being: It all comes to nothing. But this outcome also includes *us*, and all our grand projects come to nothing. Our reconfiguration of the primal ethos comes to lack any ultimate point.

And do we not experience some such coming to nothing in our knowing, our doing, our feeling for life? *Knowing*: the self-critique of reason in modernity shows reason to *tear itself* apart: reason comes to this impasse – it cannot take *itself* seriously. We shine an excess of our own light on things and the now shadowless things lose their light and weight. The more we rationalize life the more life seems to lack reason.

Doing: we may will to stamp our value on things, but we have to "psyche" ourselves up to the needed act of faith in our willing. We have to become willingly deaf to the quieter sense that such willing is in a void. The will's faith in itself must be sustained through itself alone, that is, through its own lack of faith. And then we meet the ethical relativism that is only the self-deceiving moral chatter that is penultimate to the collapse into ethical nihilism. We will show our hand, but this has no hidden aces, not even a joker, only a sheaf of null cards.

Feeling: the élan of life is drained when we lose the aesthetic feel of the agape of being. We may work ourselves into frenzies of excitement about the latest novelty, but this frenzy is the hysterical mask of a dead numbness. Feelings are the bodies of value. This anesthesia of being is this nihilism of the aesthetic. We should not be fooled by whoops of wow and floods of gush. The sincerity of sentiment is affected in the end if, in the end, it all comes to nothing.

Can we live with this coming to nothing? The simple answer is: no. Our ruses of escape are testament enough to this. We distract ourselves with "meaning." Perhaps we should live the shattering more deeply. We do come to nothing. We are as nothing: a double ambiguous conjunction of being and nothing. We are but are as nothing, and experience our nothingness as the frailty of our finitude, as the perplexity of being that resists being dispelled, as the mystery of being that remains despite our best conceptual maneuvers. The truth brings us to despair of truth, and of ourselves, and of the good. Nihilism, the truth of nihilism brings us to despair of God.

Despair may destroy; despair may also bring one to a bottom, to a crisis, hence to a turning point. What can happen then? The idol of autonomy can be broken open. The shattered idol shows us nothing, shows us our own nothingness. Coming to nothing may be the reopening in us of the porosity of being. The event of being shattered is not in itself decisive; it is more the moment of truth in which we must decide. It is critical in this exact sense: it brings on a crisis. We are brought before judgment. The ordeal is an *oordeel*, a judgment, as much on us as our being called to judgment. Equally so, the crisis is a *krinein*, it asks for a discrimination. And what then, on this sharp edge that cuts (us) to the quick? We can give the doubleness of our "being as nothing" over to nothing. Or we can live the tension of our "being as nothing" differently. The ghost of God haunts the despair of nothing.

Nihilism? Surely this is your wonted tendency to exaggeration, dramatic and postured. Tosh. Nihilism? – a posture, once à la mode, now passé for the advanced intellectuals who have gone way beyond it to the weightless delights of unencumbered irony. While for those who reckon less on these advances, surely we live in an age of comfort and air-conditioning, and niceness. Nihilism? Come now!

Yes, there is something to such a protest. And yet . . . at the bland heart of having a nice day horror can nest – and the niceness of it all, if finally without ultimate point, hints more a horror than an honest confession of horror that it all comes to nothing. Niceness can be a profane parody of the agape of being, but it grins with emptiness, if that agape is gone. And that indeed is nihilism – the faking of the festivity of this agape. Let us have a nice day, but let us not sleep too deep in the comfort of this shadowless light.

For the various projects of will to power hide failure, not on the obvious level of pragmatic successes, but at a subtler level of metaphysical basics, that is to say, estrangements from the primal ethos. Pragmatic successes may hugely crowd the foreground of our everyday absorptions but they crowd out the hollowness – in the background – of our hold on metaphysical basics. Can one carry on as if calculated contentment with the necessary pragmatic compromises were enough, as if it were in bad taste to be passionately earnest about this ultimate issue? Pragmatic compromises are essential and necessary, but gird them round with prudent rationalizations and we may reveal less our fear of truth as perhaps alarm at what might be required of us, were we truthful. Perhaps the archaic disquiet, in being startled by traces of the divine, attuned more to the primal ethos, was a more noble disquiet. (Once upon a time the atheist had to go in hiding; being godless enforced esotericism. Who now among the savants is the inquisitor – the pious or the impious? Is it the pious who now must dissemble, become differently esoteric? Query too exoterically posed, perhaps.)

Suppose coming to nothing, "being as nothing," constituted a kind of ontological ordeal. Suppose in this there is both a deepening and a sifting: deepening, since we are thrown back on ourselves; sifting, in that we may be purged of impediments blocking our release to what is beyond us. Self-knowing may come to know that self is not enough, and ask if there is an other beyond self, intimated either in the inward otherness of the *passio essendi*, or in the transcendent as other (be it inner or outer, it does not matter). Suppose the return to zero intensifies the tension in the antinomy of autonomy and transcendence, and at a certain pitch of stress, the idol of autonomy crumbles. The antinomy need not be resolved simplistically relative to one side or the other. Rather, in breakdown there may be offered a breakthrough; and not of transcendence as simply *in opposition* to autonomy, but of transcendence as communicating a quite other exigence, calling on the release of our seeking beyond autonomy.

Seen so, this ordeal does not offer a secular *nunc dimittis* which dispenses us to turn away from perplexity about ultimacy. Faced with the blank front of pointlessness, the ordeal returns us to a zero point. World, or self, or others do not vanish, but finding their immanent point forsaken, the point of it all must be sought again by us. Can return to zero resurrect a new perplexity, intensified by loss? Can it hollow out a purer space in which we can seek anew concerning the divine? Can it prepare for a resurrected patience to ultimate transcendence, a new porosity to God?

Chapter 2

Beyond Godlessness

We have looked too low
The ground beneath us
Falls away
& joy leaps up in us
Out of nothing
Leaps out of itself
Leaps out of more than itself
& the elemental world is there
Again

In the leap
Joy looks up
As well as out
We dare no longer
Look too low
More than ourselves
We look for more
Again

THE ANGEL OF DEATH, BEING AS GIFT

What is our concern now? To see if we can start on a way beyond godlessness. Can our return to zero enliven again our taste for the ethos of being and its signs of transcendence? I detect the lineaments of a countermovement to the absolutization of immanent autonomy. This absolutization shows the extreme temptation of self-transcendence (T^2): self-divinization. This happens in the flood tide of the *conatus essendi* that overwhelms, overtakes the *passio essendi*. Godlessness suggests a certain recession of the *passio essendi* and a certain accession, a "takeover" of the *conatus essendi*. Moving beyond godlessness suggests a renewed relief of the *passio*, and a qualification of the *conatus* that brings it home to its proper reserve. There is a turning in the flood tide of the godless endeavor to be. For though the return to zero can seem like the ebb tide of the *passio essendi*, it can also be a turning around which allows flow in our porosity, a new communication patient to the divine. In the inner otherness in excess of our self-determination, there are signs of transcendence as other (T^3) in our self-transcending (T^2).

For the return to zero may be the nihilism of despair, but it need not only be that. It may be a different nihilism: a nihilating of despair in despair. Does despair call us beyond our contracted configuration of being and to a new communication of the ontological promise of the primal ethos? Likewise, does the return to zero bring the I of self-insistence, even the I of ideal self-determining, closer to its own being as nothing? Can a reborn I, beyond self-insistence, beyond self-determining, come to be in the nothing, in a new release of transcending, as willing to be other, both in itself and for other-being? Is there not, as religions have often indicated, a saving despair? You object: Is this not just religious nihilism? But the point need not be intended Nietzsche-wise: that is, religion – the "bad" nihilism. Quite other to Nietzsche's "strong nihilism," this other "nihilism" can be profoundly affirmative.

One wanders a desert that bleaches with burning light, or one is exiled to a Siberia of soul that freezes, or one is fleshed together with perishing, as with one's Siamese twin; one has become as nothing, and one is kissed, before one knows it, by the angel of death. What is the kiss? It is a Golgotha of our human hubris. The kiss opens our sightless eyes. One sees the same things but sees the sameness as other. The wings of the angel beat quietly but in the unbearable terror of her approach being suddenly shows the beauty of thereness as absolute gift. Being is given, and it is given for nothing – nothing beyond the goodness of its being, and of its being given. The terror liquefies the world that one has fixed. The world configured as worthless also seems to dissolve. Something else is offered: a taste of the elemental goodness of the "to be" – abundance without a why, beyond the sweetness of its being at all. Here commences a reversal of nihilism, and a redoubled search for God, for we seem to be given to be again, redoubled in being.

Is this to speak of signs – and speak of signs in signs? Perhaps. A shadow falls as the angel of death spreads its wings over us. The shadow is shadow only because a light is cast from beyond the wings. We do not see the source of this light. We see the glow that bends around the wings. The glow communicates a startling halo to the thereness of things. One goes towards the death that crushes one; one goes down, one goes under; one is as dead; reborn to a different mindfulness, one sees beyond purpose: pointless seeing that sees in the pointlessness. The point? Not proximately a new finite teleology: neither an external teleology imposed by a specific end for us, nor an immanent teleology of autonomous self-determination. To what point then? The return to zero releases the energy of coming to be into a *new interface with creation*. Another sense of goodness matters, purposeless and purposing at once: good beyond determinate good and evil and our self-determination. The redoubled beginning: to be, to be again, and for no reason beyond the good of being, as if one were given to be anew, like a child, or as if, in another way, vouchsafed a light by the angel beyond the terrible struggle of life and death.

GOD AND POSTHUMOUS MIND

Is this too much, too intolerably cryptic? What are you getting at? Something of this. At a way of mindfulness, beyond the reductive alternatives either of being as reduced to a particular finite teleology (the kind that some attribute, not justly, to premodern views) or of being as reduced to the valueless world of modernity, be it the worthless thereness of the scientistic picture, or the purposeless being beyond good and evil of Nietzschean becoming. There is a sense of the good, not first bound up with a definite finite purpose and not merely purposeless either. It concerns the good of origin, and of coming to be as beginning again and again: being as perennial resurrection into thereness, out of nothing. This is the gift. This is being given all the time, though we risk failing to heed it all the time. The kiss of the angel wakes us to resurrected beholding that heeds the process of being as perennial re-creation.

I am speaking about what I call posthumous mind (see, for instance, *PO*, pp. 278ff.; *BB*, pp. 36ff., 40ff.,192–3, 199–200, 264, 503). I mean something like this. Suppose one were to die and then come back from the dead and now look upon what is there, beyond the instrumentalizing mind dominating so much of our first life, free of the will to power that endeavors to impose itself on being, or even affirm itself; free now to look on being as given in its otherness, loved for its otherness and not just for what it is for us? I venture that this would signal some resurrection of the agape of being, the astonishment also given to us in the first life. This first life loses its joy, falls into perplexity, seeks to recover its point in a curiosity that falls under the spell of things, though it essays to be their lord. Posthumous mind implies an outliving of the enchantments of the first spell: beyond the bewitchment of our own autonomy, come to be vigilant beyond ourselves, come to be welcoming of traces of a transcendence other to ourselves and given things (T^3). For suppose the return to zero were a death in that sense, that is, also a promise of rebirth, beyond all will to power? Posthumous mind would then entail a second astonishment before the agape of being. Would this be void of a second perplexity? No, but this would be beyond the determinate cognitions that more or less satisfy our curiosity about determinate beings and processes. The agape of being is communicated as overdetermined; ambiguity is constitutive of its manifestation. It gives rise to the second indeterminate perplexity that is not answered by any definite cognition of a determinate being or state of affairs. It is in this second dimension that God is to be sought again.

The kiss of the angel of death awakens posthumous mind to the thought of God, beyond the determinate cognition that seeks to put every finite thing and process in its definitive place, beyond the sovereignty of our mastering autonomy, beyond the erotic glory of our will to power, beyond also the despair of coming to nothing. For this coming to nothing awakens us to finitude as finitude, and thus also to the beyond of finitude in the very gift of finitude. As it turns out, it is often only at the extremity of being lost that this kind of truthfulness comes to us. No one can see God and live, the saying is. But we live more than once, we die more than once, and we must die in the right way, to find our eyes awakening, as if from the blindness of a former life. And all this, now, right now. There is paradoxically a new kind of blindness: everything seems to be in its place as before, but now its familiar face has become foreign to one, and one has to grope over it anew, suffering the unsettling communication of its strangeness. A new patience of being is needed. Learning it, perhaps posthumous mind may turn out to be a born-again mindfulness of the signs of the divine, as communicated in and through the ethos of being.

OUT OF NOTHING: POROSITY AND THE URGENCY OF ULTIMACY

Put the point another way: *nihilism strangely makes the light itself strange.* Were nihilism the ultimate truth, we would expect no light, and yet light there is. We see the "truth" of nihilism in a light that nihilism, were it true, would render impossible. What is that light? Is it something in which we are, in the more primal ethos of being, which we do not bring to be, but rather *we are simply what we are* as participants in it? Has it also anything to do with the shining that bends around the wings of the angel? Does the resurrection of astonishment in posthumous mind also imply a rebirth of what I call the urgency of ultimacy?[1]

Different possibilities are here suggested. The ultimate can be named in a variety of ways. Some of these will fix on what is not ultimate, and then our name will tag an idol. Even nihilism sings its *Te Deum*: nothing is ultimate. It seems impossible to step outside some relation to what we take as ultimate. A very revealing fact is that we humans are capable of idolatry *at all*. I take this as indirect confirmation that our being is religious. Even when we deny ultimacy, as in nihilism, our being is to be in relation to ultimacy. Ultimacy is not nothing, otherwise there is no relation, and no ultimate, and we would not be what we are.

Consider the urgency. We do not create the relation to ultimacy; we are in the relation, are what we are in it. What urgency shows is the exigent articulation of the relation in our mindful desiring. An urgent happening is not first the outcome of some deliberate choice. It may communicate from within or from without, or both. Its source may be immanent or transcendent, or both. An obscure passion is precipitated and we are importuned. Opportunity comes in the importunity. Something disturbs our more settled forms of domesticated life; something more absolute importunes us; a gap of difference opens, through which we are coaxed into a deeper rapport with the primal ethos.

Such urgency is ecstatic – it catapults us *beyond* ourselves. From within out it surges from abysmal sources beyond secure self-consciousness, and so communicates the secret intensities of our being. Its movement is also from without in: there is an opening inward – an inbreaking that is a startling outbreak of obscure intimation. In the urgency a *dawning* comes over us. There is the bite of the unbidden about the urgency that breaks up our smug self-satisfaction. It brings unquiet to our vaunted autonomy, stressing it, even shattering it. A longing springs up in a descending darkness that we do not determine, though gropingly we cast around for direction. Drawing us deeper within, it drives us further out beyond. The urgency of ultimacy can erupt any time, anywhere, from any direction, from

---

[1]   I speak of being religious thus in *PO*, Chapter 3; I qualify this now with relation to the importance of the *passio essendi*.

no one direction in particular, from no direction we can detect, in dreams and waking, in gravitas and frivolity, in laughter, in reverence, from above, from below, from the secret places of earthy immanence, and from the humbling immensities of cosmic exteriorities.

Consider now the ultimacy. Urgency of ultimacy: the "of" is ambiguous. Is the ultimacy of our urgency, thus revealing only our transcending (T^2)? Or is it *of us* only because more fundamentally the urgency is *of ultimacy* (T^3)? "Ultimacy" seems to refer us to an end, but here, as seeding urgency, it is a beginning. Ultimacy makes our being urgent, but one might say we would not be urgent about ultimacy *at all*, were not the urging of ultimacy somehow already leavening our being. The urgency brings the urging of the ultimate to desire, to mindfulness. Urging points us beyond ourselves because it communicates a source in us that disquiets, rouses, moves, and quickens. We are moved by, we strive towards, the ultimate out of the urgency of ultimacy.

Of course, often in determining the ultimate we inappropriately reduce it to this or that thing, and so we secrete a pantheon of idols. The urgency of ultimacy shows us to be participants in a process that is equivocal, reflecting our ontological situation in the middle. We cannot but reconfigure the primal ethos, and so we always risk vainly reading *our own face* into any initial intimation of the ultimate. Our condition is conducive to ambivalence, distortion, obfuscation, impertinence, and refusal. To be released to the otherness of the ultimate we have to undergo a transformation of mindfulness.

A great danger is to construe the "urgency of ultimacy" too much as just *our* urge: *our* will to be in relation to the ultimate. This is not entirely wrong – we are such a willing. But there is something more primal at the roots of this urgency of ultimacy: the *passio essendi*. Before the *conatus essendi*, our urge to be, to be in relation, there is the *passio essendi*, our passion of being, our already being in relation. The word *conatus* itself points back to this in its meaning of "born with, co-birth." *Co-natus* refers back to a being with, to generating community. One might even think of a prior porosity that is like a fructifying womb, a mother who becomes fertile. The *conatus* points back to the *passio*, as well as carrying it forward. The urgency of ultimacy is itself an expression of the *passio essendi* in which our being given to be is more primordial than our endeavoring to be. Before the seeking in which we are put in question and put ourselves at risk, there is a porosity of being which is always already presupposed by all our acts of self-transcending. Being religious brings us home to the primal porosity of being. This is the living middle between the soul in its most abyssal intimacy and the divine. In this porosity, the communication of what we later call prayer happens.[2] Thinking itself is a later formation of the self-transcending of mind which is rooted in the primal porosity: the self-transcending power of thinking is derivative from this primal porosity. Is this our being, what we are: porosity to the divine? Porosity which gifts us with the power to be beyond ourselves; porosity that allows us to be beside ourselves, for already the beyond is beside us, beside us before we are with ourselves in a self-knowing way?

The porosity of being is not a vacant emptiness but is endowed and empowered. It is a "being nothing" which is the potency to open to everything. Describing it in terms of the return to zero implies a *fertile void*, not just a nihilating one. Its endowments are important for how we conceive further the redoubled beginning beyond godlessness. I give mind to fundamental ontological endowments that make us porous to the hyperbolic in immanence: the elemental, the idiotic, the aesthetic, the erotic, the agapeic. These endowments exert various influences in different ways to God, as well as in different notions of the divine, as we will see in detail later.[3] The redoubled beginning concerns a kind of

2 In *IST?* Chapter 8 I write of a primal reverence in which religion, philosophy and science participate, albeit differently stressing it. Being religious is closest to the root of this reverence; philosophy's own roots are buried close to a religious occasion in a not merely contingent way.
3 I use the language of potencies in *Ethics and the Between*, with somewhat different variation on the fundamental endowments when I speak of the idiotic, aesthetic, dianoetic, transcendental, eudaimonistic, transcending, and transcendent potencies of the ethical. The difference here bears on our being guided by the urgency of ultimacy, without losing intimacy with the porosity.

ontological hermeneutic of the primal ethos via these endowments. They offer us signs of the origin, as communicated in the between as the ethos of being. In a way, our question now becomes: Does a Hermes surprise us in the wake of the angel of death?

REDOUBLED BEGINNING: ELEMENTAL YES

The return to zero restores us to a condition of ontological vulnerability in which we are confronted with an "either/or" between an elemental "yes" or "no." I recall that the Hermes figure – Terminus in Rome – was a boundary stone marking the space between the living and the dead. I further recall that Heraclitus said that Dionysus is also Hades (Frag. 15). The return to zero puts us in a place that is noplace. There is no "bottom"; nevertheless, we have reached "bottom" in the ordeal. And yet: though coming to nothing, we are not nothing. Though we might feel we are as nothing, nevertheless we still participate in an elemental affirmation of being at all, in that we continue to be. As being at all, we are already an affirmation of the good of the "to be" – even in the return to zero, it is good to be.

For we are first an ontological "yes" – this surges in and through us in the *passio essendi*. But we are confronted with a further "either/or": either "yes" or "no" in an elemental sense to being and the good of the "to be" in its worthiness to be affirmed or refused. If we say "no," we may go under into despair. If we say "yes," the "yes" is not determined by anything other than the rightness of the "yes," and its fidelity to the given *passio essendi*. By virtue of the latter we are already participants in a primal affirmation of the good of the "to be" – ontologically we are the living of this affirmation before we know of it, and live it more mindfully. We can live in express refusal of this prior living "yes." If here there is a second "yes" to the first "yes," it is the mindful springing up again of the affirming energy of being, in our porosity to what is beyond us, and in the finite rapport of self-being and other-being.

There is *no argument* for the first living of the ontological "yes"; it is a happening. Nor is there an argument that moves us into the second express living of the elemental "yes" or "no," though there may be arguments and reminders that condition our being brought to this pass. The second "yes" or "no" is, as we say, the moment of truth. Much may bring us to this pass, and much more may flow from it. But it is not the product of reason, since being reasonable flows from the trust in being that marks the first "yes," reaffirmed in the second. One might say that confidence in reason is grounded in a prior fidelity, a *con-fides*, or confiding that comes with the elemental "yes." There is a sense in which our very being is simply the elemental "yes," but since we have lost ourselves, we have to seek to regain ourselves. Certain kinds of life lose us the "yes," so we must think through the "yes" and its meaning again, live towards it, live in it. And just as one may live despair, not knowing it, or knowing wherefrom it comes, one may be in this "yes," live it without noticing it or its wherefrom. One might even know, in an abstract intellectual way, that one should live it, but some enigmatic block has clogged our porosity to it. Least of all must we forget that there can be counterfeit doubles of the "yes." I mean: our second "yes" may appear to be true to the first "yes," but it is feigned. A feigned affirmation says "yes" but does not say "yes."

At this level, we participate in perhaps the most primal endowment of being: no mere possibility, but the incontrovertible power of the "to be" as affirmatively singularized in our own affirmation of the good of "to be." We come *not* to be in it, only in the *relative* respect that our negation is *despite* this ontological affirmation which is our being. The negation is only because to be is already to be good. We turn from the living of consent because a determinate satisfaction or pleasure, or desire, or its violation, or frustration, turns us into disappointed being, into vain or despairing being. The living affirmation has an overdeterminacy about it; specific choices are determinate, and free, and hence consonant or dissonant with the primal overdeterminacy. Often, in fact, rejections of God flow frequently from *specific determinacies* (say, rebellion against the hypocrisy of a sanctimonious and domineering parent). But there is the more elemental level of consideration. Thus the primal overdeterminate "yes" can be overtaken by an *indeterminate* *"no"* to being, become an indefinite rancor that on specific occasions is expressed very definitely: I hate just this or that, but the specific hate springs from a more pervasive festering "no." If one is in this condition, one may be unable to consider God, or one's rejection of God *may* flow from not quarrying deep enough into the sources of one's "yes" and "no." Or one's rejection may "know" at some deeper level that what one now rejects always looks one in the face. It is at a deep down intimate level that one is clogged.

Given to enjoy the sweetness of the "to be," we participate in an affirmative counterpart to such a state of indeterminate "no." We might speak of an ontological pleasure – a being pleased with being. This is elemental: it does not derive from something else, but other "yeses" derive from it. This means also that to touch bottom with the elemental "yes," one might have to be stripped of derivative "yeses" and "noes"; at the least their potential for tyranny must be put out of play. There is a poverty here demanded: the stripping of false selves. It may be extremely difficult to come to this naked "yes." A life of counterfeits of being may cling to one like a false skin. Having lived thus and thus one just *is* that false skin. To strip it away will feel like being flayed. We may need the discipline of a new asceticism: an *askēsis* that is a "no" seeking to waken again the elemental "yes" that endows and blesses us. Any violence here, of course, is fraught with ambiguity, indeed danger. The stripping that claims to purify might secretly derive from the indeterminate negation rather than the elemental "yes." We are a mingling of opposites, and great discernment is needed to sift them. There is an asceticism of hatred; there is a purging of love; and hatred may speak the language of love. To see the difference we need love, but love may be what we most lack.

IDIOTIC REBIRTH

The rebirth is *idiotic*. By "idiocy" I mean an intimacy of being at the limit of discursive objectification in terms of any neutrally public conceptualization (*PU*, Chapter 3). One must have something of idiot wisdom (*PO*, pp. 309–11) to see that the quest of God is ultimate for us. It is idiotic in a number of ways connected with the intimacy of our participation in the original power of the "to be" as good. First, it goes to the roots of intimacy of self-being, our pre-objective, indeed pre-subjective, powers of being. Here we come alive again to the porosity of our own being and its *passio essendi*. Objectivist modes of thinking do not adequately aid us here. We have to plumb the intimacy of human inwardness. It is there that the ordeal of nihilism and despair occurs: the desert is within – or the fertile void. Nor are we to think in terms of solipsistic subjectivity. Quite to the contrary, the most idiotic inwardness reveals selving to be as communicative being: it is itself in relation to what is other to it. There is its own inward otherness, but there is another otherness more intimate than this inward otherness. This is not incommunicable, but the task of communicating it is formidable and almost impossible if one's interlocutor has not kept touch with the idiocy of her or his own being.

The language of idiocy might sound strange, but consider Augustine's classic utterance (*Confessions*, 3, 6): God is *interior intimo meo*, more intimate to me than I am to myself. The deep truth of this is not easy to articulate. If the intimacy of our being is idiotic, how much more idiotic is the intimacy of the divine beyond this self-intimacy. It is as if one entered a darkness, first to come upon a source of light, and then, dwelling with this, the conviction grows that this first light is really second, and that there is another light more ultimate and intimate. Of course, if two lights *mingle*, it is difficult even to say: "There are *two* lights." One exclaims: "There is light!" – though one is not less in the dark for saying this. Yet the idiocy in question makes one pause and wonder: "The light is not my light, perhaps even the light that is mine is ultimately not mine at all." To insist that anything, even what is most my own, is *just* "mine" alone – this now seems untrue. The idiocy is not at all solipsistic: it is the happening of a community prior to determinate subjectification and beyond final objectification.

Second, the rebirth is idiotic because there is no completely compelling path along the road of objective knowing to the place of resurrected religious porosity. Would that there was a *geometry of God* in which, one's beginning secured with certainty, one could advance by measured rational procedures to demonstrated conclusions. There is no such geometry. The beginning is wonder and bafflement. It is less the *esprit de géométrie* we need than the *esprit de finesse*. The powers of demonstrative reason need not be eschewed, but alone they lack the final discernment to touch the heart of the matter. The power of our reason takes its energy, its confidence from its communion with this heart. This heart is idiotic, though not merely subjective. One could say it is the "subject" that is in question, but the "subject" is not "subjectivistic." Nor is the idiocy idiotic, for there is an idiot wisdom. But there is no objectivist science of it.

Third, the rebirth is idiotic because we have to endure in a lack of certainty. Probing the intimacy of being, there is riskiness and hazard. One is traveling a way unsure of what one will encounter, unsure, more unsure, of oneself and the resources needed for this wayfaring. One will be put to the test, a test that is not an objective testing. At moments of faltering one hopes there will be aid. What reason does one have for this hope? Objective reasons none, in the respect in which objective reasons give us hope about the conformity of past and present *determinate* happenings to future happening. But the *overdeterminacy* of this way asks for a hope that has nothing to do with objective predictability. One might even say that one idiotically hopes for the miraculous – the miracle not univocalized as a determinate happening that ruptures objective causality or predictability, but rather as a transformation of mindfulness and manifestation from another dimension beyond determinate objectification or subjectification. Relative to objective and subjective determination this other dimension is idiotic with a necessity of its own neither objectivist nor subjectivist.

Fourth, the rebirth is idiotic for those enlightened, even those post-enlightened, who squirm at the divine intimacy. Going in, one has to be willing to go outside, risk what the more shrewd will consider, say, a suicide to a scholarly career. One may have few external props in this going in going outside. This might even seem a great arrogance, as if one were relying on oneself absolutely. The opposite is more nearly true, in that one is ushered to this place, while filled with fear that the quest is folly. One might even exclaim: "I would turn away if I could, but I cannot." Why not? Because were one to turn, one would be betraying a call that, strangely, insists on nothing, yet is absolutely importunate. One is entering wild country or virgin terrain. Though one has the presentiment that numberless others have trod these paths before, everyone who treads them does so as if for the first time. Why again then? Because the call is addressed to one's unique singularity. The idiocy of the question of God does not call to humankind in general; it calls to the singular human, even though every human is that singular. The idiocy of the singular call is not the opposite of the universal. It has to do with intimate access to the ultimate porosity, and there is a communication of the universal here, but it is not the general or the abstract class. Being religious has to do with the intimate universal.

AESTHETIC RECHARGING

The rebirth is *aesthetic*. If the idiocy is first pre-subjective and pre-objective, this does not exclude our being turned towards the thereness of being as sensuously manifest. Again the impossibility of solipsism is implied. There is an intimacy of our being with the glorious presencing of creation. This is pre-subjective and pre-objective, if by subjective and objective we imply a context determined by oppositional others. Rather there is a togetherness of selving and othering prior to their counterposition in this subjectivist or objectivist sense. Yet this togetherness is both "objective" in that *it is there*, out in the world, and "subjective" in that *it is here* in the concrete thereness of our fleshed presence to the world. I call the rebirth aesthetic, because aesthetic invokes both *ta aesthētika* of other-being and *aisthēsis* on our part. There is an immediate dynamic flow back and forth between the aesthetic things and our *aisthēsis*, a fluency richly articulated, though not acknowledged initially in our reflective categories. Our patience of being vibrates in attunement with the saturated glory of creation.

Why is this important? In a rebirth of our aesthetic mindfulness, we are offered again the charged presence of creation as other. We are brought closer to the primal ethos. Nothing like the neutral, valueless thereness of post-Cartesian objectivity holds. The qualitative presencing of the world as other is given to us over and over again. Very relevant here is the *power of art* to recharge our feel for other-being. Art woos us to attend to intimacies of nuance that our pragmatic or scientific objectifications pass over. Art and the great artist can have a significant role in renewing our rapport with creation, recharging our responsiveness to being as mystery, and hence mediately to its ultimate origin. In this light, there is always a religious dimension to art, just in its power to precipitate astonishment and perplexity. With the latter alive, our porosity is kept fresh, and there is less chance that the urgency of ultimacy will be dulled and assuaged with a faded finitude.

The rebirth as aesthetic makes us mind being-other as *incarnation*. There is a flesh of givenness, a flesh that reaches its apotheosis in the human body. You might say: this is all very well with the human being; it is mere anthropomorphism with being as other to us. Yes and no, for anthropomorphism is double-edged. Ordinarily we see anthropomorphism as the imposition on other-being of our sentimental wishful thinking. This indeed is often true, this so-called pathetic fallacy. Yet there may be *another* "anthropomorphism," at least in this sense that, more primally, there is a *community of togetherness between us and creation as other*. We seem to be imposing ourselves on the other-being, but at another more primal level, the other-being is coming to us as manifest differently, prior to the disjunction of other and us that feeds the first sense of anthropomorphism. This might as easily be reversed so as to suggest that the forms we exhibit emerge as much out of a call from the other as from an urge on our part to impose ourselves on the other. Here it is we who are patient.

If we have passed the stages above, especially the ordeal and the stripping, there is a very diminished will to anthropomorphism in the first sense. This other "anthropomorphism" emerges when one has abdicated humanistic hubris. It might better be called an *indirect heteromorphism*, indirect because it seems to originate with us, yet its origin is far more complex, coming from a pre-determinate community between us and the *heteros*, and owing its form as much to the *heteros* as to us. It may be pathetic in quite another way to the "pathetic fallacy": we do not impose our pathos, our feeling, on things other, but we *undergo a pathos*, a suffering, a receptivity to the other as other.

Our being opened to beauty is the embodiment of the ontological "yes" we encountered before. To say "This is beautiful" is to say "yes" to it. To it: not indirectly to one's own feeling, as if the other were a mirror through which one merely detoured back to one's self. Not at all: "*This* there is beautiful." I affirm *it*. I go out of myself in an ecstasis of self-transcendence. The body that feasts on the beauty of the other is simply aesthetic self-transcending, that comes to rest in the other, and that, in the rest, is energized and refreshed in a manner that seems the opposite of rest: there is a resting in the given energy of being itself, and as good, as valued for itself, and affirmed in this valuing as valuable for itself.

If we are deficient in the aesthetic "yes," what signs could be given to shake us into the thought of God? Live in a world one deems utterly ugly – would the thought of God spring up as an affirmative thought? Or would it tend to be a compensatory outlet for our feeling of lack? True, religion *per se* has been saddled with this last description, but this is clearly one-sided. There is a religious affirmation fostered in the same family as the aesthetic "yes." It is the beauty of creation as given in its otherness, to be affirmed as good for itself, that sets in motion this other moving of self-transcendence that feeds on a hunger beyond finite satiation, not on a compensatory satisfaction beyond one's present dissatisfaction. This thought of God springs from plenitude not lack.

This aesthetics of creation has significance for the ethos of being, for it affords a habitation different to what we find with the valueless being of objectivist thereness. If the latter is one of the sources of atheism, the former is both a source of premodern religion, as well as a necessary way station to religion beyond modernity. The idolization of autonomy is also called into question: the self-determining subject is *not* in charge of the aesthetic charge of creation. The pathos of undergoing makes us first suffering selves. We suffer joy in being; this joy comes to us and we find ourselves enjoying being. Joy and enjoyment are *ontological passions*, not products of autonomous reason or will.[4] Absolutize the latter, and this joy might seem like an unintelligible and incomprehensible poverty. Perhaps it is a poverty, but the nihilism of idolatrous autonomy cannot get a fix on the plenitude of this poverty.

Bear in mind an unavoidable equivocity with regard to the aesthetic "yes." Our intimate rapport with creation, and it with us, takes body in an overdetermined ethos in which opposites, in fact, are often mingled. What is "yes" and what is "no"? What is of us and of the other? What is of creation in itself and what is of the origin? None of these are straightforwardly set apart. Perhaps we can never definitively set them apart. The aesthetic "yes," mingles a "yes" to self and to other, a "yes" to world and to its origin, and this doubleness of the "yes" can tell against the fullness of ultimate transcendence that would be set forth in the "yes." Thus: self-transcending, I would affirm the other, without squashing self; but I find that, in affirming the other, it is more myself that I would celebrate. Thus too: I affirm the origin, so I say, but discover later that it was the world that I was divinizing all along, or perhaps even my own sweet self. The equivocal doubleness never entirely disappears, even when we have been cultivated into mindful finesse for the counterfeit doubles of the divine.

The most baffling and dispiriting side of this doubleness, striking at the heart of our religious porosity, comes home to us with *evil*. Evil as radical, in its roots, pertains to the idiocy of the monstrous (see *BHD*, Chapter 4), that is, pertains also to the intimacy of being. The aesthetic may seem either prior to good and evil, or beyond them, as having suspended them as moral categories. This is not entirely wrong relative to certain complex considerations, but it does not touch the present point. Just as beauty is related to ontological affirmation, the ugly brings out in us our ontological disaffirmation: we are not, cannot be, completely at home in the world, despite its overwhelming beauty. The ugly is not a "merely" aesthetic category, though it has been made that, and there are senses of the ugly that are merely "aesthetic" in the modern post-Kantian usage. More deeply, the ugly pertains to that in being from which we recoil: what repulses us, what disgusts us, what we hate in our living recoil.

That we so hate, shows us loving good; for we would love the good to be there instead of the ugly we hate. It also shows us as defective in love, and hence what is disgusting is also our own sweet selves. When we hate we show ourselves as hateful. The ugly incarnates something of the show of the monstrous. The doubleness of the aesthetics of being is also in that show. I am not talking now directly about the so-called problem of evil, but about a more primitive negative rapport, a repulsion from some of the faces of creatures: the slimy snake, the hideous toad, the fish dredged up from the dirt of the murky deep, a snarl on a human face that is pure malice, the blister we ourselves are. The aesthetics of creation both delights and disgusts us, resonates with us and repulses us, sweetens us and nauseates us. Aesthetic rebirth also quickens new senses for this second side. For the monstrous has deep significance for the question of God, though the significance is screened.

There is an equivocal plenitude given in aesthetic happening – equivocal because mingled with desolation. There is singing, there is howling. Plenitude itself urges the upsurge of an *urgent lack*. Not just nature's devastations, not the towering power that tramples all, not the sly insinuation of sickness, not the heedless hand snuffing out innocence, not the bruising wear of age, not the dementation that grinds down steadfast patience, not

---

4   A crucial aesthetic recharging occurs with music: an unclogging of the porosity is offered – powerfully prior to and beyond will to power. Music woos and opens a space in the soul like prayer (see *AOO*, pp. 47–8). Aesthetic being: the "to be" as *singing life* – inspiring we philosophers (of religion) with thought singing its other.

the corroding disappointment, the betrayal that crushes, the malice that blights, the greed that devours, the lust that leers, the pride that snorts, not the anger roaring, the envy sneering, the hypocrisy smiling; not just these and so much more too. But: the glory of the morning, the lark on high, the wind in the summer trees, the day's heat on the meadow, those swans there gliding on the lake, the glint of light on the wave, the sudden squall at sea, a golden voice, an effortless runner, the comic first step of a child, or just having a laugh, or bidding farewell, or biding with the dying, helpless to comfort but being there; these and much, much more, all bespeak the glory of finitude; and yet there is a transcending that is still *more*. Whoever says the desire for God springs up only from the deficient is blind to the mad longing that arises out of fullness itself. But this mad longing the fullness of finitude does not fully answer. There is a love of the finite that, just in its love, is made to look beyond the finitude it loves. Its love exceeds itself, even as what it loves intimates what it is not, and what it and the love both need. The aesthetic rebirth is intertwined with erotic outreaching.

EROTIC OUTREACHING

How is the rebirth *erotic*? If aesthetic show recharges our attunement to the worth of other-being (say, T^1), erotic outreaching gives wing to a fresh energizing of our own being, an energizing emergent from secret recesses in the idiocy of the intimate. Eros reaches out from this enigmatic intimacy of being. This self-surpassing potency of our desiring "to be" is replete with ambiguous signs of the divine. The glory of creation often moves us more deeply than discursive categories can capture, setting in motion our self-transcending (T^2) in ways sometimes surprising. In some respects, this erotic energizing finds form in the onset of almost intractable perplexity. What is given in creation calls forth a troubled thinking which no determinate cognition seems finally to satisfy. Now mindfulness is not oriented to a determinate, finite cognition, for one might dispose of an enormous amount of determinate knowledge and still be overcome by the perplexing thereness of creation. Beyond determinate cognition, this perplexity is in an other dimension. Just the being-there of finite beings, not what is there, calls forth this troubled thinking. Our own finite being at all troubles us.

Why trouble? And why trouble with this? Why not satisfaction with the determinate knowing we have commendably accumulated. Why not gleaming expectancy about scientific acquisitions undoubtedly to come? Something quite other still escapes one. One should be content, and in a way one is, but an intimation unnerves one that we have hardly fumbled with an outer veil of Maya. And we do not give up on thinking. Quite the opposite: we find ourselves as if standing still in a withstanding perplexity – one we cannot definitively answer or dispel, for perplexity returns again and again. What withstands perplexity withdraws from determinate cognition, but solicits from us a different mindfulness.

The self-transcending of mindfulness, though finite, seems not to be merely finite. Though I might successfully attain a multitude of specific objectives, each determinate completion, while a term to this particular search, is but a prelude to another search, and this itself another way station to further searches, precipitated again and again, in an unfolding without cease. Nothing determinate finally satisfies our self-surpassing. There is an infinite restlessness to it. This infinite restlessness is a mainspring of our quest for God. Nothing finite finally answers the self-surpassing sweep of human desire, extending all the way from delights of flesh to sublimities of spirit.

Of course, human desire can be rendered in terms of a nihilistic asceticism, and religion itself either promoted as such or attacked. The situation must be more complex, given the rich interplay between insufficiency and plenitude marking our desire. Sometimes we reach beyond ourselves in compensation for lack, but not always. To reach out testifies to affirming energy. We may need what is beyond us, but the transcending articulation of the need can be robust with the joy of being itself. It need not be the whining self-negation that revolts against the glory of creation, singing out its starved praise in a piteous hosanna of woes. Our self-transcending, as knowing the lack of our finite being, is itself testament to the very plenitude of being as given and as the promise of good. Self-transcending is not negative energy but a singularization in us of the affirmative energy of being that, though finite, shows the seed of transfinite potency sprouting in it. As thus finite, it is always beyond finitude.

Is there a *love* marking our being religious that is erotic? Much depends on recognizing the more primal affirmative energy of being that cannot be fully described in terms of lack. I relate eros to the *porosity* of our being.[5] As there is a poverty that is no mere indigence, so eros is more than lacking. Recall Diotima's myth in the *Symposium* concerning the double parentage of eros in *penia* and *poros*. We often focus on *penia* as lack; less often do we foreground the "resource" of *poros*. I relate this "*poros*" to the porosity of our being. Is there a resource of *poros* intimately related to the porosity at the root of our being religious, a resource in lacking itself that is not just an expression of negative energy but intimately connected with porosity? *Poros* has connotations of a "way across." With no way across or through, we are at an impasse, an *aporia*. By contrast, porosity enables a passage through or across. It is something that is not any one thing; it is more like a medium enabling a flow of energy, an energy itself no thing since it passes or is communicated from one thing to another. *Poros* names the making of a way. It names a transition that is no transition, since in making a way, it makes way and hence there is a withdrawal in the very opening of the way. We cannot determinately fix the passage, or passing through, to this or that finite thing, and so it seems nothing. In another sense it is not at all nothing: it enables a way being made, a making way, an original coming to be. In some such wise, the between is constituted as a space of primal porosity, and every being within it participates in this porosity after its own kind. In our return to zero, we become intimate again with this gifted poverty, and in the elemental eros of our being. To become mindful of the porosity is to come closer to the primal ethos, though neither porosity nor ethos can be approached in a univocally direct way.

The doubleness of *our own being* is here important, whereas before (with the elemental "yes," the idiotic rebirth and the aesthetic recharging) it was more the doubleness of given creation that perplexed us. This doubleness means *we are the very incarnation of equivocity*. This is why we humans, most glaringly, can turn ourselves into the counterfeit doubles of God. The equivocity is especially evident in the role *negation* plays in self-transcending. For it can happen that our participation in the primal porosity can be overtaken by a negative energy that gives powerful expression to the *conatus essendi*, to the detriment of the *passio essendi*. This can go all the way to a nihilistic negation towards determinate finitude: negation would do away with it, putatively in the name of something beyond the finite; and yet this negation has nothing to do with the renewal of the elemental affirmation of the "to be" as good. It seems to me quite wrong to portray religion primarily as having the "evil eye" for finite existence and in terms of the workings of this power of negation, whether in shameless overtness or in duplicitous stealth. We find traces of this root error in a whole host of thinkers after Hegel: Feuerbach, Marx, Nietzsche, Freud, and their multiple progeny. What is evident here is rather a univocalization, hence reduction, which deals crudely with the ambiguity of religious negation, lacking nuance enough for the porosity of being and the intermediacy of our *passio essendi*. Even these latter aside, there is a negation not nihilistic, as there is a despair not despairing, a breakdown that is constructive, a shattering that rebuilds.

We human beings can incarnate nihilistic negation, and are the more likely to do so the more we look on the world as devalued being. But the erotic power "to be" shows another way: if negation is carried by the energy of self-transcendence, this presupposes

---

[5] Is religion, in one of its roles, a therapy of *eros turranos*? There is a proximity of *eros turannos* and *eros uranios*. How to discriminate them? Perhaps analogous to the proximity of philosopher and tyrant is that of the faithful person and the atheist (recall Dostoevsky; recall Pascal: atheism reveals a vigor of spirit, but only to a certain point). Erotic outreaching – porosity from the side of self; agapeic release – porosity from the side of the other: religion allows their communication in the between.

our *passio essendi* and the porosity of being between. We "negate" what is present in the presentiment that the determinate present does not exhaust the full reserves of being; in our negating, we incarnate some intimation of the beyond of that present. Even when we negate our own determinate selves as present, and with the view to a fuller self-affirmation, the "negation" can serve as a witness to reserves of being, beyond determinate presentness, and hence reaffirm presenting, as newly seen in light of a more ultimate, giving plenitude. Our negative energy, in this understanding, arises from a more reserved, affirmative source in intimate, original selving, beyond complete objective determination. The source of transcending in us is drawn to the overdeterminacy of the origin as inexhaustibility. Even here, to overuse the language of "negation" is not only equivocal, but potentially misleading, as can be found in trying to make sense of the Buddhist Nirvana. For us, a more subtle deployment of the language of the *passio essendi* and the porosity of being would be the better way.

Much of our thinking, too much, puts the accent on *conatus* as our endeavor to be. Here the equivocity of erotic self-transcending suggests a dialectic of limit and the beyond. Self-transcending encounters a present limit, drives beyond it to a more fulfilling condition, there confronts another limit, but this too fails to halt the movement of self-transcending. To know limit is to have some anticipation of what is on the *other* side of the limit. Self-transcending is a proleptic ecstasis, already beyond limit as a fixed determinate boundary. Limit for us is deeply equivocal, if we think we can determinately univocalize where it is, there for us to come to a full halt, thus far and no further. The Kantian critique of traditional transcendence, and hence its approach to God, suffers from lack of finesse for this equivocity of limit. Hegel tried to address this interplay of univocity and equivocity relative to limit; but he does not adequately address the equivocity of erotic transcendence, especially from the side of its enigmatic and idiotic sources, and rather seeks to drive through to a self-completing end that overcomes all equivocity. Self-transcendence and transcendence as other become *two phases of a single process* in which the self transcending comes to itself in the other and through the other. Transcendence as other (T³) is made immanent to a more inclusive, singular, self-completing process of self-transcending (T²). What eventuates then is a dialectical circle of autonomous immanence. In some ways, this seems the highest thought of transcendence in modernity, assuming the face of a moralized imperative in Kant, a speculative-dialectical completion in Hegel, a revolutionary hope in Marx, a poetized rhapsody in Nietzsche. This highest point also reveals the lowest: the equivocal erotics of transcending becomes the idolatry of autonomy that, just in the self-satisfaction of its own transcending energy, is deaf and dumb to true transcendence as other (T³), and of which it has made itself a counterfeit double.

The eros of self-transcending is of immense importance, and much is to be learned by passage along its vector of surpassing: renewal in us of the urgency of ultimacy; new finesse for the energies of the primal ethos, through the erotics of being in the between; fresh mindfulness of the ambiguous signs of ultimacy itself; but also renewed intimacy with the porosity of being, and the *passio essendi*. These last are especially crucial if we are to learn from the equivocity of erotic transcending: equivocity most elementally, in the doubleness of our being as both *passio essendi* and *conatus essendi*; equivocity in a positive sense, in the doubleness of the unavoidable implication of finite determinacy with what transcends it; finally, equivocity in a negative sense, in the temptation for us to cover over the porosity, to short-change the *passio essendi*, thence to short circuit the full release of self-transcending in a self-enclosed autonomy of self-circling.

We always risk an idolatry of autonomy if we fail to clarify the relation between our self-transcending (T²) and the prior given plenitude of being, the relation of self-transcendence to the finite other – natural (T¹) or human – and its relation to transcendence as other (T³), in a further sense again, such as is religiously named by God. We can, we must, think these relations differently. Erotic self-transcending requires a *relative* autonomy, a relativization of any of our claims to immanent absoluteness (see *EB*, Chapters 10, 11): autonomy is relativized by virtue of the *passio essendi*, more primal than our *conatus essendi*; it is relativized by the givenness of the plenitude of being; it is relativized by the community with others as the home of its own inescapable relatedness to beings beyond itself; most of all, it is relativized by transcendence as other (T^3). We are alerted to this relativization in the resurrection in us of a more ultimate transcending, namely, agapeic transcending. Without this further quickening, the erotic rebirth can instead be still-born as an idolized autonomy.

AGAPEIC RESURRECTION

There is a self-transcending beyond erotic self-surpassing which yet is not the latter's opposite. It comes forth from the fertile void – in the equivocity of its plenitude/lack – unclosed in erotic self-surpassing, but it arises from an intimation that we are already given to be with (co-natus) a certain fullness, out of which we go beyond ourselves, and not always to detour through the other back to ourselves again. Its ecstasis is not from defect and as compensatory, but from abundance and from gratitude for being as gift. The ground of this transcending is obscurely felt to be a fullness in the beginning, remembered in the process of our unfolding, and not forgotten even in the determinate fullness of attained self-becoming. The fullness, given in other-being, given in self-being, is greeted with a gratitude, newly arriving out of refreshed astonishment. If erotic self-transcending tends to come forth from perplexity beyond determinate cognition, agapeic self-transcendence arises beyond self-determination, with astonishment, once prior to perplexity, now won again, at the end, out of perplexity, or perhaps suddenly simply given to an expectant soul, long burdened by perplexity without relief. It arises beyond determinacy and self-determination and rouses in us an overdeterminate expectancy relative to the ultimate source of the givenness of determinate being, and the endowed promise of our own being as self-determining.

I mark a fourfold deliverance towards the ethos of the between and its signs. *First*, release towards the *givenness of creation* as an other, not there just for us, but having its being and value for itself. Delivered to the world, one delights in its elemental being there, in the glory of its aesthetic beauty, the unstrained gift of its availability. Agapeic release towards creation is a love of the finite and mortal. This release – episodic and too rare in us – may extend to beings normally deemed repulsive. One is abandoned to purposeless admiration at the strange good of other-being, suffered as unutterably precious in its stunning thereness. Often this only happens in an extremity. A person confined beholds the frail spider daily build and rebuild her web, beholds with a love keeping alive the flame of faith in life. Laid low, one senses the same flame flare from the tiny patch of sky, barely visible through the small window high above one. Failing one looks at the long familiar tree, but the looking is a longing, exceeding every finite name. The signs are in the *incognitos* of the everyday middle.

Second, there is a certain release of the *abyss hidden in self-being*. One goes out, out of a porosity of selving that is also a too muchness. One is in excess of oneself, in excess towards the other, because the idiocy of self-being is in excess of itself. And yet one is also a kind of nothing. Selving too is a great mystery, enjoyed even more vitally when released towards the singular inexhaustibility of the other. One has opened a door to this dark abyss, too much and almost nothing, and found there many spectral residents – hideous guests, vile parasites, one's own gargoyle self. One has entered into fearful converse with the monstrous. A delivering may come, another energy of selving freed, by warring with and making proper peace with one's gargoyle shadow. The war does not destroy but bends the deformed energy into a diviner form. Agapeic self-release is a release from what one is, and a release of what one is, and was, always, though what one was and is has corrupted the purer energy of ecstasis towards the other. The abyss of inward otherness is a source within selving of radical release, out of self towards the other as another inexhaustible source for itself.

Third, there is a release towards *the community of creation and self-being*. I mean a certain agapeic rapport between us and beings. It takes places in the aesthetic rapport, in ethical solidarity, and in sacrificial love between us and other human beings. There are many forms of community, but at the best it takes shape as agapeic service in which being for the other transcends the insistences of being for self, even in the self's warranted claim to autonomy. There is a heteronomy revealed by agapeic release that has nothing to do with an *ab extra* superimposition by a tyrannical or dominating other. The other becomes the source of a solicitation that is a welcome rather than a demand, that delivers both self and other into a liberty beyond autonomy that lightly, even anonymously, is there for the good of others.

Fourth, the otherness of given creation, the inward otherness of self-being, and especially this heteronomy beyond autonomy, deliver us to *wonder about an other transcendence*, other in a truly ultimate sense. The finite other, natural or human, release us to mindfulness of transcendence as the ultimate other, and especially in the heteronomous community that is agapeic service. This service is an ethical and religious service. Given the absoluteness of availability for the other that is solicited, it is not defined relative to various forms of instrumental relativity that have their place in the economy of self-insistence and serviceable disposability, and even self-determining autonomy. Agapeic service is a transcending beyond these, disproportionate to such finite systems of finite exchanges. The service is not done from constraint or perplexity. It is the most elemental thing to do. It is done as if without thought, and yet it asks the highest thoughtfulness for the other, released from thought for self, from thought as for itself (see, *inter alia*, EB, Chapter 16). One can, of course, be released towards *oneself* in the same spirit of surplus generosity. This is true love of self.

We philosophers are sometimes poor servants of this agapeic release. It is hard to assimilate to more familiar modes of explanation. The why at all of this service, this should trouble us. It does not seek self-justification, but as a transcending of self, it is self-justifying; and yet it is not done simply for itself. It is the enigmatic reversal of self-transcendence into true transcendence of self, making us ponder if it is really transcendence as other (T^3) that is the ultimate solicitation of our going beyond self. When self-transcendence becomes transcendence of self, one goes out of oneself and counts for nothing. This "counting for nothing" is the affirmative double that in its love counterparts the nihilistic form of "being nothing." This "counting for nothing" is implicated in the becoming of our highest self-transcending. It is the porosity of being between as a love of the other. In another reversal, there is a peace to self, a satisfaction that is no self-satisfaction, rather a resting in the good because one is being true to the good, and again not because one can be happy with oneself because one had done the right thing; the peace is that the good has been allowed to be, released to become in the travail of life. One is at peace because one has been privileged somehow to participate in its passage.

See overall, then, the redoubled beginning beyond godlessness as the release of the passion of being: the *passio essendi* intimate to the elemental "yes" and the aesthetic re-charging; the *passio* secretly fermenting in erotic outreaching, despite the tendency of the *conatus essendi* to take over; the *passio* now consumed in the porosity of agapeic communication, for love's openness is not an empty lack but a passionate porosity, and at the limit gives itself as a *compassio essendi*. The sacrificial compassion: this is the *compassio* that makes sacred (*sacer facere*), and whose "being nothing" is the resurrection of the agapeics of being.

How does all this relate to nihilism and the ethos of godlessness? The ethos appears now as entirely other to devalued being. Such ontological valuelessness strikes one as profoundly untrue. It is a catastrophic impoverishment, a lie against the abundance and prodigality of life. Our perplexed wonder about God insinuates itself in this richness, in the pleasure, enjoyment, and gratitude of agapeic release for this feast of being. The release is entirely other to the will to power that rebels against, or exploits, or instrumentalizes, valueless being. Will to power might seem to make sense relative to the latter ontological poverty. It is entirely inappropriate at this feast: a greedy boy grabbing at a table with more than enough for everyone, including the greedy. There is a religious poverty of being beyond this nihilistic poverty.

Agapeic release is more affirmative of being than even will to power that affirms its own abundance (see *IST?*, Chapter 6); for the goodness of the other, as well as the self, is to be affirmed; a more unequivocal release of self towards the other is entirely consonant with the deepest truth of being. Our "counting for nothing," lived in its full paradoxicality as a poverty of plenitude, can be the abandon of self-release that makes a way for transcendence as other (T^3) and always more than self-transcending (T^2).

Will to power is conceived relative to an original ground understood as valueless. By contrast, agapeic release to the ontological worth of creation solicits a rethinking of the grounding origin, as giving being thus to be at all. This calls for a new quest of the divine ground and its relativity to the finite between. There is a kind of ontological marveling, in which thought is drawn towards its own deepening into praise. Thinking can itself be, so to say, surprised by a kind of praying. Seeking God cannot be by way of merely negating finite being; it must be by way of the surpluses of finite being. The gratitude of agapeic release impels us to ask: What it is about the original ground that gives such a release? Can we call it agapeic origin?

I stress: rebirth is still only a beginning. And I hear the snort: all this pretty talk about "beginnings" is nebulous prating; a serious philosopher respects only what can be determinately and intelligibly articulated. Yes, yes: we do need more determinate articulation. Yet, given the complex dimensions of this redoubled beginning, it is no mere indefiniteness, to be conquered by new conceptual univocities or speculative systems. Rather, it enjoins a further turn towards the primal ethos, in mindfulness of a fuller feel for the being-there of being and beings. Our opening to the surplus in the otherness of given being can be complexly articulated, even if it exceeds all the determinations of intelligibility we muster. For again, if the other to thought thinking itself must be thought, and thought otherwise, we are *not* giving up on thinking, but trying to think otherwise than along the way that dead ends in nihilism. We now turn to more determinate thinking concerning the divine, as defined by the guidances offered by the fourfold sense of being. Along a winding way the question awaits us: Can we understand the ontological potencies of the ethos as the *hyperboles of being* that, read metaxologically, communicate in the between the overdetermined signs of God?

Part II

Ways to God

Chapter 3

God And The Univocal Way

We cannot stand the face
That smiles
& withstands our beholding
It passes
& we love it so
We will not let it
Pass and go
We will take hold
& in the happy triumph of our grip
It will not be withheld

Our will be done
On earth as it is
Not in heaven
We give ourselves
Our bread today
That yesterday withheld
Evil will deliver us
From powerless good
& ours will be the kingdom
& the power
Becoming the glory that will be forever ours
Though never ours forever

WAYS TO GOD

Beyond godlessness, the fourfold sense of being orients us towards a deeper sense of the primal ethos through an exploration of immanent features of the reconfigured ethos. The fourfold opens us to different ways to think about God. This will be our concern now in Part II. We begin this exploration with the univocal way of sameness, thinking through its rationale, its strengths and limitations. In subsequent chapters we work through the inescapability of the equivocal way of difference, the mediating way of dialectic with its inclusion of difference in a "sameness" more subtle than the univocal way, to the interme- diating way of metaxology, beyond the univocal unity that fixes, the equivocal difference that disperses, and the dialectical unity that includes. A way to God is sought via a finessed, transdialectical *logos* of the *metaxu*. The metaxological way is a figuring of the primal ethos which divines the nature of the community of God and the between, heedful of the difference, not reducing to sameness the transcendence of the divine, not dispersing this transcendence into impossible difference, and not sublating it in a dialectical–speculative whole claiming absoluteness by its immanent closure on itself. The community *between* immanence and divine transcendence is ultimately more than every immanent whole. First to the univocal way.

THE WAY OF UNIVOCITY

The univocal sense of being is pervasive throughout the philosophical tradition, perhaps the major influence on our approaches to intelligibility, and not only in philosophy. When we encounter the astonishing diversity of happenings, or within happenings, our search for intelligibility looks for, looks to, constant sameness in the muchness of multiplicity.

Dominant emphasis is placed on identity in difference, homogeneity in heterogeneity. Does the outcome have to be a reductive monism? Surely not. Even seeking the one constant voice in the Babel, we find there are many voices of oneness. The univocal way to oneness yields not one but many responses to manyness – and to the One.

This way is indispensable to our configuration of the ethos of being. Astonishment reveals a happening that is too much for us, hence perplexing. We try to place determinacy where this overdeterminacy is. The univocal way is correlative with the specification of *definite curiosity* about this or that *determinacy* of being. The initial too muchness looks like a negative indefinition, to be progressively overcome by more and more definition. It will be said: To be is to be intelligible; to be intelligible is to be determinate; and to be determinate is to be univocal. There are *many* forms of determinate intelligibility – common sense, mathematical, scientific, and so on. Yet the general attitude remains constant: intelligibility means transcending the too muchness given in the original astonishment, guided by the faith that there is, in the end, nothing too much, and nothing, in the end, in excess of intelligible determination. If there is mystery in the beginning, in the end it will be replaced by determinate intelligibility. Result? Conquering of wonder, and the vanishing of the marvel of being. The neutralized fact of being will replace this marvel.

These are some general points, and they influence our thinking about God. Clearly, the univocal sense has a religious bearing on *monotheism*. Must monotheism also be a monism? The first commandment reminds us: God is God and nothing but God is God. Are we not then addressing an absolute singularity? How speak of this One, since all our speaking must be finite? How avoid at all having strange gods before us? Do we not inevitably secrete false doubles of the One? We must consider a plurality of efforts to univocalize God, premodern and modern. The worry is we tailor God too much to what is intelligible in terms of *our* determination. We determine God and end up without God. Making God determinately intelligible, we conclude by occluding God. We must explore an immanent logic here, with key historical episodes correlated with important philosophical orientations. The more relentlessly we univocalize God, the more the equivocity of the enterprise emerges. The logic of univocalizing God produces its own atheism. When the Western philosophical tradition lets itself be dominated by that logic, its shadow is always this atheism. This atheism of the univocal, we will see, turns us back on the chiaroscuro of the divine, and the further search for the God beyond our univocalizing.

PANTHEISTIC UNIVOCITY: IMMEDIATE SACRALITY

The univocal way can lend itself to a kind of "objective" orientation, relating more to the God of the philosophers, while the equivocal way allows more of the "subjective," and hence, too, the pathos of religious existence. However, to fix on this contrast would be to miss the context of origination more basic than either univocal objectivity or equivocal subjectivity. The univocal determination of sameness emerges relative to the initial overdetermination of given being. Hence one might speak of a primitive, undifferentiated univocity, though it would be unrecognizable to scientific and mathematical univocity, for it looks more like equivocity, in that definite identities are not here kept clearly apart. Univocity is only defined in interplay with the equivocal, nevertheless, there is an aura of undifferentiated unity that seeps over the borders of differentiated unities, suggesting what I call the *rapturous univocity of being*. Related to the elemental affirmation, the rapturous univocity names a relatively undifferentiated rapport with being, whether self-being or other-being, the difference seems not yet to matter.

The point is important, for initially we do not have a defined concept of God as any kind of definite unity. Initially there is more an undefined "feel" of immediate sacrality. This can be vague or overpowering, and may crystalize in any determinate thing that becomes the anchor of fascination and awe. The divine seems pervasive in all things. *The whole is the holy.* This "feel" matches religiously the ontological sense of the overdetermined inexhaustibility of being as given, but here this is not known as such; it is lived.

Just as there is an original ontological astonishment, so here, simply to be is the miracle, the marvel. Any thing may become the object of devotion, for anything in given being may serve as a hierophany. It would be quite wrong to call this fetishizing. The finite is not fetished here. No clear differentiation between finite and non-finite marks this immediate sacrality. Everything finite may be the occasion of divine presencing, for in a way there is nothing finite. There is simply the indeterminate presentiment of the divine that now vaguely, now overpoweringly, presences in the being there of beings.

Such immediate sacrality puts us in mind of a kind of *pantheistic univocity*. Not reductive of a many to a one, this is immediately *expansive*, in that any one of many things, and every one of all things, seems somehow alive in the one life of the all-pervading power. The incontrovertible power of the divine permeates and overpowers the many, even as the many themselves expansively are in a flow of transcending that carries them beyond themselves. All is One, and every one in the One is somehow also All. There is the divine, and there is nothing apart from the divine, and we too are nothing apart from the divine.[1]

Modern persons find it difficult to appreciate this orientation, for we inherit millennia of the objectification of being, and in this beginning there are no objects and subjects in their modern meaning. To superimpose our habits of thinking objectively and subjectively is to show a failure of "objectivity," that is, a lack of understanding of the otherness of any such immediate sacrality. Even today, residues of immediate sacrality survive even in extreme secularization, though its occasions not be named religious as such.[2] It can also return later, say, in mystical univocity, or in the recrudescence of paganisms of the earth aflame with a kind of Dionysian univocity. Many secularized persons feel as if just the objectfication of being had left them undernourished, if not starved, for non-objective community with being in its otherness. A strange cultural schizophrenia can result: here, the hard objectivities of scientistic, technicist attitudes; there, the innocent spirituality of a new age, seeking all in all a blithe bliss, high on its own unsuspecting narcissism.

Perhaps we should not even talk about God or gods here, since this presupposes a degree of differentiation relative to unity and multiplicity. Why take note of the immediate sacrality? Because it obscurely intimates something of the primal ethos of being, hence also of the context of our more differentiated relations to gods and God. There can be something both rapturous and unruly about this immediate sacrality, just because it is overdetermined and spontaneous. Because it is rapturous, it floods us with a sense of awe of the great power everywhere abroad in things, fills us with an indeterminate gratitude for the great abundance giving all good things. Because it is unruly, it is beyond our control and mediation, and puts us into subordination, though it need not be felt as subordination but lived as immersion in the passing of a great power. As we are thankful

---

[1] The sense of immediate sacrality is not necessarily expressed in terms of a spiritual god at all. The generative power in nature may be what surges forth and sacrality expressed in images of procreative fertility. Think of the outside of Hindu temples, crowded with images of sacred sexuality; for instance, the statues on the façade of the Kandariya Mahadev temple at Khajuraho. Or the cult of the Great Mother (*Magna Mater*), Cybele, an almost universal figure in ancient religions, great goddess of fertility, originally Phrygian, but spreading over the ancient world. Or the Dionysian festivals: orgiastic unity with pre-reflective, pre-subjective yet originative oneness of being. The phallus as sacred is carried in religious procession, but tart Heraclitus is always alert to the equivocal: "If it were not in honor of Dionysus that they conducted the procession and sang the hymn to the shameful parts, their activity would be completely shameless. But Hades is the same as Dionysus, in whose honor they rave and perform Lenaean rites" (Frag. 15). The immediacy of the sacred, as dipping back into the porosity of the pre-subjective, is invested in the fertile body with regard to the spontaneous powers of generation that are not within our control, and that live us towards a larger life beyond our self-conscious mastery.
[2] On the negative side, consider the hostile, indiscriminate incomprehension towards all Islamic energies, or to movements in the West dismissed as mere "fundamentalisms." Regarding "residues," consider: "fetishizing" of fashionable things or "celebrities"; orgiastic dancing; football as cult; crowds as intoxicants; clubbing; the flaring up of religious interests, such as the occult, the extra-terrestrial. Immediate sacrality is not yet repressed in children who are often surprised by it; it returns in our dreams; some artists make contact with it; music has special power to open up our porosity to it.

for its unbidden blessings, we are liable to unchosen trepidation before its eruptions and interruptions. The immediate sacrality is full of beneficence and disturbance.

Thus there is no purely homogenous univocity, even in this presentiment of the all-pervading power that runs through all things. There is a doubleness to this power: the rapture and unruliness cannot be separated completely. The immediate indeterminacy, precisely as an overdeterminacy, may offer a floating unifying rapport with the great power, as well as the shock of unpredictable otherness. Perplexed by this doubleness, we encounter the *inescapability of manyness within* the immediate rapport. With this, ambiguity comes forth, making any univocal determination of the divine pregnant with different *equivocities*. The point is not a primitive historical "monotheism" (claimed by a variety of deists in the seventeenth and eighteenth centuries) but an ontological "pan-theistic univocity" – meaning by "*pan*" an indeterminate pervasion of the all with a vagrant sacrality that, just as pervasive, becomes differentiated into a plurality of manifestations of the sacred, and hence into a kind of "poly-theistic univocity." The overdeterminate is not the merely indefinite, and might be said to include the indeterminate and the determinate. If this says something about the *ontological ethos* of the beginning, we can grant *both* this inarticulate feeling of the all pervading sacred, as well as the more determinate concretion of the indeterminate into determinate divine beings. With Thales, we can say: All is water. With Thales, we can also say: All things are full of gods.

EQUIVOCAL TRANSIENCE AND UNIVOCALIZING GOD

In the ontological ethos being is immediately overdetermined but also, as given, it is *transience*. Being is in passing: not just temporal but temporary. What comes into being passes out of being: now it is, now it is no longer. This difference between "being now," and "not now being at all," offers the basis of a sense of fundamental difference, on which other more relative senses of difference depend. Thus when I say: "*This* is different to *that*," the difference is relative to the fact that both *this* and *that* are taken for granted as given in being. But when I say: "*This now*" is different relative to "*this not now being*," the fact that the being is granted is not thus taken for granted. For the fact that there is a presentiment of its "not now being at all" means that any affirmation of its "now being" is made against the backdrop of the possibility of its non-being. There is a transience where we see that "this" becomes "that," and that "that" becomes other again. But there is an even more basic transience: it concerns *coming to be at all* (the "once"), and then *not being at all* (the "never"). What is here suggested? An *immediate equivocality* of transience. Immediate: transience is primitively given in the process of finite being. Equivocal: transience reveals itself as one and the other (it is and yet it is not); or neither one nor the other (it neither is, nor is it not); or again, as both one and the other (it both is, and yet it is not). *The process of finite happening shows forth just this equivocality of transience.*

This equivocality is *too much for us*. Why? The "once" and the "never" are both at the boundary of determinability. Like the rapturous univocity, this equivocal transience retreats beyond our conceptual mastery. I suggest: just that retreat engenders our desire for a univocity different than the primal rapport. I mean we now drive for determination in a far *more definite sense*, so definite, in fact, that the doubleness will be reduced to one sense, one sense in which we turn the ontological recalcitrance of beings into fully determinate presences whose very ontological "coming to be" is taken for granted, that is, not taken *as* granted, and so overlooked, and with repercussions for the divine.

A more definite univocal attitude to the divine arises indirectly from the equivocality of transience given directly in the rapturous univocity. Just that *ontological ethos* impels us to univocalize the divine. For we cannot live indefinitely with marvel or trepidation. We need to determine more familiar unities and samenesses. Common sense effects a familiarization of our "being in the midst," but the univocal way drives our restless curiosity not only *within* the between, but relative to the *whole* of determinate beings as such. The eros of self-transcending mindfulness also *outstrips* the finite ensemble of finite determinations.

The search for a more ultimate unity inevitably emerges. That One is to be sought in and through the doubleness of the immediate equivocality of given being.

In what now follows, I explore that self-transcending in an interconnected series of relations between the One and the double. Overall, I look at three variations, roughly corresponding to the search for the One in the context of ancient polytheism (sections 4, 5); to the theological determination of the One in the context of a more articulated monotheism (sections 6,7); and to the erosion of a sense of the divine One in modernity, in light of the dominance of mathematicized univocity, and of the human self considered as the one source of determination (sections 8, 9, 10). We will see the necessity of univocity and its insufficiency. When our univocalizing is cut off from its own matrix in the primal ethos, impoverished categories result, untrue to our porosity and the full intermedium of being, untrue to God as inexhaustible origin of surplus being as given to be.

BEYOND DOUBLENESS TO THE ABSORBING ONE: THE PARMENIDEAN WAY

The self-dissolving of finite unities shows their univocity to be equivocal, but is there a more ultimate univocity beyond all equivocity? The Eleatic One is an extreme answer to this question. While perhaps few thinkers have taken the univocity of being (*to on*) with such radicality as Parmenides, the Eleatic influence on the thinking of God is deepgoing. How is being described? A whole absolutely one with itself, entirely homogeneous throughout, no lack within it; Necessity (*Anankē*) always holds it (Frag. 8, 27) as resting within the firm boundaries of its own well-ordered sphere (*eukuklou sphairēs*, Frag. 8, 43), at home with itself, for there is nothing other beyond its own sphere. Other than being itself there is nothing; nothing that might constrain being in any way from outside, for the notion of the "outside" seems unintelligible. There is its eternity, for it never arose at all (*agenēton*, Frag. 8, 3), for were it to arise it would have been not, and it could not have been not (Frag. 8, 10–15). It is immovable (*atremes*, Frag. 8, 4), one (*hen*, Frag. 8, 6), continuous (*suneches*, Frag. 8, 6). It neither "comes to be" nor "becomes." It is as being eternal necessity, for there is no way to think outside of being; we are in the sphere of well-rounded truth (*aletheiēs eukuklēos*, Frag. 1, 29).

Nevertheless, Parmenides has a keen eye for equivocity: the extant poems are saturated with a plurality of doubles. Example: the many wander double-headed (*dikranoi*, Frag. 6, 5) – a picturesque image of our equivocal mindfulness of becoming. For pious metaphysicians, Parmenides ghost still roams abroad, but post-metaphysicians do not escape the sweet seduction of the same circle. Nietzsche, ventriloquizing through Zarathustra, sings his love of the ring of eternity. Heidegger, the pious post-metaphysician, was also haunted by an afterlife of Parmenides.[3] Indeed, when one begins to think of God, be one pious metaphysician or just pious – or for that matter, impious – it is hard to dispense with metaphors like the sphere or the circle. In antiquity the circle was the image of perfect motion, and hence of perfection. It offers the pleasure of determinacy – for a circle is a quite definite configuration of space. It also gives us the energy of a becoming that is no becoming, since the beginning and the end join, being on every point of the

---

[3]   Some aspects of the present discussion suggest *not* seeing the Western tradition as "onto-theology" or "metaphysics of presence." I am wary of totalizing claims that thinkers like Plato and Plotinus are *only* univocal philosophers. We need more nuance in reading the premodern reconfiguration of the ethos and its promise for metaphysics and philosophy of God. My view is less a critique of "metaphysics" as a post-Hegelian metaphysical exploration of an ascendant univocity that is asleep to significant equivocities of being. Relative to the ethos of being, there is much of reserve and resource in the longer philosophical tradition easily passed over by the postulation of "ontotheology" as the unsurpassable horizon of considerations. The enterprise of rendering God determinate is carried out in the *metaxu*, the ethos of being, whose ontological reserves do not simply come for consideration "before" Western metaphysics or "after" the so-called end of metaphysics, but are at work even in the effort to univocalize the divine. Maybe this univocalizing fails to attend on these reserves, but we also can fail to attend on them as at work *in premodern metaphysics itself*, if we characterize the entire tradition as "ontotheology."

encircling and also at no one definite point. The circle seems to communicate something of the *overdetermined* in a determinate figuration. For it is not in this point, that point, or the other point along a distended line that the circle affords something of the joy of closure. It is in the circling itself, the self-circling. We seem at home within a whole, and the whole seems our home. And yet we must ask: Is there a God beyond the whole?

Part of the majesty of Parmenidean univocity relates just to the *interplay* of the univocal and equivocal, the way of truth and the way of seeming. Parmenides is often credited with being the founder of "logic" in commanding us in terms that later will more formally take shape as the law of contradiction. Either it is, or it is not (*estin hē ouk estin*, Frag. 8, 16). Being and non-being are logically contradictory, and to think the nothing is the most basic of logical equivocities, namely, to think nothing as somehow being. To think is to think being (*to gar auto noein estin te kai einai*, Frag. 4, 3). To be is to be thought intelligible and to be thought intelligible is to be. But to try to think non-being intelligibly is to think of it as somehow being; this is absurd. To think nothing is either to think, that is, think something; or it is to think nothing, which is not to think at all. Thinking nothing is either thinking something or thinking nothing. If the former, we are caught in irremediable contradiction, if the latter we are empty of thought and can command no respect in the lists of intelligible *logos*.

But if the drive to univocal unity is energized by the desire to escape equivocity, this means there is no univocity without equivocity. *Why is there any equivocity at all?* This is not easy to explain univocally – for the univocalist. If the absolute One is the self-compacted whole, how explain those ontological considerations out of which our search for the One emerges, namely, the immediate equivocity of transience? The purely equivocal is the unintelligible, but the equivocal *is* somehow, hence also the unintelligible is. But this is itself unintelligible, nay impossible, if the intelligible is what is only univocally intelligible. There could not even be a search for the One, if all there is is the One. The search for the One means the absence of the One, at least relative to our finite mindfulness. Hence *there must be lack*, and if so, some sense of being as *other* to the absolutely One, which then cannot just be *that* absolute One.

Expressed in terms of God, if God is all there is, there is no search for God, and our search is merely illusory. But this last claim is nonsense, for even our merely illusory quest for God is itself illusory; and one seems to have an infinite regress of illusions. But then this regress is also an illusion, and there is then no regress, and no illusion. And being without illusion surely is illusory for us. But this too is *just what one should not have*, for the proposal was that all there is is God. On one side, you seem to have all but *absolute unintelligibility*, signaled by the infinite regress, not merely of provisionally established realities, but of self-dissolving illusions. On the other side, you have an *absolute univocal intelligibility* that itself generates the first outcome of the infinite regress. If all there is is God, whence the (perhaps illusory) infinite regress of illusions? Should we then say: absolute univocal intelligibility generates absolute unintelligibility? God as absolute univocal unity, in making absolute sense, ends up making absolutely no sense, perhaps making absolute nonsense of the thought of God?

These tensions, perhaps antinomies, suggest that the absolute One cannot be approached just in terms of the univocal sense. What then is necessary? Our hewing more faithfully to the nuances of middle being, for in those nuances a richer intelligibility may guide us in thinking of God. And perhaps here we notice something for which we must thank Parmenides. Even as father of *logos* he spoke from the heart of *muthos*. This philosopher wisely wrote *religious poems*. Might we call them metaphysical prayers? A career logician will shudder. Since Aristotle, the embarrassment of logic is ingrained in our professional habits; but why not praise Parmenides for being pious and not professional? Are the religious poetics that invoke the Goddess (*Thea*, Frag. 1, 22; she calls him "youth," *koure*, 1, 24) just a concession to the weakness of the many? That too perhaps, but also more. There is something of metaphysical prayer in them. They resonate with the originating context of thinking, namely, the rapturous univocity, the pre-logical communivocity, so to say, of logic and mysticism. They reflect the aura of the divine in the original overdetermination of given being. Prayer bespeaks something of praise rising up in the primal ethos. It comes as communication in the porosity of being. (I do not forget that Parmenides took active part in the politics of his city.) The Parmenidean determination of univocity was still close to the rapture of the all surrounding ether of being, the intermedium of the ethos in its astonishing mystery. That we lack such an attunement in no way makes us superior.

Esti: *It is*. This, Parmenides says, this alone is left for us to say (Frag. 8, 1–2). "It is." What is? Being? God? Is it the *ens supremum* or *ens realissimum* of so-called ontotheology? I doubt it. Is not the *Esti* rather resonant of an immediate sacrality of "Being is," a resonance impossible to fix to any determinate being, even the highest? Might one then say: all is divine as equally as nothing is divine? The all is a sign of God, nothing is a sign of God? Either everything is a communication of God or nothing is? *Esti*: remember this when, along the metaxological way, I speak of the first hyperbole of being.

The "too muchness" becomes absolute plenitude in Parmenides – but engulfing of finite differences and determinations, what I have called the absorbing god (*DDO*, Chapter 1). We might say that the mythic side of Parmenides is resonant with the inarticulate sense of the "too muchness." Absolute plenitude is a very good thought relative to the fullness of the origin, but we must understand this fullness as allowing the arising of finite determinacy, and hence also as allowing the arising of *lack*, and forms of being that are *not* marked by absolute plenitude. The origin must be such as to give rise to finite being as other to itself. The One must be such as to allow the arising of equivocity and manyness. The logic of the One must take us beyond the One, even as the logic of the equivocal must take us beyond the equivocal. Once again the question must arise: Is there a God beyond the whole?

BETWEEN THE ONE AND THE DOUBLE: THE PLATONIC WAY

The Platonic way is a further mediation of the equivocity of transience, a new way to the beyond of its double being, through a more pluralized univocity. It is also attentive to the middle space *between* the One and the many, by means of a new attentiveness to manyness. "What makes the many to be as determinate at all?" Notice that this mixes two questions, reflecting two senses of transience: "What makes them to be at all?" "What makes them to be determinate?" Because of the influence of univocity, the second form of the question tends to be more dominant, the first more recessive. The difference of these two forms is correlative to the difference of "coming to be" and "becoming" – a difference full of consequence for us.

The answer cannot be their transience simply, since this reveals a self-dissolving equivocity, and hence is more like the indefinite than the definite. And yet each thing as becoming is definite, if only for a time. Thus this question of the original ground of manyness regards just the mingling of univocity and equivocity in many things. The answer looks beyond the determinate this to an *eidetic determinacy*, beyond aesthetic thereness to *dianoetic univocity*. This dianoetic univocity that mediates the aesthetic equivocity is one but also many. For there are many kinds of things; and what makes these kinds of things determinate is not their unity as this thing, but their unity as this kind of thing. In this respect, the Platonic approach shades over the question: "What makes beings to be at all?" by seeking to answer "What makes them to be the determinate kinds of beings they are?" An answer to the second is not an answer to the first, and if taken as such, can result in a determining essentialization of the overdetermined being of the origin.

The *eidē* are univocal units of eternal intelligibility: univocal, because they are themselves and nothing but themselves; units, because they are the changeless sameness that determines the essential temporal identity of this or that kind of thing. Philosophy here mirrors, if you will, the move from pantheistic univocity to polytheistic univocity. The univocal approach results not in unity simply but a *double order of being*: the aesthetic and dianoetic, transience and the eidetic beyond. This double order is not a mingling of univocal and equivocal in the given middle, but the definition of the equivocal middle as given by another order of univocal eternity. We are not trying to determine one finite order in terms of another but seeking the original ground of determinate finiteness as such. This is its importance for the question of God. It witnesses the emergence of *a presentiment of transcendence arising within the middle*; a presentiment not brought to a stand before the middle as given, but entailed by features of the middle pointing beyond themselves to another order of being.

We are long familiar with questions put to this approach. There is the problem of the otherness of this other order, the problem of the interplay of forms and instances. Plato's answer is participation, though he knew that this answer, in some respects, puts a new face on the question (see *Parmenides*, not least on the famous third man argument). The other order cannot be so other as not to be immanently at work in the temporal order it grounds. Some account of the recessed *metaxu* must be ventured. There has to be an *intermediation* that not only goes from equivocal transience to the univocal beyond, but in the other direction also – otherwise the starting point of our transcending would simply not be at all. The whole situation would collapse were there no first intermediation from the otherness of the eternal. This, I believe, bears on the question of the "coming to be at all" of transient becoming.

A sense of the otherness of transcendence emerges in our understanding of the middle, though as emerging, it also remains hidden. This very reserve entices our mindfulness to a deeper exploration of the givenness of the finite middle. The problem of the interplay is insoluble for a univocity that simply fixes on determination. If there is to be a double mediation, it is impossible to seal univocally the orders of time and eternity both in themselves and from each other. Quite to the contrary: they must each be beyond themselves. If so, the dualism that separates is undercut by the double movement that intermediates between time and eternity as transcending orders of being, as each a dynamic ecstasis. Time may be the moving image of eternity (*Timaeus*, 37d6–7), not because time is moving and eternity is static, but because eternity is moving with its own dynamic; and what moves in the becoming of time is finite *dunamis* that images the more original *dunamis* of eternity.

Perhaps *the equivocal is not so equivocal after all*. A positive resistance keeps coming back: the equivocal keeps reappearing because there is a something above, or more than, deeper and higher than univocal determinate intelligibility. The dynamism of becoming, even as equivocal, is not a merely negative condition we must fly towards a decontaminated univocity. Equivocal transience is overdetermined: its too muchness is a double manifestation in that, though showing, it is also and necessarily concealing. Its equivocity is just this doubleness of showing and concealing. And this doubleness has much to do with the double form of the question of transience: not only of becoming, but of *coming to be at all*.

There is also the question of the "unity" of the many forms of unity. If there are many units of formal intelligibility, what constitutes the "unity" of these? Can it be just another formal intelligibility? The question is imposed by the quest for univocity, but it is impossible to solve in terms of any determinate unity, be it temporal or eternal. There must be another sense of "unity," more transcendent still, and more inclusive, and yet more incomparable, and in that sense more singular, since it is not one of a class of unities, nor class of classes, but is the unity beyond all classes of unity, and hence beyond all classification. This other sense of "unity" is suggested by the Good, as *epekeina tēs ousias* (*Republic*, 509b9): a singular "unity" and a dynamic one, likened to the Sun, and hence as shining, self-transcending, without diminishment to itself. In its shining, it makes possible the being, intelligibility and growth of what is other to itself. It is itself, and thus for itself, but as shining it is for what is other. This is to acknowledge both the question of *coming to be at all* and the *becoming* of this or that determinate kind of being.

Why is this suggestion of the One beyond communicated to us through a similitude – the Sun? Though the univocal sense is at work, it does not issue in a desiccated conceptual determination. The pregnant image, even in its ambiguity, and resistance to complete discursive articulation, shows its power. The image is a metaphysical metaphor, and shows us how we need a richer *ethos or milieu of mindfulness* than univocal thinking allows. Follow through the logic of univocity, there will arise the self-transcending of mindfulness, what Plato calls its eros. We will find ourselves moving beyond univocity in univocity itself. Moreover, there will arise a progressively richer sense of the equivocity of being, mediating a more and more complex sense of the ultimate. The equivocal is not conquered, but rather suggests reserves concerning the fullness of being that a callow univocity leaves fallow or fails to let ripen.

It is here that recessed resources of the *metaxu* ask for fuller articulation. For self-transcending eros, in fact, is beyond univocity and equivocity. It is metaxological – a *metaxu* Plato explicitly says (*Symposium*, 202b5). It is thus revealed in and through a deepening mindfulness of the interplay of univocity and equivocity, not by the absolutization of one or the other, or by the extirpation of either. We need metaxological thinking, beyond univocal mind, and addressing the equivocity of transience, to do justice to eros as self-transcending (T²). The fact that we need a metaphysical metaphor of the Good, imaged in likeness to the Sun, points us towards the One (T³) as something hyperbolic.[4] We come to the same point we found with the Parmenidean One: the resonance of the "too much-ness" of the ultimate, relative to the ontological ethos of our thought, is *not* dispelled as our thinking deepens. Even while seeking to give a determinate articulation, metaphysical metaphors or hyperboles try not to betray that "too muchness."

THE ONE BEYOND THE DOUBLE: THE PLOTINIAN WAY

Observe something paradoxical: the focus of univocity seems narrow but it yields a significant *enlargement* (something one would not quite expect from "ontotheology" or "metaphysics of presence"). By an immanent dialectic with equivocity, there arises a richer mindfulness of our being in the middle, and of the original ground of given transience. As the univocal way more complexly mediates the between, it also mediates a more complex sense of the original ground of the between, indeed an incomparable sense of the transcendent One. Here Plotinian thought allows us to speak of *the One beyond the double*.

First, the One is approached by a transcending move of mindfulness, beyond the given multiplicities in the finite world, indeed beyond the community of stable intelligibilities that ground the intelligibility of manyness. Transcending the equivocities and dualities is not a mere flight from manyness. It is a following of the metaphysical vector in manyness itself beyond manyness. Second, the duplicities in our own thinking must be transcended. We think in terms of a variety of dualisms, but these must be surpassed, not by simple suppression but through the ontological dynamic at play in the self-transcending of mindfulness itself. Passage beyond is a self-surpassing, in and by and through mindfulness itself. This is also transcending in, and through, and beyond the counterfeit doubles of God. While no metaphor of spatial directionality is adequate, we are inclined to think in terms of *height*. Metaphysical mindfulness is vertically self-surpassing. The vertical does not exclude the horizontal, nor, within its infinite range, the height from it own other side, the deep. The full dimensionalities of the between must be granted, as signs of the over-full God of the between in its granting of highup and deepdown grounding. The divine envelops, or pervades, or penetrates the very ontological voluminosity of the between. And yet it is immeasurably above the between.

Third, mindfulness is lifted immeasurably above *itself*. If it seems to lift itself, this is not quite so: it is lifted. Mindfulness transcends itself infinitely, and so is not mindfulness. It cannot be mindfulness is a more normal sense separating inner and outer, up and down. Such objectified determinations are suitable to the finite between, but the original grounding of the between, enfolding them in its incomparable over-wholeness, suspends them in a

---

4 Glaucon's response to Socrates on the Good beyond being: "By Apollo, a daimonic hyperbole (*daimonias huperbolēs*)!" *Republic*, 509c 1–2.

higher transcendence. Mind does not think; it is being thought. What it thinks is not thought; this transcendent One is other to thought thinking itself. Strikingly enough, though a certain notion of oneness is stressed, here a savor of radical otherness arises from the thought of radical unity, pointing to something beyond the unity of thought thinking itself.

The One beyond duality seems to be formless, hence indeterminate, and hence a very strange unity, for normally unity is determinate unity. It seems contradictory to speak of an indeterminate unity. I think we should speak of this One as overdeterminate, over-whole, if it gives rise to the multiplicity of determinate beings. If it is "formless," it is more than form, not less. Our knowing of it, our coming into its company, must itself look like a kind of "formlessness," and so not look like knowledge at all, if we mean a determinate knowing of a determinate somewhat or form. It is more the opening up our (more original) porosity to the ultimate extremes of the between, following the signs there communicating of what is beyond the between. Thus Plotinian "univocity" goes up to a kind of mystical night, beyond beings, even beyond being, in a "knowing" that is beyond knowing, for no-thing is known. And yet there is the energizing of self-transcendence and a transformation of our mindfulness.[5]

In Plotinus I find nothing of the raving enthusiast of the kind Kant hated, and that can arouse disdain, verging on sneering. There is an immediate dialectical finesse that balances opposites in a nuanced equilibrium. He immediately practiced a noble hermeneutics of finitude, antipodal to that hermenutics alternatively aggressive with suspicion about any "beyond," or paralyzed in immanence by its own anti-metaphysical misgivings. Nor should we be fixated by the spatiality of metaphors of height, for this only entrenches dualistic oppositions which it is the task of metaphysical mindfulness to understand, to unweave and to transcend. The following five points merit mention.

First, the unique unity of the One means that extraordinary demands are here made on the univocal sense of being. Yet mundane univocity by its own logic points us in this direction. *Second*, extraordinary demands are also being made on our mindfulness. Metaphysical mindfulness is already a transcendence of determinate univocity, even when it thinks univocally. *Third*, the overdeterminacy of the One beyond is not merely negative: from it arises everything in the "lower" worlds, either intelligible or sensible. It is hence the overdeterminacy of a plenitude from which issues what is other to itself. It is an originative One, and as originative also self-transcending, and not again a numerical or geometrical unit. This is univocity beyond the *esprit de géométrie*.

Fourth, *we* must return to the indeterminacy/overdeterminacy in our own selving to make the movement beyond; we must return to a kind of "formlessness." Though reminiscent of the return to zero, this is not a nihilating return. It is a re-opening in us of the more original porosity to the divine, and a re-energizing within selving of the source of transcending beyond self. To return to this "formlessness" is to risk being swallowed by the indefinite, or being overwhelmed by the overdeterminate. The risk has to be taken. There are no methods, or guarantees. It is beyond *nous* and *epistēmē*, as Plotinus says. There is entry into a night of mystery, and a daring journeying one knows not where.

Fifth, the problem of the *intermediation* of the One and the many is not avoided. The way up and the way down are not the same. The way up, from our side, is by way of an erotic self-transcending: we both love ultimate being and lack it; becoming mindful of our lack, the love of our being is energized in this mindfulness; we surpass what is finite, in love of what we lack. Nevertheless, we must not slight finite being, wrongly stressing its lack. By contrast, the way down, from the reserves of the One, is by way of plenitude: the overdeterminate source as over-full "overflows," giving all that is its share of the good.

---

[5] In his *Ennead*, "On Matter" (see, e.g., II.4.10.1–5) Plotinus discusses *to apeiron*, and the view that "like knows like." If we were to know *to apeiron*, would this knowing also be indeterminate? Lacking determination would it be like a porosity that is empty? What if the One beyond determinacy is over-determinate? Is there a move of mindfulness towards this overdeterminacy that is a *likeness in reverse* to the "knowing" of the merely indefinite *apeiron* – a porosity that is less empty as over-full, that empties itself to receive the over-full?

This way down is not at all out of lack, for the One is beyond all lack. If we are deficient in the *esprit de finesse*, we may be tempted to harden this lackless One into a knot of indifferent impassability, and distort the fullness overflowing, not to be separated from the Good. The Good is a giving and so any metaphor of an indifferent unit cannot be right. The danger is evident, however, when the overflow is turned into a "fall," and "fall" tainted with too much of ontological deficiency: generation from the One turns into its opposite, namely, degeneration from the One. This undermines the interplay with the between. The sense of lacking being in the upward movement is given its reduplication in the sense of the downward movement, even out of plenitude, as giving rise to lack in generated manyness.[6] Transcendence thus leads to the loss of transcendence.

We need here a more articulated understanding of the transcendence of *agapeic origination*. Agapeic origination gives rise to the other for the good of the other; and though the originated other is not the origin itself, there need be no negative judgment of ontological defect. To be finite is to be good, not to be defective, even though the finite needs what is beyond itself, and points beyond itself towards what it lacks. The arising of being as finite is not an ontological defect(ion). It is not a transgression against the origin, not an injustice demanding retribution (Anaximander). It is given being as good, and for the good of its being itself as other. I find many suggestions in this direction in Plotinus, but perhaps embedded in a tacit orientation to the primal ethos, not always entirely free of some of the above equivocities. More might be said, but we need more explicit cognizance of dialectical and metaxological considerations.

REVERSING THE ONE AND THE DOUBLE: OR HOW THE DUALISTIC DEFENSE OF TRANSCENDENCE EFFECTS ITS ECLIPSE

To recap and anticipate: in the Parmenidean mediation of equivocal transience, univocal thought recoils from the threat of self-dissolving equivocity; but this assertion of absolute univocity itself dissolves in new equivocities. In the Platonic, the pure unity of the first gives way to a qualified duality, whose own equivocities impel further the search for the One beyond duality. In the Plotinian, the One seems shrouded in an incomparable transcendence *beyond* all mediation. Further equivocities emerge, especially relative to transcendence as other (T³). For if the One is beyond all mediation, is it not relationless and beyond relation? How then does it relate to the finite middle and its constitutive manyness? What if now we give way to a dualistic approach to transcendence as other? While seeming to guard God in absolute otherness, this can lead to the unweaving of that otherness, and the loss of the God guarded under the sign of univocal determination. We turn from God (T³), turn towards ourselves as immanent transcendence (T²), and lay hold of our own power to master the flux of equivocal transience (T¹). We ourselves seek to be the univocal One to seize and determine equivocal transience. In the end, in fact, we are plunged back again into those quandaries about godlessness previously discussed.

The elevation to the One beyond the double *can* give rise to a *new dualism* between the One and equivocal many. If the One is so high, we may *fix on opposition* between transcendence (T³) and all else. This is especially likely to happen if we put all plenitude to one side, and consign all lack to the other. Then arises a dualism between transcendence itself

---

[6] Plotinus passionately rejects the Gnostic view of the material world as evil (*Ennead*, II, 9). One must hold oneself against any slander against the Father of all. The suppressed vehemence of his attack makes one wonder about his own passionate anxiety to separate himself from a position not unlike his own: materiality as the lowest of ontological lows, farthest away from the plenitude of the One, on the verge of nothingness. Plotinus rejects slander of the goodness of the aesthetic creation, and its noetic original, but does the absence of fuller agapeic resources make things difficult for him, not only about the goodness of finitude, but also the irreducibility of its otherness, and indeed the arising in finite creation of genuine newness and originality? "It does no good at all to say 'Look to God,' unless one also teaches how one is to look" (*Ennead*, II, 9, 34–5). Yes. I would add: we must learn to look agapeically.

(as absolute plenitude) and finite being (as the negative condition to be transcended).[7] Over there all good is, over against here, where all the lack is, and perhaps all the evil. The mediations between the superior One and what is finitely other become strained, just by the way the One is held supreme. The more we elevate it, the more we depreciate the intermedium of given being. Dualistic opposition thus develops out of this univocal logic: A is just itself and nothing but itself; B is also just itself and nothing but itself; hence both A and B, as just themselves, cannot be defined by reference to not-A or not-B. The determination of identity, coupled with the "not" between identities, makes us fix the two as opposed. Moreover, if the "not" between them is traversed by a self-transcending in flight,[8] the side fled is more and more lowered in estimation, as the side sought is elevated more and more beyond. As we approach the sought, its being further elevated means it always retreats, hence our flight from the first side gains on the second but the receding of its goal. The devaluation of both the flight and the point of departure become more and more extreme. The more we gain on the goal, the more we find we lose the goal, and our success is always only our failure.

This interesting result looks like a *reversal* of the seeking and the sought. Absolute transcendence in the mode of dualistic opposition seems to secure such transcendence just by making it unapproachable: itself and nothing but itself, there surrounds its unity a gulf that nothing other can cross over. Outside of the One, our point of departure is devalued as the transcendence we seem to approach is more and more elevated. This univocal determination of the One seems to imply that God has no relation to creation, either determined by God's own nature, or such as a finite being might call upon, with some expectation of reciprocity.

Picture this: the inscrutable King in the magic castle seems not to communicate with the people, and as a protective barrier forms around the fortress, the people wonder what transpires therein; in time they even begin to forget. The very inner self-security of the King makes the people outside less secure, for this inscrutability suggests something ambiguous. Sometimes things terrible happen outside the fortress. Black death descends and there is no escape from its reign. It is as if the world outside is so outside the divine that it *is* the reign of black death. Does the King within exhale an infection into the air around, whose spell enchants us only to swindle us? In the multiplied equivocities of this world outside, who is to say what is good, what is evil, since the good is sometimes unmasked as evil, and the evil proves the *incognito* of surprising beneficences? Does the poison too emanate from the high tower behind the high walls on the high hill? And yet too, has not that height risen so high that before our eyes it has vanished from sight?

What of that? This. This univocal securing of the One as beyond all equivocity becomes mired in its own equivocity. In so securing the One, we are made the more insecure about the One. If its relation to the between is one of oppositional dualism, no affirmative meaning can be given, first to the origination of the finite between, second to the promise of our porosity to the divine, third to our traversing the between as the ontological intermedium wherein our self-transcending contributes to its own destiny, and finally in relation to the good of that between and that self-transcending.

From an incomprehensible origin, we find ourselves inhabitants of a middle, involuntary exiles waking to taste the bitterness of ontological disorientation in a foreign land that can never be home. The light that should alleviate the darkness is itself darkness and we cannot tell twilight from dawn. Nor do we comprehend the point of it all, for this middle seems without end, and it seems better not to be in the between at all. After all, the between now seems less a good than a confinement. The world seems sunken in corruption. To say "It is good to be" has a mocking ring, as if taunted by king death.

---

[7] We need not attribute this to medieval transcendence, as is often done. There are aspects of it, but the rich complexity of a variety of approaches, including the Augustinian, Anselmian, Aquinian, exceed the univocal way, and are better understood in relation to the metaxological way.

[8] Flight is ambiguous: it can mean to flee; it can mean to be in flight, uplifted into the heights, "flying high," as we say.

Appeals to origin and end seem to have despair written all over them, despair not only about the corruption of the world, but despair before the inscrutability of the One.

And so, such a univocal securing of the One produces a dissolving insecurity in which the univocal formation of dualistic opposition undergoes a series of contorted mutations. Looking to the high One, seeming to find nothing, we taste the ashes of our own nothingness, and in the torment of our self-transcending a mutation begins to breed. For in the heart of the dualistic opposition is the work of negating: this can turn this way or that, devour now this univocal, now that univocal, univocals above, univocals below, even devour the secure univocity of the transcendent One. And then where do we find ourselves? On familiar territory: the *devalued world* that, as we saw in a previous probe, pervades the vain hollows of the waste landscape of modern godlessness. Not purged of dissolving equivocities, this univocal securing of the One creates the conditions in which the seeds of godlessness put forth many seductive sprouts. Transcendence on high stilts lets space below it empty for the creep of slouching atheism.

We have not been true to the too muchness of overdetermined being: the drive of dualistic univocity damps down the sense of fullness of given being. It muzzles the tongue that would exclaim "It is good to be." It drives away any aura of the holy that plays around the beauty of the world. That beauty, it might now seem, is a temptress – before us, all is come on, behind the come on, all else sluttish. The drive to univocity is not saved from its own totalitarian propensity. The very ferocity of its despair over itself renews itself in aggression against the equivocities of the intermedium of being, including the ambiguous traces of the divine there. It is not that we are finished with dualism, nor with the drive to the univocalization of being. Not at all. But in this further drive a new temptress comes beckoning us, a new slut – our own god-like godlessness. If the language seems brutal, remember that this here world is said to be a corrupted world. The beautiful mutates, but in such a mutable world, the mutation of beauty disgorges monsters.

THE IMMANENT DOUBLE(ING): OR HOW THE SHADOW OF MODERN MONOTHEISM IS ATHEISM

Where are we now? Still in the between, but with cognizance of the *heightened equivocity* of the happening of finite transience. How overcome the heightened equivocity? Heighten the univocity. But how now? By developing new modes of univocalizing that methodically here and now eradicate perplexing doubt. We can here situate the mathematicization of nature (T^1) marking early modernity, and whose reconfiguration of the ethos of being has come to dominate Western culture. This mathematicization has repercussions for the thinking of God (T^3).[9] For the exigence of transcendence is not extirpated; our immanent self-transcendence will seek God anew, or perhaps its new god, and moved by immanent mutations of negativity within its own energy of self-surpassing. I will make four main points.

First Point: Monotheism has a mediating influence in shaping our approaches to the intelligibility of nature. Even if the Most High is too high, and beyond our intelligence, the faith we upwardly direct to the One can come down to earth in an immanent faith that nature as given is marked by intelligibilities our intelligence can determine. For instance, Descartes's appeal to God's veracity is often judged as epistemologically dispensable, and yet he is not wrong in seeing the need for a ground of intelligibility, expressing a founded confidence in our cognitive powers. Were there no such ground, our confidence might not be up to its self-proposed revolutionary task. Not funded for this task,

---

[9] See *BB*, Chapter 2 on the univocal *mathēsis* of nature. John Craig, an intimate friend of Newton, wrote a book entitled *Theologiae Christianae Principia Mathematica* in 1699, a work full of complex algebraic equations that claim to demonstrate the truths of Christianity; it also calculates the end of the world 1500 years thence. See Frank E. Manuel, *The Eighteenth Century Confronts the Gods* (Cambridge MA: Harvard University Press, 1959), p. 92.

it would founder in it. We might muddle through the equivocity but the ambition radically to reconstruct the intelligibility of being would be enfeebled. Descartes's diffidence notwithstanding, his *project* shows the distinct note of world-historical ambition. If we have no grounding confidence that being can be so univocalized, why bother?

Second Point: To seek such a grounding confidence is not incompatible with a sense of the fallen world. Religious dualism can be a source of this, thus colluding in the configuration of a devalued world. The world is there, thrown out with its own intelligibility, but there as other to the origin. Think dualistically of this otherness and we are tempted to see opposition not only between world and transcendence, but in *our* dualism *with* the world. World as valueless thereness is drained of traces of community with the transcendent origin, reflecting a like lack of community between us and creation. We are strangers in the world. Though some responses to the strangeness sought to draw upon reserves of pagan affirmation, sacred power lying dormant in things, this is hard to sustain if the dominant configuration is dualistic opposition. The devaluation of creation need not come from secular rebellion against the sacred but from forms of religious dualism. Those most in favor of nature's mechanization were often those most insistent on preserving God's transcendence.

Third Point: This concerns our understanding of *ourselves*. There is a great gulf between creation seen in light of God, and nature as a valueless thereness to be univocally rationalized in mathematical ways. In the first, the halo of the origin still flares; in the second, this flare has been quenched, more or less. No longer bowing to the master on high, we rise and go on our way, hungry to become masters of what is other here and masters of ourselves. Descartes may promise we will become *comme le maître et possesseur de la nature* (*Discourse*, VI). We may soften the hubris by invoking for this a remote divine sanction. But when we have tasted the ashes of our nothingness, it is less love of life that drives our will to mastery than fear of death.

Fourth Point: The ensuing figure of God, or, rather, counterfeit double of God, is reconfigured in accord with ourselves and the valueless thereness. Like that self, God is master, master beyond equivocity, a kind of *mathematical master*. The good of creation is less emphasized as God's *absolute power to effect*. Since the connection of intelligibility to good is severed, intelligibility is itself coupled with the most efficient power to effect something. A dominant figure of this power: the clockmaker. The world is a machine: efficient power concretized in a structure that in itself has no value, indeed no life or love, and yet for all that, a structure amenable to mathematical univocalization; parts can be clearly taken apart and seen in their connectedness, connectedness not at all organic but extrinsic: *partes extra partes*. The human being? Diderot: man is a walking watch – *une horloge ambulante*. And God? Power yes, but absolute power to effect, in the special sense of making the world-machine, and perhaps having occasionally to intervene in the machine should any problems develop with its parts, or effective functioning. If intelligibility is mathematical univocity, we determine God as the absolute mathematical univocity, source of all mechanical determination, the One who engineers the clock of creation with eternal geometry.

We have come a long way from the incomparable One of Plotinus, and that way is not up. Atheism is the shadow of this geometrical monotheism. The shadow lengthens more and more as the light of the One seems withdrawn more and more on high, or sinks low on the horizon. As our geometry waxes our finesse seems to wane. The already dark earth is darkened more, though geometry may call its own darkness enlightened.

For it is *impossible* to maintain God in, or confine God to this kind of univocity. Since the will to mathematical univocity here methodically makes itself more and more effective, God must become progressively marginal and in the end redundant. The redundancy is epitomized by Laplace's response to Newton: I need not that hypothesis. God never becomes redundant, a counterfeit double of God becomes redundant, and this relative to the univocal determination of intelligibility. The scientific project may make finite being more and more univocally intelligible in a determinate way; God as the highest determinate intelligibility may become redundant, yet the question of the ground of determinate intelligibility itself is never redundant. What makes determinate intelligibility itself intelligible, and even the totality that constitutes the entire system of determinate intelligibilities is not itself another determinate intelligibility. This other original ground cannot be approached fully in terms of the univocal way. We need a God of finesse, and not just geometry.

The machine-maker God is an emaciation compared to the plenitude from which we must abstract to think it. The abstraction of the world produces an abstract of God. But abstraction is slow death. Likewise, there seems no community between God and creation. The mathematical master has less intimate communication with the world than the transcendent One on high. One might respect the astounding technical intelligence of the mathematical One, perhaps feel trepidation at its extraordinary power to effect, but one can hardly summon reverence, much less love. Deistic theism is the last halo of the devalued world – the halo whose shadow is scientistic atheism. Each is an evacuation of another relation to God, both have lost their roots in the primal ethos and its signs of living transcendence. The affirmation of this divinity is from the outset a mechanical elegy for a dying God, though this may be not known for a long time. When the realization strikes home, there is little or no memory of another God, and the undifferentiated cry goes up: "God is dead." But the cry does not know what it says, beyond the emaciated state it now dreads as its own spiritual debility.

Further, as the machine world cannot, so the cybernetic God does not, aid us orienting the very energy of our self-transcending (T²), itself beyond mathematical univocalization. That energy is harnessed to the projects of nature's mathematicization and the objectification of human being. But, of course, this energy is more than its projects, and will always remain so, since it is never a determinate intelligibility but a determining source of freedom. Freedom may proceed to make itself a crystal palace as its place of habitation, but when it takes up abode in this palace, it is not redeemed by mathematical enlightenment but finds itself the victim of unbidden forebodings and broodings, and dangerous distempers that repeatedly thwart the project of univocalizing. Desire distends itself and consumes things with a predatory greed whose voracity as quickly mutates into a deadening apathy. The more it eats, the more emaciated it becomes. The energy of self-transcending sickens in the palace of crystal, or diverts itself to the domination of others within the palace. Its palace is a cage, or a cave: a hole in which it kills its despair, as it kills with despair.

In more ways than one, our local way of being is an issue of the globalizing univocal configuration of being, and in more ways than we know, its victim. There is the remote mathematical master forming one double with the world; there is the devalued thereness in the immanent world forming our dualistic opposite; and there we are, standing in the way, opposite this opposite, dualizing the world in an active manner, out of our uncertain claim to be the One, *the* power. We cannot live with the devalued thereness and redouble our opposition to it by reconstructing it: the world has no value, we are the value of the world, and the bored God pares his nails in the crystal heavens.

This redoubling of opposition can only mean *aggression against creation*. There now seems no creation really, only the devalued thereness we cannot accept and that we must make valuable, come hell or high water. Despite all our self-congratulation about coming of age, it is the taste of our nothingness that drives us to secure our place in this valueless immensity. The univocal security of determinate intelligibility is thus wedded to our crediting ourselves with autonomy, for this securing is not for purposes of opening to creation as other but to making ourselves secure. We can never succeed totally. It is not in the nature of things. For it would mean this impossibility: the complete overtaking of the patience of being by our endeavor to be. Signs intimating the divine will continue to go unheeded, without renewed fidelity to the *passio essendi*, and without new openings to other-being, whether through free transcending towards the other, or the unwilled permeabilities that finitude often enforces. Our self-assertive autonomy fronts our nothingness, even as it affronts the otherness opposed to it. There is an autonomy hardly different to the misery of happiness with oneself. That misery must taste its own happiness more abysmally.

GODS OF GEOMETRY

I comment briefly on three important mathematically influenced determinations of the One: the Cartesian, Spinozist and Leibnizian.

Cartesianism configures the ethos of being in accord with different dualisms. Consider reason and religion. Descartes suggests that the truths of religion are too much above us, hence reason deals only with what is here to hand. But this humility is communicated with a wink to those in the know. What those in the know "know" is the mirror image of faith: namely, that faith has nothing to do with rationality. This is not a compliment to mystery. Rather univocalizing mind will seek to consummate its own autonomy, but this will be the reverse of irrational mystery, as a mirror image is a reversal in sameness. Let religion be, but with the aim of reason being let be. And where reason is let be, it will methodically *expand the circle* wherein its mathematical determination of intelligibility comes to dominion more and more. The release and self-elevation of reason is insinuated in Descartes's "submission" to the superlative height of religion, so high it is almost out of sight. But almost out of sight now, later becomes out of mind. Later may mean centuries.

Think of this elemental double: God and the *cogito*. Which of these is really the ultimate first? Soul and body are defined by a univocal dualism, favoring, it seems, orthodox views: the soul saved as immortal – a spiritual simple, a soul monad, entirely other to material atoms. Dualism also defines the whole human, and the interaction of body and mind: atoms of matter, atoms of mind, aesthetic substances, dianoetic substances, univocals each, but essentially separate. What of the self-mediation between these two in us, and the intermediation between us and the outside world? Oppositional dualism stands in for intermediation: we conquer our bodies with our minds; we conquer the aesthetic givenness of the world with the mathematical dianoetics of our science and technology. In time, we will turn these last back on ourselves, turn ourselves into objects, and seek to exert the same dominion over objectified humanity. The dianoetic dominance over aesthetic happening is nowhere more evident than in Descartes's projected therapy of a new *medicine*. Conquer the body and one might extend life indefinitely. Is there a therapy of soul to heal what is evil? Can the God of geometry help? Where is the God of finesse, when the machine destroys the good and the evil alike – with mathematical homogeneity? Is this geometrical God hard finally to separate from the evil genius, if its virtuosity with mathematical homogeneity leaves blurred the ultimate heterogeneities of good and evil?

Strangely, perhaps not so strangely, the search for strong, indubitable intelligibility of a mathematical sort inside the world coexists with the *attenuation* of God's ultimate intelligibility outside the world. For God's will as creating the laws of nature seems to be *sans* reason or beyond the law. There is much hidden here (Leibniz already was troubled) that will come out more extremely in a post-Kantian context. If the origin of intelligibility is beyond intelligibility, this will not be seen as a superluminous light beyond the natural light we know. It will not be a divine darkness at whose mystery we marvel. It will be an inscrutable will, which might as well be said to be absurd as intelligible, perhaps it may not matter which. God as the ultimate surd: a strange consequence of the accelerated will to do away univocally with all surds. We will to determine God intelligibly and end up making God unintelligible. We might learn something positive from this, but malnourished with the emaciated abstraction of deism, this is a hard lesson. We have the dying of this God or its accelerated leave-taking, ushered out by the clucking of enlightened critics.

The *Spinozistic God* seems most to exhibit the will to univocity of post-Cartesian thought; nevertheless, qualifications are needed. Much in Spinoza exceeds the horizon of mathematical univocity, though officially Spinoza will represent himself as subjecting nature (T^1) and human nature (T^2) to "geometry." If we take "geometry" as signifying the will to mathematical univocity, there is something equivocal about the Spinozistic *desideratum*. We find the trace not only of Stoic holism, but most importantly Stoic *gratitude* for the universe being as it is, being as it must be, according to the laws of eternal necessity. Of course, the laws as eternal necessity can partake of the univocalization in much the same way as the forms of eidetic intelligibility do in the Platonic context. Still, we are enjoined to *rejoice* that things are as they are. The philosopher attains not only wisdom but a blessedness. Is this perhaps a survival of the first sacred univocity in Spinozistic geometric holism? It is connected with Spinoza's ability to attract in the eighteenth century Novalis's compliment *der Gott-vertrunkene Mann*. And this as a counterpoint to the opposite judgment of the seventeenth century – not Benedictus but that most infamous atheist, *Spinoza maledictus*.

As a metaphysician in quest of ultimate univocal determination, Spinoza is more coherent than Descartes. The doubleness of two substances, thought and extension, is rendered more univocally in terms of two attributes of the one substance. There is but the One, and multiplicity follows in terms of complex modifications of the One, all, in the end, internal self-modifications. If we are reminded of Plotinus, still Spinoza's quest is so marked by the modern mechanical mode of explanation as to yield a very different impression. Geometrical method replaces Platonic eros, to the contraction of the thinking of the One.

Spinoza's definition of the One substance (*quod in se est et per se percipitur*) follows directly from Descartes's definition of substance as what is defined alone *per se*. Appreciation of the otherness of transcendence (T^3) relative to finite creation (T^1) is not strong. We must reject the vulgar picture of "creation," performed by a suitably caricatured "artisan," making the world from an "outside," itself prohibited by the definition of the One substance. For all the emphasis on geometrical determination, we risk a mediationless unity wherein crucial differentiations are blurred, a post-Cartesian version of the absorbing god of Eleatic monism.

The famous formula, *Deus sive Natura*, evidences a lack of needed differences (say, between T^1 and T^3). Among crucial differentiations needed is the idea of the origin as for itself and not just simply the other side of the same process of finite happening. The origin is not creation considered from the side of its immanent sources of generation; there is a more ultimate sense of origin, in excess again of the generative source of finite happening, that is, nature in a more normal sense. In a word, we need *more* than a distinction between *natura naturans* and *natura naturata*. To grant this would be to depart from the univocity of total immanence. Plotinus has a better presentiment of this excessive origin. Spinoza recoils from any such excess, for it must compromise the hegemony of any geometric method, here meaning the view that to be is to be determinate or determinable. There is no ultimate complete determination of this excessive source. To grant this would be to dethrone the geometrical univocity. We would not have to guillotine it, but its absolute preeminence, or sole sovereignty would have to be ceded.

The mechanical model also insinuates itself into our understanding of God, and we find it hard to avoid a kind of *theological determinism*. In our time, such a theological determinism shaped the "either/or" that Sartre proposed *vis-à-vis* human creativity: either God determines everything and there is no freedom; or we are free, not everything is determined, hence there is no God. Sartre makes a choice Spinoza would not endorse. The logic of the One entails the denial of divine freedom in any sense other than eternal necessity, and this coupled with the reinterpretation of human freedom, itself hard to distinguish from a certain qualification of necessity. How often we philosophers slide from "it happens to be so" to "it must be so," especially when we start to hit our heads against walls. The reverse also occurs: "it must be so" becomes "it happens to be so." Eternal necessity slides down the slippery slope of time to bottom on the historicist (ab)surd. Here Spinoza and Sartre have the look of cousins in the same family.

Within the immanent totality we find the network of qualified and subordinate centers of efficient power, centers of *conatus essendi*. Effective power strives to perpetuate *its own self*, to preserve its own being: this it would will eternal, were there no other interfering or qualifying sources of effective power. Such effective power, *conatus*, is like matter in motion in the mechanical context: it will continue endlessly, unless interrupted or hindered by an external intervening matter in motion. Every center of power endeavors to be absolute, and would be, but for its being relativized by other centers of power also endeavoring to be absolute. It is the totality which qualifies all these subordinate centers and as such alone is unqualified by another, hence is absolute, in the sense of *ab-solo*: from itself alone. In God as *causa sui*, we see the univocity of the unit, not just as effecting power, but as self-effecting power: God is the absolute unity of self-effecting power. *Causa sui* is absolute *auto-nomos*.

Seen in this light, the theological determinism is hard to distinguish from a kind of naturalistic atheism. God may be an honorific name to offer to nature,[10] but nature as the total system of such qualified centers of effective power seems but the cosmic machine. We should perhaps speak of a self-determining organism, since there is no clockmaker. But as a totality, "that it is at all" is a surd, devoid of any more ultimate intelligibility. Ironically, it is as intelligible or absurd as the indeterminable will of Descartes's God – only now in immanence rather than as transcendent. We wonder again if the ground of inherent intelligibility is itself unintelligible on univocal terms.

More: the cosmic machine or organism is, but there is no basis for saying "it is good" in an ultimate sense. "Good" is determined relative to what we desire. There are only the finite instrumental values the particular centers of effective power determine in their *conatus* to secure and perpetuate their own hold on being. No wonder Nietzsche admired Spinoza: *conatus essendi* is redoubled as self-affirming will to power; the deterministic monism of the whole as the eternal return of the same; the self-determining organism becomes the world as work of art that gives birth to itself; *acquiescentia mentis* becomes *amor fati*, and both these are less than charitable to (less charitably put, they turn away from) the God of the good, and creation, the one God of biblical monotheism. The sublime unity of the Spinozistic One hides enormous equivocity behind the mask of its pure, serene univocity.

What of the enigmas of the human one, and its sometimes sublime, sometimes wretched self-transcendence (T²)? What I intend by the *passio essendi* does not properly figure, except perhaps as an "inadequate" form of *conatus essendi*. Of course, *rejoicing* in the universe and Stoic *gratitude* are hard to explain without reference to the *passio essendi* and its porosity to the worthiness to be affirmed of what is other to us – this last means the ontological worth of other-being as being and as other. On that score, the porosity and the *passio* are beyond the terms of a *conatus essendi* that affirms *itself*. Spinozistic "religiosity" actually needs to draw on, draw from, the porosity and the *passio essendi*, even though its explicit philosophical resources cannot adequately deal with these.

We need not decry geometry, but its great helpfulness with univocal exactness is not the most helpful, particularly when dealing with the equivocities of the human condition. We need finesse and not just geometry. Spinoza is not without his own finesse, but overall one worries that "geometry" overtakes and usurps the role of finesse. Spinoza makes an astonishing statement: "Truth would be eternally hidden (*in aeternam lateret*) from the human race had not mathematics, which does not deal with ends but with the nature and properties of figures, shown to humankind another norm of truth."[11] If I read this right, a (quasi-)soteriological power is being claimed for mathematics. Prior to the geometrical sages of modernity, humanity seems to have been lost in the caves of night. After the new mathematics, rational salvation offers humankind the possibility of release into light, into blessedness.

What release, what blessedness? If mathematics saves us from purposes and ends (*fines*), would its knowing then be a purposeless knowing in a purposeless universe? If this is an

---

[10] Atheist Schopenhauer sees something dishonorable in this – he borders on the apoplectic at Spinoza's attribution of divinity to devouring nature. Big fish eat little fish, Spinoza and Schopenhauer would agree, but to throw flies to spiders and to laugh with glee, as his first biographer Colerus told us that Spinoza did for fun, this Schopenhauer could not stomach. See Arthur Schopenhauer, *Parerga and Paralipomena*, translated by E. F. J. Payne (Oxford: Oxford University Press, 1974) Vol. I, p. 73. When Augustine perchance watches a lizard or spider catch flies (*Confessions*, 10, 35) his response is quite different to Spinoza's: praise of God displaces the concupiscence of curiosity and of the eye.

[11] *Ethics*, Part I, appendix, in *Spinoza Opera*, edited by Carl Gebhart (Heidelberg: Heidelberger Akademie der Wissenschaften, 1924), p. 79; see *The Chief Works of Benedict de Spinoza*, translated by R. H. M Elwes (New York: Dover Publications, 1955), p. 77.

advance beyond darkness, it also seems an advance into a different darkness, darker in its intelligibility than the unintelligible darkness we have supposedly left behind. Are we given a geometrical counterfeit of saving knowing? Despite Spinoza's exoteric caution, moderation and sobriety, does "geometry" mask a version of rationality as esoteric will to power: the *conatus*, knowing the causes of nature, and becoming mindful of its own self-interest, will be better able to *serve itself*? "Rational" will to power, whether of Descartes's desire to be "master and possessor of nature" or of Spinoza's perhaps more masked form, is not quite Nietzsche's "irrational" will to power, but it is still will to power. Finesse requires a different love, before and beyond such purposeless science.

What of the *God of Leibniz*? For Leibniz to be is to be determinate, yet, under the sign of univocity, he wants to hold together two orders that transform the definition of being in terms of effective power: the mechanical order of natural intelligibility and the moral order of providential power. His critics charged Leibniz with regression for reintroducing the despised final causes, but he is more profound than his critics. Merely effective power alone is valueless, and in the end comes to nothing. Mechanical causality, as the *nec plus ultra* of intelligibility, is infected with ultimate unintelligibility. Effective power, to be effective, has to come to something. To what does it all come? For Leibniz, God has to be both supreme effective power and also power to determine events to a worthy outcome: effective power is literally worthless without providential ordination to the good.

In addition, the dynamism marking beings reveals them to be more complex than the mechanical philosophy can allow. Things reveal their natures to be defined in a process of self-becoming, as much telic as effective. Their self-becoming shows beings as becoming *themselves*. Things have no "selves" in the mechanical philosophy which offers us mathematical abstracts of things without self-becoming. Leibniz saw that determinability also involves *self-determining*. That the monads are windowless well accords with the determination of unity without its contamination by external difference. Yet their internal determination is inseparable from their *being determined* within a community of units. The doctrine of pre-established harmony follows from a more fundamental determination. The community of plural univocals cannot be effected by any finite monad, just because the determination of such units is through itself alone, and not with reference to other units. And yet they are *determined in relation to one another*, though in the mechanism of nature there is no proportionate ground for this entirely encompassing order. Who determines the communal plurality of finite univocals? The supreme determiner, the chief monad.

When we envisage the God who determines the compossibility of all the possibles, it is hard to avoid the supreme and absolute cybernet. This God possesses the *heavenly characteristica universalis*, with its "Adamic language of mystical vocables." Where there is disagreement, He will just say: Well let us calculate! Creating amounts to this heavenly: Well let us calculate![12] But surely Leibniz steps beyond the calculative divinity in stressing the providence of the good? Yes, but so much is still governed by the univocal determination of being. We need a God of finesse for providence and freedom, not just a God of geometry. Leibniz's theodicy, while in intent separating providence from fate, certainly from blind fate, seems to end in a *knowing fate*: Thus, finally, it must be so. This knowing seems to partake more of geometry than finesse, given the supreme effective and calculative power. One wonders if the shadow of theological determinism haunts Leibniz as much as Spinoza. Leibniz, one suspects, wondered himself if he was so haunted.[13]

---

[12]   Here I take the liberty of transferring from earth to heaven Leibniz's own description of the universal characteristic in *Philosophischen Schriften*, edited by H. Herring (Darmstadt: Wissenschaftliche Buchgesellschaft, 1992), IV, pp. 39–57; "On the Universal Science: Characteristic," in *Monadology and Other Essays*, translated by P. Schrecker and A. M. Schrecker (Indianapolis: Bobs Merril, 1965), pp. 11–21; see also *PO*, p. 317.

[13]   See, for instance, *Discourse on Metaphysics*, in *Philosophischen Schriften* [1985], I, sections 2 (pp. 58–61) and 13 (pp. 84–92).

This might not be so clear in the *Theodicy*, but Leibniz's later effort to summarize the essential argument in syllogistic form is so logicistic as to make one suspect that Leibniz is making God conform to the tortured constructions of his own system of syllogism.[14] Moreover, the monads all the way down are finally determinate through and through; their definition is an analytical proposition, not for us, but for the One who properly understands, namely, the infinite mind; the system of monads, as the kingdom of the whole, is determined through and through from the point of view of God. It is as if, under the spell of univocity, Leibniz could not twist free of the circumscription of the intelligibility of all being as univocally determinable. The will to make God so rational can end up with irrational consequences, when the atrocities of evil are shoehorned syllogistically into the best fitting cosmos. There is not enough of open space for freedom, and the overdeterminacy that releases it. There is too little of the surplus of the origin, and the mystery of the gift of being that stuns us, and that always stays with us, should mindfulness not fall into the sleepwalking of reason, programmed by its own constructions of determinate intelligibility.

Leibniz is cognizant of many of the most important considerations: the being-for-self of finite creatures, their "individuality"; the dynamic definition of their being, in a more organic sense, hence the inherence of natures in things of nature; the actuality of community, not first created by the things, but within which the things are created – pre-established in that regard; the recognition that to make sense metaphysically we need more than valueless mechanism. But the being-for-self of univocity closes the finite beings in themselves; their openness to others demands an overdeterminacy/indeterminacy in their dynamic that transcends univocity. We need to acknowledge an overdeterminacy in the creative power of the "chief monad," if there is to be a real creation of the other as other, and not merely the determination of God himself in the determination of creation; that is, if we are not to end with *Deus sive natura* again in which the otherness of origin and creation is collapsed.

The twistings in the *Theodicy* signal the net of universal determinism casting its toils over the best of intentions to preserve the otherness of God, the openness of the good and of freedom. The calculus of the divine will not work, and will bring God into disrepute. Inevitably to those geometrical humans under the sway of mathematical univocity, it will be the universal cybernet that will be of more relevance than the providential origin. Given what counts as intelligible, it is the universal cybernet, or the universe as simply a cosmic calculable order that will be declared intelligible, and Leibniz's invocation of the good wrongly dismissed as mere scholastic backsliding.

THE ONE AND THE DOUBLE IN IMMANENCE: KANT'S TRANSCENDENTAL ONE AND ITS HUMANISTIC DISSOLUTION

I conclude with a significant modern formation of the univocal way, emerging from the above considerations, and generating, directly and indirectly, many of the perplexities still pressing on us today. I mean the transcendental univocity associated with Kant's philosophy

---

[14] I refer to the supplement Leibniz produced to the *Theodicy* [Vol. II, 1 and 2 in *Philosophischen Schriften*] – "Abridgement of the Argument Reduced to Syllogistic Form" in *Philosophischen Schriften*, II, 2, pp. 285–313. What comes to mind is a kind of rational mania for syllogistic security. Christian Wolff, the famous rationalist, who made popular the Leibnizian philosophy, is revealing in claiming that a mark of genuine revelation is this: God must speak in clear unambiguous sentences, with no grammatical mistakes. Is this a rationalist dictation to God of the univocal grammar God must observe in order to be recognized as God by the rationalist? Who or what is God here? The rationalist philosopher himself, I fear. One meets a streak of the univocalizing tendency in an earlier logical and theological thinker: Abelard. See his interesting *A Dialogue of a Philosopher with a Jew and a Christian*, translated by Pierre Payer (Toronto: The Pontifical Institute of Mediaeval Studies Publications, 1979). Abelard's love and correspondence with Heloise are remembered more than his logicizing theology. Kant might have benefited from an Heloise.

and its offshoots. Kant addresses issues bequeathed by a mixture of Leibniz and Hume, and certainly he wished to avoid the Spinozistic One. He combines a number of approaches reflecting the modern reconfiguration of the primal ethos.[15] The rationalist approach to God proceeds by way of dianoetic univocity, the empiricist by way of aesthetic univocity. As the former leads to the suspicion of emptiness concerning a priori proofs, the latter produces skepticism concerning unwarranted a posteriori inference, or at best, ambiguous probability which can be turned as equally to the denying of God as to the affirming. This doublet of aesthetic and dianoetic univocities was to influence Kant's innovation, since it crucially reflects the doubleness between mechanism in exteriority (T¹) and self-determination in the moral self (T²). Each of these univocities can give rise to unacceptable conclusions: dogmatism and skepticism. Yet, our inextirpable need of univocity points beyond the mechanistic univocity, whether expressed in rationalist or empiricist terms. We need a third way, more original that the aesthetic and the dianoetic: transcendental univocity.

Kant's transcendental univocity does not directly refer to God, for God is and remains transcendent. In relation to transcendence itself, Kant is an heir of the dualism which sees us as trying to find a way from "down here" to God "up there"; but we are stuck "down here" on this side of the dualism. One can attribute to the univocalization of being a kind of *metaphysical spatialization* that separates and opposes the orders of the world and the transcendent. Kant, however, is cunning: he turns to the transcendental, newly defined by him, in distinction to the transcendent (perhaps closer to the ancient meaning of transcendental), and finds an *indirect* pointing to transcendence itself. In light of the failures of dianoetic and aesthetic univocity, Kant inquires about the conditions of the possibility of our knowing God, and gives primary place to the *transcending power of self-being* (T²), not the otherness of nature (T¹) or God (T³). In modern dualism God's manifestness becomes increasingly problematic; with Kant *that very problematic* itself becomes the problem. The search switches from transcendence as other (T³) to self-transcendence (T²), understood in a complex transcendental way.

This is not at all like Plotinus, in whom the *native ecstasy* of mindfulness opens up towards the divine. If one is thus impelled towards transcendence (T³), and has undergone the dynamic outgoing of the urgency of ultimacy, moved again by the reserved energies of the *passio essendi*, one might be so caught up in the movement that it will seem a paler secondary matter to analyze reflectively how the movement is possible at all. If I am in love with eternity, that love carries me. I analyze it, and the love is already grown old, or cold, or perhaps it was cautious and anemic from the start, perhaps not having taken wing at all. There comes then a suspicion of ecstasy, a suspicion already too old with time, before being young for eternity. I sang to my love, when I was in love. Now I am not in love, and so I analyze the song. And now I love my analysis, perhaps my clever self, and no longer my love. I no longer sing. Alas, my old song cannot be voiced by my new transcendental language. My new language speaks about *itself* and not the adored other that once turned my head. We argue about the possible conditions of engendering a child, while ourselves being eunuchs. We come up with a theory that engendering is not possible: transcendental eunuchism. Those who can, do; those who cannot, construct transcendental theories. Or deconstruct them. Or mount high up the pulpit of reason and preach with odd venom contra *Schwärmerei*.

Say this: a certain retardation of our transcending (T²) or perhaps senility of skepticism becomes evident in the wake of modern dualism. It is as if the unrelenting will to the *mathēsis* of nature drains the energy of transcending away from the divine, and redirects it to the immanent task of univocalizing given being. The spontaneous joy we find in someone like Plotinus is seen through the uncomprehending eyes of the retardation, or the suspicious eyes of epistemological anxiety, or the sour eyes of that senility.

Consider the continuation and strange exacerbation of Leibniz's double view in Kant's transcendental univocity. Leibniz lives posthumously in Kant – especially concerning

---

[15] I now focus on the matter in relation to univocity; in Chapter 5 I return to Kant as seeking a way beyond univocity and equivocity, relative to what I call his virtual dialectic.

the differences and relations of the doublet: nature and morality.[16] One detects a *double seeing* in Kant: "Dare to know!" he exclaims; "We cannot know things in themselves," he explains. "God is beyond cognition," he claims; "God is necessitated," he proclaims. "God is unprovable," he claims; "God must be postulated," he counterclaims. And God as unprovable proves to be God as necessitated otherwise than theoretically. One finds an oscillation between default and unavoidability; between ambiguous evidence and recalcitrance to being known; between inscrutability and moral necessity; between will to univocal determination and metaphysical perplexity impossible to silence, metaphysical perplexity itself nourished on moral sources. Kant's God: an "impossible" but necessary transcendence. To all this you might say: either a fine tissue of equivocation, or the equilibrium of a delicate balance. Or you might say: both equivocation and equilibrium.

I confine myself to how the transcendental univocity is invested in the *constituting subject* as the *ground of determination*. The active self constitutes the intelligibility that before we naively took to be there in the real: intelligibility is not given, it is constructed. This transcendental one is not transcendent. This opens an *immanent self-transcendence*, though Kant does not speak this way. The source of determining univocity has turned to the side of self-being. Other-being is the medium in which intelligibility is determined, but it does not give or determine intelligibility. This turn to self is extraordinarily important, not only in a Kantian and post-Kantian context, but in any serious thinking of God. But since Kant, the turn has *not* been mainly understood in its religious meaning. Rather as source of construction, the active self also is source of deconstruction, even destruction.

The Kantian turn to the transcendental self is less something revolutionary new as an *episode consolidating and accentuating the apotheosis of autonomy and the dubious ambiguating of transcendence as other* that constitute the longer movement in modernity. The dualistic opposition of self and other generates equivocities between the two, but now the equivocal between must be made more univocal through *our power* of determination. We become the One who mediates the double, whether immanent or transcendent. The urgency of ultimacy is then primarily defined by the self-transcendence of an activist self. This urgency is not directed to transcendence as other. It becomes our urgency to will our own will, to will to be or to become the One. Mindfulness of the *passio essendi* falls into recession, as we grow more oblivious of the porosity of being in and through which the signs of the divine are communicated.

I will come back to Kant, but I conclude the current line of reflection with two crucial formations of this will to univocity: the *scientistic* and the *humanistic*. These bring us again to our present predicament, but also point us further along the current line. Scientism is one formation of the collusion of aesthetic and dianoetic univocity, under the baton of self-autonomizing humankind. The project of science is believed to answer all the essential questions, or to promise to do so. Issues traditionally reserved for religion will cede their mystery to this will to scientific determination and technological instrumentalizing. The approach is objectifying in that being and its intelligibility emerge in a process of scientific determination of which we ultimately are the source. The urgency of ultimacy takes form in our will to the mathematical mastery of nature. We would be, so to say, the *dianoetic master* of nature. Nature's transcendence in its exteriority (T^1) is not denied; yet its intelligibility is not determined from its otherness but from the immanent resources of the determining self (T^2).

And yet, there is something incoherent about such a will to absolute objectification, since the will itself, as a transcending, cannot be completely objectified. Something about the self-transcendence of the dianoetic master is not itself objective. Hence this objectifying project *must* presuppose another sense of the self as transcending, *beyond science*. This becomes evident in humanistic form, whether expressed in terms moral (Kant),

[16] Kant being haunted by Leibniz is not surprising given his younger allegiance to Wolff – the vulgarizer of Leibniz.

political (Marx), or aesthetic (Nietzsche). For the first formation issues in valueless objectivity, and this is an insupportable outcome of the human effort to be the One mediating the double: valueless objectivity is a redefinition of dualistic opposition, because this valueless otherness can finally only evoke our disgust or contempt or rebellion. While the will to univocity is present here in diverse humanistic formations of self-transcendence, the monsters of the equivocal also await their exhumation.

Put it down this way: some of the dragon's teeth that Kant sowed spring up later as Nietzsche's monster children. For if all determination leads to human determining, aesthetic creativity merely bides its time to step forth and redeem the claim to be *the basic mode of constructing.* Our self-assertive aesthetic creativity claims its proximity to, perhaps even identity with, the origin. Moral autonomy, political solidarity seem to lead back to artistic work, as do mathematical structure and religious myth. The imperial self as *poetic master* occupies the throne, sometimes in opposition to, sometimes coexisting with the dianoetic master. Scientism of nature and aestheticism of life make a fine couple, now in high dudgeon, now stroking each other. Life is our art; gods have been and will be our art works; we will be our own works of art; we will work our way to being the gods of our own art. Once again the urgency of ultimacy is defined by our immanent self-transcendence, and transcendence as other is loathed if it places limitation on that immanence. Even nature's transcendence must serve the human self as the one who determines, hence the dianoetic master is mastered by the aesthetic master. Life is the play of our aesthetic will to power. Scientism is incorporated in a more inclusive aestheticism.

This summarizes a dominant configuration of the ethos of being in our postmodern times. It also signals the return of the equivocal. How so? The fact is this formation of the urgency of ultimacy is never quite released from an insecure opposition to otherness. For transcending (T^2) here is inseparable from negating any otherness that limits one's power of determining. Inevitably, the transcendence of nature as other (T^1) must be subordinated. God's transcendence (T^3) must be either rejected, or redefined in terms of our immanent self-transcendence (T^2). But in the process of elevating our powers of self-transcending into the ultimate, we discover inward otherness in ourselves. We would be the sovereign one, but within this one there is an immanent otherness that causes the posture of sovereignty to come unstuck.

The recessed *passio essendi* slips free of every effort to overtake it, or completely take it over. The porosity of our being can never be closed into an immanent self-completing whole. The otherness above self or outside self that we thought to have mastered reappears *within* the circling of selving. First, nature is not just outside us, for we are parts of nature, and something of its otherness will continue to erupt within us, no matter what mastery over it we claim. As nature's products, we can never be completely its masters, since as masters we must necessarily be its products. And this will be most evident in our own aesthetic being, namely, our incarnate natures. Our bodies are beautiful but they are mortal; and before death, in the energy of life itself, they are unruly in manners we cannot fully determine. We are determined as much as we determine; we cannot be the one who absolutely determines. And this is even more true of the gift of incarnate being at all.

Second, with respect to God, exploration of our own inward otherness brings home to us sources of determining that are beyond our determination, even in our self-determination. The inward otherness of selving finds turmoil and torment its lot when its urgency of ultimacy finds nothing but itself. For what is it but *radical equivocity in inwardness itself?* Anyone with even a modicum of appreciation for the inner tangle of our desire knows what a bruising struggle it is to fight free of its fetters. Art itself proliferates testimony to the dark labyrinth of the heart: beauty and brutality, eros and death, savage gods sought by us, but staying beyond their welcome to devour the harvest.

Now we ourselves are the monsters: monsters of the equivocal but deficient in reverence and in utter want of porosity to the immediate sacrality of pantheistic univocity.

The human one who would be the sovereign determining power floats all along on a sea of equivocity, and at any moment can drown. Its urgency of ultimacy comes to nothing when it is itself the ultimate. One may spend a lifetime living as if one were the ultimate, but one cannot postpone the honesty that sinks one's claim. One is not ultimate, and the urgency of ultimacy, thus directed on self, is astray. One has been astray. One has been an evasion of this moment, which is every moment and no moment in particular. Transcendence as other, the One in excess of all our determination, remains in waiting. Strangely, too, at the limits of our scientistic and aesthetic dominion of the between, and as we sink, a new porosity can open up. The rapture of being can be reborn, and we must seek new buoyancy on a sea of equivocity that washes all shores.

Chapter 4

God and the Equivocal Way

Stones thrown out as by a wanton boy
We skimmed the surface of the sea
Touching and rising, dipping and leaping
Always moving away
The fling was in the throw of the flight
& we rejoiced in our being light
An impulse passed on
An impulse passing on
An impulse perishing
Exulting, we were stones

See out there
Beyond the breakers
Sky and sea collapsed
The stones sink down
Claimed by the sea we defied

The silent world is full of signs
But is this what You wanted in the garden
When we passed among the trees
To be as now sulking
In holes of the sea
Sunk in our lost selves?

THE WAY OF EQUIVOCITY

Our urge to determine God in an absolute univocal way is enmeshed in multiple equivocities. In subduing one set of equivocities, we generate others, and just in our determination of univocity. We cannot define univocity apart from its *interplay* with the equivocal, and, in fact, it is just this interplay that our previous probes invariably revealed. We must now interpret the interplay with more finesse, that is, turn again to the between as the overdeterminate matrix, and to our predeterminate rapport with being there. Perhaps the *doubleness* of the equivocal offers more revealing guidance concerning the primal ethos, and so aids our thinking of God, or mindfulness.

We need *a hermeneutics of the equivocity of the between*, not a univocal system to master it conceptually. We need finesse of mindfulness attuned to its signs and hyperboles, something traditionally offered in symbolic theologies or the doctrine of analogy, and so on. Yet something double-edged persists. Finesse for equivocity *can* occasion our rapport with the communications of creation, and *can* release celebration of its glorious gift. The primal ethos seeds a kind of urge to sing. A great poet or musician or artist might be made intermittently porous to the return of this urgency. But all is not light, and, contrariwise, the coming on of night rocks us back on our heels, turns us round, turn us upside down, we may not even know which side is up, which side down. Equivocity puts us at sea again.

Quandaries about God are often posed in the context of a fairly developed univocalization of being, but if we lack a *poetics of the divine*, we start too late. We need such a poetics that is before or beyond any *mathēsis of God*. For if the univocal way tilts more to the God(s) of the philosopher, the equivocal way returns us to more intimacy with the passion of the religious and its God(s).[1] Our desire to univocalize often displays an

---

[1] Thinkers exhibiting finesse for the equivocal include Heraclitus, Augustine, Pascal, Dostoevski, Nietzsche, to mention a few. The interpretation of signs is crucial, and perhaps the human being is the

objectifying bent, but we do not cease to suffer perplexities stubborn to objectification. When such perplexities come over us, we cannot find our way around in an entirely objective way. Are we lost? In a sense, yes; and certainly lost, if the objective way is the only way. But perhaps there is a "being lost" that augurs the promise of other paths to God. If objectively there is no way that is absolutely univocal, it does not follow there is no way, or that no ways offer themselves. There are extremities of life that awaken us to what is not-objectifiable, both in ourselves and in nature as other, or in what, further still, is superior. The point is not a mere subjectification, though there is a path of subjectification we must pursue. *We ourselves* are essentially in question, in how we face the universal impermanence and the "not." Equivocity thrusts us along this passageway of danger and hope.

If univocity stresses sameness, equivocity attends to unavoidable doubles, even breaking our fixation on sameness. If the extreme of one is unmediated identity, the extreme of the other is unmediated difference. Such pure extremes are nowhere to be found, for they are abstractions from the mixing of the two in the between. Because they mix, we may highlight now one extreme, now the other. But just because they *mix*, there is a sense in which *the equivocal is more fundamental*. In the between, we are opened to an undifferentiated pluralism prior to our discrimination of the many into differentiated identities. There is an equivocal promiscuity of sameness and otherness, unity and plurality given in the overdetermined beginning. This pre-objective matrix can be called either the immediate univocity, or the immediate equivocity, but because it can be called both, we must more rightly call it the equivocal matrix. This matrix offers a richer rapport with the primal ethos of being.

We come once again to transience, and to another way in the universal impermanence, where the doubleness, and not just the One, calls on our mindfulness. I name some of its way stations that below will give us pause: first, nature's equivocity as mediating an ambiguous feel for the divine; second, God's own possible equivocity; third, the rupture of evil as intensifying our perplexity about God's equivocity, perhaps to the highest pitch of torment; fourth, the shift to inwardness to sift the equivocity, a shift showing the equivocity of religious inwardness itself; fifth, our trial by Gethsemane thoughts, suspended between curse and blessing; sixth, the equivocal way as a purgatorial passage through difference. In this last station, the steadfastness of our own being in the universal impermanence is strained to the utmost and our intermediate being is called to catharsis, that is, a purged porosity, between the extremes of nothing and God .

NATURE'S EQUIVOCITY

Presentiments of the divine emerge in the between, for the intermedium of being is no machine; it is the matrix of coming into being and passing out of being. There is plurality, but also there is process never to be univocally determined, even while it gives rise to determinacies of being. The process that determines beings as determinate also determines beings to be undone, and beings pass away. As process, the between shows both a *naturing* as well as a *natured*. The naturing gives rise to the natured, but it also exceeds it; in time this natured being, that natured being, pass out of being. This is the doubled process: being is given, being is taken away; things appear, things disappear.

The appearing, the disappearing show us the between as *aesthetic happening*. With univocity, we move towards the *mathēsis* of nature; with equivocity, we regain contact with the *aesthēsis* of naturing. The first is correlated with a determined nature as natured, the second with nature as a determining naturing. Equivocal naturing is closer

---

most equivocal sign to interpret in relation to what exceeds humanness. Heraclitus: "You could not search out the furthest limits of the soul, even if you traversed all of the ways; so unfathomable is its logos" (Frag. 45). On the messenger and the god: "The lord whose oracle is in Delphi neither speaks out nor conceals, but gives a sign" (*oute legei oute kruptei alla sēmainei* Frag. 93).

to the concrete happening of the ethos, soliciting an ambiguous openness to the ambiguous showing of the origin. Here we need the artist, the poet, as well as the prophet, who speaks in divine metaphors or parables. We need a poetics of the divine – for aesthetic happening is marked by constitutive ambiguity that cannot be entirely reduced to fixed determination. Why? It is the confluence of the fixing and the unfixing that itself cannot be finally fixed. There is no univocity of the world given in the full glory of its show, for not only does the givenness show astonishing thereness of being at all, it also shows what retreats from show, namely, the vanishing of beings that now are not, or that will come to be there no more. Astonishment before this showing and withdrawal puts us in mind of a more original source that gives being and takes back what is given.

The showings of nature in the universal impermanence are themselves ambiguous. They mingle creation and destruction, life and death. The aesthetic happening shows the togetherness of these as dynamic processes. Process suggests not some static ground fixed by univocity, but a more primordial origin that is dynamic power in an even more original way. The thought of God looks through the presentiment of this more primordial original. This thought of God is not a univocal retreat from becoming to stasis but arises from honesty before the equivocity of givenness, from thinking into and through the constitutive ambiguity of creation as an aesthetic happening. There need be no flight from the world. The world itself is a givenness of aesthetic show that intimates a source that is more than aesthetic show.

As the showing itself is double, our presentiment of this origin also shows doubleness. There is a show of dynamic power, power extraordinarily creative since it is creative of the ordinary, power making our minds reel with barely an inkling of the prodigal pluralizing dynamism broadcast in the world. And the power of that origin is in excess of all that. This might make our minds to stagger, as if we were drunken idiots. In fact, more than our mind is staggered, because the aesthetic show of power affects us in our bodies, and not only as if from outside. It courses through our bodies and vitalizes them, especially in an excess of erotic transcending. That eros is not just sexual eros, and the vitalizing can be as basic as the elemental delight of breathing afresh the air of a summer morning. We embody the aesthetic showing of the original powers of being, broadcast in all beings in the aesthetic show of creation. As our bodies live the vital delight of being at all, so too they are schooled in the ebb of energy and the withering of the grass.

And the origin of all that is the source of this twofold gift: gift that seems to contain its own curse when, once having tasted the sweetness of being, we feel the impotence at the oncoming of night. God is lord of life. God is also master of death.

GOD'S EQUIVOCITY

The *aesthēsis* of naturing is related to fertility and death – eros, perpetuation, perishing, and surpassing. The *mathēsis* of nature deals more with a product generated than a producing genesis; form more than forming; structure rather than structuring. God is not nature naturing, though nature naturing points more to God than does nature natured. It is not surprising, then, that the power of origin should be associated with fertility. The naturing of nature puts us in mind of the origin, and our bodies, all living bodies, live this mindfulness in a mindless way. In the flesh they are aesthetically lived by naturing. Humankind will sprout fertility cults, at once highly elaborate and elemental. The thought of the origin is not that of mere brute power but more. Brute power cannot do justice to the rich variegation of life, nor to the nuance of its aesthetic beauty, nor to the sweep of its elemental joy. Brute power would be a univocal monochromism of origination: a grey origin that would produce a grey world, and with no shades of grey to delight. The world is not grey. It is green, it is gold. The fineness of its coloration is beyond our telling, calling for a finesse so deep and delicate one might weep to have it – and to lose it. The power that paints the beauty is no brutal power. The aesthetic finesse of the origin seems also beyond all telling.

Perhaps it is when we live love, or our bodies live love, that we live an unstated sense of this divine finesse. I know this is no *argument* for the origin, no stately syllogism for God. This would be laughable. The laugh itself is closer to God. It is elemental, and erupts out of living in closer communion with the vitality of the origin. We are lived by a love, for we do not choose love first, but find ourselves in love. We fall in love, and, when lived by love, beings become musical, their music like the evanescent communication of a mysterious lover, achingly distant, strangely close. Things are not univocal units of effective power. Things now are songs. They sing the glory of the origin. The finite lover does not know this, being too caught up in being lived by love. The love and the beloved are enjoyed, and there is already too much for us in that joy.

There is more: not only the fervor of the *incognito* origin, but the fading of the flush of beauty. We are lived by the love *episodically*. Our bodies are frail vessels and pay the price of their intermittent ecstasy. The scales tip down on the other side. When that other side has its day, that day in truth is night. What is fertile sprouts from the earth that is dark, for the womb is hidden. The nocturnal passion comes on: nocturnal not simply as the ecstasy of love, but as the undergoing of what cannot be brought into the light of day, what we dare not bring into the light, what dare not bring itself. Night terrors, not *amor*. Sweats cold and with a shuddering dread. A cry of terror that shouts in the silence. A wounded pleading, but there seems to be nothing or no one there to hear. A plea beyond nothing. The groaning of creation, this pathos of the night; not the singing of things, for beings seem blighted. In the aesthetic equivocity of creation, the passion of the nocturnal also speaks of God, of God's darkness.

The resistance of the divine to univocal simplicity is evident often in its double, or Janus mask. Heraclitus: "[The] God is day night, winter summer, war peace, surfeit famine" [*koros limos*: satiety craving] (Frag. 67).[2] The presentiment of the divine is mediated by the equivocity of naturing where there is a mingling of profusion and waste, giving of bounty beyond our reckoning and suffering beyond all kenning. And this darkness of God is not just the nice complement to the day of the divine, a neat equilibrium tailor-made to console us with tame symmetry. The darkness is mysterious, but with the hint of power incomprehensible to the point of contempt for our justice. The God that laughs is also the God of wrath, and wrath here is the grim power to bring everything to nothing. The wrath laughs mockingly at flimsy finitude. The sublimity looks like power overweening, the transcendent threat in which we dwindle to nothing.

Think thus of the doubleness. First Eden: the bounty of the creator given in creation and given simply because it is good, very good; the paradisal univocity of immediate rapport with nature and naturing: no gap of alien otherness, no effort against an opposite, pure joy in being one. Can one bid adieu to the fading beckoning of Eden? One rises on a spring morning and the wind has blown away the storm, the sun sparkles and paradise is there. Once I heard a blackbird singing, with full throat pouring its praise out of a hiding tree, and suddenly I was in paradise. Was I in paradise? Why am I unable to erase the memory of that song?

Now the Flood: water is matrix of all life, but in deluge its creative indeterminacy overwhelms and swamps. Finite beings are flimsy, tossed around as flotsam. (DECEMBER 26, 2004: EARTHQUAKE BENEATH THE SEA, TSUNAMI – PARADISE ONE MOMENT, DROWNING DESOLATION THE NEXT.) Creative power is destructive power beyond our measure; the overdeterminacy brings into being but also annihilates. The garden of the world is wasted, wasted perhaps to make a clearance for a new garden, but wasted now and our child has perished. The torrent washes away the filth and freshens life, but our father has been carried across the bar and we are bereft. Can one disjoin the creative and destructive power? Power seems to be not one or the other, but both, for the opposites are together. If they are not opposites but showings of the one power, is the one power then *double in itself*?

---

[2] Relevantly again, Dionysus and Hades are the same (Frag. 15): the god of generation and intoxication is inseparable from death and the underworld. Doubleness in the myth of Persephone: flowering, death, returning to the Earth, and then the spring resurrection. Shiva: creator, destroyer. Kali – from Sanskrit root *Kal*, meaning time – Shiva's consort: goddess of destruction – intimate to all creation.

The law of contradiction that would separate out the opposites into exclusive univocal categories seems not entirely faithful to naturing. It is just this redoubled togetherness of the opposites that we live and know. The power seems equivocal in itself, in that sense, contrary in itself, indeed so in a potentially creative sense. For to destroy, or to turn against one form, is also to generate another form, to turn towards a new being. The equivocal being of the power of naturing cannot be captured in a logic of univocity. We need the myth or the image or the artwork to express something of its surfeit and its famine. (Do you notice how, as we reflect on the equivocal way, we need images and metaphors as much as ordered thought; more need, in fact, by comparison to the univocal way?) Religions, in that regard, cultivate the mythic arts which image the equivocal being of the divine power, mediated through the equivocal power of the creation that power has wrought. The power that makes the lamb makes also the lion. The power caressing the playful child has wrought the killer whale. We may shudder at the killer, we should shudder, but we should also shudder at the making source. We lack the measure of that creative power.[3]

All this places us in deep perplexity about the equivocity of both nature and its origin. Nature's equivocity is not alleviated by the univocity of the origin, because the latter is also the origin of the former's equivocity. That there is darkness in this world allows no escape from the perplexing thought that it is so because there is darkness in the origin. The mixing of light and darkness here suggests more a twilight middle than a new dawn, because when every new day comes to shine, it brings with it this darkness that is not just a darkness of the night. It is the perplexing darkness of being itself, still there even when we have shone on it the glare of our brightest objective enlightenment. We determinately explain everything and all is day. But all is night relative to the origin of the determinate, that it is at all, and that, as it is, it is inseparable from its own nothingness, whether previous or impending.

The equivocal stirs up trouble in the pit of our souls, because the stirring rumbles with the enigma of the very doubleness of finite being itself. This doubleness is a possible duplicity: it shows itself, but shows itself as hinting its own hiddenness, hiddenness quite other to the face it has deigned to show us. The smiling face – suddenly – seems to snarl and spit out what seems to us a curse. Shaken to the core, we savor the bitter doubleness of finitude. The shocking reversal from smile to snarl causes a liquefaction of our confidence. It liquidates our ontological trust and we know the sinking feeling in our bones that things are not as they appeared. This sinking in one's being makes one sick at heart. Something other, seemingly sealed behind the mask, puts one's trust to the test. One will never master that mask. "I am poured out like water, and all my bones are out of joint" (Psalm 22:14, King James Version). The liquefaction of ontological trust reveals a breach in the immediate rapport with the goodness of being, a breach that seems irremediable. A seed of suspicion has been sown, and it roots itself so intimately in one's being its source vanishes from consciousness. It is astonishing how the reversal from smile to imprecation so quickly does its work. We suddenly cease to bless. As soon as we learn to speak, like Caliban, we learn to curse.

---

[3] Think of Blake's great poem: "Tyger! Tyger! Burning bright/In the forests of the night, /What immortal hand or eye/Could frame thy fearful symmetry?" The aesthetics of happening are aflame, the symmetry is fearful, its beauty is not tame: "In what distant deeps or skies/Burnt the fire of thine eyes?/On what wings dare he aspire/What the hand dare seize the fire." Icarus did not fly on these wings. The fire might be the dangerous fire Prometheus, the thieving Titan, stole from Zeus. Among the gods, there is daring, whether in creating or in stealing. "When the stars threw down their spears/And water'd heaven with their tears/Did he smile his work to see/Did he who made the Lamb make thee?" Meekness and wrath must kiss, the stars and the spears, the smiles and the tears. "Tyger! Tyger! Burning bright/In the forests of the night, /What immortal hand or eye/Dare frame thy fearful symmetry?" Question on question must be redoubled to the great artificer, the immortal hand. *The daring of God*: we daring God, God's own daring, God daring us. The daring is ominous. The divine daring is itself redoubled: a hazard, and hazarding on the creature made: our challenge, a challenge to us – a dare: Do we too dare say "yes" – to this?

Why do we curse? We curse, not just because we think we are cursed, but because the face behind the smile remains behind. Hiddenness that retains the measure of itself causes us to curse. This measure of itself crushes our confidence. We are not even the measure of our own rapport with finite being. Its evanescence shows how much an unmeasured gift it is. When the gift does not smile, we turn against it just as gift, where before we turned towards it spontaneously in consent. Have we been "taken in" by the smile? Were the hiddenness to offer itself to us, we might accept its curse. We would be taken into its confidence again. It remains on the other side of the mask. It remains in its equivocity, and will not surrender this equivocity, either to our pleas for light, or to our rebellious provocations that would flush it from its cover. Not taken into the mystery of its confidence, our being passes into shock; recovers somewhat in diffidence; breeds in silence its own suspiciousness; and having brooded on its resentment, finally hatches into releasing revolt; a release itself false and futile.

EQUIVOCITY AND EVIL

We know evil. When the smile on the face is interrupted there is delivered to our face something like a blow. Evil is a trauma: our mindfulness becomes blurred and our souls concussed. Now our perplexity about God can never more be a matter of analytical epistemology. Having been struck, our speech ceases to sing, and comes out as a stammer, not a sleek argument. An outcry from the stricken soul, a rasping plea: we do not know what evil means at all, what it all means – this is what the stutter says, and perhaps the sleek argument too. Indeed after this trauma, there is no speech that is not the guardian of its own secret silence – a blank of spirit buried in the idiocy of the soul. And yet, it is often so that out of such secret hidings come the deliverances of the divine. Sometimes rational univocity seems the callous of mind that hardens over the porosity of our being, assuaging some hidden hurt or longing. Univocal reason: a remedial protective for vulnerability? But something is religiously answered in the equivocal saying itself, let the philosophers – those glad impresarios of univocity – go scowl at contradiction and paradox and murk.[4]

Evil has different meanings, but here I couple evil with equivocity because our exposure to baffling difference initiates our distancing from immediate immersion in the elemental rapport with being. We begin to be set apart, and this not only through immanent powers of differentiation, but through the doubleness of traumatic difference, issuing from the creative/destructive might of naturing. That might brings the determinate unities in nature to their own definition, but is also brings to us our own difference from nature's otherness. Awakening to our own difference, we know our ontological insecurity in the unmastered impermanence of being. Alerted to the *nothing* that works hand in glove with the creative power of being, this we know not only in externality, but intimately in the intimation of our own mortality. We lose intimacy with the agape of being as dark

[4] As more intimate with the ambiguity of the archaic, myth is a speaking of the divine that enfleshes the equivocity, granting the perplexing doubleness of life and death, creation and destruction. Here truth is not univocal correctness (see *BB*, 466–75). The spontaneous languages of religions, in their imagistic, mythic, representational equivocity are, in this respect, truer than the more univocal languages of philosophers. They address our religious being in a manner the latter too often attenuate. That they are equivocal is not necessarily a defect, even though it is full of danger, as many philosophers have realized. If you climb into a hell hole, or ascend a mountain, everything you do is dangerous. The perils of this saying can be superior to the cautions of the rationalizing chaperons. *Story:* There is a treasure spoken of on the other side of the meadow, but the meadow seems mined. A philosopher cautions against crossing the field, paralyzed by his foreknowledge of mines. If he moves, he might be blown to bits; he stays where he is. Or perhaps he clears a mine on the edge of his path; he ventures no further, except to show the mine, display its mechanism, and speculate about other possible mines, how they might be like this, or counter examples to this one, and so on and on; until he forgets entirely the treasure. If reminded, he may have a thousand and one arguments as to why the perilous crossing should not be undertaken; anyway, apart from the possible mines out there, no one has even come back to tell us about the treasure and univocally "prove" its real existence; it is all a tall tale; forget the treasure.

follows day, war peace, craving satiety. Our love of life is one side of the screen whose other side hides dread of death.

As there is a more equivocal poetry before a univocal literalism, there is a more primordial emergence of perplexity about evil than that defined by "the problem of evil," as classically formulated. There is an *earlier complicity* with evil. The intimation of evil emerges with rupture to the rapport, rupture first felt in a pre-objective brush with the powers of destruction. Our predicament is not first a reflective problem of giving a logically coherent account of God's goodness and power. There is a more primordial strain placed on any naive faith in the goodness of being itself by the very equivocity of the power of being. Were we only to have the goodness, there would be no perplexity about evil at all; we would simply live in the bliss of the paradisal now. With the emergence of the equivocity of difference, what bliss we live is blighted by its own death, the dominion of which robs bliss of its delight.

It is as if an invisible ladle were stirring the waters wherein we swim, all limpid translucency of life being churned to turbulence, and we ourselves carried round and round in that maelstrom. Not only churned in it, we ourselves are churned by it. We have a hold on nothing. This is elemental: You are dust, you will be blown away. You are grass and will wither by the evening. You are a breath vaporized by the dissipating wind. You are a spark engulfed by fire, feeding on its own destroying joy. The elemental knows no bound, knows no respect. Its power shows no deference in its ravaging of all limits, especially of our limits. Ravening, raging and uprooting, it carries us swiftly into the desolation of reality (I bow to Yeats's *Meru*). Elemental power: incomprehensibly generous, incomprehensibly serene, and serene in its devouring fury.

This might of nature strains the naïveté of our native faith. Henceforth we sing, when we sing at all, to appease the savage power. We might not break faith with being, yet being's equivocity puts us so off balance that we wonder if our native faith is cheated or a cheat. That faith loses faith in itself, even as its faith in being's goodness begins to slip. I want to say that this pre-determinate, pre-reflective equivocity of faith/distrust comes closer to the ambiguous matrix of our presentiment of the good or evil of being. How we approach it, at that level of the pre-reflective rapport, is in some respects more important than any subsequent set of reflective arguments about the classical problem of evil.

Often the most treasonous breaches of trust occur when we are children not yet callused. Betrayal calluses us, hardens us into adults, and we learn to be blithe about our own betraying.[5] Our later judgment is infiltrated, mostly unselfconsciously, by the heritage of our primary dealing with the distrust life itself throws up. Our aesthetic feel for the value/disvalue of being is effective prior to any determinate or self-determining thought, especially in the way our elders or friends or family, either bring us (back) to faith in being, or else reinforce, or exacerbate suspicion, even unto hostility to all otherness. In the first instance, while not escaping evil's equivocity, we might inherit resources enough to maintain an affirmative equilibrium: a chastened faith surfaces again beyond the betrayal of faith. In the second instance, a posture of dualistic opposition to other-being justifies itself, just by the other's ambiguity – it will destroy me, therefore I disarm by attack first. But how can we conquer evil by extending evil? This extension is effective in our determination to treat all other-being as potentially our enemy, whose hostility is

---

[5] *A sentimental story*: A three-year-old child is in hospital, desperately lonely and sick. An uncle comes to visit and gives the child sweets. The child is thrilled and his loneliness vanishes. The uncle has to leave, but he is too decent, too good to tell the child he is leaving. He will be back in a brief moment, he says. He goes, the child waits. The child waits trustfully in the gathering darkness. The trusted visitor does not come back. The promise of the one trusted was not one to be trusted. The child weeps and is consoled with sleep.

Strange that, breaches such as these, breaches done out of a goodness, sometimes seep beyond their definite borders, sowing a seed of an unpredictable indeterminate distrust. And this indeterminacy of trust/distrust is centrally formative of our orientation to God. Notice again the double-edge. Such breaches can occasion a turn to God as trustworthy beyond human betrayal; they can influence a turn against God, since *nothing* can be trusted, if even my beloved visitor cannot.

all that concerns us, for the rest we take care of ourselves. This hostility to evil is paradoxically a hostility to life itself, since the other it wills to disarm or destroy is just other-being, as giving and taking life. *It is a hostility to evil that is itself evil.* There is no escape from evil by this path. This very dominating of evil is a new extension of the dominion of evil. We might look in turn at evil's own equivocity, in relation to *nature* as other to us (T¹), in relation to *human being* (T²), and in relation to *God's* otherness (T³).

The *first* equivocity pertains to the destructive power already noted. No doubt, we can seem to become "reconciled" to "normal" death, but often the qualitative scale of destruction exceeds any "norm." There is no norm here. Death is a trauma, and, whatever its form, it is metaphysically shocking. Our very being recoils from it, and the recoil is ingrained in our being. True, we do prepare ourselves, rearrange ourselves in expectancy of this uncanny guest. Indeed when death is anticipated according to a certain order, we may seem quite reconciled with it, especially since it has not yet come to us. This peace is mostly secured by the expedient of small forgettings. Things, people slip away unnoticed, or are soon forgotten, and the strange persistence of simple being proceeds innocuously, and the traces of the shock are softened, as if nothing had happened, and indeed nothing has happened, but death is that nothing, and as long as it is other, we live as if nothing is happening.

What of death in excess of the "normal" order of vanishing? Famine, floods, epidemics, earthquakes, catastrophes reveal a measure of destruction exceeding our measure. You may say it is not evil, according to its own measure. Very well, what is the meaning of that measure, so pitiless with the measure of the good of finite beings? Does that other measure concern the divine? The pitiless waste troubles us, even into our dreams, about the nature of *what gives* the "evil" happening. Moreover, the ordinary distinction of "natural evil" and "moral evil" fails to console us in the face of this extraordinary excess of death. This excess may even tempt us to propose an origin of evil in the course of things coeval with the origin of the good in things, with the aesthetic cosmos as the site of their spiritual war (Zoroastrianism, most obviously, comes to mind).

The *second* form of evil's equivocity concerns less an outer dualism as *ourselves as divided* within ourselves against ourselves. Our perplexity about evil as outer seeps into our soul as bewilderment about our own relation to it, even participation in it. We anticipate the good of being; we encounter the evil, and yet we would not immediately impugn the good. So we take the evil *upon ourselves*, feel ourselves stained, and all the more so as the vastation grows inexorably within us. Exposure to evil not only makes us deeply troubled, it *makes us deep*. An abyss opens within; we are already an abyss but now are made to mind it. We are not opened into an underground below ground, we are ourselves an under-ground, even when we walk out in the air above. We are an underground whose own groundlessness comes to mind. This is perhaps what it means to be radically a porosity of being – an openness that does not ground itself but that wakes to the minding of its own "being as nothing." This is why we become *suffering beings* to a degree not true of any other animal. We suffer the equivocity of being in an unprecedented way that is not the mere continuation of animal suffering. Other animals are beneficiaries of the good and victims of evil to them, but they do not know good and evil, beyond the sleeping bliss of one and the brutal thoughtless moment of the other. We are animals who suffer metaphysically from a misgiving, or "guilt" whose precise source we cannot quite fix.

The equivocity opens a cleft in us: not only between inner and outer, but in innerness itself between the selving and itself. We *interiorize* the duality and stand in opposition to ourselves. We learn the doubleness of our desires, pulled this way and that, hither and thither, self-assertive and unsure. In trying to master our duplicitous desires, we will this rather than that, but discover that what we will, we will not do, and what we do not will, that we do. At odds with ourselves, the war of good and evil is not just that of two external principles pitching their battle in the site of self. The strife *is* the selving as at war with itself, pitched for fighting on itself as its own battle site.

What dawns on us in this strife is that we too secrete evil, almost but not quite as the tree secretes sap. We are not innocents in paradisal univocity: the power we are feels the goodness of its own power as power, and expresses itself for itself, and if this means refusal or violation of what stands in its way, let that be so. We refuse our own selves, as we thus affirm ourselves. *And so we come to our own evil, by asserting our own good.* We sniff evil in the air, but we are it, it is our own evil we smell. We do our evil in furtherance of our good, but we create a loop in which our extrications from evil are deeper entanglements. The evil we execute as good is sticky, sticky with ourselves, and we are stuck with our sticky selves.

I am not now talking about the classical discussion of the evil will – this is more in question along the dialectical and metaxological ways. Prior to explicit willing there is an immersion in the equivocity of evil, all the more difficult to pin down just because of this equivocity. There is a twilight mingling of light and dark before the explicit choice is available to us. This twilight of value – or dawning – is shown in the outer world, shown in our own being. Our being is a chiaroscuro of the good, and the darkness – or dawning – casts a long shadow over us, even before we are aware of our own being as distinct. There is a pre-objective, even pre-subjective fascination with evil that floats in our desires at the edge of all mediation. It is perhaps more articulated in our dreams than in our waking consciousness. These dreams are not mere dreams, they are expressions of the nature of being as fitfully waking up to itself in our fitful equivocal dawning to ourselves. The play of light and dark is alive in us, and we are not first its masters, if we ever are. We find ourselves living those dreams. The darkness comes to walk abroad in the day. We are that walking darkness, that daily "darkness visible."

You object that this is not easy to grasp, and I agree. But that is just what we would expect, if we find ourselves in a pre-determinate promiscuity of good and evil. Evil somehow haunts the good. Think of the night terrors of the child. A shadow appears on the wall. The child screams. Why scream? Because it is immediately in rapport with the menacing. The sinister haunts presence. The equivocity is idiotic: radically intimate, and yet quite out there. Why do we fall into these terrors so spontaneously? These fallings are not animal fears; they exceed animal fear. For there is nothing determinate of which one is afraid. It is the sinister foreboding of nonbeing and death. It is there already ingrained in our flesh. Our very flesh suffers its passion in the equivocity of the good, which is the equivocity of evil, breaking into sweat before the insecurity of being, before the threat of nonbeing to all identity, the threat at work before we shape a determinate identity.

All this is prior to the definite willing of this or that as good. There is an equivocity of evil at work before we *choose* an evil. What repulses us seduces us. (See the child's fascination with excrement, revisited in adult scatology.) What is seductive is repulsiveness itself, and hence the repulsive is not repulsive, for we go towards it like enthralled sleepwalkers. There is an indeterminate "willingness" towards evil, before this or that willing of an evil. We are already guiltily enchanted before we make our definite commitment. There is a "willingness" before willing, a "commitment" we discover ourselves to have *already made* once we make the definite commitment and find ourselves with a definite evil act on our hands. We tumble to it too quickly, as if we were destined to it. Now it is done, and yes, I am glad, and no, I am infinitely regretful, for there is no going back or revocation. Our "willing" is already in the possibility of evil before it chooses evil. In tempting us, even though we do not yield to it, evil has already seduced us (on temptation see *EB*, 282ff.). After all, in the story of the Fall, the human being does not create good and evil; the serpent, the tempter is already in evil; the temptation is insinuated by evil already at work; we respond to the equivocal seduction, and so must ourselves have already been in evil in an equivocal way. We are not evil, we are in the possibility of evil.

In the *third* equivocity, evil is linked to *God's otherness*. Equivocal evil outside and inside converge to fill us with foreboding and anticipation, with regret and expectation, with sorrow and defiance. Foreboding makes us uncertain before the unpredictability of divine power. We are as nothing in face of the reckless powers of destruction. We are as playthings in what seems a game of mockery. We are unsure if we are being toyed with. "As flies to wanton boys are we to the gods, they kill us for their sport." God played with the evil one to toy with Job. Job submitted, though his wife enjoined defiance: "Curse God and die!" The wife lived the equivocity of evil from the other side: defiance not sorrow. Job was silent. He knew in the flesh the shudder of God's power: incomprehensible power that exceeds our measure of justice. It is as violent as the killer whale battering in joy the helpless seal squealing on the shore's edge. Incomprehensible suffering that remains incomprehensible, power incomprehensibly generous, power inexplicably permissive of incomprehensible suffering, power in excess of any measure we have.

Job has his counselors who advocate the rationalization of the equivocity: take the guilt definitely on yourself! But Job is not (definitely) evil, he is in (indefinite) evil. When he revolts and questions, there is a summary release in revolt. But the voice that answers does not answer his questions. The voice puts questions to Job he cannot answer, no one can answer. What is the answer? The answer is to rock us back on ourselves in a perplexity of which there is no alleviation. The perplexity seems ineradicable, though we may learn something in consent to just its excess to our feeble rationalizations. This consent, in perplexity to perplexity about the mystery that does not answer perplexity but exacerbates it, is trust, faith. This trust is consent to the mystery of God in the midst of evil's equivocity. It is a consent beyond the measure of any univocal reason. This is why it must look irrational, if the latter measure is our ultimate measure.

Since the consent is always in the midst of perplexity, it is always precarious and must always be renewed. Being the equivocal creatures we are, consent will always be mixed with refusal. We are the struggle between consent and refusal, and not consent to this or that, or refusal of this or that, but rather consent as an overdeterminate trust in the basic goodness of being, or refusal as an indeterminate negation of, and dissent from, being as good at bottom. The mystery of God manifested in the shock of evil makes of the equivocity of being a darkness against which we may rage, or in which may dawn on us the consent to live uncertainly. These two are faithlessness and faith, and each is equivocal. For the first is defined over against the second, as the second is gained, sustained only in the face of the first. With us they are like Siamese twins, sometimes joined at the head, sometimes the flesh, always in the heart itself, and perhaps in death only do they part. For when they are parted, that is the moment of our death – and perhaps true life.

DEUS SIVE EGO? ON THE EQUIVOCITIES OF RELIGIOUS INWARDNESS

Whichever way we turn, the same lesson strikes home: we are rocked back on ourselves. We are impelled to turn to ourselves, not because we have the magic map of univocity to guide us, but because in our own being we are intimate to the deepest equivocities. Nature does not mediate God with sufficient luminescence to dispel all ambiguities rising within nature. Recourse to ourselves in the very labyrinth of inwardness may, may not, lead us to a different intimacy with the divine. So also exposure to equivocity seeds a *different selving* – the space of inwardness is exposed. We are and must be otherwise. Awareness of our responsibility in the appearing of other-being, be it of nature or God, also occurs. If the manifestation is equivocal, the doubleness comes as much from us as from the other. To respond to the appearance, to be responsible, we must call to account our own receptivity. Perhaps we have not been properly receptive. Perhaps suspicion of soul lets rot on the branch the gift of generosity. Perhaps our porosity has clogged on itself. Perhaps receptivity has betrayed us, rather than we it. There are receptions warm, receptions stony, restrained receptions hiding their open-handedness, receptions playing the game of welcome though secretly resentful about receiving the other at all. Appearing and being apparent, giving and receiving are defined by an interplay between other and self, and if each is possibly equivocal, the interplay must be multiply equivocal.

The full intermediation of this multiple equivocity moves us to dialectical and metaxological ways, but here now, in the interplay of univocity and equivocity, there is a shift to *inwardness as a way of interpreting the equivocal signs*. Nature's equivocity cannot give us univocal knowing of God, so in ourselves we seek the way beyond equivocity, and there just to the extent that we are most intimate with equivocity. We do not rely on signs from externality, we rely on ourselves. Remember the interplay of trust and distrust. What or who are we to trust in the equivocity of transience? Nature? But this seems to drown us. God? But God seems to hide, even mock us. Ourselves? But we are frail. Why frail? The moderns say: Because we have relied on these others.[6] We have let ourselves be too porous to these others. We need to secure ourselves. Henceforth we will rely on ourselves alone. We will pitch our building where our power seems to be. We seek God to find the fullness of life, not to dance with the angel of death. But can we find that fullness without this dancing? The full equivocity will make us put this question. But now we want the dance with ourselves.

Augustine rightly said: God is more intimate to me than I am to myself. Religiously, the sifting of equivocal being is most intense in inwardness. But that intimacy is *itself* equivocal. And so instead of finding immediate rest, our hearts are made restless once more: equivocity before, equivocity again in the new path chosen to deal with equivocity. And what then the result? God receding now into the labyrinth of the heart?

For there are *the intenser equivocities of inwardness as religious*. The counsel is common: Turn from the exterior way, recollect yourself. What do we find in turning? Ourselves, you say. But what is a self? A univocal center of existence? I am I and nothing but I. Yet, if so, the univocity is an idiotic one. There is resistance at this center to complete objectification, and an intimacy of being beyond final self-determination. You say, selving is a dynamic source of coming into being as this person, not that, as idiotic singular that is for itself and not interchangeable with anything other on a more general neutral scale. Very well, but this dynamism breeds desire, and the restlessness of self-transcendence, and neither of these can be univocalized. The idiotic center, even as dynamic, is again beyond determinate univocity. Very well again: this is a non-objectifiable intimacy of being that opens up the pathway to God. As sources of original being within ourselves, we are the image of a more original source. And yet this pathway to the more original source is not itself univocal, hence we can *pass along it in different ways*. Is every way here a way to the divine? The answer must be "no." And so again there is equivocity at the "center" of the original power we are. We are driven by desire but desire is pluriform, and there are desires that, satisfied in certain ways, corrupt us. They destroy equally mundane contentment and religious peace.

The very source of original power defines a selving, and defines itself as for itself; but just as so defining itself as for itself, it can set itself apart as other to what it is not. To what it is not, it stands in a *negative* relation in order to be itself. I am I because I am not the other; and I am the more I, the more I am not the other; I define my own self-becoming as *defining itself by negation of being-other*. And so the very dynamism of selving is mired in the ambiguity of its relation to the other, even when it seems to have escaped the external other into the pure inward path of itself as the way to God. There is no such pure inward path: there is ardency, longing, yes, love, but there is also a tangle of urges, a snarl of insecurities, impulses, compulsions, aggressions, rages. The inward turn is religiously significant, but it is no univocal solution beyond equivocity.

Quite to the contrary, the danger is heightened. The more we enter the intimacy of selving, the more the equivocity grows. It seems to be constitutive ambiguity all the way down, all the way up. The equivocity is emergent relative to the ground of the selving, a ground that makes us refer to the relation between self and other. But negation implies that with reference to the other, there is no foundation that is a self-foundation. We are

[6] Earlier peoples perhaps were more likely to *blame themselves* for not properly relating to the divine; we now are likely only to blame ourselves *just for* relating to God, or to seek someone or something *other* to blame. Reading, for instance, Augustine's account of evil, we notice how he criticizes those who complain that the world is not better: he sees pride in thinking one can better God. By contrast, we today make a constant refrain of "making the world a better place." Who shows more trust? Those who claim to improve creation? Or is it because we lack trust that we insist on "making the world a better place"? We certainly *think* we are better.

tangled together with the other, even when we seem to have retreated from exteriority. The other is ambiguously there before us, before we come before ourselves.

Think this. Finally, we reckon we have arrived at the last room, the last empty room, and we open the door to find ourselves at last. We enter and see the mirror of ourselves, and we look in the mirror of ourselves and we do see ourselves, but what we see is also not just ourselves but the hint of an other that was always there before us, an other perhaps that, unminded, companioned our quest in the labyrinth, and that somehow managed to slip in before us, just in that split second we took to open the door. There is an other in there before us, before we are there before ourselves.

If we are seeking the foundation of selving in self, this can be frustrating, this can be intolerable. I want to find myself, I want to found myself. But the more I enter selving and its equivocity, the more the intimation grows that only an act of ontological violence can make me the foundation, and hence I cannot found myself. That violence is just the cutting of the Gordian knot that ties me to the other. I would do away with the constitutive doubleness and establish myself on my own singular basis. I will to be single, the single one, but doubleness taunts me at every turn, redoubles its knot, even when I would that it were not.

If my will is to be for myself my own ground, I refuse to be that porosity of being that cannot found itself, and my co-implication with others will come to seem intolerable, unbearable. I can violate this co-implication, and the violence too will give expression to the original energy at work in my intimate being. For the doubleness that is in me also means that I am an original source that is for itself in relation to the other. I am the power to be myself, and free to be so in opposition to the other. If I choose the way of self-founding, the unavoidable other must be made to serve the process of my own becoming for self. The doubleness within must be turned around in this turn to self, turned into the mirror that gives back only reflections of self.

And now? Now the double mirror which shows the two faces will be silvered over, there wherever the face of any more original other peeps out. A new double mirror will be created, as the original mirror is silvered over. A new reflection is created by us overlaying *our own sheen* on the surface. But though this sheen slides over the surface, now and then, when the silvering becomes frayed, traces of a more archaic and other original appear. The traces are insinuated through the second surface. And then we have to paint another surface, and another, to prevent the archaic original coming through. And this can go on for a long time, a life in fact.

But what if the archaic original, in any case, is not at all down there, under the multiple cakings of layered silver? Suppose it is there above them all, companion to the very eyes of selving looking on the surfaces? Then I look at the mirror from which the trace of the archaic other is obliterated, but *my looking itself is companioned by the other that looks with me at myself*. It is not just *what* I see that is double, it is my *seeing itself* that is also double. *The I is always companioned.* I only see because there is a light showing me what there is to see. This light is not my own. It is other but belongs to no one. The light lets me see myself, indeed shows me to myself. I am shown myself before I see myself, and I do not first show myself to myself. What shows me myself is not myself. I see myself because I am seen.

Consider again the equivocity relative to the story of the Fall. The Fall looks like a turn from the immediate rapport with other-being that paradise represents, and in whose immediacy there is no seeing and being seen, in the guise of dualistic opposition. But the equivocity is already there: for it is not we who create the tree of the knowledge of good and evil; the presence of such a tree, even in Eden, means the possibility of some prior equivocity of evil, even in the innocence. The presence of the tree is *in paradise*, but does not corrupt paradise, though its very presence is intimately ambiguous because it is just the potentiality to corrupt, perhaps destroy paradise. Only after the primal refusal, and the will to have within one the source of good and evil, does the sleeping equivocity spring up into wakefulness. The first persons are *tempted*, put up to temptation, prior to any willed malice. We are as much *victims* of temptation as succumbers to it. The tempting to evil *befalls* us, as much as we fall to evil.

By eating the forbidden fruit one assimilates its otherness to oneself, one seeks to have a *radical source within oneself*, the source of the *primal division* between good and evil. Eating thus one thinks one becomes divine. "Having it within one" means interiorizing the difference, the equivocal doubling of good and evil; it is not outside one; one wants it within one; perhaps even with the good intention of conquering the equivocity. Yet in wanting to be master of good and evil, one has bitten off more than one can ingest; one has bitten off *the ambition to be the good*, and one falls from the inarticulate equivocity of good and evil into the forthright war of the two. And then indeed the doubleness is truly within one; for one's very being is known explicitly as being in evil. Hence one knows that one is seen. Adam and Eve suffer themselves as shame: not just their bodies, but their selves as shame-ful.

The turn to self that turns the self into an original being for itself is equivocal, because in being for itself as power to be itself, it can refuse the necessity of the other for just its being itself. You might say that the gift given is double, hence potentially equivocal, thus neither predictable nor in our complete control. This is true of all gifts: to receive this gift, any gift, is to *accept from beyond* what is beyond one's control. To receive is itself to be gifted – gifted with generous porosity. Yet the acceptance is mine, or the refusal. Just this "being beyond" may strike one as the fatal equivocity to be undone. But our claim to undo the equivocity absolutely through ourselves alone is just again the fatal equivocity redoubled. For this undoing is the will to undo gift, to undo porosity, to undo our *passio essendi. We* ourselves cannot be absolute sources of control or certainty concerning the gift and its source. Because of this, we are tempted either to try to secure it through ourselves alone, or to wish that there be no gift. In fact, to try to secure the gift thus is to wish that there be no gift at all. For we would then only accept what we have given to ourselves. But any such self-giving is a rebuff to the more original giving: everything we give to ourselves is only thus because we have first been given to ourselves. Our being for ourselves is also first given to ourself; we do not give ourselves to ourselves; we only begin to give ourselves to ourselves, subsequent to being given to ourselves.

What, then, is the temptation of the equivocity now? To will to be the source of our own given being, and hence not to acknowledge the prior gift, and to rationalize the refusal by exploiting the equivocity of gift as beyond our secure univocity: *it, the gift* is not to be trusted, just because *we* have not given it to ourselves. This is an original perversion of gift, which must be received with openness, in the very uncertainty of ambiguity. We are beneficiaries, not bestowers, and as beneficiaries we must wait on the goodness of the giving other. Not being willing to wait, and suspecting the goodness of the giver, we cannot accept a gift.

We can, of course, *take* what is given. "Take and eat, and you will become as gods." But "taking" what is given is itself equivocal. Taking can be with a consent to the gift – this taking is a partaking, as when the psalm says: "Taste and see that the Lord is good" (Psalm 34:8, King James Version). Taking can also be a graceless expropriation of what is given. Then taking is envious to possess life, ungrateful greed that will not wait on the other. There is no thanking in this taking. This taking does not consent to the other, does not wait upon the consent of the other. "Taking" like this is thus like stealing or sacking or raping. We speak of "taking in" another person, or being "taken in," that is, deceiving or being deceived. "Taking" is thus also at the origin of deceit and being false. Is this not one reason why Satan was called "the father of lies"?

GETHSEMANE THOUGHTS: BETWEEN CURSE AND BLESSING

Where is the garden now? And what suspicions has sly Satan whispered in our ears? But now what is ultimately at stake is not any neutral objective process, univocally out there, but the enigma of equivocal creation in which we participate, whose chiaroscuro we exemplify, and to which we are responsive in terms of who we are and are to become. We cannot put the question to it without being put in question ourselves, and in an extreme sense – that is, between the two ultimates of curse and blessing. *One extreme* of the doubleness of the inner way keeps us in thrall as we wander in the heart's maze. There is another extreme, as we will find, but I pause and linger some with the ascendant self, turned to itself for itself, and for itself as a source of power turned against its being given to be.

Remember this ascendancy is motivated by a turn against God's suspected equivocity. Does that mysterious face curse as well as bless? If so, how exorcise that curse and come to blessedness? Here, not by blessing, but by cursing the curse; and by cursing also the curse our life seems to become, following the fall from primal rapport with being as other. Cursing utters itself into life whose crusade we might call the sacking of the sanctuaries. I mean: first the banishment from nature of all traces of the divine; Godless nature over against us, and then no reverence with us, no awe before this double power that gives and takes what we would take; a bare ruined creation, and no angels sing. And we will not sing. We will shout our will into the silence, shout ourselves into the ruin. Nothing now of nature as aesthetic feast, intimation of the more agapeic origin. Not the first garden, not even the garden of Gethsemane. The holy waters turn black – a horror to those who see. The altars of creation are broken stones that we break lest they break us further. And as we break the stones, we exult in power. We show ourselves not to be gods, just in our claim to be gods. In the turn to self, what has turned up is the devouring worm in inner-ness itself. We ourselves are consumed by this worm, consumed by ourselves. We are the inversion: the power that dedivinizes itself in the very act of divinizing itself.

Should one speak of the vanishing of God? Does God appear and disappear in the chiaroscuro of the equivocal? What does appear is the monstrous power of man. In a way, this seems destined by the equivocity of being itself, which we cannot bear beyond a certain point. I mean, our power is free, and indeed is let be as free, even when constrained not to eat of good and evil. This free power opens our rapport with death, for we have eaten of evil. Our being is rapport with death, for power as free is also power of negation. This rapport takes on confidence when the face of God is eclipsed in the equivocal, and all manner of monsters stir. Do we create death or are we created by death? Does it matter how we answer, if death is the truth of being when the face of God has faded?

Why then be taken aback that the sanctuaries are sacked? I heard the desolation speak. Hell told me this. The greedy pleasure of unconstrained power is crime itself. Freedom to negate given being has in it the breeding of imprecation, not blessing, and impreca-tion because life is taken as betraying us. "That it is at all" is the wonder, but now it is a surd, a vile surd, for we did not ask for it, and it is beyond us, and it might overcome us, and so its thereness is threat, not welcome. Our defection from agapeic astonishment consoles itself with ontological disgust and metaphysical indictment. This turn to the self thus turns into a *turn against the finesse of the inner*. The coarser power of self-assertion celebrates itself, not the finer, nobler promise. Innocence, nobility: mere masks of coarse-ness – so the coarse self says. The outward violence comes to nothing, and the silence of the sanctuaries now mocks us – like limp bodies that no longer feed our pleasures even with a moan. What echoes back to us is *our own emptiness*. The cycle of curse circles back on the curser.

This rebound effect is evident in the sacking of the *sacker*. The turn to self returns the outward violence back to its source: inner aggression of the inner on the inner. There closes in on itself the circle of self-laceration and torment. Look what strange animals we humans have become, we who tear the flesh of our own being into strips, we who eat ourselves in this monstrous evening, we who even this bright morning went forth from our caves glow-ing with ourselves as our own sun? We are the suns whose shining dims and glooms and finally blackens the good of the "to be." To claim hell is the other perverts the whole thing. I am hell. I am the excremental self that eats excrement, myself as excrement. Lucifer, son of the morning, bearer of light, excretes not light but an infernal equivocity.

The infernal I devours that equivocity, as it is devoured by it. I come to my god in the heaven I have made, that is, the hell I have made for myself, the hell I have made my heaven-ascending self.

You say: "Tut! tut! What exaggeration! What balderdash! Has his imagination gotten the better of him?" More likely memory has gotten the better. You, tut-tutter, I fear, suffer from amnesia of the cannibalizing darkness of the century just past, caked as it is in black blood. But all times have their Gethsemane nights. The point is not just historical amnesia, but loss of metaphysical memory of the coming to nothing we cradle within ourselves. This coming to nothing can create for itself a kingdom of death that, strangely, seems to lack even the consolation of death, the consolation of there being an end of it all, for this end of it all seems like endless torment – being riveted to the infernal self one has made oneself – beyond redemption. Is that, then, the end of it? How could it be, if we are this torment?

Tut! tut! offers its counsel: "Assume instead a (dis)guise like this: no torment, and the shrewd will to live without perplexity, with a domesticated equilibrium that shuns the excess of God and the excess of godlessness; a temperate middle, where common and garden decency is prudence enough and the small pleasures that make life tolerable, no big questions and no big answers, no great suffering, no great bliss. Give up on the quest of God."

The halting reply: "Would that the middle could be made so easily mild, but it bucks. Nor do philosophical (or other) therapeutics seem quite able to quarantine us against the siren songs of the extremes. We are intermediate beings who remain in love with the extremes. The wretchedness that can follow impulsion to the extreme is the twin of the greatness also promised. We settle for the small contentments, but the price is the stifling of every tremendous reaching out. And even let the contentments be more and more widespread, the hunger for the extraordinary will rise again. Let our unpredictable fires be damped down with therapies, even religious therapies, but the fire smolders on, and the ground will break open and the glowing burning will be exposed. We simply are extravagant being; given to excess and yet in excess of every finite limit; over and above, even when mired in our own wretchedness. This is to be self-transcending. Self-transcendence will not cease to be surprised and overtaken by the excess of otherness, whether within itself or above."

An abyss opens within us, and we tumble into the pit of self. We fall into ourselves as a voracious emptiness without God. Our power of negation makes us nothingness incarnate. Does the gyre come around again, coming to nothing and the ordeal of return to zero? Return to zero can risk ruin, but as a crisis, it can also be a turning point. Can we now say: *the turn to self itself reaches a turning point*? For "being as nothing" can reveal the primal porosity of our being, and recall us to something of the *passio essendi*, sourcing anew our self-transcending, even now out of its radical disquietude with itself. Here, even here the promise of our self-transcending powers seems to be called to a sending of self beyond self, not because of any determinate lack, the lack of this or that object, but out of a more radical lack, a more extreme indigence. There is a kind of transfinite poverty in oneself that one cannot fill through ones own finite powers alone. If we tumble into the pit of emptiness we are, we do not cease to reach out of this emptiness, we do not cease to be turned by this reaching. The urgency of ultimacy does not cease to reappear, even when nothing seems ultimate. We desire death rather than desire nothing, and we desire death because what we desire is as nothing, and we ourselves are as nothing, and we are as nothing because we have turned to ourselves as if we were everything, as if we were a god, and all this to dispel the traumatic perplexity brought on by evil. There is no eradication of this urgency of ultimacy this side of death.

Put the matter this way: Was Pascal mad when his Gethsemane thoughts led him to say: Jesus will be in agony till the end of the world; there must be no sleep as long as that lasts? What could this hyperbolic vigilance be? But can we wake ourselves, or keep ourselves awake? Will we not all, like the disciples, fall into sleep, again and again (see *IST?*, 54–7)? How turn to *ourselves* to overcome the equivocity of evil, if *we are the equivocal once again*? Every such turn to ourselves repeats the dilemma. Or falls asleep. Are we then without reprieve? Can we absolutely sift ourselves? If so, we would be sieves as well as impure water; but the sieve too would be impure, so how would it sift its water? Perhaps indeed we must be sieves and porous, for a purer water than our own to pass through us, and sweeten the bilge at the bottom of the soul.

Evil can bring us to despair, but do we bring ourselves to despair by making ourselves alone the salvation from despair? If so, does this mean that to be saved from despair would be to transcend self in a radical way? Do despair of ourselves and despair of God go together? Does self-assertion as despair of God becomes despair of self, as we go under into the pit or cry out again from the depths? We now – a tortured parody of Zeus: satiety with self and disgusted craving? Riveted to ourselves, while we crave release from self, does our defiance conceal some secret appeal to God? Is despair close by prayer, parched in a drought of hope? Does its unquenched thirst bring us again to the elemental "yes" or "no"?

DEUS SIVE NIHIL? THE EQUIVOCAL WAY AND PURGATORIAL DIFFERENCE

The equivocal way, we see, often leaves us with more questions than answers. And there are more still. I leave it at this one: Can we see in the passage through the equivocal something of purgatorial difference? If we can, the between would be a matrix of metaphysical and ethical ambiguity wherein desire is enticed by, though it need not fall to, the *false doubles of God*. Purgatory would be a preparing for release from bewitchment by such counterfeit doubles. What would release require? A different dwelling in the matrix of ambiguity, at the least. It would require us to grant *the finite as finite*. This granting would not be a univocal literalism about finite facts, idolizing them as if ultimate. Quite the opposite, we would have to grant that nothing finite *is* God. For an idolatry of the univocal can be compounded by an idolatry of the equivocal. There is never anything unequivocal about the finite as telling us of the origin. If we are to be told of the latter, we will have to read the finite differently, always aware that it *cannot be identical with* that about which it tells.

Too true, in this difference of finite and God, atheism can flourish. We say the finite is finite and it tells us nothing of anything other to it; the finite is finite and that is that. The univocal idolatry would be the immanence that claims the finite fact tells us only of itself and nothing more. To make immanent finitude thus univocally the whole beyond which nothing greater can be thought would be to produce a counterfeit double of God, hence still to sleep in an equivocation about the divine, and not even be aware of this. But suppose even that such an atheistic univocity could isolate such literal fact, the fact is, the truth of univocal truth is not univocal. Certainly, when we take into consideration the labyrinth of the human heart, we cannot avoid this truth: our being in the truth is not a univocal truth. To insist that humans are measured by univocal truth is to be in the untruth, that is, to be in the equivocal that one has denied, for one has denied what human being is, namely a source of self-transcending that cannot be completely univocalized, even when it is the very basis of *just this* atheistic univocalization. The pit is not just a hole in the ground. The pit may be a crystal palace.

In a certain sense, the purgatory of the equivocal brings home to us, *in our not-knowing*, the truth of the divine as *beyond* us. I do not say impossibly beyond, but beyond such as to call our claims to account. God is never mastered. Our being thwarted by the equivocal is a sign we fought a battle on terms that could not succeed, for the terms that are true demand there be no battle for mastery. No dominion over the equivocal, but discerning habitation of it, with a mindfulness that awaits what will come, come what may; that does not force its own categories on what is there at play; that is not merely passive, but in a refreshed *passio essendi* is in a ready state of high alert for the manifestations of transcendence. We are not lords of transcending but beneficiaries. If this sounds all too somber, remember that essential to being released is learning to *laugh* at one's pretensions. To take oneself too seriously is to think one is God – and so not to think of God. Laughter itself would not be possible at all were there not deep equivocation intimate to our being.

A line is being drawn by the difference of transcendence as other (T^3) and self-transcendence (T^2). If that difference is being drawn just in the turn to the self the equivocal effects, we must turn again and retrace our steps through the labyrinth, taking note of cues and clues previously not minded. A different communication was always possible, and especially if, as we now suspect, the equivocal is really *plurivocal*. But why was the way not laid out univocally, like a string of beads to follow to the big pearl? Perhaps because there is no freedom without equivocity, and if all is univocal determination. As free, we are the acme of the equivocal: finite and infinitely self-transcending, but not the infinite. We are to find our own way and find we are not on our own; find our way to what is not our own. The equivocal mingles together what is our own and not our own; what is not our own is to be found mingled with our own.

This is not to deny that there springs up the solicitation of self-responsibility, but this cannot be a matter of absolute self-determination, for were it so, we would reduce the doubleness to our side alone. There is a given, but given the given, we have to answer for ourselves. Given to ourselves initially, once given, we have to answer for ourselves and cease to wriggle away from the singularity of our difference. It is as if the between has been let be to be itself in the doubleness of its ontological constitution, and we have to find our way to the divine in and through that doubleness. We ourselves are double, given to ourselves ambiguously as answerable for ourselves. The gift of freedom releases us to be what we are in promise, in the redemption of which we participate, as responsible for our response.

Seen so, the purgatory of the equivocal helps create a new humility. Rocked back on ourselves as not God, we step on a thorny path to God, or from. Our free openness may cease to be open to God, and be always tempted by hubris, be it atheistic or fideistic. By contrast, the humility means elementally: *I am not God*. Seen so, sifting the equivocal militates against self-infinitizing.

Our self-infinitizing is a counterfeit double of God. It tries to close the circle of self, making finite and infinite two sides of one process that, in thus being closed, makes itself its own ultimate. We make our doubleness to be just two sides of a completely self-contained process of self-infinitizing. Man surpasses himself, infinitely surpasses himself, Pascal said – but here he surpasses himself to himself and transcendence as other is just self-transcendence again. The plurivocity of our relation to the ultimate has been collapsed when we make ourselves the ultimate. This self-infinitizing has still to face the emptiness opened in the pit of itself. It soars on itself, and as long as it soars, it forgets there is no ground under it, but it will stall and plunge, for the emptiness that is infinite cannot infinitely sustain itself. It will plunge into its own infinite emptiness again, just in its self-infinitizing. It will be dizzied by the vertigo of its own sublime emptiness, but the dizziness of this height of emptiness over emptiness is the prelude to blackout and contraction back into itself as its own black hole.

This black hole is the counterfeit double of our elemental porosity to the divine. If we now need to mediate our own selves, we need catharsis of our doubleness, as both finitely bound and infinitely restless, and marking a *fork in our being* that may signal a way to transcendence as other (T^3). The purgatorial difference of our being, as both finite and infinitely restless, draws a line around finitude that encloses what is on one side of the line, but that releases mindfulness to what remains unclosed on the other side. But really there is no univocal line at all, for the boundary changes as our infinite restlessness goes to the boundary. When we go to the boundary, there is no boundary there; and yet we are bounded, bound and then released once again beyond the boundary. This is, so to say, a shifting boundary between time and eternity. We move on that shifting boundary; that is why neither time nor eternity, nor we or God, can ever be finally univocalized. One could equally say we are between time and eternity, or that there is no boundary here at all, but a fecund void, an enabling openness. For what is in play in the between and at the boundary is not this thing, not that thing, not anything at all. It is nothing and it is God.

Between nothing and God, purgatory can begin to dissolve the idolatrous doubles of the divine. It can unblock our porosity, as it also can cultivate finesse for the more intimate subtleties of showing, be they inner or outer or superior. The uncertain poetics of the divine makes us take heed, with some maturer finesse, of our inner doubling and immanent self-mediation. Will we find ourselves? Find ourselves in ourselves but as awakening to a dialogue with God in innerness; find ourselves always beyond ourselves, and in what is beyond us, even as within us? Has the purgatory of the equivocal prepared us for dialectical and metaxological ways?

Chapter 5

God and the Dialectical Way

First God
In the grave I came to myself
I did not know
That being away
Was my way
Of coming home

I spoke as man
But spoke as one away
I did not know
I spoke myself as man
Now coming to myself
In death at last
I speak as God
There is no other

I spoke as God
But did not know
I exiled my word
& now in this death
At last
I speak as myself
I speak as man
There will be
No other
God beyond me

I was first spoken as God-man
At last I answered as man-God
& at this last
Exchange of opposites
The first God falls silent

Second God
I speak myself
As the circle
Of all circles
I circle all circles
Fully
Self-encircling
Free in my absoluteness
Nothing beyond me
Sulking
In the sovereign solitude
Of the circle
Aghast at the magnificent autism
Of my absoluteness

I look in myself
And in my mirror
Make faces of myself
Man – once my smile –
Is now my grimace

I tire of man
The man-God
For love of him
I betrayed God

I long for the grave
I thought I had flown
I long to roll again
The stone
Across the opening

Third God
& voluble man
Talks himself into a death
Beyond God
Talks himself to death
He rolls the rock
Across the grave
& sees in the polished stone
His skull

GOD BEYOND OPPOSITION

Dialectic has a plurality of meanings,[1] but one meaning relevant to our search is that what stands in opposition also stands in relation. Immanent in opposition are sources of relation that, while more than opposition, are defined by passing into and through

---

[1] See *BB*, Chapter 4; also *BHD*, *passim*; "Thinking on the Double: The Equivocities of Dialectic," *The Owl of Minerva* , 25, 2 (Spring 1994), pp. 221–34; "Being, Dialectic and Determination: On the Sources of Metaphysical Thinking," *The Review of Metaphysics*, 48 (June, 1995), pp. 731–69.

opposition itself. At issue is whether the interplay of univocal and equivocal ways, as well as oppositions within each, point us beyond both ways to a dialectical togetherness. Granted that neither the univocal or equivocal ways alone is enough, is there a dynamic immanent to each and to their interplay that testifies to the unrest of a more original dialectic?

We have seen how the univocal determination of God runs to equivocities beyond univocity. Does this running insinuate a *determining beyond determination*? Does univocity not point to the dynamic ground of its own determination? Does not the passage through univocity suggest an (over)determining source as this ground of determination? If dialectic turns us toward this more original source, what has this to do with God? Likewise, equivocity suggests that the oppositions we encounter are not absolutely fixed. There is a dynamic of opposing, as there is of fixing. Does this dynamic not exhibit certain forms of "being in relation," show a certain inseparability of the opposites, as well as their inseparability from their source? Do we find in opposition a different doubleness – not the dualism of univocity, not the duplicity of equivocity but a self-doubling that unites? Passing into equivocity, dialectic also allows passage through it, showing us some way to address the *false fixations* of the ultimate. Would this be a way to dissolve, so to say, the false doubles of God?

Our equivocal predicament, we recall, ends up in a purgatory of oppositions: between ourselves and nature, between God and ourselves, between nature and God, between ourselves and ourselves. Everything seems to be so contrary. Dialectic denies this to be the last word. Complex differences, running to antithesis, give form to the determining of relations, or lack of relation between God, world, and the human being. Each is other to the other, but not so other as to be destitute of the promise of different communities of togetherness. Dialectic quickens mindfulness of this togetherness, intermediating a more faithful vigilance of the ontological promise of the ethos. We must explore dialectic's "thinking beyond" of opposition. We must also move from dialectic's "thinking beyond" to a *thinking beyond dialectic itself*. For we will be unable to avoid this question: Dialectic may help to dissolve some false doubles of the divine, but is it tempted by a new counterfeit double of God?

I anticipate. If the univocal approach is more "objective," the equivocal way more "subjective," our dialectical search is for a passage beyond the dualism of object and subject in quest of what makes both possible: something both trans-objective and trans-subjective. The modern dialectical way especially approaches this passage beyond in terms of the "subject." Recall Hegel: from Substance to Subject, from the dyadic relation of consciousness [S-O], to the triadic unitary relation of self-consciousness [S(S-O)], all the way to the absolutely inclusive Subject sublating and comprehending the (finite) subject and the object. This might be mapped onto the following movement from T^1 to T^2 to T^3. T^3 is thought primarily on the terms of a particular version of T^2: transcendence as other is conceived on the basis of self-transcending, and its putative power to include the other to itself in its own process of self-transcending. There is too much of T^2 in this, I hold, and not enough of the robust otherness of T^3, precisely as transcendent to all inclusion in "subjectivity," no matter how "absolute," or even when speculatively reconfigured as inclusive (inter)subjectivity. In the latter we revert, relative to T^3, to a "higher" univocity: for instance, transcendental univocity in Kant's case, dialectical-speculative univocity in Hegel's. We short-change the otherness of transcendence itself (T^3), and a counterfeit double of God is hard to avoid in the self-doubling of the speculative One. We find this in Hegel, as well as after him in a post-Hegelian reversion, or rather reduction, to the human being as god.

Since I have devoted a book to Hegel's treatment of God (*Hegel's God*), my treatment of him here will be abbreviated. I want to grant the family relation of the dialectical and other ways, and indeed its recessed metaxological promise. No less do I want to keep in mind the great danger of modern dialectic, especially in its Hegelian form: turning the between into the medium of God's own *self*-mediation, resulting in a philosophy of holistic immanence at best, but not in a philosophy of God which is faithful to transcendence (T^3), or indeed the hyperboles of immanent being as given in the ethos. This would be to unlearn the lessons of the univocal way concerning the excess of the divine, and of the equivocal way concerning the difference: the fact that nothing finite is God, not nature, not the human self, not humanity, not even the whole of holistic immanence.

The contrast of objective and subjective, univocal and equivocal is complemented by the contrast of the God of the philosophers and the God of the religious. Dialectic reveals some desire to mediate their difference. We do need philosophical mindfulness of the equivocity of the religious image, but is speculative dialectic really true to this equivocity? The Hegelian *Aufhebung* worries one when formulated in terms of one absolutely inclusive whole. Then the dialogue of religion and philosophy is primarily orchestrated from the side of a philosophy claiming the more absolute absoluteness. By contrast, metaxological mindfulness asks for a two-way communication. We need a new poverty of philosophy, and a new porosity of philosophy to religion (*IST?*, Chapter 3). We need a different inter-relating of religious "image" and philosophical "concept": we need ontological hyperbo-les, offered immanently in the between, but pointing beyond holistic immanence. God is not the between. The God of the between is "beyond" the between. God is beyond "the whole." The hyperboles of immanence, communicated in the between, are signs of what exceeds immanence: true transcendence (T³). This God of immanence is beyond holistic immanence. This is another reason why our overall trajectory must move from the "think-ing beyond" of dialectic to a thinking beyond dialectic itself.

KANT'S VIRTUAL DIALECTIC: FINDING DIRECTION BY UNKNOWING INDIRECTION

Why begin considering this "thinking beyond" by looking at Kant? Surely there are more overtly dialectical thinkers, like Eriugena and Cusanus, who sought to fathom the *coincidentia oppositorum*? Yet, in Kant the path of inwardness, met on the equivocal way, is taken in a crucial direction: our *moral being* provides a passage to God. This is not an objectivistic passage, nor is it through the univocalism of mechanism. It is through the subject, not any subject but the *moral subject*, viewed in light of the critical "destruction" of the theoretical and objective proofs. In all this I find a "virtual dialectic" – a dialectic somewhat recessed qua dialectic, worthy of consideration in its own right, yet allowing us access to resources that prefigure and prepare for a less retiring dialectic, perhaps even considerations of the metaxological way.

Overtly Kant has a quite negative view of dialectic – it functions as a critical safeguard against transcendental illusion. It serves to police all passing beyond, all transcendent adventures not issued with proper passports by the critical philosopher. It scrutinizes all traveling papers to transcendence (T³) with an eye suspicious for forged permits. At the boundary of immanence, Kant stands like a forbidding angel with a flaming torch, and few have dared pass beyond his border post since that torch first blazed. I find some vac-illation. Standing guard at the boundary, he permits himself some furtive peeks across it, and with the illumination of his flame. A peek at Kant peeking will advance our explora-tion. Perhaps it will also release us from metaphysical paralysis by the flaming torch. Out beyond, over beyond the barring angel of critique, we seem to have heard some other song, perhaps a piercing note of the blackbird of paradise.

Kant's approach is famous for its alleged "demolition" of the traditional proofs of God's existence. Let me pursue the point with respect to the so-called ontological argu-ment, criticized equally by believers (like Aquinas) and non-believers. We might focus on this argument, less to analyze fully the intricate logical argumentation as to understand why its "founding" moment and its moment of "deconstruction" are emblematic.

"Founding" moment: This argument seems emblematic of the search for a neutral homogeneity with respect to *the one way*, rationally "neutral" between believers and non-believers. There is a certain drive to *homogeneity* in this. Think of Anselm's desire to have *the one argument (unum argumentum)* that will suffice for believer and infidel alike, and silence the murmurings of the grumblers. Of course, the manner of argumentative explication may contain something at odds with deeper riches at work in the ethos.

Something lacking in the explication may, in the long run, contribute to the evisceration of our sense of the ethos and hence to the self-subversion of the explication itself.

"Deconstructive" moment: The argument seems emblematic in being crucial for the critique of the other ways. Kant's criticism also seems decisive for the other proofs. These have the semblance of being separate, yet finally reduce to the ontological way. So Kant says. Since his approach to this way is a linchpin of his critique, critique accepted often as extending to all ways, Kant's critique is then taken as devastating for *all* traditional ways. So Mendelssohn called Kant "the All-destroyer" (*der Alles Zermalmende*). It seems every possible way is put out of play if the ontological way proves thus deficient. A certain univocity of implication extends beyond the "founding" moment of pure rational proof to its "deconstructive" moment.

This surface of homogeneity is deceptive, but first I rehearse briefly some details of Kant's "demolition." There are three major proofs, the ontological, the physico-theological, and the cosmological. Kant claims that the last two reduce to the first, and that the first is invalid, for there is no legitimate way to deduce the existence of God from the concept of God. This is just what the ontological proof claims to do. From the concept of God, as the being greater than which none can be conceived, the conclusion is drawn that such a being necessarily exists. Did it only exist in the understanding and not outside the understanding, then a being could be conceived that also exists outside the understanding. This would be to conceive a being greater than the being greater than which none could be conceived. But this is absurd. The being greater than which none can be conceived must be conceived to exist outside the understanding also.

For Kant the illegitimacy of this is evident in the claim to existence from possibility as defined by the concept. Claims of existence are synthetic propositions, not tautologies or analytical propositions that merely elucidate what is already contained in the definition of a concept. Just as we cannot go from a hundred possible talers to a hundred real talers, so we cannot go from the concept of God to the existence. Existence is not a predicate, in Kant's famous assertion; it is a matter of positing the reality corresponding to the concept. God is not an object within experience, and hence there can be no legitimate theoretical knowing of God. Kant has respect for the other two proofs: thus the physico-theological way arises in a most natural manner; while it cannot offer us necessity and certainty, it earns our respect. Nevertheless, since every proof contains at core the illegitimate move of the ontological proof, there is no rescuing the other proofs as certain rational demonstrations.

There are many issues here, and I can comment only on some pertinent ones. First, Kant's formulations mirror the modern reconfiguration of the ethos, hence they are heir to the univocalization of being consistent with Newtonian mechanism. The matter is defined in terms of a justified rational proof (dianoetic univocity) of the ground of nature from nature so conceived, or from the very concept of God. Nature is all but shorn of traces of the divine, while God is thought of as a fixed being outside the world. God is other to the universe considered as a material totality or pantheistic whole. The ontological proof might seem to avoid that dualism by bridging, *in the immanence of thought itself*, this difference of finitude and God; however, from what is immanent in a concept all that can emerge is the explication of a concept, and hence truth of an analytical sort, not any existing reality, hence no synthetic truth at all. See Kant's critique thus as a rejection of the reduction of God to conceptual immanence. We must reiterate the disjunction between concept and existence. In this, one might hear a warning against the temptation to *hubris* of theoretical reason. If theoretical reason, purely through its own immanent resources, can bring forth God's necessary existence, it has no need to transcend itself in search of a more ultimate source. There can result an *idolatry of reason itself*.[2] Reason finds God in entering into its own conceptual immanence, and hence God's transcendence is denied. This critique of rational(istic) immanence is perhaps of a piece with a rejection of Spinozistic immanence

---

[2] This point about the ontological proof and the rational hubris of immanence could also be considered in relation to Hegel, and indeed Kierkegaard. See *HG*, pp. 93–8.

(thought of by Kant as a naturalistic determinism, even fatalism) and any materialistic reductionism. In his own way, Kant is a critic of the idols of philosophy, though tempted to create his own philosophical idol. Is there an exploration of immanence not finally reductive to immanence, one that explodes all idols, an exploration that is not just a moral one, in Kant's form? Would we not need a different ethos of thought?

Think of the transcendental anorexia of Kant's notion of existence: existence is not redolent with the fullness of being, or the astonishing fact "that it is at all," or the glorious good of the "to be." Existence reverts to the power of the self to posit, and posit legitimately in accord with the evidences of experience (itself understood in a determinately restricted sense). Clearly there never will be statements about God with the univocity appropriate to the precision demanded by the Newtonian *mathēsis*. The evidences of God are never thus univocal, always equivocal, though sometimes these equivocal traces do move the heart to exaltation and marvel. Thus, in praising the physico-theological proof Kant gives a sign of this. Nevertheless, he is *stern* relative to this uplift: given the epistemic ideal, we must not let ourselves be taken in by these exaltations. Their status is irremediably equivocal, and whatever else we say, we must deny them epistemic certitude and necessity. We might put a positive face on this and say that Kant shows the inherent equivocity in any effort to prove the existence of God in theoretical terms that claim univocal certitude. Yes. But the presuppositions of univocity (be it aesthetic, dianoetic, or transcendental univocity – see *BB*, Chapter 2) remain themselves inadequately criticized, especially in the *Critique of Pure Reason*.

Kant was the heir of the Wolffian version of the ontological proof in which the concept of God is that of the *ens realissimum*. One thinks also of Descartes in the rationalistic context in which the idea of a *triangle* functions as an analogy to the concept of God. We find no context of prayer and meditation that informs Anselm's version of the proof: no inkling that the idea of "that which none greater can be conceived" originally arises within the ethos of a religious meditation. None of this nurturing matrix is present, as we now analyze, so to say, an *orphan concept* of God. Taking for granted a concept of God as the *ens realissimum*, we reflect rationally on it, as we might reflect on the concept of a triangle. Kant is not altogether mistaken if all he finds here is an analytical truth. But too often philosophers deal with orphan concepts; indeed *we make concepts into orphans*, do not delve into their ontological sources. We should bring orphan concepts back to their family sources and connections. We should feed the orphan, nurture it, and not grill it.

What might the "concept" of God mean in a different exploration of transcendental inwardness?[3] Of course, we find in the *Opus Posthumum* a suggestion of the immanence of the divine in our moral experience ("*Est deus in nobis*"),[4] but this is not worked out, and were it so, it would require a significant reformulation of the central doctrines of the more familiar Kant. This suggestion of divine immanence is equivocal, in that it can be seen as motivated by uneasiness with God's heteronomy as threatening the absoluteness of immanent autonomy. Autonomy continues to win out in the antinomy with transcendence as other.

To return to the more familiar Kant: his treatment of the ontological way remains too much at the level of a logic of categorial abstractions – out of which it is quite clear no worthy affirmation of God could be forthcoming. Any affirmation would itself regard a scarecrow abstraction of God, not anything like the living God. Even if the logic were sound, expunged from the supreme being rationalistically affirmed would be the fullness of the God religiously worshipped. Kant gives little evidence of understanding the sources of worship, indeed it struck him as full of danger, danger to the power of autonomous selfhood, for worship must put us in a position of subordination, and Kant is obsessively

3   As an heir of rationalism Kant seemed devoid of the intimation that clear and distinct rational concepts might be shadowed by their dark other, their surface univocity hiding perhaps intractable equivocity. He seems only partially aware of the hidden depths of concepts, depths concepts tend to hide. He may have woken from dogmatic slumber; but waking up still meant going to work univocally with rationality, and this might mean a new sleep.

4   *Opus Posthumum*, edited by E. Förster, translated by E. Förster and M. Rosen (Cambridge: Cambridge University Press, 1993), p. 209.

insistent that no compromise to our self-determination can be tolerated. I would say that prayer returns us to a porosity prior to our autonomy, to the *passio essendi* before the *conatus essendi*. Such a porosity would give Kant the sweats. In *Religion with the Limits of Reason Alone*, while Kant seems positive to the *spirit of prayer* (something purely inward) he does suggest it would be shaming for us to be observed, or taken unawares, in prayer: shamed he says, not just at praying aloud but merely to be caught in the posture of prayer.[5] And yet one might claim that the ontological argument, as in Anselm, is more truly approached only in terms not hostile to the porosity of prayer.

Kant has more to say, and more to say to us. He recognizes a natural and inexpugnable metaphysical exigence to think beyond, to think the ultimate, even if we are denied "legitimated" theoretical knowing of its nature and being. Recall, for instance, his distinction between a "boundary" (*Grenze*) and a "limit" (*Schranke*) in his *Prolegomena to Any Metaphysics* (§ 57). In our search for univocal knowing, there springs up an equivocal longing for what epistemically is denied to us. I see Kant bordering on a supreme tension: committed to respect what he saw as the limit, and yet impelled to think at the boundary of the limit, and indeed beyond; pulled on one side back within the limit, driven out from finitude on the other side, but driven out without the relatively secure univocities of the former. He is *between* finitude and infinity, though he often masks that intermediacy in a manner more intent on securing coherent univocity *within* the between, and letting the equivocal darkness beyond take care of itself. In truth, however, these two sides cannot be kept from each other in an uncontaminated purity.

See the antinomic character of Kantian thinking as a kind of *hovering* on the limit in its equivocal character. But, as Kant perhaps came to know, one cannot really hover for very long, and the natural metaphysical impulse reasserts itself. We might employ a *method of immunization*, or a *critical quarantine* against the impulse, but these imply a kind of *sickness* in the impulse, and unlike later philosophers, Kant could not quite hold that metaphysics was a sickness. There might be diseased or deranged metaphysics, whether the manic metaphysics of the enthusiasts or *Schwärmerei*, or the stiff-necked dogmatic metaphysics of the rationalists. The wasting sickness of the skeptics was just as bad, worse in fact. In between, we need a different health, but it does not come easily. Kant was a hypochondriac; though he did not suffer, I think, from a "holy hypochondria," as Hamann, his friend and antagonist, might put it. There are sicknesses of spirit that are real and unreal at once, that is, entirely equivocal, and yet constitutively real, just as equivocal. Some of the most fascinating aspects of Kant are just his opening up the territory of the equivocal and the antinomic. Perhaps he might reject this diagnosis. As if he were, so to say, a recovering metaphysical hypochondriac, he thought he was making reason completely healthy to itself, at home with itself. We are all familiar with the sick person who *talks himself up* – knowing and not-knowing at once – and yet the person is still sick.

Metaphysics as knowing may be off limits, but morals as metaphysics carries us legitimately beyond the epistemic limit, and God is allowed to make a re-entrance. This approach is immensely suggestive, but also immensely ambiguous in ways of which Kant seemed relatively innocent. What to me seems blatantly equivocal in Kant is not

---

[5] *Der Religion innerhalb der Grenzen der blossen Vernunft*, ed. K. Vorländer (Leipzig: Meiner, 1937), pp. 228–9n.; *Religion within the Limits of Reason Alone*, trans. with intro and notes by T. M. Greene and H. H. Hudson (New York: Harper Torchbook, 1960), p. 183. There is a passage, for instance, in *Kritik der Urteilskraft*, ed. K. Vorländer (Hamburg: Meiner, 1954), §29 [*Critique of Judgement*, trans. J. C.Meredith (Oxford: Clarendon Press, 1952)] where Kant despises a certain praying as "cringing and abject gracebegging." Pervasive ambivalence runs throughout *Religion within the Limits of Reason Alone*. In general, Kant was wary of the power of music to *move* us involuntarily (see AOO, pp. 35, 77–8, 240), but there is a revealing footnote in the *Critique of Judgment* (§53): Kant inveighs against the "singing of spiritual songs" – "they inflict a great hardship upon the public by such *noisy* (and therefore in general pharisaical) devotions, for they force the neighbors either to sing with them or to abandon meditations." Kant lived close to a prison where, to his evident annoyance, the prisoners had to sing hymns. Forced to listen to the singing, one thinks of Kant, instead of being sweet reason, as being beside himself – against his will. Perhaps it is even funnier: Kant forced to sing along with the hymns of the convicts!

equivocal at all for Kant. Kant's univocity is often a restatement of the equivocity dressed up in scholastic distinctions. One might say that the equivocal is interiorized by his thinking, hence we get the strange impression of a *wavering effect*, sometimes an *oscillation* between opposites, sometimes indeed a kind of dizzying of the mind, one is not sure where one is, being swirled around with eyes blindfolded that see nothing in itself. See how we are turned around: one thinks metaphysics is destroyed but discovers it reconstructed on moral grounds; a metaphysics of morals brings us to God; but then this is a peculiar God, because it is not for God's sake we are brought here but to satisfy a discontent, indeed a possible torment in our moral being. God serves not as the end *simpliciter*, but as a mediating supplement, relative to our own final moral end. Do we here make of God a means, a *moral idol*?

Suppose we approach the moral proof on analogy with the ontological proof: within the immanences of the moral subject there is at work something ultimately other; by exploring these moral immanences we are driven to affirm such an other as the condition of the possibility of our own moral being. Our moral being testifies to the charge of the unconditional. Kant will concur: we are under the unconditional demand of the moral law. Whether the moral law is the ultimate unconditioned is a question, of course, and one might argue that the moral law, while imposing an unconditional demand, does so because it issues from an unconditionally good source or source of goodness, namely God. Moral law is not the ultimate.

I know, I know: Kant seems to let the moral law just dangle there; the giver of the law, as other to us as moral legislators, is and is not pursued. We may give the law to ourselves, but we do so because the moral law seems, in a way hard to understand, already given to us, and in obligation we *find ourselves under* its unconditional demand. But who gives the law as thus given to us? The natural answer would seem to be God, even if we do not know what God is. In one sense, Kant knew this, and there are passages where he gives us permission to think of religion as the "recognition of all duties as divine commands" (*Erkenntnis aller Pflichten als göttlicher Gebote*– the point is reiterated again and again in the *Opus Posthumum*)[6]. But in another sense, Kant dragged his feet and shunned the implication of such an admission. To take this view, one might have to say there is an unconditional good, or unconditional source of goodness that, while unconditionally good itself, is *beyond* the moral law. The unconditional source of unconditional law is not itself another law; it is other, precisely as determining source. Is there not something here *beyond* the law? The suggestion must send the shiver of a secret terror into Kant's moral heart, as well as making more severe demands on our need to think beyond.[7] For just that other "beyondness" would create insuperable difficulties for the entire ethics of *autonomy* to which Kant cleaved. Such autonomy is relativized in face of this ultimate other.

In Kant's own line of thought, God arises as a necessary postulate relative to the *summum bonum*. God is not the *summum bonum* (as God is, say, for Augustine and Aquinas). The *summum bonum* as the *bonum supremum* has to do with virtue, but the supreme good in the sense of the most inclusive (*bonum consummatum*) refers us to happiness in addition to virtue. Kant thinks the virtuous merit happiness, in exact proportion to their being virtuous, though they are not virtuous because they seek happiness. Quite plainly, and contra Socrates, in this world the virtuous are often not happy, while the vicious seem to be. The unconditional moral requirement obligates us to do the good: it is better to be good and wretched than vicious and happy. The antinomic character of the situation is plain: there is no resolution to this polarity in the present life. It has always been, is now, and it will always be, that the good are not necessarily rewarded with happiness in this life. Finally there is something deeply *offensive* about this to Kant,

---

6 *Kritik der Praktischen Vernunft*, ed. K. Vorländer (Leipzig: Meiner, 1929), p. 148 [Book 2, Ch. 5]; *Critique of Practical Reason*, trans. L. W. Beck (New York: Macmillan, 1993), p. 136.

7 On this in relation to Kantian autonomy (as well as Hegel, Marx, and Nietzsche), see *EB*, Chapter 4. An analogous point holds with respect to the terror of genius and the otherness of the sublime; see Chapter 2 of *AOO*.

let him hide it as he will behind the mask of pure reason. His postulate of God serves to soften this offense.

Everything points to a constitutive ambiguity about our moral being, an equivocity we cannot resolve here and now. Perhaps *we* can never resolve it. *Now* happiness and virtue cannot be reduced to a completely coherent unity; the antinomy breaks up such a univocity. The lack of this unity has about it something morally offensive, but if morals is *metaphysics*, this offense threatens the very basis of being's intelligibility, indeed worth. If the antinomy remains without *any* resolution, our confidence not only in the intelligibility but in the ultimate goodness of being is put under assault. We ourselves are the demand for their *unity or togetherness beyond equivocity*, for the resolution of the antinomy. But any such a resolution cannot be guaranteed *by us*. It is beyond our self-determination, though we intimately know of its necessity through an intractable equivocity in our immanent self-determination. For Kant we must postulate a ground of unity that guarantees its possibility, and this is God. The God we so postulate as other to our present equivocal plight serves to remove the offense from the equivocity by guaranteeing the possibility of its resolution beyond death in another life. (Does Kant here unwittingly give us a moral variation on the theme of *posthumous mind*: a thinking from the "beyond" of immanent life that releases us to see differently what is here and now before us?)

Kant denies making any theoretical, cognitive claim: we have to think *as if* the soul is immortal and God exists. Kant's view is what I term a "postulatory moral deism": if we are to think of ourselves in the moral terms as Kant claims, we must think as if there must be a moral God, the ground of unity of virtue and happiness. The Kantian indirection comes in again. Kant is deeply diffident about making a direct and affirmative claim. Yet if the indirect arising of God is meant to solve the moral equivocity, does not the *as if* reintroduce equivocity? For if there is no *constitutive* being to the ground of unity of virtue and happiness, is not the guarantee Kant wanted to secure funded with inadequate assets? Is it a matter of putting *moral noughts* after one's hundred possible talers? As *if* one has *morally* increased one's capital, but not "really"? We wonder if the "*as if* God" is a *projection, albeit moral, that we throw beyond this life* to diminish an intolerable equivocity.[8] And yet, if the inscrutability of this other is also remembered, we see that there is no escape from the equivocity, better put, the ultimate mystery, of the divine.

Why does Kant not come out and say this more forthrightly, if this is what he wanted to say? Or is it that he could not do so because this would be a severe compromise of the univocal security he otherwise works so diligently to build? Understood in the light of equivocity, the *as if* makes us face into that mystery more insecurely than ever. Something about this situation was also offensive to Kant; perhaps intolerable, or to use his own word, *unendurable*. But this is just the point: we have to endure a recalcitrant otherness not within our control, not subject to our doing and our self-activity, beyond our self-determination. *We suffer in our being* the necessity of this God; it is beyond us. We know again, in the most intimate immanences of the soul, the *passio essendi*. This being so, the moral autonomy that is the source of the postulate must itself be relativized by such an understanding of God. We are at sea.

There is also the question of the *nature* of the God thus postulated. Is not this postulated "*as if* God" too much tailored to our morality? Does this not dull us to the

8 In the *Kritik der Praktischen Vernunft*, p. 164 (*Critique of Practical Reason*, p. 150) Kant says that the righteous man can say: "I will that there be a God..." (*ich will, daß ein Gott...*) – almost, if not quite, as if the being of God were dependent on the righteous willing God to be. There are some sentences in William James's "Will to Believe," where he implies that our will somehow gives God to be: "I confess that I do not see why the very existence of the invisible world may not depend on the personal response which any one of us may make to the religious appeal. God himself, in short, may draw vital strength and increase of very being from our fidelity," *The Will to Believe, and Other Essays in Popular Philosophy* (Cambridge: Harvard University Press, 1979), p. 55. A lot depends on what we might mean by saying God "depends" on us. On this see my piece on R. Kearney's *The God Who May Be* (Bloomington: Indiana University Press, 2002) – "Maybe, Maybe Not: Richard Kearney and God," in *Irish Theological Quarterly*, 68 (2003), pp. 99–118.

terrors of the ultimate, as also to the mysteries? And since Kant's morality is modeled on autonomy in conformity with the moral law, does not this God, at most, become a giver of moral law? Kant hated despotic monarchs who make their subjects into supine, abject slaves. The God of arbitrary power and *fiat* is anathema to him, as is the religious practice that makes the worshiper a spineless worm. But does not the *as if* leave so *indefinite* the space of equivocality that into it postulates *other than his moral God* might just as easily be projected? Does not the *as if* allow an undetermined space in which others might postulate a perhaps more malign darkness at the base of things, as did Schopenhauer, or an amoral, immoral Dionysian energy, as did Nietzsche? And what of the question above, namely, that the source of moral law is beyond moral law, and is hence perhaps *good* beyond good and evil in the moral sense? Is not this just why the equivocity must always remain if we fix on the moral level, even when our natural sense of justice seems to demand that it not be there at all? Still it is there, demand as we will. Is God just beyond that demand, not because God is beyond justice but because God is not to be measured on the scale of our moral justice? Is there an ultimate good beyond moral good and evil? The question of this ultimate good returns out of the equivocality of good and evil as proportionate to *our measure* of justice. The question puts our moral measure in question.

Kant conceives God in the image of his own determination of morality: God as judge of the exact measure of justice, of happiness as merited in exact proportion to our worthiness to be happy – namely, our being virtuous. Only the virtuous ought to be rewarded with happiness; to "reward" the unvirtuous would be unjust. The emphasis on the exact measure betrays a kind of religious univocity: the moral God will calculate (think again of Leibniz) this measure; we humans cannot. Thus Kant does not follow through fully on the momentum of the virtual dialectic which suggests a God also beyond the measure of our moral difference of good and evil. He does not see the equivocity in the antinomy of happiness and virtue as pointing beyond both equivocity and univocity. He seeks a higher moral univocity in his postulated God. Hence he returns to the univocal, instead of being released beyond the wavering between univocity and equivocity. This transcendental moral univocity does not bring resolution to the antinomy or peace to the equivocity. The virtualities of his dialectic remain too recessive and need to be brought into fuller relief.

Kant wants to soften the offense in the equivocal disjunction of virtue and happiness, but does he also want to *avenge* the offense in the happiness of those not in real earnest about virtue? Does he back up this desire with his moral God, such that the projected ground of unity becomes also the God of a retributive Last Judgment (see, for instance, *Critique of Judgment*, §88). I have often pondered what Kant would make of Jesus's parable of the workers in the vineyard. The workers who enter the vineyard at the end of the day hardly work at all and get the same pay as those who sweat in the heat of the day. They have not *earned* a full day's pay, but they are given it nevertheless. The owner of the vineyard is just, but he is also more than just. "Reward" (or should we say "gift") goes to those who merit no reward. Good is given gratuitously, for no reason beyond its goodness. Would Kant grumble like those who have worked all day for their pay, worked even into the endless progress of unending eternity? Grumble, indeed find it an intolerable affront to his dignity to overhear the laggards outside the vineyard, telling jokes, laughing, lazing indolently in the heat, just enjoying themselves, waiting, not working? And they too are "rewarded" in the same measure! Is not this a measure of justice itself unjust, if justice is sameness of pay merited for the same moral work? Is this not an offensive generosity beyond the measure of even a transcendentally univocalized justice?[9]

I think this generosity in excess of moral measure *must* be offensive to the entire viewpoint informing Kant's postulated God. That postulated God is the mirror image of the rationally self-determining moral agent who deserves to be rewarded because he has

---

[9]   On how the story of the Prodigal Son might sound, as retold by a K(ant), or a H(egel), or a M(arx) or a N(ietzsche), see my "Dream Monologues of Autonomy," *Ethical Perspectives* 5, 4 (1998), pp. 305–21.

struggled and worked hard to be the good person he undoubtedly is. Kant invariably shows contempt for those who do the good not for the sake of the good but for the sake of the reward it brings to them. Kant has worked hard and earnestly, and Kant too wants his earned reward, though it will be a postulated reward in the continuing afterlife. As Kant's morality of autonomy takes too little care for the *passio essendi* that is porous to the good of the "to be" beyond our self-determination, so he is not alert to the divine *compassio essendi* that loves beyond determinable merit. Kant's moral God lacks the generosity of agapeic transcendence that may well also give beyond the why or measure of moral justification.

Kant's postulatory moral deism directs us to a divine ground of unity beyond but here on this side of the limit it leaves us with something like double vision. Kant might be taken to mean: If we look for God to know God, there is nothing to be found, no God is there where we look. Do not look for God thus; God is never an object; God is non-objective – beyond all objectification. Thus the double vision: God is nothing, no objective thing; God as non-objectifiable urges us towards a non-cognitivist, or unknowing, sense of transcendence as other to the finite. The first – agnosticism, though not theoretical atheism; the second – nescience, perhaps an unnamed exaltation of transcendence. Kant's double vision gives us now the firm stability of this side of the opposition, now that side, and both as determinately different. But then we find motion back and forth, or wavering back and forth, or vacillation up and down, when we try to face the hard question of how these two are *related* to each other at all. Clearly Kant wants to relate them, and indeed with reference to God as the ultimate unconditional ground of unity. Beyond a univocal objectivism and equivocal subjectivism, self-determination may seem to be beyond the idols of theory, but then we must worry about a new *practical idol* – a divinity projected in the image of our moral autonomy. Kant seems unable, or unwilling to go beyond this. He gives us a reluctant dialectic, reticent about its ultimate source, withholding about its final faith. Recall that Kant understood dialectic in a negative sense relative to the detection of transcendental illusion. Is his own postulation of God an exercise in *moral illusion*? I do not doubt that Kant put this question to himself. But does not the wavering back and forth in his thinking make us suspect a secret uncertainty, a terror before the abyss of God, only partially kept hidden?

A PARABLE: FISHING FOR GOD

Do we need to take a step further? Will I be forgiven if I answer with a parable? Let me call it: Fishing for God.

A fisherman stands on the shore's edge. He casts his line into the sea. He wants to catch the big fish he is somehow convinced is out there. But, alas, the big fish is just out there beyond the limit of reach of his fishing line. He will never be able to reach the big fish, much less catch it, if he stays where he is. But he believes that he has only a legitimate right to stand where he is standing; there resides his justified line; were he to step over this line, he would be trespassing, so he thinks, and so he cannot catch the fish.

Ah, but this fisherman is sly. He cannot catch the fish, and cannot quite cast as far as he would require. He will feel despair if he cannot somehow "catch" the fish. What does he do? He takes from his bag a different hook, a *moral hook* instead of a theoretical hook, and puts it on the line. And he continues to cast his line. But does the line reach any further than before? Not at all. But now it reaches the same limit but as a *moral hook*, and somehow it is *as if* the big fish has been caught. If another fisher challenges him to show the big fish, he will quickly reply: I cannot *show* you the big fish, I have drawn it towards me *as if* I caught it. That is what moral hooks will do for you; they allow you to catch big fish, as it were, but they also allow the big fish off the hook, so to say, and what's more they allow the fisher off the hook also, when another fisher with only a theoretical hook asks to see the strange catch; the fisher with theoretical hooks alone does not understand what kinds of catches are possible with moral hooks.

But suppose there is another way. Suppose the answer is not to be paralyzed by the line at the edge of the sea. Suppose the fisher should simply wade into the water, and hence get closer to the catch that way. The fisher knows he may be knocked over with a big wave, or that there may be a hole into which he may fall and drown, or a tidal current that may sweep him away, or – terror itself – be himself caught and consumed by the fish. But if he moves into the sea, he will be able to cast his line and land it closer to the big fish. And maybe it does not really matter what kind of hook he has on his line. He ventures out into the deep with all its dangers and mysteries. And of course, this inscrutable fish may never be caught. But this fisher knows the terrors of the deep, yet he thinks this is the way to fish, risking perhaps his life, for these are the terrors of God.

DIALECTIC BEYOND DUALISM: DETERMINING ORIGIN BEYOND DETERMINATION

If we swivel the Kantian equivocity slightly we begin to see a dialectic that more decisively takes equivocity by the scruff of the neck. Perhaps Kant ought to have had more courage relative to the momentous opening and excess of human self-transcendence, and not only have made an exception out of a desperation relative to moral transcendence. Our being is to be a "passing beyond" and, because we are mindful of the passing, a "thinking beyond." We are self-transcending, transcending not exhausted by its moral form. The exigence of metaphysical transcendence can reveal the robust health of the overflowing soul. Is there not a *prior* dialectic of our being, permeating all our developments and surpassings? Is this not at the source from which objectifying science emerges as one of its determinate formation, and from which our own endowment with self-determination also comes? Has this source to do with the porosity of our being, this reaching beyond with the urgency of ultimacy?

I would emphasize both the porosity and the urgency. The first recalls us to the givenness of finitude, the second shapes our outreach beyond determinate finitude. We are the living of the dialectic between the *passio essendi* and *conatus essendi*. The two might seem to be in opposition, the passion of being signifying our being given to be, the endeavor to be signifying some surpassing of givenness. Yet we are each and we are both and we are their joining. It is precisely their tense togetherness in our being that, on one side, opens us to what transcends us, and that, on the other side, urges us beyond our current limitation. Without the passing beyond, we would be only an inert passivity; without the porosity, we would be only self-inflating self-insistence. The Kantian wavering is between two hesitations: on the one hand, diffidence about the *passio essendi*, lest it weaken our claim to autonomy; on the other hand, caution about our dynamic being as driven beyond, lest it become an empty self-inflation.

The dialectical way, to my mind, tends to stress less the *passio essendi* as the self-surpassing movement, our being driven beyond opposition by opposition itself. The endeavor to be strives beyond the strife of opposites, and something about our self-transcending itself embodies both the strife and the conjunction of opposites. It is important to remember this tendency to recess the *passio essendi* in dialectical self-transcending, since it helps define the affirmative claims made by dialectic about the divine, as well as its not always granted weaknesses. The affirmative claim is that opposition, say between the finite and infinite, cannot be ultimate. These "opposites" refer us to a *determining source more ultimate* than their fixation as antithetical. There is a *determining beyond determinations*. It is not one opposite, it is not the other; it is neither and it is both; it is a kind of coincidence of opposites. We might think of Cusanus who claims God is such a coincidence. Some might judge him an incautious speculative theologian, innocent of the critical restrictions of Kant, but I would resist here any transcendental condescension. To speak of a "coincidence of opposites" is a sophisticated response to the *understood* insufficiency of finite ways of speaking of divine transcendence. There need be nothing naïve about it, except perhaps the naïveté that always will accompany bold and courageous thinking, as naïve, or as wise, as the fisherman that will take the risk, and walk into the water.

Dialectic tries to sift the chiaroscuro of the equivocal. We cannot but do that. Kant knew this. The very thrust of self-transcending, differentiated in the antithetical matrix of the equivocal, carries us further. The tension of the equivocal, once interiorized, urges us further. This tension is itself beyond antithetical determinations as antithetical, since we are the embodiment of their conjoining. Their struggle is joined in us, since we are this strife itself. The dialectical way tries to pass along the articulation of this strife qua strife, to seek in the passing some unity or wholeness more ultimate than our striving. This may sound far from Kant, but it is he who postulates God as the *ultimate ground of unity* guaranteeing the final accord between virtue and happiness. Short of postulating that ground of unity we are racked by the unresolved opposition of virtue and happiness, the intolerable equivocity we ourselves are. This ground of unity bears definite resemblance to the coincidence of opposites.[10] One might even see Kant as a negative theologian – a negative moral theologian. But do *we* have to be as negative as Kant?

Look at it this way. Suppose dialectical self-transcending recesses the *passio essendi* while bringing to the fore the urgency of ultimacy. Suppose this urgency manifests a complicated interplay of finitude and infinity in our very being. We are, but are as desiring beings, lacking what we seek, and so we are finite; but just as finite, we surpass ourselves to what as other will requite our lack; impelled beyond ourselves, just as finite we are not just finite. Were we just univocally finite, we would not move from the spot; we move, hence are more than univocal finitude. Is this movement equivocal, making our finitude a contradictory dissolving condition? In a way yes: we are what we are in passing; our hold on being vanishes before us, as also we are dissolved into self-discord. In passage along a way, we pass away. We know ourselves as coming to be at war with ourselves, and with other-being, be it of nature, of humanity, or of God. But is there more?

A certain infinitude springs up in the overdeterminate restlessness of our finitude. While this is the passion of our being, it is also the urgency of ultimacy. Indeed, this urgency is effective in Kant's scheme all along, though within the system there is no category for it. There can be no category for it, for it is trans-categorial. It is irreducible to any set of univocal concepts. Kant lived this dynamism as a philosopher *philosophizing*, but he is only partially successful in drawing our attention to its efficacy and import. It does not fit in, and yet Kant must acknowledge it, and indeed satisfy it in his inimitable equivocal way. The tense togetherness of finitude and infinitude incarnate in our self-surpassing brings us closer to the ultimate as transcendence even more original than our self-transcendence. Equivocity is inescapable because we are dialectical, because already from the outset we are more than equivocal.

You object: This is all very well if we confine ourselves to human self-transcending (T²), but thus confined, can we say anything about transcendence *as other* (T³)? The coincidence of opposites is one thing with us, but are we not supposed to be talking about God? How get from the first to the second?

Here the recess of the *passio essendi* has some fateful consequences, for the dialectical way offers an understanding of the interplay of the indeterminate and determinate that mediates our defining of being as other, including God's otherness. It goes something like this. Suppose we try to fix completely the other determinately; but the very differentiation of the other shows a process of self-becoming and self-othering which surpasses univocal identity. The process shows a double face, as both itself and not itself, at one and the same time. The other is itself and not itself, if it becomes itself. And if it becomes itself determinately, this seems to mean there is also an indeterminacy, prior to what it has become

---

[10] Hegel wants, as it were, to turn Kant around and begin not with the duality but the unity: the unity from which differences come to be, as the self-doubling of the original one, the self-othering of the One. See §59 in Hegel's *Encyclopädie der philosophischen Wissenschaften* [English translation of Part I as *The Encylopaedia Logic* by T. F. Geraets, W. A. Suchting, H. S. Harris (Indianapolis: Hackett, 1991)] where, against Kant's doctrine of the *summum bonum*, which is reached starting from antithesis, he suggests God as the third beyond subjectivity and objectivity, universality and particularity that resolves their antithesis. This third, of course, is really the first for him.

determinately. Its very self-becoming is an interplay of determinacy and indeterminacy. Its full truth is neither a univocal determinacy nor an equivocal indeterminacy but the togetherness of these two as a self-becoming. The dialectical way proposes that such an analysis might be applied even to the divine.

Rather than dualism, it seems that the *inseparability of God and world* is the more concrete thought. It is univocity and equivocity that are relatively trapped in abstraction. The paradoxical conjunction is closer to the truth than the equivocal self-consistencies of univocity. Nothing, in the end, has an entirely separable identity or difference. Ontological togetherness is all. This is not entirely untrue to creation in the universal impermanence (see *BB*, Chapter 7). All creation groans, as the apostle says. Creation is, as it were, the prayer of time sent up unceasingly to the origin. The otherness of creation as for itself is not a being for self that excludes ecstatic transcendence towards what is other to it. Its very being for itself contains within itself the welcome and solicitation of the other. If the groan turns into a howl or a curse, this too is a perverse prayer of time. The center is other, even when we see creation as centered in its own being for itself. It is always already involved in a community with what passes beyond itself. We have a presentiment of this in agapeic astonishment, but mostly sink back from it and take no note. And yet there are those days of grace that surprise us, and when the world floats above its own dark nothingness, as if its hovering were the heat of its eros for ultimate transcendence, as if a sigh of unknowing love were floating free into the ether, releasing creation into the lightness of eternity. Dualism as opposition seems to dissolve in that lightening love.

How does the point relate to the divine otherness? I put it pedestrianly: God may be the absolute other, but the absolute other is not absolutely other. This other is absolute, but just as absolute it is for the other of itself, and hence not absolute, in the sense of being purely for itself alone. This is the agapeic ecstasis of transcendence itself. God is not a One retracted in lone identity with self: the "identity" of the divine is a kind of infinite self-othering, and self-othering towards the finite. As finite being refers beyond itself to the infinite, the infinite communicates beyond itself to the finite other. Creation itself is the original communication of the "coming to be" of finitude, the very happening of the between. We cannot elevate the absolute other into an otherness that is just the absolutization of opposition. Were this the last word, we would have to pack our bags and shut up. I agree, a reverent silence may be needful, but we can only speak of the absolutely other, even as absolutely other, because in some mysterious sense that other is communicated. The real question is the character of the communication. Is it dialectical, or only dialectical, or is there more? Dialectic points to more than our way of thinking toward the divine; it borders on the issue of the divine way towards us. It calls attention to the mediation of the two, and not just need, but the already effective work of an enigmatic intermediation in the given between of finite passing.

DIALECTIC AND THE SELF-DETERMINING GOD: ON SOME HEGELIAN WAYS

To situate Hegel, I recapitulate Kant's views in terms of the determinate, indeterminate and self-determining. Kant "deconstructs" determinative proofs: no univocal certainty can come either from the dianoetic evidences of theoretical reason or the aesthetic evidences of empirical experience. Both these evidences are equivocal. Beyond these efforts at determination, Kant reconstructs a proof drawn from moral self-determination, one claiming a kind of practical univocity beyond aesthetic and dianoetic equivocity. But there is still some equivocity in this: relative to the *summum bonum*, God is a "supplement" to our moral autonomy. Beyond determination and self-determination, there is no overdeterminacy of God, more a relative indeterminacy bearing on the ambiguous *als ob* character of his postulated God.

Hegel, by contrast, is a provocative speculative dialectician who points beyond univocal determination and equivocal indeterminacy, addressing the antinomic character of finite thought, and claiming to surpass it, even beyond Kant's God postulated out of moral self-determination, to God determined constitutively in terms of *God's own immanent self-determination.* Not entirely unlike Kant though, Hegel is not true to divine over-determinacy. Here are some brief remarks. Lest I seem to shoehorn Hegel into a constricted space, the reader can consult my more extensive treatment in *Hegel's God.*

The Hegelian critique of Kantianism addresses the claim that the noumenal is unknowable. How claim this at all, since to claim it is to know something about the unknowable, albeit something minimal? Even Aquinas will grant that though we know not *what God is,* we can know *that God is.* This is still something. In affirming even radical transcendence, we know something of that transcendence, hence it is not just only transcendent. Is not, minimally, some intimation of the unknowable already "known," hence always already presupposed? Why is the grounding unity only on the other side, as it seems with Kant, and not on this side also? And if we *speak* of the absolute other, we draw the absolutely other into proximity with what is not other, and hence it is no longer absolutely other.[11] Should we counsel silence? But how then exonerate our silence? If we do exonerate our silence, is not the exoneration informed by some perplexing immanence of the absolutely other? In such a light, some qualified form of the Hegelian critique seems unavoidable. But all depends on the qualification.

Suppose we grant the absolute other as somehow at work in immanence, must this compromise its otherness? In its being manifest, must otherness be deprived of its otherness? Metaxology leads us to deny this. There is a reticence of reserve in communication itself. Kant's *instincts* may be right here, but his *arguments* are not always up to Hegel's reply. If we are to second such instincts, we cannot do so without granting something of the rationale of the reply, while going further to reinstate the otherness differently. Hegel wants not an intimating dialectic but a fully self-determining one. The *porosity* to the divine that intimation requires is overtaken by the *conatus* of a speculative thinking that would gather the presentiment of divine otherness into its own systematic self-determination. Our patience to the divine is entailed by "unknowability," but Hegelian dialectic wants to supersede such patience and claim fully articulated "knowing."

Hegel's speculative dialectic, I hold, is not properly qualified by the ontological porosity and patience more primordial than self-determining thinking, but is encouraged to exfoliate, without proper measure, on the sense of inescapable presence. Once having granted *some* immanence, he proceeds to totalize this, while asserting that claims of absolute transcendence are simply incoherent. Beyond fixating God as a univocal determinacy, God will be the absolutely self-determining concept. Speculative dialectic will claim to bring what is going on in immanence to more and more comprehended presence; so much so that its overriding impetus will be to see ongoingness itself as the very process by means of which absence is progressively converted into comprehended presence, transcendence into immanence, differences into more and more comprehensive unity. Hegel's speculative dialectic will grant determinate identities that run to ambiguity at their limit; it will notice differences running to oppositions that, in turn, turn against each other, and so notice opposition running to togetherness in strife and beyond strife. But it will see in all this the inexorable *process of the ultimate itself* whereby it becomes more and more comprehensively present – indeed not just present, but present to itself, comprehending of itself. The being of the between, or the absolved relativity between God and given being, thus speculatively interpreted, becomes the process of absolute self-comprehending, inclusive of anything that from less comprehensive standpoints seemed merely other.

Hegel presses the point from *both* our side and God's. *Our side:* Our self-transcending seems to epitomize just this movement from transcendence to immanence, from absence to presence, from patience to self-activity, from heteronomy to autonomy, from distraction abroad to self-presence at home with itself. Remember again the inward way. It might

---

[11]   Some arguments like this have been used against Levinas, for instance by Derrida (in "Violence and Metaphysics," *Writing and Difference*, trans. Alan Bass (Chicago: University of Chicago Press, 1978), pp. 79–153), with one or two Hegelian tricks thrown in. Levinas's privileging of infinity over totality clearly has implications for Hegel. In Levinas there is the suggestion of a dualism, reminiscent of master and servant; I would prefer a pluralism, beyond dualism and dialectic, in terms of agapeic service beyond sovereignty and servility.

now be renamed as the *dialectically intensive way*. We are the intensiveness of dialectical inwardness. The intensification of dialectical inwardness brings us to the infinitude working in our finitude, the divinity fermenting in our humanity, the absolute effective in our relative state. The consummation is just to be absolutely in the mediated return to self out of its own otherness. Out of the alienation also necessary for self-differentiation, the self is both same and immanently different, for its differences have passed through the cauldron of strife, and are now held together in an inclusive self-mediating unity said to be unsurpassable. This (it will be said) is the absolute in us, or equally, us in the absolute.

God's side: We seem not to "know" God at the beginning. In fact, the inchoate origin, first mere intimation or presentiment, has to develop to the point of difference and opposition. In Hegel's conceptual reconfiguration of religious figures (*Vorstellungen*) the created world is the self-othering of the divine origin, self-othering to the point of radical opposition, yet this hostile antithesis, indeed evil, is not the end, but only the mediation by which the opposition is reversed, or the opposites are turned towards each other, turned because dialectically each is what the other is not, but as not the other they discover their inseparability. Hostility turns us dialectically to the other as not other simply. And this turning to other that is a returning to self is the divine life *discovering itself again*, in the antithesis of evil; not merely discovering, but *redeeming itself by becoming itself* more fully in what seems absolutely opposed to its secure self-identity. *God's redemption of finitude is God's own self-redemption.*

The claimed recognition of self in other and other in self means now that *both sides of the divide are at bottom the same*. Recall Hegel's definition of the absolute as the "identity of identity and difference." He speaks of the highest knowing in terms of "pure self-recognition in absolute otherness," but the first and last accent falls on pure self-recognition, the otherness is its own, and hence Hegel's reference to absolute otherness is dialectically disingenuous. It makes no sense to speak of an absolutely other any more. God becomes fully God in returning to Godself and in returning the otherness of world and self to Godself, a return not really the return of an irreducible other but of the othered-Godself. If this is Aristotle's thought thinking itself in speculative–dialectical form, the content of this thinking of thinking itself is nothing less than the "totality."[12] Most importantly, this consummation from the divine side is the same as the consummation from the human side. There is no way to keep the two apart. Their doubleness is speculatively transformed into their at-oneness. The first transcendence of world (T^1), our self-transcendence (T^2), and transcendence as other, God's transcendence (T^3) are all speculatively incorporated in the absolute immanence of the whole of wholes.

There are unstable and potentially corrupting ambiguities in all this. What kind of a God could possibly have to redeem *itself*? This ultimate oneness beyond opposition is said to *develop from* the opposition of the opposites. We might say: humanity's ascent from finitude to infinity is not antithetical to divinity's descent from infinitude to finitude. Ascent and descent, seemingly opposed, are two moments of a more unifying process of the mediation of finitude in infinity, or infinity in finitude. It does not matter which way we put it, because finitude and infinitude are themselves two moments of the *absolute process*. Beyond any dualism of finite and infinite, Hegel speaks of the "self-sublating" infinity which contains finitude as a moment of itself. As, previously, dialectic emphasized continuity over discontinuity, here, in the intermediation of God and creation, it is the *self-mediation of a total process* that receives priority, with otherness a subordinate, subsumed, albeit necessary moment.

---

12 Of course, Hegel's invocation of *noēsis teˉs noeˉseˉos* suggests more than the Aristotelian form, enriched as it is intended to be by everything essential in history (notably the development of Christianity and the revolution of transcendental philosophy) which is dialectically sublated into the divine life. One might also call Hegel a transcendental-speculative Spinozist: God may be the name religions have for the "whole of wholes," but there is no God beyond the whole. The Parmenidean One is dialectically resurrected: redoubled as redoubling all otherness and negation within itself. I will say more about the whole of wholes, when I discuss the pan(en)theistic God in Part III. For fuller discussion, see again *Hegel's God*.

The return to sameness we are here witnessing shows the *reinstatement of a transcendental-speculative univocity* within dialectic: not univocity at the level of fixed determinacy, but in terms of the very fixing of determinacy, namely, determining as absolute self-determining. This reinstatement can short circuit the lessons of equivocity. The equivocal way rocks us back on ourselves, returns us to ourselves, but in the realization that we are *not* God. It asked finesse for the porosity of being, for the *passio* in which ambiguous signs of the divine remain tokens of mystery, and reminders of "unknowing," even in our most finessed mindfulness. As the univocal fixation of God can turn into the vanishing of God in equivocal indetermination, the self-determining "absolutization" of God can lead to a kind of dialectical eclipse of the divine. The occlusion of transcendence as other (T^3) is achieved, one fears, by the systematic fronting of a conceptual counterfeit of the living One. The metaxological way will try to reopen this occlusion.

Hegelian dialectic determines the togetherness of God and world in terms of *inclusive self-mediation of the absolute One in and through its own self-othering*. There is no One beyond the double, no double other than the One. Hegel's One *becomes itself* in the return to oneness *with itself* through its own self-doubling. God becomes absolutely self-mediating being in and through the world as its own other. The One is the dialectically self-reconciled One. The One comes to itself as realized oneness with itself, out of its own self-posing, self-opposing, self-othering.

Is this a block eternity without dynamism, an Eleaticism of the divine once again? How square this with finite manyness, indeed the nothingness we have tasted and the horror of evil? Is this a retreat from the equivocity of good and evil that threw our ontological confidence off balance? It is not so simple. I see Hegel's God as an erotic absolute: the eternity that loves itself in time. Inclusive self-mediating in and through the owned other is seen as the very self-structuring of transcendence itself (T^3). We see signs of this with self-transcendence (T^2): the self as source transcends itself towards the other and into the other, but in thus being out beyond itself, it is still itself and complexly with itself. Self is itself in redoubling itself outside of itself in relation to the other. How or why apply this to God (T^3)? Only if God is *self-determining eternity that determines itself in its own temporal productions*. Time is eternity's other, but as eternity's other, time is the medium of eternity's self-completing mediation with itself. Rather than a block, static Eleatic eternity, time and eternity are in love with each other, though in loving the other each loves itself, for indeed the whole love is the love of the whole, the whole that, in embracing time and eternity within itself, loves just itself.

What kind of love is this? It is love disporting with itself, a phrase Hegel uses and qualifies to name his absolute *Geist*. While Hegel admits that this description would become insipid without the work of the negative, finally this work also turns out to be within the love that loves itself in and through its own self-othering.[13] Why does divine transcendence redouble itself beyond itself? The metaphysical metaphor serving us here is love as a kind of *eternal eros*. The self-mediating transcendence is a kind of erotic transcendence. This dialectical transcendence puts into recess the *passio essendi,* while putting to the fore a self-energizing, self-positing *conatus essendi*. This *conatus* is also self-othering just in its self-positing, but both self-positing and self-othering constitute its absolute self-determining, by which it entirely overcomes what is held to be the merely undeveloped indeterminacy of any *passio essendi*. It is *causa sui* at the level of absolute *Geist*.

The true is the whole, Hegel said. For the beginning is nothing without the end, hence the beginning in itself is nothing. With this dialectic of divine eros, the beginning is a lacking indeterminacy, but this drives beyond itself; it is no ordinary lack; it is dynamized with the energy of self-transcendence in search of what is lacks, and that is just *itself*. The lacking beginning seeks the completed end, and in finding it constitutes the consummated

---

[13] I believe that Hegel does not entirely escape from the shadow of Eleatic Oneness (see *HG*, p. 111). See *PU*, Chapter 6; *BB*, Chapter 6 regarding the attractions of the erotic absolute; though one must also insist there is a perversion of the union of human and divine for purposes of humanistic hubris; there is the degrading of the erotic absolute after Hegel, into the *eros turannos* of Schopenhauer's will or Nietzsche's will to power.

whole. The middle is the between as medium of the self-completing of the whole. Claims of the otherness of the between to eternity are untrue. Rather, the origin becomes its own end in passing into the between which is *its own medium* of self-transcendence. The end is the eternal love that is in complete self-possession and not in flight from the negativities of time, but just in and through them. These negativities, it is said, are its own negation, and as its own negation they are its affirmation. This dialectical-speculative God affirms all such negativities as in the end only itself and necessary for itself as the consummate whole of wholes, greater than which none can be conceived.

DIALECTIC, COMING TO BE, BECOMING

While dialectic often addresses the continuities of immanence more than the discontinuity of transcendence as other, nevertheless, it exhibits metaxological promise. I offer a sketch of dialectic transformed through a commitment to fidelity to this promise in the intermediation of first (T^1), second (T^2), and third transcendence (T^3). Divine overdeterminacy outstrips Hegel's self-determining God.

T^3 – *World*: It is there, and as there, determinate, but as determinate not self-sustaining; it is determinate because determined, and determined because the issue of a determining. The world is there as a happening that becomes, and this and that becomes in it; "before" it becomes, however, it *comes to be*. It is the issue of a more primordial determining that it itself is not: the world as becoming points to its coming to be from an origin that gives it to be; world is what it determinately is and becomes, as already having come to be, through this origin.

T^2 – *Human being*: We are there within this world as coming to be – our becoming presupposes our coming to be: both our being at all, and our being this or that, are defined by relation to a more primordial determining. This determining is not *our own* self-determining, it is our being given to be, by a source other to our being, whether determinate or self-determining. The dialectic of our being suggests an interinvolvement with a more ultimate giving origin.

T^3 – *God*: If we say God is this other origin, do we *leap beyond relatedness*? No. We approach the other from where we are in the between, and we cannot escape entirely seeing it as it seems to be for us. *What* we see *we* cannot entirely disentangle from *how* we see it. Even God as this other origin is defined *for us* in a relativity *to us*. But this is inescapably ambiguous. It might seem to mean: *only* as for us. Or it might mean: for us, but in a manner that is *not only* for us; but for us as released into our own being; and for us to see it as other *for itself* and not *for us alone*. This last difference points beyond a dialectic for us to a metaxological way as for the other as other. What is other in its otherness remains other even when it is for us.

In the intricate intermediation of world (T^1), human (T^2), and God (T^3), if we think any one of these, or the One, we find ourselves also thinking of the others. Why so? Because each is as communicative being, or a communication of being. How think of communicative being? Transcending is at work in each. None is a fixed univocal unity closed back into itself in fallow identity. Each is a happening of communication that is other than univocal. But why communicative being? Consider human being: other than univocal, it goes beyond self and manifests itself, but the source of manifestation is a determining energy of original being never coincident with a determinate manifestation; the otherness in sameness of source and its manifestation is the basis of the equivocal in that no determinate manifestation is absolute showing. This difference of source and manifestation thus determines the doubleness of the manifestation as also a *remaining in reserve*. The very determination of the determining source casts before itself the reticence of a reserve that is not determinately manifest. Hence the *doubleness* of determinate manifestation makes determinate manifestation itself equivocal, as an appearance itself impossible without non-appearance, even though this non-appearance is broadcast as the reticence of reserve. *There is a togetherness of manifestation and non-manifestation, in manifestation itself*. This doubleness of self-manifestation constitutes something of what it is to be communicative being: being that is itself not just for itself, but is itself in coming out of itself towards the other, even as it broadcasts, in its coming out, its own reticence of reserve.

Can something similar be said, granting the necessary qualifications, about world and God? Think thus: suppose world entails an "open whole" (not "totality" – this implies closure) of determinate beings, such an "open whole" itself is not a determinate being. There could be no final univocal determination of "totality" with respect to such an "open whole." For though we are driven to determine the character of the world, in order to determine the intelligibility of its conditionally determinate beings, we find we cannot quite so determine it as a determinate whole. What is within the "open whole" of world may be exquisitely determinate, but something more, not just determinate, remains in reserve, and is communicated as reserved. Perhaps something of this might be read into Kant's claim that the unconditioned was a regulative, not constitutive principle. We are driven to unconditioned "totality" by the conditioned intelligibility of finite determinate beings, but we can never make that unconditioned determinate. In fact, to do so would be *not* to have the unconditioned totality, since everything determinate is conditioned. If a sense of the indeterminate is necessary, Kant thinks of it as a negative limit, but something more profoundly positive might be seen. The unconditioned is not constituted in the way determinate beings are, but it is constitutive in being at work in the determination of the determinate; and this, even though its reserve always means it cannot be identified with determinate beings, not even a "totality" of them.

Is this what a more positive dialectic seeks to understand – the unavoidability of, and need to make intelligible sense of, that interplay between the more original determining and determinate being? World as "open whole" suggests what is beyond determination, but if this is something positive, it is better called an overdeterminacy. This "over," this "beyond" must be more than a univocal *ens realissimum* or *ens summum* beyond the world, but an original source in communication with the indeterminate "totality" or "open whole" of finite being. The world as "open whole" is open to the origin that gives it to be a whole that is finitely for itself. It is a community of beings that communicates, in the openness of its own transcending finitude, with the origin as "over," as other.

And what then of God (T^3)? The "open whole" of communicative being suggests a *God beyond the whole*, where now communicative being entails the *communication of being* in a radical ontological sense. If the communicative being of the human being (T^2) and world (T^1) communicates opening to their other, is that other merely the recipient of that opening? But how could that be? For are not the human being and world themselves given to be? If so, would not the original other be communicative being as "over," as in excess of what is given in finite transcendence? Were not this other a source of communicative being, hence a source of giving out beyond itself, the result would be the fixation of God in a frozen impassivity, and we would return to dualistic opposition. We would passionately transcend to this other, but we would speak with a wall. There would be no communication. Or, the difference of the participants in communication would be irremediably antithetical: ontological indifference at best, hostility at worst, not a more ultimate community between others. The ontological situation must be more than this one-way communication from finitude to its ground. The very ground of such a one-way communication cannot itself be one-way, for otherwise it were no communication at all. Here, I stress, it is crucial to bear in mind the difference of *coming to be* and *becoming*, when trying to address the communicative being of God. I mean the ultimate other communicates in the most radical sense of giving determinate being its being. It not only determines being as determinate, it determines being as to be at all. This is a determining source that can be called ultimately other, just because of this character of its grounding originative communication. We must think an overdetermination more than the indeterminacy we find in a process of (self-)becoming. (This "overdetermining," we shall see later, is not a determinism, nor a self-determining, since it releases the finite other into its own being for itself.)

What does this mean? Here is a first sortie. Consider what is involved in the *becoming of something*. For A to become B, there must be more than complete determinacy to A; it must be open to further determination, hence "indeterminate," as yet open with respect to that further determination, B; hence becoming something is a dynamic transformation of this antecedent indeterminacy (which is not absolute but relative) into a subsequent determination B (which itself is not completely determinate, but open to further determination). But – and this is the point – *this* process of determining the indeterminate in a becoming is *not* the more original determining. Something more original is reserved relative to becoming, while being communicated in the coming to be at all of becoming, just as finite happening. There is a more original overdeterminacy that first grounds *coming to be* and not just becoming. *Coming to be and becoming are not to be identified.* For becoming already grants the givenness of determinate beings and happenings, whereas coming to be is just about the original arising in being of such beings and happenings. God concerns first the question of the coming to be of beings, and not the becoming of beings. Hence the question is not one simply of the ground of becoming. It is the origin of coming to be, which itself grounds the promise of becoming as a determination, or even a self-determining process.

All of this seems to indicate the excess and radicality of the ultimate communicative source of coming to be. But one can see how such a communicative source is compatible with a more *affirmative* sense of equivocal becoming. For what is manifest in this communication is not *directly* the origin itself; what is communicated is what is originated, and this as world in becoming is marked by its own creative indeterminacy. We have difficulty enough in reading the meaning of this creative indeterminacy and our relation to it. But the communication of *the more original source* is an even more enigmatic creating and giving. The giver may be suggested by the giving given, but there is no immediate line of direction that will brings us face to face with this origin. We will always move through signs and indirections, that is, through the multiplication of intermediations. These intermediations are double, hence ambiguous, hence never such as to dispel the equivocal completely. Is the origin dark? Yes, but dark as communicative source of light, for what is communicated bears with it the reticence of reserve, broadcast by the communicating itself. And this reticence of reserve, or excess, is mystery which will eternally be mystery, even were we come into the company of the angels.

Clearly, there is no univocal clarity about this at all. It is so exceedingly perplexing that one often thinks one is compounding rather than transcending equivocity. And yet the dialectical way does transcend mere equivocity, if only in the help it gives us in seeing the point of why equivocity at all makes sense, and what we may begin to glean from the tangle of ambiguous signs and our own being entangled in such signs.

GOD BEYOND DIALECTIC: ON AVOIDING A COUNTERFEIT DOUBLE OF GOD

Among the attractions of Hegel's view are: it takes us beyond static dualism; it proposes a dynamic God implicated in time, a God transcending, even "becoming" in time, realizing its own end, in the becoming of time; it seems to suggest a God that becomes in the alienations of the temporal, effecting a dialectical redemption of the evils of time, even if its redemption is *self-redemption*. But if this love of time and eternity is the self-love of eternity, do we only *seem* to see the God of the between? Is it all, in the end, *only between the absolute and itself*? Is it between the One and *itself*, doubling itself, via the medium of finite otherness, such that there is *no between other than the One redoubling with itself*? If so, there is no true finite between in the metaxological sense. This is absorbed into the dialectical One rather than genuinely released into its own being for itself. If there seems to be a "between," is it not rather a dialectical double of the between? If there seems to be a "God," is this too a dialectical double of God? Are we not then in danger of bowing before counterfeit doubles of the between and of God?

Hegel's speculative dialectic avoids the full implication of the equivocal that we are *not* God, and exploits the Christian story to blur the difference. His speculative unity

---

[14] See *HG*, Chapter 8, where these reserves are more fully discussed. I draw on some main points here.

of opposites produces a dialectical equivocity: seeming to transcend the equivocity, it hides the equivocity and leaves us worse off, in the recurrence to a sameness that is the speculative univocity. In the eyes of those more honest about the equivocity, dialectic *tout court* is thought (wrongly, I believe) to be discredited. Rather Hegel's inflated claims of speculative univocity bring it into discredit by asking us to invest an incredible credit in his hyperbolic claims concerning self-determining reason. After this inflation, we have suffered a long deflation.

I come to what I take to be major reservations about the dialectical way, reservations not unconnected to what I call the reserve(s) of God.[14] To fail in mindfulness of them may mean to construct dialectically a counterfeit double of God. These reservations and reserves are linked to an understanding of the absolved relativity of religious community as the intimate universal, not the homogenous generality, beyond the terms of holistic immanence. God is not the whole but communicates porosity as the ultimate love of the infinite beyond the whole. We must wait on, be patient to, the reserve(s) of the divine. How patient? All reservations imply we must pass beyond dialectical passing beyond.

First Reservation: Evil and the Reserve of Divine Patience Speculative dialectic deals with the equivocity of evil and good in terms of more and more inclusive wholes said to redeem the refractoriness of the less inclusive parts. The absolute whole of wholes will "sublate" the equivocity. Is that so? Granted, in some instances, from the standpoint of a larger whole certain evils are relativized. The death of the lamb is evil for the lamb but good for the wolf; relative to a more encompassing ecological community, this death can be relativized as an evil, for clearly it serves a good. Good comes out of evil: an evil relative here is a necessary condition for a good relative there. This seems immanent in the equivocity of evil: by an ontological irony it contributes to the furtherance of its opposite. But can we make this the truth of the whole? In the so-called aesthetic theodicy, the whole is compared to a painting whose beauty is not transparent to those in the painting, especially to us, over there in that hook of brooding, of foreboding, of suspicion of the sinister. To the God on a par with the whole, the whole itself is good, but what of this darkness thickening about us? We commit or are exposed to evils that seem irreparable nihilations, at least relative to any power we can muster. Are there losses of the good that even a God cannot *dialectically* redeem? Is there radical evil such that, even in the good of the whole, which we might grant, its horror is not dispelled? Is there evil at the edge of all mediation, dialectical or otherwise (*BHD*, Chapter 4, *HG*, Chapter 6)? Must God be such as to let such radical evils be, just in their transcendence of mediation? Is there an idiotic monstrousness to radical evil that shatters mediation? A violence of the singular as in the intimate universal, but not just a particular set against the whole, or included in it? An equivocity of the evil that resists being unknotted, for the truth of this knot is just that it would not be unknotted, eternally turned in a posture of "not" to the goodness of the source? Is there a divine letting be that allows not only our free "yes," but also our radical "no"? Does this letting communicate something of the reserve of divine forbearance, signaling an unsurpassable *patience* beyond the comprehension of dialectic and hyperbolic to the terms of holistic immanence? Is there a divine forgiving that is in the dimension of the hyperbolic – an "intermediation beyond all mediation"?

Second Reservation: Singularity and the Reserve of the Intimate Many forms of dialectic favor less singulars than wholes, relative to which the singularity of the singular is finally an instantiation of a more inclusive universal. The singular in the irreducible sense is defined as the *recalcitrant particularity* that comes to stand against the whole, and as such it is the very evil that dialectic wants to overcome. To reach the absolute unity of the whole is to overcome the singular: to surrender itself or be surrendered. I give myself over to God, but, in this giving over, I come to myself, at home with myself in a way impossible when I cling to myself. Fashionable rhetoric about singularity might deride this view, but we need not. There is a giving over, and a giving of the self back to itself, in its being given over to what is beyond itself. Yes, but one must still ask about what one is as giving over, to what one gives oneself, and the character of the giving.

What one is: The singular self is a unique incarnation, a "world" rich unto itself, not just an instance of more encompassing universal. There is an ontological intimacy to singularity that is, in truth, fulfilled in participation in community, and most of all community with God, but that community and singularity cannot be described in the standard dialectical languages of a more absorbing inclusivity. In being in community, the reserve of the intimate is not violated, even when there is a coaxing open of singularity that has closed back into itself, hugging its own precious selfhood. The latter is the curvature of singularity back on itself in opposition to its own being as communicative self-transcendence. When this curvature is turned around again, we may witness the breaking through of singularity in the released power of its self-transcending. The *religious* release of this singular transcending never turns the reserve of the intimate in the direction of a neutral, homogenous universal, but rather intensifies the porosity of the singular to communication with the divine. It intensifies the passionate betweenness of the singular as singular.

To what is one given over: I give myself over to the inclusive whole, but is this to give oneself over to God? If singularity is personal, one might be giving oneself over to impersonal powers at a lower level of ontological richness. The other is as much in question as the I that gives itself over. Giving oneself over to an impersonal whole suggests flight from singularity rather than fulfilling the life of its self-transcendence. This death of singularity might seem to transcend the suffering of being, but also denies its highest flower: its flourishing as this astonishing personal being. We have to do justice to both sides of the giving over, self and other, certainly to what we know of human singularity, even if the other side is shrouded in mystery. Perhaps the God that answers the personalism of the reserved intimate singularity is a God beyond this immanent whole?[15]

The character of the giving: There are different ways of giving singularity over. Some are just the accentuation of singularity as self-affirming. This seems true of the seemingly superior giving of Zarathustra's "gift-giving virtue" (*die schenkende Tugend*). Real giving over must break the subtle secret circle of "me" and "mine"; be broken from without, or break from within; and let self-transcendence follow its dynamic as breaking out to the other as other; or perhaps regain a porosity lost to it through a hypertrophy of self-affirmation. Beyond this "me" and "mine," there is an *erotic* giving over, in which I go towards the other, but in finding the other, I am given myself as beyond the lack I underwent in being broken open. The lack breaks the circuit of self-enclosure, revivifies the passion of being, and the giving over breaks forth. But the other to whom one gives oneself, lets one be given back to oneself. This giving meets an allowing of the other who, in returning the porosity to the giver, serves less the other as other and more a different possible fulfillment of self (not necessarily hostile to the other), beyond the self-absorbed circle of "me" and "mine." But there is a *further* giving over which inhabits the porosity between self and other with a different generosity of giving and receiving. This is a giving over of self not for self-finding but for being with the other. For generous giving in the porosity is in bond with generous receiving, though no demand is made that the other give one back oneself, or indeed that it give itself. Such an *agapeic* giving asks us to have free regard for the other in the light of its promise of being agapeic.

Dialectic tends to give prominence to a variation of erotic giving, so we need another way to deal with agapeic giving over. The first is tempted to accentuate the *conatus essendi*, the second is nothing without a *com-passio essendi*. Both awaken the question

---

[15] The reserved depths of human singularity make us ask about the analogous character of the other to whom one is given over. Indeed surrender to the impersonal could be supplemented by, say, Nietzsche's view of the other as will to power: *Amor fati* as surrender to the ultimate ring of will to power in eternal becoming. I call Nietzsche to mind because he was very well aware of the claim of singularity, too aware some think, yet he too will give himself over. Is the will to power what answers to singularity? Is there a disjunction that is bridged by a violence to human singularity? Is "God" will to power? And notice that the other to which one surrenders could also be Hegelian *Geist*, obviously not the same as will to power. I will take up the question of the personal and the transpersonal in Chapter 9. There are certain senses of the transpersonal that need *not* be strictured, once we are mindful of the fullness of singularity in the between, and the plurivocity of the giving over.

of the personal and impersonal other. Does agapeic giving promise more, if eros remains ambiguous about its end, as its intertwining with thanatos seems to indicate? Or is it that a different "yes" can come to be when our own participation in agapeic transcending, be it halting or heroic, must also face death? For one can be given over to death differently, as one can be differently given over to creation. Is being given agapeically, or being given over agapeically, impossible without a certain divine reserve, that is, without the divine giving the finite creation its otherness as other, *making way* to let be the finite as finite? Is this reserve also a re-source of goodness surpassing finitization? One might wonder if this making way of the divine is less a withdrawing from the finite as an opening of the space of porosity wherein can come to be constituted a communication between the creature and God, a communication marked with its own agapeic promise.

Third Reservation: Plurivocal Otherness and the Reserve of Communication When speculative dialectic describes otherness as a sublated moment of a more encompassing whole, its way of immanence immanentizes otherness also. This raises a huge question about God's otherness. But suppose that otherness, even in the superlative Oneness of the divine, is plurivocal: a community of the full, of the (over)full. Plurivocal otherness is a sign of a communication of the (over)full that cannot be contracted to univocal unity or speculative-dialectical totality. In this light, dialectical immanence is too much the reactive heir of seeing divine transcendence in terms of dualistic opposition, relative to which dialectic proposes itself as the inclusive solution. If divine otherness is plurivocal and (over)full, it exceeds the full circle of absolute self-mediation in its own otherness. Just that excess may signal not its dialectical unintelligibility but the limit of dialectical intelligibility and its immanent way. Transcendence as other hovers on the permeable border between mystery and mediation: mystery violated when immanently mediated without reverence for its reserve.

Dialectic reminds us of the togetherness of God and world, but this reminder needs its reminder of God's transcendence, even in this togetherness: transcendence that retreats beyond the comprehension of speculative dialectic. Divine otherness is other to the otherness interiorized in any holistic self-mediation. This other otherness is "beyond," but not in the derisory sense of a heteronomy that tyrannizes over the between. It may be a *heteros* absolutely necessary for there to be any self-transcendence, any self-mediation, any autonomy in immanence, in the finite between. If this other otherness is not a lack of determinacy but the plurivocal reserve of the full, of the (over)full, we must acknowledge properly the "beyond" of the immanent whole.

If our granting of *some* togetherness of the human and divine disrespects that otherness, or disregards this reserve, we invite a new "higher" univocalism in which we say the human "is" the divine, the divine "is" human. Despite claims about the inner complexity of this "is," we are inclined to override the otherness as a reserve of the (over)full divine. The latent legacy of dualistic opposition resurfaces in the following alternatives. *Either* the human is swallowed up in the divine as an all-devouring absorbing god; *or* the divine is interiorized by the human, and the human declares itself as the one, true, holy absolute of history. Mystical absorption has not been to the tastes of modern man, who wills his own autonomy, but the second option has been chosen in a variety of atheistic forms. The choice is really the result of our being victimized by, or the willing victims of, the equivocity of a speculative dialectic that is still itself victim to univocity. We pay the price for this equivocity in an atheistic univocity that violates the difference of human and divine in its hyperbolic promotion of the human as the One. The human god, if you will, the man-God, claims the right of the (over)full, but it is too full of itself: its fullness – on the heights – is in fact its fall.

We learn from this that we need more than a univocalized form of dialectic. Dialectic is pluralized, just as otherness is plurivocal, and always entails that the beings in relation are irreducibly different, even in their dialectic. The one form of inclusive self-mediating dialectic cannot cover what God, creation, man each is, either in itself or in its relation to the others. Certainly one might venture that God is absolutely self-mediating, but that is not all that God is, especially with regard to what remains in reserve of God, both in Godself, and in relation to creation as other. Grant this reserve of the (over)full, then there is a both a different intermediation *within* the divine, and *between* origin and creation: an intermediation still a togetherness even in otherness, and allowing in finite creation for happenings at the edge of mediation, allowing even of the free power that turns to evil and against all mediation, including divine intermediation. All this makes more sense if we think of the porosity of the between, our own primal *passio essendi*, and the "intermediation beyond self-mediation" as metaxological. If there is an immanent otherness in self-mediating itself, and if there is *more than one* source of infinite self-transcending, then the intermediation *between* these sources cannot be self-mediation once again. And if we were to speak in the figure of the *coincidentia oppositorum*, this would not undermine difference but be a paradoxical sign of the (over)full origin that creates, communicates, and sustains originative differences beyond dualism and holistic immanence.

Fourth Reservation: The Overdetermination of Origin and the Reserve of Transcendence
The reserve of the (over)full points to a notion of the origin as overdetermined, not just indeterminate. Here, too, something is communicated of the excessive reserve of God. How does speculative dialectic understand the origin? It conceives the movement of *all* being and thought as ordained to a more inclusive self-determination. The beginning is an indefinite lack to be overcome by a transcending, itself impelled forward by opposition, undercut and overcome by dialectical process, consummated in the *absolute self-mediating whole*, itself the end of the indefinite lack of the beginning. With regard to God, this means that any mystery in the origin must be dialectically displaced, as the process of (self-)determination becomes more and more complete. We see a dialectical teleology of (self-)determination, the end of which (as we see with Hegel) is the conceptual conquest of God's mystery.

We might also be tempted by a progressivism that sees earlier peoples as, say, given to a superstitious wonder, easily struck by marvels, taken in by them because ruled by the indefinite, in the form of lacking ignorance. Their wonder at mystery is their *not understanding* and an escape hatch sanctifying mystification. Religious infantilism is progressively overcome by more and more complete dialectical (self-)determination. As it turns out, this move from the primitive to the advanced finally means the evaporation of the religious, since a certain imperial reason dictates the terms on which progress is judged. Rational philosophy arbitrates the rights of the divine to any claim to be ultimate. What is wrapped in enigma is thrown out of court; it comes unprepared before the tribunal of reason with its case unripe: "Send it back to the cells, where maybe it will mutate, 'mature' into rational knowing!" Putting behind ourselves the indefiniteness of beginnings, coming of age, we determine ourselves, give an account of ourselves. We would like the divine to return the favor and account for itself. Our demand is not exorbitant, not hubristic. We have sweet reason on our side as we demand that all the reserves of God declare themselves. (Why do I think of Squirrel Nutkin provoking the silent Owl? He got more than he bargained for.)

This, I know, is not the only possible outcome, and while Hegel is not always so overt, he is still in the business of dialectically generating a speculative double of the God of religion, a counterfeit double, in my argument. Of course, I grant our need to determine the indefiniteness that bogs us down in the merely nebulous. Yet there can be a disastrous oversight in the will to determination that mistakenly thinks the absolute teleology moves from the indefinite to the determinate, thence from the definite to the self-determining. If there is "more" to the origin, the enterprise is misconceived. If the origin is overdetermined, not merely indefinite, we are not dealing with a beginning lacking in determination and whose defect further determination must provide. We are dealing with a surplus plenitude out of which everything definite, and even every definite lack, comes to be. The origin may be the wonder of fullness itself, (over)fullness which, as the reserve of the hidden God, deals out the being of, and the deep promise of, finite happening, be it determinate or mutually determining or self-determining. This overdetermination accompanies every stage of determination, and mutual determination and self-determination, from beginning through the middle to the end, which cannot be an end but a return again of the overdetermined to which no finitely determined end can be consigned.

Fifth Reservation: Questioning the Primacy of the Whole over the Reserve of the Infinite Perhaps the above reservations find their point of concentration in this: the reserve of the infinite. The exalted dialectic of the absolutely self-mediating whole places in a secondary position the infinite as overdetermined and as transcending all wholes. This infinite is reduced to a mere "beyond," perhaps suitable for religious representation, but not ultimate for speculative dialectic for which God is the whole of wholes that includes all subordinate wholes. Indeed the togetherness of finite and infinite with the "self-sublating" infinite is within the absolute self-mediating whole. But what if God is beyond the whole? What if the God of the whole is beyond the whole, reserved relative to the overdetermination of the infinite?

First, for dialectical holism, there will be no final otherness to finite creation, for this otherness will be ingredient in the inclusive self-mediation of the dialectical One. It will be the self-othering of the One, such that the world is the self-creation of God, not a creation of other-being that has its own constitutive being for itself. Why should we accept this view? Does it do justice to our being in the world as an intermediated between? Creation is given with its own integrity of being. The first passion of finitude is its being created, and in this also lies the promise of its primal porosity. The integrity of finite creation may not be absolute, but why see it as the absolute in its self-othering? The world is not God; this we indelibly learned along the way of equivocity. Further, their *difference* is not to be rendered in dualistic terms; it is, rather, the basis of their community. We have to grant not only God's otherness, but the very difference of creation as exceeding monistic holism.

Second, what of our own otherness as centers of finite self-transcendence, albeit infinitely restless? We are not just self-mediating wholes or parts of larger wholes, but infinitely beyond ourselves in our being in relativity to everything other. Our self-exceeding witnesses as much the *passio essendi* as the *conatus*, and both refer back to a primal porosity in which we are given to be as open to both other-being and our own being. Our difference is not a vanishing moment in the constitution of something more inclusive. Our infinite restlessness exceeds every holism, both in terms of the reserves of enigma out of which it emerges, and that towards it nesciently yearns.

Third, is this also not true of our communities? They are not to be modeled on self-mediating wholes, since this holism truncates the singularity of the singular, the otherness of the other, and is not mindful enough of the porosity between self and other. How dialectically comprehend this porosity as porosity? The excess of the overdetermined is hinted at in *finitude itself*, in terms of certain excesses resistant to self-mediating dialectic, excesses that suggest an infinitude not fully exhausted by an inclusive whole, be these excesses the affirmative overdetermination in the being of singularity or the community of being, or the more negative indeterminacy in the happening of evil. Something again remains over and above, or below and beyond.

Fourth, to insist on the dialectical priority of the whole over the infinite, and in a way that denies the infinite as over above, or even below and beyond, is to court atheistic repercussions. In the resulting "unification" of God and humanity, the subsumed otherness can mean less the mystical absorption of the human into the divine than the anthropological reduction of the divine to the human. We can generate a kind of *temporal mysticism of the human* as absolute being itself. The legacy of a certain dialectical identification of the human and divine turns out to be an atheistic humanism that produces the rupture of human and divine, and rupture that recourses to previous dualistic forms. For this rupture, *after speculative-dialectical identification*, takes the form of hostility to the divine, especially in transcendent form. In our being full of ourselves, there will be no *other* (over)ful, no divine fullness over us. More than any other, just that divine (over)fullness stands as the ultimate bar to any self-apotheosis of the human being, any absolutizing of the human as untrammeled self-determining being. That bar will not be let stand.

This dialectical atheism proves to be more than an intellectual position when it posits itself as a political project or existential demand: we will ourselves to be as impatient gods. There can be no other god left remaining to remind us of the sin of hubris, here celebrated as our creativity. The overdeterminacy of the other becomes the overdeterminacy of our own otherness, which we must exalt into the heavens. Subsequent to Hegel, the rupture of the human and God, after speculative identity, can be traced to a reductive dialectic, greatly influential in shaping a projective theory of religion.[16] We meet the dark twin of the identity of God and man. We have dialectically reconstructed ourselves as the false double of God. In truth, this is a return to the equivocal, a return dissembled and dissembling, hence a return to evil, though it announces itself as the final liberation of human creativity.

Transcendence still remains over and above, reserved, if we remain faithful to the overdetermination of the origin and the signs of the "too muchness" immanent in the finite between. The problem of transcendence is not, then, fundamentally a matter of a dualistic opposition. It is more a new accession to the reserves of porosity in our being at all, a revivification of the *passio essendi*, and a rethinking of self-transcending being that, allowing for erotic self-becoming, so relates to the marvel of otherness that it moves beyond erotic to agapeic transcendence. While preserving the otherness of the other as bound up with the origin's overdeterminacy, it is also bound up with our caretaking of the integrity of the between. If there is an "ontological way" it must delve more deeply into the hyperbolic resources of the between. And perhaps the contrast of the ontological and other ways will prove to be not as radical as has been claimed in the past.

---

[16] Perhaps the seeds of the atheistic gods in Schopenhauer and Nietzsche, and in the legacy of the coarsened dialectic of Feuerbach and Marx were sown in what Kant calls the "transcendental subreption" in *Critique of Pure Reason* [*Kritik der Reinen Vernunft*, ed. R. Schmidt (Hamburg: Meiner, 1952] with respect to transcendental illusion (see A583, 611n; see also A509, B537; A619, B 647; A643, B671). "Subreption," among other things, suggests our imputation to the object of what properly belongs to the subject; hence "subreption" is the word also used with respect to the sublime in *Critique of Judgment*, §27. Its logic simulates what I call a dialectical self-mediation in and through an other that is no other finally. Such "subreption" allows the reduction of the hypostatized, even personified (Kant's words, 611n.) other to the self that has hypostatized it. Kant's transcendental subreption harbors the gene of later mutant dialectics more reductive, more negative, and more unruly.

Chapter 6

God and the Metaxological Way

A brimming tide
Wet with desire
People promenading
Along the verge
Of the bay

A jet in the blue
Above
Traces a white line
To somewhere
Unknown
To those wandering
Below

A cormorant surfaces
& devours
A small fish
The sea smells
Brackish
& bracing

In the midst of all
A man limps by
& pretends
He does not need
His cane

A wounded creature
Has passed by here
For I have followed
The traces
Of its blood

I am grateful
For the benches
That let me
Rest and write
Of these saturations

Soul a dripping sponge
Medium of a meaning
Whose message
It cannot pinion
As it passes

There among the passing
I am nothing
Impinged on by the passing
As if I myself had passed out
Not there I am more there
By abstention from grasping
What passes

Things offer themselves
In words
They consecrate themselves
They do nothing
They are consecrated
I do nothing
To merit it
I ask for nothing
I have already received
Everything

FOUR WAYS: GOD AND THE METAXOLOGICAL

All ways seek God and may be opened differently to God, in and through mindfulness of being in the between. Each is attentive, after its own manner, to the ontological potencies of the primal ethos. Each allows passage towards finite beings and passing beyond. Each opens metaphysically to what is beyond finite beings. Each encounters hindrance and bother. What marks out the metaxological way? Among other things, the six following distinctions. First, a presentiment of the promise of the primal ethos in and through the second reconfigured ethos. Second, vigilance to the ontological surpluses of immanent being. Third, fidelity to these surpluses expressed in a new being true to our self-surpassing as a metaphysical transcending. Fourth, care not to compromise divine transcendence as it is intimated in the surpluses of immanent being. Fifth, mindfulness of the immanent between as showing forth the milieu of the absolved relativity. Sixth, concern for the dialogue of philosophy and religion, in which religion is not a mere representational prelude to philosophy, and in which the philosopher essays intelligible reflection companionable with the enigmas of religion. But, perhaps a brief digest of the four ways is in order.

Broadly put, the univocal way stresses definite sameness rather than indefinite difference. Seeking determinate solutions to determinate problems, impelled by curiosity, God is made a problem, even if the highest or ultimate. This does not "solve" the "problem," it, rather, makes God more deeply problematic – problematic in the paradoxical sense that the question here exceeds what can be fixed as a determinate problem. By contrast, the equivocal way is attuned to what cannot be thus fixed. It accentuates the shock and provocation of ambiguous difference, sometimes steering into unmediated manyness, sometimes even being wrecked on extreme opposition. Result: We are overcome with restless perplexity about God. God is not just a determinate problem but troubles us with a more intractable enigma. Driven out of the houses of incontestable surety, we are exposed under the pitiless and serene sky.

Our loss of univocal certainty may become, though there is no guarantee, our gain of mindful finesse. The dialectical way can help with refining this finesse. Generally, it emphasizes the mediation of the different by the conjoining of opposites. There is a more subtle "sameness" than the univocal way accesses. Beyond the normal binary oppositions defining finite knowing, there is a mediated togetherness of God with finitude more than the univocal unity that fixes or the equivocal difference that disperses. Modern dialectic privileges an inclusive sense of the "same" in this conjunction of opposites. The "system" of the same is given ultimacy over the "systematics" of togetherness, as well as priority over finesse for what exceeds system. Finessed dialectic can engender truer mindfulness of the togetherness of the human and divine, *perhaps* even a taste for their absolved relativity. But given recessed equivocities in the dialectical sense of the "same," we must refuse just this temptation: to hold that this togetherness lets us reduce the difference of the two. The togetherness is crucial, the reduction perilous.

And now the metaxological way? It lives between peril and crux. As a figuring of the primal ethos, it divines the nature of the togetherness, the absolved relativity, with heed to the difference, and without forgetting the transcendence of the divine and its reserves. We need a finessed, transdialectical *logos* of the *metaxu*. The community of God and the between concerns us, but as *not exhausted* by any dialectical self-mediation of the same, nor any whole claiming absoluteness by its immanent closure on itself. This community is *between* immanence and divine transcendence, as ultimately more than every immanent whole. The fourth way tries to think this divine "more" by calling on a metaphysical mindfulness finessed for the surpluses of being manifest in the immanent whole.

This fourth way opens to a pluralized intermediation, beyond self-completing self-mediation, yet hospitable to the communication of what is transcendent to us, out of its own otherness. Beyond any self-totalizing whole, however dialectically or speculatively qualified, in the community of immanence and transcendence, otherness in the between remain open, as does otherness between God and the between. Ruptures shake the complacencies of finitude at the limit of the dialectical way, and we are as a reawakened receptivity to mystery, intimated in the overdetermined givenness of immanent being. This givenness regards not some bare fact of being but the ontological worth of what has been given to be. Beyond univocal determination, beyond equivocal difference, beyond self-mediating totality, God is to be thought through the between as given to be, and given to be as good.

Here we gain a richer sense of the primal ethos of being. We do not create the between, nor does it create itself. As given, it is not absolute; it is given to be, and as coming to be in the absolved relativity. It is not a neutral given, or valueless thereness but charged with the good of the "to be." This is communicated in a pre-objective community of mindfulness and being, inarticulately given to us in original astonishment. The *metaxu* is first a happening, then we try to articulate it metaxologically. All three other ways participate in this happening, but do not manage to articulate it metaxologically. The fourth way shows the fuller truth of the other three, seeking the right words for what is communicated in the primal ethos, and what is given in the overdeterminacy of the original astonishment. The other three ways are conducive to, even as they truncate, the truth of the fourth, but we cannot absolutize any way, as if it were the absolute. We must abdicate the claim to have categories to determine finally what itself outstrips every categorial determination.

Let me first outline four participations in the between which revealingly define our rapport with the primal ethos, the ontological milieu wherein mindfulness of God arises: the marvel of the middle, the familiar middle, the perplexing middle, the (renewedly) astonishing middle. These participations will lead us to venture the hyperbole of God as the agapeic origin, via mindfulness of different ontological potencies of the primal ethos, something of whose sense has already being intimated in the redoubled beginning beyond godlessness (see Chapter 2).

The marvel of the middle

We are given to be in a manner opaque and astonishing; we come to ourselves in the midst of things, between an origin and end we cannot completely determine. This between is determined in terms of definite beings, thus also made intelligible; we are shaped by, and contribute to, selvings and communities in the between; we are called on to be both true and good. All these – being as given, things, intelligibilities, selves, communities, being true, being good– can occasion different emphases in our approaches to God.[1]

We are roused into mindfulness of the intimate strangeness of the between. This first occurs in an unpremeditated porosity to the givenness of being. The wonder that eventuates is a patience to its otherness. Overcome by its "too muchness," its being there is not a burden for us. In the first marvel of our patience to being we are released and lightened. There is something celebratory about our inhabitation of the middle. There is elemental joy in being, though the joy seems without a determinate why. It is not that we make this an object of thought; it is pre-objective; which does not mean it is subjective; the thereness of beings is not univocally objectified, their very being there is a marvel. It is the freshness of the morning, the morning that was not just once back in some long ago beginning, but is now, always. The *passio essendi* is offered its given participation in the freshness of the morning, and in this morning the *conatus essendi* surges. If we cease being roused by this astonishment, lose this trans-objective, trans-subjective joy, our power to ponder God wanes. The morning fades, and day does not bring light brighter but sight greyer. There may seem nothing divine to see, and that is why the second morning is differently strange: strange but now not quite intimate.

Without astonishment there is no seed for the thought of God. We are that very seed in our being as mindful. The marvelous middle is not a nebulous indefiniteness but overdetermined: trans-determinate, more than any determination, whether subjective or objective. It is the overdeterminate community of beings, in which we have a presentiment of the "more," as even more than the too muchness of what is given to be in the finite between. The world is too much for us, but our satiation with this muchness puts us in mind of something more excessive still, perhaps even God, though we do not yet speak that name, or have no name, or even say it is nothing.

We cannot endure the too muchness. We wake from astonishment through astonishment itself. Having been struck by the otherness of being, mindfulness finds itself surging out of itself, as self-transcending to beings that are there and other. Our fascination makes us beings seeking to know what their being is. We move towards beings, wanting to know their strangeness, in this process converting their strangeness into something known and more familiar, and in this too the original intimacy is dimmed. Thus arises the familiar middle.

The familiar middle

The familiar middle, as a reconfiguration of the ethos, begins to crystallize with the conversion of astonishment into perplexity. What astonishes us also perplexes us, just as, likewise, we want to be more definite about what is given in the initial overdeterminacy.

---

[1]   These correspond to creation, things, intelligibilities, selving, communities, being true, being good – each discussed in successive chapters in *BB*, Part II.

Perplexity is a child of astonishment, when mindfulness grows more determinately aware of the *difference* between us and what is given. This difference must be granted: the very otherness of being is given in the beginning. Perplexity is a becoming thoughtful about that otherness, as now beyond us, but, as beyond us yet calling forth our desire to make its determinacy more definite. Perplexity seeds a troubled thinking in the porosity that makes us patient to given otherness. From unquiet troubling arises the will to familiarize ourselves with the beings in the between, to surpass the overdeterminate porosity by means of determinate cognition of this and that. From perplexity arises specific curiosity, reformulating the given between as a totality of definite beings and determinate happenings.

In this, of course, being's intimate strangeness is easily overlooked. We take things for granted, and fail to think what grants them to be at all. We are familiar, but there is a familiarity deadening us to the intimacy of being together, offered in original astonishment. Too familiar, we have betrayed the family, as it were, or at least the deeper intimacy of being has been allowed to lapse into silence, or deserted in favor of our claimed supremacy over the determinate.

We might even *welcome* a fall into the familiar middle from *dread of the too muchness* of original givenness. There is something of *suffering* in astonishment, as in perplexity. Being in the between is first a suffering; we undergo our being given to be. We are pathetic to being: recipients of an endowment, not rulers of a realm; creatures of God, not sovereigns of creation. This is too much. We cannot put up with this, just because it is too much. We leave these heights where equilibrium is arduous and descend into the lowlands where the exploitation of resources is more proportioned to our powers. For it is in proportionate power that the intermedium is first familiarized. This is again to turn from the too muchness: we address that to which we feel proportionate, addressing it through our power, and so seeming to prove we are above it. The familiar middle is proportionate to our power only because we are disproportionate to it, in staking out our preponderance over it. In familiar determinations proportionate to our power over beings, we come to betray our increasingly disproportionate power.

This process of familiarization produces the occlusion of the truly disproportionate: the excess of the gift of being is always disproportionate to us, because we too are gifts of it. Only the giver could be relatively proportionate to it, by being in excess of it; we are disproportionate to it as its recipients. When we familiarize the granted we slip into amnesia of the gift as gift. It is now a determinate object or totality of objects to use or exploit. If this familiarization were total, the pondering of God would peter out in disregard.

This familiarization seems to put us in sight of everything as on a par with our power; but as we see everything, it comes to be that we are seeing nothing. We do not see, we use. Use: in making the others mirrors wherein we want to see ourselves, our power. Use: in turning the beings in the middle into means to secure our self-satisfaction. The familiar middle thus can well become the dominion of serviceable disposability (*EB*, Chapter 14): things are serviceable so long as they serve us, but disposable when they no longer serve us, or have served their use and are used up. What we use thus becomes invisible in its being, and in the strangeness of its being. We serve nothing beyond ourselves, and in our sleepless care we are sleepwalkers in the feast of being. Staring wide our calculative eyes are sightless, not resting on other-being with the peace of festive community with it. There is a counterfeit peace and a sluggish stupor about God, far removed from the divine exhilaration of astonishment, or the perplexity harrying us into troubled thinking about transcendence.

The perplexing middle

The familiar middle strangely becomes unfamiliar, the more familiar we become with it. In this unfamiliar familiarity *the intermedium of being again becomes perplexing*. This is the third conversion. Think of living with someone for a long time, so long, so close they have passed into the invisibility of taken-for-grantedness. And then the familiarity passes a certain threshold and, behold, the familiar takes on the face of an enigmatic stranger. The presence of the familiar becomes the absence of the familiar. This absence to mindfulness becomes a strangely different presence that exceeds familiarization and becomes newly perplexing, indeed astonishing once again. New mindfulness: as if one suddenly woke up from the stupor of obviousness. One is not waking up to *anything determinate* in the familiar. *It is the whole presencing of the familiar that has become strange.* There is a new wonder, shading into a new perplexity that transforms the familiar, jolting one into a disconcerting unfamiliarity.

As I was awake to all that, I was asleep to all that, from this other dimension of the newly unfamiliar. I saw your face every day, and I thought I knew it to its most intimate details, and yet in knowing everything I knew nothing, because I had fallen into stupor relative to this other strangeness. This has now roused itself into wakefulness, and I see my seeing was unseeing. The familiar as *intimate* comes to intimate a strangeness that no familiarization process as determination will ever destroy. The familiar is new, and it is not new at all; it is what it always was, because it is just what it is, and may always be; but in our sleep of determinate knowing we knew nothing at all of this. The between is perplexing again, in this reawakening of a *second perplexity* in a dimension beyond determinate knowing.

It seems to me that the fallow seeds of thinking God are seeking to germinate freshly in this second perplexity. How seeking? Perhaps here only through the wordless intimation of an as yet nameless God, so nameless the name "God" might not even yet come to mind at all. The porosity of our being is coming unclogged but one does not know what passes in the porosity or is communicated. The intimation calls for divination. What is the meaning of divination? It is a medium of mindfulness, patient to communication in the bright dark of the equivocal. It has no apodeictic certainty, but as a patient minding, it is also a venturing, a "probing" into the unknown, an uncertain fathoming of the unfathomable, a plumbing of what cannot be sounded.

When you say something perplexing to me, I divine your meaning, I get some of its *gist*.[2] It is like listening to an unfamiliar language: one gets a word here, a phrase, a feel, and then darkness and one is at a loss, like driving and hitting sudden fog, and the road vanishes, and one is fearful of driving off a cliff. One must get *into the flow* of the unfamiliar language – divine the gist even when uncertain of details or determinate particulars. The latter is the later univocity; the former the unavoidable ambiguous overdetermination of earlier beginnings. One starts there; one ends there; more determinacy is possible in the middle. With God one is always divining. There is no point at which divination of the gist gives over entirely to clear and distinct determination alone. One is always in the dark even as the brightness grows. One listens for the unspoken in the spoken, and the spoken beyond the unspoken, and the silence reserved in both the spoken and unspoken.

The astonishing middle resurrected

The fourth conversion comes with the resurrection of astonishment. This astonishment is not the first native gift we joy in, and come to squander blithely. It is engendered out of and beyond perplexity: the perplexity that puts one off balance; sends one to the outside of easy obviousness; exiles one from thoughtless domesticities; mourns the ingratitude unappreciative of the miracle of a child; sorrows with descending darkness, darkness darker for having once tasted morning joy. This perplexity grows into unknowing the more growing into knowing. It has passed into being at a loss. It is lost before

---

[2] Gist comes from Old French *gésir* to lie (from L. *jacet*), but I guess gist also suggests some relation to guessing – getting the gist: being porous to the essentials of something, or spirit (*Geist*), though not master of the letter. Guess, gist, *Geist*: one is minded also of the (holy) ghost, as the (hair-raising) ghastly, or of yeast (*gist* in Dutch) that ferments, likened to the kingdom of God. To guess the gist: intimation of a leavening power, hard to fix, that yet opens porous space, like nothing as like en-livening breath, offering risen bread and wine that heartens.

the impermanence of the between as itself loss and perishing, as giving being and as passing away.

In the fourth conversion, our configuration of the ethos yields to transfiguration – calling forth the fourth figure of indirection: the hyperbolic. The second refreshed astonishment is born out of the *known and knowing pathos* of the between. In despite of our being stressed by the extremities of receiving and loss, the gift of an overdeterminate joy in being flares up: primal *passio essendi*. Whence it comes, we do not know. It comes in the darkness, and it is dark to us, and yet it lightens our despondency. It is something that breaks through episodically. There is no method, no technique to guarantee its visitation. Sometimes there is waiting and hope and expectancy. Other times there is exhaustion, bitterness and cursing. We call upon it, we cannot command it. Calling upon it is prayer; commanding it idolatry, but perplexity makes patient, and suffering opens the eyes. When this joy comes it is offered as a godsend.

What is this sorrow of joyful passage in the universal impermanence? Does it intimate a constancy in passing, perhaps a fidelity to finite being, even in all perishing, and offered from beyond finitude? Does loss make us know our want of, our wanting for, a different way? The surpluses of immanence are much, but is there more beyond immanent surfeits? We are exposed to the darkness the world is, the darkness we are. We strain in the gloom, expectant for the edge of a visiting light that etches its cut on the arrested night. The waters rise to our neck, and above it; the words of appeal we would were prayers come out instead as gurgled mumbles as we drown. In being shattered, is there ingression? In breakdown, breakthrough? In dying, life?

We ask, and there is no univocal answer, and we ask again. We are thrust again into that place/noplace earlier visited with the return to zero: there we know intimately we come to nothing, and yet a new porosity, a new interface with creation is made available. There is more than coming to nothing. What then is the resurrected astonishment? Is it not the "yes" to being as other that always did and always will now pass beyond us, but that, just in its passage, intimates itself as good? The new astonishment is the "yes" for the simple elemental gift of being. It is a gratitude, won from suffering; a "yes" purged of complaint; an affirmation that has wept, as there is a mourning that is blessed.

Can we be completely sure we have come clean of any counterfeit double of "amen"? Who can answer "yes" without prevarication? And then there are those philosophers who want their pound of universal proof. But cut that pound from the flesh of the religious, will it not, must it not die? And even granting this "yes," it is not at all clear that is can be universalized without ado. How could it be, for it is a consent that comes in the openness of freedom itself. It may be universally solicited; it is not universal as imposed by univocal compulsion in the guise of rational necessity.

We are put to the question as to whether this "yes" and this astonishment make sense finally outside of relation to the divine in its insuperable mysteriousness. Of course, one need not overtly invoke the name of religion, even though, evidently, we are addressing something that recalls the intimate universal. And yet the promise of this "yes" is with us as what we are, and with us at the impasse to which we are brought in the radical idiocy of our being, name it as we will, religiously or otherwise. The soaring constructions of the *conatus essendi* totter. They totter on high because prior to their soaring there is our patience to the gift of being, and the received energies that enable us to be at all and to become. We are brought to a place of radical breakdown, even as we may have spent a lifetime fleeing the more original patience of our being. How we go into that place/noplace will be shaped by who we are, how we have lived, how we responded to what we were given. How we come out of it, no one can say in advance. (What point here some rational argument claiming universal necessity?) Some come out broken, some transfigured, many more come out a germ of battered hope, still seeking to be rooted again and to sprout. The place of breakdown is not elsewhere; the between itself is the cemetery of loss; we ourselves are that noplace. Can we be resurrected to astonishment before the extraordinary enigma of being at all? Can we utter a "yes" of gratitude? What meaning can this gratitude have, outside of the goodness of God?

THE INDIRECTIONS OF TRANSCENDING IN THE BETWEEN

These four configurations are not like four fixed frames stacked on top of each other, or placed side by side. They reveal our dynamic reconfigurations of the primal ethos, showing diversely our participation in the ethos and interplay with it. I set them forth with a somewhat formal character, unavoidably so, given the nature and need of communication. But they are formings more than fixed forms, open to reformings and intercommunication. They are not to be understood purely chronologically, though phases of human self-becoming may dominantly give prominence to one rather than the other. They give expression to orientations to being, communications from being, potencies of our being in the between, each with a promise that can be more or less realized or developed. As formings they have their own dynamic but they can pass into each other, appear and recede, interrupt and continue, diminish and augment each other. The promise of one or each may be recessed but is not necessarily negated by the overt predominance of another.

They might be described *musically*: a theme is stated, developed, it can be overtaken by another theme, go into recess, re-emerge in a new variation, like and unlike, with resonances over the whole of unfolding, and moments of stress sounding a note of crescendo whose emphasis is not lost when the music recedes into silence. Thus, while the marvel of the middle may be noteworthy in early phases of life, it can visit any time of life. Or one might be more or less engrossed in the familiar middle, only unexpectedly to find it interrupted by intrusions of extreme strangeness. Or, for long periods of time, one might be oppressed by the perplexing middle, weighted down without relief by "the burden of the mystery," made bearable only by lightenings offered as godsends that hearten one to continue. Or there may be stretches of unasked serenity when one walks on air as if enfolded by beneficences from the green world. We ourselves are in the music. We cannot tell the singer from the song, and we ourselves are both sung and singing.

These configurations suggest we need *figures* to address transcendence as other. For the *difference* between our transcending (T^2) and transcendence itself (T^3) entails an essential *indirection* to our transcending. There is no direct univocal pathway to God, and we must heed what the equivocal way has taught us. There are indirections directing human transcending. These indirections are *figurations of transcending*. Perhaps certain configurations of our own transcending may also reveal (pre)figurations of transcendence itself. Religions can be ambiguous here, either domesticating our transcending or intensifying it. Religions can mollify perplexity, they can renew sacred astonishment. If the latter, they can effect an irritation of the urgency of ultimacy; they set on edge the between, vex the familiar, impel us through war to the extremes of peace. Transcending is energized in search of transcendence as more than our own self-transcendence. These indirections, we might say, orient us in freedom to transcendence as other (T^3), through the transcendence of creation (T^1), and our self-transcendence (T^2). In that there is a *difference* between origin and creation, and we inhabit the pluralism of creation, we must find our way to the origin by indirection.

Why will no univocal literalism do? Because this contracts the ontological charge of the aesthetics of happening, makes too determinate the porosity of our being, fixes the urgency of ultimacy on objectified beings, and overall enfeebles the feel for transcendence as non-objectifiable. Are we lost then in equivocal erring? That can happen, and has to be contended with, but transcendence as other is also non-subjectifiable, and there are further possibilities beyond equivocal self-transcending. Indirections that are directions can be (pre)figurations of that to which they are directed. They can be figurings in and through the primal ethos of what in the between is intimated as ultimate. The middle equivocities cry out for more intensive interpretation. Without some seeking of intermediation, the celebration of equivocity, even though it not cease from babbling, will finally be indistinguishable from mute autism, connecting nothing with nothing. We must speak of the ultimate via a metaxological discernment of the between and its equivocity. The transcending of the urgency of ultimacy might be said to come to some discernment in these four indirections: the metaphoric, analogical, symbolic, and hyperbolic (see BB, 207–22). In all these figurings, our mindfulness is patient to a communication of ultimacy we cannot either univocalize or dialectically sublate, even as we are in passage towards the hyperbole of the ultimate as the agapeic origin.

The direction of metaphoric indirection

A living metaphor has the power to stun us into surprise and open our receptivity to unexpected otherness. It makes us porous, but also takes us outside ourselves in that surprise of otherness. The metaxological approach to God is metaphorical in being a "crossing" and a "carrying across": *meta-pherein*. We are crossed by a difference, and ferried across that difference. As carrying one from here to there (*meta-phora*), immanent in metaphor is a *poros*, a way making us porous to the surprise of otherness. Relevantly, "*meta*" can mean both "in the midst of" and yet also "over and above." Thus a metaxological metaphor of God will communicate something double: from the "midst" of immanent being a passage (*poros*) is opened, and we may become porous to something communicated of what is "beyond" or "above." The "above" is not "beyond" as a dualistic opposite or a void inaccessible transcendence; the fullness of the immanent middle is already opened to what exceeds it, and its signs of fullness serve to enable some metaphorical prefiguration of what transcendence as other might be.

Of course, metaphor can accentuate the "is" in a certain way. "God is the rock of ages," we say. Obviously God is not a rock; nevertheless, the "is" does name a "being together" of rock and God, of what they signify, of what they are signs. The "is" is complexly qualified. How qualified? First, immanently, by means of our twofold sense of transcendence in the middle, namely, the transcendence of beings and the self-transcendence of human beings, each of which suggests something "more" than itself. Second, by the absolved relativity that keeps a space open between immanence and transcendence as other. We could then say: the "is" is metaphorical of transcendence, but not in a manner that univocally reduces to these two senses of transcendence. If these are "in the midst" (*meta*), transcendence itself (T^3) is "above" (*meta*), as suggested by the richness of what is given in the midst, what is "more" in the middle. This "more" is also more than the speculative sublation of immanent transcendences (T^1, T^2).

If metaphor refreshes our porosity to otherness, it is not at all a unidirectional projection of ourselves onto otherness. Living metaphors startle us into surprise, but one cannot "project" startlement. Surprise *hits* us. We are patient. Yet metaphor also shapes the articulate unfolding of our transcending as the urgency of ultimacy, and so there will *always* be some risk of anthropomorphism. Our speaking from the middle is complexly qualified by just the granting that first transcendence (T^1) and second transcendence (T^2) *do not* exhaust, *cannot* exhaust what is signified by third transcendence (T^3). The possibility of surprise is matched by the fact that we always face a hazard in naming the divine, a hazard we still must chance. How chance? On the basis of the richest energizings of transcending in the between, and the communication they incarnate of the surplusses of being. These, I believe, come to be most fully embodied in agapeic self-transcending and communicating.

Our caution against reducing this metaphorical "is" to univocity names a temptation of the metaphorical way itself: in crossing differents, it may forget the difference, or at least so temper it that we distort the togetherness, moving it closer to an identity than a community. Properly, metaphysical metaphor addresses a community of differents rather than an identity. This community is not a matter of the speculative sublation of the differents. This is important because the metaphysical metaphor of the "unity" of the divine and the human, improperly qualified in certain religious contexts, can corrupt the community between them, and indeed lead to a reductive anthropocentrism such as we find generally in post-Hegelian thought. The question is, of course, the nature of this community.

The direction of analogical indirection

Owing to such considerations, the metaxological way is attentive to analogical indirection, as reminding us of differences even in the togetherness. For an analogy is a relation of likeness, and likening clearly keeps open the space of difference. Hence, if univocity is not absolutized, neither is equivocity. Equivocity absolutized would entrench the difference, and there could be no intermediating togetherness of differents. Were we to be so equivocal we could land back in a dualism of the between and transcendence (T³). Or, since transcendence seems to have nothing to do with the between, we could turn from transcendence (T³) and immerse ourselves in an immanence closing on itself. Or, again, we could flee immanence, and negate it totally in a flight beyond the given world. The analogy of likening guards us against all these in suggesting a togetherness of others that cannot be collapsed into a univocal identity, dissipated in a flux of equivocal difference, or dialectically sublated in one immanently self-closing whole.

We say: "God is like (as) the joy of the morning." What is the meaning of the analogy? It is *both* the joy of the morning and the being of God. There is an "is like (as)" that is complexly qualified by a sense of intricate, elusive, and subtle community. What joy there is in the morning is like God, though God is not morning or not just this joy. The analogy borders on the equivocal, but if we have entered with purer mindfulness into the joy of the morning, the sweetness of its sheer being puts us in mind of the ultimate as ever freshly good: eternal joy in being, being eternal joy. We partake of the joy of the morning in our first porosity to the good of the "to be."

It is hard to say exactly how different this is from equivocal speech, for one thing seems *to be as in passing* towards and into another. Indeed, there may be a *constitutive ambiguity* to all our speaking about the ultimate. A constitutive ambiguity is not a merely disabling equivocity. There are fertile equivocities that just in their resistance to complete determination or self-determination impel us to the edge of ultimate mystery. The joy of the morning is itself astonishing, and when we are gifted with it, we are transported to another dimension beyond objective determination and our own self-determination. We must be transported ("be crossed," "carried out" of ourselves, "carried across") to have an intimation of the divine. Transport – being beside oneself – makes one fluid to the other beside one. Surpassing oneself one passes to an other sur-passing one. And just such metaphorical transport in the between restores some of its original marvel, and we are astonished. The person who has lost this capacity for astonishment and transport is perhaps the true atheist.

Analogical indirection is not without its difficulties. As I have put it more fully elsewhere (*BB*, 211–16), there is a danger that its quasi-mathematical form will be preponderant. (*Pros hen* analogy is recurrently tempted with the consolation of a more fixed univocity as a stable reference point: this has its reasons relative to a likeness of finites, but what is here at issue is the likening of finites and the transfinite.) After all, analogy has its root in mathematical proportion, and in that respect one is also inclined to a kind of univocity: the difference of the between and ultimate transcendence is mapped as a ratio on a quasi-univocal grid of relations. Such a grid easily freezes into a two-tiered system of otherwise unrelated terms, and hence risks the dualistic opposition between "here" and "beyond," between immanence and transcendence as other (T³) that it is the great power of analogy to circumvent. The transcending that is testament to the togetherness of the terms is a dynamic connecting, not a static connection.

This dynamic is the passing of one towards and into an other, as well as the receiving of the communication of the other that passes towards and into one. This dynamic expresses our wayfaring to transcendence; in a deep sense, it is our wayfare. We must follow its signs, for they are not just our signs, since the way is shown in the faring. The togetherness of the divine and the human, the connecting, is not an analogical structure, but an analogical likening, where likening carries this faring between the divine and the human, a faring both receptive and energetic. Take our faring – this is not a static likeness but a creative likening: I liken myself to you, but my imitation is not at all "passive," even when I am nothing but faithful to the original I am imitating: it is receptive in an originative fidelity to the original. Porosity becomes creative love in this fidelity.

Our self-surpassing calls on us to be related to the *disproportionate* in what is proportioned to us. Rather than analogy tilted towards (quasi-)mathematical proportion, our focus is on the analogy of origination that we find, for instance, in the Platonic likeness of the Good to the sun.[3] There is a likeness between an origin and its offspring. There is the origination of the between; there is origination in the between; and there is a likening between that second origination and the absolute origin that gives the between to be. Whether uncreated or created, transcending is original: it gives out of itself and goes towards the other. Likewise, the originality of the other is a going outside itself. Thus their togetherness is not their being statically side by side; it is being beside self in being beside the other, and this redoubled from every side; it is the plurivocal conjunction of the ecstasies of originals. The double, re-doubled likening is transcending, original, communicative, and ecstatic. It is on the basis of communications of ecstatic originals in the between that we seek analogies of the absolute origin. *The very relating of analogous likening must be seen as invested with the original energy of self-transcending being.*

The analogy of God to the agapeic original serves to qualify the community of being, dynamize the relativity between origin and creation, preserve what is original about the creation, and at the same time keep open the original transcendence of the origin as it is for itself, and not just in its relativity to creation. For such an analogy may also be a relation that releases the terms in relation from an encapsulation in the relation; it is a releasing relation, itself an agapeic relating. Such an analogy may be a sign of the absolving relativity that not only gives the creation its being but inspires it in its otherness.

The direction of symbolic indirection

Why not stop at this? I think because two further recourses are necessary, each of which answers to two sides of analogy; one which recurs to the togetherness, the *sym* or *syn*; the other which recurs to the "over and above," or the *huper*; one the symbol, the other the hyperbole. These also reflect the two senses of "*meta*" as both "in the midst" and as "further beyond." Both are requisite, though all indirections finally seek direction "in the midst" to what is "over and above."

First to the symbol. The symbol is a throwing together (*sumballein*) of the differents; it is the sign of a "being with," a *sun-ousia*. A broken ring is divided and shared by two lovers, each half a token of their original togetherness and in their separation a sign of their promised and renewed togetherness. No doubt this sign risks the equivocal mingling, the promiscuous togetherness of the differents. Yet this promiscuous togetherness needs our attention. We cannot approach God purely, not only because we ourselves can never be pure, but because God, so to say, never stands on haughty ceremony, holding everything other at a distance, holding Godself alone in lofty aloofness. Such divine autism is corrected by the symbolical sense of God's immanence: God, for all we may know, does mix mysteriously with the finite, indeed with the dirty and disgusting. Within the filth of creation, the sign of God is there, even there.

Traditionally religious symbols have tended to elevate God, though involvement with creation is the point. Even elevation is an involvement, for creation is in want of, and wants, a perfection above it to draw it upwards. There are also symbols that signal descent into the grime of finitude, even into the valley of bones. God is united with death; Dionysus is Hades; Jesus descends into hell. The symbol brings us to an equivocal

3 See again *BB*, 211–16. Also *AOO*, Chapter 1, on how the between can be distorted by a wrongly static understanding of *mimēsis*, a distortion perhaps a source of the caricature of "Platonism" that is now quite common. We need a dynamized *mimēsis*, as well as proper attention to eros and mania, to appreciate the dynamic of the between, beyond static dualism. Analogy (especially the analogy of origination) points us towards a dynamized *mimēsis*, also towards the dynamized between beyond static dualism. Such dynamized *mimēsis* is more coherent with the porosity of being and our *passio essendi*.

promiscuity, where the mysterious and the horrifying lie down with each other. In the dead look of the ugliest man the eyes of God look out.[4]

Suppose we take the erotic absolute as a symbol of God. (In Greek *sunousia*, "being-with" also has the meaning of sexual intercourse.) This symbol is one major way of trying to name the involvement of the divine with immanence.[5] God is in love with creation, passionate for its good, zealous for the realization of its promise and integral wholeness. Is God then dependent on that immanent wholeness for God's own fulfillment? We might be tempted to think so, but serious questions must be raised about taking erotic love in that direction as the ultimate symbol. There is more to the *sun-ousia* of the divine with immanence than is captured by the symbol of the erotic absolute; there is in eros itself the porosity of *poros*, as well as the being nothing of *penia* that makes a way for the other; there is the *hyper-ousia* of the divine figured by the hyperbole of the agapeic servant.

That said, the symbolic indirection can be taken in a sense relevant to the agapeics of the divine: the infinite immanent in the finite, passing *incognito* in its festivity and travail, intimating the willingness of the ultimate to be involved with the ultimate in negation – the nothing of death. Fire burns, it may temper, it may utterly consume, it may cleanse of cataracts our squinting souls; suffering often simply shatters us, sometimes purges us, but these consequences are exceeded immanently by the divine *compassio essendi* that offers anew the promise of life. The astonishing surprise of this agapeic symbol: God, the suffering servant; God, resurrection again and again of the good of the "to be." The symbol maintains a kind of *immanent disproportion*, or *disproportion in immanence* irreducible to any univocal or dialectical concept. Through the symbolic indirection, the ever present overdeterminacy of the "being given" of immanent finitude serves as a perpetual reminder of the unsurpassable surplus of the divine in its equivocal presencing. And this even in iniquity, malice, and squalid vice; for some sin not simply to defy the divine but to test, to taste the intimacy of the divine, in their horrifying defiance. (Did Luther know something about this? *Pecca fortiter!*)

The direction of hyperbolic indirection

Here we have stepped to the edges of the hyperbolic, though in monstrous form. The monstrous is sublime, but there are diviner sublimities at that edge, diviner ways of crossing, or being crossed. Generally, by contrast with the symbolic, the hyperbolic indirection

---

[4] See *PU*, pp. 162–3 on the ugly man of Clonakilty. There are other eyes, of course. One looks to the beloved but the beloved, now lover, looks to one. One is beheld. This is like the icon, recalled by Nicholas of Cusa: the divine gaze rests on us, wherever we are: moving with us, as we move, resting in itself, unmoving. If one brother moves from east to west, it rests on him and moves with him; if another brother, simultaneously, moves from west to east, it rests on him and moves with him; the icon of the divine gaze moves in opposite directions simultaneously and rests unmoved beyond the oppositions of movements (preface to *De Visione Dei* [*Concerning the Vision of God*], trans. J. Hopkins in *Nicholas of Cusa's Speculative Mysticism*, 2nd edn., [Minneapolis: Banning Press, 1988]). Note the doubleness: beholding and being beheld: God seeing and the seeing of God. There is a doubleness above dualistic opposition. "He will marvel at how the icon's gaze is moved unmovably."

[5] The symbolics of divine erotics might be linked to the analogy of origination, in human terms, the *likening of generation*. Consider family likenesses: a variable mingling of like and unlike across many generations, and both likeness and unlikeness are defined by reference to common, though often hidden or unknown, origins. Family likenesses are sourced in the transcending energy of erotic generation, but are embodied relations that transcend generations, relations also not just erotically defined. The energy of generation becomes incarnated in resemblances between originators and offspring, some more expected, some more surprising. Such analogical likeness of origination is defined by the communication of a community with all its promise. When we call God "father" the analogy of origination is not just a matter of biological engendering; nevertheless, a kind of generational likening is suggested, as well as this promise of community. Divine erotics are more to the fore when God's love for humans is less likened to a family as to a lover and beloved, or bridegroom and bride, as in the "Song of Songs." The love broadcast by familial likening shows a communal extensiveness, while erotic likening can stress the intimately, passionately intense.

turns us to the *excess of disproportion*, but this time in terms of transcendence "above" rather than immanence "in the midst." The hyperbole gives us a figure of the overdeterminate in the determinate and the self-determined, the overdeterminate that cannot be exhausted by determinacy or self-determination, the "beyond" of immanence in immanence that cannot be immanently (self-)determined and that "throws us above" immanence. The symbolic throws together, but stuns us with disproportion *in* immanence; the hyperbolic "throws us above" (*huper-ballein*) in the disproportion *between* immanence and transcendence, just out of that being stunned with excess of being here.[6]

Though we may have an equivocal sense of the divine immanence, we always are nagged by its too muchness for us. This divine disproportion intimates that it is, *at the most, that side of the ultimate transcendence turned towards the immanent between.* There is intimated an *other side*, turned into the mystery of its own being for itself. This is the reserve of the divine. The agapeic origin is nothing but its giving to the other, but it is also more than any of its determinate gifts, and hence the heart of the agape is both poured forth into finitude and reserved in itself, reserved perhaps just to let the finite be as finite. The finite let be as finite points back beyond itself again, and in its given inexhaustibility points to the radical excess of the absolute origin, reserved in itself in its light inaccessible.

This is why we need hyperboles to say what we mean, what indeed *we alone* cannot mean. We feel we need to pile excess on excess, and then some more, and then we are not any closer to what we do not even have to approach, because it is there always, though not always there, just because we are not always there for it. For we cannot get any closer to that which is absolutely close. Being absolutely close is also being absolutely reserved: close but not closed, rather resource of absolving communication; utterly intimate always, always further intimated; never passing, ever passing.

Hyperboles call to mind excesses of praise. Both symbols and hyperboles bring our saying nearer to the rich poetics of religious practice. In their own way they might be, so to say, prayers of thinking and indirectly redirect us to the ultimate superiority. This is no squashing heteronomy but a releasing transcendence drawing us upwards. The hyperbole gives shape to the arc of ascending thinking like a kind of praying that can descend into its own depths, know its own excessive nature, know the fragility of its reaching beyond, because it does not proceed through its own will (to) power alone. It is being thrown beyond, rather than throwing itself beyond. Its being beyond, its altitude can be as much in the dimension of depth as of height; for "*altus*" (like "*meta*") is metaxologically double, meaning "deep" as well as "high." As with praying, there is an ultimate patience in being in the throes of hyperbolic thinking. The *passio essendi* comes to the fore in the throw of the hyperbole, which cannot be just a matter of the exceeding of our own striving to be, a hypertrophy of our *conatus essendi*. Being thrown by the hyperbolic is being in the throes of an undergoing which is an overgoing, an abovegoing in receiving, or being received by, the *huper*. The hyperbolic is not a hypertrophy of will to power, but a poverty in extreme porosity that is filled full with richness from the superior other.

Religious utterance, we say, is not only a "carrying across," but is "carried away." Is it just "carried away" with itself? Or does it get "carried away" by an other? The agapeic hyperbole (we will see) implies the second rather than the first. Though, again, there is

---

[6] The analogy (of origination) and the hyperbolic run together strikingly in Plato's *Republic*. Socrates does not venture an account of the nature of the good in itself, his surmise of which is above the impulse winging his present flight. Instead he offers us the indirection of the offspring of the good (*ekgonos te tou agathou*) most nearly made in its likeness (506e). The story of the father (*patēr*) must be left for another occasion (506e). The offspring of the good stands in analogy (*analogon*, 508c) with the good itself, yet the non-identity in likeness is stressed (508a–b, 509a). The excess of this difference of the good is expressed in the famous *epekeina tēs ousias* (509b9). Responding to Socrates Glaucon bemusedly exclaims (509c1–2): "By Apollo, a daimonic hyperbole (*daimonias huperbolēs*)!" Eros as daimonic is to be properly elevated to the highest, but its improper pretension to be the highest is to be deflated. Plato brings us up to that middle space between mortals and divinities, ventures boldly an iconic saying about the ultimate, and relativizes the ultimacy of our saying, without relativizing the ultimate.

no claim that the equivocal has been entirely dispelled, and sometimes our being "carried away" by ourselves is taken for a divine "being carried away." We must dwell in these religious equivocities with precautionary mindfulness against being "carried away" in the form of our own transcendental bluster, or self-effusion, or existential overreaching into nothing. Do not worry. The discipline of finitude will keep us in check. What is this discipline? At the least, it is proper metaxological mindfulness of the ontological sources and resources of the between, its richness and its snares.

In what now follows, I attempt a more intensive discernment of the divine by way of the between, and in a movement which approaches the ultimate hyperbole of God as the agapeic origin, through the indirections of different hyperboles of being. The movement is from the idiotic to the aesthetic, through the erotic to the agapeic. It passes from an immediate givenness of ontological community, through the glorious aesthetics of happening, through the exceeding energies of human selving, towards the releasing of free community, all the way to ethical community and beyond. The idiotic, aesthetic, erotic, and agapeic give articulate expression to the ontological potencies of the primal ethos and their metaphysical promise. While none of these potencies is to be neglected, and while a properly ample philosophical mindfulness must find the just place for all, undoubtedly for many the question of God takes on its most intensive form in relation to ethical community. To this we will come, though there is more.

Coming to this "more," we will also resume with more intensive mindfulness the deeper promise of the other senses of being. I mean that univocity is metaxologically resumed with the hyperbole of the idiotic "that it is," equivocity with the hyperbole of the aesthetics of happening, dialectic with the hyperbole of erotic selving, while the metaxological itself comes to fullest showing with the hyperbole of the agapeics of community. Likewise, just as the metaxological way resumes the other three ways, so when speaking of the hyperbole I mean also to resume in this figuration the indirections of the metaphor, analogy, and symbol. These four indirections and what they figure might be resumed through these four words: "is," "like (as)," "with," and "above." So also through the four hyperboles the passage of (metaphysical) mindfulness is moved in and through the between from the "is" that is immanent to the "above" that is transcendent.

GOD AND THE BETWEEN: FIRST HYPERBOLE – THE IDIOCY OF BEING

A first metaxological approach takes its direction from the excess of given being. Call this the *first hyperbole*. Being is given before any of our conceptions and remains always in excess of our determinate categories. Can one address God out of wonder at the sheer *givenness of the given*? How to understand this givenness? Is it the sheer fact that is, and that is all? Anything further we cannot ask. It will be granted: it is presupposed by all efforts to make sense, indeed by all forms of life, but since all questions take place within it, there is no question about it; we must accept it, and again that is that.

Yes, there is a consent here, but of what kind? A tendency here is to conflate the familiar middle, reduced to a surd thereness, with the astonishing or perplexing middle. Then meaningful questions only regard connections between determinate beings or happenings, or an origin as first or ultimate determinate cause. The univocal sense of being then reigns, with God perhaps denominated as the first or highest being. Against this, however, there is an astonished perplexity about the "that it is" which is not itself such a determinate question. One is not asking about how *this* relates to *that*, or how determinate beings relate together in some totality the sum of determinate beings (Kant inclines to think thus of the unconditioned). Rather there is the excess overdeterminacy of the "that it is" of all finite beings that are there. The issue of God then is: Why the "that it is at all"? not why this or that, nor how and why some total sum of determinate beings.

If this question addresses an overdeterminacy, so the answer, if we can call it such, is *not a determinate solution to a determinate problem*. It too is overdetermined: excess calls to excess, relative to the superfluity of the "that it is." There is something surd about the "that it is," for it is not self-explanatory. It happens, and does not explain itself. The question is whether this surd is absurd. If it were a mere surd, we would say, it is finally absurd. It is there, and either it makes no sense, or there is no further sense to be made. Either way, there is given being, finally in itself senseless and groundless. But what if there were a surd not absurd? Suppose the "that it is at all" is such a surd? Suppose God, as source of that surd happening, might also be a surd not absurd, and hyperbolic to the surd of finite happening as such? Of course, the language of the surd is deficient language, the language of a remainder, a residue. In fact, the "that it is" is no mere residue but given being as gloriously rich and enigmatic. It is this surplus of finite being that puts us in mind of the source of the given. What gives the surplus happening of the between? This cannot be defined in terms of any determinate being within the happening of the given between; the source is other, but not other such as to destroy intimacy with the gift of being itself.

This surplus surd can be correlated with the *idiocy of being*, in the complex sense I mean by this.[7] To reduce this idiocy to senseless thereness would be to lose its intimate insinuation of sense beyond objectification and subjectification. Just the intimacy of the given "that it is" is on the edge of all objectifiable and subjectifiable determination, hence extremely resistant to determinate conceptualization, and so we either forget it, or live as if there were no idiocy. This forgetting is itself inseparable from the intimacy of being it ostensibly denies. Were there not the "that it is" in its idiocy, there would be nothing of the more public determinations that allow all our more manipulable communications. The "that it is" is known perhaps most intimately in the idiocy of our own being, though sometimes even more so in relation to the given being of the beloved other. But we can know it also in relation to the being of nature. Self, other, non-human nature can strike one as receding from complete determination, even as they come forward into determinate manifestation. As beings proceed, they recede; as they show themselves, they reserve themselves; as they manifest themselves, they hide their being.

We are here on the boundary of determinate intelligibility, but this idiocy of the "that it is" directs us to the living ground of communicative being, as centered in this being and that being. Often we think of that centering as the selving of the being, a selving which takes a more personal form with humans. This idiocy of the "that it is" might serve to metaphorize the *idiocy of God*, and the resistance of God's being to any determinate statement, beyond perhaps "that God is." The "what" of the divine recedes into hiddenness, just as the "that it is" shows itself forth through the surd of the idiocy of being in the between. (Aquinas: we know *that* God is, not *what* God is.) Nevertheless, this showing is ambiguous, hence opening itself to the opposite claim that the whole story is completely absurd. We come to the surd of being as it just is, and we reiterate this surd, and then we make no further move. Why and how must we make the further move? Because of, and on the basis of understanding this surd, just in its idiocy; an understanding inseparable from how one understands the meaning of being in the between. We have to be awakened from the sleep of postulatory finitism. All things considered I would venture the following.

The primal givenness of the "that it is" is not a matter of the "becoming" or "self-becoming" of beings. There is a "coming to be" prior to "becoming." The latter presupposes a prior "that it is," even granting that this "that it is" is given with an open promise, and not as a static and completed fact. Granted, there is the openness of (self-)becoming, but there is granted a "being opened" to be, prior to determinate becoming. This is idiotic, since all determinate sense presupposes it, and no determinate sense can exhaust it. This "being opened" is the primal giving of the porosity of being, the between as enabling an astonishing diversity of becomings, self-becomings, and together-becomings. There is an *ontological passio essendi* which gives beings to be before they can give themselves

---

7   See especially *PU*, Chapter 3: this idiocy is not a "what," not a neutral generality, and is not defined by formal determinability; it is elemental, but it is not the horrifying *Il' ya* of Levinas, nor the threatening, nauseating viscosity of Sartre's *être-en-soi*; see *BB*, pp. 270–8 on the elemental.

to themselves in their diverse self-becomings and together-becomings. The gift of being at all is more primordial than every endeavor to be: it may enable striving, but it is not strife. The idiocy of being points us towards an overdeterminate porosity of giving and being given, of creating and coming to be, of offering and receiving. When we are turned to it in the mode of marvel, there is intimated an overdeterminate generosity of being, giving before and beyond strife.

Our metaphysical movement beyond takes form in this "being opened," but it does not claim to offer a "scientific explanation" for something that truly is not self-explanatory. It, rather, testifies to the intimation of something trans-objective in all objective determinacies, and to something trans-subjective in the self-determining of the human being. We witness something of the latter in the infinite disquiet of human mindfulness, and something of the former when the disquiet will not rest with any surd less that the final surd beyond which there is nothing. Why stop with this final surd? Because as one comes to understand it – all things considered – there is noplace else to go or be. Does it bring peace? It depends. If the final surd is chance, or necessity, or fate, or will to power, and if how we understand these offers no response to what is most intimately deep in our between-being, there is no peace. If we call that final surd God, there may be peace beyond understanding that deepens understanding. But why call that final surd God?

Some of the reasons for this might be approached by correlating the hyperbole of the idiocy of being with some traditional "proofs," and their metaxological reformulation. Thus the "movement further" is related to the fact that the "that it is," albeit a surplus, is not an absolute plenitude such as is Parmenidean being. Nevertheless, recall Parmenides's "It is" – all we can say, he says, is *Esti*. Perhaps this is his way of naming the first hyperbole. (Hegel did not appreciate what is at stake here.) The "that it is," just as a happening, might not have happened. It is, but it might not have been, and indeed we come to know the shadow of death that hovers over its stunning being there. It is the "not" of its being, and the further possibility, indeed certainty, of its not being, that shows the ontological character of the happening of the "that it is" as itself *equivocal between being and nothing*. As happening to be, it comes to be, but it might not have been; it now is as passing, even as it has its being; and it will have passed at some time into not being anymore. The idiocy of being is not just our failure to take a grasp on it conceptually; the very ontological process as passage is itself always an escaping from beyond all grasping; it cannot be grasped by itself, for it always is as passing in the porosity of the between, passing away from itself, even as it comes to be itself. Its security on being is at the same time a loss of being, just as its loss of being is a provisional re-securing of its place in the sun, till it die.

It seems to me that many approaches to God do not face deeply enough this double face of happening, as coming forward into determinate being, and being withdrawn into nonbeing. They, too, secure the familiar middle, screen us from the return to zero, clog our porosity, and dull us to a new interface with creation. But the pull of nonbeing is in the being, and the equilibrium of finite happening is a poised balance of present ontological power that rises above just that pull. The equilibrium is lighted up by the threat of toppling into death. The light of finitude is outlined starkly against the backdrop of nothing. And the backdrop is not back there behind it; it is, so to say, in the light itself. Finitude is itself ontological mixture. That is why the idiocy of being can be seen from the two sides: taken for granted as the final surd, just senseless idiocy; or taken as granted, though as disquieting us with its radical ambiguity, and in that ambiguity tantalizing with a light that is not its own light. It is the second way that leads to the thought of God.

I ask again: Why go this way? Not to escape oblivion, but to grant, to acknowledge, to praise, the origin of the light. Idiotic happening might itself be called a light, in the sense in which "coming to be" is a "coming to light." Givenness that is something and not nothing comes to light. The light of the happening is not given by itself; the happening comes to be, comes to light, coming into the light, before it shines with its own light. Not to escape oblivion, but because in intimately knowing the idiocy of being it is impossible to place into oblivion the intimation of the origin and our wonder about its goodness.

There is not first a "proof" of this, an argument; it is a matter of a living and a mindfulness turned towards ultimate sources. Arguments come out of this turn; arguments alone do not get us there – and in that sense there is no argument for God. Yet there is a sweetness to being at all, known even in face of the horror of nothingness that is also brought home to us in the intimacy of idiocy. This idiocy is most intimately known by humans, and hence humans alone have religion, explicitly. We live the taste of the goodness of being; to be at all is to be good, in some all but inexpressible way; that is most undeniably shown in our spontaneous shunning of death. I know we can choose death, but this does not controvert the point; in a perverse way it amplifies it. We may choose death rather than horror, but our horror before the horror of choosing death is a more primordial affirmation of the simple elemental "it is good to be."

The "that it is" recalls Kant's discussion of the *cosmological proof* (called by Leibniz *a contingentia mundi*). As Kant describes this, here we argue from a concept of *indeterminate [experience of] existence*, whereas the ontological proof argues from necessary being, and the physico-theological proof from *determinate [experience of] existence*. In Kant's summary: "If anything exists, an absolutely necessary being must exist. Now I, at least, exist. Therefore an absolutely necessary being exists." I suggested before that Kant's understanding of existence is thin. He is right to touch on the indeterminate here, but the meaning seems little more than the indefinite. Further, he defines the necessary being as the *ens realissimum* which is completely determinate.[8] Moreover, when claiming that causality cannot be used beyond the limits of experience, those limits are understood in a clearly determinable sense as what can be objectified in accord with the transcendental conditions of possibility. The overdeterminations within "experience," that is, within the intermedium of being, are not noted by him (one finds hints in the *Critique of Judgement*). The "horizon" of the between is excessively defined in terms of the univocally determinable. "Causality" is itself understood determinately as a determination process which connects an antecedent condition to a consequent effect. Clearly God cannot be a determinate cause like that at all, for this would make him just one determinate being within the between. It is wrong to apply such a category of causality beyond objectifiable determination. To apply it to God is the more deeply wrong, because God could not be that kind of a cause.

Rather than Kant's indeterminate existence, the idiocy of being points to the overdeterminate, suggesting the analogy of the origin in an overdetermined, indeed hyperbolic sense. Kant strikes one as having been terrified of everything hyperbolic. A deeper sense of the nothing of finitude and contingency would have helped, as would an understanding that there is crucial difference between "coming to be" and "becoming." In "becoming," the happening is already given as having come to be, and, within the happening of becoming, we can use the notion of cause and effect. But "coming to be" concerns the ontological arising of happening. It is not a determinate becoming, but rather what determinate becoming presupposes as giving it to be at all. That is why stress on the "that it is" of being is very important, and not to be reduced to Kant's use of indeterminate existence, which dissolves into a mere vanishing indefiniteness in the face of the will to univocal determination, also operative throughout Kant's entire discussion.[9] Almost always our search for "proof" is tempted with falling under the bewitchment of univocity, and so with ending up as a rationalistic idol. "Proof "becomes a means of connecting, in the end, the determinate with the determinate, or the indefinite with the determinate. I think there are "probes"; probes

---

[8] *Critique of Pure Reason*, A604–6, B632–4; also A572, B600: Kant's connecting of complete determination with the *ens realissimum* differs from my emphasis on the overdetermination of the primal ethos, and the suggestion of the hyper-overdeterminacy of its giving source. The primal ethos is not exhausted by a totality of determinate beings, nor is the giving source the *ens realissimum*.

[9] Consider Kant's invocation of the "I exist," as the minor premise (repeating Leibniz). One recalls the question about what is really prior in Descartes, the "cogito" or God, and which of these is more truly ultimate, if God is proved on the basis of the "cogito." Which is minor, which major, indeed maximal? The "I exist" does have a certain idiocy, though this idiocy is not confined to the "I." There are also singularly *existential* aspects to this that exceed Kant's understanding of existence.

that take form out of our "being opened," out of our antecedent porosity, antecedent to all the striving of human self-transcending. The probe at issue with the metaxological concerns the overdetermined, out of the givenness of the "that it is" in the between. If it probes a "connection," this is more like the porosity of the between, or absolved relativity, in and through which its ultimate source is sought.

In some respects, *Aquinas's third way*, called by him the proof from possibility and necessity, has a deeper meaning than Kant's version. How might this third way run? Putting it most concisely, in terms not Aquinas's: *If all being is possible being, ultimately all possible being is impossible.* Here is a reconstruction.

The finite world is contingent: things come into being and pass out of being. In the endlessness of becoming, there is one possibility that would be realized at some point: namely, that there would be no contingent being. After all, everything finite might not be; and at some time, in the infinite time of endless becoming, the possibility of everything *not being* will be.[10] If this possibility of everything *not being* is possible, then nothing could ever come to be; for nothing comes from nothing; hence nothing could *now* exist. Thus, if everything is contingent, not even contingent existence now is possible. This is absurd, because the world of contingency is actually given. There must be another being, not contingent, to make contingency intelligible, possible, actual. If some necessary beings are through themselves or another, a plurality of necessary beings as ultimate is subject to the rejection of the *regressus in infinitum* – analogously to the rejection of infinite regress relative to endless becoming through another. One might interpolate and say that Aquinas claims we must come to an Other that *is* not through another, or does not *become* through another, but through whom all others *come to be*. One might call this an other origin, hyperbolically necessary. This origin is necessary in a sense that has neither come to be, nor become; rather it is the reserved source of all coming to be and becoming. This other origin, the ultimate necessary being exists – that is, God.

Thus Aquinas somewhat metaxologically reformulated. Of course, one worries that in speaking of the necessary being one objectifies it as one determinate being among others. Here the hyperbolic dimension saves us, in that we are addressing the overdeterminacy of an other origin, beyond the objectification of determinate being, and the subjectification of self-determining being. One worries also about how Aquinas's scholastic formulation displays a kind of forensic univocity in the mode of articulation. This displays the legacy of the univocal sense of being effective in the philosophical tradition, indeed dominating most forms of saying and thinking. Scholastic philosophers strove for as much determinacy

---

[10] *Image*: think of all contingent beings as doubly possibilized coins; one side of the coin is being, the other side not-being, or zero: if we flip all the coins of contingency, at some point in endless becoming – finite becoming without origin or goal – all the coins will come up zero, or return to zero; there would be nothing – something absurd given the incontrovertibility of given being. Here I see a surprising connection with Nietzsche's argument for eternal recurrence! If time is infinite and the set or combinations of possibilities is finite, then all the possibilities would have come to be, and come to be again and again. Thus we get the circular movement of becoming – again and again – eternally (see *Will to Power*, p. 1066; also p. 55 for the horror and paralysis it can induce). How then, in this scenario, can a determinate becoming or self-becoming *come to be again*, if one of the possibilities in the total combination is *nothing*? This I mean in a sense analogous to what is suggested by the ontological game of the flip of a coin – or perhaps the throw of a dice, or even Heraclitus's *pais paizon* (Frag. 52) – ancestor of Zarathustra's child and its sacred self-circulating wheel. A singularly crucial combination of possibilities in infinite time: *All the zeros come up.* Clearly finitude entails the happening of given being as a contingency that might *not be at all*, even though it is, in fact. Nietzsche is oblivious to the difference of "coming to be" and "becoming." The consistent thought of finitude as such points to this difference. If Nietzsche's philosophy is honest about finitude, and if there is to be anything at all, then his thought of eternal recurrence requires reference to *another source* of *coming to be*. This origin, hyperbolic to becoming, Nietzsche's philosophy only seems to avoid by closing the circle of a *cosmic becoming*. Heraclitus's *pais paizon* becomes Zarathustra's child, with its sacred "yes," and self-circulating wheel. Thus seen, eternal recurrence proves to be less an unreserved consent to what is, as a dulling of our astonishment before the "that it is at all" of finite being, the marvel of its irreducible "*once*."

in their articulations as possible; but the will to determinacy rubs against some of their better intuitions that God could not, could never be a determination or determinate being. Aquinas obviously knew this deeply: we can know *that* God is, not *what* God is. But his form of articulation seems sometimes more suitable to a legal disputation than a theme which calls also on meditative, even prayerful mindfulness.[11] Forensic univocity is not finessed enough for the idiocy of being, or the intimacy of the mystery of the "that it is." Yet it is just the latter that is most at stake in this third way, metaxologically reformulated.

I say something more. This way has to do with being struck (as I think Aquinas was struck) by the incontrovertibility of being. There is the bite of otherness in thus being struck. There is no way to sidestep being, and the inescapability of its givenness, even if there is something overdeterminate about being as thus given. Moreover, the dynamism of being is very important; being is be-ing. Further, there is a beautiful delicacy of ontological fineness about finite being; it is, and might have not been, but it is, and that is extraordinary. Can we see Aquinas's third way as a thought experiment that tries to stun us into astonishment about the "that it is," despite the nothing? If so, this awakening to nothing and contingent being is no regress to an empty time before "real" time. There is no linear regress, but an intensive dwelling with the now of being in its ontological depths: the nothing is now, just as is the incontrovertibility of being there at all. In that mindful dwelling the incontrovertibility shines out in the given, outlined as gift before the nothing that is also now always possible. The "proof" is this intensive, "probing" dwelling in metaphysical mindfulness on the "that it is at all," though it well might be nothing. This double possibility of finite being defines its contingency, what Aquinas calls its possible being, as not necessary. It is not merely possible being, but being that as finitely actual might possibly not be, and hence carrying no inherent necessity that it must be. The lack of the latter is the mark of a kind of surd for Aquinas, in so far as he held to the disquiet of mind short of an absolute "limit" at which it comes to peace. Minding does not come to peace here, but its very affirmation of possible being, its joy in contingent being, in creation, points it beyond givenness in the givenness itself.

Were we to think of this as a regress or progress, whether determinate or supposedly infinite, we would not get the point. In a certain sense, there is no way of *getting from* finite being (creation) to God, as if we were going somewhere else. We are going nowhere. We are simply mindfully dwelling on being as given. This is to be opened to the ontological promise of the ethos of being. The mysterious hyperbole of the "that it is at all" is the first thereness that calls for an origin that would be, not merely on a par with, but over and above, more than this there "that it is at all." Such an origin would have to be one that enables beings to come to be, and come to be as we know them to be, that is given to be and striped with nothingness.

In relation to the latter, there arises some presentiment of the creative process of coming to be out of nothing. I will return to this in a later chapter. Here it might be taken to mean our intimation of the nothing, relative to which the being of the possible, or the contingent, is constituted: every being, arising newly at the interface of creation, is the possibility of return to zero, hence also, simply as being at all, arising out of zero. What is shown here is a *constitutive nothing* relative to finite being – not that the nothing constitutes the being, but that the being is constituted with a nothingness intrinsic to the qualification of its coming to be. The "that it is" of the origin is not just analogically like

---

[11] In fairness, the highly formalized manner of scholastic disputation might be seen as a *dialectic* containing within a compact order of exposition a *plurivocal dialogue* of many contending positions. The forensic univocity can camouflage this dialectic, this hidden dialogue. Of course, the ways are only a beginning for Aquinas, and later in the *Summa* explicit religious and theological concerns come to the fore. The itinerary of spirit of the whole work exceeds, is hyperbolic to, the form of forensic univocity, though the latter helps us to be as determinate as we can. Aquinas transforms Aristotelian metaphysics, and the influence of the biblical picture is crucial, if disputed, in relation to notions like *esse*, *actus purus*, *esse ipsum*, and so on. Here I cannot dwell on the power of being relative to the contrast of the God of creation and Aristotle's self-thinking thinking. See chapter 12, Part III below.

the "that it is" of finite being; it is *hyperbolic* relative to it. It is *more* than the coming to be, and the nothing, and the finite becoming of the determinate and self-determining beings that have come to be, as more than nothing, at least for now.

I find it relevant that Aquinas calls on the analogy of origination when speaking of God as an "analogous cause." This phrase makes no sense in a Kantian context, but perhaps Kant was the victim of a certain univocalization of causality. If a purely "univocal cause" issues in simply the same (Parmenides), a purely "equivocal cause" in the sheerly different (Nietzsche), an "analogous cause" issues in an originated other both like and unlike the origin. Aquinas is closer to the truth than Kant, even if the language of causality is inevitably equivocal with respect to divine "causality" (creating), as other to finite determinate causing. This cause is a because, a be-cause, a cause of being, in the radical sense of original source of *coming to be*.[12] The hyperbolic sense of the origin is belied by the quasi-univocal character of Aquinas's language and the sentence that seems so straightforward: "and everyone calls this God." What seems so simple is deeply ambiguous, in fact, and betrays bewitchment by univocity, perhaps itself influenced by the incontrovertibility of the "that it is at all," once it is given to be. There is perhaps greater truth in his final words about his own words about God: Not "*et hoc omnes intelligunt Deum,*" but "*videtur mihi ut palea.*"

In sum: there is a deep idiocy of being which we must think. If this seems paradoxical, this is so and not so. It is not so: thinking always faces what resists it, especially initially, what is idiotic. It is so: this thinking does bring us to something that always resists us, remains idiotic, but now in a paradoxical sense of intimation of the origin of the "that it is." In that intimation something of the character of God now comes into view. God is the hyperbolic original of being in its radical coming to be. A radical origin is absolutely original power bound by nothing. Could "anything" be more hyperbolical? What more could be said about the "being" of that origin? We move to the second hyperbole.

GOD AND THE BETWEEN: SECOND HYPERBOLE – THE AESTHETICS OF HAPPENING

Our second turn is directed more towards the determinate character of the givenness: not the "that it is" but something of the "what it is." From the primal ontological promise of the givenness of being as given, we turn to something of the determinate promise of what is given, approaching the divine from the *aesthetics of happening*, the second hyperbole.

By "happening" I mean not only the idiocy of givenness but the fact that this givenness shines forth with its own intimate radiance, coming to manifest its own marvelous intricacy of order. Radiance: but we are not confined to sight only, for one might consider things musically, and speak of a resounding of givenness that sings in the hum of thereness. By "aesthetic" I mean the sensuous showing that (keeping to sight) shines from itself in the happening of being. The "aesthetic" signals a sensuous figuration or figuring forth of the ontological potencies of the primal ethos. This is not just relative to our perception, but communicates the self-showing of the given; self-showing as marked by radiance beyond fixation, by singularity, dynamic form, and ordered, open wholeness; self-showing also intimating a reserve of ontological promise, promise not shown in a completely determinate way in the reserved showing. The ethos of the between is charged with aesthetic effulgence that comes to be embodied both communally and singularly.

---

[12] Should Heideggerians pounce with the ready-to-hand accusation of "onto-theology," I confess I do not recognize in that accusation the hyperbolic origin. The accusation risks being, so to say, a case of mis-taken "identity." In any event, how are *they* in a position to *know*, whether I speak of God, or of a counterfeit double? See *AOO*, Chapter 7, on Heidegger's failure of finesse in assimilating creation *ex nihilo* with making as a technical imposition of form on matter.

Aesthetic radiance shines from beings, passes in and through and between beings. Mostly, for humans, there is too much to this radiance, which, just as excessive to our complete intake, retreats into the background of showing. Within this more enveloping effulgence, the aesthetics of happening comes to showing in the singularity of things. This is consonant with the idiocy of being, but the bite of determinate existence manifests itself here. And while this singularity is determinate existence, it is at the edge of our determination in univocal or dialectical categories. The "that it is" becomes "it is *this*," and there is something excessive about, not only the "is," but the thisness of the "this." That beings should be given with this singularity resistant to univocal objectification and dialectical encapsulation strikes one into a wonder about the communicative character and source of such singularity. Does such a communicative character suggests a source supremely attentive to the singular as singular?

This singular is not a pointillistic particular. To put it in terms of hearing: it voices itself, it utters itself – though there is more than self-voice. It is porous to a more universal communication between itself and other beings. Yet in itself it is not devoid of internal articulation. It is not an inarticulate autistic "this," but manifests its own inherent self-mediation and order. It is as becoming; as itself in becoming itself it is a dynamic forming of itself. This, its self-mediation, is held within the bounds of the open integrity of the "this." The singular being shows itself as a harmonious integration of its own powers of being as they dynamically crystallize its own promise of being. An integral open wholeness marks the aesthetic show of the beauty of the being.

Drawn in further, one heeds the passage of the original radiance, exceeding final fixation. But this does not vanish into nebulousness, since this singular is as transcending itself towards the others, each self-transcending and offering to other singulars, in a network of intermediation, the constancy of communal support. Aesthetic happening shows the enabling ethos as a togetherness of splendid beings. Beauty here is not something subjectivistic: aesthetic show communicates the beings themselves and their togetherness in terms of integral harmony and community with others. We are invited to wonder about the world as aesthetic happening on the analogy with the art work. The ontological work of that art configures a togetherness of beings that communicates something of the source that brings the beings to be, and as, astonishingly, aesthetically fit.

The aesthetics of happening awakens us to the glory of creation – offered both in given beauty and sublimity, and in what we ourselves create. Think of how some music comes to one almost as a praying, for instance, in listening to Bach's Cello Suites. Or, hearing some of Mozart's divine music, one is stricken and the unwilled conviction wells up: God is. Music moves us, without asking permission from determinate reason, or self-determining will. It moves us without a why, but when we are moved, we have the feeling there is a why, though one could not say it is this, or it is that. It moves the *passio essendi*, makes us so porous that we feel transported, as in a uplift of praise. The singing of transcendence as other seems to come over the singing of our self-transcending.[13]

Beauty is revealed in the intimate order of immanent wholeness, but something hyperbolic to the immanent whole is also intimated. The stupendous prodigality of the between comes to pass in equivocal transience, but beauty is *fugitive*: it shows itself, it eludes us, and flies away; it is revealing and shy; wanton and concealing, forward and withdrawing, coming forth and reserved. There is a rich wholeness *there* – but something *beyond wholeness* is intimated in the showing there. There is a *saturated* equivocity to the aesthetics of happening. This is something "meta": something crosses us, something carries us across. The fugitive nature of beauty invites us to the *boundary* of the sublime. On the boundary we pass more unreservedly into the movement towards the hyperbolic. The aesthetics of happening is metaxological: in beauty we behold a self-mediating wholeness, wholeness open and opening; in the sublime an intermediation of the transfinite,

---

[13] Beyond the profanities in instrumentalizing matter, something as stolid as a building can become a soaring prayer in stone, as we see in some of the great cathedrals.

the overdeterminate is communicated. The overdeterminate in the determinate and the self-determining whole calls us to the boundary, calls us beyond the boundary, between the sensible and supersensible, the visible and invisible, the hearing and the call.[14]

The sublime more extremely indicates the hyperbolic: in sensuous happening there is the breaking in of something beyond, or our breaking beyond which contests the ultimacy of finite and determinate form. There is a breakdown of the finite form, and the release of or invitation to what exceeds finitization. This rupturing communication of the beyond of immanent form can be terrifying: it calls our securing of life into question and can bring disarray of mind. The thunder disordered the regal mind of Lear on the blasted heath. There is disturbance of immanence within immanence and from beyond immanence: finitude is exceeded by an other that visits it unexpectedly and uproots us from immanence as our absolute home. (Mind, I am talking here about a certain orientation to T[1].)

The sublime in nature is beyond our determination and self-determination. It is an excess appearing as excessive to appearing. It scorns the pretensions of our projects. It mocks absolute claims made by our *conatus essendi*. It occasions an initially involuntary revelation of the *passio essendi*, a revelation that yet may mutate into a wiser patience and consent. Before this sublime otherness we are tempted to retreat, though there is exhilaration in our terror, and we are lifted up to being more than ourselves. The passion of being is released in a movement towards heights, or in a descending into depths that dizzy the downgoing soul. Along the way, the *conatus* staggers and we are exposed: exposed to a show of what exceeds us and what exceeds show. Note again the doubleness: the excess is both "in the midst" and yet "above, beyond." Modern, self-mediating autonomy muzzles the voice that would proclaim the glory of creation in its otherness, for that otherness relativizes our autonomy: we are not the superior power. (Kant's moralization of the sublime bends this away from its true meaning.)

This is not to underestimate the hyperbolic *in us*: the sublime in the inward otherness that breaks out, for instance, in moments of inspiration. Artistic creativity must take form to be communicated, but the sources out of which it comes to form are beyond fully formal determination. Creativity's transcending of technique indicates a coming to form out of a being beyond oneself, being beside oneself. The hyperbolic in us is, as it were, an inward sun making us melt, making us sweat. The sweats bring a porosity wherein the very pores of our being are opened from within out, from without in. The sweats are signs of the exposure in us of the primal porosity of being.[15] We can refuse these signs, we can see them as portents of what exceeds humanness. If we consent to the porosity, there can come a breakdown of the too self-insistent *conatus*; and a breakthrough of the *passio essendi*, elemental in us and opening us to the elemental in being.

The hyperbole of aesthetic happening can cause a reversion to self, but not for purposes of securing subjectivity at home with itself. More likely, reversion stuns us out of our stupefaction with ourselves and our torpor before what is other. The sublime breaches our defenses against transcendence as other. We are not safe through ourselves, and yet, in the face of the destroying power, there may be a saving power beyond ourselves. Dismay passes into one; everything we normally hold dear is disturbed. One counts as nothing, one is as nothing. One's self-justifications are swallowed up. One is as naked as Job on the day of birth, or the day of death, or the day his flesh felt the unmerited affliction. This shattering is the unclogging of the porosity. A "yes" can come in the silence of being as nothing. Being as nothing is a boundary of the between, the other side of which is haloed with the radiance of the givenness of being as gift. There is nothing we have done to merit

---

[14]   There is an aesthetic mixing of the senses and the sensible, an equivocal synesthesia which is an intimation of what cannot be sighted or sounded. If *to kalon* resonates with a calling, we may not know what calls us, but we know we are called beyond ourselves.

[15]   This becomes more overt with the hyperbole of erotic selving: we move beyond the ordered likeness of *mimēsis* towards the transcending energy of loves, and the disturbing communication from beyond of the mania that places one beside oneself (see *AOO*, Chapter 1). In relation to otherness, *mimēsis* is perhaps more analogical, eros and mania more hyperbolic, though there are also metaphorical and symbolic indirections in them.

this gift, and yet it is given, and we ourselves, otherwise nothing, are not only recipients of this gift, our very being at all is this gratuitous gift. Religious porosity is born in this being as nothing, and there too it may be reborn in a resurrected gratitude, posthumous to the shattering of a lifetime of dissembling configurations of the *conatus*.

In the fittingness of beauty there is something of the religiously fitting. In our shattering in undergoing the sublime, there is also something fitting in what does not quite fit our finite frame. Philosophy here requires more than system: it asks for the finesse of a religious poetics. With such finesse, one detects various expressions of the call of the beyond of self-contained immanence in some of the traditional proofs. One might consider Aquinas's fifth way from the governance of the universe, or Paley's argument from design, and its many variants, or Kant's discussion of the physico-theological proof. Here Kant focuses on determinate existence rather than the indeterminate existence of the cosmological way. In Aquinas's case, providential order is at issue relative the unconscious teleology of nature. Paley's version most famously, or infamously, uses the analogy of the watch. This is not the best analogy, since it reductively configures the intermedium of being as a mechanism. Mechanical design is a sign, but as a configuration of the ethos this sign is designed to (re-)make the ethos as proportionate to our powers of making. This sign resigns the hyperbolic.

Nevertheless, we can grant the main reminder: structure of order in the artifact calls to mind analogously an artificer. Plato gives one of the most beautiful versions in the *Timaeus*: the image of the demiurge calls attention to the divine artist who wants to make the most beautiful cosmos possible, the most perfect. This cosmos itself is called an *aesthetic god (theos aesthetikos)*. Interestingly, and illuminating the equivocity we cannot here escape, resort to the aesthetics of happening can seem to lead to an *atheistic god*. Ecce Nietzsche! Earlier Nietzsche: the world-artist in the *Birth of Tragedy*, and its "aesthetic theodicy." Later Nietzsche: the world is a work of art giving birth to itself. Art alone justifies existence, but art here carries the ontological charge of will to power. Redeeming art is sacred. Early or late, "aesthetic theodicy" is the only "justification" of life Nietzsche contemplated (see *AOO*, Chapter 6).

Suppose the aesthetics of happening is seen to suggest an origin figuratively to be likened to the artist. The art of this source would not just be the technical imposition of form upon matter, but a more radical bringing to be from which both the elemental good of matter and form are themselves derived. Its *poiesis* would originate a coming to be: not just a self-becoming or selving of beings, not a mechanical ordering, not just a "forming" or self-forming, not just an organismic self-organizing, not a work of art giving birth to itself. Given this likening, this origination would be *unlike* any artistry we could adequately conceptualize, since our artistry always operates in the context of the givenness of being. This other art is hyperbolic to our artistry. We make something, we do not create it in the hyperbolic sense of bringing beings to be. Yet we can have care for the singularity of the work, and this can show something of the hyperbolic. Great art has a singularity which resists an exhaustive univocal analysis or dialectical encapsulation. In it shines forth a freshness and inexhaustibility. Mostly we think of singulars in terms of their classification by generals: human beings, not this singular, for instance. To look at the world with this love of the singular, we would have to be the embodiment of agapeic mind: loving the singular for the sake of the singular. In its love of the singular, our art can show something of agapeic mindfulness and its hyperbolic import.[16] Looked at this way, the aesthetics of singular happening puts us in mind of a source of agapeic origination.

We encounter a great work of art. We are struck by it. It seeps into our souls and makes us marvel. It frees a surge of light in us. This light is often dark, but we feel gratitude to

---

[16] See *AOO* p. 288: the artist finds access to the *passio essendi* in its promise of agapeic power to create: the artist unselves, as it were, but is also more than negative capability in drawing on the surplus of agapeic origination, giving rise to the other as other, releasing the artistic creation into its own otherness and being for itself, whereby it communicates something inexhaustible beyond itself.

the creator of this work, though we do not know this creator, though we may never meet. Still we are thankful, and would that we knew something more of the creator, perhaps more than what the work shows. We wait further revelation, as analogously we antici- pate further work from a living artist whom we have come anonymously to love. Love is the true word here. We are talking about the opening of agapeic mind to the otherness of the aesthetic happening, itself a show of agapeic creation.

An astonishing order arises within singulars and between singulars. Their commu- nity as being together is inherent in the becoming of aesthetic happening. This order is more than a dead mechanical fit. Seen with the tonic of astonishment, the beauty of that order calls forth our admiration and celebration, not just the calculation of mathemati- cal connections. Of course, the beauty in the mathematical connections transports even the *esprit de géométrie* beyond itself towards its own latent *esprit de finesse*. The *esprit de finesse* enjoys rapport with something finer, more subtle in the nature of things. This celebrating attunement to the sublime beauty of the between is on the verge of offering its prayer to the unknown creator.

Even so uptight a critical philosopher as Kant knew the power of the "physico- theological proof": it evokes the highest respect, following, as he says it does, the natural movement of our mind (*Critique of Pure Reason*, A623–4, B651–2). We walk out into the starry night and the heart is filled with longing and strange peace. We know we are almost nothing, but we do not fear. Kant responded to nature's beauty, and though later he will make of beauty a subjective formal universal, there is always the suspicion of more, indeed it becomes the symbol of the moral, and this, we know well, is the prime way he willed God. I do not slight this way, but the beauty of being shows a *more robust ontological significance* than Kant allows. Under the dominance of his transcendental turn to self, he does not do justice to the other as other, and our opening to the other in agapeic minding. This opening occurs with the aesthetics of happening, though the curve of self-transcending does not cease at the aesthetics but rises above the shown to what is suggested beyond all showing. Is this God as original source – analogical artist as above, as *huper*: God of the aesthetic whole as God beyond that open whole?

We might situate here the *appeal of the mathematical*. Mathematics has often lured thinkers by an order of being and truth, it seems, beyond equivocal transience, and not dissolved by the opinions of the day. Not surprisingly, God and mathematics have frequently been linked, and not only by modern thinkers such as Kepler and Galileo.[17] I would say: the showing in the aesthetics of happening suggests something more, not just aesthetically shown. A figuration of mathematical order is taken as a sign of a math- ematicizing source. Notice mathematical order is not the opposite of the aesthetic: math- ematicians – now, as of old among those of Pythagorean pedigree – have intimations of a surpassing order of beauty in the mathematical intelligibility, and will speak of music, or the elegance or beauty of a "proof." Thus in univocalizing, they step out of univocity.

The mathematical can reveal what we might call the *(dia)noetics of the aesthetic*: the manifestation of the beyond of the sensible in the sensible itself – the noetic in the aes- thetic. Our perplexity: *Is the intelligibility of finite intelligibility itself intelligible in finite terms?* Does it require reference to a source of intelligibility beyond itself that gives rise to the determinate intelligibles? This suggests a variation of the argument from *coming to be*: intelligibility as determinate is there as having come to be, and cannot make its own

17 Remember the interplay of the aesthetic and dianoetic relative to univocalizing God (Chapter 3). Recall Plato's artful god: he draws on both the dianoetics of geometry and the aesthetics of finesse. The artful god calls on the uses of geometry but for purposes consonant with finesse. The whole point of the making is the beauty and goodness of the cosmos. Finesse calls on a deeming of the beauty of things, and on an esteeming of their good; deeming and esteeming are more than geometrical structure. Artistic finesse and geometry, aesthetics and dianoetics, are joined in the cosmos itself as a certain icon (*eikon*, *Timaeus*, 29B). This is not far from the Pythagorean cosmos as communicating the companion- abilty of music and mathematics. The world itself is a kind of music: a song that is in being sung, and in whose songlines, sung into being, the singer is heard, unseen. Singing structures are companions of the aesthetic and dianoetic: structures of intelligibility that resonate with the (unseen) singer.

intelligibility intelligible; to make intelligible the intelligible means to appeal to a further determining source; since this cannot be our intelligence, relative to the cosmos as the aesthetics of happening, it must be other.

This consideration also tells against the mere reiteration of the surd of being: the so-called surd is not surd in itself; it is marked by highly intricate intelligibility, not explained by an ultimate surd. We have to appeal to the *huperintelligible* to throw light on the finitely intelligible, and the huperintelligible, while not completely determinable in terms of finite intelligibles, makes them to be intelligible. The intelligibility of intelligibility is an overdeterminacy in the ontological situation. As Einstein suggests, that the world of experience is comprehensible is a miracle.[18] *That beings are intelligible at all* rouses astonishment and perplexity that cannot be answered in terms of a determinate intelligibility.

A danger here is this: missing the point in getting the point. We fixate on mathematical order to the forgetfulness of perplexity about its ultimate source. Then eternal truth becomes as dead, hence ontologically incapable of doing justice to the singularity of being and especially human beings. (Shestov inveighs against *this lifeless eternity* as beloved of, idolized by philosophers. Consider Spinoza.[19]) This order points beyond to a source that, to be truer to the intelligible givenness of singulars and their community, must be hyperbolic to such a dead eternity, and is perhaps more to be likened to an agapeic origin. This would be a God who not only thinks but loves, or whose thinking, as agapeic minding, is love of singulars, of living communities, love of the intimate universal not just of the abstract. Eternity would not be a lifeless mathematical order but living, trans-temporal *energeia*, to be imaged, at the very least, in terms of what the ancients called "soul." Contra eternity as stasis, the chief characteristic of psyche was movement, indeed self-movement. We should look to communicative being.

There is nothing univocally clear about this, nor could there ever be. This follows from the nature of the aesthetics of happening. Because this is an aesthetics, it is always equivocal to some degree, and always will be. This is true even when the figuration taken as a sign of the divine is an eternal mathematical order. The poetics of the religious is at the boundary of systematics, even when systematics brings us to this boundary. There is no complete eradication of the ambiguity in clear and distinct univocity or dialectical encapsulation. Were there this eradication, there would also be the erasure of reverence and esteem for mystery.

This is what we know of a great work of art: we esteem the enigma that abides. The artwork is always, in some measure, equivocal. So is the intimation we have of the artist. We can never be absolutely sure if things are to be taken completely this way or that. Sometimes this looks like a joke (without ambiguity there is no laughter or indeed festivity). But there are also jokes we do not appreciate because they throw an unflattering light on us. Sometimes we suspect the artist is not inviting us to festivity, but laughing at us, as victims of a spectacle of cruelty. (God makes a pact with Satan to test Job. This smacks of sporting in another's suffering. What is betrayed just by allowing the test? Has Satan succeeded in sowing suspicion in the mind of *God*?)

That the aesthetics of happening never completely escapes equivocity can be understood *positively*: it allows the promise of fecundity that comes with creative ambiguity. Without this fecundity, there is no festivity, no generation beyond ourselves, no self-transcendence. A condition of the continuation of our self-transcending is the continuation of the fertile ambiguity. Perhaps the source of the aesthetic happening made it

---

[18] A. Einstein, *Sidelights on Relativity* (New York: Dover, 1983), p. 28: "How is it that mathematics, being a product of human thought which is independent of experience, is so admirably appropriate to the objects of reality?" Also A. Einstein, *Ideas and Opinions* (New York: Bonanza Books, 1954), p. 292: "The world of our sense experience is comprehensible. The fact that it is comprehensible is a miracle."

[19] See my "Philosophical Audacity – Shestov's Piety," in *Lev Shestov Journal*, 2 (Winter, 1998), pp. 45–80. Also, "God beyond the Whole: Between Shestov and Solov'ëv," in *IST?*, Chapter 5.

such, put us into the equivocal to free self-transcending that could only come alive in the chiaroscuro of the good. Were we too directly in the brilliance of the origin we would be destroyed, consumed by light. We would not be the intermediate beings we are. Mystery is a constitutive condition of being in the between.

The aesthetic configuration of the ethos may well mean that design is a sign, but this may exceed the figure of the machine and the organism. These figures may be ambiguous signs, but we must not forget what we have learned along the equivocal way (Chapter 4): the testing interplay of good and evil, sometimes their promiscuity, that also rocks us back on ourselves. Symmetry of beautiful mathematical order does not let us forget the fearful symmetry of Blake's burning tiger. Its terrible beauty shocks us into perplexity: What immortal hand or eye dare frame that fearful symmetry? Beyond God's geometry, we must find God's finesse, in and through the equivocal art of creation.

Again there is no univocal "proof." "Proof" is the misplaced demand for a univocity that betrays what is most powerful and suggestive in that aesthetics of happening, what keeps open the space of transcendence, whether that of nature as other, or our own self-surpassing, or that of the ultimate transcendence as other to us. I think the usual arguments for design make wrong claims to more univocity than is possible. This is especially evident with the analogy of the machine.[20] If the world is no such machine, our analogies cannot hitch without ado a ride on the geometrical figuration of the mechanical. Instead of seeking an inappropriate univocity, we need mindfully to read the signs. Mindfulness of signs is not the same as a mathematics of design.

The design is also a sign, but the design is itself double: constructive and destructive power together, coming to be and passing into nothing all together, intelligibility with recalcitrance to intelligence all together, goodness immense with horror unimaginable all together. This doubleness allows a Hume to exploit the skepticism inevitably bred by a misplaced univocity. This skepticism turns the doubleness of design upside down, or turns around the analogy of the artwork and infers from the immanent destruction or horror the incompetence, if not ill-purpose, of the artist. The signs of design are said to suggest a botched work, the universe the misshapen try of an apprentice God, and so on. Hume is quite right to show that any analogous argument can be turned around this way. A metaxological mindfulness of analogy knows this doubleness already, knows no way around it that escapes it completely. Unlike Hume, however, a different skeptical deciphering can serve our humility before transcendence rather than the debunking of transcendence (T³). In the between, we are in the aesthetics of happening, and there is no escape from the doubleness of the aesthetic. Even at that, the eros of self-transcendence is to be carried on that aesthetics towards openness to the origin, though we cannot univocalize that origin. The release in the aesthetics of happening signals less the failure of univocity than the freeing of further potencies of mindfulness and being, and, with this, our passage more deeply towards the enigma of the source. (Are Shakespeare's works beaten out blindly by a screeching monkey or authored by a sublime artist? How know the latter? In the end, only by love.)

There is no apodeictic certainty, Kant is right. Apodeictic certainty might be appropriate if the aesthetics of happening were univocal, but they are not. What of the moral assurance Kant claimed? Or do we need another kind of "faith," not Kant's moral faith? Relative to our moral being, more is demanded than the play of the equivocal.[21] Before turning to this, one final word about reading the signs and Aquinas on governance.

---

[20] This mechanical model has implications with respect to the counter attractiveness of pantheistic, panentheistic models. These take wing on organic generation, and are closer than mechanism to the equivocal matrix of genesis (as described in Chapter 4), thus closer to the primal ethos than the univocalizing of mechanism. Cybernetic analogies now have replaced earlier mechanical models.

[21] Hume's skeptical query cannot be answered on the level of the aesthetics of happening without taking into account the ethical, and the religious, though the aesthetics of happening has more power to move us than he acknowledges. There are bleak passages in Hume in *Dialogues on Natural Religion* suggestive of the emptiness, almost horror of existence. One thinks of Sartrean nausea.

Aquinas seems to suggests that this is more determinate than, in fact, it is. The harmony of the whole, and the teleology, seem a little too neat, the artist too efficient a creator with not enough justice done to the equivocities of aesthetic happening. Is this because the determination of teleology is too univocally held, the end an objective too firmly in the grip of certain anthropomorphic images? The overdeterminations of the between make us diffident in subscribing to such a determination of governance. We have to think of *the point of it all* metaxologically – think it out of the chiaroscuro of the between. This means thinking in terms of an overdeterminate purposiveness beyond definite purpose – an overdeterminacy often appearing as merely indeterminate to us, struggling to read the equivocal signs of aesthetic happening. Some light will be thrown on this with the further hyperboles, now to follow.[22]

GOD AND THE BETWEEN: THIRD HYPERBOLE – THE EROTICS OF SELVING

In us the doubleness of the aesthetics of happening assumes an extraordinary urgency. The human being as self is idiot, then is unfolded in aesthetic selving, and further moved by erotic selving and agapeic communicating. These latter are decisive in making us mindful of the porosity of our being, participating intimately in the passion of being, and articulating the urgency of ultimacy. As forms of self-transcending they occasion different hyperboles of the ultimate as transcendence itself. We come to the third hyperbole of erotic selving when we turn to ourselves as media to surpass the equivocity of aesthetic happening.

We risk being overwhelmed, even traumatized by this equivocity, but turning to ourselves, where is the univocal assurance of overcoming the equivocal? We too incarnate equivocity, indeed more so than any other being. Yet this is not merely negative. In us the overdeterminacy opens up an indeterminacy which allows of the freedom of self-becoming, as well as the potential for greater chaos. Look at natural happening as other: there is ordered stability to its processes, and a beauty of constancy, though the traces of God be equivocal. Look at ourselves: we are plunged into an agitated maelstrom. Where the order, where the constancy? Behold the feverish multiplication of craving, beyond the measure of nature. Behold turbulence and roil. And the field of our endeavor? A panorama of folly, extravagance, waste, soured expectancy, disgust, grim glee in the infliction of death. We heap equivocation up to heaven itself, even unto a provocation of the ultimate. Surely we should stay with nature's innocent equivocity? Equivocity become hyperbolic – such is the being of the human.

And yet this hyperbole of self-being impels us further. The excesses of "objectivity" are never enough, and bring about a rebound on the "subject." There is no escape from selving, though there may be disciplines that transform its hyperbolic equivocity, and in this mark a pathway to the divine. In and through the inner excess something more is traced in this path than can be richly enough articulated relative to the idiotic and the aesthetic. I will offer first a general, then three more particular considerations.

Or of a Pascal – but without God – such that the world becomes a "fallen" world but without a "fall." Is Hume constructing rejoinders to the design proof, drawing on, without really drawing attention to, a kind of Gnostic disgust for a broken world, a valueless thereness?

22 Our movement so far, and overall, suggests a move through the aesthetic, the dianoetic, towards the transcendental, the eudaimonistic, the transcending potencies of being. It also mirrors a move from elemental givenness, through aesthetic happening and intelligibilities towards selving and communities in which the exigences of being true and being good are mindfully served. In the first instance, the progression is presented in more simplified form than were one to articulate all the potencies, such as I outlined in *Ethics and the Between*. In the second instance, the same point holds, though here the movement is outlined more fully in Part II of *Being and the Between*, from origin, to creation, through things, intelligibilities, selves, communities, being true, being good. Could one correlate the four hyperboles with the traditional transcendentals such as being, beauty, truth, good? A good question. I could write a book on that.

General consideration: human desire and hyperbolic transcending

Human desire is sourced in transience, but, in coming to mindfulness of the equivocities of becoming, something more and other is communicated. Our selving is rooted in, as well as roots incarnately in, the equivocities of aesthetic transience. Eros reveals an upsurge of selving from these carnal roots. What surges up in selving also exceeds selving. Though eros is more than sexual desire, we see the point with sexual desire, namely our dark intimacy with aesthetic transience and our surge beyond. We are drawn to sensuous beauty, but our sensibility of living is also our being sensible of death. Out of the equivocal transience the impulse to generation reveals a passing beyond self, a will to further life beyond oneself. Our endeavor to be wills life beyond death, even one's own death. And yet all this upsurging of selving is carried by those ontological energies given as the *passio essendi*. In given creation, the creature becomes generative, but in the case of the human being the creature becomes creative in a finite form. Thus *all human exceedings beyond finite determinability* are at issue in the hyperbole of erotic selving. The equivocities of aesthetic transience are not only sensible in our bodies; they come awake in the heart, the intimate in the carnal. They offer signs of the intimate universal in our carnal selving, in our bodies beside themselves.

We turn to ourselves to mediate external equivocity and read the double signs, but we, as mediators, as readers, prove also double. Our transcending equivocity proves also equivocal. How come this second equivocity? It arises from the *overdeterminate in our being*, as creatively effective in the open indeterminacy of our freedom. The openness of our transcending cannot be fixed to causal univocal determination, or to dialectical self-determination, but reveals a resistant doubleness when it seeks to know itself. I come to stand out of the indeterminacy of becoming, but I cannot stand univocally, or just dialectically, for I can understand my own overdeterminate indeterminacy in either an affirmative or negative light.

If I view it negatively, I turn it into an indefiniteness in which I may luxuriate, or will to overcome. *Luxuriate*: I pursue its feverish equivocity, but merely drift in the indecision of indefiniteness. This luxuriating remains closest to the aesthetic, reaching its apogee in diversion with endless possibility, deeply explored by Kierkegaard to its outcome as despair; despair deplored if no further step is taken beyond the indefinite disport that will not earnest itself. *Will to overcome*: I toil to dispel my indefiniteness as a lack that, through my own powers of determination, I strive to turn into a satisfying outcome. Now I am driven erotically forward in a self-becoming that progressively becomes a self-determining, and in which I seek my goal(s) as giving me some more articulated wholeness of being. This latter way of erotic self-transcending goes beyond self as lacking towards what is other, through which it seeks to be fulfilled and come into its own wholeness. Seeking God thus, I think I will find God in the future, or perhaps postpone the seeing until the other world.

If I view the (overdeterminate) indeterminacy more affirmatively, I may be either taken up with the equivocal plenitude of presentness or seek in that plenitude signs of the (over)origin of the given surplus of being. The first possibility suggests a kind of *mystical hedonism*, in which the kingdom of heaven is just the right dwelling in finitude. The sweetness of its pleasure passes finite saying: a sacred "being pleased." The second possibility, by contrast, offers more fully the intimation that my own indeterminacy is an overdetermination, but one that points back to its (over)origin in an overdeterminacy that cannot be called my own. Instead of driving forward out of lack to the end of wholeness, I dwell with the present in heed of its *(huper)archē*. I read the doubleness of my own being as an equivocal sign of the surplus of divine overdetermination. I am put into question: Am I an overdeterminate indeterminacy just because I am a pointer to the *(huper)archē*; an exceeding of selving beyond self, because selving is pointed towards the *archē* as overdetermined in a hyperbolic sense? If so, neither selving nor *archē* are a lack of being seeking its own fulfillment through transcending. There is an other transcending not from lack but surplus, and that communicates out of itself, not for purposes of mediating with itself, but for going to the other as other. This transcendence is not lack completing itself, it is surplus giving out of self, giving for the other as other, as well as for selving. This is the way of agapeic self-transcending.

Given the doubleness of selving, both the erotic and agapeic ways are needed: the first negative way as an apophatic transcending through lack and nothingness, aided by meta-phor and symbol; the second affirmative way as a kataphatic transcending through the surplus of pluperfection, carried by analogy and hyperbole. These two are not entirely on a par: as the overdeterminate is more ontologically primordial than the indeterminate, agapeic transcendence is more ultimate than erotic, just as also the negative way is not possible without some implicit actuality of the affirmative. Both these ways are *beyond objectifiable determination or subjectifiable self-determining*. Neither is intent on reducing God or selving to any objectifiable determination or subjectifiable self-determination.

I try to put a more human shape on this. I face the world and am aroused to celebrate its source, but when I encounter the ambiguity of the happening, I cannot be sure I see the face of the source there. I take heart from the possibility that through inwardness I will see that face, but when I turn to the heart, I find this even more equivocal. If I do not give up and try to see it through, in the heart I am made porous to the work of love. What is this strange ferment of secret love? Eros drives me beyond my own lack in an urgency seeking the ultimate other. Agape draws me more deeply into the heart to find the effective work of a source more ultimate that I am myself. What does the heart metaphorically name? The most intimate reserve of our self-transcending – in search of transcendence as other; and yet companioned within by an *incognito* communication of the other transcendence it seeks. We could not erotically seek at all, were not the effec-tive urgence of the other transcendence already wooing in selving, calling to selving, and bringing back selving to transcendence itself, itself that never left and that always was available for us as other to it. We divine the doubleness as not only our own immanent duality, but as intimating the absolved relativity of our transcending to transcendence as other. And this, whether we are oriented beyond our present limited form, or returned more intensively into our own original ground. The immanent equivocity of our inti-mate being is a plurivocal sign of an immanent community of human self-transcendence and transcendence as other; an immanent community that can never be reduced just to immanence. In the inner equivocity of our own immanent selving we find ourselves awakening to what is beyond ourselves, awakening in the communication of the intimate universal.

First particular consideration: the ontological way and immanent excess

Think of the above with reference to the *ontological proof* in its "Anselmian" more than Cartesian or Kantian form. Remember the milieu of Anselm's "proof" as one of prayer and meditation. This is the inner way, qualified by the discipline of religiously educat-ing the maelstrom of desire. Consider our thinking as a continuation of this discipline, and not as something strange to it. Prayer and thought can pass into one another. *Fides quaerens intellectum* might reflect an urge of prayer to become thought, but perhaps equally there is an urge of thought that, at certain limits, becomes porous to the passion of praying (see *IST?*, Chapter 3).

Consider the transcending power of *reason itself* as one expression of the hyperbolics of selving. Reason is a self-transcending power to be beyond itself, in openness to what is other. It is not self-determining simply: there is a *passio* of reason, an erotics of reason. The Greeks knew this when granting the eros of philosophy itself. Yet reason's equivoc-ity is the equivocity of the human being itself: its *conatus essendi* can seek to overcome its *passio essendi* and *assert itself hyperbolically* as absolutely self-determining. From a metaxological perspective, this is untrue to selving and reasoning, since it sends into recess what the *passio essendi* communicates: the being given to itself of thinking, and the excess of the enigmatic origin in the immanence of thought itself. The "Anselmian" ethos is truer to the human doubleness here important, and to the original patience of our reason. Prayer keeps open the elemental porosity and even can be like the advent of astonished thought: thought so astonished by what it thinks it seems to be laid asleep in reverence. Such thought is like prayer become perplexed at the mystery before it. What does perplexity here find unavoidable? The thought of that which nothing greater can be conceived. Thus Anselm's definition of God.

I rephrase the matter. Suppose thought thinks itself, and explores the inner abyss of itself, what does it come upon? The thought of what is in excess of all excesses. In the exploration of thought thinking itself the thought of what is other to thought emerges. The overdeterminate thought of what is radically other to determinate thought emerges in the immanent self-exploration, even self-determination, of thought itself. If you call this other a being, this is equivocal. For us a being is a determinate existence, but this could not be that kind of other being, since it surpasses all finite determination, and is unsurpassable by anything at all. One temptation with the ontological proof is a transcendental univocity in which we determinately reduce to self-determining thought both the overdetermination of the thought itself and of the other thought by it. The logical facility with which the argument can be turned this way and that, in this regard, can be a distortion of what is ingredient in the truer import of the argument, namely, to destroy the pretensions of that kind of logicist facility.

Whether or not my rephrasing is identical with Anselm's intentions, it does not coincide with Descartes's. Did Kant have some repressed inkling of it that returned as moral earnestness? Hegel had some feel for the movement of the argument, but, instead of dwelling metaxologically with the equivocity, he constructs his own dialectical equivocation concerning immanence in his speculative inclusion of all otherness in thought thinking itself. The thought of God revealed by the immanent exploration of thought shatters any logicist or panlogist illusion. (Did this tempt Anselm? Certainly it tempted Hegel. By contrast, consider Augustine: *Si comprehendis, non est Deus.*) The thought of the unsurpassable humbles us as it exalts us. Just as unsurpassable, the thought makes impossible that transcendental or speculative univocity in which we think we are identical with the divine. This latter is conceptual hubris, not the hyperbole of the being greater than which none can be thought. *The hyperbole of this thought of God shatters in immanence itself the illusion of self-contained immanence.*

Otherwise expressed: the ontological proof, just in its truth, shatters the illusion of "proof," whether determinate and self-determining, whether univocal or dialectical. It brings us into the company of the incontrovertibility of the divine excess, an incontrovertibility that is never the outcome of any proof because it is the *incognito* necessity that precedes and exceeds every proof. The ontological proof is right about the incontrovertibility of the thought, but even this incontrovertibility remains shrouded in enigma, just because of its unsurpassable excess, and hence for us it is never entirely free from the equivocal. Even in the inescapability of God, we find no escape from the equivocal.

Nevertheless, something does seem to call to us beyond the merely equivocal, and beyond the aesthetic show of happening and inwardness. I mean *the difference of good and evil* and the charge we find laid upon us to be good to the utmost extent possible. Dwelling in this perplexity is not just aesthetic, as it is not logicist or panlogist; out of the ambiguity of mystery the incontrovertible call of the good emerges. Considering this as an ambiguous manifestation of the agape of being, one ventures: The overdetermined origin gives itself as good, and gives being as good, even in the aesthetics of happening; in the aesthetic equivocality of our own transient being, this presentiment of the agape of the good begins to wake up in us; we become aware of the call of the agape, though we more normally call it the moral sense, or some such. This is not just something that we experience, it is already given as constitutive of our being, by "nature," not by "convention" simply, though nurture will shape the call – in fact, sometimes smother or corrupt it. Even though we are free to controvert the call of the good, the call is incontrovertible, for every fidelity or defection takes places within the broadcast of its original givenness. The character of such an incontrovertibility that frees us is important for how we see the moral way.

Second particular consideration: the ethical exigence

How see this way? We find ourselves before, or in, the incontrovertible call of the good. There is a sense in which the difference of good and evil is irreducibly given to us; we find ourselves in this difference, we do not first produce it. We may not originally know what it means, but it makes us to be the kinds of being we are, before we make ourselves into this kind of person or that. We may come to determine this to be good, or that, but our determination takes place in the space of a more original difference of good and evil. This more original difference is communicated in the porosity of our being to good, in our reception of the good of the "to be," indeed in our very being itself as received from and into the good of the "to be." Our original patience here to the good-ness of being is spontaneously lived by us, in that our living at all is itself an affirming of the good of the "to be," a good prior to and more original that this good or that good, whether determined as such and such by us, or not. This more original difference points to a sense of good (and perhaps evil) in excess of determinacy, for it is not this good or that good, and in excess of our determination and self-determination, for these are empowered in the ethos of its original givenness. Communicated in an original porosity that endows the openness and exceeding of our self-transcending, it is in excess of our self-transcendence, even as it emerges to be minded in our self-transcendence. We are in the communication of the good, but not at all the ground of our being in the good. We are called to be good, and we are good, but we are not the good, the good that endows us and calls us to be good.

What is this other good over which none has mastery? Not easy to say, since it exceeds objectification and subjectification. But it is not nature as aesthetic happening: nature as aesthetic happening does not give *this* call. There is something disproportionate about this other call as emergent in the porosity of immanent selving, and as summoning beyond the equivocality of aesthetic being, even as it emerges for us in that equivocality. Further, we are not the source of that summons for it sources the kinds of being we are, as called to be ourselves in ethical selving. If our ethical self-transcending is something hyperbolic, there is something even more hyperbolic about this solicitation of the good. There is an other origin of this call, an origin that to be proportionate to the summons of the good must be disproportionate to what it gives. Can that source be called God?

The givenness of the original difference of good and evil and the vocation to be good reflect an ethical qualification of the porosity of the between: its openness to what gives it to be, and its "to be" as good. There is an original patience and receiving in this, but it is fitting to remember that *the urgency of ultimacy* takes noteworthy form with the ethical. The ethical is beyond just playing with possibilities; we are not dealing with any-thing optional; there is an urgency about the ethical that is ultimate; there is no side-step-ping it. Contemplation of nature, aesthetic cultivation, seem less exigent, can sometimes be taken up or not, but we cannot avoid the ethical, its urgency of ultimacy. It is not incidental that with modernity's devaluation of nature, and its elevation of praxis over contemplation, this moral way should have recommended itself more than before. I do not endorse the devaluation or the elevation, but that the moral way is of great moment I do not deny.

There is a related urgency of ultimacy about the enigma of evil. It stuns us into thought – thought that cannot be the measure of itself, or of the evil. There is an inescapable sin-gularity involved in this urgency: I am called, not mankind in general. This is the idiocy of an existential importunity. Yet all are thus singularly called – in the intimate universal. This is the idiocy of an existential opportunity. This singularity is very important regard-ing the idiocy of evil as monstrous. Finally, this monstrousness tortures our hearing of the call of the good. It implicates our agony over the agape of the origin, forcing from us the cry: But is the origin good? We each may have to sweat blood with this torment-ing question, urgently and as singulars, each of us suffering, like Jesus, our own night in Gethsemane garden.

I approach the point from a different angle. Suppose some sense of inherent good is emergent with human selves. How account for this inherent good? The world of nature does not answer, for though nature is not devoid of value, it is not *this* value, though it is hospitable to this value. There is no answer to the question, if being is not inherently hospitable to value. Yet this value is not any value, it relates to the infinite worth of the singular self. This infinite worth is hyperbolic and unsurpassable, surpassing as infinite even the good of finite nature. Can the human being be the answer? It seems not. For the being of the human is already given the charge of this sense of the good. An other transcendence itself good seems to be the only source on a par with the value at issue: only an unconditional good that as disproportionate can offer a proportionate way to think the ground of this good – though these very proportions are themselves analogies, hence also disproportions. This point will come back.

I try again. I do not say so much that morality leads to God as that the exigence of the ethical, in the unconditional requirement made, is hard to make sense of short of invoking God, and not just at the end but anonymously at work all along. How else make sense of the unconditional requirement? If we only think of the end, we will stress an erotic seeking of God as the goal of morality, and thus of morality as leading to a religion, perhaps like Kant. If we think the other way, we ponder an *incognito* agapeic effectiveness of the origin, as giving us our being as free, though free to revolt against the origin, and the good of given being, as well as our being as free to revolve back upon the origin as surging into its call, both in our freedom and the charge of the good that is effective in our freedom. Out of this second way, a different ethical eros emerges for us to be freely good, to be ourselves sources of agapeic origination towards the other. It is hard to make any intelligible sense of the hyperbolic dimensions of all this if our ethical being is entirely out of community with the nameless goodness of God.

I emphasize that none of this is to be proved abstractly. Such "proof" would be an abstraction from a process ongoing in ethical selving and the secret communications of the intimate universal. In that process elemental affirmations or refusals are involved in our most intimate willingness. These elementals bring us back from the heights of speculative reason, merely theoretical, so-called. So far Kant is not wrong. But the matter is not just practical. For ethical practice is mediated by mindfulness, just as mindfulness is shaped in its openness by ethical integrity, and just as the integrity of both the openness and mindfulness is nourished by living fidelity to the original patience of our being. A corruption in one infects the other. We must do justice to this original patience of being: a "doing justice" that is a prior fidelity neither merely theoretical nor practical.[23] At stake, at one extreme, is our keeping unclogged the more original porosity of our being, and at the other extreme, the fullness of selving, expressed in both our being ethical and in our being mindful. Metaphysics and ethics cannot be separated.

These remarks show the ontological and moral ways to have something in common, namely reference to an origin in excess of what can be determined by the given powers of immanent self-transcendence. There is an excess in inwardness that is not of inwardness. There is a transcendence in self-transcendence that is not of self-transcendence. It is more, it is above, it is hyperbolic. While it is "with" (the *sun* of symbol) the selving, it is still not completely proportionate to selving (analogy), and yet what we try to say of it comes from what is richest in self-transcending (as metaphorical, as carrying across). Normally, the ontological way is said to be theoretical, the moral way practical. This opposition cannot be final with respect to the intimation of excessive transcendence emerging either in thought or in the charge on our willingness: in thought – the other to thought thinking itself; in willingness – the other to the will willing itself. This other other is communicated in the summons of the unconditional good that is not our good or the good for us, and that can never be completely determined in any relativization for us.

---

[23] "Doing Justice and the Practice of Philosophy," *Proceedings of the ACPA*, Vol. 79, 2005, pp. 41–59.

Once again there is a fidelity to the original patience of our being prior to the normal contrast of theory and practice.

This "reading" of the moral way has a rebound effect on the ontological way. The presentiment of the hyperbolic good brings us closer to the sense of "being greater than which none can be conceived." The notion of the "greatest" is most richly concentrated in the being of the unconditional good. Suppose this is the "concept" of God that is to be found within thought, and not just as an abstract idea but as an absolving (hyper)origin immanently working in the ferment of human selving in its own being for itself? What is at issue is the being of the good at work in our being and in excess of our being, such as we come to know in the agape of being, as intimated in the between, marvelous in the "that it is," sung in the aesthetics of happening, energized, communicated, and loved in our erotic transcending. We as mindful, as thought, can be woken up to this companioning good, most unavoidably relative to the ethical, but not confinable to the ethical, and asking of us a refreshed religious willingness.

This is to take a different tack to Kant, not only on the moral way, but also the onto-logical. Kant's moral way points to God as the postulated ground of coincidence of happiness and virtue. This coincidence means that we are to enjoy happiness in exact proportion to the merit we have earned as virtuous beings. Moral earnestness must earn its merit, and God will reward it with its due happiness. It has paid its dues, it will be paid its due. Kant insinuates here a troubling instrumentalization of God. Like many, he was horrified that the wicked in this life often are quite blithe, while the virtuous toil and endure. Is this not an offense to reason? And is it to stand? Kant's postulates serve to soften the offense – over on the other side of death. In Kant's motioning to the other side, I detect the erotics of practical reason, the hyperbolics of moral selving, as exceeding the bounds of finitude. Still one has to ask, why should God underwrite the *proportional justice* Kant takes to be the proper measure? Such a God must be reasonable according to the Kantian measure. Indeed, this God risks being a means for the implementation of *our* proportionate measure. If so, in Kant's way of thinking, the hyperbole of our ethical selving serves *morally to reconfigure* the hyperbole of God, and there is to be *no more divine hyperbolics*. We moralize the disproportion of the divine, and there will be no more scandal of disproportion. Then *our* demurral comes: Why should the divine finesse be confined by our rationalized measure of proportionate reward or retributive justice? Is this judge the eternal surrogate for the resentment of the virtuous, robbed now of their reward here, compensated then with recompense there? Is divine justice, then, the revenge of wretched virtue? Nietzsche claimed to smell such vengeance: "the categorical imperative *reeks* of cruelty." Nietzsche's judgment reeks of its own cruelty, but whatever else, Kant's God is not a God of mercy, and even less a God of the festive agape of being. Kantian reason, whether human or divine, keeps the ledger of merit and demerit, and the day of reckoning will come, reckoning calculated according to an exact proportionate measure. Kant's God governs the moral order according to a strict and righteous univocity.

This means that the hyperbolic in goodness is shunned. Kant cannot grant God as agapeic transcendence who gives according to a measure beyond measure, a measure not proportioned to our measure of moral reckoning. Jesus's parable of the vineyard reveals to us something superior. It witnesses to the hyperbolic good. The master of the vineyard gives to all according to a measure of justice, but his giving is not exhausted by the measure of proportionate justice. There is a giving in excess of proportionate justice. This is an agapeic giving that offers no why for itself, beyond the goodness of excessive generosity itself. And this is not just mercy, as the setting in abeyance of the strictures of justice. It is in excess even of that mercy, for it is nothing but generous giving, even when the other is sunk in radical evil, not sunk but snarling at the giver in profane provocation.

There is horror to this thought – not wonder, not perplexity, but horror – that the ultimate measure of the good so exceeds our measure that goodness looks like an almost reckless disregard of justice. We would prefer a God more measured to our measure. In seeking a way to God through ourselves, we can end up with God measured to our proportions. But if that way lies via the hyperbolic in us, we must make way for a measure not tamely proportioned to us. This way seems to risk a dangerous anthropomorphism, even the righteous anthropomorphism of Kantianism. The way of the hyperbolic rather issues in a reversal: a turn back, a return that becomes a turn about, a being turned upside down. The sense of the excessive measure turns the human measure outside in or downside up. This excessive measure is the measure of our exceeding. We are ourselves an excessiveness, but we are not this measure. Instead of projecting ourselves into the heavens, we find ourselves creatures of a heaven that, in being with us, always exceeds our finite measure, even our potential for infinite self-exceeding. The heavens are not just in us, we are in the heavens, embraced in the excess of the divine that cannot be called inner or outer, higher or lower, for it is everywhere, and it is nowhere, and perhaps even in hell.

Third particular consideration: excess and evil

Hell brings me to my third particular consideration. One might speak of the "proof" from evil, though there is no proof, only a way of metaxological mindfulness that shows us to be always in extremis and, so to say, tethered to God. For there is something hyperbolic about evil. The horror of evil floods into mindfulness and we humans alone are devastated with this. Even if we do not do the evil, we are wasted by the evil power of humanity. It is a shame on us all, though that is not the present point, but rather a perplexed horror, suffered at the edge of despair relative to what we are. Normally, evil is said to be the great stumbling block to religious faith. The arguments are well known. How could a good God tolerate the evils that happen? If all powerful, God could prevent evil. If all good, God would prevent evil. Yet evil happens. Our choice seems to be: power without goodness, or goodness without power. And is it often not the seeming impotence of the good that drives many to despair about God, or to suspect malice? Is it not often that the same despair drives others to embrace power without goodness, and usurp the right of might in the world? The disjunction of power and the good states an equivocity that can engender the despair of faith or the revolt of defiance – itself a despair, continuing the first despair.

Can we finally make sense of the horror, the perplexity, the despair outside of the unavoidability of God? Is it only because God is, that evil is the monstrous perplexity it is? Were God not, would there be a problem of evil at all? If there is a determinate problem, the solution will be also determinate. Evil is not just a determinate "problem." Something about it exceeds determinacy and self-determination. Is this not why there is something hyperbolic about it? Here the hyperbolics of evil have everything to do with a *self-absolutizing* of the erotics of selving: a hyper-activation of the *conatus essendi* that absolutely revolts against any given patience of being. Instances of the extreme: Satan is sublime – Milton's Satan – sublime in revolt – and revolting, even if sublime. Satan: the sublime evil of the erotics of selving, in the usurped sovereignty that counterfeits God. Ahab is sublime – Melville's Ahab – erotics of selving bordering the infernal in Ahab's monomaniacal hatred of the hunted Moby Dick – Moby Dick, the white monster, the blank Leviathan, also hyperbolic and sublime, but whether in evil or innocence remains in mystery.

Evil as hyperbolic is not a problem at all, in the sense of a determinate difficulty. It is a fundamental mystery, an enigmatic perplexity, unavoidable for us yet in certain respects insoluble for us. Still evil calls us to deeper, troubled, mindfulness again and again. Even then we cannot think it: we flinch from it. It fills us with dread. Not only are we afraid of evil, we are affrighted about *even thinking* too much on it, for the mind can be overthrown by the pondering of its crushing burden. And yet we must think and be crushed.

Something about evil is idiotic in its monstrousness. Even if we are the source of evil, or one of its sources, we are not proportionate to it. It reveals a dark excess at work in us, ever beyond our complete mastery. Sometimes we seem in the grip of evil: we cannot shake off its sinister equivocity. The recoil of horror before evil is disproportionate to any finite determinate happening. Our being in evil, our recoil from being in evil, and – it must be confessed – even our relish in evil, have an excessive character, on any measure of natural finitude. Does our knowing of the monstrousness of evil find anything like a fitting analogy in the serenity of natural violence and death? Why then wear oneself thin with despair about evil? Animals do not despair; they are defeated. We are not defeated, and yet we despair. We seem supremely successful, and still we despair. Why? Why relish the power of life and death, and especially the power of death? Animals do not relish the power of death. We do. Why? There is no problem of evil in the animal kingdom. The problem of evil is much more than a problem. If evil were a finite determinate problem we could solve it with measures appropriate to us. There is no solution to the problem of evil, for the mystery of iniquity is hyperproblematic. The only solution, it seems, is salvation, but we cannot save ourselves.

The horror is secreted in the *inward otherness* of our selving – here the excess in self of selving that turns to the infernal. Who doubts that human beings can be infernal, but can we make sense of the infernal outside of religion? Is being mindful of evil inseparable from being mindful of God: God as either violated, or horribly turned away, or withheld in the midst of being we otherwise would think of as good? This is sometimes secretly so, secret even to most determinate formations of selving. Evil is a spoiling and despoiling, but were there no good to be de-spoiled there would be no question of evil at all. It is said evil is a refutation of God, but it rather seems that without God there is no enigma of evil at all – evil certainly in the hyperproblematic, hyperbolic sense. One does not say God is, because evil is, but rather because evil is, one must say God is. One recalls Aquinas: *Si malum est, Deus est.* Said succinctly in reply to the pointed question of Boethius: *Si Deus est, unde malum?*

Further: even if God is, we cannot sidestep the question of the power of the good, or its impotence. Evil seems to show us the impotence of the good, or the indifference of the divine amounting almost to an evil itself. Should we then turn from this divine impotence and grow our own power, such that we willingly will to be power – without the good? That option has been taken up. The issue looks otherwise from an agapeic viewpoint and the letting of freedom that marks its giving. There is a freedom of the good that, from a certain point of view, looks like impotence – and yet such forbearance from force is not powerless. Highest power might not be unilateral self-assertion but an empowering of what is other: an agapeic letting be. The letting be might seem to look like an indifference, amounting to evil, in the sight of mortals. Yet the mystery of the letting be is of the same (hyperbolic) order as the enigma of evil itself.

Agapeic letting be creates a space of openness for finite freedom: finite freedom is empowered with the highest possibility of self-transcending, and so is itself the promise of being agapeic. That space of empowered openness witnesses to the porosity of the between and the allowance of both the *passio essendi* and the *conatus essendi*. In that space the multiple possibilities of the equivocal germinate, including the being for itself of the finite. As let be for itself, the finite being can stand over against the source that lets it be as free and other. The finite human being can turn against finite creation and will to be the mastering power over it, and out of the known insecurity of its own equivocal finitude. Its *conatus essendi* overrides its *passio* and it revolts against any patience to an ultimate other than itself. Its very urgency of ultimacy can turn into the hubris *to be God*. Let be as free, our freedom in the equivocal is potentially monstrous, indeed infernal. The extremest freedom is the freedom to will to be God, and this freedom is itself allowed or let be by the agapeic origin. This allowance is the highest daring: a hyperbolic endowment of the finite creature. It is a freedom that always tempts us: as idiotic selves we taste the deepest intimacy with our own being, and we would that our being were itself divine. It is, in a derived way, already divine, but it is not God.

This is the hyperbolic paradox: *it is out of greed for eternal life that hell is created*. The gift of being is not wanted as a gift; it is willed to be by the being who is first let be, and always given to itself. Hell is the will to be one's own creator and creation in one, and by the denial that anything at all is given to one, least of all one's own self. Hell is the fiction of absoluteness that ontological ingratitude secretes. It is the figment of nothing such ingratitude creates for itself. This is the counterfeit redoubling of God's creation: the construction of a nothing masquerading as a world that would be devoid of agapeic self-transcendence. The divine irony is that this very construction is given allowance by the gift of agapeic transcendence spurned.

Does this agapeic transcendence suggest a source that is beyond good and evil? Yes, in this regard. The agapeic origin cannot be fully determined in the terms of a determinate morality of good and evil such as is generally proportionate to our finite measure. Kant was averse to this transmoral possibility. There is a power of the good that possibilizes beyond good and evil, but it is so beyond because it is an excessive good relative to the moralization of the good. We cannot be the measure of it; we are measured by it, even though we mostly do not know this and are oblivious to the way we are let be by this excessive good.

What I say might seem reminiscent of Nietzsche, but it is very different. His rejection of the Kantian moral God shows the obverse inability to think the origin agapeic. I do not urge: Pray, bow now to Nietzsche's monster, that something we know not what, that nothing perhaps, beyond good and evil. Nietzsche's monster of will to power – this is another *parodia sacra*, produced in the dimension of the hyperbolic. Did Nietzsche prefer to love a self-produced "nothingness" rather than the agapeic good? By his own proclamation, Nietzsche's origin is a monster of will to power beyond good and evil. There is a priority of power to the good: the good is an instrumentality of will to power, and will to power knows no good, no evil; the latter are human constructions, themselves products of secret will to power. What if the origin is not will to power beyond good and evil, but agapeic power beyond our good and evil, power as agapeic that is itself good in an excessive sense? Agapeic power, while hyperbolic, unlike the monster of will to power, makes possible the freedom of the finite other as other; indeed in that transcendence of the origin to creation, it makes possible a community of the good in creation itself.

Will to power wills nothing but will to power: it wills its own self-augmentation. There is no radical letting be of the other as other; there is no goodness to the creation as other and for itself; it too is the self-augmentation of will to power willing itself; and the human being is will to power become incarnate, and wills itself in willing its will to power. As a transcending, such will to power is an erotic self-absolutizing process, turned into itself, turned from the agapeics of being, such that the good of the other finally is dissolved back into the will to power that wills itself. When we seek nothing but hyperbolically to augment ourselves as will to power the otherness of the divine must also be enfolded back into our will to power willing itself. In the vanishing of this difference, we seem to become God, but we really implode and are shattered into a thousand fragments. "I am not a man, I am dynamite" – this is the buffoonery of the sacred: the self-deifying duna-mis alone, exploding into nothing. The counterfeit doublings of these *parodia sacra* are heroically unhinged. This divine madness is just mad madness – perhaps infernal. For the soul can be stunned, and not always with sacred astonishment. We seem to be beyond good and evil, but we have stepped beyond into amoral evil. We have missed or betrayed the divine agape that is the good beyond moral good and evil.

GOD AND THE BETWEEN: FOURTH HYPERBOLE – THE AGAPEICS OF COMMUNICATION

I come to the *fourth hyperbole*. The false self-absolutizing of the erotics of selving is evil, but evil itself brings us to the boundary of erotic selving where, to save the goodness of being, a renewed patience to the agapeics of communication is solicited. While the erot-ics of selving testifies to the urgency of ultimacy, the agapeics of community witnesses to the porosity of being between, but with the stress on a *com-passio essendi* whose ethical promise is redeemed in the service of being good. There is a surplus generosity in being good which is the *incognito* promise of all ways of being good, most redeemed as a promise when human beings give themselves over to the living of agapeic service. In that this surplus has something hyperbolic to immanence as such, is there something about it that communicates of the divine as the *nec plus ultra* of this redeeming promise?

In a general sense, the fourth hyperbole bears on the *metaxological relativity of community beyond immanent self-mediating totality*. The communicative intermediation between self and other manifests an *excess in relativity* which is irreducible to any *ex post facto* aggregation of a many or to any holism of inclusive self-mediation through others. This excess in relativity means that the intermediation between self-mediating beings cannot itself be just a more inclusive self-mediation when these beings have the inexhaustible promise of infinitude. The between as a togetherness of such beings is likewise inexhaustible because these beings are *communicative in excess of self-mediation*. Granting such an exceeding community, beyond subjectification and objectification, beyond any immanently self-determining totality, what endows its possibility, what originates its promise? The overdetermination of this communication of inexhaustibility also communicates to us something of the primal ethos beyond our finite determinations and configurations, beyond our self-determinations. We find ourselves here in the hyperbolic dimension of absolving relativity. We are called not only to mindfulness of this relativity but to what exceeds even its excess, its endowing origin.

I remark first on the general point about being between as community. Second, I revisit the ontological way, as suggestive of such a community as incarnating a sign of transcendence as other. Third, I ask about God and the worth of being. Fourth, I ask about God with respect to ethical community and its ground (this is different to the worth of being *simpliciter*). These considerations are connected to what is immanent in all the other hyperboles but which is here most overt – namely, the good of the "to be." This is communicated to and in finitude; its promise is ethically and religiously enacted in our being good in the community of agapeic service. Does the community of agapeic service – as the hyperbole of the generosity whose giving *is* goodness – incarnate an overflowing sign of the overdeterminate God?

What/who endows community?

First, the metaxological sense articulates being in the between as a community of the plurality of open integrities of self-transcending being. This community is not a formation, after the fact, of beings first given to be as fully for themselves. They are given to be for themselves, but the first giving is a communication of being, and from the first giving they are communicative beings, and hence in immediate rapport with beings other than themselves. Community is elemental, not a derivative. Even if it points to a further fullness to come, it is still elemental as given. If it were not so given, how could any further promise be redeemed? Beings are not monadic but communicative; their selvings are self-transcending and embody communicative power, more or less extensive and intensive, depending on ontological endowment. The togetherness of beings in the universal impermanence of creation and the inherent communicative being of the beings who are together, these do not *create* the elemental community. Rather they are created as and in the elemental community; this community is given with the being given of the beings to themselves. But if nothing finite in the between gives the elemental community, and the community is, who or what endows this community?

To use a language not altogether right: this community is *a priori* – it is given from the origin. In Leibnizian terms, again not altogether right, there is an enigmatic kind of pre-established harmony. This language is perhaps too determinate, for the givenness of the community is overdeterminate, hence hyperbolic. That things are communicative in their being, that they are together, this is astonishing. What gives this overdeterminate community of finite beings in the between? Any answer in terms of finitude itself which makes this community an after the fact togetherness, or an adventitious collection, or the random emergence of order from chaos starts too late. Community is "being with," given from the origin. Community is an ontological happening, always already at work in the universal impermanence, where what is opposed is in relation, where things hold together even in falling apart, where being together is also an absolving letting. There is a more universal togetherness in the becoming of beings, pointing to a more original communication in the coming to be of being.

Does this community of the between then speak of another hyperbolic communication of the between by its origin? What then is this origin as a giving source? Must the origin be itself communicative being, at the very least proportionate to, though really disproportionate to, the community as given, given as the between, indeed given as hyperbolic in some of the senses above suggested? For community is a cum-unity: a "being with" of unities, a togetherness of integrities of being, not just one whole. Such a kind of togetherness points beyond immanent holism in every whole of immanence. The community of the between is the togetherness of open wholes, sustained as integral in an absolving letting, rousing for us astonishment before the openness of the immanent "whole," and making us wonder if the togetherness of the community of immanent being reveals a primal porosity to the communication of an origin or good hyperbolic to the immanent "whole." In the points to follow I explore this further.

Community and the ontological way

Second, I revisit the ontological way, but my point is not quite traditional. For it is just with respect to the meaning of *community* that this way might be understood otherwise. The traditional view often sees the ontological way as not really getting beyond a kind of subjectivity, albeit one engaged with an exalted concept of God within its conceptual thinking. This is not quite it. Before, I suggested we reconsider the thought of the excess of the "greatest"; now, and more importantly, we must reconsider it in relation to community. I mean that the power of the ontological way is just *its dwelling on a consummate relation, or an ultimate togetherness*: the ultimate togetherness of God with the mindfulness that comes to wakefulness in human selving. It is the being of the human to be communicative, but its communicative being finds itself in an inescapable community with ultimate communicative being. We come to the community in the ontological intimacy of human being, community given in the intimate soul but calling us beyond ourselves, above ourselves. Such a community is fitting for being religious as dwelling in the intimate universal, beyond merely isolated subjectivity and merely neutral, homogenous universality. The intimate universal is hyperbolic to self-enclosed subjectivity and any objectifying universality. The ontological way does not *establish* this community. Rather, it wakes up to mindfulness of community already always in play. That is why there is porosity and patience in this way: we awake to something excessive being given. (Something religiously analogous happens in the porosity of prayer.) In that regard, this way does not appeal to so-called "empirical experience," for its truth is not pieced together after the fact, *a posteriori*. If there is "experience" here, it is a hyperbolic undergoing in the intimacy of immanent inwardness, and in virtue of what we are as given to be. In language not quite right, an ultimate *a priori* community is entailed by the mindful communicative being of the human being.

Mindfulness is itself in a communication of being, a community with what exceeds our self-determination. Here the metaxological emphasis enters: it is never to the point

---

[24]   The Hegelian rendition of the ontological way does not always guard enough against this, and so contains the recessive genes that will engender Feuerbach – a true son of Hegel, not a stepson, a son who not so recessively constructs the paradigm of many approaches to religion since Hegel. It is not that Hegel directly reduces God to our self-mediation, it is that our movement to God and God's movement to us both instantiate self-mediation in and through their own other, hence both movements are speculatively the same, as expressing the full life of the absolute as the absolute self-mediation of the Whole mediating with itself through its own other. Hyperbolic transcendence evaporates in this absolute Whole of wholes. On Hegel and the ontological argument, see *Hegel's God*, pp. 93–8.

to reduce God to our self-mediation;[24] rather the reverse, it is to show that we are always in community with the ultimate other, community not the product of our self-mediation, indeed always disproportionate to our powers of constitution. We do not constitute this community, we are constituted in it. This strikes home when we think about communicative being in terms of metaxological intermediation. The ontological way calls for a kind of metaxological rumination and anamnesis. Rather than the reduction of the ultimate other to our proportions, metaxological anamnesis undergoes the reverse: what is at work in us always exceeds our proportionate constitution. (This "reverse" will come back to haunt us again.)

The ontological way is a way of immanence, but *this immanence itself turns out to offer us an intimate symbol/hyperbole of transcendence as other to our own self-transcendence.* The meaning of the most intimate immanence is just transcendence as communicative being. But this transcendence is communicated in excess of our self-transcendence. We do not think of God and then, after thinking, try to make up a community with God. The thinking is always and already in that community, though it may not know that, and even though it may not recognize that, or may indeed entirely reject the suggestion of being in that ultimate community. The ontological way is a waking up to the "yes" to disproportionate transcendence in the intimacy of immanence. Even more, perhaps it is our waking up to the "yes" of transcendence as other in the immanence of the intimate universal, and revealing there not the immanence of any isolated subjectivity, for there is no such isolation. That is the point: the deepest intimacy of subjectivity reveals selving as essentially communicative being, in community with the sourcing original that communicates its being given to be. There is no "subjectivity." I am nothing – nothing if not in communication with the ultimate in community. The porosity of being is opened in an ultimate communication, and the passion of our being is our passion for God. This is perhaps what the mystic undergoes religiously (see Chapter 13). What this also might intimate is that thinking can be, as it were, a kind of sleeping praying. Praying is thought awakening to its original ground, waking in the intimate universal to its own most intimate being as a love of the endowing origin.

Community and the worth of being

Third, how does this community relate to the *worth of being*? This question invites us to gather together the significances of the other hyperboles. To recur to the first hyperbole: Does not the marvel of being astonish us with the given good of the "to be"? To recur to the second: Do not the beautiful and sublime call us to a deeming of the fitting, and indeed the surprise of what we cannot quite fit in? To recur to the third: Does not the erotics of selving passionately summon us to the inherently lovable, what for itself is worthy of being loved? Beings are in the between as a community, but a community cannot be thought apart from some notion of the worthwhile. Beings as together fit together; the being of community is a *fitting*: it is fit. Another way to say "it is fitting" is to affirm "it is good." Is there a certain fundamental rightness in the nature of things as being fitting? What would allow us to say that? We could say: Community is the good for beings – but the community we here name is not any specific community of this or that; it is the togetherness of the finite creation in the universal impermanence in which each being participates. What, if anything, allows us to say that this community is somehow right, that somehow it and all that participates in it is good?

We cannot say "it is fitting" in the sense at stake if we are obsessed only with its fit *for us.* Nor can we with a kind of Schopenhauerian outlook. There is a nobler kind of Nietzschean who *wants* to say it, but on what grounds? Nietzsche is himself a complicated case: one doubts not his desire to say "yes," but what (re)sources this "yes"? If will to power, is his "yes" only a counterfeit double of the true "amen"? For what is inherently good about his will to power, good in the hyperbolic sense at issue? Nietzsche's *amor fati* echoes a Stoic awakening to the rightness of the community of being; the Stoic calls us to gratitude – not gratitude for this or that, but gratitude for and towards the "whole." Does not such gratitude implicate something hyperbolic to the immanent whole? I think, too, of Spinoza's *acquiescentia mentis*. Is this a consent beyond the endeavor of every *conatus essendi*? If so, it is hyperbolic to the immanent whole. But how make sense of the worthiness of being to be affirmed, to be loved, without invoking the *goodness of the source* that gives it to be? Here, someone like Sartre leaves us in a hopeless situation. Despite the hyperbolic talk of the other in Levinas, one hesitates when here and there he speaks of *le mal de l'être*. Whether one is atheist or not, one's entire sense of the goodness of being is placed in the scales. To one who looks at the world with love, the world looks love-ly – not because he looks but because he beholds, and wakes to find himself beheld and beholden. Being beholden means being the recipient of gift, means being beholden from, where the initiative is with the other that gives.

Recall earlier considerations (Chapter 1) concerning the modern devaluation of being and the dark origin. The metaxological understanding of the hyperbolic community of being wakens us differently to the ethos, and to a very different mindfulness of being in the between: an intimation of inexpressible good breaks through, inexpressible because overdeterminate, as beyond specific determination and our self-determination. Beyond this and that good, beyond our self-determination, the overdeterminate good of being shines in the fittingness of the community that is the metaxological between. If the source of that shine is overdetermined good in a further hyperbolic sense, has not this good also been called God? What is at issue is a hyperbolic "amen" to the good of being. Such an "amen" to fittingness raises this thought of a hyperbolic God: as inexpressibly valuing the being of what is, loving it down to the singularity of the hairs upon the head. This means: *We* can say "it is good for itself" only because first *it* is loved in the glory of its created goodness: it is love-ly because loved, and not simply by us. For us, this answering to the question cannot be merely theoretical, though it can be shaped in relatively neutral generalities. This answering mobilizes all the resources of a human being, asking one to exceed these finite resources and wake up to one's ultimate community with the ultimate. *We must be woken up to the reserves of the ultimate relation.* This is also to be awakened to the reserved promise of being good in the finite between. A fitting way of life, keeping reverence, cultivating finesse, devoted to serve, is as needful, as is the thoroughness of one's reflective thinking. More needful. Logical argument alone certainly will not awaken one.

Community and ethical good

Fourth, what is the implication of hyperbolic community, not just in relation to the ontological community of beings, but to the ethical community of moral beings? I have touched already on the ethical, but without placing emphasis on community. The issue is evident with the hyperbolic erotics of selving, but now the stress falls on a hyperbole beyond erotic sovereignty: the community of agapeic service. It is not the erotics of selving that has the ultimate word but the agapeics of a service of the good as other. While the human being might be a kind of measure of things external to himself, and while he might attain the measure of some sovereignty of himself, he is not, and never will be, quite the same measure of himself as participant in the ethical community. The solicitation of something unconditional emerges immanently in ethical community, but there is also something hyperbolic to ethical community, pointing beyond moral and human measure. The ethical community of agapeic service makes us cross unconditionally the boundary of morality into the religious, where our love bears on the hyperbolic measure of the measureless good – God. The agapeics of community is intimately related to the other three hyperboles, but here there is also something more hyperbolic and most fully communicative of the divine overdeterminacy. We are what we are under the call of the good, porous to the surplus generosity of being good, but *we are so as participants* in an ethical community that is both elemental and ultimate.

Elemental

The point comes again – we do not first constitute this ethical community; rather because, already, community for humans is elementally ethical, we can ethically contribute within community. This ethical community is not to be identified with any specific human community, or exhausted by any particular tradition, though specific traditions and communities may manifest that community in a variety of ways. *There is an ontological solidarity that is not neutral but ethical.* This elemental community is sometimes most evident when all the markers of specific communities have been stripped and we are with others in terms of our elemental humanity. We are with each other, as if prior to specific objectifications of our human being; to be human is to "be with" in this way.[25] We are in communication by being participants in the intimate universal.

One might say that there is a community of elemental compassion. This would be a communication of a *compassio essendi* in which we are opened to each other, before we come to ourselves. Here we live the porosity of being between as ethically qualified, not only relative to the good of the "to be," but the good of the being of the other, and indeed of selving. This communication of the good of the "to be" is not dominated by the *conatus essendi* but, rather, derives from fidelity to the more original *compassio essendi*. This is often hard to realize, since we are from the start defined in, sometimes overtaken by, more specific objectifications of our human being, even as the *conatus essendi* over-rides the more subtle insinuations of the *passio essendi*. Yet traces of this elemental community are evident in the silent language of bodily thereness which qualifies a space of meeting with the promise of ethical presence: I smile at you and the bodily gesture can become a mute sign that rearranges the space into an ethos resonant with the promising hospitality of the good. I salute you, and not in terms of a specific language or tradition or encultured courtesy – this incarnate greeting of the hand outstretched is a communication at the edge of definite communication. This (so to say) pre-communal communication is an elemental, and in a way, hiddenly overdeterminate community of solidarity. It is an ethos, in one sense indeterminate, in another sense very determinate, even overdeterminate, since there is an immediately recognizable surplus of communication when we encounter it or find ourselves in it: the unmistakable surplus presence of the human, the communication of the human that as "there" is also elusive and mysterious. You wash my wounds, and behold me beyond or before the fact that I am a leper.

In such an elemental ethical intimacy we are coming closer to the primal ethos of being as hospitality to the good. For this pre-communal community is a togetherness steeped in a good, not named or determinately known as such, nowhere to be fixed to this or that, and yet saturating the entire communication. It is not merely indefinite, but overdetermined, in that it both precedes determinate communications and exceeds them. It is most often revealed to us when certain given social determinations release their absolute hold on us: we behold the poor, or the hungry, or the sick, or the bereft, or the tormented, and the steady, everyday determinations of social conventions fall by the way in the face of the overdeterminate appeal of the other. There is the resurrection of community beyond determinate community. Even though there is a surplus here, strangely we have to strip ourselves of the surpluses of determinate social fixations to let it be released. The destitution of the other is a surplus summons to a poverty, a porosity on our part that is full with the promise of an agapeic generosity. There is such an ethos saturated with the promise of the good, even in the desolation of the desert. Sometimes the desert brings us closer to the primal ethos than the sophistications of the city of man.[26]

25 See, especially, *Ethics and the Between*, Part IV, for a more extensive treatment of different interme-diations of ethical community from the idiotic to the transcendent, including the family, the dominion of serviceable disposabilty, and the communities of erotic sovereignty and agapeic service. See also "Doing Justice and the Practice of Philosophy."
26 What has this to do with philosophy? But think of Bonaventure and the "poor man" who is the subject of self-transcending in the *Itinerarium Mentis ad Deum*. Through poverty, *Il poverello* was brought into the festive community of the primal ethos, and what he sometimes called "the table of the Lord." See *IST?*, Chapter 3.

This is the question that perplexes us: If there is this elemental community of ethical solidarity which is not constituted by us but which constitutes us within the communicative call of the good, how is this elemental community constituted (see *BB*, Chapter 13; also *EB*)? How do we name the source in which and through which it is constituted? We cannot account for it through the human, nor through nature. Not the human, for we are given to be as ethical and become ethical in and through this ethos; we presuppose it; its character is such that clearly we do not make it. Not nature, since the sense of the ethical good here at stake is disproportionate to the sense of ontological value we find in nature – it exceeds the measure of that ontological value, which in any case, as we saw, does not account for itself in entirely immanent terms. Why not give to its originary ground the name God?

Of course, just because of the overdetermination of the good at play, we name this origin with trepidation. There is again something too much for us. This is fitting, given our approach via the hyperbole. We will always feel the strain of the hyperbolic, given our wanting to remain in the more comfortable humanization of being that is our reconfigured ethos. Someone will advocate that we boldly side with Kant and speak of the kingdom of ends. Nevertheless, it is quite clear we do not constitute the kingdom of ends; we are constituted within the kingdom of ends. There is much of Leibniz transmuted by Kant, though he is more diffident about naming the divine, just as he is very diffident in naming God as the ground of the moral law in a more specific sense. I am talking about an ethos that is prior to law: the agapeic ethos of the ethical solidarity of humans – the elemental ethical middle as an agapeic milieu that cannot be completely objectified or determined or subject to the measure of our self-determination. There is no humanistic or naturalistic account adequate to the fact that we are ends in ourselves, and of infinite value. Such an end or value as infinite cannot be exhausted by any determinate value, or aggregate of such values: it too is hyperbolic. Being an end of infinite value, and indeed being thus as a member of an ethical community transcending every determinate and self-determining community, suggests an infinite source in excess of all finitude, and that we ourselves cannot make.

Ultimate

The gift of the elemental community summons us to realize the promise of the hyperbolic good. Our participation in ethical community is a call to the fullest realization of the agapeics of community. This is shown in the community of agapeic service (see especially *EB*, Chapter 16; also *BB*, Chapter 12). This involves not only a good elementally given, but a summons for us to give beyond ourselves: to be agapeic. Being agapeic is not just elementally given but freely comes to be in an elemental giving, in which the ultimate generosity of being is communicated. This may extend from *incognito* acts of everyday consideration all the way to sacrificial love, in which one lays down one's life for another. In excess of the erotics of immanent sovereignty, there is a community of agapeic service which enacts our being for the other in the most ultimate sense possible. The community of agapeic service is a hyperbolic sign of transcendent good. Our participation in agapeic transcending is our fullest self-transcendence: our love, in transcending self, transcends to transcendence itself. We find ourselves in a love that not only passes beyond self, but more ultimately passes *between* ourselves and transcendence itself.

If there is a kingdom of ends, it is so not just because of the ends, but because of what gathers it into a community. Kant does not give due attention to the gathering power. The saturation of the kingdom of ends with infinite value suggests the gathering power as hyperbolic to the kingdom of ends. Must the ground of the value of the kingdom of ends be the unconditional end beyond all ends, namely, God as the absolute Good? If so, I reiterate the different, hyperbolic dimension in which this other community and its original ground has to be thought. It cannot be completely objectified or determined; nor can it be reduced to our self-determination, not even dialectically qualified in terms of an immanently self-completing totality. At stake is the surplus otherness of the good to both our determination and self-determination, and to immanent totality. This is the good as transcendent, even as that good also creates the immanent space of ontological and ethical availability which is the elemental ethos of the good in creation.

Might the kingdom of ends better be called the kingdom of God? It has been so called. Even Kant slips in this call. The hapless Fichte got into hot waters when he identified the moral world order with God. Considering the hyperbolic dimension of the agapeic of community, such an identification is ill-judged, at the very least, it cannot be the last word. What the kingdom of God means is very elusive. Its surplus good cannot be identical with, or exhausted by any determinate human community, though it can be at work in any determinate human community. Perhaps Augustine meant something like this in talking about the City of God which, in the between, will always mingle with the City of Man. We live in the middle of this mixed togetherness, where beings are both in harmony and hostility, but where the mixture points us further. The mixture is metaxological: in the midst, and yet beyond. In time, the wheat and the tares will always wind around each other, and we humans do not always have the finesse wise enough to tell the difference. The last judgment will not be our judgment, though it will be our judgment.

We are first called to fidelity before being called to judge or to judgment. I round off with two considerations bearing on this. First, the *agapeics of community and truth are inseparable*. Being true is a communicative togetherness of knower and known, knower and knower. It is a fidelity to the togetherness of beings; a fidelity of self-transcendence (T^2) to itself and what is other, and ultimately to transcendence as other (T^3) [see *BB*, Chapter 13]. Being truthful testifies to our being in the call of the true. Our privilege to be truthful is granted in the happening of a more primordial community.[27] What accounts for this prior community in being true? The simple answer, enigmatic though it is, is that truth itself is the ground of being true, and hence also of the community in which the truthful being finds herself participating. Two illustrations: First, Plato's Good, imaged in the sun, not only shedding light but making possible the relativity between our mind and being. Lighting is a communication of the ultimate relativity sourced in the origin as the absolute Good. We are involved with an excessive transcendence in all that involves us. Second, Augustine: we see the truth, and we are truthful, but the light by which we see the light is not us, and the light wherein we enact fidelity to being truthful is again not of us; it is intimate to us but it is not us; in us, not of us; and if of us, of us in a manner qualified by our poverty as incapable of being the possessor of what is most deeply intimate to our beings. Augustine's argument from truth to God (in *De Libero Arbitrio*) might be reformulated as a metaxological argument *from the community of being in the truth, to the Truth that communicates the promise of being in that community.*

The second consideration concerns *the good as the endowing ground of being good.* Being good is defined metaxologically as participation in community. We are given to be in the surplus givenness of metaxological community, which reveals an overdeterminacy that we do not constitute but within which we are constituted (see *BB*, Chapter 14). Being true and being good are forms of self-transcending within the between, forms ultimately energized by agapeic self-transcending. They are forms of communicative being, possibilizing definite relations between self and other, possibilizing relatedness in which the other as other cannot be subordinated to any form of dialectical self-mediation, no matter how speculatively inclusive. Being good is a form of agapeic service of the good within a community of servants of the good. But we do not determine this community; it "determines" the promise of our freedom to be self-determining. Our self-determining

27 See "Pluralism, Truthfulness and the Patience of Being," in *Health and Human Flourishing: Religion, Medicine and Moral Anthropology,* ed. Carol R. Taylor, Roberto Dell'Oro (Washington, DC: Georgetown University Press, 2006), Chapter 3.

is given first as a promise, and only later accomplishes itself more fully. There is a predeterminate communication of the promise of the good. We are what we are within the givenness of this promise. We become what we are to be by realizing this promise in the community of agapeic service. We have to ask once again: What ultimately (re)sources the endowment of this community of agapeic service? Can it be called the agapeic origin? Is this what God is: the good as agapeic transcendence itself?

Chapter 7

God Beyond the Between

Along the shore's edge
Bent into the gale
Buffeted by the wind
Blowing from out beyond
Struggling to stay in place
Almost at a standstill
Unable to go further
I am turned

& I turn
& am borne
On the way
In balance and quick
Running
Effortlessly
Home

THE HYPERBOLE OF THE AGAPEIC ORIGIN

Given rumination on the four hyperboles in the between, can we venture on their basis a hyperbole of God *beyond the between*? But perhaps I have already so ventured by speaking, maybe too assertorically, of the agapeic origin? Any further venturing must needs be speculative: not just a *hypo-thesis*, but, so to say, a *hyper-thesis*. Call this an adventure in speculative metaxology (not speculative dialectic in Hegel's sense). Given our indirect direction to God via the hyperboles, a hyperthesis would be a "placing or being placed above," a "putting or being put over." Of course, it may be the case that divorcing the *hyper* and the *hypo* is not finally important, if what is above is also below, what high also deep. For what is full seems sometimes also void; what is (over-)all seems nothing (at all). Let me try anew for some further finesse. I will address considerations with broad correlation to the four hyperboles: God's absoluteness and relatedness; creation and the worth of the finite to be; agapeic origination and nothing; overwhole infinitude beyond the whole. And if the air higher up seems thinner or portends nausea, best stay closer to the finite base, for further on a little, we will come down.

Divine idiocy – absoluteness and relatedness

The "is" of "That God is" is hyperbolic as exceeding finite determinacy, hence exceeding determinate intelligibility such as we know it in the between. This suggests an *idiocy* to the divine, but in an affirmative superplus sense: not the absurd as falling below intelligibility, but the mystery itself, as exceeding all finite intelligibilities. This idiocy is not a divine autism. The intermediated character of the metaxological way allows us to venture that the hyperbole of the agapeic origin might be seen to entail a *double mediation*: an immanent self-mediation and a transcending intermediation with the genuinely other. The first self-mediating would refer us to God's *absoluteness* in self, the second intermediating would refer us to God's *relatedness* to finite creation as other.

The idiocy of the divine would have to do with its own immanently communicative being. But metaxologically speaking, can it be entirely right to refer to a divine *self-mediation*? Is not *inter*-mediation more primordial than *self*-mediation? Yes. I would say yes, especially so if the inner life of the divine is like a love that is communication: an immanent community that is also a self-communication. This would be an agapeic community whose self-communication is superlative love of the exceeding good of the "to be," itself as the absolute "to be" of goodness. There is a generosity of giving which *is* simply being good: communication not from the full to the lacking but of the full to the full, which as itself full is generous giving of the full to the full, and generous receiving of the full by the full. This would be agapeic intermediation in the superlative sense. This indeed, as hyperbolic, would be the communication of the overfull, and of the overfull to the overfull, whose goodness as agapeic giving is itself simply in giving on and giving back. It is hard for us human beings to think this, since normally we tend to contrast self-mediation and intermediation with an other. But if the immanent otherness of the divine is agapeic, it is loved by itself for itself, loved by itself for its otherness, goodness loving and loved for its goodness, as intimately immanent and immanently other, and these all "all at once."

Dare we liken the immanent absoluteness of God to our self-mediation? Yes and no. *Yes*: What the likeness suggests is an infinite inexhaustibility that opens up immanently in selving. I try this: Out of infinite reserves, unsurpassably intimate, God mediates with self, but in another sense does not mediate, because there is an infinite simplicity to the divine intimacy also, hence there are no reserves at all, for there is no reserve at all between the divine and itself. There is, so to say, a divine overdeterminacy that, being overfull, immediately converts itself to the most limpid being with itself. Yet there is no conversion from one thing to another, since this overfull communication with itself is simply what it is. And it is not at all indeterminate in the sense of the indefinite or potential; it is not converting itself to definition in its self-mediation. It is overdeterminate goodness. It is inexhaustible reserve of its own power to be as good, absolutely at home with itself. And there is more again, in that there is still a "side" that reserves itself in light inaccessible, relative to us. This reserve releases a communication of finitude and to finitude that, remaining reserved, is paradoxically unreserved.

No: "selving" is a *misleading* likeness, if we see selving only as other to communicative being. The metaxological way dissolves any fixed disjunction of selving and communicative being. This infinite inexhaustibility, as much overdetermined as absolute simplicity, might be likened to communicative being, in all plenitude of agapeic surplus. The immanent self-mediation is an intermediation with the immanent otherness of this surplus, a communication out of goodness, from goodness, and loved as goodness. This intercommunication from (over)full to (over)full to (over)full would be an absolute self-communication, in that it would refer us to an absolute surplus, or pluperfection already effective through itself, before anything finite as other is effected. Its primordial effectiveness would be just the communicative actuality of its absolute being with itself, a "being with itself" that could not be captured on any model of univocal self-identity, or indeed dialectical. This excess of the infinite reserve of the origin, just as completely at home with itself, would be the infinite serenity of goodness. There would be no ripple of disturbance in its inner life, for even its immanent otherness is also absolute goodness, and hence the infinite serenity would be a radiance of goodness, at once, and paradoxically for us, if one could say it, both centripetal and centrifugal. It is not that the turbulences, indeed evils of finitude are nothing or irrelevant to it; rather, the embrace of the infinite serenity is ready to take the disturbance to itself and restore it to the peace of goodness.

What other characterizations God might be consonant with this? Power in excess of all finite confines, but as empowering rather than unilaterally overpowering and determining. Absolute self-knowing that dissolves not the mystery of God, since it is the mystery. The divine "self-mediation" must be mindful, though this divine self-knowing would not be as an autistic self-thinking thinking but as agapeic mindfulness where knowing and loving are intimately one. Nothing more? Infinite simplicity, as in itself the resolving of oppositions, as prior to oppositions arising, and superior to oppositions having arisen, though no opposition does arise in the divine life itself. (Hegel and others like him make a serious mistake here, in thinking of the divine life in terms of a self-becoming through immanent opposition.) Inexhaustible richness, and in that sense a kind of infinite complexity. But also: a kind of infinite poverty, as the pure porosity of agapeic love, and the compassion of being that is pure readiness, even to the point of kenotically making (a) way for what it brings to be as other to itself.

The intimate process of divine "self-mediation" would be the eternal arising of infinitely intricated surplus, communicating itself in a pure porosity that is absolutely itself in not insisting on itself, loving its own otherness immanent to its intermediation, enjoying its goodness in an eternal peace that is the absolutely limpid simplicity of its being.

Just this simplicity suggests to us the agapeic idiocy of God. Is it not strange that we humans often have greater difficulty thinking the full rather than the deficient? The splendor of the surplus or the (over)full non-plusses us. The shine of the (over)full appears to us like an empty mirror. What appears disappears, and we seem to see nothing. The empty mirror is the smile of the infinite serenity, the infinite simplicity, the pure porosity.

Divine aesthetics – creation and the worth of the "to be"

The pluralized mediation of the metaxological way requires that we not conflate this first immanent self-mediation, which is also a first communicative intermediation, with a second intermediation, which has bearing on God's relatedness to finite creation. The endowing origin is hyperaesthetic, yet it gives the idiocy of finite being and the aesthetics of happening. Through this second intermediation, not to be reduced to the primal immanent divine intermediation, the agapeic origin brings to be the absolved relativity in which the finite between is originated and let to be. This second intermediating would not first be constituted by the already existent being of finitude. It would be a *creating* intermediation that brings into being the finite creation as other. This coming to be (understood as an agapeic origination) would be a coming to be of finitude as genuinely other to the origin. This would express, if you like, the divine *poiesis*, the creating art of God. But this creating art is not creating God, it is God creating finite creation as other.

Here we must advert to a further pluralization of intermediations. For the creating intermediation gives the between to be, and hence possibilizes a further, *originated relativity* between creation and God. A primal originative "intermediation" gives rise to the between; this is the elemental communication of the "to be" of beings, not mediation with their being as already having their "to be." This is more like an original *poiesis* (in the sense of a bringing to be) rather than a technical making. Then again a further intermediation allows a communication between God and given being as already being. This further communication is not to be reduced to the first giving, and neither are identical to the intermediation or communication of God with Godself.

The hyperbole of the agapeic origin here connects creating and the worth of the finite to be. The aesthetics of divine *poiesis* brings to be the aesthetic marvel of the material world in all its plurivocal goodness. To be as mattered is to matter: it is good. It is not a fall. Its otherness as other is good and appreciated as such. God's own goodness is not only good in self and for self, but good in a transcending and communicative broadcast. The broadcast issues in the aesthetics of the divine turning toward the second "intermediation." The surplus of the origin as communicative goodness would communicate being to finitude, and do so doubly. More primal than the originated relativity of God and given being there is the first absolute communication of being at all: this we call creation, or radical origination. Why does it arise? For no reason beyond the being agapeic of the origin. It is good to be, it is good to give to be. This is the ontological giving generosity of the origin.

The origin communicates being as finite; it amplifies good in giving rise to the finite other. It "augments" the good; though, in another way, at the level of the excessive pluperfection, the meaning of this "augmentation" has nothing to do with any model of quantitative addition. To "augment" the good is not *that* kind of addition. Nothing is added to anything in that sense – except that, astoundingly, the being of the beneficiaries comes into their own being. They are brought into their proper good; just as, equally, the being true of the giver is in its bringing all beings into their own proper good. Example from base in the between: if I do another good, is this not at bottom what I am doing: bringing the loved other into the neighborhood of their own good? Agapeic creation would be a bringing of beings into their proper truth and good, by bringing their truth and good into being.

Divine erotics – between nothing and agapeic origination

Does it make sense to speak of a divine erotics? Not if we think of the divine communication as necessitated by lack. Yet something comes to be that before was lacking, and it is called to be out of superplus goodness that "wants" it to be. If we speak of the divine erotics as this wanting of God, this is a wanting not wanting, since as agapeic it is always in excess of any lack.

Does it make sense to call such a communication of being an *origination from nothing*? To answer yes, as I think in some sense we must, would mean something like this: The erotics of the divine is not driven by a lack in God that creation must fill; it is given from surplus generosity – a generosity beyond need that loves the finite creation to be. Divine erotics is hyperbolic in giving to be and wanting the good of the finite. Out of nothing it brings finitude to be by surplus generosity. Given finitude exists in an openness, a porosity that is like a kind of no-thing. It is not nothing that originates, but the origin as superlatively more than nothing. Since the agapeic origin of creation is not the self-origination of the origin itself, creation is the arising into being of an other.

Creation from nothing would name a hyperbolic origination of which we have no finite analogue. When we turn to any finite analogue of creative activity, all presuppose the being-there-already of finite beings. Perhaps inspired *poiesis* by a finite original offers a partial analogy, but technical making does not. By difference, this hyperbolic origination is prior to there being finitude there. It would be an absolute *poiesis*: the arising of being and beings such "that they are at all." Why coming to be at all? The divine erotics is not wanting – not wanting in ontological generosity. But this generosity wants, without wanting, to give being. It is good to be, it is good to give to be, it is good to be given to be. The beneficiary of the gift can resonate with all of this in its own erotics of being and in thanks rendered to the giver.

This agapeic origination would presuppose nothing of finitude, since it would be the absolute presupposition of the being of finitude. "Nothing" here also means that the otherness of origin and creation frees the finitude of creation as marked by its proper being and order. This given order is the interim of time. The being of the finite is not unconditional: as it was brought into being, it will pass out of being. Thus the "nothing" also signals something of the equivocity of transience that finitude undergoes. It betokens contingency: nothing in particular might have been, and all that is might not have been, but for the radical origination. Contingency is possible nonbeing, and the possibility of nonbeing is constitutive of all finite being. Yet "that it is at all" means we must refer to creation and not just to nothing.

It is important not to conflate these two communications: on the one hand, the original "coming to be" of finitude, on the other the "becoming" of beings in finitude. Beyond the communication of being at all, the open promise of creation to its own good is communicated. There is the elemental ontological community of being in finitude itself, and between finitude and the origin, but the between itself constitutes the promise of its own community of being. In their own erotic transcending beyond lack, finite beings are called to be beyond themselves by the erotics of God. The wanting of God for the finite is not symmetrical with the want of the finite for God. The erotics of the divine is more than erotic, its wanting beyond want.

Divine agapeics – overwhole infinitude beyond the whole

A fourth speculative consideration could be ventured by contrasting the erotics of divine selving and the agapeics of divine community. The first can be seen as oriented more to the self-determination of a whole, the second towards the overdeterminacy of a community of (open) wholes. In line with the pluralized mediation of the metaxological, we must rethink the notions of *wholeness* and *infinitude*. As "self-mediating," God might be called an absolute whole but not a determinate whole: as "intermediating," God would communicate infinity in excess of every whole. Finite beings are determinate wholes, and some beings, like humans, can become self-determining wholes, but God, it seems, would have to be thought of as an "overwhole." Does this make any sense: an overwhole in excess of being a determinate or self-determinate whole? For does not being whole imply a determinate, or self-determining boundary that, so to say, closes the circle on itself? There is, it seems, no such closure to an "overwhole," hence it seems no whole. Must we choose between the whole and the infinite? Or must we think an overwhole that as infinite is inexhaustible?

Do we not get glimpses of something like an "overwhole" with, for instance, a great work of art, or more so with a human being of great ethical integrity that exceeds even moral self-determination? Do we not see this especially with those who are holy? Each of these may make manifest an inexhaustibility beyond determinate and self-determining fixation, and this just in the (over)wholeness of being they communicate. God's "overwholeness" would refer us, on the one hand, to God's immanent absoluteness, yet, since such an "overwholeness" suggests its infinity, just in its inexhaustibility, on the other hand, we are impelled to the paradoxical notion of an *open whole*. Such an "overwhole" we cannot close, and it does not close (on) itself. It seems we have to think an absolving "open whole," an "overwhole" that opens beyond the whole. One might say that such an "overwholeness" would be the releasing of freedom, such as we find, again, in the presence of a great work of art, or a holy human.

See here the connection of infinity and "overwholeness": the movement of the infinite is in excess of all finite wholes, beyond determination and self-determination, but it is shown, with all reserve, in finite wholeness as the inviting power of what draws us on to the "more" beyond our self-determination, to transcendence itself. The opening of God would be the releasing of the creation as a finite whole, a bringing to be that is a release of the creation. The divine overwhole would be an infinite releasing of which, again, there can be no adequate finite analogy, except perhaps the compassion of the saint. (Beatitude(s): The agapeics of the suffering servant.) All finite release is another entanglement; there is no absolutely pure release in the finite as such. The equivocity of finite freedom: outside of the agapeic infinite there is no absolute freedom. And yet we know something of absolved freedom. A taste of this is in prayer: we are offered an absolving release, hard to name, even as one feels the lifting of constraint, and it is all but nothing; offered in an instant, one is placed in its "presence," and then it is gone, or else we are distracted back to our familiar selves, our cells. The unbearable serenity of this release is offered, often with allowance, so it seems, for our ability to "take it in" or surrender to it – offered with consideration for what we can bear. The offering is unbearable, we cannot bear it, and instead we are borne by it.

Would this overwhole infinitude beyond the whole make God so transcendent that no divine immanence would be conceivable? I think the response must be more complex: not a dualism of immanence and transcendence; not a speculative sublation of transcendence in holistic immanence; not a God so utterly other as to be for us indistinguishable from nothing, since no communication to finite immanence would be possible.

I answer in terms of a sense of metaxological doubleness. The first immanence of the divine would be its inaccessible light, as absolutely at home with itself: absolute intimacy of agapeic being, absolute idiocy. This hyperbolic immanence is the mark of transcendence itself: the divine immanence at home with itself is just its being other to the whole of created finitude in its absolute "overwholeness." This is not known as such but religious finesse has an intimation of it in relation to the reserves of God. Then the second immanence: the agapeic transcending of the origin as giving rise to finite creation in the good of its "to be." This second immanence is also a granting of *otherness* between origin and creation. The issue it raises: What then of divine *immanence in* creation itself?

I respond to this also in terms of a metaxological doubleness. First, there is the primal communication of origin in the elemental ontological fact that creation is at all. Second, there is the communication as giving to creation *its own promise* of agapeic being. The overwhole infinitude of God endows the agapeics of community in finite creation. This means: the communicative origin does not give and withdraw; rather it gives and *gives way* to the integrity of the creation. This giving way is no indifferent withdrawal, but the giving of the porosity of the between and the endowment of the space of freedom. It is a letting to be that is intimately immanent in granting the space in which the promise of a more agapeic freedom in finitude might be redeemed. The agapeics of a *divine making a way that gives way* entails both transcendence and immanence, of being other and being intimate, or letting to be and yet being there absolutely available.

Put hyperthetically: first, the agapeic movement of releasing creation would entail a coming to be, not just a becoming. This would be the given agapeics of communication between the origin and creation. Second, the energizing of the promise of agapeic community in creation itself would not be just a becoming as moving from a defective to a less lacking condition. Because of the first given agapeics of communication, this "becoming" would be from a fullness already effective, as well as a seeking of what yet is lacking. Agapeic energization has more to do with the "becoming" of a promise than a mere potential. A promise is already an endowment with effective goodness, at work before the promise is fully redeemed, and a participant in this redemption to come. This coming is not just a becoming from lack to fulfillment. For a promise of goodness is an open happening that always already is leavening given being with an intimate empowering power: power empowering of what is other, and let to be as other. The redemption of the promise is for the good of the beneficiary, not the donor. This is agapeic promising, for the good of the creation, not for God who wants nothing but the good of the creation.

Finite beings concretize the promise of agapeic being, and this most evidently in the ethical and holy lives of human beings who most intensively incarnate the promise of agapeic transcending. And so not surprisingly, it is with relation to such an ethical/religious community that a likeness for the life of the divine is witnessed most consummately: the community of agapeic service images the agapeic origin. It is true that sometimes a religious community will claim to be *the one and only* image, but the overwhole original cannot be confined in any image. Agapeic communication is catholic and can occur as much on the margins as in the middle, as much in the night as the day, as much in the recesses of intimacy as out in public expanses, as much in the fall of the yellow leaf as in the joyous surge of life that revels in playing the game or running the race.

When *all goes well*, we take for granted what is (as) granted. "All going well" – this itself is participation in the quiet festivity of agapeic being, at home with itself, though perhaps all but asleep to itself. We must be very diffident with any judgment about where and when and how the community of agapeic service testifies to the communicative being of God. Nor need we slight the community with non-human otherness. One recalls one's rapport with a particular place, or beholds a flower dangling outside the skylight hatch, or one is taken by hatched chicks freshly scattered in spring, and on a sudden one finds oneself porous, and summoned into the agape of being. There is no knowing where and when this happens. We have to be ready and patient, both expectant and repenting our unripeness.

REVERSING THE HYPERBOLES AND THE RESERVES OF GOD

Everything I say above I say under qualification: it is spoken from the between. It is a venture of hyperbolic thought, and as thinkers we know nothing of God, save what we glean from the ambiguities of being in the between. The hyperbolic startles us with a reversal of directionality: more than our erotic self-transcending from below up, a reverse way down is suggested in the agapeics of communication. This way down is *not symmetrical* with our way up. Given the asymmetry, can we think, even in our not-knowing, *the reverse movement from the origin*? Would this movement really be the reverse (as if it were the second), since it is we who are (as seconds), if anything, in this "reverse"? What if we were to venture this: liken this movement to a kind of reverse of the movements present in the four hyperboles that above led us up? This would be to try to think the absolute/absolved relativity from the other side: from the origin towards us.

First "reversed" movement

The agapeic idiocy of the origin is mirrored in the idiocy of creation itself. I mean the intimacy of profound particularity of things. This first "reversed" move from the origin to the "that it is at all" cannot be accounted for in terms of any determinate structure or general explanatory principle. For these structures and principles are themselves the products of the original coming to be; they may be appropriate for a finite becoming, but not for a radical coming to be. We cannot finally have a *determinate explanation* of the "that it is at all," but the absence of such explanation is perfectly *intelligible* given the nature of what is at issue. The first move to finite concreteness has this singularity of idiocy which is not reducible to any more general condition. The universe, the universal, are themselves the issue of a singularity of event that is all pervasive and that yet cannot be merely generalized. Something of this is suggested to us in being religious so far as this is porous to divine communication in the intimate universal.

Put otherwise: the happening of being is universal and singular at one and the same time; it is the singular creation that itself is universal, and the singularity of the creation gives rise to the universal. This universal cannot be a generality in any more usual acceptation, such as a class concept which is for the most part, more or less, applicable, without reference to the singularities then put into parenthesis as the perhaps merely accidental. Thus, at the origin there is nothing accidental, just as there is nothing generally necessary. It is not fitting to speak in this way. There arises the absolute singularity of contingency, but this is not an accident. And there are intelligibilities coming to arise, but these are not necessities determining the origin only to this, or only to that. Such a univocal necessitarian determination is false to the overdetermination of the origin, and also to its agapeic being as a free release of the other as other, and of communicative being towards the other. The normal antithesis of necessity and freedom does not operate here. These usual notions are too much defined in relation to finite determinations and self-determinations.

Second "reversed" movement

This is from the singular idiocy of being to creation as aesthetic happening. I mean the materiality of creation – creation as sensible and sensuous work. In the *poiesis* of coming to be the beauty of the incarnate world comes to stand. This aesthetic happening is not a neutral materiality: it is worthy in being affirmed, worthy to be affirmed. When we turn to its being there, there is a leap of joy in the eyes, in the ears, in the flesh, and we feast on the world. The aesthetic show shows also the origin, but like all aesthetic show it does so ambiguously. Released into its own being for itself it constitutes its own world, and so can be seen just as for itself. And we do indeed often forget the fact that it would be nothing outside of the gift of the origin. Creation lives in the sleep of the gift of being; it is itself the gift, but it does not know this, a beneficiary that does not know the benefit that it is and has received.

Third "reversed" movement

This has to do with the awakening of erotic selving especially in the human being in whom this doubleness of the gift of being is not just sleeping. We are the mindfulness of the gift, just as we are the mindfulness that turns to itself and lives itself as free being that it thinks is supremely for itself. With this, our own intensively double character – gifted beings who can refuse being gifted – we are prey to all the agonies of ethical and spiritual freedom. These are the freedoms that come to be with selving and being in community. As double, finite beings are equivocal between being-for-self and being-for-the-other, and so they *cannot be* the ultimate good: finite beings are good but not absolute good. All the travail that leads to God or that is lost to God finds its home in human double-ness: the intensive incarnation of the equivocity of the finite between. Here the highest and the lowest are possible. Only the human can fall so low to baseness and iniquity, as rise to extraordinary heights of nobility, even sanctity. The powers of self-mediation and intermediation are most intensive and extensive in us. *Most intensive*: as leading into the interiority of being as radically idiotic, into the hiddenness of mystery, across the thresh-old of the abyss of self. *Most extensive*: as turning to all being beyond self, and sometimes turning with a love that exceeds every circuit of self-love.

Fourth "reversed" movement

This has to do with our being awakened to the gift as gift when we are solicited beyond ourselves in agapeic transcending. For our *"intensive"* powers lead to the way of inwardness in which we discover the deepest lack in our being: horror of existence with-out God, and yet horror itself as a pull of reminding. This lack, beyond all finite satisfac-tion, takes us back to the primal porosity and flowers into the urgency of ultimacy in the form of our erotic self-transcending. This urgency sleeps and wakes in the equivocity of human desire. What temptation and bewitchment can consume us here! Our infinite lack, full with itself, cannot be filled with itself. It shows itself as a child of the primal poros-ity of our being. Meanwhile, our *"extensive"* powers show the unavoidable need of the other, and now not just as a need, but a love that is not in need of the other for the self, but that loves the other for itself as other. Being in the between shows itself as the promise of agapeic communicability. Erotic self-transcendence is itself equivocal in not knowing that the tide that carries it beyond itself is the giving of being out of agapeic generosity.

In sum: the hyperbole of the agapeic origin is consonant with metaxological intermedia-tion *in* creation, where communicative being shows itself in plurivocal manifestation. It is not that God must mirror our being or our world, but God must be such as to help us acknowledge mindfully the fullness of promise offered in the between, as manifesting the ontological power of the primal ethos of being. Our entire search has been to understand something of the divine by understanding something of that ethos, itself understood through the different configured forms of ethos as shaped by the univocal, equivocal, dialectical, and metaxological ways. Through the metaxological we find ourselves in creation, itself a universal impermanence, a dynamic aesthetic happening, ever ongoing, and where any wholeness is open. In the between things are singularized; intelligibilities come to manifestation and are not just superimposed on an ontological ooze; intelli-gent mindfulness reveals the self-mediating powers of singular being, most intensively concretized in human selving. Here we find continuation and rupture: the equivocities of aesthetic happening are doubled over and tangled. In the untangling of this knot, we weave something of our own integrity of being. This is inseparable from intermediating communities which practice the truth and are servants of the good. These communities give us the richest hyperboles to envisage the being of the origin. In the communal prac-tice of truth and the service of the good, we try to live agapeic being. This life makes us mindful of the life of the origin as agapeic. It is hard to be pervious mindfully to that origin if we do not try to live as agapeic, hard to have genuine thought of God if we do not live godly. The gift of spiritual freedom solicits us into a thinking of God, a thinking hard to separate, at a certain point, from a kind of praying. We do not think of God. Our thinking is itself something granted.

BRINGING THE HYPERBOLES BACK TO THE BETWEEN

The hyperbole of the origin must be brought back to the between. Though ventured *from* the between in relation to what is *beyond* the between, the hyperbole of the origin must have relevance to what ultimately is revealed *in* the between. It must reveal some crucial ontological connection with our being in the between, or illuminate crucial concretions of the power of being in finitude. Once again I will name four connections or concretions.

First: the otherness of origin and creation

Agapeic origination names the giving rise to the finite other as other. The arising or arisen other is not a means by which the origin comes to itself or mediates with itself. Origination of the other is not self-origination. God is not creating God in creating the creature. The first divine intermediation means the origin is already whole for itself, over-whole regardless of relation to creation as other. No lack needs to be filled by an other to itself. It is from the overwholeness of surplus, or from the second intermediation, that this arising of creation comes. God is God apart from relation to creation. God does not need the world to be God.

Since the agapeic origin is for the otherness of creation, this arising is genuinely an arising, it is not a fall or degeneration from the One. It is the "augmentation" of being and of being as good – "augmentation" not "additive" in a quantifiable sense. Hence while the creation is "less" than the origin, the "less" of creation is a "more" that is a good for itself. The arising of creation, and its possibilizing of many forms of being must be appreciated affirmatively. We are far from thinking of the arising as a decadence from the One. If the origin deems the creation good, so must we who are gifts of that origin. We can do no less, though we often do much less.

Second: the pluralism and becoming of creation

The meaning of agapeic origination is in the giving of the pluralism of being as good for itself. This pluralism is not a dissipated many, for there are forms of togetherness in the universal impermanence. These qualify the many as possibilizing different kinds of community, ontological, ethical, and spiritual. The assertion of mere diversity is not quite to the point. The pluralism of creation itself harbors the promise of agapeic being, from very primitive beginnings all the way to the community of agapeic service with ethical and religious humans.

In the pluralization of creation, the *becoming* of finite beings follows the *coming to be* of finitude. The finite being *comes to be* as a happening, hence as a contingency not marked by inherent necessity. Because it is not absolute being, it must become what it is; becoming what it is, it is not fully itself, and so there is a lack, even though there is also the elemental fullness that it is at all. Thus there is this interplay of coming to be and passing from being in becoming: *becoming is a qualification of coming to be by the possibility of not-being or nothingness that is the mark of all contingent happening.*

The affirmation of the agapeic is not at all a sentimental sigh of sweetness, for the nothing it recognizes exceeds the negative lack more at play in erotic self-encircling. As the affirmative surplus of original being is hyperbolic, so also is the nothing. The nothing is too much for us, and too much for us because it is just nothing at all. There is a nothing that completely passes beyond us. We divine it in creation as universal impermanence, and we are not at all on a par with it. We are perhaps on terms with this or that determinate negation, but not the absolute nothing that qualifies the coming to be of finite creation. As the too muchness of creation puts us in mind of God, so also does the appalling nothing intimate in the universal impermanence. And yet that nothing cannot have the final word, for after all creation is, and hence the surplus of affirmative being is more than this nothing. God is more than all, as the transcendence greater than which none other can be. The agape of being is most intensely outlined against the horizon of the ultimate nothingness which is not the ultimate. Death returns us to zero. We suffer the *passio essendi* that no *conatus essendi* can overcome. Every endeavor to be is dissolved in an ultimate porosity to the ultimate that exceeds us. Is this porosity of death the way of truth (*slí na fírinne*) that opens us to God? If death has a meaning, the meaning is not death.

Third: the singularity of beings and the promise of freedom

The origin is not for the world *in general* or creation in the mass; it is for the intricacy of the singular in the intimate universal. How else think a coming to be that in creation itself shows such an astonishing intricacy of individualized definition? We humans lack the agapeic mind really to be discerning on this level of singularity. This is a mind of finesse we humans lack. Now and then an artist reveals a hint of it in showing us the charged presence of singularity. Perhaps we feel a brief flare of it when we love someone. Perhaps we elusively encounter it in a holy person, released to love of the singularities of the earth as sacred gifts. Scientific and philosophical knowledges tend to be diverted from the singular as such towards the general, and they find it difficult to conceive the agapeic mindfulness of the singular. But even this diversion can be a potential form of agapeic mind (see *PU*, pp. 105–13 on science and agapeic minding). Singularity itself is a communication into being of the finite. At its most intimate and idiotic, the singular is a concretion of a communication, and hence there is no absolute aloneness of the singular: the ontological ground of the singular is the communication to it of its being; its relation to the origin frees it into its singularity in the community of the intimate universal.

Once again the openness to creation is not the univocal determination of the origin. The origin is not block being and does not give block being. It gives plurality and the promise of agapeic being appropriate to the form of finite existence. Creation as universal impermanence is a world that is still in the process of making, and of making itself: there is no ready-made completeness. Agapeic pluperfection endows a process of perfecting in finitude itself. This is just the gift of time: with time we come to be, and come to be ourselves. And so we are also let to be on our own, and at times may seem to be abandoned, bereft of oversight. But the origin makes way, makes a way. "Making a way" of being is not determining the coming to be from the outset and in view of the outcome; it is a coming to be that is free, issuing in a determinate becoming that is free to issue from itself.

Fourth: the infinite value of self and ethical-religious community

I relate this infinite value to the interiorization of free being for self that, in its power to say "no," shows itself to be potentially infinite. What is our power to negate infinitely? It is the antithetical show of the power of an infinite valuableness that is our being. Why infinitely valuable? Because infinitely valued. What being could be on a par with this infinite value of the human being? Not the human being, not nature, no determinate being, not even creation as a whole. This infinite value, as known in inwardness, is idiotic relative to the creation. Do not our characteristic forms of self-transcending show us as exceeding the measure of creation, sometimes to our shame? Must we not venture that within the finite whole the infinite value of the human being images an infinite good beyond the whole? How we answer will depend on how we understand the fact that the value of our self-exceeding freedom is, in the end, ethical and ultimately religious. Freedom takes on a plurality of forms, depending on how deeply we have understood our being, or been transformed into ourselves, or how we understand our community with others. I note briefly three forms.

First, there is the *community of equivocal desire* (see *BB*, Chapter 11). Here our self-transcending is seduced by an equivocation between its determination to univocal finitude and its restlessness that exceeds finite measure. We want every thing but want the energy of excitement that comes from exceeding every thing. But we remain in bondage to things and to our own excess; so we do not properly value things, nor our own exceeding self-transcendence. Second, there is the *community of erotic sovereignty*. Erotic self-transcending is more than manic flight from self; it knows the lack of finitude, but it can know it wisely, as the disquiet that impels its own self-becoming to its own more full realization. The community of erotic sovereignty can communicate the nobility of immanent excellence (see *BB*, Chapter 11, and more fully, *EB*, Chapter 16). Third, there is the *community of agapeic service* (see *BB*, Chapter 11, and more fully, *EB*, Chapter 17). It communicates the highest release of the promise of freedom, and it endows the highest ethical-religious community. There is no reason for its being good other than that it is good. It is the incarnation of the good in creation. Otherness gets transformed into an infinite value for itself; pluralism proves to bear the promise of a togetherness more than any mere manyness; singularity takes on its greatest intimacy of being; the freedom of becoming is released into its own most creative coming to be, the coming to be of good; the infinite value of self also becomes an infinite valuing of the other as other; and the enigmatic passing of the world is celebrated, as much as its astonishing arising into determinate being.

The utmost limit is approached in an agapeic service that is not only an ethical service in which good humans try to do the good. There is a mystery beyond human community which is more fully religious. Agapeic service brings us to the border of the mystical, when the mystery of the intermedium of being, and the mystery of the divine origin resurface with absolute power. In the universal impermanence, the borders of the between are porous to what is beyond the between: be it the coming to be, be it the passing out of being, the borders are the tugs the divine makes on us, in all commencement and in all cessation. No one knows the answer to the enigma of destiny, and yet we are nothing but the fullest question about it. Nor do we know the answer to the agonies of tragedy and evil, though they fill us with torment. No one knows the answer to the exceeding love between singulars which may mark human communities, be they spouse and spouse, or parent and child, or friend and friend, or lover and lover, or indeed a person and a place. The universal impermanence passes, and all this passes beyond us.

And it is not just the turmoils of this sudden and fugitive creation. It is the gloriously common, the ordinary: a glass of wine on an oak table; a shine of sunlight through a shutter; a blossom on a bush swaying; a squall of sudden rain; a crow cawing on a twilight tree; a girl giggling behind hiding hands; a saucy rogue winking; the last sigh of a man dying; the bawl of a baby born. All passing into being, all passing by, all passing away. And as the origin has, so I too must love it all.

I name the strange love of the singular for the singular. There is birth, ripening, suffering, perishing. There is rage that is oddly in love. There is sweetness that itches to despoil. There is the *béal bocht* that purses its lips at life's sweet bounty. There is simple gratitude for the sweetness of being that no one merits and that no act of thanks can ever repay.

Part III
Gods

Chapter 8

God(s) Many and One: On Polytheism and Monotheism

It is One
It is many
It is the sea
Circling the globe
It is no sea
It is of the air
There is nothing
That encircles it
It gives the flood tide
It withdraws to let
The cleansing wind
Turn things around

The ebb tide
Has drained the strand
The earth will revolve
The spring tide
Will flood the land
Drown the parched inlets

Between ebb and flood
Our hearts
Are stretched
& parched

Say nothing
Pray for nothing
Walk in the sun
Let the wheeling world
Pass by
Pass into
Your emptiness
Your earth

It will come again
For it has never left

GODS

Beyond godlessness and ways to God we now try to take further steps and say something about different gods and God. The fourfold way throws light on different ideas of God and the divine that have been influential in various ways and at various times, such as polytheism and monotheism, Gnosticism, pantheism, panentheism, theism, mysticism. Ludicrous would be any pretense to comprehend the numberless details associated with these views, or to the specialized erudition here exercised so estimably by the scholar of religions. Yet the fourfold way and the hyperboles can help us understand something of their essential lineaments, allowing us in immanence to address the God exceeding immanence. The point is not to pit one view against others, though there is undoubtedly conflict, sometimes to the point of war. Nor is it to put all claims on a par, for this would be untrue to differences. The notion of God truest to the being of the metaxological between offers, I believe, the richest understanding. This also offers us a plurivocity that is no mere scattered manyness but bespeaks a community of togetherness. A philosophy seeks to understand and, on the basis of its best understanding, does not shrink from advancing some view as the truer. Philosophical understanding also entails an advocacy of the strength of what seems weak. It seeks to be an agapeic mindfulness of different possibilities in their truth, let this be partial as it may. Such agapeic mindfulness must extend even to those possibilities the philosopher does not finally endorse or embrace.

   Being is plurivocal; being religious is plurivocal; the fourfold way allows a plurality of configurations and reconfigurations of the primal ethos of being, allows a plurality of ways of thinking about the divine. This plurivocity is not to be univocally reduced in the eradication of this possibility or that; nor to be speculatively sublated into one totality. The plurivocity persists in its overdetermination – it is a communication in many-meaninged signs. These signs are often equivocal but not merely equivocal, since they communicate something of the mysterious surplus of God. There remains something enigmatic about the divine, yet we are not lacking resources to come to some appreciation of the rationale, power, and limit of different ways of being related to that divine surplus. There may be many ways to try to name the absolute, none absolute, though some more true. We need mindful discernment of the inner rationale of the different possibilities and their relation to each other, a discernment as much sympathetic as critical, as much receptive as exploratory.

The movement from chapter to chapter that follows in Part III will reflect overall a movement of mindfulness from the idiotic to the aesthetic to the erotic, and to the agapeic. It will also be a movement between many and One, to mediated manyness in terms of the whole, to intermediated manyness in terms of the One beyond the whole, and finally to the agapeic One communicated in the intimate universal. This mirrors a movement between monotheism and polytheism, through the personal and the transpersonal, the Gnostic, the pan(en)theistic, to the theistic and the mystical. This last brings us to the intermedium between the human and divine in the community of the intimate universal, for mysticism is potentially idiotic in an agapeic sense: the agapeic God beyond the whole communicated in the intimate universal, and calling the human to a life of agapeic service, whether in psalms of lament and praise, or in devotion to ethical service.

RELIGIOUS IMAGINATION AND POROSITY TO ARCHAIC MANIFESTATION

I speak of archaic manifestation in terms of the plurivocal communication of the *archē*. By manifestation I do not mean univocal presence but plurivocal showing. Manifestation here implies less being grasped by the hand (see *Begriff*, *be-greifen*), and more something of the medieval religious resonance of *manifestare*: inviting to touch or being touched, more like a caress than a grab – an intimate palpability. By *archē* I do not mean one determinate principle or univocal beginning within a process of manifestation, but the (hyper)origin that creatively possibilizes manifestation in the between. *Archē* is hyperbolic in being neither reducible to the first principle in a series of manifestations nor exhausted by any one determinate manifestation or pantheon of manifestations. Of course, since we speak of *archē* in and through these more or less determinate manifestations, we always both risk, and must guard against, the identification of the derived manifestation with the originating *archē*.

Polytheism seems the most archaic manifestation, in respect of the manyness of the gods with earlier peoples (archaic in another sense). My suggestions bear primarily on the religious significance of the ontological potencies as shown in the hyperboles of being. With the more archaic ontological potencies no clear and fixed distinction between plurality and unity can be said to hold. This bears on the rapturous univocity: a saturated immediacy impossible to separate from its own equivocalness and a relatively undifferentiated sense of differences. Thus, in the archaism of polytheism there may float a vague and equivocal sense of a one and elusive power whose names are various. The immediate promiscuity of the rapturous univocity means that differences are also melded together. We could not say that there is a definite sense of an absolute One, and yet the rapturous univocity does not preclude some vague, equivocal drift of the One. This is quite compatible with the striking feature of polytheism, which is, namely, its ability to hold together often completely opposite gods without any hint of transgression to the law of contradiction. In this "holding together" that logical law of univocity seems not to hold. This fact often provides the pretext for rationalistic critiques of polytheism, yet such critiques can be misdirected: they impose on such archaic beginnings forms of univocal rationalization not at all fitting to the form of the manifestation. This manifestation is inseparable from our place in the between: there what is manifest may be *other to us*, yet the manifestation of this other is *still for us*; it is hard, initially, to separate *what* is being manifested from those *to whom* the manifestation is offered. There is a promiscuous mingling of the divine being manifested and the beings to whom the manifestation is manifest, namely, we human beings.

Primus in orbe deos fecit timor, the ancients said (Petronius fragment XXII, author unknown). Should this surprise us? Much depends on how we interpret it. Fear is inseparable from imagination, for to fear is to have an image of threat, an anticipation of harm. Fear is born together with imagination, for imagination inaugurates express differentiation, allows us to be beyond ourselves in the between, in allowing the beginning of our envisagement of what is other. Imagination is at the source of our articulating power, *prior to fixed definition* in terms of inner and outer, self and other, lower and higher. It reveals the spontaneous ecstasis of self-transcending that opens to what is intimate to inwardness, as well as placing us in a space of possible otherness beyond ourselves. These openings are saturated with ambiguity: the other portended may be ally or alien; the space of inwardness may be startlingly divine or darkly demonic. Sweet surging delight is twinned with grim flooding wrath, monstrously devastating. Just as the daimonic can be directed downwards, directed upwards, the sacred seems double – both dreadful and fascinating.

Why then baulk because our images of the gods are carriers of our fears and hopes? Could it possibly be otherwise? If there is a manifestation to and for us, what is manifested will be blended with us, and its articulation will show what we are, as well as what is other. The porosity of our being, so to say, speaks its first words with imagination. Imagination is a threshold power between what is recessed in dark inarticulation and what comes to express utterance, whether of our own immanent otherness, or of what is more originally other than ourselves, and even nature. At its deepest this porosity marks our being as a *passio essendi*. This is no gust of empty nothing. In the porosity, the energy of our "to be" takes (on) form as imagination, desire, fear, hope. In all these, there is the incipience of metaxological mindfulness, first more as promise, later perhaps more as redeemed or betrayed.

Incipient metaxological mindfulness means plural intermediation: our mediating with ourselves, our being in intermediation with what is other. Is this *only* our own self-transcendence, or must we take into account an other transcendence not reducible to our self-transcending? The metaxological suggests the second, yet not exclusive of self-transcending: in our self-transcending there is the *incognito* companionship of an other transcendence. The double mediation is first articulated inarticulately in the ambiguity of manifestation. In archaic manifestation, there is a mixing of the two, such that in one light they seem one, in another light, utterly heterogeneous. At one extreme, an almost seamless continuum of the human and divine; at the other extreme, a discontinuity of the powers disconcerting to all mortal desire.

From the outset manifestation is implicitly metaxological, and so already intricately overdeterminate. To take it only from the side of our porosity, it seems less than proportionate to account for the opening of our imaging as just the aftereffect of primitive stimuli-responses. Not only uncomprehending of the hyperboles of being, this model cannot even account for aesthetic appearing, considered as an event of sensation; much less can it address the idiocy of being, the outreaches of the erotics of selving, and the agapeics of communication. In the porosity there is a spontaneity to the upsurgence of images, generated from idiotic sources that enable some later self-conscious mastery but not first under that control. There is also a more primal rapport with the other-being of aesthetic happening. Equally with desire: a restlessness, potentially infinite, manifests something of the idiot source of the desiring to be beyond finite determination. This "being beyond" takes shape in the different forms of "being besides oneself": we live in the erotics of selving and the agapeics of communication. Hope is not "added on" as a predictive inference after a rational survey of the world; it is more a relatively inarticulate confidence that good will come. We may have determinate reasons for thinking this or that good will come, or evil, but hope here is an indeterminate expectancy of, a possible porosity to a good itself not confinable to this or that good. The porosity is a kind of exposure, and so there is *more* than definite fear in fear; there is nameless dread, intimation of the nakedness of our assured death.

Since around Kant's time a predominant view of imagination sees it as *projective* of self on the other. I have discussed elsewhere the connection with religious imagination (*IST?*, Chapter 4), but I note these two views. First, the more empiricist: imagination as an aftereffect or shadow of more vivid and original sensation. Imagination is all but emptied of the energy of transcending – a passivity without passion. Second, the more idealist and romantic: imagination is our original power to project images onto an externality otherwise void of significance. We are originals of projected otherness, not images of received otherness. This reversal of the first view risks evacuating the communication of the other, in thus elevating our original projective powers. This doublet of views is equivocal between empty fantasy and truly transcending imagination. One view risks reducing the porosity to a univocal determinate passivity; the other is tempted to cover over our *passio essendi* by making imagination the rhapsodic herald of our unbound *conatus essendi* – an activity hyped beyond all patience.

The metaxological view requires finesse for the deeper sense of the doubleness of passion and endeavor. Our transcending energies are in communication with an *incognito* source more ultimate than the abyssal self, as its own source of self-transcending. For these energies are given to be, not self-given; the source of their being given to be is an origin beyond themselves. Their own power of origination does not originate itself; it is only self-originating because it has already been given to itself as the power to be self-originating. There is an other origin beyond the origin in the self in its own inward otherness. This source is a transfinite origin – transsubjective, transobjective. We might be tempted to call it the divine, God, the origin, nothing, you name it. There are many names, and perhaps no name entirely proper. But one thing we are not doing – even as we ourselves come to name – is just naming ourselves.

Given the tangled equivocity of this implicit metaxological condition, is it then surprising that this other origin is denominated in many different images, some of them vague namings of mysterious powers, some of them with the rounded character of more completely formed beings, such as the gods? It would be surprising if there were *not* a proliferation of names, images, beings. Since the transfinite origin in itself is excessive to determination, and since in manifestation it interplays elusively with the between and us, many determinations will spring up to give articulation, not only to it but to the ambiguities of our being in the between, our own intermediate and double nature, as well as the prodigious pluralization of beings in the aesthetic happening of nature.

In this regard, polytheism shows the spontaneous efflorescent of such pluralized manifestation. Pluralized – there is the proliferation, and the many together, human, nature, the divine; manifestation – not just of the divine, but of its being enfolded together with nature and the human being. The pluralized manifestation is thus not any simple serial unfolding of determinate naming following determinate naming, like an analytical explication of predicate following predicate. Each naming of manifestation is rather complexly enfolded into itself, with power on power of participants, some of which are not immediately recognizable as divine to more reflective, analytical late-comers. The naming is compacted into itself, with a more than finite character, even when overall it stands before us with a definition harmonious and serene – behold, for instance, Greek sculptures of the gods. The naming is the finite sensibilization of sources of being, and the origin, that are beyond sensibilization. And there are names that also try to name that "beyond" of sensibilization.

SACRED NAMINGS AND THE HYPERBOLES OF BEING

I briefly remark on naming(s) as taking idiotic, aesthetic, erotic, and agapeic forms. The hyperboles are evident in both the process of selving and in the showing of the other as othering. It is just this, their *intertwining*, their communicative togetherness, that we encounter in plurivocal manifestation.

Naming the Idiotic God(s)

Archaic manifestation is idiotic in emerging from the intimacy of being and its primal porosity. This means it is on the other side of normal fixations into inner and outer, up and down, dark and light, eternity and time. It is also other to reason as determinate. As beyond determinate reason, it might seem irrational, but this is not the best way to put it: it is more in excess of determinate reason than merely irrational, and may have a deeper rationale than determinate rationality. The idiocy of manifestation has to do with the suddenness of happening, the opening of recesses of being, the hidden beyond the fixed.

A hole opens and no one asks it to open itself. Sacred space, at least initially, is not unlike such a hole. Mystery and horror mix there, fascination and recoil. Primal wonder is twin to primal terror. The secret intimacy of manifestation is also overwhelming and frightening; one might as well meet with demons as with angels. Heroes and giants mirror each other from opposite extremes. Becoming porous we seem to dissolve in the formless, as if falling down a well, or being swallowed by a whale. The inviolability of the sacred can become the tempting of the blasphemous; holy terror can turn to imprecation. Fear of the Lord is the beginning of wisdom, it is said, but this "fear" is not afraid of this or that, it is an idiotic terror shaking us to the foundations, for there are no foundations, only this porous hole.

Custom and habit cause us to forget this idiotic intimacy. Life settles into routine. The roiling beneath it all seems no longer to shift. Even religious habituation can serve to make us oblivious. The sacred idiocy tells us of the foreign that cannot be warded off. Is it an enemy? We are not always sure. It is an intimate, but it is not just our own inward otherness. It is intimate communication from an other origin. This idiocy can erupt at any time, without warning, in domesticated determinations, even in highly rationalized and moralized life. Instance: Socrates's daimon irrepressibly surfaced in a life dedicated to the rationalization of the moral, and the moralization of the rational. The recesses ask their due: the intimate strangeness is with us, within us, and we become oblivious to it at our peril.

Religious frenzy surges from this idiotic source: one finds oneself seized or overcome. (Panic is idiotic: overtaken by a contagion of dread.) Of course, this frenzy can also breed hubris and wrath (the surge is orgic): these too are unloosed daimons, or angels turned daimonic. There is a divine mania whose sacred idiocy must be treated with care, just because it carries its own opposite within itself – namely, mad madness and the evil pride that stands for itself alone against the very source of itself, as if it were it own source. Since the other origin is beyond univocal reason and differences, hubris and divine mania can be easily confused, as can damnation and blessedness, for damnation is to make oneself the absolute source of one's own blessedness. Absolute self-saving, blessing itself, becomes a counterfeit of being blessed. By contrast, religious renewal has to regain intimacy with the idiotic porosity: die to what one has determined, allow the overdetermined source shake one free, allow manifestation to pass without let, relative to the *passio essendi* purged of the wrath of a devouring *conatus essendi*.

How do the One and the many look here? There is some intimation of One beyond determination, as well as a sense of the indeterminate many. The divine is difficult to pin down, since there is a promiscuity of divine and human, and also the divine and the dark, the mysterious and the absurd, the glorious and the excremental. There is oneness that may drown us, as much as oneness that floats us free. There is plurality that might dismember us, plurality that might release us to good things of creation. The overdeterminate One and indeterminate manyness are more than merely univocal, because charged with the equivocity of sacred value. And perhaps the extremity of this equivocity will be our uncertainty whether to call the One overdeterminate or indeterminate, the surplus full or the empty nothing; since, after all, our intimacy with the porosity, be it renewed or fresh, is also a kind of return to zero.

Naming the Aesthetic God(s)

Beyond the idiocy in its pre-objective, pre-subjective overdeterminacy, there happens a more definite expression of the sacred. Manifestation becomes aesthetic, it becomes sensibilized, made to be there in terms of definite incarnations. In one regard, all manifestation is a kind of incarnation, a fleshing of the divine, but, as aesthetic, there is no one regard whereby completely to stabilize manifestation in this or that incarnation. This is notable with polytheism: aesthetic image after aesthetic image will try to pin down some intimated

---

[1]   Inanimate presences as sacred: a black stone, a sacred mountain;organic beings: the sacred oak; animal powers as divine: the bull. All "more" by being other to the human, though some would say less.

sense of the divine, or indeed the daimonic, but none will be final.[1] Just because the idiotic source is overdetermined, it could never be aesthetically determined, while it must always be so determined, in its interplay with us in the between.

Doubleness is evident again: the impossibility of an exhaustive aesthetic manifestation, the absolute necessity of manifestation, nevertheless. This is simply our condition. This is not to reduce manifestation to what it is for us. The very intimation of excess in the aesthetic presentation speaks against that. Reduction puts the finite images in place of the more than finite source. Instead of introducing the sacred, it shows itself off. In every aesthetic manifestation the balance of showing and secrecy is delicate and can be tilted oppositely: towards an aestheticism that keeps the sacred from its secret source in favor of a mere play of outward form; towards an idolatry that turns aesthetic presencing into a self-contained absolute. Aestheticism and idolatry are uneasy cousins. Hence their avenger: a rampaging iconoclasm that would smash aesthetic presence as either unserious or only an idol. Such smashing is lacking imagination. For as aesthetic presencing, sacred manifestation is more than aesthetic presence: there is the intimation of the inexhaustible surplus it cannot objectify, or subjectify. Incarnation is never objectification, or subjectification: it is the flesh of the intimacy of being. Otherness is non-objectifying, the face of presencing is not merely subjective. Flesh here is manifested sacredness, but, of course, exposed flesh can be reduced or traduced or tortured or turned to stone.

How do the One and many look here? There is a manyness to aesthetic manifestation, and we may be tempted to see manyness as the essence. Indeed, aesthetic manifestation does celebrate the plural; one manifestation, because it is other or even contrary to another, is not thereby unacceptable, or to be crushed. There is a tolerance of otherness in aesthetic manifestation. Consider the openness of polytheism to different manifestations. And yet in aesthetic manifestation some sense of the *familial togetherness* of the plural is intimated, though not necessarily spelt out: a presentiment of a togetherness in the idiotic source; of beauty in creation as holding together in an elusive aesthetic harmony; of sublimity as ominous of a divine excess beyond pure aestheticization. Aesthetic equivocity suggests this togetherness and transcendence beyond equivocity.

Naming the Erotic God(s)

The flesh as sacred shows forth features more passionately intimate and more urgently concrete. This is clear with the erotic: not only sexual eros, but the outstripping sweep of transcending. Obviously, sexual erotics, in its biological urgings and ceremonial rituals, offers a richly suggestive aesthetics of the sacred, and one that draws up from secret recesses of the idiotic intimacy. One thinks of earlier peoples – generation and fertility take us back to hidden sources: birthing gives rise to the flesh of new creations; flesh must wither into the wintering nothingness; life will be quickened anew in the interface between creation and nothing.[2] One thinks of the Song of Songs: as much the prayer of eros, as the eros of prayer. Much of mystical praise is saturated with erotic tones, the woo and swoon of love. This is not unexpected, since the idiocy of being is at its most intensive just when it takes on a more "humanized" form. The source shown in the intimacy of human flesh is not a merely subpersonal power, nor is it merely personal. It is in excess of personality, as other to its inward otherness; yet, it is beyond the impersonal, in being closer to the ontological powers of the "to be" in selving itself. The erotics of selving tell not only of the communication abroad of generative powers, but the gathering to some fulfillment of diverse

[2] The mother as matrix, as porosity between below and above: Cybele – *Magna Mater*. Demeter and Kore/Persephone/Demeter: mother/goddess/virgin of the corn/queen of death. Baubo: Orphic goddess. Sheila na nGig: obscene vulva shown, said paganly to precede Brigid – presiding, protecting spirit, patroness, saint of Bealtine. Gaia: mother of the Titans who fought the Gigantomachia: strife between Chtonic and Ouranian powers. Leda and the Swan. What of Mary, virgin mother of God? On Egyptian goddesses and gods, see Karol Mysliwiec, *Eros on the Nile*. Translated from the Polish by Geoffrey L. Packer (Ithaca: Cornell University Press, 2004).

creative powers. The *selving of being* happens in the between. It does not seem wrong to venture that *human selving,* communicated abroad in the splendor of its mystery, is a more manifesting aesthetic image of the ultimate, and of the ultimate in its intimacy. Just as for us eros can be an aesthetic sign of divine excitation and bliss, the divine itself might seem to be erotic, and erotic just in the manifestation that seeks out the mortal other – creation and the human creature – in a process of courtship, or seduction, or seizure. Manifestation might be this love of the god, or God, for the mortal.

How do the One and many look here? The One here might seem to be mediating with itself, even while in relation to the many. There is the sweep of the many, yes, but perhaps the One turns things towards itself, in its relation to the many, perhaps even out of its wanting for the many to be fulfilled in it. Dynamic recurrence to self in all differences might thus serve as a metaphysical metaphor of an ultimate ontological holding together in the unfolding of plurality or proliferation. This we see more expressly with human being, where selving is intensively erotic, and the return to self can be as deep in itself, as it is expansive to plurality outside itself. Such a re-turn to self also points to mystical possibilities of the "being together" of the human and divine. Mysticism suggests one of the most intensive forms of erotic manifestation. In this "being together" of the divine and human, there is a homecoming to the idiot, but appreciated with absolved mindfulness, where the sense of difference as dualistic opposition falls away, and the reversion to self is a restoration to God. Of course, return to self might also seem like a return to zero, if we think of the porosity of being in terms of the lack of eros, but even then the nothingness we are seems to be in some secret communion with the God who is no-thing.

NAMING THE AGAPEIC GOD

Just as the outsides of the Hindu temples, say of Khajuraho, proliferate stone cuts of erotic bliss, chaste in its wantonness, so there is an antechamber to divine peace, and when we pass out, or pass into its intimacy, all frenzy fails, and the erotic devotee falls to the ground in service beyond servility and sovereignty.

Plurivocal manifestation, I said, has to do with the intertwining of selving and othering. Given the intertwining, does our naming the divine also show the divine naming itself – naming itself as entering into communication with us – endowing the open porosity of community? Would this reversal of our naming the divine be most evident with the agapeic name – the self-naming of God as the agapeic giver?

The agapeics of community calls to us from the utmost in divine porosity. It communicates to us of the goodness of being, calling us to service of the good of the other in an abandon of self. The porosity of being is inseparable from an excess of generosity that perhaps most names the idiocy of the divine, idiocy in that the generosity is without a determinate why, and hence, in its own way, beyond all finite reason. This naming is the most elusive, often the most *incognito*, and can sometimes seem quite mad. The image of the God has a hiddenness passing beyond finite fixation: the porosity of goodness that appears only to disappear in its passage towards what is other. So where is the image and of what is it the image? Nothing finite is on a par with this passing: this hyperbole of agapeic communicating of goodness that is too much for us, and that seems all but nothing. Is there such a thing, such a no-thing, such a more-than-any thing, as the agapeics of community? We know the answer only from life, from knowing love, either our being loved, or our being in love. We know, if we know at all, only from the hazard of generosity and the exposure to goodness.

How do the One and many look here? The unity of the God, if it has a "unity," would be more like a community: manifestation of agapeic love of the plural as plural. There is a metaxological togetherness of One and many, in which the many is given its being as good, in which the One, while hidden in its own intimate reserves, yet is manifested in the aesthetic glory of the world, and in the loves of being. I call this a metaxological monotheism. I do not mean this in a sense *necessarily* hostile to the pluralism of polytheism.

There can be an appreciation that all manifestation, and not just polytheistic, bears always its own form of equivocation. The ontological truth of plurality follows from an understanding of the One as more than self-returning: as an excessive One that transcends itself, beyond itself, giving finite plurality out of surplus. God is exceeding towards creation, and the exceeding is a giving rise to the between and its original porosity, as itself communicating sacred manifestation.

This means that metaxological being, as intimating the agape of the origin, can be thought of as an intermediated manifestation of the sacred. This is why the hyperboles of being in immanence tell us of what is hyperbolic to immanent being. The manyness of creation, though it is not divine, is not de-divinized; the pluralism between origin and creation is upheld. Within creation itself there is the promise of community as exceeding the measure of self-returning eros. For this agapeic naming is, in an important sense, "personal," though it also exceeds mere "personality." There is an excess of generosity that is both radically personal and yet, as such, is more than merely personal. This community of agapeic service is the ethical-religious image of the agape of divine being. If this is a prophetic community, it does not desert the earth, nor is it necessarily antagonistic to the mystical relation, for its prayer is participation in the intimate universal that ceaselessly asks an absolved porosity between the human and divine.

FROM POLYTHEISM TO MONOTHEISM

Our stress is on the religious significance of the hyperboles, but they can be a resource for interpreting a diversity of claims of divine manifestation.[3] Archaic manifestation is often more idiotic, aesthetic, and erotic than agapeic. It is not devoid of the latter, but this is first lived equivocally, not known as such. From dark hiddenness there is a springing forth, from secret reserves, of divinities themselves dark. One thinks of Chthonic powers: Titans, Giants. One thinks further back beyond the distinction of earth and heaven. There seems a yet more idiotic source – the very origin of earth and heaven – a void, sometimes called Chaos from which all seems to spring. Chaos is idiotic: pre-objective, pre-subjective, pre-determinate, an origin older than determinate earth and sky gods. Chaos is porosity: a void, a gap, a gaping chasm (*khaino:* to gape, be wide open). Thus, too, there was named an original generative Eros, along with Gaia, twin first-borns of Chaos from which also emerged Nyx and Erebus?[4] Images related to procreation, or sacred metaphors like the primordial egg, serve the mythic naming. Sometimes the first is said to be self-generating (later rationalized as *causa-sui*): this reflects the third name of the erotics of selving, but divined in the idiotic origin, and with no clear distinction of self and other, same and different. There this "void" or "nothing" is not void or nothing – it is the anterior self-generating source, original beyond determinate generation and beings: a "void" beyond void and being; "being" beyond being and void. The idiotic God is the *nec plus ultra*: it is elemental full/empty, and there is nothing beyond, for it is the beyond out of which heaven and earth, Chtonic and Uranian gods come. The movement from the idiotic and aesthetic and erotic to the agapeic can be seen as a movement between elemental gods and the One. Here is a sketch of that traversal.

Looking at the *theomachia* between Chtonic and Olympian gods, the springing of the divine from the secret earth has much of the idiotic about it, mingled with the aesthetic and erotic. There is something Dionysian about such an *Ursprung*. A kind of madness of

---

[3] A small sampler of the extensiveness and complex detail in the study of ancient religions might be *Religions of Antiquity*, ed. Robert M. Seltzer (New York: Macmillan, 1989).

[4] See Hesiod, *Theogony* (116, 123–32) on this: Pre-Olympian Eros as a primordial generative power (overdetermined); the Olympian Eros as one god among other gods (determinate divinity); see the first speech of Phaedrus in Plato's *Symposium*, 178a6–180b12. The Tao is also a "mother" or "uncarved block" or "unborn child" prior to heaven and earth. In Egyptian mythology the creation myths hold that in the beginning, only a primordial, stagnant ocean called Nu existed.

desiring to be is manifest, a sacred idiocy, rooted in the intimacy of aesthetic happening. *Phusis*, or *natura* not only reserves its secret resources but also springs forth in all the glory of blossoming. The idiotic process of being flowers into aesthetic show. Dionysus is a vegetable divinity: he images the vine as it withers as if to nothing, into Hades, but also the power to come back to life, to fructify and revitalize, even out of laceration and dismemberment. There are, one might say, sacred porosities between what is below and what is above, between the underground and what grows on the surface of the earth. This vegetable resurrection is passed to us in the fruit of the vine, but the godly wine releases more than vital powers. It releases a *theia mania* in us, lifting vital powers to another height. The intimate ontological power of the "to be" redoubles itself aestheti-cally, first blossoming in us as begotten of nature, and further blossoming in the begetting in us of art.[5]

That the gods of paganism are many is consonant with aesthetic manifestation as a passing forth into equivocal proliferation. Aesthetic being celebrates the equivocal gen-erativity of pluralism for it is charged with erotic power. Not surprisingly, we find a kind of "personification" of the divine in different guises, from lower to higher. I doubt one should call this a "projection" of human attributes onto an other. Such a one-sided sub-jectivism simplifies the *intricated redoubling* in the process of manifestation. For what is here to be interpreted is just the *promiscuous mingling* of human powers as selving with the shown otherings of the other-power(s). At an elemental level, *the powers of nature* appear as aesthetic energies, often full of generative élan, erotically at play in the living milieu of air, earth, fire, water. A later rationalism will determine them as quasi-personal powers evidencing the "pathetic fallacy," and reduce each to an impersonal "it." But what if the immediate rapport with the charged otherness means there is no projection of a "thou" onto an "it"? For there is no "it," as understood in an objective or post-objective way. All is alive in an ensouled way. Animism, one might venture, would be a kind of immediate porosity to an enigmatically manifesting origin as trans-subjective and trans-objective. The intricated redoubling of the process is a passage in the between, and first there is no fixed distinction of subjective and objective, and no projection of subjective onto objective. In truth, no "side" determines the between (there are no sides – not yet in the porosity). In the ethos of being, closer to the primal porosity, the origin is not any "side" and is not the between either, nor the togetherness of the "sides."

If we traverse further, we can discern something of the inter-involvement of selving and othering in *the gods of the family*. Aesthetic pluralization takes communal shape through the generative power of flesh itself. Flesh embodies *relativity*, being in com-munity. Ancestor worship, for instance, marked the fleshed community that gathers a family, a *gens* into a togetherness, not merely trans-subjective and trans-objective, but perhaps beyond death itself. (See the *Lares*, spirits of the family ancestors, coupled with the *Penates*, spirits of the larder.) The living and the dead, bound first in the flesh, are bound beyond death, in a life that extends beyond the boundaries of the manifested mid-dle. To be of a family was to be a member of a religious community, not product of a contract, not child of a romantic love, but concresced in a relativity where the intimacy of being is in the flesh itself. Given the intimacy of the blood in familial *religio*, it is not surprising that our bond with the ultimate origin should be described in terms of father

---

[5]   Such an art is not merely aesthetic in a post-Kantian sense. As a celebration of Dionysus, it is a sacred art, that is, myth and religion. Nietzsche, the herald of Dionysus, understood this about Greek trag-edy: a religious art which is nothing outside of the power of myth. The persistence of the idiotic in tragedy makes it resistant to univocal rationalization, hence its suspect nature for many philosophers. The tragic god – idiotic, resistant to rationalization, its darkness dubiously divine, perhaps other than divine. Are we philosophers up to thinking this idiocy? More often than not, we are not. More gener-ally, aesthetic gods bring us bother. I except – and accept – Heidegger's appeal to renew dialogue with the poet. The poet is engaged with the divinatory rapport before and beyond the calculative intellect – rapport with the "holy," with the "daimonic," perhaps the accursed. The daimonic is between. Heidegger appreciated this intermediary role of the poet, especially Hölderlin.

or mother. Parents, the most proximate worldly source of our being, image the most intimate origin of our being at all, without which we would be nothing at all, and no "that it is."[6] (A soldier falls, fatally wounded, and many such a one calls for his mother; a person dying calls on God; each event remarkable, yet not remarkable, if we think of the child and death as the advent of the idiotic.)

Traverse further, and consider now tribal gods, *the gods of the gens*, something more communally erotic. These are the gods of the people or race, or simply of those who are one's own, and not confined to the family. Modern Westerners, disenchanted heirs of monotheism, may claim not to bend the knee before such gods. Sometimes, however, what we deny we denominate differently and even instantiate. Attachment to one's own is evident in the modern racisms (Germany under National Socialism is only the extreme example), in the ethnic animosities that sprung up with the demise of communism, even in visceral tribal allegiances to a football team, replete with emblems, animal mascots, or totems. One thinks of Rilke: the dark guilty rivergods of the blood. The flesh of the race is mediated with itself through its gods. The people comes to its own, comes to itself as claiming *erotic sovereignty*, in its celebration of its gods. In the erotic self-mediation of a people, the otherness through which it mediates with itself may be seized on as *its own otherness*. In that seizure the sacred *as intermediating* is contorted, for the *inter* of this intermediation is plurivocally open, but here it is univocalized to *one's own* people. Here we are dealing with the gods of the community of erotic sovereignty.[7] What is perilous here is that the unholy work of the community will also be seen as the manifestation, indeed indwelling, of the divine, for it is enough that this work is ours alone. As we know too well, holy evils can be committed in the name of the god of the tribe.

Such gods of erotic sovereignty express the truth that there is nothing isolated about the divine. The divine is manifested in the intermedium of being; communities of humans are extraordinarily rich concretions of being between. Clearly such communities are themselves equivocal, hence any form of erotic self-mediation through the other is inherently risky. The propensity to bring the interplay with the divine back to oneself, and hence the people back to its own, can become so predominant that what remains other is turned into an opposing alien. The people make themselves an encirclement of "God."

This intermediation of the divine in community is evident in ways not immediately recognizable as religious by modern Western man. I mean the final inseparability of the social-political and the religious. The manifestation of the divine in the between comes in everywhere, not only in the intimacy of the family but also in public acts done on behalf of the people, acts the bearers of religious as well as political significance (see *EB*, Chapter 15). This is clear from the plurivocal meaning of piety in the ancient world. It cannot be confined to religious worship, for in addition to familial piety, there are local and political pieties, bonds no less sacred than the familial.

In perpetuation or protection of one's own, the gods of erotic sovereignty are often marked by virtues associated with the warrior-king: mastery and decisiveness in battle, generosity to loyal supporters, contempt of enemies, extravagance in victory, indomitability in adversity, jealousy of other gods standing in the way of dominance, yet willingness to respect powers of equal measure, and in some cases offer a subordinate place to vanquished gods. The peoples of warrior gods are themselves worshipers of the warrior spirit of erotic sovereignty. They will to subjugate peoples of lesser power, they see the hand of destiny in that subjugation: they are on the side of the god, the god is on their side, it matters little which; the god is with its people. The erotic people finds its power swelling,

---

6   Plato speaks of the Father of all, hardest of all to find, even harder to tell if found (*Timaeus*, 28c). In the metaphysics of Neoplatonism the metaphorics of the father refers us to eternity, and our longing for home (Plotinus). Aquinas speaks of the life to come in terms of our true *patria* (see, for instance, his discussion of the beatitudes in *ST*, IaIIae, ques. 69).

7   On the charisma of power, the connections of social power and the sacred, the community of erotic sovereignty, and the intermediation of the general eros of a people, see *EB*, Chapter 15.

and it is not its own power merely: the power goes into deeper sources that it cannot univocally call its own; it is given to it to be the bearer of the destiny of these powers, which are only its own because they are not simply its own. From there its imperial confidence comes. When this confidence deserts it, its destiny is no longer manifest.

As we know from the ancient world, the extension of imperial erotic power can pound the distinctiveness of the plural powers into a subordination in which the many come to be assembled under a sovereign one. The many are not extirpated but subjugated and subordinated, and can continue a qualified role, under the gathering of the one power. The process reaches a culmination, I suppose, in the figure of the emperor, who is god incarnate on earth. This cannot be the end. The erotic sovereign is more *conatus essendi* than *passio essendi*, and if we do not acknowledge the latter we can betray the primal porosity that is intimate to our being and to our being religious. There is a further reach to transcending which is patient to deeper sources of ultimate power, though it will appear as an abdication of self-affirming power to those totally in love with the gods of erotic sovereignty. The erotic sovereign can be a king though he can degenerate into a tyrant. The sacred king becomes the tyrant when he forgets the sacred, and then, as earlier peoples knew, he is no longer a true king and nemesis will come.

To say that the emperor is a god is not to say that the emperor is God.[8] Imperial pantheons, of course, may also embrace national or tribal gods, when an empire like the Roman, as a community of communities, seeks to realize a more universal openness or inclusiveness. Gods hostile to the transcendence of a closed particularism turn us away from the universalism promised intimately in the community of the between. That promise may first appear as nothing more than an inchoate ideal. In the Hellenistic empires and then the Roman empires a less particular sense of community extends to a togetherness of many peoples under the emperor. Interestingly, with this burgeoning of universalism human beings are driven more into themselves to regain contact with the idiot and to emerge with a strengthened appreciation of the singular. The acme of this idiocy is the sense of the singular as of infinite value. We are pointed to true religion as bringing together the singular and the human community in the *intimate universal*. This comes out most clearly with the God of agapeic intermediation. But in the gods of paganism there is *the emergence of a One among the many*.[9] Zeus may not be the One, but Zeus is the name closest to the One, and the others revolve around this one.[10]

Aid was offered by Athens in another guise, namely, that of the philosophers. Their questioning of the traditional gods involved a sifting in which there emerges the call of *the universal beyond family, or city, or tribe, or empire, indeed beyond nature*. The universal

---

[8] To read (after the regicide of the French revolution, for instance) just the ideology of human self-assertion into the situation is to misread the living togetherness of human and divine power. For human power is an endowment of divine power, gifted to finitude for its provisional span, within a more opaque providence we can hardly discern as angry armies clash by night. The pagans and Augustine are more deeply in agreement with each other here than with the modern post-Enlightenment political theorist who thinks in a horizon that contracts the notion of the power of being, be it human or natural or divine.

[9] In his *Civitas Dei* Augustine's discussion of polytheism and the many gods of the Romans is interesting. His engagement with the philosophers, the Platonists, bears on the discrepancy between their more refined monotheism and the popular polytheism. Augustine applies arguments to the polytheistic gods modifications of which later atheists were to apply to the Christian God: product of fantasy, if not the connivance of dark, daimonic powers (with modern atheists these powers are often psychologized as stemming from (im)potencies of the unconscious). Augustine tries to "demythologize" the pagans; the atheists of modernity claim to demythologize Christianity, as of course do some Christians. There is a tendency in postmodern thinking to oppose monotheism and polytheistic paganism, to the detriment of the former as "totalizing" and to the complement of the latter as pluralizing difference. This contrast is overdrawn. See *Pagan Monotheism in Late Antiquity* eds. Polymnia Athanassiadi and Michael Frede (Oxford: Oxford University Press, 1999), on monotheism in late paganism and Hellenic society.

[10] *Vide* the fact that Zeus had many names, manifesting a plurality of powers that overlapped with the powers of other subordinate gods – these names testify to idiotic, aesthetic, and erotic potencies.

is the uni-versus: literally, *turned towards the one*; the call to be universal turns us thus to the One. Philosophers have been servants of this turn: they sought a *logos* that ran through all things: a *logos* not of here or there, but of here and there, and elsewhere, and everywhere, and yet of nowhere as a confined this. Stoics will speak of cosmopolis. Who or what governs this polis? Not human power, and not any determinate thing in nature, but more a guiding noetic providence, to be discerned intermittently when our own noetic powers have been properly quickened. Though the Stoics counsel a return to soul's inner fastness, there need be nothing "subjectivistic" about this: *nous* within us is in community with the universal *Nous* without and about us, above us. Deeper appropriation of inner mindfulness offers the release of self-transcending power that opens to what is other to ourselves: not other as hostile but as in community with what is most intimately ethical in us.

We are here on the boundary between the gods of the erotics of selving and the God of the agapeics of communication. We are both drawn out beyond ourselves and yet returned back to ourselves, even as we are drawn above ourselves. A more universal porosity turns away from closure on ourselves, but here being drawn deeper into the idiocy of innerness is not at all the opposite to being drawn out beyond self. It is in a more intensive openness of the infinite innerness of selving that a potentially infinite openness to othering becomes more marked. That infinite restlessness shows erotic selving to be more than infinite lack, even as it also is the lack of the infinite. There is an affirmative power at work in our lack, a secret surplus of promise that drives us beyond our present partialities. There is the seed of agapeic self-transcendence at work in erotic selving, a memory of divine festivity that is there at the origin of eros itself, and without which eros would be nothing but a nothingness, lacking even the wherewithal to make any effort to overcome the lack.

Becoming discontented with what is our own, *there is a (re)discovery, in the surplus of ourselves, of an essential poverty*. This poverty would make itself available to what may come, what will come, come what will. In our porosity, a seed of agapeic mindfulness germinates, mingling richness and poverty, and paradoxical beyond dialectic. Poverty here is a divestment of false attachments to finite things when they prevent, or we prevent in them, the shine of what exceeds them. Of course, finite things can also come to be released unto themselves, as they let the shine of the origin appear in finitude. We have to *become as nothing* to let the divine other be there as more truly communicated. Our being nothing is not nothing. It is the dying of erotic self-sovereignty and the resurrection of a new passion of openness beyond sovereignty. In the release of a form of posthumous mind, I mean a mindfulness posthumous to our will to power, a truer self-transcending is called forth.

METAXOLOGICAL MONOTHEISM

The religious intermedium is not univocally determinable, nor dialectically self-determining, and not irredeemably equivocal. It is an occasion of metaxological discernment of the intimated signs of the *agapeic archē*. The claims to ultimacy of the previous namings must be relativized – not so much rejected as transformed. Each is to a degree in thrall to the circle of itself, and not thrown fully enough beyond or above itself.

First, the relativization means a new mindfulness of what comes out of the intimacy of being; a guardedness against formations of power turned away from the origin, despite their surge of energy; a vigilance struggling with angels and demons, coming from beyond consciousness, speaking in tongues, soothing and sweet, snarling and stenched.

Second, it means a shift in our love of the glory of creation: the aesthetics of happening is something beautiful, but it is good as given and is not ultimate; the powers of generation, marvelously proliferating, are gifts of the divine, not God; nothing in creation is God, and yet all is there as gift of God. *A love of the mortal* is released, for the mortal is given being because it too is loved in its otherness.

Third, the relativization means a conversion in our understanding of power: we are not to turn on the world as if God-forsaken, as if it were given its value through us, and our will to power. We are not sovereign gods anointed for the seizure of creation; pause is given to any *conatus essendi* that would divinize itself. The world stands before us differently. This difference appalls us when we behold the wasteland our will to power has produced. We have lifted ourselves to divine status, the garden of creation we have fouled. The inflation and the fouling are not different.

Fourth, the relativization reorients our relation to ourselves and our otherness. We are not time's master but its beneficiaries; nothing we own is ours, it is from another, and not, we sense, given grudgingly, but as freeing us into the promise of that gift, and hence also into the freedom to exploit the gift in ways not generous, not agapeic. If there is a critique of anthropomorphism here, it should not be directed at God's deflation in our own inflation (as with Feuerbach and his heirs), but at the chastising of our hubris, its bubbling and abuse.

What now makes the relativization also a *transforming*? First, with regard to the *idiocy of being*, it brings home to us the intensive depths, indeed innerness of being in all beings. This is especially so with the singular human self: the poverty of the singular self as idiot is its infinite worth as valued in its being itself and not for its being of use for something else. Its goodness for itself is its uselessness for anything else but to be itself. This uselessness, this poverty, is what makes it rich in promise relative to its own ability to be agapeic for the other.

Second, in relation to *aesthetic manifestation*, the glory of creation draws us towards itself with a refreshed feel for its mystery. It is there for a good we try to divine, though often we come up blank. The poverty of that blankness can oppress us; it can also release a strange sense of purposiveness beyond any definite purpose we can fix. Creation is an ocean in current; streams come from sources unknown, far and near, perfumed with their origin, carrying ships somewhere, to undreamt harbors, elsewhere and here, who knows where exactly. The current seems to stream with overdetermined purposiveness and with no definite purpose the poverty of our souls can comprehend. Even to be able to see that the gift is a gift is itself a great gift and a release that brings relief.

Third, in relation to *erotic sovereignty*, eros awakens beyond sovereignty in a further stirring of lack. The satisfied self is not satisfactory. Even in its noblest self-satisfactions it is ushered humbly before mysterious otherness that brings it to a stop and draws it on. The stirrings of the restless heart sometimes are so faint as to seem as imagined voices: a faint breeze whispers in rooms back there not visited for years, perhaps not ever opened; the memory of something never seen appears for an instant, and one was not sure if one dreamt that instant or not, does it matter, for one is unsettled and unsure, and the self-contentment of sovereignty is taken from one. For one has the presentiment of a presence behind one's shoulder and one turns sharply to confront it and demand its name, but there is nothing when one turns so, and as one turns away and back, the absent presence is again there, where, nowhere, somewhere. And now one cannot settle again confidently to one's pursuit, for one is pursued.

The heart is restless; there is no rest in it; it cannot bring itself to rest. A loneliness arises that is not alone but hungry, and lonely because of that rustle of the wind, or the air of music that strayed through an open window and caught the soul off guard, or because of the arresting glimpse of children caught in play, and the stab of foreboding that suffering will come, and the voices of play will all fade away into their appointed hush. Loneliness that has no name, hunger that has no food: the erotic sovereign is returned to its own idiocy, and there turned over, its mastery revealed as not the possession in which it possessed itself. The self-possession was a child shielding itself. The intimation of the agapeic *archē* pierces to the *passio essendi*. Vulnerability to the suffering self and the suffering others brings a new longing that fits no finite world, nor finds any final home, though creation be loved exorbitantly.

Where, or in whom, find *manifestation of the agapeic God*? The opening of the universal, the opening to the other, the opening to the singular, all in the goodness of creation are acknowledged in the monotheistic religions, Jewish, Christian, Islamic, but Christianity makes the most extreme claim: the agapeic God is shown in a singular incarnation. But let us take these three points in turn.

In relation to the universal: The One is not just power. God may be called Father, and though equivocity is always possible between the punitive father and the father who embraces the prodigal son, this second father points us to the agapeic God. Recall the parable of the vineyard, already mentioned in relation to Kant. The Father of Jesus gives in excess of the measure; there is no measure that is proportioned to human exactitude; all are given their due, and more again – and in a sense, nothing is due, for all is gift.

In relation to the other: The respectable ones are loved, for they are lovable, but what of the reviled others? To love them would be too much – excessive to the human measure; exceeding the bonds of solidarity defined by the roles a particular culture imposes. One walks the streets among the crowds, and many, so many, look ugly, but there is to each a worth of being that ugliness, even evil cannot expunge entirely. The posthumous minding of agapeic love sees the ugly, there is no squinting, but it knows there is more. See the father's embrace in Rembrandt's rendition of the prodigal son: tender compassion beyond all finite measure, and yet there it is in care of the finite other in his woebegone singularity. A sign of the absolute is written in suffering, even in sinning finitude, accepted beyond the measure of its defection from good, beyond all measure. There is no measure here, except the good of the mortal, and this is measureless in the agapeic origin.

In relation to the singularity and goodness of creation: Audacious claims are made about care for the sparrows, or the lilies that neither weave nor spin. What is all this? It does not tell of a vision surveying the world from afar, like an astronaut looking down on earth from far off space, where the suffering cries of tortured humans do not reach. It tells that agapeic engagement is there in the midst, there in the torment chamber where the suffering cry out and torture us with their torment. Agapeic mindfulness loves the singular in its intimate thisness. It is idiotic in extending into the deepest recesses of the singular, recesses the singular might not even know of itself.

And the goodness of creation? Have the lilies of the field more splendor than Solomon in finest attire? To answer "yes" would mean that the elemental aesthetic happening of creation offers us beauty beyond finite measure: man-made beauty cannot touch it; the touch of the elemental, the very flesh of the world, is charged with worth from the origin. We are not unlike Dostoevski's Ridiculous Man: we have seen and yet do not see the shine on creation, having filtered out the shining we awake to life as a dull half-light. The dream of the ridiculous man tells of an awakening from the sleep of finitude, awakening into a porosity to finitude that cannot be just finitized.

What of death and God as agapeic? An almost impossible question that brings us to a stillstand, or a stand. The matter is more than a cyclical return to life after death, as spring recurs after winter. Beyond the immanent guarantee of such a cyclical recurrence, there is something singular about death, in the dimension of the hyperbolic: the "once" of singular life is matched by the singularity of the "never," perhaps "never" again. Once and once only is life given here to us in the finite between. Never again? Our great agony bears on the "yes" to being, in the greatest extremity of suffering, and sometimes even more hyperbolically in the enduring of evil. We return to zero and face a blank, but will something be communicated in the last passion, the ultimate porosity? Will the godsend of an affirmation come – the hyperbole of a great amen? Such a "yes" would be the final faith that the goodness of the origin is the truth of being, even when the time comes for the gift of our time to be withdrawn, and sometimes with an extremity of violence to the singular. Simply to be is so good we cling to it, we recoil from death, but we have no claim on being and its gift for us. This gift of our being, it lasts a finite span, and the clinging to be must be released from its clinging, and then not cling but be released into a thanking of the unmerited gift. It was given for no reason beyond its good, and now it is over, and I must give myself over to the origin again. Is this being given over a passion that transfigures – where we must live the agape of being in consent to, in patience of, the goodness of the origin in death itself?

Golgotha is the place of porosity between death and God. The outcry from the place of skulls comes out of the most intimate depths and shows the extreme idiocy of suffering: a return to zero, where the porosity between life and God is even in death itself. Death returns the *conatus essendi* absolutely to its most intimate *passio*: death is absolute patience to God, finding us (out) at extremes either of refusal or absolved trust – for there is finally no middle between that is unresolved – unless purgatory allows another middle between this life and heaven and hell.

What of Christ's return to zero, his passion? Might it not be seen as the complete kenosis of any usurping *conatus essendi*, and its restoration to the *passio essendi* – absolute passion, hence also absolute porosity, absolving porosity – and in the ultimate undergoing, giving himself up into the "yes" to God? This absolute passion absolves the *conatus* of its false being God and is given back to the one God. The humiliated Christ is the absolving poverty, the porosity that is also an absolute patience to evil. This patience is an enactment of divine redemption. Patience is redemption: not to say "no" even to the absolute "no" of evil; "yes" to the promise of good, even in the absolute defection of radical evil. The last moments of Christ suggest that in the desolation of abandonment, and in being bereft, there is release beyond abandonment, a different abandon to the good of God. His life is given up to another, the final "yes" releasing self from clinging to its own absoluteness, giving itself over to the Father.

What is asked of us? Giving back – in the ceasing of given life. But what have we now to give back? Nothing except our "yes." Yes: that our dying be our birth into gratitude for being as gift, gratitude no matter what comes in the narrow grave, perhaps nothing, perhaps resurrection, perhaps transfiguration. Love is entrusted to the goodness of the origin in trusting beyond the measure of finitude. The mystery not only remains, it is deepened in this entrusting. Love's hope is that the taste of peace comes in this trusting.

THE PRAISE OF PAGANISM

Why you seem to preach like a pious Christian! Perhaps. But perhaps in any event, it is not at all a matter of thrashing paganism. Is there a worthy praise of paganism? Need our turning to the agapeic One be a turning against the many, if no one has a monopoly of this One? The situation is ambiguous to say the least.

First, paganism has been criticized as divinizing what is not divine, and for some the superiority of monotheism is its dedivinization of such putative idolatry. There being only one God, all others must be impostors. A sacred imposter is not a neutral simulacrum, it is temptation to apostasy from the One. War must be made on polytheism, which is polyidolism. Yet there can be a *univocalizing* monotheism which risks a kind of light pollution: we cease to see above us the stars in the sky or feel the earth beneath us. A *polemos* against the pagan is generated by an *exclusive One*: it is either the One or it is nothing, and the many as other to the One must be either nothing or made into nothing. Thus can come a monotheistic totalitarianism which issues in hatred of claims other than *its own*. By contrast, one might claim that true attendance on the agapeic One is not closed to strange showings of the unmeasured One but is alert for any unexpected revelation.

The dedivinization of the world is true in that creation is not God. The dedivinization is untrue if it extirpates every trace of the divine in creation. The violence towards the polytheistic many can become the worldly assault on the neutralized earth now arousing in us no reverence but only greed. There is a religious rage that readies the earth for our predation. But the earth is passing strange. We feel the strangeness, less and less in the great cities we light without cease and fill with never subsiding noise. We endure in spiritual poverty. We should we go outside and pass through silence. We would know who the intruder was, and it is not the wind or crow. We break the silence. Strike off, take to wayless fields, see scrub and mud, and the earth like rough flesh has a touch of realness. We cover the earth but it withdraws into unreached recesses of patience, in waiting, and as if abiding with an abandoned mystery.

Second, polytheism determines the divine in terms of a plurality of divine figures, powers, persons, but complex relations pertain in the network of these figures and powers. The pantheon is a community of plurality, and yet the gods are often shown in the splendor of individualized thereness. Greek religion: We behold the statues of the gods, each a unity for itself – a resplendent integrity of being, univocal in being a one, more than univocal in that no fixed finite measure will fully contain the reposed radiance that has sculpted itself in showing. The pantheon gathers the familial plurality of such resplendent ones, under the one who comes to be the father: Zeus.

Third, the free play of human imagination is given release and not contracted into a vanishing point of self-enclosed unity. Such free play, of course, can run to excess, even madness. The release can let loose depths of richness – and monstrous darkness too – that a constraining univocity would merely stifle. There is something to the view that certain constraints of monotheism can be disciplinary in a stifling way towards the some-times wayward upsurge of the urgency of ultimacy. Tares and beautiful blooms grow up around each other in this upsurgence. A monotheistic *univocity* can cut down all the crops before the flowers of earth surface for harvest. It may lay a blight on the ground of immanent manifestation such as to produce godlessness and then atheism. Is the fertile soil of manifestation to be sterilized just because it also produces monsters? Sterile soil brings forth not God but nothing. Could one live in an antiseptic world, a world without perfumes? Is reaction to such perceived sterility an ingredient in current attractions of polytheism to some postmodern thinkers?[11]

Fourth, polytheism *may* foster a kind of tolerance for diversity. It can also foster the opposite: our gods ally with our destruction of your gods, and you. Depending on the play of one and many, and how we inhabit this interplay, encounter with plurality can give us pause to be perplexed about the *other's* gods, and hence about *our own* gods, and hence about the God that is neither mine nor thine. Diversity invites diffidence about an even more ultimate One. Diffidence mutes our crowing about our small divinities who, after all, may not be the ultimate. Perplexity may precipitate a rush to premature convic-tion – it may also rob us of our say-so certainty.

Fifth, polytheism suggests there is no escaping *mixture*. Perplexity granted can yield a porosity to manifestation as enigmatically plural. Is the other's god the resented source of my distress? From whence comes the divine? No one knows. Who can comprehend its mystery? No one. What certainty is given us? Not easy to say. Riddle on riddle may bring some breach to the soul's closure on itself. Strangers whirl to savage gods: Is this manifestation? Yes and no. Sparrows twitter in the hedges: Is this manifestation? Yes and no. A boy grips his father's hand as the plane lifts off: Is this manifestation? Yes and no. A child howls hearing his mother is dead: Is this manifestation? Yes and no. Is it weaseling to say yes and no? Yes, it may be. No, it may also be startlement before ambigu-ities that will not fade away and that yet for us make a way. To be on a way we need not go away, for home is intimately strange. Being at home in not being at home; not being at home in being at home: this is our intermediate condition. All being in the between may be porous to divine communication, but you could not prove this univocally, for

---

[11] Postmodern polytheism is associated with Lyotard, though Nietzsche seems to be the patron saint of post-Enlightenment paganism. Unlike Nietzsche, some New Age postmodern paganisms seems more like aesthetic Hellenism washed of the furies (not much sticky evil here). The elemental is sanitized of the sinister. Out of the games of babes at Halloween comes more of the truth: porosity to the dead. *Et in Arcadia ego.* We celebrate a Sabbath of the earth but are unsuspecting that the earth can give back monsters. *The earth is ominous.* See Heinrich Heine's conclusion of *Zur Geschichte der Religion und Philosophie in Deutschland* [*Philosophy and Religion in Germany* (Albany: SUNY Press, 1986)] regarding modern pantheism and its ominous tone concerning any resurgence of German paganism.

we cannot appoint its where or its how or its what. We can make ready. We need not be foolish virgins.

Sixth, if the divine is spoken of in many ways, must this plurivocity be confined to *our* speaking? Suppose God communicates in the equivocal signs of the permeable ethos? The manifestation may be to us, it is not just effected by us. The plurivocity of the metaxological is not just *our* speaking. Being bespeaks itself plurivocally. Why not the divine also? And yet, there may be an order of relations in the many sayings, with some more ultimate.

Seventh, what of the danger of totalitarianism? It is wrong to think in terms of "total-ity" here because in a polytheistic milieu the world has neither been *demythologized* nor *remythologized* by "totality." The question is anachronistic in so far as totalitarianism is a modern phenomenon, born in the wake of Christendom's triumph over paganism, then of the secularization of Christianity, then of the divinization of secular politics wedded to the stupendous powers readied for exploitation by modern technology. The politics of ancient paganism were never secular. Though the character of those politics was often imperial, and in that sense potentially "totalizing," their sacral character contained many chastising rejoinders to the worldly will to power of the human lord. A sacred king is not a tyrant. Hubris there might be, but nemesis there also was. Every lord of the world forgot this at his own peril.

Modern totalitarianism is the outcrop of enlightenment reason turned away from the divine as instituting human power, turned towards a systematic, secular will to power that would have a *philosophy on its side*, and if necessary to justify its degradations. The Leviathan, as Hobbes reminds us, must be a mortal god, monstrous enough to cow the plurality of competing wills to power. Leviathan makes us drink the wine of an old wisdom in new, very different bottles: fear of the Lord is the beginning of wisdom. But there is no divine lord, only humans lording it over creation and each other. In these new bottles the wine of the old wisdom must become a bitter gall.

I agree: the religious urgency of ultimacy must be tempered socially and politically, with due respect for its different expressions. The *passio essendi* must never be forgotten, nor the religious meaning of our porosity of being. The urgency of ultimacy is *always* danger-ous. It may erupt into a mania not divine. Filled with one's feeling of being granted the ultimate truth, one cannot abide the other dissident to one's dispensation. To impute our notions of individual freedom back into polytheism is wrongly to mingle the religious premodern and the a-religious modern and postmodern. There is no return to polythe-ism possible, but there is possible a tolerance for plural ways of divine manifestation. Postmoderns prefer their paganism without the blood. We can never sanitize the plural-ism of its potential for *mischievous equivocity*. Evil sprouts from dark sources – sources badly understood and miscalculated by the naïve, sources malignantly manipulated by others not naïve, the modern princes of darkness. They stir the pot of equivocity to stew the sour juices of their witches' brew. We do well to be on guard religiously – about reli-gions, especially political religions.

There are enchantments some malign, some benign. There may be also magicians, magi who, in seeking to be wise, do not entirely fail. Think of Prospero in the *Tempest*. Remember in exile his aesthetic intimacy with the elemental powers – this means Caliban as well as Ariel. His destiny: political power usurped by his brother, then exile, and ambition to reverse the usurpation. But on the enchanted island, a different wisdom is attained, even a realization that a certain pursuit of truth can neglect wise order in the kingdom and allow usurpation its chance. There is a different power beyond will to power. It is beyond servility and sovereignty. Prospero, able to command the elements, abjures this his ascendancy and breaks his staff. There is a vision beyond political power and enchanted aesthetics. These our revels now are ended. A song bids adieu to domin-ion and consents to the sleep that (sur)rounds our life, the sleep of the idiotic, its intimacy now more than half-hidden from wakefulness. There is a sleep deeper than wakefulness, where wakefulness is an enchanted dream, and perhaps we will wake up in that other sleep beyond all dreaming by fitful finitude.

We do not return to polytheism, there is no return, but pagan love of the earth is always asked, love of the good of elemental being, astonishment before the river that runs, the surf that pounds, the clear blue of the ether, the blinding dazzle of new snow, the musk on the fields in spring. The ageless earth waits in its dark mystery. Its dark mystery is in our very flesh, flesh that is the earth come to mindfulness, the humus inspirited with the breath of God. The love of God's breath on and in the dark humus, that is why we are human. To be true to our humanity, to know the breath in our flesh, to know the earth in our inspiration and expiration, is to be true to God's even darker spirit in all things and above all things.

Chapter 9

God(s) Personal and Transpersonal:
On the Masks of the Divine

Between the intimate silence	I am behind the window	I do not hear it
& the hearing of love	Of the moving train	But see there
It sounds and recedes	Outside by the wayside	In the residing motion
It sings its face	Something there (– a ghost,	The unseen wind
& it is always	a gust)	
More than what faces us	Tickles the bluebell-topped weeds	
Beyond all faces	& the grass shivers	
It is never faceless	Into a passing of laughter	

PERSONAL GOD(S) AND PLURIVOCAL MANIFESTATION

Should we speak of the divine as personal or nonpersonal, or both, or otherwise again as transpersonal? The meaning of manifestation is again in question. Certain essential considerations make the personal unavoidable. The more we move from univocity to metaxology, the more we find an intensive sense of communicative being as selving within community. To be is to be in relation: to be personal is to be in social relations, to be at all is to be in community. In that light, being as personal is ontologically richer than being as impersonal. There is also an ontologically richer personalization in the movement of naming from the idiotic to the agapeic. Consonant with this movement one might say this. First: person is idiotic as singular and irreducible – in one sense incommunicable, in that no substitute can absolutely replace a person, and yet person as idiotic is also an original of communicability. Second: person is communicated aesthetically in its bodied thereness – personal incarnation shows more than fixed univocal determinacy. Third: person is erotic as self-transcending, showing forth a dynamic integrity of being, an open wholeness more than any self-enclosed identity. Person is ecstatic: the "more" revealed in self-surpassing is both a desire to be more (oneself) and a desire for more than oneself, a desire for inexhaustible being. Fourth: person is agapeic, at least in promise: its being is a love of inexhaustible being; its communicability is to be in a community of goodness with others, a community beyond finite fixation, wherein the intimate reserve of goodness is never depleted by being given away.

And yet there are indicators beyond "person" evident in metaxological pointers to an otherness not simply subpersonal but transpersonal. The transpersonal must come into consideration, if "person" is confined to the human being as *a finite integrity* of mindful life. The divine intimates more. Person itself intimates something of this "more." My line of exploration will again reflect how the hyperboles of being communicate something of this "more." Agapeic being in metaxological community points to the transpersonal that less suppresses the personal as fulfills its release into a more ultimate communicative transcending beyond self. The agapeic origin at once suggests the acme of the personal God and also the transpersonal ground that cannot be confined, without further qualification, to the "personal." In this light, even our images of the divine as "impersonal" (God, for instance, as the *rock of ages*) might be seen as (indirectly) hyperbolic to the personal – and this, even though we do sometimes identify, too closely and questionably, the transpersonal divine with the less than personal, say, with the "blind" forces of nature.

The notion of "person," as is well known, took on some of its present meaning somewhat late, in Roman times.[1] The "*persona*" (*prosopon*) was originally the mask the actor wore in enacting a role; the persona was the enacted being, the presented identity of the character on the stage. *Persona* is manifestation, through an acting one, of an other, such that while this other seems to recede as the acting one appears, *this receding is also the coming forward of the other*, in and through the mask of the acting one. *Persona* is the happening of an ambiguous aesthetic show in which guise, dis-guise, even *incognito*, are significant. An other faces us in and through the mask: expressiveness that is recessive and excessive at once. A visage is a face: a presencing of intimate being sur-faces but there is more than surface. Again we encounter *plurivocal* manifestation. The movement is to make manifest the other in the one, or the one in the other: there is a passage between character and enactment, between the reserve of the role and its dramatic incarnation. The acting person must be porous to the reserve of the role and let the incarnation of the character be there as manifest. Person is mask, hence partakes of the doubleness of mask as at once both revealing and reserving, manifesting and intimating. This doubleness seems to be equivocal in one guise, but perhaps in a truer guise it is metaxological. Yet even the truer guise for us humans is not absolutely separable from dis-guise, perhaps a certain *incognito* of the divine. Person has to do, we might say, with both the manifests and masks of God.

How understand this double movement of personal expressiveness – both recessive and excessive – in relation to the fourfold sense of being and the hyperboles? Could we speak of God "being personally" *between* full reserve and full communication? Speak of the first reserve as the intimate source of full communication, and the second communication as in no way exhaustive of the full reserve, for the divine would be inexhaustible, superplus agape?

Revisit the fourfold correlation: first, the idiotic is correlated with the person as singular and incommunicable, in the sense of being irreplaceable. This incommunicability, for instance, is noted by Aquinas, referring to Richard of St Victoire (*ST*, Ia, q. 29, art. 3). I understand this not as an autistic univocity, but as a singular oneness of being that is an original of communicability, and communication. The intimate incommunicability is what sources the singular communicability of this person or that: the personal original one is both reserved, incommunicable and yet in communication and expressed.

Second, the aesthetic correlates with the more overt communication of the singular person: there as embodied expression, but as such not mere body – the body is a sign of the soul; the body is the soul in aesthetic communication with what is other to itself. The spiritualist evaporator of the body is as unsatisfying as the physicalist reductionist: aesthetic communication of the incommunicable person is always more than finite univocal determinacy. This "more" is plurivocal, though often encountered as equivocal in that we are not sure how to read the signs of incarnate communication. Something inexhaustible is communicated in the mode of plurivocal excess.

Third, the erotic correlates with the self-surpassing character of this plurivocal "more." The personal energy of self-communication is both centered and decentered: centered, for someone communicates; decentered, communication is the exceeding of any center closed on itself. The person is a living whole but an open communicating whole, hence beyond the terms of holism, in a manner which does not destroy the whole but intensifies it in a self-surpassing movement. What passes through person passes beyond person as this person, and yet intensifies the singularity as a happening of passage, as a porosity of being that becomes creatively self-transcending.

[1]   The term becomes humanized relative to Roman legal usage (the person as one before the homogeneous law), and in wake of the Trinitarian conception of the inner life of God: the three persons as manifestations or hypostases of the One at home with itself, the immanent intermediation of Godhead.

Fourth, the agapeics of communication correlates with the emplacement of the person in the metaxological community. This emplacement is most fully an emplotment when this community is ethical and religious. The intimate communicability here, as agapeic, shows the person as in generous communion with the other, without violence to the reserve of the intimate. There is a fullness of communication but it echoes and calls to, even as it calls out, the reserve of the full already there at the origin in the intimate idiotic. This communication shows itself to be from surplus plenitude. Here personal communication is never a depleting of what is reserved in the intimate. Quite to the contrary, the possibility of the intimate universal suggests itself: not the neutral, not the homogenous universal, but one addressing the deepest reserve in the person. Being religious most intensively participates in this intimate universal; prayer is our porosity in and to the intimate universal. Person in this fourth communication is also most radically porous, in terms of a renewed opening of the intimacy but also ethically in being willing to place itself in the compassionate service of others. In its very irreplaceability it makes itself available, even to being a replacement for the irreplaceable other to the extreme of sacrifice.

MONOTHEISTIC AND POLYTHEISTIC PERSONALIZATIONS

The interplay of monotheism and polytheism, One and many, comes back again, now marked with the doubleness of the mask. The anthropomorphic gods of paganism are personal, but there are powers that cannot be easily humanized. *Moira* is not personalized at all, for it is above all gods, even the highest. Yet there is likeness to us, down to our mischiefs: Homeric gods as wayward, as lovable, as risible, as we their human doubles. Catastrophe is not attributed to impersonal forces in an impersonal cosmos ordered by impersonal intelligibility. Catastrophe shows the offended gods in need of propitiation; a pollution must be cleansed in a ritual reordering of the cosmos. We *do* image the gods, and while that imaging often is trapped within the limits of our self-understanding, there is a dynamic beyond self in it also, a dynamic perhaps never entirely free from self-entanglement. As in an equivocal intermedium, self and other mingle, and it takes a long purging to see that the other *is other* to the self, and so not just like but also unlike and perhaps in some measure so unlike as to be in another dimension entirely, and not to be measured by our standard. This asks for our *patience* to hyperbolic manifestation, when we are slowly made permeable to extreme otherness and the communication of the inexhaustible reserve of the divine.

In monotheism, by contrast, the personalization of the divine is both more contracted and more universalized. Contracted, in that the One God is likened to an all-mighty source of personal solicitude. Universalized, in that, there being only one God, this God is God of all of nature and history. And if this God is for a special people, such as the Jews, God is also for all creation, and hence the God of all peoples, and the God of none exclusively. If His favor is a people favored, they do not choose Him, He chooses them. The initiative is His revelation to guide them in time's twilight or its dawn to the promised good prepared for them. This God of all is the supreme Thou. Thus Pascal's famous contrast of the God of Abraham, Isaac and Jacob and the God of the savants. The personal names of the ancestors, their very singular identities, have to be named, as does the singular history that defines their identity in covenant with God, because the divine other is also to be worshiped in the spirit of what is deepest in humans: their being together as ethical persons in community.[2]

---

2   Moses to the Voice: Tell me who sent me: "I am who [I] am." The Voice names itself; we do not name it. Of course, the meaning of the name is disputed – it seems personal, as a voiced name, but not finitized or finitizable, hence in a sense, transpersonal, if we think of personal in our own terms: this doubleness of the name: personal and transpersonal – not at all impersonal, for the impersonal does not have a voice, does not bespeak itself singularly to the singular human being. Intimate and universal: known and beyond knowing; named in not being named; not named in being named; absolutely immanent and immeasurably transcendent. Being in self (transpersonal): being for (personal: I am for you – though "being for" is personal as *trans*personal); being there with, *con-stans*, standing there with: absolute constancy that was, is and will be there – and there for . . .

The personalization is contracted even more radically in Christianity, but also more universalized. More contracted: the singular person Jesus is the incarnation of God – God as singular human being undergoing the time and mortality of the human, and divine even in the death that is the last suffering of our sojourn in the between. More universalized: the God revealed in this singular human is not the God of any people or any person but of all, and all here includes the reviled, the outcasts, those twisted in the deformation of personal being that is sin. What does love of one astray mean? That the deformed selving is still kept as a personal promise of community. God keeps promise, in hope that our singular good will be consented to anew. This God has no favorites, because this God has only favorites. The God of the Christian is not the God of the Christian. This is a God neither of Jews nor Gentile, Greek nor barbarian, male nor female. The personalization is so developed that, already, the passing of the dynamic of transcendence beyond finite personalism is suggested. But the passing beyond of the finitely personal is an accentuation and intensification of what it passes, not its negation.

In the Christian vision, the death of the singular Jesus is also the coming of spirit which is personal and more than "merely" personal. Spirit is the power of the good dwelling in a community whose members are personal singulars but whose community is not a more inclusive whole but the porous between of giving and receiving, of service and togetherness, of empowerment and availability, of ethical solidarity and worship, beyond servility and sovereignty. The spirit of community is a kind of metaxological idiocy of being, its intimacy broadcast into all and not confined in any, for it is something more than the "merely" personal that yet enlivens the persons together. Could you call such a community the mask, the (mystical) persona of the exceeding power of the hidden God? But we would have to be careful to be clear about what is appropriate to different communities, especially those of erotic sovereignty and agapeic service (see *EB*, Part IV).

It is the likeness to us of the personal God that impresses us, and likeness thought of in terms of what is potentially richest in our experience of being in the between, namely, the agapeic servant. God is like us, we say; though we also think we are like God. If the two are thought convertible, we have the basis either for religious hubris or for the demythologizing critique that reduces the divine to the human. If the two are not convertible, then the question of the otherness of the divine persists, and it is not clear that the divine can be put on a par with the human. If we say, we are like God, though we are personal, then the unlikeness of the relation means that there is an other side to the divine that is not to be imaged in our terms.

Likening is a relation, but the relation is always a play of likeness and unlikeness. Absolute likeness would be identity without difference, hence no likeness, hence absolute unlikeness. Likening as a relating is always between these extremes. The most important likening is how we live our lives; this is *imitatio Dei*. The doubleness of likeness is capable of being looked from one side, and from the other. If we are dualistically oriented we will end up with either a theological dualism of humans and God, or a humanistic dualism. The first leads to estrangement, the second to secular reductionism. Both distort the double relation of likening, which, as pluralized, is metaxological rather than dualistic. This means, the participants are internally self-mediating in such a way that a dualism of image and original cannot work; for the image is original, and the original images itself, that is it manifests itself to the other. The two are not subordinates images of one more inclusive original whole. There is an open intermediation between different originals: God the absolute original and the human being the created original.

In a communicative relation it is not always easy to disentangle one side from the other and determine unequivocally which is the image, which the original. There are communicative relations that do not exclude asymmetries, but even the asymmetries do not exclude the movement of the superior that makes itself available for the other that is not up to it. The superior may then look like the inferior, and we may be deficient in discernment to see the superiority in this. The agapeic relation goes beyond equal symmetry, even as it allows the superior to be given to the other who is beneath it. The abdication of erotic sovereignty equalizes, in the sense that the superior, the fuller form, shares in the condition of the poorer form. It gives its superiority over for the other; its superiority consists just in its abdication of superiority, for the good of the other. This is a divine nobility.

If God is an original that images itself in the world, the image of the speaking origin is not inappropriate. The connection of God and the primal word is to be found in many traditions as an image of the original coming to be. Hence also the divine original as *logos* bespeaking being to the creation. This logos is communicative being. Surely it is also connected to the personal, in that our own experience of the speaking being is preeminently the human being. All beings articulate themselves, but we do so mindfully and with a release from self that is self-transcending. Our speaking sends words out to the other, words that are intimately our own and yet other to us, expressing who we are and yet shaping a world of communication beyond ourselves. Speaking is communicative selving in transcendence of self, selving constituted in being communicatively together with others beyond itself.[3] Receiving the word, hearing from the other, is the *passio essendi*. To be personal is to listen patiently.

If there is such a language of God, and such a communicative being together, there need be no exclusion of an idiotic relation to the divine, a personal relation, for it is in the intimacy of singularity, and within the communities that support such intimate singularity, that we can find the deepest relation to God. Such idiocies would be nothing other than communities of prayer. Prayer would be the highest form of listening speech, even though it be speechless. Praying would be idiotic community with God. One cannot speak of complete estrangement of the human and divine as long as the possibility of prayer is there. In a sense, this is impossible for us alone. This possibility is not just a human possibility. We can will to pray, but that will does not constitute prayer. That is the paradox of an idiotic community: never constituted by one alone, though it appears as one alone, and though the non-participant suspects only autism. The paradox extends to the fact that the participant will be troubled by a similar misgiving: Am I only talking to myself alone?

In the traditions of biblical personalism, this misgiving is offset by the conviction that the language of God is communicated in history, hence public, not idiotic in a merely private sense. Not surprisingly, these religions of revelation are those with the most developed sense of agapeic communication. The personal God makes his story a drama of service of the good of the people, a plot of salvation. Its major acts: goodness gives rise to creation, an agapeic gift; we creatures, given integral being for ourselves, are tempted to absolutize that finite integrity and stand over against the source of the gift; we turn the vector of our transcending into a closed self-assertion of erotic sovereignty and renege on the full communicative being of agapeic service. This is the sortie of pride and fall: self-will dominates the more catholic willingness that will let other being be as other, and free in the proper good of its own being. The result is absolutized being for self, instrumentalized being of the other. The sweat of work rules us, a punishment in one sense, though not in another, since the sweat is just the expression of the closed self-mediation that has set itself up and set itself against the other. We cannot solve our confinement to ourselves through our own will, for this will is our confinement. We need the aid of a source beyond ourselves to restore us to the community of being. A will to restore oneself merely continues the hostile opposition.

There is God's enduring agapeic care for creatures in their predicament. The covenant with the Jews is the sign of that enduring service. This is the personal God, of special relations with this special people. But, of course, this God is not just the God of that people;

---

[3] I mention one complication here about Trinitarian speculation. There might be a conversation, a communication, within the divine itself; there might be a communication between the divine and the finite creation, a creative communication that gives finite being to be, but we do not want to conflate these conversations in the manner which I think Hegel's dialectical-speculative Trinitarianism does, and just because of his inability to do justice to the difference between an erotics and an agapeics of the divine. God "being personal" is between a hidden origin and a fulfilled communication, without the latter depleting the reserve of the former: for the first is full, overfull, as is the second "being personal," as is the third fulfilled communication. All this would suggest an agapeic communication from overfull to overfull to overfull. Call this agapeic Trinitarianism. See *Hegel's God*, especially Chapters 4 and 5.

no one owns the divine. The personalizing of God can be dangerous when it becomes a claim to the exclusive possession of the divine. Religion as the intimate universal is of great importance here: true religion allows the singular intimacy of relation to God, without monopoly, and hence without prejudice to the universal availability of the relation.

The Christian view is perhaps the most extreme personalism of the divine. Something astonishing is claimed: namely, that in incarnation God becomes absolutely intimate with the flesh of time: the divine speaking is singularly personal as concretized in the person of Jesus. The personal God is intimately porous to the glories and torments of time, not a jealous eternity that cares nothing for transience. Time and its passing is the immanent porous intermedium wherein can be redeemed the promise of community between the divine and the human, the human and creation. This promise is not in denial of evil; rather the service of agape expends itself as offer and to restitute the goodness of being.

In the between, there are evils we suffer, and do, for which no finite deliverance is possible. There are evils in the dimensions of the hyperbolic, exceeding all our best efforts at finite restitution. No finite deliverance: if there is to be justified life beyond evil and suffering, there must be an infinite saving, that is, redemption. The promise of being is in the process of being redeemed. What is redemption? Living the service of agapeic being, even in the undergoing of the ultimate suffering of death. God shows the living of agapeic being, in the "yes" to the good of being, even in the nihilation of finite life which death brings. There is a "yes" beyond death. Redemption is living beyond the threat of death: life beyond death, in life itself, in death itself. The meaning of this posthumous life is not simply posthumous to life; it is in the life itself that we die and are reborn in the life of agapeic service. The frail bark of the finite person floats of a stream of mystery, and what lies beyond the roaring waterfall is wrapped in unknowing. What there is beyond death we do not determinately know. That is why in the face of its enigma there is called for the most radical trust in the goodness of the ultimate. In life we undergo many deaths, and many rebirths. We are weaned from false gods in these many deaths. To die thus is to be born as prayer: the offering of the *conatus essendi* in an amen to the origin, and the release of the pure porosity of the *passio essendi* and its love of the ultimate God.

BEYOND PERSON, BEYOND MASK

The Christian view is perhaps the consummate personalism of the divine, but what of efforts to *unmask* that personalism? If person is bound up with mask, and there is nowhere in being where manifestation is not offered, what could it mean to unmask the divine? The masters of suspicion execute this unmasking and find the human being and nothing other. The double metaxological character of manifestation is skewed towards a humanizing univocalization of what is in truth plurivocal. What can unmasking taken to the end mean? Beyond every mask another mask, and another, on and on. Does unmasking then point towards the transpersonal not less than the personal? Or does it expose less than the personal: beyond masks the non-personal, perhaps the sub-personal, finally perhaps nothing. There is only the movement from manifestation to manifestation, from mask to mask, and there seems nothing more. The "more" is "nothing." Every image, even our image, is the image of nothing. And yet something is being shown, and shown not only as excess to nothing but as hyperbolic to finite determinacy. In something being shown, is there a mediated presentiment of the source of all the "somethings" that exceeds the shown: the giving showing of that source that is also a reserve of showing? Unless the nothing is absolutely creative there would be nothing at all. But if the nothing is creative there is no reason to call it merely nothing. We are impelled again to consider the original source as hyperbolic, but in an affirmative sense: God the hyperbolic creating counterpart to the nihilating nothing. God would also be no-thing, but we would rather relate this to a transpersonal porosity that makes possible personal communication.

When we reflect on this "trans," we see that personal communication is transpersonal, in that communication is itself a transcending between person and person. We get a hint of this if we emphasize the acoustics of person (*per-sonans*) rather than the optics (*pros-opon*).[4] Is there not something transpersonal in per-son when we think of this per-sonans, this sounding through? The person is as an acoustic passage. The person is as a porosity of transition, in which an energy of being more original than itself passes in communication, and it is spoken or sung into being. A strange song: it is as long as it is sung, but as long as it is as sung it too can sing – its own song, and in its own voice. We hear this perhaps more clearly with the extremities of this middle of passage, this intermedium of passing; with the idiotic and its reserves, that is, and the agapeic and its overdetermined excess. But it is also sounds and resounds within the aesthetic and the erotic.

If there is something trans-personal in per-son, we can understand this "trans" as a between of communication. The "trans" is also an "inter," hence there is no person as trans-personal without the inter-personal. We might also understand the acoustic passage as *wording the between*: a *logos* of the *metaxu*. If God is personal and transpersonal, we might think of the word in the between: trans-personal as wording the divine between; wording as itself the divine between. I do not mean just our wording. God would be trans-wording, while we word the between in virtue of the original gift of the divine wording of the (finite) between. Our wording of the (finite) between, our *logos* of the immanent *metaxu*, would participate (inter)mediately in the more original wording of the divine between.

Perhaps I can rephrase in somewhat more familiar terms. A first point: if there is a personhood to God, it must be peculiar. In the monotheistic religions, God is not physical, even if there are incarnations that tell us of the divine. Our notion of "person" is hard to separate from embodied selving. But there is also a hiddenness to this. If so, this must mean that the divine is also concealed. How then think of a communication more universal than can be confined to any singular person? Does such communication point to a transpersonal source? Does the hidden "side" of person bring us to limits in personalizing God?

A second point: this concerns anthropomorphism as double-edged. If God is like the human, God is also unlike. The hiddenness of what is not manifested must make us diffident about the anthropomorphic likeness, and hence of certain personalizings of God. If God is unlike, "person" must also mean something other: either a meta-personal or non-personal otherness beyond all finite manifestation. This makes us very uncomfortable, for this otherness cannot be faced directly. We cannot put a face on it, and this renders us deeply insecure. Because of this "beyond," the face opens just by guarding a hiddenness. And further: why should only the faces of beauty show the divine, and not the faces of the repulsive? Startling us, sometimes monstrous faces seem truer masks of the divine, for even in the revulsion they call forth a reckless consent. The divine is there in the grotesque, disproportionate to our sense of finite harmony, shattering the concord of our finite measure of love. There is excess to the repulsive we cannot stand, but the ultimate stands with the monstrous too, and we must look at the monstrous differently to be with the ultimate differently. We need agapeic beholding of the beauty in the ugly, the eyes of God in the scabby countenance.

A third point: our sense of "person" is dominantly tied to *finite centers* of mindful life. How think an *infinite center*? In the line of Cusanus and earlier thinkers, would not such a center be also circumference – not here, not there, but here, there, everywhere, hence nowhere, but then how determine this as a *center*? But is not this what a personal God would have to be: an infinite center of mindful life, absolutely integral to itself, but not closed into itself. But if not closed into self, it is as if there is no "circle" and hence no center either, for again the difference of these seems to vanish, and we seem left with an indeterminacy or pure openness.

Response ventured: the agapeic (trans)personalism of the origin would be in excess of every finite whole. If the agapeic origin is an infinitely self-exceeding energy of being

---

4   Richard Kearney's interesting phenomenology of person in *The God Who May Be* stresses the optical, as in the Greek, *pros-opon*. If we take the Latin persona as *per-sonans*, what sounds through? And from what source is this sounding through sung or played? We see the cognates in something that is *resonans* or *consonans*. A sounding strange and intimate, startling us from mere personality and yet personalizing us more deeply – as great music paradoxically does. It calls us: we ourselves are as coming to be in being called to be, and being ourselves the person we are (to be), in answering this call; though, again, the sounding of the call cannot be fixed since it is manifest in its passage, its passing. *Per*: sounding through: the person as *per* is a medium of this passing of sound(ing): resounding – consonant with the source of the sounding.

it is, in one sense, whole unto itself, but, in another sense, it is not a whole closed into itself. It is communicative being in the superlative sense: absolutely one with self as the exceeding One that pours forth its goodness in the giving of finite creation to be. But this pouring forth exceeds the measure of person as a finite center of mindful life. In that sense also this broadcasting surplus is centerless and a nothing since it gives passing into being and endows porosity and cannot be pinned to this thing or to that person, even though it is absolutely immanent in this thing and that person as enabling them to be at all. Even the finite person floats on the transpersonal, on a hyperbolic otherness within every immanent integrity, and given to human mindfulness in an inward otherness that exceeds inwardness in inwardness itself. The overflow is not only externally beyond defined boundaries, it is communicated in the intensive self-exceeding that opens the person into the immanent abyss of the transpersonal in itself.

A fourth point: such transpersonalism rouses perplexity about evil. Evil seems at odds with a personal providence solicitous for the good of the singular as singular. How can a personal providence tolerate evil we find intolerable? The question unsteadies the conviction that God faces us alone with goodness. As we saw along the way of equivocity, there is a pre-articulate intimation of the fragility of finitude, its being threatened by its own possible nothingness, its being under threat from powers not themselves good, powers perhaps malicious, perhaps merely impersonal, and as such other to our humanized definition of the good, and hence for us potentially evil. At this level, the "problem" of evil is not really a "problem." A problem is a determinately stated difficulty that calls for an equally determinate answer. But the original intimation of evil is not thus determinate, and hence is a perplexity rather than a problem. Again and again it comes back to anguish us.

Evil is thus like the question of God: unanswerable in terms of any univocal determination, but unavoidable in terms of the hyperbolic perplexity that stings mindfulness out of the sleep of finitude. Both make us tremble with dread, not fear, for there is nothing to fear: dread is the beginning of a wisdom that is not scientifically determinable. We know in our bones we are not on a par with these questions, and yet these questions are more important than any specific curiosity we put to any definite happening in the between. These most important questions well up from recesses of the idiocy of being over which we do not lord. They are in us as coming to us from beyond us, and yet they are the most intimate to the lives we live. Failing some rejoinder to them, human life is mutilated of meaning.

The pre-articulate intimation of evil is correlative to the pre-articulate rapport with the good of being when we are carried into life by an immediate ontological festivity: joy of being, play of the child, glint of the wave on the shore. The intimation: immediate presentiment that the good of being is under a threat we cannot specify; vague, undefined foreboding that death too is in Arcadia. This is the ominous equivocity of the earth. Shadow of nothing: shadow there in the bright sunshine, there in play, there in the joy of feasting, there in the glint on the seashore and the glower of the darkening wave. Standard accountings of evil often arrive too late to address this idiocy of the sinister.[5]

With the personal God of Christianity we find less this intimation of the sinister as a story with a definite line: evil emerges with an original transgression, but God through his Son, takes the punishment on himself. This is hardly a God of vengeance if the price is exacted on the *offended* party. True, this can become an ignoble exaction in terms of *equivalences* proportioned to a finite measure of merit, retribution, and compensation. Does such a divine calculation of equivalences dip deep enough into the idiocy of evil – or God? If the divine pays the price for the offending party, one rather sees the agapeic excess of goodness. You are insulted by me, I should seek forgiveness, but it is you, the insulted, who takes the atonement on yourself. You are forgiveness, since you say "It is nothing." That God should be this acceptance of the refusal makes no sense on the scales of a proportioned retributive justice. It is in excess of such justice. It says of the evil: "It is nothing." Forgiving sets

---

[5] I mean the standard posing of the problem relative to the attributes of the monotheistic God: all-good, all-powerful, all-knowing, and so on, yielding views of evil as *privatio boni*, or incumbent on free will (Augustine), or connected with teleologically oriented theodicies, such as the so-called virtue theodicy (Iranaeus), or the aesthetic theodicy (Aquinas, Hegel, even Nietzsche).

it at naught.[6] Evil is exposed without violence, even in subjection to violence, and the quiet gentleness of reconciliation opens a new day as fresh with promise as the first day of creation.

Idiotic evil will strain our personalizing of God, and we will feel a darkness in the divine idiocy, even as it mirrors our own darkness. The haunting of the sinister is not simply the product of human will but somehow "there" already, before we enter into evil or will evil acts. Paganisms were sometimes more attuned to this pre-determinate sense of evil, giving some articulation of it in a variety of myths[7] If we do away with myth, we blank out of mindfulness something that does not any the less effect us for its being sent into recess. To the extent that monotheism rids us of myth, it rids us of the feel for the pre-determinate evil, making everything depend on the determinations of free will. But in the biblical story there is the serpent – already evil, or the temptation to evil, before any choice or act by the original humans. Does this not transcend the personalized evil of the human? Does it make one ask about the transpersonal character of the good God? Recall the archaic image of the wrath of God: the dark side to the divine comes out in such awful catastrophes as the aboriginal tsunami. What does the flood face us with? Destructive power sweeping away all personal being. You may call it a cleansing violence and personalize it as wrath, but the scale of the wrath exceeds all personalizing. In this personalizing of the wrath of God is not another seed sown in our souls, either of a transpersonal God, or an impersonal power?

This seed may grow up under different skies, and one of them is a personless sky that turns us away from any heaven of the divine. For if an impersonal order is more ultimate than any personal one, the personal seems childish. The deluge faces us with indiscriminate destructive power. It inflicts on us the indifference, perhaps hostility, of the ultimate power. "As flies to wanton boys are we to the gods, / they kill us for their sport." Who is to fight this sport? God or man? But our prayers seem to leave us in the lurch. Not prayer but human power, and work to master the impersonal conditions of life – these *will personalize* our world indeed, humanize the sport, but on our terms. And now we work for ourselves, we do not wait for God – or serve. This is a cleaving to ourselves that issues in cleavage between us and the divine. Our human self-mediation, in the impersonal intermedium of the indifferent whole, will place the divine as personal under erasure. Catastrophes will be exorcised of their charge in being called "acts of God" – meaning contingent happenings with no meaning beyond the contingency of happening and the meaningless bad luck of the mortal that finds itself crushed. The earthquake is "nothing personal." (But do not tell that to the mother weeping over her lost child.) The sun rises and warms, but cold to our loves, it is a mere burst of blazing gas.

"Demythologization" was a fashionable theological movement in the earlier twentieth century but something like it recurs in different times and places.[8] It reflects the depersonalization of world and gods: the myths as anthropomorphic are too "personal." But the disappearance of the divine is not the only outcome possible. We can come to appreciate more deeply God's otherness to nature as a finite whole: God is beyond this whole, and not determinable in univocal objectivities. There is a skepsis that frees in us a purer receptivity to what might be coming towards us from divine otherness. There can be a purification of porosity to the divine. This can looks more like a poverty than a power, but it is a passing of power into patience. Transcendence as other comes towards us, as if for the first time, and does so even when our powers are astray. The critique of anthropomorphism is a sifting of the equivocal mix of the ethos and puts us on guard against all our human-all-too-human images.

---

[6] "Sin" hardly makes sense outside of some reference to a personalism of the divine or the ultimate; one might speak of some kind of evil perhaps, but it would lack the bite of ultimate intimacy or idiocy; the same holds for "forgiveness."

[7] Consider, for instance, the Orphic myth of the origin of evil; see Paul Ricoeur, *The Symbolism of Evil*, trans. E. Buchanan (Boston: Beacon Press, 1967), Part II, Chapter IV.

[8] A sample: in ancient Greece with the philosophers such as Xenophanes and Plato; in Judaism, and its ban on images; with Spinoza, historical criticism, modern Enlightenment; with the Left-Hegelian demythologization of Hegelian *Geist*; in various hermeneutics of suspicion, Marxist, Nietzschean, Freudian. The diverse practices of mysticism religiously embody disciplines of the deeper discernment of images.

If skepticism turns mind against mind's own anthropomorphisms, can it do so completely? I doubt it. New anthropomorphisms are often surreptitiously reintroduced, like the anthropomorphism of the "machine." And then demythologization betrays its own danger. When the ultimate ceases to be "like" us, in however minimal a sense, and looks like a cold "it," our bonds as *humans* with "it" are warped. They become as cold as the ultimate so coldly named. The urgency of ultimacy is not cold, and sooner or later will seek more "warm," that is, more passionate, perhaps even more fanatical expression, and sometimes without the purification of our porosity such as comes from being genuinely religious. We humans dehumanize the ultimate and the world, and finally we dehumanize the human – and with a reductionistic zealotry whose passion persists in being human-all-too-human. What then? The will to power, *our* will to power, flares up claiming to redeem the icy ultimacy of thereness. We are the blaze that kindles the meaningless cosmos. We are the fire in the stars, and the star that is the earth we will set on fire, but the fire will be infernal because godless.

Of course, there will be milder outcomes, less consuming outbursts of life's flare. On the one hand, we will be disillusioned and claim there is no grand narrative, no epic story. On the other hand, we will be edified with the realization that we are all makers of our "historical narratives," or more simply our own (little) stories. Does not this mean that demythologizing must end with *new myths*? And this, even when we so modestly announce that our new small stories are not grand stories? Lyotard announces the end of metanarratives, and then draws lessons, with touching postmodern earnestness, from the telling of the myth(s) of the Cashinahua tribe. We are consoled with a "paganism" without any absolute – a postmodern "polytheism" that is oddly "impious" since it is not to be lived in *religiously*.[9] Religious myths take on the tonality of aesthetic possibilities. Can one take this seriously in any genuine religious sense? Does postmodern discourse, unsatisfied heir of Enlightenment demythologizing, play aesthetically with new "mythologizations." There are ironies here, perhaps salutary warnings. The project of demythologization prides itself on surmounting naïveté, but there come to be new naïvetés in demythologizing itself. We cannot live without stories about the ultimate. The mythless impersonalism of the whole (but there is no whole) is also in its own way a story of the ultimate, that is, a myth. To be without myths is itself a myth.

THE GODS OF PHILOSOPHERS: MASKS OF THE IMPERSONAL OR TRANSPERSONAL?

Beyond the above reductions and self-assertions, beyond their deconstruction, there can be a mindful response marked by a considered fidelity to religious imagination. We may have to go beyond imagination, either to complement its strengths, or compensate for its limitations, but this "going beyond" need not be a univocal reduction, a dialectical sublation, or an equivocal deconstruction. It can be a plurivocal dialogue in which there is two-way communication between religion and philosophy. Philosophical reflection on anthropomorphism need not be just a destructive critique. It can be a purgatory of mindfulness. Mind may be a sanctuary of idols, for idols can be made from thoughts as well as wood or stone. Mindfulness can also expose its own idolatrous formations.

Religious people have not always warmed to philosophers, and are not always wrong in this. There is such a thing as obtuse cleverness. Mirabile dictu, mindfulness does desert clever philosophers when religion comes in question. We ask for the bread of reverence and are given the stones of concepts. A small dose of sympathetic imagination might cure many a sterile doubt, open many a pass beyond petrifying rationality. There are philosophers who do nurture the familial bond with the religious. This bond has been under censure for

---

[9] See, for instance, "Lessons in Paganism" reprinted in *The Lyotard Reader*, ed. Andrew Benjamin (Oxford: Blackwell, 1989); also *Just Gaming*, trans. Wlad Godzick (Minneapolis: University of Minnesota Press, 1985); *The Postmodern Condition: A Report on Knowledge*, trans. Geoff Bennington and Brian Massumi (Manchester: Manchester University Press, 1984).

centuries now, but the lasting bond is there and its subterranean persistence. (The critique of ontotheology: beware of Germans bearing gifts.) Hostile philosophers critical of religion, religious critics hostile to philosophy together opt for apartheid to preserve their respective homelands. Peremptory scientistic annexation, or conquest by easy cultural assimilation, or uneasy segregation that relieves the tension by means of a stand-off – such resorts have not been favored by the most interesting philosophers. As with many familial bonds, they have sensed a double relation of philosophy and religion: tense in likeness, and loving in unlikeness; agonistic at times, but intimately so, and not necessarily antagonistic.

Openness to the ultimate, receptivity to astonishment, honesty about perplexities exceeding complete determination, metaphysical shock before the singularity of the human and the tragedy of suffering shaking all humans at some time, appreciation of the praise of contemplation, these and other things make the philosopher a religious person, but oddly religious in that the desire to seek articulate understanding is also there, and this issues in complex explorations of the meaning of all these things. (How is one to credit the silent condescension of the fashionable academic preening himself on being entirely untroubled about the ultimate? There were times when an endowed chair honored by such self-advertised thoughtlessness would have shocked finer sensibilities. In a time of godlessness there seems nothing shocking – except perhaps that one would want to understand the ultimate with all one's heart and mind.) Self-transcending openness to transcendence as other to the self: this describes an ultimate porosity giving birth to the urgency of ultimacy, shaped now in more recognizable religious terms, now in less familiar philosophical fashion. The name of the transpersonal emerges in religion itself, and some of the best philosophers have been servants of transcendence as pointing to a transpersonal principle, and in such a fashion that neither intends nor entails any violence to the personal. The agapeic origin is also an effort to name this "*trans*."

To the honor of philosophers, they have traditionally sought names for the ultimate; and, though the names be impersonal ones, there is nobility in so seeking to name what exceeds finite naming. The impersonal ultimate will be called the One, the Idea, the Absolute, the Whole, the Infinite, Being, Substance, the Void, Nature, Will, Origin, Ultimacy, Transcendence, and such like. This is quite a list, and something different is being emphasized with different names, yet notable is the absence of personal names, or names relating to more personalized events of life, such as motherhood. These abstract names are not connected with singular events and people and places. The Gods of the philosophers tend to be Gods of erotic sovereignty – with the eros expunged or disguised or transmuted into reason. The eros of the personal God is transubstantiated into the self-cause or the autarkic absolute. This is tied with the drive to impersonal universality in the philosophical quest: the truth of the event or person or place is the universal that is not this or that event or person or place. This introduces *dislocation* into our thinking of the divine. It strains against our particular embeddedness in this time or place or people. Positively speaking, such dislocation might be seen as pointing to a form of *posthumous mind* – outliving the immediate participation as thoughtless, but reliving it with mindfulness, intermediated by love of what shows itself worthy of ultimate affirmation in the singular occasions of being.[10]

One might argue the necessity of this: the ultimate God cannot be confined to particular times and places or peoples but is the God of the whole who is beyond the whole. The philosophical drive to the universal is compatible with the drive of monotheism to the One God, even though this God is highly personalized also. A God beyond the personal God is suggested in this drive, for the One God has to be more original and ultimate than all forms of finite being, including the personal. The limits of the personal revolve around its potential restriction to the human as the image. But there are other images, and at a certain point there are no images at all, and we must tap our blind way in the night of the invisible.

---

[10] Being at home in not being at home; this can also be contracted into simple alienation – not being at home. But there is an alienation that allows one to see the truth of the other, the alien – exiled, sent to the outside, suffering a Golgotha of mind, unhoused yet strangely at home.

What temptations beckon with the philosopher's universal? There is the matter of the allegedly homogeneity of the universal: its neutral objectivity seems at odds with the passion of lived singularities. We are tempted to fix the universal as so other to the singular and personal, making it hard see the second as an epiphany of the first. We dualize the universal and particular, look for a univocal relation between them, and fail to appreciate plurivocal manifestation. Manifestation suggests that the universal is not the antithesis of the singular, nor indeed simply the univocal truth of the singular, if we think of universals as more general categories. Singular showing is itself not just a univocal "this-here-now." There is no neutral being in general, nor autistic particularity, especially so if the origin is agapeic – a God for the singular as singular. The singular is a concretion of communicative being, communicating with its own being, and with what is other to itself.

The significance of this is evident for religion, which one might claim to be a primary space of significance where the singular and the universal are in communication. I mean that religion is concerned with what is most intimate to the singular soul, the living porosity between the human and the divine. And yet this cannot be confined to this or that singular, since it is communicated to all, and hence religion, as the intimate porosity, is in promise open to universal communication. The religious communication is both intimate and universal. Philosophy tends often towards the universal and masks the singular intimacy, art often tends to the intimate singularity and masks the universal. Religion is their older sister, closer to the mother, and bears most fully the promise of the intimate universal.

I admire Pascal, but I cannot accept as the final word the contrast of the Gods of the savants and of the religious. The contrast is real, but it states a further problem, which it does not solve, and indeed it points further than the contrast, for this cannot be sustained as ultimate. What is the problem for the non-philosophers? It is that their hearts find only husks in the philosophers' abstractions and they miss the spirit of thinking that can be a way of transcending in rapport with religion. What is the problem for the philosophers? It is their failure to remain intimate with the religious sources out of which reflective seriousness about the ultimate emerges. There are other dangers for philosophers. There is the danger of an idolism of concepts. There is the danger of being taken over by the negating power of thinking: thinking tears God apart, thinking it is taking apart an idol, intoxicated with its own amazing energy of negation. There is the danger of weariness when the trail grows cold and the light dims and thinking turns out the weaker in its combat with the jubilant night, and steals away into accommodation with the duller solidities of the quotidian, though, there too, flashes of transcendence never cease to blaze and to startle. Too much thought can be too little thought. Needed is not less thought but more thought of the right sort, thinking astonished and perplexed, thinking that hardly seems thinking at all, for it seems in suspense over its own nothingness, as it awaits a new porosity to what is greater than any of its own thoughts. The eagle must fly from the angel's crag.

It can be a breaking thing to be cast by thought into a desert of expectation, there where the philosopher's names lack all the ceremonial compensations of ritual. These names do not dramatize our relation to the One in a liturgy that recalls the great events of God's disclosure from the glorious past. No myth entices the soul's unfolding and touches its secret recesses, disarming it to shudder and laugh and strangely speak of enigmas half apprehended, half shunned. There seems no story of consolation with the philosopher's One. There is the secret life of the absolute power towards which we gesture in dumb signs on the periphery of the holy.

We are that thing swaying in the wind, the thinking reed that knows that flesh is grass. The philosopher may not fall on his knees before the One, or send up prayer, as if caressing or pleading with a lover. Nevertheless, there is a kind of philosophical thinking that seems *bestowed*, and not unlike the gifted energy of praying. Both the thinking and the praying are accorded to persons like a music out of the blue. Surprised by a melody of insight, suddenly a person's thought seems as if transported elsewhere, overtaken by a knowing one cannot command, for it is what calls. Philosophical thinking is on call. One was always there in range of hearing but one shut oneself out from the calling, in forms of thinking so determined for oneself that one clogged the porosity.

The more we are in the praying, the more we intensify the personal, and the more paradoxically there is a divesting of personality. The opposites are no longer opposite. Praying, one is oneself, and yet one does not know or own self. There is an intimate porosity, not cloying but freeing, cooler than the most impersonal, sometimes hotter than the maddest passion. Is there a thinking that is thus both personal and transpersonal?

The philosopher's names rarely if ever denominate any special intervention in human life. They seem indifferently to support the "whole" – disease as well as health, pests as well as persons, a louse and a king.[12] This seems an affront to our cherished sense of specialness. Of course, there can be a cherishing of our specialness that fixes into a higher narcissism, a superior closure on one's being for self. Suppose, then, that the ultimate, named as agapeic origin, cherishes all being, and since beings are marked by differences, cherishes some differently to others, and suppose human specialness is a basis for special cherishing. Can we then insist on an exclusive claim on the agape of the ultimate? Would this not be to miss the point of the agape? Suppose we need to abdicate any specialness that closes us off from the love of the ultimate for the "whole," love that, because it is of the whole, sometimes looks to us like indifference to the singular. Is this indifference not rather a generalized regard for indefinite generality, not the agape of the ultimate which is singularized in the fullest concrete sense? Perhaps it is *we* who too fix the contrast between our own specialness and such a generalized regard for indefinite generality. Perhaps it is *we* who make being in general into nothing in particular. With God the "whole" of being cannot be abstracted from everything in particular. There is no special intervention in a sense we can determine univocally, because all is special in a sense beyond finite determination, and not in an indefinite generalized sense but in the particularized singularity that escapes the discernment of our best mindfulness. At times our proper love is an agnostic adoration.

The philosopher's names tend to be esoteric, not exoteric: for some and not for all. With the esoteric, there are masks too, and the "impersonal" can be a different *persona*. How does one read this mask then, this esoteric *persona*? The unexpected can happen here too: the universal claim seems to name the impersonal for everyone, hence it is *exoteric*, not esoteric. Exoteric, yes, but exoteric only to those who have staggered under the burden of metaphysical perplexity and tried to see the matter through; universal at the level of common thoughts that being true seeks, common as constituting a community of mindfulness beyond common befuddlements. The universal is for all – but not for all is that intimacy with the universal given through thought but in particular images that charge our feel for the divine with special and singular significance. The gift of reflection slows the hurry of time and allows a subtler regard of what is constant in transience. Busy practical people with little time for thought are sometimes the inconstant, even godless ones, despite their loud disdain of philosophy. Mindfulness that is reverence for the ultimate is not of worth to them, not worthy of a life of thinking about the ultimate. Some philosophers are devoted in that sense. They are esoterics, hidden ones, who truly live out under the open sky. There are exoterics, open ones, who live in the confines of their own cells.

What of the fact that the ultimate, philosophically named, tends not to be a moral power in any ordinary sense? It is not the Lord, not the Judge. Does it do anything? But life is dynamism, is energy, is act. We must think of the ultimate in the image of life, hence in terms of act and dynamism. What dynamis? Highest power: but then the ultimate will have to be more than just blind power; it will have to be ethical power; it will have to be the good, and the good is nothing if its being is not to be and do the good. Fructifying in all that is, if agapeic being is the richest form of ethical being, the ultimate will have to be ethical in such a hyperbolic sense also. So hyperbolic as to seem not moral: the good beyond good and evil, but as an en-acting, as a be-ing good, as verb rather than as noun.

---

[11] See *Sophist* 227a7–c5: In the search for a definition under one common name, the qualitative differences between the art of lice-killing and the art of the general do not matter for the Eleatic Stranger.

Is this to moralize the ultimate? Would this be another idolatry of "person" which feels comfortable with the mask of God as acting only within the measure of *our* moral standards? Agapeic ethics is already a breach of self-absolutizing morality, a breach that does not destroy the moral but releases into a religious freedom beyond autonomy. The agapeic breach de-moralizes the ultimate – not to the submoral but the transmoral. It is to the ultimate as other than, more than, our moral ultimates that we must hold, not the ultimate as beneath the ethical, as an amoral power that offers no ground at all finally for making sense of good. The good beyond good and evil is not made to our moral measure, and yet it is the superlative transmoral measure that is, as good, for us.

Philosophers have often been accused of atheism, such as Spinoza or Socrates. Each of the cases is different, and the accusation is not necessarily without its justice. There can be an atheism of philosophy, and not just of the post-Hegelian variety. There are different atheisms. There is the subtle atheism which has invested itself in a false double of God. Philosophers can produce counterfeits of the divine. There is the atheism that is carried by the very elevation of self-transcending thinking that is seduced into hubris on the heights themselves. One participates in an ecstasis of enthusiasm, masked as rational sobriety, and thinks one is that divine dispensation itself (Socrates [*Philebus*, 28c]: In making *nous* king, philosophers elevate themselves). This especially can happen with philosophers of erotic sovereignty, and at opposite extremes of the rational and the nonrational: Hegel and Nietzsche.

There is another intimately related "atheism" that yet is distant to these atheisms: what looks like the philosopher's hubris in criticizing the gods is a humility in service to a God that is no god. This seems atheistic in seeking beyond every human image of the divine, including the philosophical names of the ultimate. No name is the name. One is a-theist because every effort to name must fail. Many efforts to name the highest think too highly of themselves. We lose our grip on God, we lose God, we must let go of God to come again to God, for God to come. This letting go is release, because a religious porosity has already been unblocked in a new poverty of thought. Because that release may be the most secret drama of life, hidden even from our self-knowledge, we must grow hesitant in any easy ascription of atheism. The release may be happening, but the thinking naming it may not happen or may miss. We have to think beyond the overt thoughts and their manifest masks.

The atheism of the philosophers can well be the mask of a piety of the ultimate.[12] One might agree with Heidegger that questioning is the piety of thinking, but of course the same question can be posed in very different spirits, for instance, with love and reverence, or with aggression and disdain. "What is truth?" asked Pilate. We philosophers revere this question, but we would hardly grant to Pilate the piety of thinking.[13] For the *how* of the posing is as important as the *what* of the posed, and indeed the *who* of the one posing the question. In the how and the who of the questioning, the *person* of the philosopher is in question. We need not mean this mushily, for we still have eyes in our heads. In our godless time, the silence of the philosophers can strike one less as a divine abandon as the abdication of a responsibility. There are other silences and they are more finessed by the needful reverence. We are in a time where silence about the divine must be broken, for there is an irreverent atheism that is too coarse for the deeper religious truth of atheism which is to show us we are not God, and to show us the horror of life without God. Though Nietzsche desired a new reverence, his masked piety spawned a host of graceless impieties, but I concur with him this once: Atheistic life is now the life of what he called – appalled and thrilled by what he saw – the ugliest man.

---

12 I have discussed this in a number of places, for instance, in Chapter 1 of *PO* (on priest and philosopher), and Chapter 2 of *BHD* (philosophy as "God-service"), and recently in "Consecrated Thought: Between Priest and Philosopher" *Louvain Studies*, (30) 2005, pp. 92–106.

14 Nietzsche, I know, calls Pilate the only person with integrity in the New Testament, but then he also attributes to him the attitude: "One Jew more or less what does it matter. One would have no more to do with them than one would with Polish Jews. They smell too much." The who of Nietzsche is revealed in the what of this his utterance.

Chapter 10

God(s) Gnostic: On Passing through the Counterfeit Doubles of the Divine

Between earth and heaven
The empty air
Relayed the prayer
of the dead Jesus
From hell

When at last I gave up
My breath
The emptiness
Did not want it at first
So at first I had to offer it
To hell

My descent began
I moved among the dead
I saw what none should see
Heard what none should hear
A great grimace
Congealed in malice

A howl blasting hearing
Beyond all airing
Fires of frozen craving
Burnt dry of all desire

I wept
I watered the dust
I cried out
Who hears us here?

The humus did not heave
The compost gave forth
No exhalation

I knew then
Why heaven did not take
My first breath
It had to be
The second offering

I wept breath
Into the dust
It heaved
In suppressed appeal
& I accepted
The second torment
& every appeal was recreated
As a promise –
To be redeemed
And not more betrayed –

I am born again among the dead
Older than age – always
Newer than time – always
Younger than tomorrow –
    always

The fig tree I cursed
Will give moist fruit again

GNOSTICISM AND RELIGIOUS PLURIVOCITY

We now pass from God(s) One and many, personal and transpersonal to a religious ethos marked by equivocal doubling relative to the divine. Gnosticism reflects the plurivocity of being, the plurivocity of being religious. This plurivocity speaks to us in a space of overdetermined communication where signs are perplexing and many-meaninged. Gnosticism often baffles us with a proclivity to persistent shape shifting. It takes shape in the overdetermination of the ethos, and in the interplay of determination and indetermination, but it is the equivocity of that interplay that we most notice, such that the intermedium of the between is multiply filled, filled by imagination, by myth, by ritual, by magic, by story, by speculation. Gnosticism reflects a diversity of reconfigurations of the ethos, but, throughout, one divines certain exposures to the equivocalness of given being, with a certain heightened apprehensiveness about evil to the fore. It would be impossible to give a univocal definition, reducing it to one clear, distinct and essential feature. Irenaeus, referring to the Valentinian school, uses the comparison of a Hydra.[1]

---

[1] Irenaeus, *Against Heresies*, in *The Anti Nicene Fathers, Volume 9*, ed. Allan Menzies (New York: Christiain Literature, 1986), I, 30, 15; see Hippolytus, *Refutatio* V.II; see Kurt Rudolph, *Gnosis: The Nature and History of Gnosticism*, ed. Robert McLachlan Wilson (San Francisco: Harper and Row, 1987), pp. 53ff. This is not unrelated to the importance of the serpent. See below on the Ophite diagram, footnote 25.

A kind of creative confusion is more likely, in the literal sense that things run into each other and fuse together (*fusio-con*). This con-fusion is intimately related to the fertile possibilities of the equivocal.

Gnosticism is commonly associated with a variety of sects active in the Hellenized near-East around the first and second century of the common era. Some of the sects were related to Christianity, though the relation tended to be tense and sometimes hostile. Much of our previous knowledge originated with early Christian critics, the heresiologists, such as Irenaeus and Tertullian, and Clement of Alexandria. They have been criticized as providing only "propaganda," hence distorting the original, the "enemy." Others defend their portrayals as not devoid of truth, even granting the polemics.[2] The modern discovery of the so-called Gnostic Gospels have introduced intriguing detail to the story, allowing us to read some of the texts directly, as well as adding complexity to the story of early Christianity. The situation is again a rather con-fused plurivocity: many religious voices vie with one another, at a certain point none is entirely dominant, sometimes there is a kind of a community in the plurivocity, sometimes an air of cacophony, sometimes those hostile to each other tend to mirror their opponents, but with divergent spiritual intents.

Gnosticism has been called "the religion of dualism," and while not wrong, different kinds of dualism require further definition. I prefer to speak of *doubles* and *doublings* rather than simply dualism, which can too easily become fixated on rigid binary oppositions. There is something more fluid and metamorphosing, even protean about Gnosticism. The notion of doubles or doubling qualifies dualism by the equivocal sense of being, and thereby offers more supple means for dealing not only with dualisms but with the subversions of dualities and the surpassings of oppositions. It also allows us to underline the crucial significance of the *counterfeit double*.

An initial instance of its relevance: Orthodox Christians and Gnostic tended to be doubles of each other, but because of factors added or omitted, or transmuted or distorted, they were doubles in intimate opposition. Similarly with non-Christian Gnosticism, defined by considerations closer to neo-Platonism: Plotinus's wrath against Gnosticism shows something of this hostility to the *intimate double*. Gnosticism makes the best of this con-fusing plurivocity by being an eclectic mixing from different sources and many ancient cultures. In the religious equivocity there seem many voices and no apparent unity or community in the many. The lack of community is perhaps most evident in the struggle with Christianity over the question of orthodoxy. That the notion of the heretical now appears at all reflects as much a struggle for the ascendancy of a world-view (that is, a reconfiguration of the ethos of being), as of the truth of that view. The Gnostics did not win ascendancy; hence the need to hide their documents, the possession of which was perilous. In this equivocal situation, the will to power is never entirely quiet – a point that now is perhaps overemphasized.

Such an ethos of religious plurivocity has some similarity to our own time: fresh possibilities seem to open up in a time of ferment and transition; the old has lost its immemorial stability, and in the atmosphere of a new age, there is a search for saving knowing, often coupled with dissatisfaction with public, institutional religion. In Hellenistic times people turned to mystery religions for a relation to the divine more personal and immediate than was to be found in the public religion with its institutionalized, that is, non-personal rituals. In the equivocal manyness, pagan, Jewish, Christian, Iranian, Hermetic, and occult considerations, and the Lord knows what, may all be thrown together and stirred in the melting pot of religious imagination. The babble may shout of multiple possibilities, but Babel also can generate its own heterogeneous fecundity.

[2] Hans Jonas makes such a point, confirming Irenaeus and others, in the second edition of his *The Gnostic Religion: The Message of the Alien God and the Beginnings of Christianity*, 2nd edn., rev. (Boston: Beacon, 1963), p. 295, after having consulted the Nag Hammadi texts. English translation, *The Nag Hammadi Library in English*, James M. Robinson, ed., (San Francisco: Harper and Row, 1978) – abbreviated hereafter to *NHL*.

Such a fertile con-fusion of equivocal difference reminds us of something like post-modern pluralism. We find a mixing of many styles, parabolic, speculative, incantatory, oracular, and so on. In some Gnostic texts (for instance, *The Sophia of Jesus Christ*, *NHL*, pp. 206–29) it is startling to hear Jesus Christ speaking in tones reminiscent of a neo-Platonic philosopher.[3] Not a few of the Nag Hammadi texts remind one of the discourses of Nietzsche's Zarathustra. The tone is often hieratic: full of proclamation and higher say-so – obscure, but laced with hints and insinuations of deeper meaning – delivered to insiders but meant to impress, to awe, outsiders: gospels for everyone and for no one. Zarathustra is himself often a parodist, even mocker, of Christianity. Gnosticism is often a double of Christianity, other than orthodox in many of its utterances: a double very like and yet very unlike in the way a parody is very like and unlike at once. You might suspect it of being a *parodia sacra*, but with the Gnostic texts one detects little intention to parody. To the contrary, they seem to be deadly serious about themselves, as the true utterances of original and last secrets. Nietzsche's own Zarathustra slips in and out of that kind of seriousness. Zoroaster is one of the figures of praise in Gnostic discourse. Nietzsche's Zarathustra is an equivocal double, very like and very unlike the original. For Nietzsche the original Zoroaster was the inventor of the moral distinction of good and evil – the fateful double that sets in motion the moral counterfeiting of the world. Now the truth of immoralism is to be announced and becoming restored to its innocence. There is a reminder of Gnosticism in the superior announcement to the few of the world both restored and transfigured, in the going under of its old corruption by Jewish Christianity.

The scholarly study of Gnosticism is almost an industry entire unto itself, but our concern throughout is a philosophy of God. It is not a history of religions, or a philology of sacred texts, or a hermeneutics of holy narratives.[4] A metaxological philosophy of God requires attendance on the plurivocity of what communicates itself, but sometimes in that plurivocity different voices become so promiscuously intertwined that it is hard to discern and fix differences. Then we may have to attempt a portrait that, to a degree, reconstructs what is communicated in the plurivocity. With Gnosticism it is sometimes like trying to catch the face of a recurrent orientation to the divine, where sometimes diverging, sometimes converging lineaments of this face come forward and withdraw, as when we try to see likenesses to family relations in a child or a grandchild, or in the image of an ancestor. Many similarities might appear and fade; family resemblances to a number of relatives might be persuasively invoked; a plurality of profiles might need to be sketched; nothing absolutely definite might be fixed such that we could say "*That* is it." And yet we are cognizant we are addressing relatives of the same family.

One has to enter into the spirit of a religious orientation, even if the letter of the orientation is fragmented or incomplete or even self-discordant. Philosophical finesse beyond philology is needed to read the physiognomies of the sacred. A metaxological philosophy

---

[3] One recalls, too, that genre of comic literature of late eighteenth-century German philosophers, including the younger Hegel, where Jesus is made to speak in the language of Kant's categorical imperative.

[4] I have learned much from many writers, including Hans Jonas, Kurt Rudolph, and Cyril O'Regan. O'Regan's work is compelling in addressing the question of Gnostic return in modernity, with reference to a narrative view in which the structure of Valentinian Gnosticism is central: *Gnostic Return in Modernity* (Albany: SUNY, 2001) and *Gnostic Apocalypse: Jacob Boehme's Haunted Narrative* (Albany: SUNY, 2002); see my review of these in *Tijdschrift voor filosofie*, 64:3, 2002, pp. 607–11. On connections with Platonism, see Richard Wallis, ed. *Neoplatonism and Gnosticism* (Albany: SUNY, 1992). O'Regan addresses the relation of Hegelianism and Gnosticism in *The Heterdox Hegel* (Albany: SUNY, 1994), as do Glenn Magee, *Hegel and the Hermetic Tradition* (Ithaca: Cornell, 2001) and Gerald Hanratty *Studies in Gnosticism and in the Philosophy of Religion* (Dublin: Four Courts, 1997). Michael Pauen, *Dithyrambiker des Untergangs: Gnostizismus in Ästhetik und Philosophie der Moderne* (Berlin: Akademie Verlag, 1994), includes discussions of Schopenhauer, Nietzsche, Heidegger, Bloch, Adorno, as well as *Pessimismus* and *das ganz Andere*. The question of the dark origin since Hegel – in Schopenhauer, Nietzsche, and others – has been important in my own work (see my *AOO*, for instance). The question of nihilism arises here with respect to the metaphysical judgment "Better not to be."

of God must be sympathetic as well as questioning, discerning as well as critical. Even if a view is not endorsed, the view must still be understood. This would be a practice of agapeic mindfulness: acceptance of what is other for what it is in itself, even if what it has made of itself is not acceptable or accepted as the final word.

There is something heterogeneous about Gnosticism but also something transitional and intermediate: an ambiguous mix of religion and philosophy, One and many, personal and transpersonal, monism and dualism, speculation and myth, concept and metaphor. This transitional intermediacy need not be understood in a merely negative sense. We can find a strong dualism in some versions, yet also a movement towards the God of the whole. Yet again we find a sense of a God beyond the whole that is, on the one hand, not the God of biblical personalism and that, on the other hand, makes remarkable use of elements of a more personal soteriology with certain Christian tonalities. The diverse forms of Gnosticism are characterized by certain styles of response to the equivocity of the between. I say styles of response, not a univocally homogenous set of doctrines, though there are diverse constancies of doctrines evident in these styles.[5] We find a strong sense of the aesthetic equivocity of finite being to the fore, as haunted by exposure to evil and marked by a certain doubling between One and many, tending now downwards to dualism and now upwards to recuperated oneness. In the remaining chapters of Part III that aesthetic equivocity will yield first to a more explicit dialectical sense with the pan(en)theistic God of the whole (Chapter 11) and then to a more metaxological sense with the theistic God of creation beyond the whole (Chapter 12), to turn us again to the intimate universal of the mystic God (Chapter 13), to be rethought in terms of the idiotics, aesthetics, erotics, and agapeics of the metaxological.

DIVINITIES DOUBLED BELOW AND ABOVE

A summary of some main tenets will help. The stress is on a saving knowing, but we can look at this gnosis from the perspective of the divine or the human. One might start "above" with the God beyond all; one might start "below" in our darkly equivocal world; we might start in the middle between "above" and "below" in the pleroma where powers between high and low go about and about, moving up and down.

Seen as if from the view of the divine above we begin with an absolute God beyond all – nameless, hyperbolic to the Father, a Forefather, with names like "abyss" and "silence" also needed to describe this hyperbolic transcendence.[6] This hyperbolic God is above the

---

[5] When resemblances are familial we find a mix of like and unlike, recurrent patterns of constancy and unanticipated waywardness, black sheep and shining heroes. A familial gene can mutate or recur many generations later with similarities to previous generations but no sameness, no univocal essence. One thinks also of cross-fertilizations in that Gnosticism can also be a quite syncretistic way of being religious, mixing aspects from different traditions: mystical exploration, spiritual alchemy, Christian Gnosticism. Many of the second century Gnostics saw themselves as Christians. St Paul uses the word "gnosis" frequently, though not quite in the "Gnostic" sense. Dan Merkur in *Gnosis: An Esoteric Tradition of Mystical Visions and Unions* (Albany: SUNY, 1993) offers a chapter on defining Gnosticism. He seems to accept some distinction between Gnosticism as defined by the Messina conference (1966) and gnosticism (small g) which is an esoteric tradition of unitive mystical practices. See also Michael Allen Williams, *Rethinking "Gnosticism": An Argument for Dismantling a Dubious Category* (Princeton: Princeton University Press, 1996).

[6] This hyperbolic character is very evident from the first part of *Tripartite Tractate* (NHL, pp. 54ff.) dealing with "The Father." *Trimorphic Protennoia* refers to "the immeasurable Silence," (NHL, p. 462) and the "Silence of the Ineffable One" (NHL, p. 463); also *Apocryphon of John*, NHL, p. 100. See *Allogenes* (NHL, pp. 443ff.) on the unsurpassable superiority of the One, the ineffable God. Also *Eugnostos* (NHL, pp. 207ff.) where the beyond of the Blessed Forefather and the emanations is laid out clearly. When the Gnostics refer to the *prote-pater* – unbegotten Father beyond father – they are not lacking awareness of certain difficulties in this referral. For we are pointed beyond finite relation. The pleroma seems itself to be hyperbolic and idiotic, for there is a Silence too to it. If the pleroma is all-full, this our world is as lacking and defective. If the pleroma beyond points to hyperbolic transcendence, there is still the gulf

pleroma which is its hypostasis, and within the pleroma there are further hypostases or emanations descending in hierarchical grades to the world we live in, itself reminiscent of an equivocal labyrinth through which we stray. One might call this God beyond all idiotic, in being in itself reserved for itself alone, intimate with itself alone. But there is more than incomparable divine autism, for from the Forefather the aeons or powers emanate, understood as a noetic uttering rather than an aesthetic: The first emanation, source of further emanations, referred to as First Thought (*Protennoia*; *Ennoia*), Providence, Fore-thought (*Pronoia*), is a female principle: "Barbelo." She is described as "The first power, the glory, Barbelo, the perfect glory in the aeons, the glory of the revelation" (*Apocryphon of John*, NHL, p. 101). There is a doubleness here: not only between herself and the lower Sophia, more derivative source of erring, but within herself : "This is the first thought, his image; she became the womb of everything for she is prior to them all, the Mother-Father, the First Man [*Anthropos*], the holy spirit, the thrice-male, the thrice-powerful, the thrice-named androgynous one, and the eternal aeon among the invisible ones, and the first to come forth" (ibid.). Double within herself, as male–female, and sometimes describes as the "male virginal Barbelo" (see *The Three Steles of Seth*, NHL, p. 364), she is a unity of opposites. Anthropos does not mean the gendered man, but the human being as male–female – somewhat like the Cabbalistic Adam Kadmon, the primordial Adam. The Anthropos as androgynous suggests a double being, meaning primal completeness, of male–female in one. Further, then, the aeons as divine powers are hypostasized (often in "Syzygies," as the Gnostics called male–female pairs) in a descending order of ultimacy the intriguing intricacy of which need not detain us. The last is Sophia, the lower double of the higher feminine Fore-thought, and also like the feminine double of the Forefather. With her, disarray comes to be in the pleroma, since she initiates the stray powers of dubious doubling. In the dubious doubling of the divine Sophia all our woe comes to be unloosed. If the higher Feminine is fore-thought, this seems lacking in the lower Sophia: evil emerges in the erring of this divinity. Somehow misguided, in thinking herself to be free of the Forefather, and wanting to create like the Forefather, she tries to create through herself alone, but gives rise to something like an abortion: the *hulē* is foetus-like (something like *protē hulē*?). She cast this abortion away from herself, outside the pleroma. Matter is the extremity of fall from the Fore-father and the pleroma, verging on nonbeing.

To dissimulate the erring, Sophia calls forth "Yaltabaoth" (*Apocryphon of John*, NHL, p. 104) the second "God," the demiurge said to work on the misbirth or miscarriage to create the world as we know it. In the work of this second "God" the *pneuma* comes to be trapped in the *hulē*, the divine spark in the matter. This second "God" boasts of being the only God, of their being none above it. He is also called "the God of the blind" (for instance, *Hypostasis of the Archons*, NHL, p. 153), identified with Samael. Far from being God and alone God, he does not even realize that he is far below the Primal Adam. The second "God" wants jealously to guard his power from humans. In some versions, the Adam and Eve of this lower creation below are imitations less than true doubles of a higher androgynous Adam (hence both Adam and Eve). The second "God" is a possessive lord of all dissimulating seconds, master of a world of counterfeit doubles where the lower makes claim to be the higher, and the higher is degraded to the lower. The second "God" is the God of the seconds; and each second is a counterfeit double of

between the pleroma and this our world of creation. This gulf can lead to a dualistic between on the other side of which is the God beyond world, the Godhead beyond god. Were *some* of the Gnostic writers aware of the difficult questions of *the trans-finite protocols of naming the divine*? Some were quite sophisticated intellectuals – other perhaps just speculative dabblers, even fantasists, and babblers. A speculative fantasist might pass as a sophisticated intellectual in a world full of the babble of counterfeit doubles. In this way we find a mixture of the systematic and non-systematic, the conceptual and the poetic, the formal and the erotic. Along this way, the knowing that is said to come, if it comes at all, is in the *performance of a saying*, perhaps of a kind of inspired say-so. Hence this knowing comes to delivery as much by incantation as by argument, as much by intoxicated song as by sober statement.

something more ultimate than itself. For instance, in line with the jealousy of the secondary demiurge and narrative of his tyrannizing, the serpent is misrepresented as the father of lies. By contrast, in the saving reading of this narrative, the serpent is more truly the symbol of a withheld wisdom. "The Female Spiritual Principle came [in] the Snake, the Instructor" (*Hypostasis of the Archons*, NHL, p. 155). The serpent tells rightly, rightly foretells, that knowledge of good and evil will make humans as gods. This knowledge is kept from, forbidden to created humans below by the jealous "God" of false seconds. What is called "fall" in this "God's" counter(feit) narrative is really the beginnings of a recovery of the truer knowing, as promised by the serpent. Release of the divine *pneuma* in the *hulē* will restore us to what we truly are: divine. The world below, as a fall from what is truly higher, is a dissembling world which tries to mimic the more ultimate.[7] The world simulates the divine in a material mime that allures but mocks, that seduces but also betrays. We must back away from this show, this feigning, to be restored to the true God, the Fore-father beyond the counter(feit) second "God."

Seen as if from the human point of view below salvation is effected by a saving knowing that releases the divine spark from its being hemmed in and trapped by matter. This means struggle with the dualism of the counterfeit world, dominantly expressed in the duality of good and evil, spirit and flesh. The difference of the few and the many is important, and the few are those initiated into saving knowing, the *gnostikoi*. Otherwise, and more generally, there are three kinds of human beings: the pneumatics, the psychics, and the hylics (see *Tripartite Tractatus*, NHL, pp. 89ff.). The *pneumatikoi* are those with the essential promise of becoming *gnostikoi*; the rest are either the psychics or the hylics and not in the same class. For the pneumatic have in them the true spark of the divine. The psychics may come to have something of it. The hylics seems to be defective in it.

Saving knowing is accessed and expressed by secret knowledge. Sometimes there seem to be magical names that allow passage from this world to the beyond through the different spheres where sacred passwords must be recited to allow exit and further progress. Passing through and beyond the spheres was thought to be, or be symbolized by the seven spheres of the stars and planets of ancient (Babylonian) astrology. We might understand the passage beyond either cosmologically, with reference to the whole, or pneumatically, psychologically, with reference to the inner man, the absolute God immanent within the human, and with whom the true human is said to be the same. We are dealing with escape from the low world below to hyperbolic transcendence above all. The divine spark must be released from its imprisonment, either by going beyond the material creation, or beyond the human body itself.

We find doubleness in the practice of saving: here extreme asceticism, doubled there sometimes by antinomic liberty. More often, strong ascetic practices are courted as disciplines to effect the release. We can find negative attitudes to the body and its snares, say, in the interdict against the marriage of the elite, though the mystery of the spiritual bridal chamber is not ruled out (*Gospel of Philip*, NHL, pp. 139, 149). Among Christian Gnostics, we find docetism: incarnation is not the Word made flesh but the Word assuming an appearance, an instrumental mask or persona that is a kind of impersonation. The divine man is only making use of a body, not ontologically intimate with it: Christ laughs above the cross at those who think he suffered there.[8] Admittedly, since the second "God" of the Old Testament is identified with the inferior principle of law, there can be a tendency to antinomianism in which the privilege is claimed by the initiated of

---

[7] When we find talk in the *Tripartite Tractatus* of "beings of the likeness" (NHL, p. 74), what is intended is, as it were, *mere* likeness, that is, *unlikeness* from the true God – more like a counterfeit as a "likeness."

[8] On the Savior "glad and laughing on the tree" see the *Apocalypse of Peter*, NHL, p. 344. On laughter as contempt, see *Gospel of Philip*, NHL, pp. 144–5: "And as soon as [Christ went down into] the water, he came [out laughing at] everything (of this world), [not] because [he considers it] a trifle, but [because he is full of] contempt for it. He who [wants to enter] the kingdom of [heaven will attain it]. If he despises [everything (of this world)] and scorns it as a trifle, [he will come] out laughing . . . The world came about through a mistake."

being beyond good and evil, understood here in terms of the moral law. This is the elite liberty of those beyond the law.

Release is also bound up with a kind of inner way: the divine spark is sleeping within, freeing it is making it to be awakened. Remember how (in Chapters 3 and 4) the turn to the inner is connected with the movement from the univocal way to God to the equivocal, from disconcertment about the lack of univocity in externality to recourse to what is immanent within us, as perhaps a surer measure of that external equivocity. We find a variation on this theme here, as the soul takes flight from external determinism, in the form of iron fate or arbitrary *fortuna*, towards what is more truly immanent to itself. Astrology shows the fated course of the stars as imprisoning us; beyond them we must escape. The equivocal power of evil rocks the soul back on itself and it must traverse the inner labyrinth to an appointed goal where self-knowing and knowing of Godhead coincide.

One can wonder, of course, if this inner exploration is isomorphic with a sense of the cosmos as a kind of ontological labyrinth. If the fallen creation is a first cave, there is within the soul a second cave.[9] In this second underground what is other to dissimulating equivocity is to be found: other in the inner otherness, other beyond all external otherness: God hyperbolic and beyond the demiurgic "God." Return to self along the inner way must needs be more "personal" than "institutional." One understands the attraction of the Gnostic and the Hermetic for currents of thoughts like that of Jung. These are the fascinations of the inner labyrinth. Ancient Gnosticism sets all this in highly metaphorical cosmology, but metaphor is a way of naming in which the inner and the upper might coincide. Going down into the inner cave we ourselves are, we come out above the cave the cosmos is, and we rejoin the sky above. Here this is so, since the release of the divine spark is ultimately the self-restoration to the primal absolute. The ultimate God might be first hyperbolically One, but then there is emanation and fall into a world of counterfeit doubles, then again struggle through equivocal dualism and release through saving knowing and restoration to the hyperbolic One in which the God beyond all seems only restored to itself, only self-restoring. We find a startling coincidence of opposite: hyperbolic monism in one sense, hyperbolic dualism in another, with saving knowing offering passage through the between fraught with equivocal evil, and its counterfeit doubles of the divine.

GNOSTIC EQUIVOCITY AND THE FOURFOLD NAMING

What of the One and many? We come across One God beyond the immanent many that both includes all as itself the absolute All, and yet One in a kind of antithesis with the opposing manifoldness of the immanent creation. Gnosticism offers the possibility of a kind of hyperbolic monism and yet a strikingly strong dualistic sense, while the multitude of intermediary powers suggests a transposition of the impulse of polytheism.

What of personal and transpersonal divinity? We find a mixing of a speculative style of impersonal philosophizing, with high abstractions, wedded to a plethora of personalized beings, divine and semi-divine. Speculative-theological concepts are combined with stories and parables: speculative theology bearing on the One beyond all names, coupled with an at times exuberant, even wild mythologizing, itself blended with a non-abstract style of parabolic narration such as we find in the New Testament.

What of the four namings? We find traces of all. With respect to the *idiotic*, there is the silence of the Fore-father, as absolute monad (*monas*) and as abyss (*buthos*). There is something of the idiotic in the turn to the inner way, in the superiority of the pneumatic over the psychic and hylic. This inner way is plastic and fluid, and not unrelated to the porosity of our being. Hence, again, the attraction of Gnosticism to Jung and

9 One thinks of, so to say, Mythraic caves, with worship taking place in underground basilicas, catacombs. See Rudolph, *Gnosis*, illustration 9, pp. 24–5

his admirers: the myths reveal archetypes of the unconscious where we encounter the double: animus, anima: the soul and its shadow. Is the idiotic intimacy sifted well enough? See Gnosticism as a sifting of the promiscuity in the porosity, an equivocal sifting of its equivocity, hence still captive to the equivocity while struggling to be free of it.

With respect to the *aesthetic*, despite the generally negative attitude towards the flesh, the indispensability of the aesthetic is evident in the sometimes striking images we find in Gnostic texts, as well as the penchant for paradox. This, of course, reflects something of the parabolic narrative of the New Testament, but there is something Zen-like in the provocations addressed to the more quotidian univocities of Aristotelian logic. In some respects, this indicates a station on the way towards a more fully developed dialectic (one thinks of the attractions of Gnostic themes and sources for Hegel). Importantly there is the pervasiveness of doubles in the literature: Forefather God and Feminine Sophia; the doubling between the upper world and lower; doublings within the upper and lower worlds (for example, Adam Kadmon and Adam); aeons above at whose head the Forefather, archons below at whose head the demiurge; Jesus and his twin; the male the female; the child the old man. It with respect to aesthetic naming that perplexity about the counterfeit double comes up: the doubleness of divinity, as well as doubles of divinity.

The beginning of Irenaeus's *Against Heresies* (preface, 2) is redolent of the theme of the counterfeit double: "Error, indeed, is never set forth in its naked deformity, lest, being thus exposed, it should at once be detected. But it is craftily decked out in an attractive dress, so as, by its outward form, to make it appear to the inexperienced (ridiculous as the expression may seem) more true than the truth itself. One far superior to me has well said in reference to this point, 'A clever imitation in glass casts contempt, as it were, on that precious jewel the emerald (which is most highly esteemed by some), unless it come under the eye of one able to test and expose the counterfeit.'" The orthodox believer and the heretic are very close to each other, yet very distant: close in that both make claim to the true teaching, both views overlap to an important degree, distant in that something crucial in one is altered or missing in the other. The *same* thing might be said *otherwise*, that is, invested with a significantly different spiritual meaning. The difference, sometimes all but invisible to the nonpartisan outsider, constitutes a space of spiritual contestation. The contestation is all the more intense, given that the two are too close for comfort. Each claims to be the true original, each doubles the other, but each for the other is a counterfeit double of the true Christian.[10] The counterfeit Christian is all the more dangerous: the enemy within, the intimate enemy who shows the face of the friend. The discernment of the doubleness is a challenge for both sides, bound up with what is to be deemed authoritative. The counterfeit double reveals an intimacy of the opposites, difficult to disentangle – we are on the threshold of a dialectic.

The issue extends also to the agonistic, even antagonistic twinning of *philosophical* visions. A philosophical position can be so intimately close to one's own as to risk being mistaken for it. Thus Plotinus's own philosophy comes close to Gnostic concerns on some points, for instance, regarding evil and matter. From his attack (*Ennead* II, 9) one sees that some of his own disciples had gone over to certain Gnostic tenets and practices. Plotinus's inoculation of his own students has not entirely worked. They have become apostates from the wiser affirmations of Greek rationalism. Even "friends" once touched by gnosticism so continue (II, 9, 10, 3–6). And the blast of reaction comes. Plotinus shouts: Plato knew the cave but he also showed us the way out of the cave. Plato did not slander the Father of it all. "It is not enough to say – Look to God – One must also know

---

[10] Reminiscent of the counterfeit double, O'Regan offers us a "figural Irenaeus" in terms of his notion of metalepsis: "Irenaeus is the Christian thinker who has the clearest conceptual grasp of metalepsis as essentially consisting of disfiguration-refiguration of biblical narrative. Moreover, in an interpretive move whose genius can be fully appreciated in light of the Nag Hammadi texts, as essentially consisting of disfiguration-refiguration of biblical narrative, Irenaeus indicates how disfiguration-refiguration of narrative has surface and depth narrative dimensions" (*Gnostic Return in Modernity*, p. 230; see also pp. 16ff. on O'Regan's own work as Irenaean).

how to look" (II, 9,15, 33–5). See here the intimate double in the likeness yet inversion between the evil demiurge of Gnosticism and the good demiurge of Plato's *Timaeus*: one makes an aesthetic cosmos that entraps spirit, the other an aesthetic cosmos as beautiful as possible. Against the insinuation that his own metaphysics of a fall from the One justified contempt for the material world we behold Plotinus stung into a different amen, a "yes" to being that includes the material world as good. Perhaps most intensely in all his writing, here we find the passion of his philosophical eros affirming the goodness of the world and its maker. Plotinus is stricken into singing the glory of the material world. The aesthetic cosmos is not the same as the noetic cosmos but it too is good. Plotinus cannot conceal his contempt for the impiety of the Gnostics, yet an unease remains for us that these intimate others do bring out something of the "no" to materiality latent even in Plotinus's own hyperbolic "yes."

With respect to the *erotic*, granted Gnostic asceticism can be negative towards the erotics of human sexuality, there is an erotic character to Gnosticism evident in both the "passing beyond" of our quest for saving knowing, and in the relation of divine to itself and the world.[11] The latter is suggested by the coupling of the paternal and maternal, the male and female as sacred metaphorics for divine reality itself, but also in the androgyny of the primal *anthropos*, complete because both male and female. This androgynous completeness suggests that no external power or principle is needed for generation to take place. We move within the sacred symbolics of erotic self-generation. This is evident in the rejection of demiurgic making, for instance, where the maker and the material are external to each other; there is not between them the intimate erotics in which the shaper and the shaped, the begetter and the begotten are blent, even in their doubleness, into one. An erotics of sacred begetting is evident, for instance, in *On the Origin of the World* (NHL, pp. 161–79). Instead of the extrinsic imposition of form on matter of demiurgy, erotic theurgy suggests a fluid porosity between the originating and the originated, where again we return to a promiscuous *con-fusio*, one in which there is a circulation of the divine. The erotic circling of the divine is one and two, passing from one to the other, and, though falling from the all, also restoring the all, and in the circle restored to itself in its own self-begetting.[12] Thus the dynamic doubleness, the fluid doubling of Gnosticism points to a more fully dialectical self-mediation of the divine in and through its own otherness.

The intimate double is bonded to a kind of erotic self-doubling with the erring Sophia. See the erring Sophia as auto-erotic: self-willing to be a mother without a father – without the Forefather. In the erring she engenders a misshapen matter, but matter echoes of *mater* – a matrix indeed, but a double here, a bad mother. The bad mother of matter is engendered by the erring auto-eroticism of Sophia's self-doubling. See further her response to this bad material double as calling forth the bad father, the demiurge. And see this bad father, a counterfeit double of the true Father, reversing the auto-eroticism of his mother: rather than mothering without a father, he fathers without a mother, albeit in

11 See the striking metaphor, in *Tripartite Tractate*, NHL, p. 59, where the Son (eternally) generates innumerable offspring, the Church "before the aeons," in the manner of *the kiss:* "His offspring . . . have, like kisses, come forth from the Son and the Father, (like kisses) because of the multitude of some who kiss one another with a good, insatiable thought, the kiss being a unity, although it involves many." *Gospel of Truth*, NHL, p. 48: All the emanations of the Father are pleromas and, as it were, "participated in his face by means of kisses."

12 On the erotics of the Gnostic divinity (especially in *On the Origin of the World*) see Patricia Miller's interesting contribution in *Neoplatonism and Gnosticism*, pp. 223–38. See O'Regan's view of Böhme in *Gnostic Apocalypse*: we find a decisive "swerve" towards a more erotic God in which kenotic, and agonistic movements serve a teleological completion of divine self-becoming. While this God is not devoid of agapeic registers (see, for example, p. 190), finally the erotic figuration is in the dominant. The erotic, kenotic, and agonistic divine becoming places the God of the end as higher and more "complete" than the God of the beginning. In between beginning and end is the fall of the divine, figured in such a way that points backwards to the Valentinian narrative and forward to successors like Hegel where the erotic motif dominates far more inclusively. Böhme prepares the erotic refiguration that a speculative thinker like Hegel completes.

the matrix of matter – and the counterfeit creation of the aesthetic cosmos is engendered. Behind the backs of this mothering without the father and this fathering without the mother, the creation of this world is the equivocal offspring of a kind of divine incest. All the auto-erotic coupling, the self-doublings of the divine perpetuate *con-fusio* – a covered over sacrilegious promiscuity smelling on the whole of sacred incest.

With respect to the *agapeic*, one might have mythological or speculative views about the worlds "above" and "below," but how they relate is all important. Gnosticism seems to have a monism above, a dualism below, and an equivocal doubleness between "above" and "below." This scheme might be accommodated to some erotic terms, but it is debatable if it can extend fully to properly agapeic terms. One cannot just get to the agapeics of the divine by simple addition to the erotics. The erotics will have to be entirely rethought as itself the promise of the agapeic. This would require a significant overhaul of terms.

Consider the case with reference to Plotinus. Plotinus is not a Gnostic, but he does have a hyperbolic sense of the One, the ascent to which he makes dialectically intelligible in erotic terms. But the "way down" is not explicitly articulated in terms of an agapeic origination, more an emanation which drops off into the language of a fall from the full (sur)plenitude of the One. The surplus of the One as the Good calls for agapeic terms, and one senses that Plotinus is much closer to this than his Gnostic rivals. But, relative to the "way down," there is always the danger of stressing the defective being of the derivative – the seconds as merely secondary, "mere" likenesses tending to a loss of the plenitude of the original. Porphry, in his biography of Plotinus, tells us he was ashamed to be in the body – Porphyry who was himself tempted by Gnosticism, as well as magic practices and theurgy. But in his own offensive against the Gnostics, Plotinus tells us it is shameful to say the body is shameful. The Gnostic derogation from the beauty of the material universe, and the slander of its maker, sting Plotinus into defending the goodness of the Father of the created world, the goodness of the created world.

There is no doubt that there is stress on a love, in its erotic form and sometimes in its agapeic. One thinks of how the Christian Gnostic Marcion stressed the God of love in contraposition to the God of law, drawing attention to the superiority of the former, though the latter is not evil. How explicitly agapeic is this? The Gnostic style of articulation evidences an aesthetic equivocity in which there is often a blending into one another of the four namings. The blending of the erotic and the agapeic is complemented by a sense of roots darkly hidden in idiotic intimacy, as well as by aesthetic expression putting forth shoots of religious imagination with sometimes striking paradoxical doubleness. Attention to the maternal, feminine side of the divine, whether with Sophia or the primal Eve, evidences all four.[13]

Given what was said above about erotic self-begetting, overall the stress is not fully agapeic, in the respect of giving the difference and otherness of finite creation as such, and hyperbolically affirmed in its goodness. This would be a reconciliation too far with the God of *Genesis*, otherwise identified with the blind God, the inferior demiurge. The hyperbolic "yes" of this bungling God now seems more like a counterfeit double

---

[13] Admittedly the savior is masculine (with a feminine side). This is not congenial to New Age appropriations: much is made of the passage in *The Gospel of Philip* (NHL, p. 138) where the Savior kisses Mary Magdalene often on the mouth, and the disciples ask why? (See the success of Dan Brown's fiction *The Da Vinci Code*.) Less is made of *The Dialogue of the Savior* (NHL, p. 238) where the Savior speaks with Mary about the "dissolution of the works of womanhood." One recalls the problem posed in early Buddhism: Could a woman become a Buddha? Answer: First she needs a body change into the masculine form, and then can move on from there. See the Gnostic *Gospel of Thomas*, NHL, p. 130. "Simon Peter said to them, 'Let Mary leave us, for women are not worthy of Life.' Jesus said, 'I myself shall lead her in order to make her male, so that she too may become a living spirit resembling you males. For every woman who makes herself male will enter the Kingdom of Heaven.'" Analogous problem: Could a Gentile become a Christian? Directly? Or only first by becoming a Jew, being circumcised? In the *Gospel of Thomas* (NHL, p. 124), Jesus denies the importance of circumcision.

of the true Gnostic "yes" to the truly good God beyond the dubious, even evil creation. The guarded, if not hostile attitude to incarnation also points in a different direction to the agapeic – if we understand this as a surplus love of the mortal. The agapeic God loves the finite to the point of a *compassio essendi* with its mortal passion. If we think of the docetic interpretation of Christ's passion, namely, that his body was only a mere appearance, his death was not a real death.[14] It was an impersonation of death void of radical *compassio essendi* in the agapeic sense revealed by the singular love of the mortal creature. The divine remains untouched and untouchable. It seems to be involved, but a love that only *seems* to be involved with the mortal is not a love of the mortal, for its hidden trajectory is always flight from the mortal as such.

THE EQUIVOCAL WORLD AS A COUNTERFEIT DOUBLE?

Compared to the overall rational confidence of Neo-Platonism and Plotinus, on the one hand, and the affirmation of the goodness of creation of biblical theism, Gnostic orientations to the between seem overshadowed by the equivocity of evil. There is felt to fall on the intermedium of being the shadow of a baleful light, a light darkening rather than enlightening, for it generates counterfeit doubles of the divine that entrap the true light. We have to take seriously, in a religious sense, the view that there is a fundamental equivocity to immanent being, haunting the human condition, touching us in the flesh itself. It is not univocally clear that being as given is good. To the contrary, it seems unequivocally clear that it is not absolutely good. There is war, suffering, disease. We are frail. We know our frailty, disturbed as to why we are thrown upon the surge of life, given no univocal pledge of home or harbor. Storm, shipwreck, and drowning threaten to overwhelm us, careless of our ineptitude. Sinister powers seem rampant, trampling out their grapes of wrath. What reck do they give us? We seek for God but then equivocal being squats there stopping us short, spreading like dark matter a malign spell that paralyzes our transcending powers. Recoiled on ourselves, our cries go out beyond ourselves as if like pointless appeals from a prison with no outside, for turn which way we will, we are balked. There seems no outlet, nothing but this tight coil of equivocity that winding over all holds all in thrall.

Immanent discord proliferates in many directions: the union of opposites reveals itself as radical opposition nested in all union (example: *The Gospel of Philip, NHL*, pp. 132–3). The ultimate discord is between the finite between itself and the true divine, the God that is other and beyond and always transcendent. The intermediate world is itself the ontological double that blocks free passage between us and the God beyond. The world is "in the way" and we must do away with what is in the way to find ourselves truly on the way. Seen thus, the given world is a medium of adversity hindering us from community with the God beyond. The equivocity might seem redoubled again, for the intermedium seems itself to be perfumed with the allures of seduction. It *appears* as beautiful and so seems to temper its interposition between us and the divine. But then, in an evil reversal, the interposition breaks the promise of beauty. For the appearance of tempering seems less to suspend the hindrance as to enforce more effectively the point of hindering, which is just to stand in the way, to intercept communication. It is an old, elemental story: successful guile can be more hostile in its hidden effect than overt aggression is in fact. The beauty of the world calls to us achingly, tempting us, winning us, making us tarry with the gloriously mortal. These sweetenings of life are only secret springs: sweet nothings. How can we love the world, when its beckoning loveliness insinuates its lie? This beauty is the swindle that ensnares.

---

[14] Christ only *used* a body soteriologically but did not suffer. If we fixate on the body, we will be taken in by a double of the Son of Man, the primal spiritual being, and hence be deceived by the counterfeit. Something of this is at stake in the *Gospel of Judas*: Judas's betrayal is no betrayal but a cooperation in the work of saving by enabling the death of the body of Jesus.

One understandable response in these perceived circumstances is that as medium of adversity the world is an intermedium of the adversary.[15] It must not be allowed to betray us further. We must be hostile to this world, because its beauty hides hostility itself. We must hate ourselves as of the world, for it is our being its creatures that is repellent. Being a creature is to be between: *torn* between evil and good We love the beauty of the world, and ache for its good, but we are betrayed by our love, and end up aching as bony decrepitude called at the last to the embrace of mocking death. To be, to be created is to be cheated by death itself. Being created is the first guilt, the guilt that hides itself in everything else seductively second. Is this it then: life grooms us for death?

PASSING BEYOND THE COUNTERFEIT DOUBLES

See the following as an understandable rejoinder to creation as the domain of counterfeit doubles. The given world shows itself as double – as both hospitable and hostile – and we can respond to this doubleness with a "yes" or a "no": a "yes" if we find the hospitality sufficiently welcoming, a "no" if the hostility proves too sharp. In the concrete, there is mixture, and much of "perhaps": we open ourselves, we protect ourselves; we surrender ourselves, we secure ourselves; we give ourselves, we grab for ourselves. Nevertheless, we still seek a "yes": perhaps not to the double world, but to something worthy to be more ultimately affirmed. Seeking this "yes," we see the "no" here, and seek and seem to see the "yes" elsewhere, there other, transcendent, utterly transcendent. Equivocal creation need not be *per se* dualistic but it can foster a mentality of dualism which seeks unity in a hyperbolic One, beyond the world, beyond equivocal creation. The absolute Forefather of the Gnostics answers to this hyperbolic One. But the saving search for this One can fix its terms in a variety of dualisms (perhaps inherited philosophically from Platonic sources, religiously from Iranian sources). The upshot can be a redoubling of immanent creation as a domain of doubles. Counterfeit doubles – not univocally hostile but equivocally: hostile but as hospitable – like the welcome of a seducer who leads us to woe through perilous pleasure. ("Samael" can also be translated as "seducer.")

Why is the seducer attractive? Because the seducer doubles what is attractive. The seducer shows an image of what is good, perhaps what is divine. A seducer shows love – the show of love without the spirit of love, the show of love that mimics love but does not love. Such a show redoubles the equivocity: it offers an image that mimics what is not there – love – by presenting it as being there, but all in order to conceal that what is most of all not there is precisely love. The divine is evacuated in the showing that seems to present the divine. Such self-concealing equivocity, self-concealing in revealing itself, constitutes something of a showing in the modality of the counterfeit double.

How see through the seducer? We need a knowing of finesse rather than of geometry or system. Which is the double that counterfeits and which the genuine image? We need religious finesse to discern the difference. We need to be awakened to differences to see through the counterfeit double. Gnosis is said to be this awakening and this seeing through: we awaken to the divinity imprisoned in ourselves, our flesh, gnosis inaugurates our passage through and beyond the counterfeits. Awakening sees that the redoubling of equivocity, as it were, reverses the locus of the counterfeiting: it is not the "above" world that counterfeits but the "below" world of the fallen.[16] Equivocal creation is itself the seductive but misleading double of the true God.

[15] See *The Gospel of Philip*, NHL, p. 140: "Either he will be in this world or in the resurrection or in the places in the middle. God forbid that I be found in them! In this world there is good and evil. Its good is not good, and its evil not evil. But there is evil after this world which is truly evil – what is called "the Middle." It is death. While we are in this world, it is fitting for us to acquire the resurrection for ourselves, so that when we strip off the flesh, we may be found in rest and not walk in the Middle. For many go astray on the way. For it is good to come forth from the world before one has sinned."
[16] This is the reverse of the post-Hegelian reduction of theology to anthropology: the "above" world falsifies the "below" world; there is no "above" world, then there is no "below" world, and supposedly we

We have to recall once again certain sacred mimicries between the "below" and the "above." The fallen Sophia mimics the higher. The divine Sophia herself mimics the Forefather, seeking to bring to be through herself alone. The false creation, the abortion, plagiarizes divine emanation. The demiurge counterfeits the Forefather. Material making counterfeits spiritual emanation. Hylic creation parrots pneumatic. The lower Adam apes the primal Adam. A counterfeit Adam and Eve mime the true Adam and Eve, the archetypal Male–Female. The fullness of lack – the fallen creation – counterfeits the fullness without lack – the pleroma. The father of lies mimics the serpent of wisdom. Bishops and deacons – "dry canals" (*Apocalypse of Peter*, NHL, p. 343) – impersonate the initiated *gnostikoi*. The orthodox are forgeries of the true, though they brand the true the heretic. The false visible church substitutes itself, like a cuckoo's egg, for the true invisible church of spirit.[17]

Or is it the reverse? For sometimes, of course, we are visited by a reversal of the counterfeit double and we are not sure which is the double, which the original. Gnosis sees through the counterfeit double, awakening to the true original. Awakening does not come by system but by a "blow of the light" (*Tripartite Tractate*, NHL, p. 75), or by a kind of counter seduction – for instance, by magical formulae that get the exact sacred words right to release the spirit. We are as if under an enchantment: the right magical words or rituals release one from the bondage of being spell bound. Seduction works by magic charm; escape needs a counter charm or magic. Knowing is a release from the false charm of equivocal creation and its counterfeit doubles. Escaping to the utterly transcendent One, the absolute original is reached by struggle through the opposing energies of the doubles, and ascent above the spheres, for the higher redoublings of the One are less and less counterfeit.

It is worth remarking that the counterfeit double takes somewhat opposite shapes in ancient Gnosticism and more modern forms. In ancient Gnosticism the absolute One is utterly beyond the counterfeit creation, for this world here and now is the domain of the mimicry of spirit, hence the need of a world-denying flight. In more modern forms, it seems all but the opposite, in that the absolute One as utterly transcendent must be redoubled in *absolute immanence*, which is now the pleroma to be realized through the self-becoming of the absolute One. In one, flight to the hyperbolic transcendence as world denying; in the other, flight from transcendence to utter immanence. In the latter, the inward way becomes utterly immanent: history becomes the dialectical process of realizing the divine spark initially implicit in, sleeping in the process of equivocal becoming. Ancient form: an ascetic "Platonic" response to the suspicion of the given world as a counterfeit double. Modern form: a non-ascetic "Hegelian" response to the counterfeit double of an alien transcendence. One, a version of "Christian" gnosis as world-denying; the other, a version of "Christian" gnosis as world-affirming. But the terms in both are more or less set by dualism and dialectic, with the equivocal double as a fall from, or immanent self-alienation of, the absolute One. One wonders if there is agapeic creation

---

are released to the innocence of becoming. But even then there is no escape from equivocal becoming, and no escape into innocence either. This can come to be a kind of reversed Gnosticism: in which the human being is the Primal Being: Primal Adam more ultimate than any Primal Father or Fore-father.

17 See *The Second Treatise of the Great Seth*, NHL, p. 335 on Adam as a "laughingstock" and "counterfeit type of man," on Abraham and Isaac as "counterfeit fathers," Solomon and Moses as "laughing stocks," the 12 prophets as "imitations" and "counterfeits." One thinks: with the false God, goes the false prophet, the false Messiah, the false Church, the anti-Christ (see *IST?*, Chapters 4 and 6, also pp. 183 ff.). The *Gospel of Judas*: Christ and Judas as twins, intimate doubles. The Bogomil belief: The Devil was the eldest son of God: God had two (twin) sons, the devil the oldest, Jesus Christ the younger – see Yuri Stoyanov, *The Other God: Dualist Religions from Antiquity to the Cathar Heresy* (New Haven: Yale, 2000), p. 158. When, in his *History of Philosophy*, Hegel comments on Jacob Böhme, he seems to endorse Lucifer as the first born of light – Lucifer "falls" – the necessary moment of being-for-self – to be replaced by Christ. There is a paragraph to that effect also in his *Phänomenologie des Geistes*, J. Hoffmeister, ed. (Hamburg: Meiner, 1952), p. 538; *Phenomenology of Spirit*, trans. A. V. Miller (Oxford: Clarendon Press, 1977) par. 776.

in either form. The God beyond creation of Gnosticism seems like a dualistic version of the God of the whole of immanent pan(en) theism which can take more overt dialectical form (as we will see in the next chapter). To what extent is, or can be, all this true to the agape of the origin?[18]

AGONISTICS: DIVINE AND HUMAN

The world as a counterfeit double or dissembling medium is coupled with an equivocal agon both *within* the divine as such and *between* the divine and what comes to be relatively "outside" the divine.[19] Immanent divine agonistics: Sophia, emanation of the Alien God as absolutely pleromatic, beyond pleroma, so hyperbolic in light as to be, in a way, a dark origin; Sophia, one of the beings of light, self-willing, tries to originate through self, brings to be something *outside* the region of light, a shadow, a miscarriage (*Origin of the World*, NHL, p. 162). The second agonistic "below": the *divine itself* in the spark of light has become trapped in the dissembling medium of matter; hence the lower agonistics is a continuation of the higher breach within divinity. While the first break has something of a fluid equivocity, evident in the watery language (*NHL*, pp. 162–3), this second agonistics begins to emerge into a more explicit form of dualistic opposition. The second agonistics is still a divine agonistics, described in terms of the second "God" of the lower immanent world, with characteristics like the God of *Genesis*, turned in a counter direction suggesting an evil God. The aesthetic cosmos is a counterfeit double of the noetic cosmos, brought to be by this upstart "God."

God's in his heaven, all's unwell with the world. There is the One God, the true original, Godhead beyond god; there is the God who claims to be the one God, the counterfeit double. The counterfeit double is proximately the source of the given aesthetic cosmos. As the second "God" is not good, so is the creation essentially, divinely tainted with evil. Everything appears as in a mirror that reverses left and right, above and below, good and evil. It is as if Descartes's evil genius were the "God" of the world below, but now fair is foul and foul is fair The demiurge is a derivative "God" emerging with the primal Fall. Ignorant of the higher God and forgetful of Sophia, the female principle, thinking there is none but he and none above him, he is himself bewitched by the equivocal snare of counterfeit doubling as such. He is sometimes associated with the God of the Old Testament, but there the Creator celebrates the creation on giving it to be, seeing that "it is good, very good." If fair is foul and foul is fair, this "It is good" cannot be taken at face value here. There is no face value, for every face is a mask that might be the opposite to what it shows itself. This divine affirmation becomes a counterfeit "Amen." The face of affirmation is itself a duplicitous mask. The "It is good" is a ruse of the equivocal to tempt and entrap us.

If we too are caught in an agonistics "below," would it be easy to mark the difference of the two Gods? How could it be, if all our discerning is in the medium of "evidences" that might well be counterfeit doubles? This thought is not so outlandish if our sublunary certainty is itself a bewitchment, unknown to itself snared in the reign of the counterfeit double. And does not the "élan" of the Gnostic orientation come from this: our agonized encounter with the equivocal face of the between, stressed by an immemorial memory of the good God? From the transcendence of God, but now made close to inaccessible in the equivocal intermedium, where we toil to trace the outline of the good? From our need to decipher the equivocal face, without sourcing the evil in the good God? But the finite

---

[18]   The theme of the double can be linked with a more dialectical holism: it can lead to a God of the whole: dialectic beyond equivocity. Thus the Gnostic traces in Hegel – though transformed by speculative dialectic. Chapter 11 turns to the God of the whole, Chapter 12 to the God beyond the whole.

[19]   In *Tripartite Tractate, NHL,* pp. 68ff. there is an intriguing version of divine agonistics (it puts one in mind of Hegel) not in terms of the erring (female) Sophia but of the fallen (male) Logos and its conversion and recovery. Intending good, the Logos begets "in shadows, models, and likenesses." In his "self-exaltation" he went beyond himself but "self-doubt and division" followed (*NHL*, p. 68) – "he became weak like a female nature which has abandoned its virility" (*NHL*, p. 69).

between is attributed to an other God, not the good God, now utterly beyond the finite between, and separated from the between "below" by a higher between "above." This hyperbetween separating "above" and "below," coupled with inaccessible transcendence, turns the equivocity of immanent being at best into the mask of a deluded "God," at worst an evil "God," not the chiaroscuro of the good God who agapeically originates finite being and communicates to it its inherent goodness.

Hemmed in by the dubious, even evil whole, the human being still knows intimately the religious urgency of ultimacy, but the porosity of its most intimate soul has been touched by despair, and the cry that comes out for deliverance itself reveals a desperate need to be saved from the perils of creation, the dissembling of its source, and everything of them in oneself. The outcry of religious despair is still for the good God beyond all derived or counterfeit doubles. There is a deep doubleness about the human being, but we do not always understand this metaxologically. Gnosticism does reflect possibilities of our metaxological being but as deflected in a certain direction, impelled there by our own ontological ambiguity, inflected by its encounter with the equivocity of evil. We are participants in the struggle of powers, sometimes seeming to be instruments of powers, sometimes the very epitome of their struggle. We too assist in the agon marking the counterfeit whole of the world "below" in its war against the perfection of the higher divinities, and the highest God. We are the rivals of God. The pride of the dubious "God," the demiurge, is redoubled in the wrath of the domineering human.

The double human is a site of struggle. We can double ourselves, double back on ourselves, redouble ourselves again. Our agonistic doubleness is the coincidence of higher and lower powers, and their being twinned with each other here and now. The site of strife is the ground of a togetherness that itself is war. Our agonistic doubleness allows war on our own counterfeit doubleness, for the opposites together are not absolutely on a par, for one power or group of powers are higher, the other power or powers are lower. We are drawn into the war of the good and the evil, but this is more than a human struggle. God is lost in man: human agonistics participate in divine agonistics. The war is a dreadful divine war. The conflict is sometimes presented as cosmic. If and when the war is won there is the release of the divine in the human, but this is more than the return of the human being to God. For the Gnostics, it is the return to God of what is his own, and the doubling back of the divine to itself. Our salvation is nothing apart from God's own salvation. We save ourselves as much as God saves himself. In a way, we save God as much as God saves us.

DOUBLING BACK, BACKING OUT – REVERSING RELEASE

One detects a certain extremism at work in Gnosticism: it calls to a kind of reversal of values, a turning the world upside down. Release from the equivocity of counterfeit doubles asks revolution: a revolt against the evil, a revolving back to God. This is spiritual not political revolution, along a pathway of saving knowing: gnosis brings awakening from duplicitious equivocity and freedom for the divine within the self. This return is a reversal back to the primal original. We might see this reverse release as a *doubling back* to the true God, and a *backing out* of the evil creation, dominated by the dubious "God." Doubling back: countering the movement of fall and entrapment. Backing out: unweaving the equivocal enchantments of the counterfeit doubles that keeps us in a sleep of spirit, and so passing beyond their evil spell and awakening. Sudden sobriety, as if awakening from drunkenness, and the dreams of the night are nothing (see *Gospel of Truth*, *NHL*, pp. 42–3, *Tripartite Tractatus*, *NHL*, p. 71).

I find something of this reverse doubling in an expertise practiced by some Gnostics: producing "alternative readings" of canonical scriptures. These scriptures are marked by constitutive ambiguity, hence against "normal," orthodox views, heterodox versions might be ventured. Consider the story of the Fall. The "normal" reading claims a fall *into* evil with eating the forbidden fruit; the reversal claims this eating begins our release from sleep in equivocal creation. This "fall" is the beginning of the *real reversal* of a Fall, even more original when the divine *pneuma* is entrapped in matter. The *serpent* solicits humans to knowing as a spiritual awakening.[20] By contrast, "God" is the figure of envy – the hoarding demiurge who begrudges us the divine knowing rightfully ours. Accepting the serpent's solicitation to release from the jealous "God" initiates the reversal: divinization through self-knowing. Here too, in reverse, our pride is good: we stand up, over against the despotic "God." Hence the element of anti-Judaism in some forms of Gnosticism. Moses is not the great prophet but the one who enchains human kind with law. The law oppresses spirit; the divine spark is beyond the law.

Consider the reverse doubling in an "alternative reading" of *the Tower of Babel*. The tyrannical "God" views with alarm as human beings, with one language, grow in power, and scale the heavens. The "God" of the lower world, threatened, sows confusion. This world is not awash with agapeic surplus; it is an economy of antagonistic lack and possession, deprivation and repossession. When "God" waxes, man wanes; when "God" wanes, man waxes. What man takes is taken away from "God"; there is no surplus of generous giving or allowance. The Tower of Babel read thus is like a repeat double of the Fall. Divine envy is repeated in the second sowing of discord after Babel. The self-elevating power of man is divine, but it is cast into confusion, to perpetuate the dominion of the jealous "God" over the counterfeit doubles.[21]

Could such an "alternative reading" be offered of the story of Jacob's ladder. Like the Tower, the ladder ascends to heaven; at the gate of heaven, angels go up and down. But Jacob's ladder is a gift from God of a vision in a dream. It is an opening up of the dreaming idiotic spirit by some other power, a received porosity. The *passio essendi* receives communications in divine dreams, and these are not of an assault on the heavens, projected by the *conatus essendi*. As suggestive of our own self-divinization, the Tower is also suggestive of our aggression on divine otherness. By contrast, the ladder gives a gateway between heaven and earth. On the basis of the gifted dream, a vision comes of the community of all things with God. Then a house of God is set up: the stone that was previously a pillow and placed horizontally is now set vertically in the ground as a pillar. The house shelters an ethical, religious community. The gate, this is a given opening beyond to transcendence as other.

The Gnostic reversal as a doubling back also suggests an "alternative reading" of the Creator's "It is very good." To the contrary: it is not at all good, it is blighted.[22] Aesthetic exteriority has the tinge of evil. How think finite being as an evil, how think of an evil whole? Not easy. I am put in mind of the night in *Macbeth* when the king is to be killed. The night is thick with sinister threat. The dark space around is full with foreboding – closing in, closing us in. The thickening night is stifling, congealing into a kind of evil stickiness. One has to strike back, resist the encircling darkness. We are struck by dread that the equivocity of being itself is *threatening and under threat*. Threatening: ominous, foreboding, as if over things an abysmal darkness sat brooding. Threatened: the life in

---

[20] See *Apocryphon of John* (NHL, pp. 110ff.) for a counter narrative of creation of Adam and Eve; also *The Hypostasis of the Archons* (NHL, p. 155) where, by contrast with the carnal woman, "the Female Spiritual principle came [in] the snake, the Instructor; and it taught [them] . . ."

[21] Compare Aristophanes's original wholes in the *Symposium*, 189c2–193e: plenitudinous double humans who challenge Zeus with their power and audacity. Zeus cuts them in half. Presently as humans we are halved, half and half beings, and threatened with being quartered – a fourfold fall from the fourfold into a flat univocity.

[22] "Awakening" might recall what I call the resurrection of agapeic astonishment, but Gnostic awakening is *turned away* from the good of creation, hence from the "It is good." The postlapsarian opening of the eyes of Adam and Eve is not quite what I mean by posthumous mind, since this "opening" is a partial blinding, an obscuration of our porosity to the divine, and calls for a saving knowing which is posthumous to this fall: posthumous mind, recreated life after the death of our fall into evil. Posthumous mind is called to agapeic love of the mortal and the singular. Void of this love, there are doubles of agapeic astonishment and posthumous mind that might be counterfeit. On the sleep of finitude and the sticky evil in *Macbeth*, see *IST?*, Chapter 1; also "Sticky Evil: On *Macbeth* and the Karma of the Equivocal," in *God, Literature and Process Thought*, ed. D. Middleton (Aldershot: Ashgate, 2002), pp. 133–55.

which we are tempted to take joy seems radically insecure: held out to us, snatched back from us, when we reach to it and give our hearts over. As the ambiguity of the sacred is intensified, so also is our sense of ontological insecurity, all the way to the last apocalyptic war of the adversarial powers.

(You say: *Macbeth* – that is fiction, literature. An evil whole? Excess of imagination. Something "made up." But go tell that to prisoners of the concentration camps, or to inmates of the Gulag. They lived and died in the belly of the beast. It is not feigned. This world is a corpse-eater.)[23]

What then is the between? Not the porous opening of communicative being, but the block that clogs communication. Not the promise of the togetherness of transcendences, but the barrier between what is transcendent in us, *pneuma* (T^2), and transcendence itself (T^3), God beyond all. Earth is distance from God, but distance is not now the intermedium of communication but the trapped space of estrangement. In between earth and God there are many intermediate layers, spheres, each like a wrapping that swaddles or smothers us, stopping us from getting out. *Pneuma* wants out. The layers are circles upon circles of enclosure, dominated by different powers that keep us in, we who, having had enough, want out. As a picture of the extremity of our enclosure, one might usefully consult the *Ophite diagram* – it depicts the spheres and the beyond, at the top of which in the Kingdom of God there is a small circle of agape between Father and Son, but below them and Paradise the spheres are enclosed by Leviathan, the snake biting its own tail, and within whose belly is the Behometh which encloses earth and Tarturus. We are, so to say, doubly in the belly of the beast. For the aesthetic cosmos of earth is in the belly of the Behometh, but these and the spheres beyond are devoured by the malevolent Leviathan, beyond which lies the circle of the fixed stars and paradise and the Father on the utmost outside periphery.[24]

Under such a dominion of the counterfeit doubles, the prison we are in seems far worse than Plato's cave: for we are not in prison, we ourselves are prison, and we are in the prison of ourselves. The divine spark is prevented from escape, but we do not know it, bewitched as we are by the enchantment of the counterfeit doubles. How wake from such a bewitchment? Can we awaken ourselves? If in an enchanted slumber we are under the *spell of ourselves*, prisoners who are themselves the prison, something must deliver us from *beyond* ourselves. The redeemer must come from outside, passing from "above" to "below." From "above" something or someone must *break through* the promiscuous mixture in which "above" and "below" are imbricated and deliver the spirit to itself. The redeemer will guide the passage of spirit through the enemy territory of exteriority.

This Gnostic view has much in common with other religious views. In almost all religious traditions the inner way is seen as more suitable to the soul's journey to God than is nature's exteriority. Everything turns on the interpretation of the self-recovery and the precise relation of the inner to the divine itself. The Gnostic path journeys from the external to the innermost self, and if from the external we have no knowledge, the messenger can break through, as if through the ramparts of a siege, and bring from beyond the light that lifts the siege. The way out is a way in and a way upwards. Esoteric names, magic formulae, alchemical practices, and so on may aid us along this way, but the essential point is that the return to the divine in self is the return of the divine to itself. In the end, this is not the self gathered together with the divine, not even the self gathered into the divine, but the *self-gathering of the divine in itself*. Ancient Gnosticism looks to this as

23 *The Gospel of Philip*, NHL, p. 144: "This world is a corpse-eater. All the things eaten in it themselves die also. Truth is a life-eater. Therefore no one nourished by [truth] will die. It was from that place that Jesus came and brought food. To those who so desired, he gave [life, that] they might not die."

24 See Rudolph, *Gnosticism*, pp. 68ff. on the Ophites and the serpent. Behemoth and Leviathan form in the Gnostic system of the Ophites and others two of the seven circles or stations that the soul has to pass in order to be purged and to attain bliss (Hippolytus, "Adversus Omnes Hæreses," v. 21; Origen, "Contra Celsum," vi. 25). See Job: Behemoth (40), Leviathan (41). It has been speculated that the root of Leviathan denotes "coil," or "twist." Behemoth is plural of "behemah," that is "beast."

absolutely beyond and other, but in the modern Gnosticism of someone like Hegel, this self-gathering of God into Godself is the absolute whole of wholes and the end of time in immanence.

Gnostic esotericism enables a claim to be *beyond* the equivocal while still being *within* it. It witness to – or impersonates – the *meta*: as both "beyond" and "in the midst." I, enlightened one, comprehend the truth of the equivocal, the others are subject to its confusion. If I continue to live in the confused place, my comprehending the confusion lets me be above it, beyond it. Being beyond it, I am not contaminated by it. At the exoteric level the appearances seem to be just the same for all, but to those in the know, the same is not the same. It may not show, but the *gnostikos* is in the know. Esotericism *vis-à-vis* the equivocal communicates an elitism, amounting to a kind of aristocracy of knowing – an erotic sovereignty in the sphere of spirit. Of course, such an attitude is not confined to Gnosticism but there it takes on a strong religious charge.[25]

Of course, a *further* doubling of reversal is possible, beyond the reversal from dark matter to the light of divine spirit. Let the divine spark be delivered from its slavery "below," is there still not possible, so to say, a higher slavery to evil "above" – and just in our claim to achieve spiritual sovereignty? I mean that while separating the mixture of spirit and dark matter "below," we risk tempting a new promiscuity "above" – one inseparable from the fact that ultimately the human and divine are not separate. The redeemer or messenger may claim to bring deliverance, but given Gnostic elitism and its pneumatic esotericism, how avoid being delivered over to a higher hubris, now claiming an unbounded spiritual sovereignty? First reversal: from slave of the lower to master of the higher, from being servile to the flesh to being sovereign of the spirit. Second reversal: this higher sovereignty as a fall into spiritual evil – not now "below" but on the heights? We say the sinner is transfigured into a saint, but why is this not the sanctity that is spiritual sin – the spiritual pride that claims itself to be divine? Does release from the counterfeit double of God "below" create its own counterfeit double of God "above"? Create a "higher" counterfeit double, that is, a more evil counterfeit double, just in the claim to be beyond all counterfeit doubles and all evil?

Possible here is a pernicious parody of agapeic release.[26] Escaping evil's equivocity is so fraught with ambiguity that the escape from evil seems just another evil. Beyond good and evil, we might meet a higher innocence, but we might also hear a new hiss of hatred – defiance of the hateful demiurge. Ethical law is for those in thrall to the law-giver; the superior libertine tastes the thrill of freedom in an outlaw refusal. There is, as it were, a lawless salvation that loves itself as an unlawful salvation. And so this being beyond the equivocity of moral good and evil can invert into evil masquerading with an equivocal

---

[25] Aristocracy of knowing that recoils from the messiness of the many-too-many, secret irritability at the mess itself, antipathy to the otherness of the world as one mess of a place: combinations of factors like these make one wonder at a family resemblance to Gnosticism. Atheistic politics: the inner circle of dominant revolutionaries are those in the know. The scientistically-minded: they believe their scientific precedence licenses them with superior knowing *vis-à-vis* the whole of life. The revolutionary terrorist: he must operate in secret in enemy territory, the land of the foe, but he must look normal; in a dangerous land, he must counterfeit the foe to defeat him. Think of a spy: he must lead a *double* life: be what he is not, not be what he is – a double agent: a traitor who is faithful. The *Gospel of Judas*: Judas the double agent: the "betrayer" who is the truer "insider," whose "treachery" intimately furthers the higher work of salvation. On Gnosticism and politics, see Eric Vogelin, *Science, Politics and Gnosticism* (Chicago: Henry Regnery, 1968).

[26] The heresiologist, Epiphanius of Salamis (b. 310–20 d. 403): "Carpocratians, derived from a native of Asia, Carpocrates, who taught his followers to perform every obscenity and every sinful act. And unless one proceeds through all of them, he said, and fulfils the will of all demons and angels, he cannot mount to the highest heaven or get by the principalities and authorities." Clement of Alexandria (d. 215) claims that in their agape they "have intercourse where they will and with whom they will." How much credence is to be granted to such claims is contested, of course. But see the incident embarrassing to Yeats and the Order of the Golden Dawn: the rape of Daisy Adams, in the name of "spiritual advancement, " by Mr and Mrs Horos (masquerading as Mr Cornish and Swami Vive Anandi) – Stephen Coote, *W. B. Yeats: A Life* (London: Hodder and Stoughton, 1997), p. 209.

face that absolves itself from the call of the good. In a kind of reversed Gnosticism, it is the darkness that is released, not the light.

Behold the sleek savant who does not what he dictates his devotees must. The exception makes an exception of himself. Like his God above all, he absolves himself from all, excepting himself outside the law of all others. Backing out, his saving becomes self-serving – a spiritual narcissism, a mystic greed to be God.

GNOSTICISM AND METAXOLOGY: ON SAVING KNOWING IN THE EQUIVOCAL MATRIX

Gnostic saving is an "awakening" to one's identity with the divine: a release from the evil world, a return through the inner to union with the divine above, a union itself a self-relation of the divine. It is to be saved from the world, not to save the world; to be saved from one's fleshed humanness not to save that fleshed humanness. We are *lifted off* our condition, saved from that condition, not saving that condition. Consummation is not the completion of creation but its dissolution. The spirit ascends above the world into worlds beyond, passing through the danger zones of in-between circles where powers await their prey, passing over and beyond, and beyond again, like a ship passing out into illimitable space where the flesh of the earth dwindles to a dot and vanishes. Saved from the enemy, secure at the last, one cannot be touched anymore.

Is this untouched untouchability secure against its own dialectical reversal? The posture of purity easily turns the other into the impure, on whom, in turn, pure power can be unleashed. Does the divine human metamorphose into a demonic human when the flesh of creation ceases to touch it? The sweet will to power ferrets out wily ways to serve itself, even as it avers it serves its God. This can occur in *any* religious orientation. The degeneration of erotic self-transcendence, itself the highest possibility of dialectical self-mediation, and here in the form of spiritual sovereignty, into religious will to power is certainly a release, but what it releases is the urge to dominion of the higher creature over the lower. It does not release the divine, does not release us towards the divine. To be truly released, it must give way to agapeic transcending, and its service of the good, beyond both servility and sovereignty.

What is an agapeic release? It is a freedom delivering the shut-in self, not seeking to be saved from the world but to save the good of the world: save in the sense of safe-guard, keep, revere, renew. Agapeic release is consecrated for the good, of the others, of oneself. It is the freeing of generosity towards the vulnerable flesh of human others, but of other creatures too. It is also a release – harder than one would expect – of generosity towards oneself. It is to be "in the midst" differently: to remain in the between, but to transcend self in the between, with no protection of an untouchable sacredness. To the contrary, there is commingling, hence touching and being touched. Such commingling is consecrated to saving the porosity of communicative being. Opening the untouchable enclosure of shut-in selving is like a death, though sometimes the death is unnoticed, like a gentle wooing, and imperceptibly one comes alive again. One hardly knew one was dead, but that death now has died. One is naked, as on the day of a birth, and one can be touched and can touch. Agapeic "awakening" thus might be likened to a kind of posthumous mindfulness: delivery of willingness beyond will to power; deliverance towards the beholding in love of what is there – as given to be and good for itself in its otherness to my willing it so. Posthumous mindfulness would be a saving celebration of that goodness of the "to be."

To end: An ambiguous truth glimmers in Gnosticism, in its equivocal response to an equivocal condition between good and evil. Its search for a transforming knowing is both a mediation and attempted transcendence of that equivocity. Gnosticism arises from a response to genuine dimensions of our middle condition. It is primed to the counterfeit doubles that can crystallize there. But it sees these in terms of an interplay of paired opposites and the overcoming of their duality, in terms of a secret dialectic, not itself thematized with full enough finesse for our metaxological condition. That fuller finesse requires a transformation that gleans differently the traces of the divine in the equivocity of the between – as itself the chiaroscuro of the good, rather than the thick night of a counterfeit creation that, as counterfeit, seems beyond saving, for saving lies only beyond it. The chiaroscuro shines with the dark light of the marvel of the middle, and its beckoning to resurrection of agapeic love. If creation is good, what is not divine of it is to be redeemed in it. If agapeic saving corresponds to divine intermediation in the *metaxu*, one worries that Gnosticism lacks the *gnosis* of this, since it seems to want release from this between, not the "yes" to it that affirms in its finite goodness the gift of the divine. Saving knowing is inseparable from this agapeic "yes," and the life that lives this "yes."

Chapter 11

God(s) of the Whole: On Pantheism and Panentheism

If the earth has as many hands
As this tree has branches
& if each branching
Was a hand stretched
Out in appeal
Each would only touch
A small segment
Of the sky's
Encircling emptiness

Touch it
& transform it
For every touching
Would be a boundary
Between itself and what lies
Beyond

Touch it
& be transformed
For every point of outstretch
Would be an opening
Inward

& the emptiness
Beyond would pour
Its secret fullness
Through that boundary
Between
It and all trees
& into the numberless laces
Of the branching world –
Lightning's descent
Through leave and lace
  and trunk
& earthing itself
In the reclusive root

HOLISTIC IMMANENCE AND THE GOD OF THE WHOLE

The idea of the whole has been central to philosophy's traditional ambition to give a rational account of what is, as well as to the manner God has been understood. *Das wahre ist das Ganze*, Hegel famously said, and the claim embraces both philosophy and religion. "Totality" is now a much criticized concept, perhaps in deflationary reaction to overinflated claims about the whole, not least Hegel's. Nevertheless, a holistic approach has not lost its attractiveness. The attraction is also expressed in the pantheistic or panentheistic God of the whole. As with the Gnostic God(s), our focus is on a way of figuring the divine; this is more clearly developed in some thinkers than in others, such as neo-Platonists and Hegel. In general, we find that while there is no simple univocal "either/or" between immanence and transcendence, in modern pan(en)theism a certain view of immanence is privileged over against dualistic transcendence. In this light, pan(en)theism can also bespeak a certain attunement to given being, often more implicit than not, such as we find in "green" philosophy, or in the Romantic love of nature, or the pagan love of the earth, or its Dionysian celebration. Strains of this can also be found in those who hold to the superessential mystery of absolute transcendence, for the glory of creation tells of the glory of God, and we cannot divorce the one from the other.

If this holistic figuring is a further variation on the interplay of one and many, the stress falls on the mediation of equivocal manyness in light of a One which includes all within itself as the absolute whole. The doubleness percolating in Gnosticism seemed to point beyond itself to the self-return of the divine, and its consummate wholeness. But we might well so put the primary stress on such absolute wholeness rather than on the equivocity of counterfeit doubles that there occurs a significant shift in religious register – from the darkened world of Gnosticism to the bright shining totality or pleroma in which God is or will be "all in all." The darkened world and the shining totality as not opposed to each other in the end. God as the whole plays a more immediately prominent role in the pan(en)theistic views than in Gnostic. Divine self-return does not point us beyond a fallen world but is seen as now being effected in the *immanent world* itself. Fallenness and restoration both are immanent in one inclusive whole. Divine and human agonistics are also included in one whole such that now the completed divine pleroma is rather immanent than transcendent. As the equivocal way infiltrates the Gnostic God, so the dialectical way does the pan(en)theistic. This is not always explicitly evident – or comprehended. In light of more overt dialectical considerations, we can make sense of important connections of pan(en)theism with dualistic transcendence, the religious blight of scientistic modernity, and more ancient ways of approaching the One and the all, emanation and creation, eternity and time, the whole and the infinite. I will have something to say about these matters.

I offer an interpretation in light of the fourfold way, and a critical taking stock from the metaxological standpoint. Connecting pan(en)theistic concerns with the different namings, it is less the idiotics and aesthetics of the divine that are to the fore than the erotics of selving. More precisely: first, there is an idiotic moment in that in naming this absolute whole reference is often made to a "first" moment in which the absolute seems wrapped up in its own implicit unity and immediacy; second, there is an aesthetic moment in that this otherwise idiotic absolute must outer itself, give expression to itself in sensible creation, which is indeed its own body or finite embodiment; third, finally and most comprehensively there is to be recognized in these first two moments an erotic self-surpassing of the divine that creates itself in creating the world – the world as the embodiment of the divine is the immanent other that allows this erotic self-surpassing of the divine to be an embracing self-mediation of the whole with itself. We drive dialectically forward to this last self-completing erotic mediation of the divine with itself. What of the agapeics of the divine? This is not easy to locate in this way of thinking, even though a metaxological thinking through of this way will bring us around to such agapeics.

PANTHEISM CONTRA THE WORTHLESS WORLD

The relation between the dialectical way and the God of the whole is diversely recurrent in history. There is a line of inheritance from Eleaticism through the entirety of the philosophical tradition that privileges the notion of the whole, but the resonance of the "whole" varies with the particular configuration of the ethos of being. In premodernity there was more porosity between religion and philosophy. In modernity, philosophy asserts an autonomy, and its porosity to the religious mutates. If we can call Plotinus the height of premodern pan(en)theism (I have hesitations about this), he strongly affirms the superessential mystery of the One. While if Hegel is the high-point of modern pan(en)theism, such premodern transcendence is reconfigured in terms of a different sense of the immanent whole, and there is no more mystery. First, I remark on pantheism and the modern reconfiguration of the ethos of being.

The term "pantheism" is a relatively modern one, coined by that Irish enigma, John Toland in 1705. The term "panentheism" is even more recent. The second term was coined, in part, to deal with a recurrent criticism of the first, namely, of reducing God to the world. While pantheism's commitment to a form of unity is not abrogated in panentheism, it is qualified to a degree said to avoid some standard charges against pantheism.[1] Modern pantheism is tied to the twin it rejects, namely, the mechanistic world view.

---

[1] Granted differences between pantheism and panentheism, my focus is on the God of the *whole*, hence I will use the locution pan(en)theism. Modern panentheism tends to see itself as beyond pantheism and dualistic theism. It tries to defend itself against the charge that everything of divine transcendence is abrogated in pantheism, by claiming some transcendence other to determinate finitization, as implied, for instance, in the distinction of *natura naturans* and *natura naturata*.

This latter is a particular re-configuration of the primal ethos with strong stress on univocalizing all being, whether of nature, human beings, or God, a reconfiguration encapsulated in the metaphysical metaphor of the machine. Pan(en)theism emerges in the struggle for a more organic sense of the whole, seeking to be beyond the reductive univocalization of the totality and responding to perplexing equivocities about our place within it. Is not this mechanistic world-view now surpassed, at least in some qualified ways, in post-classical science? Perhaps. However, the type of configuration in question has not vanished, and the cybernetic machine can come to offer a new metaphysical metaphor, more powerfully univocal in its own way, though it calls itself the matrix, and calling forth new equivocations, and indeed for those who long for more, new pantheisms.

What of God and the earlier mechanization? In the later middle ages and early modernity a voluntaristic God seems to have become predominant, coupled with a nominalistic view of the things of creation. The world is defined less in terms of an intelligibly mediated cosmos and more as a contingent happening in which a plurality of individuals are sustained in being by God's absolute will. The ontological situation is filtered through a basic orientation to being as *effective power*. God as absolute will implies absolute power to effect anything God decrees, for God's own reason, for any reason, or for no reason we can understand. In tandem, nature as an aggregate of entities is defined by the effective powers of things, themselves to be scrutinized in terms of the mechanisms defining this or that particular functioning order of effective power. Finally, the human being is the most important natural center of effective power. *Mind in us* affords us the greatest range of effective power: reason is the instrument by which human will extends its effective power over things, in a manner not unlike the God of absolute will. This instrumentalization of mindfulness, coupled with the apotheosis of willful effective power, fuels the technological drive which articulates humans as the highest worldly will to power in a world itself a reserve of power, governed by a God who is absolute power to will what God wills.

I have remarked before on how the mechanical philosophy recommended itself to many who strongly wanted to defend God's transcendence. God is removed beyond the world, for were God within the world God's absoluteness might seem compromised. The slippery slope is patent to the more pensive: if we thus absolutize God we make everything so dependent on God in such a wise that nothing finite is other in itself, and yet, to sustain just that dependence this God has itself to be made so radically other that any more *intimate connection* with the world and the human is radically weakened. This we detect in the metaphorics of the machine and its maker. There is no intimacy of communication between maker and machine beyond the functioning of effective power. That lack of intimacy cuts the tie binding maker and machine. In due course, the machine will seem to usurp the effective powers of the immanent totality; then the between will be lost, as will also its agapeic origin.

This is evident in a certain dialectic of the personal and impersonal. We need both: the personal points beyond itself to the transpersonal, just as the transpersonal needs its reference to the personal to prevent diminishing the transpersonal to the subpersonal. But here we find the following. On one hand, we note in early modernity a robust *personalism* in Renaissance humanism: the human person, microcosm exemplifying the powers of the cosmos, the glory of creation, touching the divine in creative promise. On the other hand, a reductive *impersonalism* grows apace. For if the absolute God of effective power is beyond the world, radically other, then the world is Godless, though again, ironically, the world is the image of the absolute effective power by itself being a machine. On one side, *elevation* of the human person, on the other, *reduction* of nature to powers indifferently subpersonal, absolutely other to the human and its anthropomorphisms, and, who knows, *spoilers* of human aspiration.

This peculiar combination is inherently unstable, and each side might be taken in different directions. Where the second line of development dominated it produced a mutation in humanism *away from* any aesthetic/religious/philosophical form towards a mathematical and scientistic form: the apotheosis of the human forms itself in the dominance of the scientific *mathēsis* of nature. Hence the second line of development rejoins the first, for we do not surrender the model of *humanity* as effective power but rather secure it more powerfully. Any dominion in art, religion and philosophy seems too "contemplative," but there can be genuinely effective, namely, technical and mechanical dominance with mathematical science and its univocal *mathēsis* of nature. Effective power *works its way in us humans*, as destined through mathematical science to come into the mastery of nature. Nature reduced to effective power, human being elevated to the most effective power, mirroring his transcendent God – and all that remains is that we stay true to the destiny ordained by the inner logic of absolute effective power itself. Reduction and elevation amount to the same thing.

What does that destiny decree? The progressive *redundancy* of the transcendent God as the absolute effective power, and the increasing assumption of power by the world's effective power par excellence, namely, the sovereign human. Strangely enough, the "death of God" Nietzsche proclaimed merely fulfills this *absolutization of God* in terms of willful effective power decreed by late medieval theology. The intervening five centuries witness various evacuations of the between of the signs of transcendence as other (T^3), with increasing claims made for human self-transcendence (T^2), with circle on circle of usurping sovereignty massing in the between, scientistically vacated of sacred signs.

It is in this vacancy that a certain face of "pantheism" comes to form. Despite all reductions we remain porous to the divine, though how to understand this, we are not sure. In the vacuum, human self-transcending turns back on itself. Sometimes it finds resources to celebrate being, and especially its own being; other times, just in its more acute self-consciousness, it becomes conscious of the emptiness it inhabits. It is as if we have seen ourselves as a flare of glorious light, but when the flare lights up we finally sees that the world around us has been reduced to grey ash, and there ceases to be consolation in our being that flare. Our very greatest power reveals our greatest emptiness. Our extraordinary singularity serves to reveal our bereaving aloneness. A melancholy descends on us, sorrow without a source, for we would the world were to us an intimate partner in noble work, not a subjugated subservience from whose store we tear the raw material for our predatory will to power.

The mechanical impersonalization of the world and the creative personalization of the human cannot be finally married in genuine community, for the impersonalized world of mechanism is dead. This latter world is one in which life itself seems the anomaly. If the universe is an impersonal mechanism it should be more dead than – surprisingly – it is. Melancholy is only the feeble form of religious despair. The grey of the world casts its pallor back on our triumph, and in the ashen light we apprehend emptiness in our victorious smile. Behind the smile the grin of death, mocking us with the meaninglessness of our triumph. Absolute effective power: it comes to nothing. Our self-glorification is incubated in, as it incubates, this despair of emptiness. It hatches peaceless anguish.

Thus pantheism, in some measure, is a reaction to the emptiness of the deistic divinity that hovered meaninglessly over a world at bottom meaningless, especially relative to the urgency of ultimacy always stirring soundlessly at the heart of our humanity. Our porosity has become like a hunger that nothing can assuage. Who would or could live in a total machine? If being as a whole is a machine, if we are totally machine or of the machine, the anguish should not even arise. The anguish is something hyperbolic to mechanical terms. In fact, we all may live lives dependent on machines, but these we prize because they free us into an *other life*, they release powers beyond the machine. We use a machine, but there is life beyond use, and what we use, we use for that life beyond use, for release into that life. If one's world as a totality is a machine, even one cybernetically absolute, such release is senseless. For every release is into this totality, itself a machine, and hence no release from the machine.

We might insist that "release" is just another mechanism, perhaps not yet fully understood, but it will be understood in the future, for it must be so, it will be insisted, since we already know the totality as machine. Such insistence, I think, is *itself* hyperbolic to mechanistic terms. No machine can *insist on itself*. Self-insistence shows a stress of selving that is more than mechanical. Not entirely surprising is this paradox: insistence on the deterministic chains of mechanism tends to breed defiance and rebellion in us. Total mechanism may be so, but if it is so, I will it not to be so. I will run my head against this wall, for I am more, even in the perverse banging of my head. I destroy myself in the blades of the machine, just to demonstrate I am not a machine. That self-destruction evidences the working of the urgency of ultimacy that will not subscribe to its own slow asphyxiation in the total machine. If we are caged in a mechanism, and if mindfulness of the cage strikes through, the result is torment. Machine man is a freak, a futility, for no machine rages and lacerates itself and breaks upon the bars.

Purely mechanistic terms make nonsense of torment as such, but torment is our exceeding pain and our privilege. This torment is the suffering greatness of a self-transcendence driven to cannibalizing itself. If the final truth is the machine, our self-transcending would be like an impossible tumor that should not even exist in the first instance. In truth, this torment betrays some *persisting vigor* in self-transcendence. It is true that we can also become, as it were, anorexics of self-transcendence; we starve and enfeeble its energy, hating even the word "transcendence" for its merely being uttered. An anorexic machine, of course, is also a nonsense. Are we then that nonsense – the living dead? To be living becomes sinister when it is life that is made the anomaly. Is this what a culture of death is?

One wonders if an oppositional dualism in the late Middle Ages produced a pessimism about creation, as if it were sunken in corruption, not unlike the Gnostic's view of the darkness of unredeemable creation. One wonders if the alien God incubates the conditions for a new Gnosticism, perhaps not of the alchemical and hermetic sort (as in very early modernity) but of a scientistic sort: the gnosis that will engender a new knowing – science as voiding creation of given value, science as granting salvation from creation thus voided. Is not pantheism a rebound from this devoid nature; a recoil from the alien God, the dualistic opposite of the world; and a witness to the foreboding that totalizing mechanism is in deep collusion with the neutering of the cosmos of any sacred charge?

This is very evident in the Romantic pantheism that was reactive to scientistic Enlightenment. A new sensibility for the immanence of the divine arose. This was due, in part, to a reawakened porosity to the divine, and a need for ultimacy that scientistic enlightenment is incapable of supplying. There are many variables here, but it is important that pantheism shares something with scientistic Enlightenment: resort to God as transcendent becomes interdicted. In the eyes of this pantheism just that transcendent God is the alien divinity that robs the creation of immanent worth. Whether the vampire deistic God or the voyeur God supply the only possible meanings to divine transcendence as other is not the issue now. Obviously, they do not. But so the old God of transcendence as other tended to be rendered by the pantheistic movement and by scientistic Enlightenment.

AFFIRMING THE WORLD AND THE IMMANENT GOD

At issue is an intended affirmation of the worth of this world, in light of an intimation of an immanent divinity. Glance on some noteworthy figures. Cusanus: God is *non aliud* (not-other), yet there is no intent to abrogate God's transcendence. The intimacy of finite and infinite is dialectically intimated, as we approximate the coincidence of opposites. Giordano Bruno retains his fascination especially, I find, for the argument that an infinite God gives rise to a world itself infinite in its own way. An exclusive opposition between finitude and infinitude is insufficient. A pluralized sense of the infinite seems initially strange, but if we are dealing with agapeic surplus, the idea is not so odd. Spinoza is perhaps the most well-known of the "pantheists" who rejects a transcendent and personal God. God and nature are one and the same. This might be called pantheism or atheism: atheism in Spinoza's own time; pantheism with his revaluation through Lessing and the early German Romantics. Spinoza *maledictus* becomes Spinoza *benedictus*: the *Gott-vertrunkene Mann* in Novalis's intoxicated words. This atheism of pantheism appears as such relative to an orthodox theism for which the personal providence of a transcendent God is not negotiable. Rather than this, Spinoza shows the influence of mechanistic science in his desire to geometrize the whole, including the human being. The *Pantheismusstreit* of the late eighteenth century was fought over this issue of whether bringing God and nature into intimacy, even identity, actually dispensed with God. Was God-drunkenness really God-dismissiveness? *Nunc dimittis?*

Is the doubleness here equivocal? Spinoza scientistic enlightener: geometer of the whole, including humankind. Spinoza pantheist: all is God or nature. I think we find a virtual form of the dialectical togetherness of the two sides, scientistic enlightenment and pantheism. We find a coupling of geometrical univocalizing and something more holistic intimated in the univocalizing. Thus freedom is only ignorance of causes (Spinoza's epigram), yet there is a third kind of intuitive knowing (*scientia intuitiva*). There is no personal immortality, yet we feel and experience ourselves to be eternal. Mechanistic and organismic univocalizing seem joined like Siamese twins.

Sometimes the equivocity of pantheism relative to traditional theism centered on an esoteric way of writing: overtly in the traditional manner, covertly intending something non-traditional. Not surprisingly, there were suspicions of the religious motives of the pantheists. In the guise of being god-drunk, were the grounds being prepared for a more thoroughgoing materialistic "sobriety," atheist to the core? The case is equivocal, for one detects genuine reactive efforts to renew a lived intimacy with the ultimate, an intimacy out of the question on the mechanistic model, and its alien, cybernetic divinity. One is reminded of efforts by process philosophers to foreground a notion of divinity more in harmony with post-Newtonian science, a notion yet more than science, some cognizance being taken of the fact that science itself alone can never deliver the view of the whole which satisfies the urgency of ultimacy.

Pantheism seeks a recovery of transcendence, not "beyond" the world but immanent in nature itself. Nature is the embodiment of the divine, God's body. It is an immanent transcendence: all the roots of life come up from a unitary source and to it return. We humans are grown out of these roots, hence participants in a living whole, not strangers in a machine. Nature is a living organic whole, a divine totality whose immanent transcendence is in community with human self-transcending. We must not direct transcending (T^2) away and beyond for fulfillment; here and now momentous tasks are to be undertaken, constituting our own wholeness as contributing to, or partaking of the fullness of the whole.[2]

I add three observations. First, one can connect pantheism with the sensibility of the sublime. This is more than simply an "aesthetic" experience. Prior to its fashionable "aestheticization," the sublime bore on a more religious encounter with an indefinite divinity in the power of nature, exceeding the determinable bounds of mechanism.[3] Beyond the univocal mathēsis of nature, the sublime shows the aesthetic happening of an undefined illimitable power. This is chastening to us, yet strangely elevates us into another dimension, not merely personal, not merely impersonal. The sublime is something hyperbolic that rears up in a dimension of height within the aesthetic happening of the between. This terrifying and exhilarating height hints at the immanent transcendence of the divine. Relative to the aesthetics of happening, we can see it as a *lived and living counterpart* to the standard "argument from design" presented in a more univocalizing, mechanicizing mode.

Second, pantheism is often associated with Romanticism, a movement now sometimes dismissed, though the denigration is cheap. Often the denigration is inferior in spiritual level to what it dismisses. Romanticism was a movement of the whole and towards the sense of the whole; a movement from the fragmentation of modern life towards a

---

2   In the language of different transcendences: T^3 (God) is not sharply separated from T^1 (Nature/World), and T^2 (the human being) seeks to be at home in this immanently divine totality (*Deus sive Natura*: T^3 is one with or interchangeable with T^1). T^3 as *other* to nature and human self-transcendence is attenuated or denied.

3   The sublime now is taken with a new postmodern fashionableness, not least due to Lyotard's influence, though postmodern sublimity dare not name itself as religious, perhaps since Nietzsche, the Moses of postmodernism, announced here an equivocal taboo. I mean his remark that now God is not to our *taste*.

new construction of integral life; a movement as much political as poetic, religious as ecological. We still survive off its legacy. Nor was it simply an irrationalist movement; one of its intents was to amplify reason beyond calculative and mechanical reckoning. At best, there was an honesty: the nocturnal side of things inhuman, human, and transhuman must be acknowledged. This is true also of the surrational darkness of God. Much of contemporary life would be inconceivable without the courage of honesty the best Romantics brought to our place in nature. The same applies to our place in society: not a few, take Blake, had an acute sense of the squalor of cities spawned by the industrial revolution; a voice prophetic of justice was raised on behalf of the down-trodden without voice.

Third, pantheism reveals our eros for vital integrity in the whole of creation, and for a God who is not the elsewhere underwriter or "backer" of our own devaluation of that creation. Creation is not God-forsaken. As the aesthetic show of the divine, nature is as if it were the body of God. We are grown by nature and in nature, and as exemplars of creation we too are like the body of God become mindful – mindful of the God immanent in the whole. Are we the self that is knowing of God (some said: the self-knowing of God) in the body of the whole? Is it our destiny to bring the divine in us to full wakeful mindfulness? Is our creativity sourced in divine creativity, which itself finds its focus and most intensive expression in the genius of the human, and in the human genius? Modern pantheism recalls us to perennial perplexities, suggesting that God and the whole are never to be sundered. Yeats asked: "How can we know the dancer from the dance?" But Yeats's great question does not have one answer only.

GOD AND THE WHOLE

Suppose we return to an old view, older than Christianity and its heritage: *Hen to pan*: One the All.[4] This very ancient attitude, profound with meaning both for philosophy and religion, is not only ancient: it names a perennial possibility, resurfacing in modernity and not only in relation to Spinoza. *Hen kai pan* was the spiritual rallying cry of the youthful Schelling, Hölderlin and Hegel, the sign of their fidelity to their new "Church Invisible." None of them ever really was apostate to this Church. Much of contemporary panentheism has more of a family relation to this Church than it realizes, or seems willing to acknowledge.

What sense of the ontological ethos shapes this figuration of God? First, there is perplexity about what, if anything, holds the multiplicity of things together? The question is not, Why being or beings at all? The perplexity is the how of their "holding together." The many as many are intelligibly together, they constitute a kind of community. Is there a fundamental unity in relation to this community, a unity not another finite whole? Further, things are not seamlessly together but endure in strife. They are drawn together in antagonism itself. Together plurality and disunion precipitate perplexity about a One power that unifies and resolves and that runs through all things. For one thing is with another despite disunion, and that other with another again, and again despite further discord, and so on . . . This seems to portend an unending succession, leading to the scattering of things rather than their gathering. Yet something more fundamental than scattering recurs in the scattering: what perdures is a coming to be that is more than all dissolution, though it be streaked with dissolution. Is there a One that runs through all? If it runs, it is not a static substance but a power that possibilizes all beings, though it is not itself a being. What is this One that is in all, and yet is not all or the sum of all? The word "whole," or "Whole of wholes" is a response worth pondering.

---

[4]   Thomas Kinsella has a fine poem "Hen Woman" informed by astonishment about worlds coming to be, like an egg from a hen. This is a poem on the occasion of a woman scooping up a hen, from whom falls an egg just being born, only to fall to the ground and smash. And then the wry ending: "She stood staring, in blank anger. / Then her eyes came to life, and she laughed / and let the bird flap away. / "It's all the one. / There's plenty more where that came from!"/ Hen to pan! / It was a simple world." *Contemporary Irish Poetry: New and Revised Edition*, ed. and intro. Anthony Bradley (Berkeley: University of California Press, 1988), pp. 186–7.

Consider again the many. They all are, hence reveals some community of being. Each, so far as it is at all, has a certain integrity of being – otherwise, it would be disintegrating and in a perpetual tailspin of passing from being. This is not what beings are. All are relatively intelligible, for there are recurrent orders of togetherness that we can come to know. None is the One, but all partake of integrity and togetherness. It seems natural to think of them deriving from and being encompassed by a more absolute One in which they participate and perhaps finitely express. We must make a movement into an *other* dimension of unity, since the absolute generating and gathering whole cannot be reduced to the level of any finite whole. This idea is one of the most natural, and the most problematic – and problematic because so natural, and hence liable to be conceived in terms of the unity of *being in nature*, not the unity that gathers nature into an inclusive togetherness.

Do discord, opposition, and negation stand against this? The whole is other to these, if we think of unity only in univocal terms, but we know the limits of such terms. The crucial importance of the *dialectical way* is evident here. This allows us think about the many without tarrying with merely dispersing diversity. It lets us address differences and oppositions without trapping us in dualism. It opens a mediated pathway into and beyond dualism in the direction of the togetherness of the opposites, and hence towards a more encompassing integrity of being that embraces manyness within itself. It encourages comprehension in terms of wholes not reducible to the sum of their parts. At the same time it allows us to view the partiality of limited wholes as themselves contributions to more encompassing wholes, all the way to the Whole of wholes, the absolute unity of the many. This is not a denial of manyness but a placing of manyness within its fuller context. The true context of all contexts is, for this view, the Whole of wholes.

Who or what is God now? God is identified with the Whole of wholes. God is like the last ring surrounding all the rings of finitude, and hence the ultimate Whole, the ring of rings completing all finite integrities of being. Of course, we must also speak of *origin* in appropriate terms. The ring of rings, the Whole of wholes revolves us round to the origin where we find a complex mingling of the erotics of the divine and the agapeics. In the Neoplatonic tradition the One generates from itself by a series of emanations or hypostases from *Nous*, Soul . . . and on down to the world of matter. Details aside, it is important that the reason for the emanation is the goodness of the origin. This is not unconnected with a feeling for the agapeic origin, though I do not mean to conflate this with the Neoplatonic One, for an important question is the coming to be of finite difference as good.

In Neoplatonic thinking, the descent from the One is by overflow from the fullness of the One whose goodness is necessarily diffused. *Our way up* to the One is by way of self-exceeding and also negation: this is more erotic than agapeic. This ancient tradition did not always find the coherence of these two ways, in so far as the goodness of being exists in tension with the lack of finiteness and the thrust of our erotic self-transcending beyond finiteness. The deeper truth of the agapeic One is connected with the goodness of the between. If we exaggerate our own erotic transcending from *lack*, our appreciation of the finite will not be properly positive.

We must not overstate this point, as has been done repeatedly in mimicry of Nietzsche's reckless pronouncements. I simply recall the splendid goodness of the cosmos, as imaged in Plato's *Timaeus*: the most beautiful possible. The vacillation between the agapeic and erotic is important because in modern versions of the One I find a shift in thinking the origin, bound up with a failure fully to think the archaeology of the good, and a faulty redirection of the entire search towards a teleology of the good. The One becomes an erotic absolute.[5] The eros is not always *eros uranios*. Without an archeology of the good, it quickly becomes *eros turranos*, and then, too, the teleology of the Whole is denied. There is a line of continuity from the One of German idealism to the dark origins of

---

[5] Whitehead speaks of the divine eros and "the eros of the universe," (see above Chapter 1, note 5) calling his view "the philosophy of organism," and speaking of "the self-creative unity of the universe" (*Process and Reality*, p. 47), as well as the "process of transition from indetermination towards terminal determination" (*Process and Reality*, p. 45).

Schopenhauer and Nietzsche, thus to darkness and unreason at the base of things, and then it is too short a step to the loss of the Whole, and of God.

HOLISTIC EMANATION AND PLURALISTIC CREATION

One can couple holistic emanation with pan(en)theism as the mode of divine origination and self-return, with consequences for the ontological status of finitude within the whole.[6] Holistic emanation and pluralistic creation are not to be taken as univocal hypotheses: they do not proximately concern a finite being or process but are metaphysical metaphors or hyperboles concerning the ultimate coming to be of the happening of the between. Modern pan(en)theism (say, in post-Spinozistic form) is not always as metaphysically daring as premodern speculation (as in Eriugena or Cusanus), perhaps because of fear of the accusation of extravagant, unverifiable notions or false science. But it wrong to think we are dealing with some determinate finite explanation. This happens, for instance, when "creation" is reduced to an empirical hypothesis rivaling any theory of determinate beginnings in scientific cosmology. Premodern speculation was less liable to this mistake, and hence more bold in its metaphysical venturing; though it too did not always distinguish a metaphysical metaphor or hyperbole of ultimate coming to be from a determinate explanation of a finite causal happening. If it made that mistake, it was because the distinction, while operative, was not self-consciously firm. If the moderns made an analogous mistake, it was because they were overwhelmed by the power of determinate explanation, and forgot the distinction.[7]

With holistic emanation, the world, in one respect, is the self-externalization of the originative principle, in another respect, it is its self-actualization. Originated from the essence of the One itself, the world bodies forth the One. This is a kind of *dynamized Eleaticism.*

---

[6] "Emanation" can be linked with the metaphorics of the circle, and the self-becoming of the whole, and be used to refer to the modes of origination of a God for whom self-origination and the origination of the world cannot be separated: where creation is inseparable from divine self-creation; where something like the Neoplatonic scheme of *monas, proodos, epistrophē* defines the circular being of the divine (another triad from the same tradition: *ousia, dunamis, energeia*) For example, Scotus Eriugena: divine self-creation in creation; the dialectic (division) of universal nature as a whole is God, or manifestation of God. *Eriugena: Periphyseon (The Division of Nature)*, trans. I. P. Sheldon-Williams, corrected by J. J. O Meara, Cahiers d'études médiévales, Cahier spécial, 3 (Montreal, Paris & Washington DC, 1987), I.3[443A9–D4); III.2 [628B–C]; God includes the world in self and in a sense deifies the world, II 23[577B], IV.4 [749A1–6]. The Trinity is referred to this triad – father/*ousia*, son/*dunamis*, spirit/*energeia*. Eriugena was deeply influenced by Dionysian theology.

[7] Is there a revealing analogy between the modern move from the clockmaker God of deism to pantheism (Spinoza and descendants) and the ancient move from the Demiurgic maker of Plato's *Timaeus* to the holistic One of Plotinus and neo-Platonism? With the model of the technician, indeed one who geometrizes, "transcendence" (T³) seems rendered as an "outside" principle of making, lacking intimacy with creation – though with Plato's Demiurge there is an intimacy with the good, and greater intimacy with the aesthetic beauty of the fabricated world. The reaction of the monists/pantheists: the model of craft or artisanship is nothing like the divine art, where there is coming to be in which origin and issue cannot be thus separated. One is not what it is without the other, and this applies to the One too, since it is not what it is without the many, and in that sense the origination is a *necessary coming to be.* It is not as if it were up to a craftsman to do or not to do; it is the necessary being of the One to give rise to what arises. The idea of absolute unity is here so overriding, that one cannot be separated from the other. Result: again a kind of *higher transcendental univocity* rather than the dianoetic univocity of the deistic God, or geometricizing Demiurge. This peculiarity of *trans-demiurgic origination* is evident in the more radical monism of Plotinus's One (for instance, his rejection of the craftsman analogy, see *Enneads* II, 9.4; IV.3.10; IV.8.8; V.8.7 – *Nous* as mastery without toil; V.8.12; VI.7.1). Compare with how the German Idealists radicalize Kant's transcendental univocity, move beyond his dualisms, ending up with a position that raises Spinozistic wholeness to a higher speculative self-mediation. A complex dialectic of dualistic transcendence and monistic pan(en)theism is evident in both, and in both mediated by a philosophical strategy of return to self, or self-mediation. Heidegger criticizes the model of *technē*, but what are we to make of his origin? Is he the unprecedented original some have claimed he is, and that he himself insinuates? As I have just indicated, the technical model has been more than once criticized in the Western tradition. See *AOO*, Chapter 7 for discussion of Heidegger's origin from a metaxological viewpoint.

The traditional idea of God is often attacked as a block eternity, dead as a rock. Apart from how fair this is to the Eleatic view, the origin is never really conceived in static terms. The world wells up from the divine source, and while the source is not exactly the same as the dynamism of worldly becoming, it is still a dynamic generative source. The hyperbolic energy of eternity comes to shape itself as the extraordinary cosmos, and we too are startling shapes of divine energy. For if there is a Whole of wholes, what we take as the separate world, or human being, are really nothing apart from the Whole, are what they are in virtue of being participants of the Whole. To be participant is to be a "part" of the Whole, and in the part itself is a contraction of the Whole into a definite finite integrity of being.

"Emanation" is not the same as "creation" considered as a mode of divine origination. Hegel will use the term "creation" as if it were synonymous with God's self-externalization, and hence interchangeable with "emanation" but the conflation is mistaken.[8] This is revealing about Hegel's insight – as well as oversight. Emanation stresses the continuity of the world and God, creation underscores their discontinuity. In the first, it is the immanence in the world of the divine or of the world in the divine, that matters; in the second, it is the transcendence of the divine that matters, hence the non-divinity of the world. The danger of the first is the conflation of world and God; the danger of the second is the finite deflation of the worth of world, as we infinitely inflate God. In the first, there is sameness of substance between world and God, while there is difference in the second.

The *sive* of Spinoza's *Deus sive natura* will be seen by some as the deflation of God to the world, and by others as the inflation of world to God. Sameness will be an identity robbed of any sense of dialectical difference From the pantheism of such an unmediated identity Hegel took pains to disentangle himself – the later Hegel, that is, while himself under attack as "pantheistic," that is "atheist," by the more orthodox "theist." Hegel is perhaps right that no thoughtful person ever was guilty of "pantheism" in that sense. Still, hard questions remain. In particular, the question of transcendence does not go away, never goes away. Just as there is an unsophisticated pantheism which lives off an undiscriminating identity, there is an unacceptable sense of transcendence which lives off an unsustainable dualism. But to *identify* transcendence with that dualism does as little service to the truth as to fasten, from the opposite direction, on the identity of pantheism. The metaxological view of the double seeks to go beyond that dualism, just like dialectic, while counteracting the latter's tendency to privilege immanent identity at the expense of otherness beyond dialectical self-mediation.

Overall in holistic emanation *the between is within the being of the One*. At a limit, this is the divinization of the world by the holistic God said to be "all in all." There is nothing finally "outside" that One. To be radically "outside" is to be absolutely nothing. To be "outside" is only a relative condition which signals *more internal relations* within the divine whole, rather than any external relation between the divine and the finite creation. Being "outside" is being "inside," but "inside" in a manner that does not fulfill the truth of being "inside." It is being within that does not recognize that it is within, and that, as within, is nothing apart from being a part of the absolute divine whole. One detects again the Eleaticism: "outside" of absolute being there is nothing, and it makes no sense to speak of that nothing, for just as nothing, it is nothing. Hence, speech about it is speech about nothing: empty sound. And yet, astonishingly, the sound said to be nothing is yet something.

Hegel's doctrine of negation reveals a sophisticated Eleaticism: the nothing is not "outside" the whole; there is nothing "outside" the whole; every nothing is a negation within the whole, but negation within the whole is the means by which the *dunamis* of the eternal passes from its state of indeterminacy to progressively more complex determinations. Determinations might be called emanations (Eriugena calls them divisions: *divisione naturae* – divisions reenacted by dialectic). But these are all "within" the self-determination of the One. The series of emanations are determinations by which the One negates itself and produces itself as different hypostases that are the One's own eternal self-determination. The Hegelian One (in a phrase that might win a Heideggerian imprimatur) is *the wholing*

---

[8] See *Hegel's God*, Chapter 5 on creation.

of the whole. Hegel describes his *Logic* in the metaphor of God's thoughts before the creation of finite nature and spirit. One thinks of the progressive dialectical emanation of the circle of necessary intelligibilities that define the life of the divine: God's thoughts, as they generate themselves in the circle of all circles, the whole as the truth of being, and by dialectical passage along the eternal ring, or eternal circling of divine hypostases.

Holistic emanation tends towards a dialectical interplay of finite and infinite: *both* finite and infinite turn out to be the dialectical self-mediation of the infinite with itself, through the finite as its own other. Thus Hegel's sublationary infinitism: the true infinite is the circle that returns to itself, the self-sublating infinite that as a *single* process includes finite and infinite, considered as one-sided opposites.[9] By contrast, with "creation," the interplay of finite and infinite is *between* the actual infinite communicating the being of the finite as other and just that finite other gifted with the promise of its own kind of infinitude. This intermediation of different infinitudes points in a more metaxological direction. Admittedly, some views of "creation" tend towards a dualism of infinite and finite, undermining their interplay and togetherness, such as is discerned by a dialectical holism. This dualism does not do justice to the truth of "creation," but this truth is not the One Whole as the self-sublating infinite.

In the outgoing and return of the holistic God, there is a circular process which constitutes the *energeia*, actuality of the divine. Different shadings are possible here. One might say time is illusory, or perhaps only relatively real, for time is nothing outside of the life of the circle of eternity, arising like a wave on the ocean where it is nothing in itself, to vanish again into the engulfing Whole. Or one might hold a circular view of time itself. In premodern times, the circle imaged the perfect motion wherein the end returns to the beginning. A more complex view incorporates time more positively into the eternal circle. Time itself shows the egress and regress of eternity: the outgoing and homecoming of the absolute. This view is found in Hegel, though he also assumes the legacy of the revelational religions as providential stories of salvation history. What is salvation history for Hegel but the exoteric manifestation of the esoteric love of eternity for time, or time for eternity: the love each of them has for the other as *its own other*? Hegel wanted to reconcile time and eternity as each other's own other, and hence both are assumed into the self-sublating Whole which is the very erotic selving of the absolute itself.

Nietzsche's eternal return of the same falls within a not dissimilar horizon. Nietzsche swears off the moral God but by no means closes off a new pantheism (see *Will to Power*, 36; sect. 55). The coming god will be a divinity of immanence. We are reminded of the great cosmological year of the Stoics, as well as earlier cyclic mythologies. The marriage of love of fate with the circling of eternity is crucial – nothing is accidental, in the end. Yet Nietzsche is more pickled in the solutions of post-revelational historicism than he always acknowledged, and these are not always congruent with his ring of eternity. He asks (*Will to Power*, pp. 549–50): Do you want a *name* for this world – this "monster of energy" – "a *solution* for all its riddles?" He answers: The *world is will-to-power – and nothing besides!* And you yourselves are also this will-to-power – and nothing besides! But he also sings a song, ventriloquizing through Zarathustra, about the ring of rings, in which everything is *in love* with everything else.[10] How monstrous will to power is married with this love of the Whole, and this love of everything with everything within the Whole, remains a mystery wrapped in a riddle.

The enigma of time in its arising again and again, and its sustaining of each being in being, and in its own being, and of time's support for the shape humans put on their own self-becoming, and also the excess of this arising to human shaping such that we make

9 This is how Hegel's describes the true infinite (*das warhhafte Unendliche*) in *Wissenschaft der Logik* I, in *Werke in zwanzig Bänder (Theorie-Werkausgabe)*, Vol. 5, ed. Eva Moldenhauer and Karl Markus Michel (Frankfurt am Main: Suhrkamp Verlag, 1970), p. 149; *Science of Logic*, trans. A. V. Miller (New York: Humanities Press, 1969), p. 137.
10 *Zarathustra: Das Nachtwandler-Lied [Das trunkene Lied]* 10: *Alle Dinge sind verkettet, verfädelt, verliebt.*

our trace but the trace is but for a time, it is a provisional marking of our presence and then it begins to fade and vanish, and the fact that this vanishing itself discloses time as a *dunamis* that must be repeatedly renewed in being for becoming to be possible at all, all these just stated happenings give a presentiment of a nothingness in the arising of finite time, an intimation that, from one side, can be heard as the call back to the origin (for arising and perishing are the masks of relative being) and that, from the other side, can be seen to show the difference between the origin and the creation, for again the finite is ineradicably finite, since its temporary gift of being, in the interim of the between, destines it to be mortal, and the end is that in the human shaping of time, time itself points to a source that is not itself time, and our great struggle is to find the right words for that other origin, and if we say that time is merely illusory becoming, or that time is the story that humans have stamped on becoming, baptizing this stamp with the name of "history," neither of these sayings is true enough to arising into being and passing from being in the between, for each cocoons itself too much from the enigma of eternity and its showing in and through time's enigma.

GOD BEYOND THE WHOLE?

If the metaxological way is truer to the ethos of being than the dialectical way, if the agapeics of divine communication are more ultimate than the erotics of divine selving, the following questions arise for the holistic God.[11]

First, how are we to look at the arising of difference? If difference is a fall from the One, or even its self-alienation, we see it too negatively, or at most as a provisional reality, vanishing as it is arising, a dissolving moment of the Whole. Then we see too negatively the prodigious plurality of the world. The plurality that roused us to thought of the One is put into the pale by the One. The agapeics of the One lead us out into the sun, and give us to affirm, reaffirm the plural. Do we not need to question the Eleatic legacy in the holistic way?

Second, why the alleged fall or self-alienation into time at all? Does not this too degrade the temporal, instead of elevating it as the gift of finite coming to be and of the becoming of what has been given to be? Why does the One have to alienate itself at all, if it is the absolute it is? Why temporal differentiation at all? Instead of fall or self-alienation, suppose there is the giving of being to the other, being-other as good? If time is supported on the love of eternity, what kind of love is this? Is it the love of the agapeic origin that frees time into the goodness of its own otherness? Is it the erotic origin that needs time to be itself the consummated absolute? The holistic view tends to eschew the first, for it introduces a doubleness not reducible to a monism of the whole. In so far as it favors the latter, it reinterprets the divine life as the eternal process that needs time to mediate with itself and hence raise itself from an indeterminate beginning to a fully mediated consummation. But this again raises the question of why the need for time at all in an origin that is said to be absolutely whole: how comes the arising of need in the absolute? Is not this also incompatible with the language of "overflowing"? There is no need in the One, hence time must be gratuitous.

Of course, there are different kinds of gratuitousness. One is the giving that is for no reason beyond the goodness of the giving. Another is a happening that is merely a surd, and that has no reason. The agapeic origin suggests the first. For do we not talk about the *arising* of being in the between: not falling, it arises, it is an elevation, a floating on nothingness, a lifting up to be. Arising is as if every moment were a resurrection from the dead, or a preserving from the threat of death, a guarding the goodness of beings; as if God were torn by grief for every death, and yet on the instant resurrected the beloved this into the goodness of life. We do not see this steadily in immanent life, but we do get glimpses of it.

---

[11]   In the following I draw on, while amplifying and modifying, some reflections found in *IST?*, pp. 192–9.

Third, what of the necessity of the arising of the many? Are our terms only univocal determinism and equivocal indetermination? Is God simply identified with an impersonal necessity that must be as it is, and such that things must be as they are? In many traditions, God has been defined as the necessary being: the being who cannot not be, the being whose essence involves existence. If the arising of creation were necessary in a sense either univocally or dialectically the same as that in which God's being is said to be necessary, the contingency of beings in the between becomes highly problematical. If acknowledged, it becomes redefined relative to the more encompassing necessity. The suspicion is hard to quell that contingency is being short changed. The very between as a *happening* ceases to be a happening; it becomes a necessity that could not be otherwise. The love of being might find expression in *amor fati*. But if life becomes a fatalism the more sinister possibilities of contingent happening seem also consecrated as themselves the fated expression of the eternal laws of necessity.

There are repercussions in human existence. How make compatible this divine necessity with religion as the intimate universal? Does not all the intimacy of being become scattered on the icy winds of indifference? Indeed, why do anything which might upset the ways necessity rules? Indeed how *do* anything? Things are as they must be; what we do counts for nothing beyond expressing the necessity of which we too are manifestations. Should we become quietistic or fatalistic? These responses can be too easily dismissed as they can be too easily endorsed. For there can be an acquiescence marked by an obscure recognition that there is a power in the deeper course of happening whereby things "come to right." This obscure recognition has to do with the intimate universal. Consent to the fateful is not wrong, but it is wrong if it excludes our being co-operators in our destiny, which must be as much chosen as find itself in being chosen. Destiny is the promise of a gift, but we must accept the gift, and, since the gift is itself a promise, we must serve the good to redeem its promise. Otherwise, the promise is crushed in a resignation not reconciled but merely cowed or apathetic, just as certain sufferings take the light from one's eyes and make one want to die. Such necessity does not "come to right" but offers the poisoned chalice of death.

Fourth, where is the space for freedom, the allowing of the open? Is there enough allowance for the porosity of the between? With the holistic God, is not the indeterminate engulfed by the self-determining Whole? What of the overdeterminate, as more than the indeterminate, more than mere indefiniteness? What of the allowance of self-transcending that realizes its full promise in the community of agapeic service: transcending to the others as the fullest freeing of human possibility, beyond any circular self-realization? One might reply that there are spaces of openness embraced *within* the holistic God. But the question concerns *another* freedom not so within but released into its difference with all its hazards, as a parent frees the child to walk on its own feet, even as it watches with love as the child stumbles.

We cannot separate our understanding of freedom and God. Here freedom tends to become rational consent to necessity. Is there not a freedom beyond holistic necessity? This may look like perverse anarchy to the rationalist, but it has the greatness of the idiotic in it. In holistic views there is a tendency to defined singulars through a network of differential relations with others, and hence the singularity is idiotic in a bad sense, that is, merely idiosyncratic relative to the Whole and its encompassing context of relational intelligibility. The holistic God does not quite know what to make of the idiotic; it seems merely idiotic. The agapeic God loves the idiotic and delights in the sweet singularity that dances or dares before it. The idiotic singular is the loved child of time at play.

Fifth, the community of being also arises in connection with the question of the intimate universal. The holistic way *does* think in terms of community, but as the more inclusive whole, all the way to the most embracing Whole of wholes. The community is the whole that mediates with itself through its members. Ultimately community is ("organic") self-communication, even if the "self" in communication is the divine. Is this adequate to the communication *between* beings in the finite middle? or between the origin and the beings in the between? or indeed between the divine and itself? The other as standing in the integrity of its otherness is necessary for community as more than self-communication. If so, there is a community of metaxological togetherness that is beyond dialectical self-mediation, and hence beyond the embrace of divine holism. Holism does not deny the oppositions in relations, indeed it turns them into the opportunity of a more reconciled community. But all otherness is not opposition. There are othernesses even in the community of reconciliation that are not merely provisional; they are essential to defining the communication of reconciliation itself. The agapeics of communication are both self-communicating and more than self-communication.

A traditionally noted difficulty is that holism suggests the absorption of the world into God. The world is "within" the divine, and both the independence of world and the transcendence of God are weakened. What "within" means is hard to say, as hard or as easy as "independence" and "transcendence" – themselves terms we do not have to conceive in dualistic fashion. Our choice is not between a dualism of the two, or a holism which asserts an identity more fundamental than their difference. There can be a community of the two which neither negates their duality nor fixes it as a dualism. There is a metaxological pluralism resistant to absorption into a one, but not for all that a source of alienation from the One.

The absorption of world into God is only one side of a general problematic of holistic unity, the other side of which is the reduction of God to the world. That unity can be tilted towards a worldly evaporation of God or towards a mystical worldlessness which evaporates into God. Spinoza's *Deus sive Natura* is again instructive. This *sive* is equivocal between the two sides due to a univocity in approach that lacked something of the dialectical equilibrium we find, say, in Hegel. The theists who saw only Spinoza *maledictus* saw the reduction of God to the world, the rejection of creation, personal providence, and deliberate free will, and in the final reckoning, the one substance seemed hard to tell apart from the mechanism of the materialists. But, in something like a *Gestalt* turnabout, the pantheists who saw Spinoza *benedictus* reborn as the *Gott-vertrunkene Mann* saw also the rising sun of immanent divinity not the reduction of God to world. Whether this was the absorption of world in God, or God in world, was secondary, for nature now seems divinized. Beyond the godforsaken mechanism, we can celebrate the sacred organism, the living body of the divine. This absorption of world into God shapes a new naturalistic piety of the whole, believed to be free of the discords of traditional transcendence and its dualisms. That Spinozistic religiosity could engender these opposed responses, and continues to do so, shows both a versatility and instability in the unity which tells against the equilibrium of the whole. The metaxological way seeks to avoid both reduction and absorption, with a sense of the One and the plural beyond both dualism and the self-mediating totality.

THE HOLISTIC GOD AND EVIL

What finally of evil? Relative to the holistic God, the singular tends to be associated with estrangement from the Whole, in some cases as at the center of evil. In Hegel, for instance, the singular qua particular is correlative with evil. The singular claiming absolute independence as turned against the more encompassing universal – this is the evil. One sees the point: the singular as a being for itself can set itself in opposition to all other being, and hence deform the community of relations that still actually binds it to all the others. But this is barely half the story.

This is the crux: the power of evil shows a freedom from the whole hard to interpret entirely in holistic terms. How can a part within the Whole set itself against the whole and assert itself as the true Whole? To do this, it cannot be a mere part. The language of part and whole is not enough. Evil testifies to a recalcitrant power that, looked at from the side of the singular's promise, is the power of a freedom to be for itself, and to be for itself rightfully. Singular selfhood entails being a kind of whole unto itself, not a mere moment of a larger whole. The holistic way evacuates the fullness of that singular wholeness, turned in a different direction to the profound abyss of its ontological intimacy, that is, to its divine idiocy. We need a God who can turn the other way. We need metaxological terms articulating the community of open wholes in the between.

The point is not the typically Western emphasis on the individual as standing over against the other, often with a willful self-insistence. The holistic view rightly sees a certain willful self-assertiveness as a block on the true mindfulness of the divine. The assertiveness hardens singularity into a mere knot of resistance to otherness beyond itself, or, worse, it exploits the powers of being given to it to lord over creation, or other humans whose very existence offends its usurpation of absoluteness. Yet singularity is not a moment of the Whole to be superseded for the truth of the Whole to shine through. Its true idiocy involves granting its porosity of being, its being as a communicative integrity of existence in communicative togetherness with others, even in the deepest intimacy of its inwardness. In that intimate idiocy the communication of the divine other is most deeply undergone in the deepest porosity of one's being. Communicative being is not outside one. It comes alive just in this ultimate porosity that is both inside and beyond one: most intimate to one, most solicitous that one be delivered from selving that is curved back on itself. We must give up a certain willfulness. Willfulness may have its qualified glory when it is one of the masks of singularity, but here its promise is diverted from community into hollow self-glorification. The porosity of being has been overtaken by a *conatus essendi* so self-insistent it has violated and betrayed its own *passio essendi*.

Relative to the beginning: the holistic God shows some inculpation in evil. If God is the Whole of wholes, and evil is part of the whole, in some sense God is complicit in the origin of evil. If all flows with divine necessity, evil also arises with dialectical necessity, God is necessarily involved in the genesis of evil. Unlike the Gnostic view of a good and evil God, here within God is the principle of evil, as well as the good.

Relative to the middle: the arising of the between as *over against* the God is evil. This is not quite Gnosticism, but each comes to choke on saying of creation "It is good." If the togetherness of opposites is given a dialectical justification, the between becomes the working out of their strife governed by a teleology of completeness, and evil is deemed necessary to the self-development of the good of God. Where is the surplus good of God hyperbolic to all development?

Relative to the end: a redeeming teleology regards the end as the consummated whole sublating the evil of opposition. Evil is necessary for the reconstitution of this final whole: without evil no development, no reintegration. Evil is holistically exonerated in the final at-onement of the absolute Whole. As with the aesthetic theodicy, the equivocity of good and evil only holds for those ensnared in the parts of the whole picture, not for the one surveying the Whole. The whole is divinely overlooked, and there is a majestic aesthetic univocity beyond and inclusive of all evil equivocity. One looks down on the planet Earth from a great height above it, and it is of extraordinary beauty, like a blue jewel suspended in space. At that great height one does not hear the screams in the torture chambers. The holistic God, like an aesthetic contemplator, purrs with pleasure. But we need a God who hears those screams and wipes the face of the weeping and does not abandon the crucified. This God is a God of the Whole, who is not evil, yet who is not indifferent to evil, and who is not the Whole.

Is this the (in)famous *coincidentia oppositorum*: the purring God who also is the self-lacerating God? In theodicies such as the Hegelian, God seems to have to *redeem itself*, by dialectical passage from its impoverished beginning to its consummated end. *Deus sive historia*. If evil arises, somehow, in God's self-alienation, God seems to have to visit evil on itself in order to come into its own final goodness. The whole of finite becoming, in nature, in history, would testify then to a kind of self-cannibalizing of God, and all with the end in view of redeeming God's own immanent torment. Self-sinning God, self-crucifying God, self-resurrecting God. The hand that heals is the hand that wounds, Hegel said. But what God would so wound itself, in order to heal itself? When humans tears strips off their own flesh, we suspect a hell within, not a heaven or its promise. The God that is the Whole seems to raven the body of the Whole to come into its kingdom. But that body it also itself. The self-loving God and the self-hating God seem one and the same, and when we bow down before God or nature or history we must wonder if some malign genius has been perpetrating a speculative swindle. (One recalls to the honor of Schopenhauer his anathema to the God honored by Spinoza as Nature – this goes beyond a bad joke.)

I come round a *second time to evil*, not now in terms of the holistic God. Evil is not in God but in the relation of God to creation. That relation is not of whole and part, but of whole and whole. What character these different wholes? Absolute good, finite good. Whence the evil? In the relation of finite good to absolute good. This is a relation of otherness, and otherness given for itself, hence not a moment of a larger whole, hence capable of standing against the absolute good. Why? The finite good, in its endowment of freedom, takes itself to be the absolute good. It determines itself as a counterfeit of the absolute whole: by willing itself to be that whole it falls into evil. How deep does the power of opposition to the absolute good go? Infinitely deep in the case of the human being: idiotic singularity goes all the way into the abyss. And this too is a noplace without a home in any immanent whole.

We know our being as nothing absolute in the intimacy of our primal porosity. There we are naked to the communication of the divine, but also tempted to seize oneself to secure oneself. In this seizure the usurpation of evil begins. Evil "happens" in a usurpation of being as gift – by a being who is given to be. This is a beginning that begins nothing, but the usurpation is itself given as a possibility from the beginning. The beginning that begins nothing wills to undo the communication that comes in the porosity: uncreate creation as given by the divine other. Why? Just because it is given by another, and I am not that giver. I cannot be self-given, I ungive the gift in counterfeiting absolute self-giving. To be uncreate: this too is an *imitatio Dei*. I look like God but I am nothing. I imitate God but I am the counterfeit whole.

The agapeic origin allows evil, radical evil, just in its creation of the between as other, with the promise of its own self-being as other to the origin. Mysteriously, transcendence is at the origin of evil. Evil is not thinkable outside of relation to God, but it is a relation that is "outside" that relation. There is an enigma to that "outside," to that placing oneself "outside." One is placing oneself noplace, but in another sense, there is no "outside" to be so placed – there is nothing outside the communication of the gift of being, and hence outside the gift of God.

The idiocy of the monstrous sleeps – and wakes – deep in the ontological roots of selving, in its singularity, and in the elusive intimacy of being that constitutes a community. There is no objectification, nor any completely dialectical account of it. Here we get a sense of the nothing that is other to determinate negativity, and not subsumable in terms of a dialectical *Aufhebung*. The holistic God is hard to square with motiveless malice or demoniac iniquity or spiritual evil. Evil is in claiming to be the absolute whole. Satan: *parodia sacra*: a parody of absolute wholeness – I am God, and there shall be none others beside me. But how can a whole counterfeit the Whole?

Of course, there are relative evils that do not thwart recovery of good. There are also losses, or deformations, or corruptions, beyond redemption, curses on the good beyond recovery. There are turnings against the light that turn away into the land of darkness. What of damnation? Milton: "darkness visible." A coincidence of opposites, yes, but a holistic view has no answer to the meaning of this damned coincidence. For, willy nilly, we are all parts of the Whole, and the cold outside of spirit that is hell does not fit into this view. As there is a *nihil* beyond determinate negation at the beginning, there is a cold absolute nothingness, or nihilating that, at the end, is "outside" the Whole. Holistic pan(en)theism has no way of addressing this icy "outside" – though it be right here now in the intimate heart of immanent man. Holistic pan(en)theism is still a child of Elea. Elea is a state of spirit; among its taboos, the thought of hell.

Chapter 12

God Beyond the Whole: On the Theistic God of Creation

A pregnant woman is round
She does not give birth
To perfect circles
There are no circles
Except those we weave
Around ourselves
Porosity being within us
& without
Void womb permeable
To surprising life

Say it is beyond
& the inquisitors of
  immanence
Turn their stony faces away
& hear only echoes of
  themselves

It lets them be

Nothing is withheld
Everything is in the open
Open it retains its mystery
Given it keeps its secret love
We need only look

Between nothing
& something
What happens
Is the pure surprise
Of everything
That is

Intimate to the between
Never captive to the between
The beyond
Springs surprise

Surprised in the wood
Upstart of the deer
The man

An early morning intruder
Startlement of the animal
Met by startlement of the man

The deer leaped away,
Leaped and stopped
Stopped and looked
& turned away
To disappear into the
  camouflage
Of the green

I, caught
Stare into the emptied space
Of disappearance
While in the distance rises
  the hum
Too near by far
Of early morning traffic
Ferrying the metal men
To the successful city
Of the grey

WHAT HAS PHILOSOPHY TO DO WITH CREATION?

Worries about the God of the whole make us wonder about a God beyond the whole? Need such a "beyond" be a dualistic beyond, fixed in a frozen spatiality, void of intimacy with the immanent whole? The metaxological response must be no. Agapeic origination is communicative giving to be, intimate to the being given to be, an intimacy that comes again in the woo of mystic love. Moreover, there is this striking singularity about God: God is God and nothing but God is God. If this is so, we are addressing something absolutely singular that cannot be dealt with wholly in terms of any immanent holism. Are there any terms at all then? Does creation *ex nihilo* merit attention as addressing God's singular and hyperbolic transcendence? This singular God contests the primacy of the whole.

God as creator is central to the Western tradition, though now placed in question in a number of ways. For instance, in the wake of evolutionary science, "creation" seems a discredited scientific hypothesis about determinate cosmological beginnings. But surely creation is not a scientific hypothesis at all, with a claim to determinate scientific cognition. It has to do with astonishment and perplexity about the ultimate, expressed in a metaphysical metaphor of origin that shapes our religious sense of the ontological ethos. We are dealing with the thought of something hyperbolic in excess of univocal, scientific determination. Some religious people can be as confused here by a univocal literalism as are their scientistic counterparts – and nemeses. Can we make any intelligible sense of this hyperbolic thought?

If creation is not a scientific hypothesis, is it then a non-reflective myth or a merely naïve "representation"? This question branches out in different directions. If creation is a hyperbolic thought, it cannot be a mere "representation" in Hegel's sense to be *aufgehoben* in the *Begriff*, wherein conceptual thought is said to be at home with *itself*. Creation, rather, points to something *other* to thought at home with itself – which yet asks to be thought. If creation is a "representation," as hyperbolic, it points to what exceeds all "representation" – and all conceptual thought at home with itself.[1]

Likewise, if creation is not the *determinative making* of a demiurge, it cannot be aligned with any sort of *technē*.[2] It is disproportionate to any finite making. What makes it thus disproportionate? Its radical origination of the new; its giving to be of the "never before" into its unique "once." But if creation has to do with the coming to be of the determinate, it cannot be grasped in determinate representations or concepts. This means that creator as origin is not a *first being* whence other beings become: the ultimate source of coming to be cannot be a being in that determinate sense. It cannot be assimilated to the terms of Heidegger's critique of "ontotheology." The projects of *Aufhebung* or overcoming "ontotheology" cannot be appropriate to creation understood in the hyperbolic sense. Far from being captive to an idol, creation shatters all idols. It is, so to say, a "representation" of hyperbolic transcendence that shatters "representation," in so far as the latter is liable to be a dissimulating figure of transcendence in immanence.[3]

---

[1] For Hegel creation is a religious *Vorstellung* to be comprehended in the logic of his concept; hyperbolic thought there is none, for any reference to an irreducible beyond is a defect; see *Hegel's God*, Chapter 5. In *Totality and Infinity*, trans. A. Lingis (Pittsburg: Duquesne University Press, 1969), p. 293, Levinas says, rather indiscriminately, of "theology": "Theology imprudently treats the idea of the relation between God and the creature in terms of ontology. It presupposes the logical privilege of totality, as a concept adequate to being." This is neither adequate to the hyperbolic thought of creation nor to origin beyond holism, nor to the difference of coming to be and becoming (see below). Rosenzweig devoted some more extended reflection to creation, by contrast with idealistic emanation, in *The Star of Redemption*, translated from the second edition of 1930 by William W. Hallo (Notre Dame: Notre Dame Press, 1985), see pp. 134ff.

[2] Such as we find in Plato's *Timaeus*, and that Heidegger seems to impute to Christian theology (whether unwittingly, or wittingly, or willfully, I will not presume to say).

[3] Jean-Luc Marion wants to go beyond Heidegger (from being to God) whom he accuses of a second idolatry, though his discourse on being is shaped by Heidegger's terms – terms I cannot accept. One worries about an "either/or" between being and God. When Marion points to agape as beyond being, the stress on the agapeic I endorse. My efforts at thinking being metaxologically are open from the outset to the promise of *agapeic being*. Marion describes a task at the end of his chapter on the double idolatry of Heidegger (*God without Being*, trans. Thomas A. Carlson [Chicago: University of Chicago Press, 1991], pp. 46–7): "To think God, therefore, outside of ontological difference, outside the question of Being . . . what name, what concept, and what sign nevertheless remains feasible? A single one, no doubt, love." Thinking God as agape: "This task, immense and, in a sense, still untouched, requires working love conceptually (and hence, in return, working the concept through love), to the point that its full speculative power can be deployed" (p. 47). I agree, especially if this means we must think what it means to *be* agapeic. The task he proposes reflects some of the aims of my work, here and elsewhere, but not as added on at the end of philosophy, rather as permeating the thinking from the outset. Without a resurrected sense of the agape of being, one wonders how one can venture to think the agapeic being of God. For what if we were to reverse the phrase "God without Being" into "Being without God," would we not come perilously close again to the devalued being of modern nihilism? Instead of the gift of creation, a dark Gnostic double: being without God? If we cannot talk of God's *being* as agapeic, how avoid this reversal? Speaking of God beyond the whole is a way of meeting the issue differently.

In many mythologies we find something like "creators," but it is within the monotheistic religions, stemming from biblical inspiration, that the hyperbolic notion develops.[4] Our concern is philosophical, but this religious source is not irrelevant. An idea of religious provenance becomes the occasion of a more radical philosophical reconsideration. That "creation" has religious origins does not mean it is philosophically illegitimate to engage with it. You cannot put up "No Trespass" signs over religion and order philosophy not to step across. Nor should philosophers themselves erect the "No Trespass" sign.[5] Who is giving the orders here? Anything can become the occasion of philosophical thought; philosophy might have to revisit and revise its cherished ways under the impact of those others, like religion and art, which contest and challenge it. Some ideas are migrants without official passports. They wander extraterritorially from Jerusalem and shock into new astonishment the settled lucidities of Athenian minds.

Creation is said to be one such idea (by Gilson, among others). The claim is something like this: Since in the Greek view of cosmos, existence was eternal, the philosophical question concerns not *why anything is at all* but rather the *what* and *how* of things, as *already given* in being. Creation arises relative to our astonishment about the "that it is," not curiosity about the "what" of what is. Thus, by contrast with Aristotle, Aquinas is said to take seriously "that things are at all." While beings are intelligible, and intelligible perhaps in ways basically described by Aristotelian discourse, that they are at all is not simply an intelligibility; there is no unconditional necessity that they be at all; their being is not self-explanatory; their ontological character shows them as possible or contingent being. Hence the question "Why being at all, why not nothing?" takes on momentous significance.

Some have made the objection that if the idea of creation, accepted on extra-philosophical grounds, determines how we philosophize, there is no real philosophy going on, philosophy as autonomous inquiry, for we always come back to these religious ideas and only end up where we begin. This seems to suggest separate, sealed boxes for religion and philosophy. In truth, some views sourced in religion prove very perplexing; even if philosophy tries to make sense of them, it does so with limited success. Yet, there is hardly a philosophical idea without sources in extra-philosophical considerations. This is to be expected. Philosophy is the thoughtful engagement of the sources of intelligibility immediately at work in the between, sources not languishing for a Johnny-come-lately rationalization to confer on them their certificate of respectability. Moreover, the modern idea of philosophy as autonomous self-mediating reason risks emptying itself of seriousness if it does not engage its others. Postmoderns who are unmoderned attend with humility to other practices of philosophy, and suffer fewer worries of influence. The matter itself is perplexity enough.

Today "creativity" is among words most abused in being most used. It drips from every lip. Indiscriminately democratized, it becomes vacated of meaning. This descent of creativity into kitsch occurs in poorly understood metaphysical shifts in the modern turn to self, and particularly its transcendental radicalization with Kant and his successors (see *AOO passim*). And yet this humanization of creativity occurs within hearing of religious resonances in the word "creation" which carry us back along theological songlines to God as the creator. Our "creativity" has lost or snagged its metaphysical moorings. Unanchored creativity can become so hollowed as to leave it unguarded against its inversion into destruction (Picasso: "A work of art is the sum of destructions"). It is all the more needful to be memorial of these other songlines, now unsung.

Recall the startling fact that Aquinas restricts creation to God alone. Creation is unique to the divine. This is something absolutely singular. It exceeds the immanent whole.

---

[4]   It seems that Clement of Alexandria was the first to state the doctrine of *creatio ex nihilo* in the form that was to take its more settled form with Iranaeus. See Gerhard May, *Creatio ex nihilo: The Doctrine of Creation out of Nothing in Early Christian Thought* (Edinburgh: T&T Clark, 1995), pp. xiv, 180.

[5]   Pascal's distinction between the God of the philosophers and the God of Abraham, Isaac, and Jacob, is turned by some philosophers, and for diverse reasons, into an injunction to *spiritual apartheid* between religion and philosophy.

This should stop us in our tracks, and make us pensive, we today who only have to perm our locks in a special fashion or whip up a soufflé or do some creative accounting or, best of all, attend a creativity workshop one weekend, to know that (clap your hands with joy) we too are now "creators." The idolatry of artistic genius turns into the religion of "creativity"; except that, since everyone now fortunately is a genius, unfortunately there is nothing now more lacking than genius.

CREATION BEYOND UNIVOCAL INTELLIGIBILITY

Just as the dialectical way has an elective affinity with pan(en)theism and the God of the whole, creation and the God beyond the whole can be aligned with the metaxological way. Can we make any intelligible sense of creation from nothing? Consider the venerable problem of thinking about "nothing." If we think of nothing, we are thinking, hence thinking of something, hence not thinking of nothing. The effort to think nothing seems self-subverting; it ends up with some thinking of being. This is Parmenides's point. Something about being shows itself as incontrovertible, even in thinking "nothing." Moreover, if to think intelligibly is to think *determinately*, "nothing" is not anything determinate, and so not anything intelligible. What intelligibility can we make of what is other than a determinate something? Are nothing and creation then irredeemably absurd?

But is it a matter of thinking (impossibly) the world *out* of existence? Even if this were possible, surely this is the opposite of what is at issue? Is the "nothing" a matter of determinate negation? For reasons that will become more evident, we must consider a more radical sense of indeterminate nothing. Something of it is "manifest" in our encounter with radical evil. It is intimated in the mortality of beings, beings marked by the extraordinary singularity of their "once." We are touched by it when we despair: everything seems to "come to nothing" and we ourselves "are as nothing." Beyond all determinate intelligibility, we experience a radical "being at a loss." To yoke all these to a determinate negation, or a "something," fails to be true to them. We cannot make them fully determinate, hence fully intelligible in that way. Does not something like this also apply to the "nothing" of creation *ex nihilo*? Perhaps our "failure" points to a truer truth, in the limit such "failure" draws around finite intelligibility?

It would be astonishing were the "nothing" to yield to univocal, finite intelligibility. From a certain angle, finite being, so far as it shows univocal intelligibility, might be said to lack intelligibility: it is *not* absolute, even as it puts us into perplexity about absolute intelligibility. Finitude fails, not for us, but in itself, so far as its passing into nonbeing shows its essence to be inseparable from nothingness. (This does not mean its essence is nothingness.) If we seek for intelligibility beyond this passing into nonbeing, we must look beyond intelligibility defined by univocal determination. (Many will forsake the search.) One might call *hyperintelligible* such an intelligibility that is more than determinate. Though the hyperintelligible seems a surd and enigmatic, it may be a necessity for there to be determinate intelligibility at all.

I do not mean that only "negatives" bring us to this limit. They can do, but the fullness of finite being can do so too. We are suddenly surprised by unbelievable joy – that is hyperintelligible. And then even such fullness can be trailed by a sorrow that too makes no sense, if all intelligibility is determinate. Something other is shadowing joy, other and beyond, "something" that might seems "nothing." Sorrow over the unintelligibility of finite intelligibility can settle into longing for this other: it is joy that is shadowed by nothing, as perhaps it is by eternity. The charge of lack of intelligibility can be turned around in directions other than the most obvious one, and no univocal absurdism need follow. There may be a homecoming of reason to a wise humility free from vain claims to have plucked the heart from the mystery.

Similar considerations apply to the intelligibility of "creation." Mostly we are familiar with "making something from something." Determinate being, in some shape or other, is always presupposed. The identification of intelligibility with determinate being here arises again. If we make from something, how "make" from nothing, hence how conceive of radical creation? If we operate with a simple contrast of the intelligible determinate and the unintelligible indeterminate, we will not get much further. We will oscillate back and forth between univocity and equivocity. Were we to go beyond this and look at the matter dialectically, it also would not be enough: we favor a "making" as a process of self-determination in and through an other (and so a complex interplay of indefinite and determinate via a dialectical self-determination in the other). Metaxologically, it is easier to acknowledge the affirmative surplus of the overdeterminate, beyond determinacy and self-determination.

The creation of anything is certainly unintelligible if we cannot acknowledge the energy of being that *passes* from a source to an issue. We must underscore the *passing*, and not only the "terms" of passage, a passing that is a *coming to be*. Finite "terms" themselves come to be, and by their very being are in passing. In passing, the very energy of coming to be is in excess of each determination that it precipitates in the process of coming to be. In other words, a finite becoming turns us towards granting a coming to be, and a surplus energy that is overdetermined as ingredient in the intelligibility of the finite passage. *If* we take our sights exclusively from the determinacy of finite intelligibility, this passage is made unintelligible. We need the hyperintelligible.

What, then, would it mean to say that creation is a hyperintelligible? Think of it this way. If we link intelligibility to determinacy and ask what grounds determinate intelligibility, the answer cannot be another determinate intelligible, for that too would be in question. If there is such a ground, it must be *a determining in excess of determinate intelligibles*. Suppose we link creation to such an overdeterminate grounding. Then, to call creation a hyperintelligible would be to say it concerns the beyond of intelligibility that sources the possible intelligibility of the determinately intelligible. If you like, the law of intelligibility is sourced in an origin beyond the law, an *archē* that is anarchic but not necessarily absurd. Such an origin would have no origin but makes all origination possible, would have no beginning but from it might flow all definite beginnings.

The limit to determinate intelligibility looks like a defect *if* we demand that God's intelligibility be absolutely continuous with the determinate intelligibilities of the finite between. If the above considerations have truth, it looks as if that continuity will not do. Whiteheadians insist that God cannot be an exception to the system of metaphysical principles. But if God is God and nothing but God is God, we are dealing with the *absolute exception*. To insist on metaphysical homogeneity to uphold integral intelligibility would have something unintelligible, if not obtuse about it. If it is God they are talking about, we do not know what they are talking about. For if it is God they are talking about, then they are not talking about God.[6]

Does this mean that the divine uniqueness necessitates a discontinuity so extreme that *any approach* to the otherness of transcendence is undermined? There can be an insistence on an extreme difference that makes difference impossible, and any affirmation of difference, and so such extreme difference can collapse into sameness. (One worries about this with Kierkegaard and Levinas.) But in the between there are many reminders of the insufficiency of equating intelligibility with determinacies. Were we rigid about that equation, we could not make sense of many things, especially the most important

6 See Robert Neville's ambitious *God as Creator* (Albany: SUNY Press, 1992) 2nd edn., which moves through and beyond the Whiteheadean inspiration. God is nothing until God creates, for Neville. There is an indeterminacy before creation which creation brings to determination. In my view of creation as agapeic origination there is an overdeterminacy to God that is not made determinate by creation, but that is surplus in itself. The between and its porosity is given, but there is something prior to this; one cannot speak even of the porosity as only a kind of indetermination, since as a resource making a way (*poros*) it too requires superplus terms. See the difference of Gregory of Nyssa and Augustine. Gregory reads *creatio ex nihilo* as *creation ex Deus*: from God's *own* nothingness, hence as a kind of "emanation." For Augustine (*Confessions*, 13, 33) *creation ex nihilo* is "*a te, non de te facta sunt.*" But see Part IV below on God and nothing. Kenneth Schmitz has a fine book, *The Gift: Creation* (Milwaukee: Marquette University Press, 1982).

things of life – like love or the favor of creativity itself. There are creative acts or lives that show the work of a certain inexhaustible surplus – surplus to determinate intelligibility, *surds full of significance*, so to say.

There is something surd about the upsurge of this energy of creation in us. It comes unbidden. We can prepare, make ourselves ready, but it comes as if out of nothing, comes as a godsend. Like the caressing breeze of warmer days, it softens the soul and makes it yearn, as if bathed in an unearthly light, now, right now. Time is graced. Sometimes we receive in suffering, but there is no generalization: it is idiotic.[7] The limit of determinate intelligibility is the frontier of mystery. Why not call this the edge of the hyperintelligible, not the unintelligible? You object I am baptizing a mystery, not solving one. But this matter is not a *problem* to be solved. Sometimes to give or receive a name may open entrance into a community of redemption, where to be redeemed asks consent to mystery.

CREATION BEYOND HOLISM

As a sacred story of divine origins, religious myth offers an elemental ontological orientation in the between, bounding it by the primal whence from where we come, and the ultimate whither whereto we go. Philosophers displace this mythic concern from divine origins to *logos,* seeking the sources of intelligibility, and indeed of the very arising of the happening of being. Beings as coming to be, and coming to be such as to be intelligible to mind – these have driven them to inquire about origin and its nature. This is true whether they be dubbed religious or non-religious. This is the most natural thing in the world, be we philosophers or not. It is not insinuated by some fatality of "ontotheology." The spontaneous opening of mind is to a world that shows itself as coming to be there. We are naturally struck into astonishment before this being there at all, and wonder about its source.

It is something astonishing that we have such hyperbolic thoughts at all. They are *disproportionate* to our finitude as things in nature. Nothing in nature, in us, in other things, seems proportionate to such hyperbolic thought. From the standpoint of finite things in nature, and ourselves as such things, there is something excessive here and out of place. Are we anomalous surds? Freaks of nature? Or are there sources other to ourselves and nature. And if *only* in ourselves, do we not then become the freak, the anomaly? Do we not become monstrous? But then we cannot even make sense of that monstrousness: we are not absurd, we are the absurd. Without God do we become either flat-souled or monsters – or both?

Beings arise, and arise dynamically. Do they carry signs of their origin in their arising? If no, we stop before their surd fact. Why then the anomalous wonder that overreaches the surd fact? We do not stop. Is this wonder more than our overreaching into nothing, or some sign of the origin coming forward in this arising? If the latter, what arises is not the origin of arising but the happening that has come to be in arising; hence the origin, in coming forward, also seems to retreat into its own reserve, as it intimates itself in the signs of things. Things are there – robust presences, though also frail and evanescent. They are poised between appearance and dis-appearance. Just that double tenseness suggests the show of the source of arising, intimates what does not exhaust itself in the coming forward of things. Things there shimmer with an elusive intimation of the source of arising.

As we can learn from the work of great artists, this double tenseness, this intensive ambiguity may be shown, intimating an inexhaustibility that cannot be shown directly or univocally. That the origin cannot be shown directly may be essential to its truth, and have nothing to do with a failure on our part to think it, or a failure on its part to be

---

[7] The positive overdeterminacy of creativity is a source of a defined order and determinate intelligibility without being a mere irrational absurd; as the genius gives the rule to art, without being a rule, and not by rule, but by favor of another origin, be it nature or God.

what it is. If it is origin, then we who are not origin but originated are always other than the origin in such wise that we can only approach it indirectly. Every issue of the origin can only relate to it *via* its own difference from the origin. Just that *via*, as ambiguous, allows different approaches, including the dualistic one, or alternatively a variety of communicative interplays between origin and originated finitude.

If it is the most natural thing to think of origin, it is also the most difficult, for naturally we are more at home with the determinate beings that have arisen. In the indirection of the *via*, we are always tempted to think more in terms of *the arisen* than of *the arising*, of the originated not of origin. The determinate beings in the between can facilitate but also occlude our approach to the origin beyond determinate beings and our determination. Thus, many myths of origin speak in relatively familiar metaphors, taken from significant happenings in the between: for example, the relation of offspring to mother or father; the splitting of a primordial egg; the image of craftsman or demiurge. Notions like imposing form on chaos seems more abstract than the splitting of the primordial egg, or the marriage of heaven and earth. Monotheism suggests considerations even *more other* to our familiar being in the between. With the notion of one absolute source, a source that originates *ex nihilo*, it is hard to get one's bearings, since our thinking is *after* the origin, in the middle of determinate beings that always already have arisen or come to be.

If there is one absolute source, then it might originate from itself, or from another, or from nothing. If from *itself*, creation is self-creation. If from *another*, this other must be derived from the one source if it is absolute, and then creation from another is first a self-creation before it is the creation of another as other; or one might give up the one source and posit another in quasi-Gnostic fashion. If from *nothing*, then creation is not simply self-creation but *the arising of another as other*, but in such a fashion that is not reducible to mediated self-creation, and that may also give rise to doublings, though not necessarily the Gnostic alienation of two ultimates. If there is one absolute source, our major choice seems to be between holistic self-creation and creation from nothing – that is, if we are intent on affirming the One as absolute source.

Monotheistic traditions clearly are intent on that affirmation. They raise the stakes in reflecting on God, given that these ideas are both notoriously intractable and impossible to side-step. Is to ask about such a One to forget about the many? Quite to the contrary, the stakes are raised here too. Such a One must do justice to the robust plurality within the world. Pan(en)theism offers us an holistic God in response to perceived difficulties with a creator God (certainly demiurgic divinity), a supposed extrinsic relation of world and God, for instance. The opposite might also be claimed: questions posed by the holistic God lead us towards renewed reflection on creation (and not any deistic or demiurgic divinity).

Consider how this might follow from an extreme emphasis on, or hyperbolic absolutizing of, the One: the One seems to be all in all; the eternal Ideas are not outside the One, but within it as its Wisdom, or *logos*; nor is there any ultimate other to stand against it – not matter as in demiurgic making nor an evil principle as in Gnosticism nor necessity as the ultimate unchangeability that God must respect or persuade, or perhaps be identified with, as in some pantheisms. Such would be a radical monotheism. The peculiarity here is also the radical granting of *the finite many*. There follows the great question of how such an absolute One gives rise to finite manyness without its own hyperbolic absoluteness being infringed? How accommodate this One – more extreme than the One of holism – and the many with a difference more finitely robust? More radical notions of origin and nothing are needed to account for a creation that lets a space of radical difference come to be without obviating God's absoluteness, the ontological robustness of finitude, as well as the community between God and creation.

The Hegelian view of the dialectical self-becoming of origin, just in its coherence, provides a foil to think this other origin more deeply. This is the question we ask: If the origin is, as Hegel seems to think, merely an indeterminacy, and must produce its other which is itself as other, and do so in order to be itself, in what sense is it itself at all in the first place? And if it is not itself at all in the first place, how then can it be an origin of what is other to itself, much less itself? *An origin that has to become itself to be itself must first be itself in order to become itself; else it is nothing, and there is no self-becoming.* And this is to say nothing about the "creation" of what is other to itself.[8] How must it *already be itself*, in order to further effect itself and what is other to itself?

In a word, is there not an origin prior to the dialectical beginning? Hence beyond any dialectical completion? And beyond holistic immanence, in the first and last instance? Does dialectic go deep enough into this already effective energy of being, that must be presupposed for something like a dialectical self-becoming to be effected at all in the first place? Is there an origin beyond the Hegelian whole that circles around itself in its own dialectical self-becoming? And is the world of plurality as the other of this origin to be equated with the Hegelian One as dialectically self-othered? Given that the between we inhabit is not a closed whole, are we not pointed beyond every immanent whole? For such wholes show themselves as open, in that their self-becoming presupposes a more primal coming to be, without which their becoming would not be at all.

It is worth stressing that "creator" focuses, at least initially, less on the whole, as does the pan(en)theistic view, as on perplexity about origin. If pan(en)theistic holism stems from the dynamism of becoming towards a perfecting consummation, the hyperbolic thought of creation stems from the enigma of the arising of becoming itself, in the first place. The former relates to a teleology of becoming, the latter to an archeology of coming to be, more ontological primal than becoming. The need of the latter is evident in the former, in connection with the question of what makes possible the movement from beginning to end that seems to constitute the process of the whole. "Creator" addresses the mystery of *archē* that gives rise to the whole of finite process itself.

As we shall see, there are equivocities in defining that *archē* in either affirmative or negative terms, or perhaps in both, or perhaps with a mixture of each, with diffidence about the adequacy of each and all. Depending on our archeology of arising into being, or primal coming to be, we will have a significantly different teleology of finite becoming. Indeed, we may have to make a sharp distinction between God's immanent "self-becoming" and the becoming process of the finite between.

CREATION, COMING TO BE AND BECOMING

Creation concerns the kind of beings we find in the between, in so far as they show themselves as *coming to be*. The most insistent showing of coming to be is intimated in the *becoming* of such beings, but it is very important to distinguish "coming to be" and "becoming." The becoming in the between is important, not because traditionally becoming was counterposed with being, as beyond all becoming, but because of the ontological dynamic of things. To think of origin by means of an escape from becoming risks depriving origin of that dynamic openness necessary for an origin to be an origin at all. Rather, the ontological dynamic shifts our attention to an *originative* source of dynamic being, an origin dynamic in a surplus sense to what is given in the between. The finitely dynamic does not arise from the static but from a more primordial *energeia*.

Becoming puts us in mind of coming to be, but coming to be is not identical with becoming. For in becoming, one becomes a *determinate something*, out of a prior condition of determinate being and towards a further more realized or differently realized determination of one's being. Coming to be, by contrast, is prior to becoming this or that; for

---

[8] Scotus Eriugena: "We ought not to understand God and the creature as two things distinct from one another, but as one and the same. For both the creature, by subsisting, is in God; and God, by manifesting Himself in a marvelous and ineffable manner creates Himself in the creature, the invisible making itself visible . . . the infinite finite and the uncircumscribed circumscribed and the supratemporal temporal." *Periphyseon* (*The Division of Nature*), Book III, 678c–d, 305. As I indicated in the previous chapter (note 7), Plotinus has interesting things to say about *Nous* beyond demiurgic making.

one must be, and have come to be, before one can become such and such. Becoming itself suggests something more primordial about coming to be. Creation is connected with this more primordial coming to be – a coming to be that makes finite becoming itself possible but that is not itself a finite becoming. In every finite being that becomes, which is all beings, there is intimated this prior coming to be which is not a finite becoming: "that is it at all" is here in question, and that it has come to be this at all.

The point is not a dualistic opposition that claims being is prior or antithetical to becoming. There is a "coming to be," an origination of the "that it is at all," presupposed in every being that becomes this or that. This prior coming to be is like becoming in its dynamic character, and yet it is other to becoming in that it exceeds finite determination or self-determination. Nor is it the finite realization of an initially unrealized potency. For the creative possibility of unrealized potency is also "power to be" that has come to be, and in a way prior to determinate becoming.[9] Coming to be is hyperbolic happening. What is suggested is an overdetermined source of origination out of which coming to be unfolds. To speak of "creator" is a way of putting us in mind of this other source that is not a finite determinate source of beginning or becoming, for that would be to make determinate what exceeds determination. It is extremely difficult to think in this *huper* dimension on the other side of determinate beings. Our thinking is more convenient with finite things – convenient with this, that, and the other in becoming, less convenient even with the *becoming* of this, that, or the other, and even less again with the more primordial *coming to be* in becoming.

We might consider this inconvenience from the other side, namely, *passing out of being*, coming to be no longer. (This inconvenience can be the source of much sour thinking about finite becoming.) In finite becoming these two sides are wedded, mostly wedded uneasily. Some philosophers, Eleatics, will consider it a bad marriage and seek divorce in favor of the side of being. Others, say Nietzscheans, will declare a bad marriage from the other side, and place the children of time totally in the custody of innocent becoming. Either divorce is untrue to the tense doubleness of finite being. That beings in becoming also pass out is very important, in defining not only the limits of finite being but also the character of the coming to be. For the coming to be is shadowed by non-being, which finite entities live in their own mortality. This passing out of being can startle us into mindfulness of the source of creation, as much as can the surge into being.

Some traditional thinkers have so stressed the metaphysical jolt of mortality that they look primarily like nihilators of being in the between. This is a perennial temptation, but it too loses the doubleness of finite becoming. I think the point is not to avoid becoming as passing out but to ask: What must the origin be like given the doubleness, both the arising and the transience, in all the passing? Is the origin beyond both arising and transience not beyond sans the *energeia* of being as manifest by finite being but beyond as giving us ontological orientation relative to the happening of nothing and being in the between, and, again, not beyond as causally linking a plurality of determinate forms of being but as showing how the determinate in its twofold character is the issue of a source itself not defined thus by that twofoldness?

Say this, more humanly: the gift of life puts us in mind of absolute life; the jolt of mortality puts us in mind of nothingness, but also jolts us back differently to life with refreshed appreciation, refreshed both in astonishment and perplexity. The jolt puts us on edge on a tightrope, one side nothing, the other side exceeding life. And as we now thread the edge of the "that it is at all," we prize newly the excess of life we also lived before mindfulness, and which is the absolute sweetness of simply being at all. We are roused to posthumous mindfulness of the strange source of the "that it is at all" – double because wedded to its own possible not being at all. This strange source some religious people call "creator."

---

[9] BB, pp. 335–9 on the possibility of possibility and creative possibilizing.

CREATION AND NOTHING

What of the rationalist dismissal of creation: *ex nihilo nihil fit*? There is a family connection with the holist for whom outside of the whole there is nothing; being comes from being, comes to be from being as already always in being. True, holistic Hegel knew the need for negation *within* the whole, short of a return to block Eleaticism. The following considerations are important.

What must the origin be like for it to give rise to an ontological milieu marked by the pluralism such as we find in our world? Such a pluralistic milieu shows negation, in that for manyness to be many there must be a difference of one from the other, and the one and the other must *not* be the same. The togetherness of the many also is the difference of the many, and this difference is as much defined by the fact that each is what the other is *not*, as by what each is, as also by the togetherness of each, just in their *not* being each other. We must look at creation relative to these "nots."

The doubleness noted above does not say creation *ex nihilo* as if it were the *nihil* that were giving rise to being; rather, it names the origin as giving a coming to be out of nothing; there is being, in a superlative sense, at work in relation to nothing. It is not *ex nihilo nihil fit*; but *ex nihilo* the origin brings finite being to be, and the origin is not just the *nihil* (apart from the fact that the origin is no thing, and in that other sense, nothing). If creation *ex nihilo* is correlated with the doubleness of finite being in the between as arising into being and subsiding into nothing, the nothing is not just at the end but is ingredient in the kind of dynamic being the finite is. What more can we say?

The finite being exhibits a kind of nothing; it is a relative non-being, in so far as it is; and this relative non-being is also the determination through negation that shapes the finite entity in the differential network of relations that we find in the intermedium of immanent being. The holistic view will see nothingness primarily in terms of this relative non-being, and so situate it *within the whole*, and perhaps make it ingredient in the dynamic differentiation of finite being in their self-becoming. Is this relative non-being the end of the matter? Is there a more primordial sense of non-being? Just as there is a coming to be that is not the same as a becoming, is there not a non-being that is not just relative non-being?

We do not quite get to this when we ask: What makes A not to be B? Negation here is ingredient in a process of determination, given already the being of A and not A. Given already that being, that is, given the primordial coming to be, here is a dynamic becoming which is *taken as granted*. We get closer with this question: What makes A to be at all, what is its "that it is at all," given that it might *not have been at all*? For "that it is, given that it might not have been at all" is *not a determination of another given being*. Nor is it answered for in terms of what it is, which is defined, in part, through negative determination in relation to an other. You might object: "that it is at all" – that is eternal. But then why the fact that the "that it is at all" does not exhibit the necessity traditionally associated with eternity: it is so and so and could not be otherwise? The "that it is" is qualified by "that it might not be at all." It is so, but it might not be so, or have been so, might not have been at all.

This is its *contingency as happening*. And its contingency is not just relative to other finite beings but inherent in the very being there of this being, indeed of all thises, of *all finite happening*. It is but it might not be; it might be otherwise, and it will not be, when its mortal term expires. And not just nothing at the conclusion of its mortal span: nothing at the beginning, middle, and end. That it might not be at all – nothing present at its origin. That it might now be other than it is – nothing present in its between. That it will not be – nothing present at its end. There is a nothingness that enters the "that it is at all," and this is not a relative nothing marking a finite process of determinate becoming, for the whole of the process is streaked with this nothingness. And likewise, the process of the whole,

This sense of nothing is a hyperbolic thought, almost always overlooked, just as we overlook the astonishing gift of the "that it is at all." Both are together, and often the exposure to one opens up the other. I am exposed to a death, and suddenly the astonishing "onceness" and preciousness of life is made manifest. Or one enjoys the preciousness of life and there is a strange sadness in this pure joy, since the death of the creature is also intimated in the joy. Joy makes one as aware of nothing, as of the agape of being.

If this nothingness is constitutive of finite being as such, the archaic perplexity comes back: Why something rather than nothing – why being at all? This question is frequently dismissed because it refers to nothing in particular. Sometimes it is misinterpreted to refer to a determinate beginning like the big bang or like the creator god construed as a determinate fabricator. This is not the archaic perplexity at all but a definite curiosity about the finite process of becoming; it neither regards the more primordial coming to be nor the nothing prior to determinate negation. There is an indeterminacy about the perplexity, but this is no mere indefiniteness; it is the whole point, for it orients us to a sense of "the whole," but now not the whole interpreted in holistic terms. The point here is that *our sense of the whole seems to point beyond the whole*. For the coming to be and the passing out of being *are not events within the whole*, but the originary issuing of the happening-to-be between as the finite whole.

The question "Why being rather than nothing?" orients us towards a way of understanding God other than the holistic way. What is the relation of the finite whole to being? and to nothing? If the finite whole is the between, it is not a closed but an open whole. Onto what does it open? Onto the origin? But should we not ask: What opens the wholeness of the between? Yes. For it is not only that the finite whole opens to the origin but that the origin opens up the finite whole not as the self-externalization of the origin, but as given a wholeness that is not that of the origin. And this "not" of otherness is the medium of creative possibility in which the finite between comes to be. The "not" names an origin that is transcendent, other than the creation, but for all that most intimately involved with what it brings to be.

If finite being exhibits its constitutive nothingness, what is the relation of its being to nothingness? To all appearance, finite being is not absolutely self-supporting. You might say that this or that finite being is not self-supporting, but is supported, nevertheless, in the network of relations binding finite beings into the whole; it is the whole that alone is self-supporting. The question remains: If *that whole* exhibits also the nothingness, does not its self-supporting show itself to be only relative, and not absolute? Does it not refer to something other than itself? No finite whole is absolutely self-supporting as a contingent happening. It evidences its dependency on a source or sources of being other than itself, without which it would be nothing. Even if we can say nothing much about that origin, nevertheless the ontological dependency does raise issues that point beyond complete determination and immanent holism. The notion of God as creator gives some articulation to this ontological dependency of finite being as a whole, even as it also tries to name something of the originative being of God beyond immanent holism, originative in a radical unique way,[10] since it is not the determinate genesis we find within the between, but the primordial arising into being of the determinate between itself. As the origin is unique, so the origination is unique to it. Hence, perhaps, the traditional view of God's action as absolutely unique. Creating is a name for that absolutely unique originating.

CREATION AND AGAPEIC ORIGINATION: DUALISM AND THE "NOT"

If we accept some sense of mystery, and say God is transcendent always, always other, can we avoid an unbridgeable *dualism* of the between and the beyond, and the equivocity

---

[10] Aquinas: God's essence is existence, to be. *Deus non est in genere, Summa Contra Gentiles*, I, 25. Again we must not forget the *uniqueness of God* and God's action, or the insufficiency of any metaphor from creation, nor yet lack a diffidence about any monism of explanation which would white out the uniqueness.

of a sundering into difference beyond mediation? (A question for Levinas?) If the "not" of nothing defines an absolute difference between God and world does not this undermine divine mystery, in the long run?

I mean, we affirm one God, but absolutely other to the world, for the two are *not* each other, ever. Then the world is dedivinized; nothing in the world is God; without God, world is nothing, and has nothing to do with God. First consequence: war on polytheism, earthly traces of the divine are extirpated. Second consequence: earth appears as the godless place of our mastery: we image in the between the One outside who rules with absolute dominion. Third consequence: as the godless earth earns less respect, we are tempted to be its tyrants. Fourth consequence: creation is made our means, mere matter for exploitation; in itself nothing good, we impose our value on it. We are God's gift to the world, the world worthless until we give ourselves, but our gift is equivocal, mixing care with pillage. We become agents of the "not" – the little god of a thisworldly dualism – the otherworldly dualism turned upside down – dominating the "over againstness" of things.

Is it fair to the hyperbolic thought of creation to accuse it of harboring such potential for (ecological) devastation? Equivocities in some formulations might suggest this possibility, but this is a warped parody of its deeper power. Creation need not generate oppositional dualism but a different sense of plurality, a communicative enabling of others as others. That the world is not God need not mean the "not" yields overwhelming negation. In creation as *agapeic origination* the "not" is defined in agapeic transcending, for it allows an arising of the other that is there for itself: origin is not the creation, but creation is not at all without the origin. Nor is world void of traces of the divine, as a work is not without signs of its originator or speech without some signature of its speaker. Transcendence is not nugatory, if the limit is with respect to the enigma of agapeic origination out of which the "It is good" is addressed to creation.

Thus, too, for us to be endowed with the earth's "stewardship" is not to be the bearer of dictatorial power. Stewardship is the call to agapeic care for creation as other. It is not a matter of bettering creation in a project of besting God. Any use of creation knows gift to be more primordial than use, as is also the gratitude that answers generosity. Creation is not a mere re-source to be treated in terms of its serviceable disposability (*EB*, Chapter 14) – serviceable as serving only our use; disposable when it has served its use and been used up. There is an agapeic service beyond servility and sovereignty. This is to be entrusted with an endowment that asks a husbanding with reverence. The God of jealous power breeds, or is bred by, humans, themselves wielders of jealous power. The image of *nonpossessive dispensation* is more appropriate to agapeic origination. This is just the opposite of what is divinized in the suggestion of the absolutely possessive God (rather than the blessing "It is good" such a God might gloat "I own it, it is mine"). Creation as agapeic origination transcends possession, even self-possession. Its richness is its own willing poverty, in willing to be nothing, that the genuinely other may be endowed as something and as good.

CREATION, HYPER-TRANSCENDENCE AND DIVINE INTIMACY

Is all this too metaphysically abstract? What of more familiar emphases? For many religious people creation is associated with *Genesis*, but there we find no formula of creation from nothing. Nevertheless, the world is not God's self-extension. World is other, and good as other. God beholds that "It is good." To behold requires "standing back." This is a seeing that says "yes." The divine song of esteem is not a song of self, or even a self-congratulation on work well done. The work is well done, but it is the work that is good, deemed and esteemed so by the creator.

If the world is not God's self-doubling, God is not touched by the nothingness ontologically constitutive of the finite being. The origin is in excess of, over and above the most extreme negation, *huper* the absolute nothing. The creative act issues from the *nec plus ultra* of generously affirmative power. One might say: This power to give being from nothing is that greater than which none can be thought. Creation is not from something, hence it is not demiurgic making, limited by being as already given to be. Creating is sheer giving to be. It is heterogeneous to any human making which produces from something already existing. The power to create in this unique instance is absolute.

Why create at all? Because it is good. Creation is not arbitrary fiat, modeled on the capricious finger snap of some oriental despot. The metaphor of originative speaking is suggestive. God says "Let there be . . . and there was . . ." Creation is an original speaking letting be. Speaking brings the word to existence. The word, speaking, lets being be. A word is not a roar. The roar would be more like the diktat of the despotic divinity. The word, spoken originatively, is the expression of communicative being. The originating word issues from the goodness of generosity. The word is the creative expression of being as agapeic and as communicative transcending. Word brings a world to be, word communicates a world, lets it issue into a space of sharing with others. Wording the between (*logos* of the *metaxu*): not thought thinking itself, not even thought thinking its other, but thought singing the other (see *PO*, Chapter 6). Wording the between: a sung world – a song not only sung, but a song giving rise to new singers. The originative word would be the primordial "yes" that gives coming to be, a word that is also a blessing with being. We know this elementally in our own being given to be, lived as an affirmation of being that first lives us before we live it. The agapeic "yes" not only blesses with being, it blesses being: It is good to be.

If we say God's creating is not constrained by any principle of external limitation – be it matter, *Moira*, chaos, an evil god, *Anankē* – we aim to preserve God's *absoluteness*. If we say that this creation is continuing, we want to insist on God's ongoing *relativity* to the world. Creation names a tense doubleness in affirming *both* absoluteness and relatedness. How is this possible? It turns on the *absolved relativity* communicated by the origin as agapeic. This turns on the connection of absoluteness and the good, and this latter not simply at the end, but in the origin and the between. Agapeic origination is the communication of the good of being in the coming to be of beings. The origin as unconstrained creator is absolute in itself; as absolute good, it is communicative transcendence; as agapeic, it brings the world to being as other, and other as good for itself. Continuing creation points both to absoluteness and providential relatedness: the God of the origin is the God of the becoming of the between. The becoming of the between – reconfigured by some as "history," though it is more than that – is the interim between nothing and eternity, the interim we call time.

The metaxological double of absoluteness and relatedness suggests God as both radically *intimate* to beings and as *hyper-transcendent*. Intimate as radical immanent origin of being's coming to be; hyper-transcendent as beyond all finitized becoming. This hyper-transcendence suggests an *asymmetrical* relation of God and world: world is God dependent; God is not world dependent. Is this asymmetry a dependence which diminishes the world? Not necessarily. In one light, one might say the holistic view diminishes the world more as a part of the divine. Here, given creation is not a part, but as apart, it is its own whole. It is not the absolute; it is a finite whole.

This hyper-transcendence is connected with divine freedom. Nothing constrains the communication of true goodness – its free release is its free giving. It is also connected with divine power, but we have to be careful of the notion of external compulsion that often strikes us first when we reflect on power. Agapeic reserve will not quickly cross our minds as power. External compulsion is related to univocal determination of one thing by another: I order, you obey, and there is an incontrovertible line of command and effect from source to action. Some defenders of a transcendent creator love such power – unequivocal dominion of being. But there is no univocal line with agapeic origination: freedom is given in the between as a space of porosity, between origin and all creation.

There is no ultimate univocalization of that porosity. Unequivocal dominion of a unilateral sort is not the point, in that the gift of free being is richer in promise, though more dangerous, than univocal determination.

If we are fixed on the magisterial God of despotic power, or the erotic sovereign who masters all he surveys, the agapeic God can look impotent, just because it lets be, lets freedom be. Hyper-transcendence is releasing power, hence some will see no power here at all. That is not the fault or default of agapeic reserve. This reserve makes way, makes a way to allow the power of freedom of what is other to come into its own. Agapeic power is absolving power, releasing others beyond itself, without insistence on the return of the power of the others to itself. It does not bind but unbinds. And it binds by unbinding, in that the deeper bond of agapeic togetherness and service is only thus allowed. Absolute absolving power is agapeic as power that gives the power to give. Only if absolute power is an absolving agape, is the absoluteness of the divine together with the relativity of the finite.

CONTINUING CREATION, AGAPEIC SELF-RESERVING

Does this hyper-transcendence reintroduce dualism? If creation is other to God, does not creation limit God, hence undercut divine absoluteness? Alternatively, if creation is continuing, how is God transcendent? How meet the double requirement: God's absoluteness in self and relatedness to what is other?

Dialectical considerations of limit enter here. The dualistic way of opposing transcendence inevitably leads to *aporiai* that undercut its best intention of posing transcendence. One could still argue that manifested transcendence is no bar to transcendence preserving its otherness. The dualistic way implies that we climb up to heaven and we pull up the ladder, but then there is no way down, we have so fixed transcendence as utterly beyond. But what is a transcendence if it does not transcend – verb and not thing? Transcending is just its being, its being beyond, not just finite beings, but being beyond itself, and hence in relativity to finite beings, just in its transcending. To pit transcendence as transcending in opposition to relatedness is to misunderstand the divine as being communicative of itself, communicative of being to the finite other. Everything points to an affirmative giving of otherness as itself affirmative, and not as the negative barrier separating two terms of a dualistic opposition.

What of the possibility of *God's self-limitation*? I would prefer to speak of *divine reserve or self-reserving*. "Limit" has too much connotation of spatialized determinacy, while "reserve" retains something of the secret of the overdeterminate. The giving of creation is a self-reserving relation in that sense. There is an original "abdication" of unilateral power. This is an agapeic abdication: absoluteness does not disappear in its reserve, for this abdication shows just the absoluteness of the agape of the giver. Absoluteness as self-reserving becomes an absolution, a letting go and free, an unconstrained release. Self-reserving allows a real relation to be, a relating of bringing to be, of empowering to be, in that what is given to be is empowered to be itself as other and free. The agapeic conception of origin, thus, does make possible the preservation of the double requirement. God is not reducible to the creation, while also being in communicative involvement with creation. If it were not the first, it could not be the second. And were it not the second, God's transcendence would not be transcending.

Does this require some correction to the classical view of creation in which the absence of a real relation of God to world is claimed? This is partly the legacy of modeling absoluteness on enclosed self-sufficiency – the circle at home with itself in eternal *autarkia*. In Aquinas, for instance, creation is an asymmetrical relation: world is effected by God, but God is not affected by world; it is a one-way communication; world contributes nothing to the being of God. If there is this asymmetry, how then a real relation of God and world? Yes, one sees the relation as one-way radical ontological dependence of the creation, but what of relation as a community *between* God and world, a between that to be between must be more than one-way? Is the one-way relation connected to a dualism that forces an "either/or,"or is a "both/and" possible: God both absolute and related?

Dialectic affirms a "both/and," but tends to compromise God's transcendence in favor of the inclusive whole's self-mediation through its own other. It seems to allow a two-way interplay, but the terms in mutual interplay tend to become moments in the inclusive self-determination of the One. We might have the erotic absolute at home with itself, instead of the quiescent substance that is unaffected by what is other, but the asymmetry of hyper-transcendence is speculatively whited out.

Metaxology allows two-way interplay but acknowledges asymmetries in that interplay, hence avoids a "both/and" which puts the two terms on a par as necessary moments of one inclusive whole. God and world are two but not a dualistic dyad, and not moments of the One at home with itself. There is a community between them, and the basis of that community is the agapeic giving of the divine, but that community allows the granting of what the creature gives to the between. The divine agapeic giving is superior, in the sense that nothing finite is on a par with it, but as superior it is not the dominating one. Agapeic communication takes the ultimate One beyond substantial self-enclosure. Agapeic reserving allows community as a porous between, in relation to which divine power seems as nothing, though it has freely reserved itself to make way for the finite other to be itself as free.

What is it to "make way"? It is a surprising creativity that is not actively subordinating of anything. The Unequal does not flatten itself but reserves itself, placing itself on the footing of the creature, equalizes itself for the sake of the other. This is the divine patience or *(com)passio*: entry into all that the finite undergoes, including poverty, abjection, despair, and death. For love of finite life, the agapeic God harrows even hell. This is the opposite of the self-enclosed transcendence that the dualistic way proposes. The porous between is nothing static, but the ongoing milieu of divine absolving: absoluteness in relativity, relativity in absoluteness.

Clearly also, an agapeic self-reserving God is not deistic, like the clock-maker who makes the clock and then stands off and lets the clock tick on according to its mechanism. As we saw, this means an extrinsic relation to world which itself lacks organic self-development. Not only is holistic inter-involvement slighted, so is any intimacy of communication between origin and creation. Dialectical holism is beyond this deistic determination of God by univocal *mathēsis*, stressing immanent self-becoming and self-determining. Metaxologically there is more again: divine self-reserving is not the same as divine self-determining; it is beyond this, as making way for the creature's otherness it has brought to be. Agapeic self-limitation is a self-reserving letting be of a between wherein freedom of the other is possibilized, and hence community between beings both self-mediating and transcending of self-mediation. Creation avoids the false closure in immanence tempting the holistic model while surpassing the merely external transcendence of deism.

CREATION AND ARBITRARY (WILL TO) POWER

The suspicion that God's transcendence implies arbitrariness of divine power persists, nurtured by biblical stories such as the awful command to Abraham to sacrifice Isaac, the Voice from the whirlwind silencing Job. How distinguish the divine from irrational will and avoid making creation just the absurd surd that atheists like Sartre have affirmed finite contingency to be and where the master of the world exchanges place with the slave master.

A dualistic orientation can yield this view, a metaxological approach need not. Certain forms of religious dualism do tend towards tyrannical divinities. Certain dualisms, we saw, can darken our attunement with creation, fostering a pessimism of corrupt nature overseen by a voluntaristic God that expresses and reinforces the radical precariousness of worldly being. The divinely arbitrary God produces an arbitrary deconsecrated world; produces its human image in a will to power, basing itself on the arbitrary will at the base of all being. What does it matter if it is this or that, thus or otherwise, so long as I will it so? All the better that I will it strongly and with sovereign say-so, instead of feebly and with the ontological blahs. Tyrannical say so-ing Gods both reflect and produce tyrannical say so-ing humans.

What we have here is a degeneration of the erotic absolute. The agapeic God is not to be defined in terms of such arbitrary will, nor indeed can richer versions of the erotic absolute. When the erotic absolute coexists with an accentuated feeling of ontological lack and a clouding over of the "It is good," eros itself tends to change from *eros ouranios* to *eros turranos*, thence into will to power. We need to be cautious of speaking of "will" in God, modeled anthropomorphically on a determinate agent determining between determined options. This is closer to the demiurgic model than the creator view. If we are to speak of "willing," we must think of a more primordial "willing" than just a matter of determinate will that wills this or that. Our willing wills a determinate realization of a possibility, or a self-determination of one's own possibility. Divine "willing" as creating cannot be thus determinated or self-determined. We must think agapeic willing, as opposed to a determinate free will, or self-determining willing, or will to power. Determinate will in us, as well as self-determining will, are more proximately formations of the endeavor to be, the *conatus essendi* in us, but more primordial than this is the *passio essendi*, and the porosity of being. It is relative to the latter that a more agapeic sense of willing needs to be thought: an overdeterminate willing(ness) as much patient as active, as much letting be as intimately involved, as much self-reserving as self-communicating.

If the origin is beyond essence and determination, this does seem to ally its being with will, in so far as the movement of willing is itself not reducible to a determination or an essence: it is an open determining, an initiating determining that opens. Arbitrary will cannot be the way to talk of this superessential determining; arbitrary will is already in the space of determinations between which a choice is made. If there is a meaning to divine "willing" it is beyond this determination. It must also be a willing more than self-determining, since the willing of the good of the created other is the issue of its initiative. Beyond determinate will, beyond self-determining will, beyond will to power there is an overdetermined willing(ness): this is wise willing, the good willing. This exceeding willing(ness) is because its willing *is* goodness. There is no disjunction of this willing and the good being good. Good willing, highest willing is, wise will: the integral intimacy of being truthful and being good.

CREATION, HYPERBOLIC EVIL AND TRUST

What again of the torment of *evil*? Evil too shows a monstrous idiocy that demands hyperbolic thought beyond the whole. Gnosticism saw the problem of evil as the problem of the creator God: the tyrannical God of jealous power. Classical monotheism's manner of putting the problem is continuous with the question of "wise willing" – *disjunction* seems to eventuate if we make a *conjunct* of God's goodness and power. If God is all good, he would will all to be good – but evil exists, hence he is less than all powerful. If he is all powerful, he could will all good; again, evil exists and hence he is less than all good.

If the creator's power extends to all, is the creator not responsible for evil? Creative power becomes coercive determination, and evil itself is one form of that coercive determination. And yet one of the deepest sources of holding God as creator is a *hyperbolic trust* that nothing but good can come from God. Even if God is agapeic, is he not complicit in evil by letting it be and enacting a divine self-limitation? Is this last different from a complicity that inculpates God: self-reserving is self-absenting, hence a benediction on malediction? Does not the goodness of the creator evaporate in the very effort to affirm the goodness? If absolute goodness lets evil be, absolute goodness seems not absolute goodness. For there are sins of omission as well as commission. Unlike Pontius Pilate washing his hands, being good sometimes means – getting one's hands dirty. To be and do good is to go among the evil. Is this what an agapeic God would have to do, give up the invulnerable self-congratulation of the beautiful soul?

Does the story of the Fall answer the enigma? It names it, it does not dispel it. It gives heed to disruption in the order of creation, in our will to be as a god, possessing knowledge of good and evil. We will to be master of being's equivocity, and in the process fall deeper into the equivocity. We become subject to it in the will to make it our subject. It is our will to elevation that produces our degradation. We do not throw ourselves down, rather we seek to be our own self-creating source of full transcendence, and the lack in our erotic will to be thus sovereign turns back into itself and becomes subject to its own void. This sovereignty makes void. Genuine sovereignty points to partnership with the divine other. It gives itself up in obedience to goodness.

Even if we make some sense of moral evil by attribution to our will, the issue is evil relative to creation, not just the human creature. Does the story of the Fall name the malignancy, the sometimes demonic energies unloosed, energies other to human will? There seems evil in excess of the moral evil we can impute to any human agent. Do we invoke a more than human agency (not quite as the Gnostics do, but not entirely unlike)? There seems no *a priori* reason to rule this out.

The lion devours the lamb, the spider the fly, the fox the hen. The cat plays coldly with the captive bird our human kindness would let go. There is something amoral in that play of life that is death: bored supremacy teasing the trembling bird with cruel illusions of being free, pinioning at the kill its flight in careless claws: love loving to disport with life, with death. Did the God creating the cat's cold eye decree too this disport?

In originating creatures, God communicates but reserves power to allow their power to be. God's power is *absolute* relative to the coming to be, but it is *cooperative* relative to the becoming of created beings. Since world is not God's self-doubling, for there to be creatures as other, God must let another be as other, and in that grant of freedom freely abdicate univocal determining power for cooperative communication. In the reserve of divine patience, the gift of freedom sometimes means allowing by doing nothing, sometimes secret rejoicing with the creature, sometimes anonymous coaxing, sometimes persuading silently. The reserve of the divine cannot be separated from the finesse: intimate companionship with the mortal creature, devotion to its good, courtesy to its singular integrity. God is esteem for the gift, honoring the promise that we are come to redeem.

The unconditioned activity of the divine is conditioned relative to the world as the creation of the unconditioned activity. The conditioned relation goes with the act of creation, and hence to act in oblivion of the gift given would be to rescind the creation as other. So long as the world continues to be thus conditioned, the relation is not rescinded. Its rescinding would be the end of the world. Till then freedom is open and the redemption of its promise possible.

The primordial origin is not abstract or indefinite, not indeterminate, but overdetermined as overfull. And so, regardless of what the world comes to be and affects God with respect to the conditioned relation, there is the prior fullness of eternal life, and nothing changes this. Yet this fullness relates to creation, and its intermediating work is to bring this to fullness also. It does not always succeed, and in this there is a loss of promise, perhaps failure beyond redemption, perhaps damnation. This does not deprive the primordial fullness of its fullness; the fullness is overfull just because it alone has the power to take into itself the most devastating of losses and destructions, and what happens then, we do not know. Only God as absolute can suggest to us that perhaps, perhaps, what is damned for us, I mean absolutely lost, is given reprieve or another chance. Who among us can say?

"Perhaps": the very word keeps open the chances of life. Despite the darkness undoing the light, a hyperbolic trust can come: trust in and through and beyond the equivocities of the between. Hyperbolic trust leaps in the void that faces us when all life's chances seem to close on us. Our passion comes again, and we are offered the chance to be porous. All determinate expectations come to an end, but there can be an expectancy beyond all expectation. This is offered in the abeyance and recessing of all our endeavors to be. Reserved in the porosity is the pure trust, the true "yes."

Now comes from beyond the whole something absolutely intimate: the gift of the hyperbolic willingness in us. God will be God come what may in the between. Because God is and will be God, what happens in the between has hope that it may come yet into its fullness. Only because God is and will be what God is can God will that the between be what it is and will be. In this generosity for the other, the generosity of the giver is not diminished if the gift is spurned or despoiled.

Chapter 13

God(s) Mystic: On the Idiocy of God

Gazing blankly at the
  blank sea
Empty of all things
Except the line of difference
So far out there
It is as if it were here
& near

There is nothing there
Between the looker and
  the line
Nothing
The emptiness porous
Between here and there
Between there and here

The horizon does not retreat
Shimmers as if nothing
Could endure to be there
On its pitiless boundary

The bob of a black something
& the head of a seal
Breaks the line
Churns the surface
With its far out silence

It is nothing
& it is there

Why then is the heart elated
At this elemental thing
& its entreaty carried up
To the lowering skies
That never recede?

There is nothing at all
Nothing to it at all

Why do I gaze blankly at the
  blank sea
Empty of all things
Expectant of all things
Standing here so long an age
As if my flesh were beyond
  all age
& coagulated with the dark
  rock
On which – in wave on wave –
It founders?

THE IDIOTICS OF THE MYSTIC GOD

The woo of the mystical

The pure trust, the true "yes" lies buried deep in the determinacies of finite life. It surfaces episodically through life, coming through and receding, on and off, visiting and gypsy, like a wayward love. One cannot just will it, though one must be willing. This is the willingness before will. But one can woo it. The devotion of the mystic, and the discipline, witness the courtship of this woo.

We misunderstand God's transcendence beyond the whole if we dualistically oppose it to divine immanence in the finite whole. The "*meta*" is not only "beyond, above," but also "in the midst." The friendship of the "beyond, above" with the "in the midst" is at issue in turning to God and mysticism. This is again an extraordinarily plurivocal matter. Not only is it difficult to pin mysticism down definitively with univocally fixed markers, it shows a fluid latitude of variability, depending on different traditions shaping its expression, Hindu, Jewish, Buddhist, Christian, Islamic, archaic religions. We come once more to the idiocy of the divine, the intimacy. At the beginning the Tao is said to be as an unborn baby, but as we move through the middle, in the end we are to become as the child again, and speak its sacred "yes," whether, say, with Jesus or Nietzsche we need not now say. We pass from idiocy to idiocy. At the beginning of our quest, idiocy is not dissolved but rather intensified towards the end, especially with respect to the absolute singularity of the God who is not the whole. Our passage through life takes firm form, but our passing makes fluid again the forms, and the abiding porosity prior to form and beyond form offers again its never closed off chance: chance of ultimate communication between us and the ultimate. Mysticism has to do with the chance of the divine woo.

The woo is furthered through meditative practices, contemplative prayer, the retraction of untoward attachments. Drugs, we know, can artificially induce a sense of intimacy with the porosity, (en)force a chemical patience, making the doors of perception seem purged. The body being bruised to pleasure the porosity, this is not the patience of the true "yes." The porosity too must be purged. Breathing with measure – this can help begin the emptying of mind of determinate contents. Sensory deprivation: closing the eyes, retracting into floating darkness – this awakens the idiotic prior to the aesthetic. Woo: we close our eyes on darkness when we kiss or are kissed. (Mystic comes from *muein*. *Muein*: to shut the eyes, to stop the mouth.) There can be mystical tinges to certain intense physical activities: dervish dances; long-distance running – not alone the body, but the soul too might get its second wind – breaking through the barrier of pain into another zone, effortless in full effort, calm in absorbed agitation, beyond suffering in suffering.

Mysticism can come in nameless visitations and in all the registers of transcendence: nature mysticism (T^1); soul-mysticism (T^2); God mysticism (T^3). It can come in various blendings, or as if from nothing in particular – because of the porosity, there is the flowing and mixing of communicative energies. A shining stone can set something off, a forbidding mountain, a surging sea; a face, the luster of the eyes, can spark a nameless love; darkness so thick there is nothing to see, but something nameless stirs; the hyperbolic breaks into our solitudes – of a sudden one is the space of the divine porosity. The porosity is not God, but God passes into and through the porosity.

Not only is the happening of mysticism pluralized, the scholarship on it is multitudinous. Does the philosophical outlook here developed aid comprehension? Is mysticism hopelessly diverse? Is the reserve justified of those who keep their distance? Is the hostility warranted of those who deride it? One notices the recurrent gesture towards unity in a variety of mysticisms, expressed now as a vision of the unity of the world, with a tendency to pantheism; expressed now as the unity of the finite and infinite, the relative and absolute; viewed again as the indwelling of the divine in the human, the dwelling of the human with God. It is striking that such strong claims made for ultimate unity generate such a diversity of interpretations, diversity often discordant. We must conceive the "unity" as giving rise to plurivocity, allowing a metaxological approach to the plurality of interpretations. This does not mean that one is as worthwhile as the other, that is, one is as worthless as the other. Discernment is all.

Our considerations are structured according to a now familiar order, namely, the idiotics, aesthetics, erotics, and agapeics of the mystical God. There will be a double focus: reflection on major issues that constantly recur; rethinking the plurivocity of the mystical, guided by the fourfold sense of being. The following is a philosophical reflection on mysticism, but it is also, to a degree, a philosophical reflection in mysticism. All this takes place in the dimension of the hyperbolic: finally beyond univocal determination and dialectical self-determination, but through the immanent equivocity of the sacred, seeking to come to metaxological discernment of the intimacy of the divine overdeterminacy.

Univocity and mysticism

I try a first approach following the univocal way. We find ourselves in the middle, already shaped in various determinate formations of life, before we become mindful of ourselves or of happening as happening. We become mindful after the fact of determination. Univocity fosters the perpetuation of stabilized determinacies, but our waking up to the middle cannot be so fixed, and as it becomes more nuanced it becomes aware that being as other now glaringly, now subtly resists univocal fixation. With this dawning we find ourselves *between* determination and overdetermination, between univocal being and being as more. Mindfulness has the inchoate sense that the second is always at play in the first, such that the second is really the first, even though a wrong univocity would try to reverse the priority, perhaps with the intention of dismissing or hiding or reducing entirely the excess of the overdeterminate.

The univocal fixing of determinate unity might seem the mystic's paradise, but the unity of the mystic is more like the rapturous univocity of immediate dwelling in metaxological community. This means that, to gain access to it, the fixity of univocal determination has to be made fluid again. Our univocal determining sets one thing against another, sets selving over against othering, sets finite being against the divine. Otherness as dualistic opposition emerges from this fixation. This fixation is already made possible by a prior coming to be, more evident in the fixing than in the fixed. Fix on the fixed and we forget the fluid original power that gives rise to determination in the first place. Our fixations must be dismantled. We need something like a negative way relative to determinate univocity: not this, not that, not the other; and yet, as we will see later, just this so, just that as such, just the other as thus so.

We are returned to a kind of fertile formlessness. This we especially know in human selving itself. This is one reason why mystical passage to the divine is aided by turning to inwardness rather than by fixation on the determinate stabilities of external being. There is nothing absolutely stable in the external world, but we can easily fool ourselves that its relative stabilities are safely out of the surge of the universal impermanence. With ourselves we more intimately gain access to dynamism beyond form, though here too we can be beguiled by a univocal fixed self said to remain static in the flux of the inner impermanence. There is no static univocal substance in that sense. If there is a unity, it is an idiot one. This is a "unicity" prior to determinate univocity, and as idiotic it partakes of the dynamism of the overdetermined. The return to formlessness in inner selving is a return to this idiocy of intimate being.

The mystic claim: in this intimacy the togetherness of the human and divine is "known," and not known by a determinate cognition of a determinate being. The "knowing" is more like a "being in love" wherein the fluid medium between human and divine is the open space of a wooing, a space that seems as much empty as full. We cannot fix it in non-paradoxical terms, for just its transcendence of normal univocal determination entails this. It is in the depths of idiotic intimacy that the deepest drama of converse with the divine happens. It happens, but we, as in the happening, are also partners in an exchange wherein we hardly know who gives and who receives. The divine is so bestowing that we think we are giving when we are always gifts, gifts to ourselves.

Philosophers sucking lemons

Philosophers have shown mystical influences: Hegel and Schelling by Böhme, Schopenhauer by the Upanishads, Heidegger by Eckhart. Indian philosophy, from Shankara to Aurobindo Ghose, has had no problem with crossovers. But, often, let the word "mysticism" be barely uttered and the look of many a philosopher will quickly assume the soured expression of someone with a sweet tooth dragooned into sucking lemons. Mysticism's otherness to normal rationalizing is greeted with distance, if not distaste. Philosophy has prided itself on seeking a *logos* of the whole, hence it has less difficulty with the God of more holistic views. The God beyond the whole raises difficulties of determinate intelligibility, and similar difficulties hold for mysticism. Now the difficulty is less relative to the "that it is" of the world than to the intimacy of being, in particular the "that it is" of selving and its astonishing inwardness. This intimacy of being is idiotic, hence recalcitrant to determination in a more "public" and general intelligibility – intelligibility accessible to the neutral understanding of "mind in general." And yet this intimacy has everything to do with mystical permeability to the divine.

One could argue that this recalcitrance by no means makes the idiocy into an irrational absurdity. Rather, we come closer to the matrix of determinate intelligibility, full with significance but other to determinate intelligibility, as a lived intimacy with the primordial energies of being itself. We must go into and through determinate intelligibility to the idiotic intimacy to come closer to the more original source(s) of intelligibility. An indicator here: mystics often stress something "experiential." There is an undergoing, often with an aesthetic flavor. Abstract knowing is not enough: in the well-known refrain, we must "taste and see."

"Experience" might seem too subjectivistic. Think, rather, in terms of the porosity of being: "experience" as the happening of original being in us, happening in us in our incarnation, but happening which wakes to itself as happening, as it wakes to the happening of being other to itself: mindful being, mindful of being other than itself as it is mindful of itself. Mindful being or being mindful is first immediate and not analytically or pragmatically or reflectively articulated. There is a pre-determinate happening which we undergo, and we do not fix it as subjective or objective. Our porosity of being, our porosity to being, is first pre-objective and pre-subjective. The mystic undergoes this happening as a mysterious *pathos Dei*, a suffering undergoing of the divine.

Mysticism, one might say, takes form in staying true to this happening, or in struggling to be returned to it, if it is lost, or overlaid with determinations which falsify it, or enfeeble it, or dry up the flow of the overdeterminate origin in us. The later determinations prove ambivalent: some genuinely shape the energy of origin in us; others congeal an outer crust of dishonesty, or evasion, or laziness, or hatred, and that crust must be broken or dissolved, and this dismantling is part of the frightful suffering. The interplay of determination and overdetermined origin creates problems for philosophy's penchant for determinate intelligibility. Neither the overdeterminate origin nor this interplay are just determinate, though they make the determinate possible.

This sheds some light on commonly noticed aspects of mystical undergoing. For instance, mystical "experience" is said not to be any doctrinal information but an immediate encounter with the divine. Sometimes this comes at the end of prolonged discipline, sometimes suddenly (*exaiphnēs*) out of nowhere, vanishing too soon into the void again. It is different with different people. Some *ways of life* offer better houses or sanctuaries for the mystical. More hospitable, the guest from the wild abides longer. The wild might itself become its home, and wild humans more hospitable to its visitation. Some ways of life, some of us, turn it away, and later might come over us a regretful wonder about what secret guest did then visit and was not welcomed.

The undergoing is also an encounter, given the sense of rupture in the suddenness, or in the resistance of the visitation to domestication. God comes, God goes. When God comes, the separation of God and self goes; when God goes, the separation comes again, though perhaps with the glow of visitation lingering. There is a complex intermediation in the coming and going, easily misunderstood by the too easy reiteration of well-worn phrases like *unio mystica*. There is an unblocking between selving and the source, but there is no block merging. Merging such as there is can be called a "loss" of self-difference, but the loss is also a finding of self in God, and there is the return to self when the coming of God then goes.

Plurivocity and mystic univocity

The mystical happening can reflect different ontological possibilities in the between. Not always does an "experience" of *God* have to be named. Mindfulness of happening can be occasioned by the external world, and we are "nature mystics." It can concern the self itself as other; the soul is released in its return to itself. Mysticism might be called a religious self-knowing, even though the self-knowing might not call itself religious, given the stress on self as a world unto itself. By contrast, either self or world may be passages to the divine source, and the divine can be either internal or external, immanent or transcendent or both together, theistic or non-theistic, and God may not be called God at all. If there is mysticism without God, as is said of some forms of Buddhism, why talk about a mystic *God*? The Buddhist will speak of form being emptiness; I would speak of the porosity. The porosity is somewhat like the emptiness, but God is not the porosity and not the emptiness and not a being within the porosity or emptiness but beyond both in the hyperbolic dimension. The agapeic origin: beyond the whole, beyond emptiness, beyond the porosity and the between.

There is nothing "univocal" about mystical univocity. Mystic undergoing: is the suffering of God, a matter of our patience to God, or God's own patience? Responses are often equivocal between these two. The "experience" allows many interpretations, including those that reject or reduce any religious claim. A certain naturalistic view will claim it to be a state of the organism induced by breathing practices or ritual behavior or fasts or drugs or magic mushrooms. A theistic approach will tend to a more personalist interpretation: the singular soul in love with God. The pan(en)theistic view may be more impersonal: transcendence of personal love into interrelation with the whole. The agnostic may grant the experience but suspend the interpretation: mysticism without theology, shy to dream its own name. There may be an atheist mysticism: what one comes to is "nothing"; God does not "exist"; finite beings exist; God is nothing.

This "nothing" is itself ambiguous. It can be the univocal nothing of the common or garden type of atheism; this is outright rejection of any mystical claim. It may be an other than univocal nothing – an equivocal nothing, the nothing is not just nothing; it names something more than negation: something full and yet not full, for it is not full like a finite solid thing – a fullness that is emptiness. It seems like a dialectical nothing which conjoins nothing and being. I would prefer to say, the porosity of being may be becoming unclogged, and with this be a metaxological nothing receptive to the excess of the divine in its nothingness for finite being. Not only with "nothing" but with many other crucial notions, what seems *one* thing at one level of considerations means something *other* at another level.

Being that is no-being is most clearly evident with human being. Here too, in subjectivity itself, the idiocy of being is not merely subjective. Subjectivity is a determinate formation of the more than objective or subjective idiocy. The idiocy itself is beyond the division of subject and object; but as non-objective, as transobjective and transsubjective, it is perhaps more fully reached *via* a certain passage into and beyond the "subjective." The granting origin of subjectivity is not subjective, nor is it objective either. The idiocy of being exceeds determination in either of these opposites. Their granting origin might be called the unity or togetherness of both, out of which the difference of the two sides takes shape. This sounds more idealistic (Schellingian perhaps) than what I mean. What do I mean? We must look more closely at this idiocy, continuing to follow the path of the fourfold.

THE AESTHETICS OF THE MYSTIC GOD

Mystic doubling(s): The rose without a why

The aesthetics of the mystic God are evident in the refrain "taste and see," indeed more generally in the sapiential (even salving) register of mystic knowing, in whatever tradition. Something of the ultimate is offered for enjoyment. Mystical aesthetics have to do with the showing of the divine: a showing of what cannot be shown that yet is shown. There is an *aisthēsis* of the divine, more than sensuous *aisthēsis*, though expressed in terms often redolent with the saturated sensuousness fitting for love.

Consider the claim of *ineffability*. Is mystical speech any more "ineffable" than the language of poetry? Would one not expect this with words of aesthetic richness and elusiveness more akin to the language of love than factual description? The rational univocity in the West is a curb on this score, false to the full concreteness of the happening. The East seems more accepting of contrariety, of the conjunction of polarities, of porous betweens, of language that goes with the flow of happening, less fixated on univocity, less alarmed by plurivocity.

With respect to ordinary common sense, there is a doubleness here: discontinuity and continuity. *Discontinuity*: One, the mystical is said to be uncommon, unexpected, even if more common than expected. Two, singular privilege is granted to an uncommon few. Three, ordinarily it says it surpassed the ordinary. Four, it melts the common *difference* between human and divine. Fifth, it distantiates itself from common consciousness: the wall into which I have crashed is not ultimate, let my bump on the head say otherwise. Six, orthodox religious images may mislead: what these images fix, mysticism unfixes. Seven, the quotidian self sleep-walks, going through the motions without mindfulness. Eight, the orthodox worry about heterodoxy and heresy: they are not entirely wrong. Nine, the mystic can claim superiority to the pride and joy of common sense, its no-nonsense pragmatism. Brushed aside, Martha resents Mary, lectures her for wasting time, for getting nothing done. Mystical renunciation seems a waste: wherever and whenever and as long as possible, the undefeatable negative is resourcefully skirted.

Continuity: One, like common sense mysticism is "intuitive"; its life blood is "seeing," immediate knowing (*noēsis* as a higher *aisthēsis*). Two, mysticism has to do with a self-evidence: you either "see" it, or you don't; to those who have not tasted, one might as well go whistle. Three, there is the understanding that passes understanding; much of ordinary life is understanding that does not understand. Four, mystical claims are recalcitrant to complete analysis, but much of common sense is also a matter of finesse. Five, dealing with "nothing," it retreats before the logic chopper. Contrariwise, its full roundedness might be picked apart by logic, and to no point. Six, it is a knowing "that it is," without exactly knowing why or what or how it might be possible. That it happens is fundamental, though it be perplexing to say what is happening and why. It happens, and there is afterwards no question of possibility. Love sweeps aside the well-prepared protestations of the clever eunuchs. Seven, it is at home in imaginative discourse, carried by suggestive metaphors, never cold concepts. Eight, common sense can be as frustrating to the logical rationalist as is the mystic – neither abide by his univocal norm. Nine, what if Eckhart is right about Martha: not resentful of Mary, but worried lest she not take the true step back from contemplation, the transforming step back into the busyness of the everyday?

What is the ordinary anyway? It has much to do with an order of stabilized recurrences and reliable expectations. There is nothing ordinary at the start. The ordinary takes shape for us as we leave primal astonishment and perplexity behind and as a more definite anticipation of predictable happening takes over. A spade is a spade, and that's that. As we know more or less what is happening, being astonished before the "that it is at all" of happening comes to count for less and less. We tolerate the child's wonder but do not indulge it beyond early fantasy. Religions, too, may serve as missionaries of the normal, domesticators of the divine. An orthodoxy becomes a sacred common sense; an institution endows a sanctioned sameness; organization rules contain the outlaw bestowing of grace. We banalize the urgency of ultimacy, meet with alarm any communication truly out of the ordinary, we excommunicate the maverick mystic.

Normalization fixes a more or less stable foreground, but the underground and the background are not nothing, though they are not minded. They make possible even what, once possibilized, denies their possibility. To recall the charge of the extraordinary in the ordinary is to find oneself in the switch from foreground to underground and background. To switch is to come upon the overdetermined; to switch back is not to come again on the normalized determinate, it is to be in an interplay which shimmers with what is excessive to determination in determinacy itself. Mystical initiation has something to do with learning the discipline of passing back and forth between the overdeterminate and the determinate. Then a spade is a spade, but it is also more than a spade: everything is just itself and also other. This is breach to the logic of Butler's univocity. This is famously expressed in Zen: first there is a mountain, then there is no mountain, then there is a mountain.

A rose by any other name would smell as sweet. What of the mystical rose? Angelus Silesius: *die Ros ist ohne warum*. Is the extraordinary the mystic name of the ordinary?

The rose by its other name? Does the fixation of the ordinary finally hold up? The ordinary: not necessarily the forgetfulness, more the namelessness of the mystery of happening? Does what is *incognito* ask to be named? To find a name for the mystery of the ordinary, this itself is not ordinary.[1]

The unweaving of identity

Logic is exigent and will lay down its litany of imperatives. Justify the special claim, the privileged intuition, the weakened differences and plurality; justify sacred suspicion, the contradictory metaphors, the occult image, the oracular insinuation.

These imperatives have their force, but what if the ordinary is beyond encapsulation in univocal categories, its saturated equivocity already informed by dialectical and metaxological articulations? Taking these into account, it is the sheer insistence on univocity that looks dumb. Dwell with the ordinary, the unruly erupts, the extraordinary long dormant. This is especially so with human-all-too-human ordinariness: a slight switch, a displacement by a sorrow or a shaft of love and the long familiar begins to sway in unsteady strangeness. Our passage in the universal impermanence passes beyond us. The diurnal mind, sovereign of its clarities, drops down into sleep, and from deep within it horror floats up from bourns beyond the boundary of all definition. The sweating relief to which one wakens chastens one's daylight certainty. A flame flares up, a rush of exhilaration, and suddenly one has no boundary of identity, and one is like a line on the sand washed out by a rogue wave. Joy breaks out, and against the grain one hums, one does not choose this, it is as if one were chosen. The overdeterminate otherness comes out, comes upon one, overtakes, takes over, ruptures, surprises, raptures, silences, utters itself in singing. There is an idiotic excess that crosses over every fixed boundary.

The heart of common sense knows this, even if the head of univocal logic counsels caution. Univocal logic can breed its own madness: it takes its convinced line, and it will continue in that line to the bitter end, though it topple off a cliff. Common sense has more sense – happy not to have everything spelt out, watchful for signs and hints, willing to listen to its secret intuitions, though it fails miserably to explain itself and is shamed in the argument. It knows in its bones and that's enough for it when it comes to the edge. Its intimation of the inarticulate will still stay its mind.

There is much of a kind of divinatory creativity in the ingenious intelligence of daily life: inventive intelligence, a "knowing that" and a "know how" that cannot account for itself discursively. In social life we divine a person, sizing them up, knowing what's what and who's who, and knowing it before a nod or a wink confirms one's already quite sure intimation. Mystic mindfulness has something in common with this divinatory character of common sense. Its sense of unity is outside the univocal principle of identity, just as its sense of otherness is not explicable in terms of separated difference. Intimation and articulation are not necessarily at war. An intimation may be the first immediacy of what we later struggle to articulate discursively. An immediate communication is not opposed to mediated expression. We wrestle with an intimation to bring what it divines into distinctness: crystallize a clearer view of what is communicated in suspense; make determinate yes, but not such as to discolor what is divined in the intimation. The divinatory character of common sense is intensified in the richest articulations we find in great art

---

[1] Of course, the Song of Songs is a paradigmatic source of the aesthetics and erotics of the mystical. One thinks of Robbie Burns's: *My luve is like a red, red rose.* Or Keats's *To a Friend who sent me some Roses.* Or Yeats's: *The Secret Rose.* See also Augustine's *Confessions* (10, 6): "What do I love when I love Thee? Not the beauty of the body . . ." and then Augustine goes on to name God as loved in terms drawing on *all the senses.* Thus too in the renowned chapter (*Confessions*, 10, 27) "*Sero te amavi, pulchritudo tam antiqua et tam nova, sero te amavi . . .*" all the senses are invoked in his laudation of God. Is this sensuousness turned to hyper-sensuousness – both the erotics of the mystic and the mystics of the erotic?

and religious myth. These express the ontological richness of the ordinary as the *incognito* of the extraordinary.

Skepticism and mystic esotericism

We find this further doubling in the mystic's claim: the claim of ineffability is itself a *spoken* claim. Words announce what words cannot fully announce. Words announce that words cannot announce what words would announce. The claim need not be absurd – though absurdity has sometimes been glorified – and yet there is announced a claim to be on the other side of what cannot be announced as a claim. One sees why philosophical skepticism will come: what cannot be articulated cannot be intelligibly appraised, hence can be treated as not intelligible. The skeptic will bespeak Wittgenstein's too much bespoken aphorism: Whereof we cannot speak, thereof we must be silent.

Is this an impossible equivocity or has it to do with a double position: standing at the limit of one form of intelligibility and seeking to make sense of what is beyond that limit, but in terms of what is communicated on this side of the limit? What is on the other side is not necessarily absurd, though it looks so from this side. Is not this speaking at the limit a speaking from a between: between the exoteric and the esoteric, between domestic solidities and uncertain intimations of a secret significance? Are there not analogous betweens in "ordinary life"? What looks unintelligible from one side looks exactly right from the other side, but one cannot see the rightness until one has crossed from one side to the other. The mystic seems to be *on two sides at once*, immersed in determinate intelligibilities, but as transcending, touched by the overdetermined origin, only enabled to speak of that other origin in terms immersed in, yet straining beyond, determinate intelligibilities. The latter cannot be fully true to the former, but instead of an absurd equivocity, this is a kind of unavoidable antinomy in which the soul is torn between two sides. There is safety and familiarity on one side, terrifying otherness on the other, and to go to the other side is to risk the death of the first security, a death without any guarantee of a resurrection. This might seem an assault on the normal sense of fixed determination ending only in madness. It might also mean we have to go with the flow – allow again original fluidity between the two sides.

Equivocity and the forlorn mystic

For the forlorn mystic the divine other is so other, so beyond saying and silence, as to be nothing. I univocally fix the god, and so fixed, the god as other vanishes, and so I fix nothing. Thrown back on myself by the utter beyondness of what I sought, I am driven deeper into myself, and in the immanent darkness of myself I taste the loss of the divine. The mystical way is the risk of an atheism, for the seeker finds its own lack and nothing, just in the rebound from its ardor for the divine other. The emptiness beyond it mirrors back its own nothingness, and turns it back to itself with the taste of its own nonbeing. God is nothing, I am nothing. In being nothing – an utterly equivocal condition – I must plumb more deeply the non-being of this condition of being.

There are a variety of ascetic practices that follow through this encounter with nothing. Some of these practices can grow from or into self-hatred, or can spring from secret rancor against life, against the God who is not there where we expect him, against the self that has not had itself confirmed in its yearning for the absolute other. This is not the only necessitated outcome. There can be a dissolution of a false fixation of selving, as indeed of its expectation that the divine will just be there as we would fix it there to be. The blind must pass more deeply into the vacancy of their own most intimate abyss.

Besides this oppositional equivocity of the forlorn mystic, there is the *promiscuous equivocity* of the released mystic: the unmediated difference of the first becomes the unmediated flowing into one other of the divine and the human. Passing into the strange and startling country of innerness one enters a hyperspace beyond the diurnal duality of object and subject. This hyperspace is a *liminal between* in the dimension of the hyperbolic: a boundary of passage, in and out, back and forth, down and up – all beyond finite univocal determination. There is unification there, but as flowing it is a *confusion* – a *fusio-con*: a "fusing with," a fluid passing from one to the other. The porosity of one to the other makes it obscure who gives and who receives, and whether one and the other, as both porous, are now most truly there as living presences, or absent like permeable holes of nothing. In the confusing porosity, intimate doubleness again.

This liminal hyperspace is a land of desolation. One picks ones way through a place of skulls. Thick night invades the valley, turning the soul into itself as into fetal security – the shape of an idiot question. As yet the porosity is not purged. Out of the inturning selving black questions to oneself materialize in the air, as out of nothing. A repulsive rat, a toad, a slithering snake – one is that and worse. A barrier has been breached, and the netherworld one is rises up. What crawls below and out of mind comes violently to mind. (Zen Buddhist *makyē* – literally "world of the devils.") We spend our season in hell, and not once. The melting of fixed selving, confusingly, makes us undergo again our extreme fixations: riveted to ourselves, wrapped into shrouds with oneself as one's own corpse, inescapably intimate with one's own being dead, one's flesh wound together with itself as its own corpse. The darkness that one is is unspeakable.

This liminal hyperspace is also a land of spring. As long as the porosity is given, the Siberia of spirit, in the coldness of its unbreakable embrace, cannot be everlasting. Hints stray in the air, a fragrance that should not be here, a stirring in the ground, a rune of "perhaps" upon the rock. The hints are prompts of life having passed, or passing, or about to pass. A shiver in the ice and the water weeps. A tear is born. Something flows – tears of Orpheus wrung from death as songs. The sorrows of this Siberia are the griefs of God. Lamentations born of love warm the land. Heart break, break heart, break. And take heart. A kiss – and a breath passes. Shoots of growth will green this land. Harbingers of a harvest, a golden field of wheat, a sea ruffled by a wind we cannot pin down, are abroad on creation, not like a dead ghost but like a breath of goodness. One is borne up or sinks as the breath now nears, now drops. The divine comes to sorrow and song, but the divine, like the darkness, is also unspeakable.

Multitudinous presencings in the vacancy: father, mother, brothers, sisters, spirits of lost friends, of children departed into their adult bodies, early faded loves never entirely evanescent. We would find the porosity a pandemonium of presences did we not make firmer borders in it, or find ourselves shielded by the balm of forgetfulness. The fragrance of the mystic rose arouses into life again what was sleeping. The risen are beautiful, even when they are ugly. In the hyperspace there is an echoing otherness that perplexes one with the voice of another, other beyond all echo. That voice is not the voice of any human. (The Irish speak of *Anam Cara* – friend of the soul.) It is that strange intimate voice of the other beyond human otherness that is the hardest to hear, the most honest with our conceit, the most considerate with our truculence, the most willing to let be. There is the otherness of selving in inwardness, but an other otherness that is not the selving's own inward otherness.

The equivocity of the mystical is to find itself in the promiscuous togetherness of many others. The discipline of the mystic is the strain to listen to the different voices, to hear these others as different, not to let them meld into a buzz of chatter. Attending: To hear in the burning buzz the high voice of the divine, unbearably beautiful and arresting beyond belief, turning the twittering into a silence that is full with presence though there is nothing there.

Remember the mystic selving is itself a buzzing, and it is himself or herself that is sifting, and being sifted. This sifting is not just an activity, for there is a receptivity, a passion to it. A chink is cut in selving to the suffering of the divine. The cleft is felt in a kind of anguish. The heart is being enlarged beyond its human measure, and there is something inhuman about the strain placed on it. To reject the tear or cut is to become the victim of a different torment, a sorrow without remedy outside of suffering the anguish. We are often spared; for we cannot bear much. Forgetful relief offers us merciful release. But the suffering and release will be offered again, unexpectedly, with an inhuman peremptory, you are more ready now, now you can bear it, which is not to say we do bear it.

THE EROTICS OF THE MYSTIC GOD

Mystical sovereignties

Claims about the promiscuous porosity of the human and divine are full of danger. The dismantling of fixed differences can be seen either as elevating the human to the divine or communicating the divine to the human, but either way the human being will be tempted to affirm it *is* the divine. Almost ritually in discussions of mysticism we find invocation of the Hindu, Atman is Brahman – "Thou are that." Connect this with the erotics of the mystical: in selving becoming the ultimate, the selving is the ultimate. The mystic wooing, begun in emptied desire, seems to end in fulfilled desire, with the mystical lover the erotic sovereign of the sacred. Is this true? Is it enough? Is it too much?

The erotics of the mystical can be allied with the dialectical, following through on the idiotics and aesthetics. Once again, discernment of an equivocal between is crucial. There are mystics and there are mountebanks. How tell the difference? There are paradoxes running against the grain of univocal logic: *todo y nada*; God everywhere and nowhere; I nothing and God-like; I empty and full; God nothing and all in all. Logic sets the opposites apart, does not mingle them. The verbosity of some mystics breaks logical prohibitions in saying the unsayable. The univocity of logic is no match for the equivocity of desire. The sexual undertones of some mystic language psychoanalytic thinkers have deemed less divine than displaced libidinal. Is this not to be expected, if desire for the divine is here in play, desire erotic, desire than may become agapeic? It has been claimed that the reverse is true: the language, say, of courtly love was borrowed from mystical erotics.

Mystical claims, like the importunities of eros, are not easily institutionalized, for institutionalized forms have to be averaged down, to a certain extent. The extremism of the urgency of ultimacy can be at odds with the more manageable medium. In the yearning to dissolve the difference of the human and divine, the danger is that, the difference dissolved, the exalted devotee will feel itself divinized by superior knowing, and court all the perils of spiritual hubris. "Glory to me, how great is my majesty!" – so Abu Yazid (d. 875) famously said, with worries of blasphemy to follow.[2] As an extremist, the mystic can become driven by religious will to power. Thus the attenuation of difference is greeted with caution, if not hostility, by the established, more domesticated views. Rightly, for the equivocity of the urgency of ultimacy must be treated with great diffidence, and with a mindfulness as much attuned to possible perdition as to glory, indeed to perdition possible in glory itself. The same holds for every inward turning way: the perils of equivocity may conquer us while we seem to conquer them. Hence the necessity of meditative disciplines to mediate that equivocity as much as possible, opening passage beyond peril, into a more intimate sanctum of the sacred.

The tendency to the extreme, and recalcitrance to institutionalization, are related to the fact that we do not primarily speak of mystics as *groups*, though there are traditions of different spiritualities. Mysticism, even in its schools, is often associated with more singular individuals: Augustine, Rabi'ah al-Adawiyya, Francis of Assisi, Ramanuja, Ibn al-'Arabi, Eckhart, Isaac Luria, Teresa of Avilla, John of the Cross. The singleness of the soul in its converse with the divine is hard to harness to a school philosophy, though this is not impossible: vide, the spiritual exercises of Ignatius of Loyola. There is a singularity to mystical selving, though paradoxically there is a reversal of attributions of achievements to the individual as such, for there is a gift that comes to selving. The singularity is important, however, for it brings religion back from the neutral public general to the inwardness of "me" and "mine," even though the discipline will be to deconstruct the "me" and the "mine." Times when public institutional religiousness wanes tend to be times when

---

[2] Abu Yazid (d. 875) developed the idea of *fana*, the passing away of the empirical self, an idea that can lead to unorthodox and controversial results concerning a claim to divinity. Al-Hallaj (854–922) was put to death for blasphemy – he seemed to claim identity with God.

attraction to the mystical waxes. Yet in both instances what ultimately is at stake is the intimate universal. Mystical singleness is tied to the idiocy of the intimate. And yet the trans-singular possesses the singular as the privileged tabernacle of its presencing.

There is a favor given, selving is passive to the gift, and the charge of quietism often follows. The charge is not entirely just. Those mystically favored have sometimes been doers of the most engaged and practical efficacy – Teresa of Avila. Clearly there can be forms of spiritual narcissism in which one is indulging one's vain self-satisfaction under the mask of godly favor. This can occur with every human thing, including noble activism itself when it has nothing to do with helping the other and everything to do with the self-importance of the helper.

The temptations of erotic sovereignty beckon the mystic holding that I and the divine are one, I am the divine. Satisfaction in the divine may mask too much of the self-satisfaction of our endeavor to be divine and not enough of religious porosity, of patience to the divine. Thou art that – one was always already that, it might even be said. But if one has come to be, this cannot be. One once was nothing, before coming to be. And, coming to be, one is as porous to the origin, but not the origin. And one will never become and be the origin. One is to be always in the middle space, though there is a mystical passion in this porous intermedium. Thou art not that.

Being (as) nothing – erotic deaths

In mystical erotics there is something that escapes possession – even if the soul is possessed. We cannot say *what* God is, we can approach the *that* of the divine idiocy. Here the way of negation is important. The expectation of positive information is confounded, and one must speak as if *saying nothing*. How say nothing, since to speak is always to say something? By enacting a negating *process:* We do not know what God is, but we can say God is *not* this, *not* that, *not* the other, and so on to infinity. The process empties out a space beyond determination which can become a receiving opening to the divine. Wittgenstein warned about language going on holiday, but this is a linguistic vacation which, emptying out our determinate cognition, prepares that holy day which is the Sabbath of the soul.

In the negative way, we vacate all the finite predicates, just as an *askēsis* in life strips off the falsely infinitized finites. One might claim the mystic interiorizes the negative dialectic of the skeptical way in regard to the truth of our relation to God. There is a skepticism here which can match, say, that of deconstructive thought, but the destructive power of skepticism is turned to an affirmative end, namely, unclogging the relation to the divine. In one tradition, there is a triple process: purgation, which strips away the inessential and prepares the opening for the divine; illumination, in which some vision is vouchsafed; union, offering a conjunction of the human and divine, and the preferred language again is that of desire and love. If the goal of the negation is union, the pathway to union is by way of an archeology of selving: the *archē* of self is sought in the inward otherness of selving, and the *archē* is not self alone.

This pathway might be mistaken for spiritual narcissism, but remember the state to which we have come: *being (as) nothing.* One is, but one comes to nothing, one is (as) nothing. This is a return to zero which interfaces with its radical other, namely, the continuing coming to be that is more than every nothing and every determinate being. This interface communicates, through coming to be, of the origin that is beyond all coming to be. Being (as) nothing: we must take seriously the desolation described in some traditions as the dark night in which the soul enters emptiness and touches the rim of despair. The despair can rinse and freshen and deepen the self towards the abyss of its own original ground, a ground that is no univocal foundation, for as an abyss it cannot be so determined. Self-knowing is thrown out of selving into the intimate abyss of the mysterious God.

Being (as) nothing: break, breakdown, breakthrough. Break: we must be divested of unfitting attachments to finite things. Breakdown: false formations of selving have congealed us into opposition with God rendered alien; the congealing must be melted down, burned to fluidity in fire; divine alienness is in the intimacy of being, hence not alien. Breakdown is like a dying, many false selvings must be shattered, or made to melt. Breakthrough: communion, like erotic love, is a kind of dying. Erotic dying is a passing out – the swoon of woo(ing).[3] This being (as) nothing is our passing over, through the portal of negation, into the hyperspace of recreated porosity. The dying of erotic love opens into our being born again in the empty space of this full beyond where the nothingness of the divine breathes. This nothingness of the divine is overfull beyond the emptiness of all beings.

Again the between ceases to be defined by dualistic opposition: this is surpassed in the flowing of selving and the inflowing of the divine (influx: a word John of the Cross favors). Infusion becomes (con)fusion in surrender to the other, a giving over that asks no return to itself, and this too is a kind of death. For it seeks to be true trust, and hence no longer to hold on to itself, and cling to its own power. The surrender also means that there is no detached or spectatorial knowing here: there is the purer porosity.

Negating representation: figurative ecstasies

The *skepsis* of mysticism, expressed in a *via negativa* is evident in relation to *representation*. I would connect the mystical attitude to representation with the dialectical way. I would also connect it with modes of figurative articulation less metaphorical or analogical, as tending often to the symbolic, though sometimes to the hyperbolic, and as sometimes (given the intimacy of excessive transcendence in immanence) bringing the symbolic and the hyperbolic into con-fusion.

Religious language is imagistic and double: the double image can both reveal and conceal, manifest and harbor mystery. Religion can be criticized and be its own critic, relative to mistaking the image for the original, or reducing the doubleness of the image to the singleness of complete univocal manifestation. The mystic embodies this critical approach also, in that the discernment, born along the way of negation, is the issue of mindful discipline that thinks in, into, and beyond the image.

This orientation in, into, and beyond the image again is marked by dangerous ambiguity. For the surpassing of the image in the so-called *unio mystica* might well be taken to mean that the doubleness of concealing/revealing, manifestation/mystery is overcome in the univocity of an absolute transparency. But the religious image's doubleness can serve crucially in being the shepherd of difference, without being the provocateur of oppositional dualism. The doubleness is ultimately metaxological, hence even in the negation of the image, the necessity of the image remains ineradicable for us. The religious image is liminal: both a *limit* between the human and divine and a *showing* that enables communicative being together between the human and divine. The image is a mediator in the porous between – making the between porous to what is beyond the between. The transcendence of images finds itself in images again, on the other side of its purification of a previously less mindful dwelling in the images.

Does the representational approach presuppose a non-representational mindfulness of the divine? Mystical vigilance can claim a non-imagistic mindfulness prior to determinate images. The path of negation serves release from the determinate images while letting emerge just that more primordial knowing. The passage in, into, and beyond the images serves the deconstruction of the images and the release of mindfulness of the more primordial unity. One does not say: The human and the divine are as one. More primordially: The human and divine are one. (Consult Eckhart, for instance.) The way of negation releases this primordial oneness, this "is" that is not of one or the other, but is itself both as one.

But what can this "is" be? It cannot be merely univocal, for then there is a simple unmediated unity and the process makes no sense, indeed could not be at all. Nor can it

---

3 *Durchbruch* – a favored word of Eckhart and the Rhineland mystics. Yeats: Blackout – heaven burning into the head.

be just equivocal, for then the coming together that the "is" expresses would be sundered by unmediated difference. The major trend is to conceive of it in terms of a more dialectical "is": a coming together of the differents, and in terms of a unity more fundamental or comprehensive than univocal identity or equivocal difference.

We must redouble our vigilance here, for there can be dialectical counterfeits, as well as univocal. There can be dialectical idols. Recall that the figurative articulations of the mystical tend often to the symbolic: the throwing together of the opposites: the *sun-ousia* of erotic relating. In the erotics of this symbolic *sun-ousia* there is a hyperbolic dimension: the *huper-ousia*, the transcendent too-muchness of the divine beyond all immanence. That is why sometimes, as I hinted above, given the intimacy of excessive transcendence in immanence, the mystical figuration can bring the symbolic and the hyperbolic into con-fusion. This can be a fecund con-fusion. But I want to claim also that the dialectical claim about unity is itself equivocal. It rightly calls attention to the coming together, but it shares too much with the univocal and hence sees the togetherness in the light of unity, to the underplaying of the difference. This indeed is the limitation of the *via negativa*: it sets out in search of what transcends finite limitation but it leads to a unity which, in transcending limitation, risks appropriating transcendence inappropriately. The "is" is rather metaxological. This is actually to restore the significance of equivocity, but also to keep open the truth of the *via negativa* as that exodus into transcending that never comes to rest in itself, or in unity either with itself or the divine. There is always something more and other. The original is always more. There is no identity that is the measure of the original. Metaxological mysticism is the acknowledgement of that shattering of all claims for absolute identity.

The image's doubleness is restored to its truth: this is not seen as a dualistic opposition that separates finite from infinite, but a name for the excess of the infinite in the infinite transcending of the finite itself. Thus the paradoxical character of the mystic's speech: a highly imagistic speaking, bespeaking what purportedly is beyond all speaking and images. It is not that there are images in the beginning that are negated and transcended in the end but that in transcending and negating the indispensability of images is restored again. This is even true of mystic silence: silence here is *full* with significance and hence is a speaking image.

Dialectic and mysticism

When separation is found to be underpinned by a deeper togetherness, the difference of the human and divine is not a difference that must finally alienate. The doubleness is there in the very term dia-lectic: the dyad, the twoness is also a speaking between (*dia*); it is dialogue, not monologue, even when it is said to be, as with Plotinus, the flight of the alone to the Alone. If there is a flight from one to an other, there is an interplay in which the two are not fixed over against each other, but are as passing over one to the other and the other to the one. The promiscuity of the equivocal relation is mediated not as the collapse of difference into unmediated oneness, nor of the rendering impossible of relation through unmediated difference, but of a process of (erotic) passing from one to the other and the other to the one. The truth of the relation of human and divine is just the passing between them in which neither must be absolutely separated from the other.

Here the negative way receives some of its deepest meaning. We must give up or surpass the too stolid dwelling in the fixity of determinate finiteness. The *via negativa* is the process of passage in which this fixity is unfixed. Turning to things, the seeker asks: Is this the ultimate? The answer will be no. The answer may not come in the instant, and may have to await the best part of a life of seeking, or even much of a life lost in things. I have given myself over to things and loved them as if they were the ultimate. I fell upon them, slaked my desire with them, and, unknowingly, this was an erotic seeking of the ultimate. But my nothingness opens up in desire's lacking, persistent even in its slaking.

A wound opens in univocal self-sameness and cries out to be filled, fulfilled. Self-surpassing is driven beyond finitude, but what is this beyond? It is empty air, it is nothing. It is a nothing answering to the nothingness welling up within. Nothing calls out to nothing, the energy of self-transcendence being called in one nothing, the elusive face of transcendence as other being sought in the other nothing. Mystic selving is strained in this redoubling of nothingness. Of course, there will be those who come from their season in nothing and say there is nothing, merely the overreaching of human emptiness into emptiness beyond the human: God is nothing – nothingness projected out of the poverty of human self-negation.

But there is no escaping the equivocal possibility: it may be exactly the opposite, even in the very *via negativa* itself. That is, human being is a nothingness, and the divine is a nothing. But these appellations also mean the opposite of what they mean: nothing is not nothing, it names, transobjectively and transsubjectively, the overplus energy of self-transcending and communicative being. It means too much, even as it dwindles into too little. It is expansive into everything, even as it contracts into nothing at all. At this limit, once again the negative way is dialectical in that the opposites are their own opposites. The maximum is the minimum, the highest the deepest, the greatest the least, God in divine excess is indeed nothing. The human exceeds the human because it is the indwelling of the transhuman. There is something divine about us but we are not the divine.

The erotic way of dialectical self-transcending can be called an ascending passage from finiteness to what is beyond finitude. This ascending is less envisaged as a flight up above to transcendence as an intensive descent into the intimacy of immanence. The going down of the selving into itself is the ascent of its own finitude beyond itself and into the transfinite in the finite itself. Ascent might first seem to be thrust outwardly, in that the moving of self-transcending is toward the things that are there. The *via negativa* discovers that the idols of externality crumble into dust. The universal impermanence in its perpetual perishing is itself this crumbling. The investment of the finite with infinite ultimacy slips through the fingers of possession, and there is nothing left in the hand that crunches its fist on an embittered emptiness. Frustration with the vanity of its investments rebounds selving back on itself and ascent becomes a descent into the darkness of the inner abyss that in selving is more than self.

THE AGAPEICS OF THE MYSTIC GOD

Mystic communion and selving beyond self

I connect the agapeics of the mystical with this realization that there is *more* to selving than self, and this we know in immanent selving. We are already in communication before we communicate with ourselves. The truth of absolute solitude is that from the first we are always absolved from solitude. There is a plenitude more primal than lack, communicated in immanence itself. Even if we understand mystic inturning as a re-awakening of the primal porosity, the primal porosity is not mere lack, even though we undergo it often as an emptiness. The between as a porosity is an open field of communication; and there is something more than the porosity that communicates the between in which we are, the between which we are. The agapeics of the mystical refers us to this superplus source of communication that attends the porosity, and to which we must attend in the porosity. The agapeics refers us to this exceeding source of the most original and ultimate communication.

Often mystic selving is said to embody a movement in immanence to union with the indwelling God. The union is both sides and not just one: God is in self, self is in God. Sometimes this union is conceived of as an impersonal power, sometimes as personal spirit, sometimes as transpersonal, perhaps in the sense of the nothing or the emptiness, as in Buddhism. Sometimes deification is said to follow. Eckhart suggests something uncreated to the soul in its apex or ground. There is a Platonic tendency to think of the soul as eternal, only barred from its divinity by the body.

Mystics influenced by *creatio ex nihilo* see the whole human as created, soul and body. The nothingness is not that of the body but of the entire integrity of self: the soul too is created, and hence has the mark of nothingness, as well as the image of the origin. The struggle is not to be freed from the body but from the darkness alienating one from the divine origin. There is no return of uncreated soul to uncreated origin; there is the opening to a communion of soul and origin, a communion ultimately a gift of the origin, since everything that is, though finite, is also such a grace.

Aristotle said that "somehow the soul is everything." How somehow? Is there a sense of the agapeic "more" here? One might reformulate in terms of the porosity of being, here connected with the opening of the soul's dunamis as self-transcending. Our soul can become everything not actually, but sympathetically, so to say. *Sumpathēs* is a "suffering with." I do not say "intentionally" become one – this is too directed and too active. The priority of the *passio essendi* to the *conatus essendi* is mystically important. (The Stoics spoke of *sumpathēs ton holon* – could one say *compassio essendi* of, or with, the whole?) Religious porosity to divine communication is prior to the religious urgency of ultimacy. "To become the other" then means to "be with" in the mode of being open to undergoing the other. Nothing is what it is other than by "being with" what is other to itself. Only by being nothing, an expectant porosity, can one be filled with the divine other.

There is a receptivity prior to and beyond the doublet of passivity/activity. This primal receptivity is not a passivity, if by this we exclude an energizing of selving in the most intensive and concentrated way. Quite the opposite: the latter is enabled by the porosity, prepared in discipline that looks to the point of poise, of energized equilibrium, in which there is nothing static and yet all is perfectly still, as if in consummate harmony with itself by being in harmony with what is more than itself. If there is a knowing by becoming the other, this is not a dominating identification in which I lay the mark of my identity on the other. Becoming one with the divine is an identification by love, a knowing that is a loving. This is communication in the intimate universal.

The agapeics of the mystical means we must speak of the union as a communion, for this keeps the openness of the "being with." Communion does not reduce to a mystical monism. If it is a unifying as it is an ecstasis of communication which is the lived between as traversed from this side, from that side, and so traversed that it seems there are no fixed sides anymore (this is why union is named: the fixity has vanished in the traversing). If there is an agapeics to this knowing it is an excessive knowing, and hence one might not call it a knowing at all. It is not a univocal cognition for it is not a determinate grasp of a determinate somewhat. Nor is it a self-determining knowing. The excess of the other strains the limits of self-determining and makes the knowing an excess extending beyond itself. This is an agapeic mindfulness. One hesitates even to call it a knowing lest one imply one has grasped a determinate somewhat, mastered through oneself alone. This communication will be an unknowing knowing, a *docta ignorantia*, in Cusanus's words, in a cloud of unknowing, as Julian of Norwich calls it.[4]

Metaxology and mysticism

Dialectic reminds us of the ascending movement of self-transcending as a descent into intensive inwardness, but there is another ascent and descent. The erotic ascent to the divine which is also descent into the depths of selving has itself to be purified of a clinging to self that prevents the release towards transcendence as other. At the point of intimacy with the deepest ground that this togetherness is primordially a gift can become blurred. The passage back and forth between human and divine is not passage between us and ourselves, not between the divine and itself. It is not the self-love of the divine in the human, not the self-love of the human in the divine. The eye by which I see God is not the same eye by which God sees me. There is a further negation required: the being of

4 Gregory of Nyssa speaks of light (*phēs*), cloud (*nephelē*), and darkness (*gnophos*); see Andrew Louth, *The Origins of the Christian Mystical Tradition: From Plato to Denys* (Oxford: Clarendon Press, 1981), pp. 80–97. Think of the night suggested even by the homely metaphor of Aristotle, master logician, echoed and approved by Aquinas: with the highest things we are like bats in sunlight. Nocturnal souls find the daylight itself a nighttime illumination.

selving as gift makes it realize its nothingness at an even deeper level; everything that it is from the ground up is nothing, were it not for the gift of the origin.

The released *askēsis* must come to this nothing, and know that the passage back and forth in inwardness itself is always sustained by the giving of the origin. The genuine other and integrity I am is itself sustained as gift. The result? A humility hard to describe for it seems to make the soul dwindle to nothing and yet it expands the soul with a serene exhalation, for it rejoices just in the divine generosity, melting in its glory even as it undergoes the suffering that delivers it over to nothing. In the undergoing of this patience, so much of what seems of ultimate significance fades to secondary significance. Previous importances can taste of insipidity; compared to this other sweetness, they are bland, even repulsive.

It is as if one suddenly heard coming from nowhere a ravishing music, and then it fades, and now there strikes up the more familiar symphony, now sensed more than before as disturbed by strident discord. Once having heard the music, the rest is noise – and one only heard it for a transporting moment and it was gone. The normal song resumes and it is no mere cacophony. The cacophony is itself a communication, but one has to listen differently. I said it before, I say it again: I once heard a bird sing in a bush, I did not see it, only heard it, for only some arresting moments, and I was taken out of myself, and I knew that for the instant I was in paradise, and I later rubbed my eyes and shook my head in disbelief and hardly believed it, the memory of that instant was indelible.

The *askēsis* takes one down into a togetherness that must be further purified, and the last release makes the self into a kind of nothing, not a nothing full of rancor before its own lack but a nothing that has emptied itself out of the self-clinging that blocks the passing of the divine through it. The soul waits quietly in itself as in a nothing, but a nothing that is readiness and expectancy. This reminds one of the Buddhist no-self, though non-oriental mysticisms have their knowing of it too, even if the language tends to be cataphatic rather than apophatic. Openness such that it seems there is nothing there, but the nothing is the silence into which the fullness of the reserved divinity is worded.

Erotic selving risks resting with its own sovereignty, be this even divinely self-affirming. The agapeics of the mystical between goes further: one is to be released from that sovereignty, not to become a servile slave but to be that readiness of emptiness, that opening of nothingness to what will come from the origin. There is self-transcending, but when the agapeics of communication overtakes one, there is no insistence on return to self. There is more of transcending than self, instead of more of self than of transcending. In passing, the soul goes out of itself, for it can go now, for it is nothing, and has been let go, it is in the music leading it through the labyrinth of itself, out into the darkness of the world lit with creation's glow, and beyond this into a darkness not the world's or the soul's, and the soul cannot name the love that radiates in that darkness, it cannot even name itself, for it is darkness, motionlessly transported in its motion of pure passing.

It is right to speak of the metaxological here because the last word cannot be with the union of opposites, if this means the vanishing of difference. There is the last vanishing of difference as opposition certainly, as the soul is released beyond its own clinging to itself. But one can as insightfully use the language of otherness here as of sameness. And, more insightfully, since our language of sameness inexorably tends to bring the other towards our self, whereas here it is the divine other that is taking us out of our sameness and identity. We are being othered, but this self-othering is not just the doing of the selving, for the self knows that doubleness within selving in which the passage between human and divine is ongoing. And it is the passing of the divine within it that doubles it and that draws it out of itself as other to itself, and other to itself in aspiring to an other that is not again simply itself.

We are drawn to agapeic selving by this passing of the divine within us, and a passing that no longer makes it possible for us simply to be within ourselves. Even when most deeply within ourselves, in the most radical interior recollection, we are not within ourselves, we are outside ourselves, drawn out by the solicitation of transcendence. Mystical communion is a between in an extraordinary complex and extraordinary simple sense. Beyond unity and opposition, beyond the unity of opposites, the community here is something more again. The frequent image of the mystical as a marriage keeps open the difference better than unqualified *unio*. Marriage is a union that sustains otherness in togetherness and is not a self-mediating unity but an intermediating *metaxu*. The mystical communion is an intermediating *metaxu*.[5]

The passage of one into the other and the other into the one is a between – a *metaxu* redeeming the promise of the agapeics of being. True marriages are erotic and more. The doubleness of the between allows the togetherness of immanence and transcendence. If the *via negativa* of dialectic leads primarily to mystical immanence, with equivocation on transcendence, the metaxological way is one of mystical eminence, restoring the excess of the transcendent not by reinstating dualistic opposition with the immanent but by shaping a different community in the middle space of interplay. The *via negativa* points to the within "in the midst"; the *via eminentia* to the beyond, the hyperbolic "over and above." So far as the mystical as metaxological includes both it is the unison of the two, for it guards the "*dia*" of dialectic without returning us to a univocal unity, without straying on an equivocal opposition, and without closure on an immanent self-determination.

The mystical between as a *double ecstasis*: not an ascent solely on our part to the divine, not also only a descent into the inward otherness on our part; it is also an ecstasis from the side of the God beyond the between. God gives in an agapeic ecstasis in the middle. The meaning of transcendence gets its character from that ecstasis: transcending is being beyond; God too is being beyond, beyond into the middle as ecstatically related to the created other. Transcendence meets transcendence in the rich community of immanence. This is the most intimate community of immanence: the coming together of a plurality of transcendences in a field of agapeic love.

Agapeic descent is sometimes spoken of as a "condescension." In English the word suggests the hint of a slightly haughty, otherwise hesitant involvement with an inferior other. What the agapeic means is more like the exact opposite: the making way for the other as other and the offer of good from an overflow of generosity. Agapeic making way is free offering – ecstatic bestowing that places itself at the ready of the beneficiary. There is a reversal and crossing between human and divine transcending. We erotically ascend, descending into and out the poverty and promise of our own most inward abyss. In the inward abyss we find the divine descent in our most ready poverty, in our very nothingness. Our opening meets that descending ecstasis, and in receiving it, welcoming it, it finds itself caught in a movement of ascension: the human heightened not through its own self-determination but through the largesse of an agapeic gift. In itself it is carried beyond itself, by what is "above" it that yet is "within" it, in a radically intimate way. It is carried in a life it does not own, and its being carried is also a gift. And the new ecstasis is not the self-surpassing of the *via negativa*; it is being uplifted beyond what any self-determined self-surpassing could achieve.

One does not will what happens here, for one cannot call it up by will power. Yet one must be willing, perhaps as close to pure willing as one can be, a willing so pure it seems to make one as like to nothing. This is the pure trust, the true "yes" with which we began. This *willing beyond will* is a giving over, a release of the promise of agapeic enabling power that one would not call one's own and yet is what makes one most to be one's own. At the same time it unselves into poverty and it most richly selves. One has no self, and one is just selving as for the other, and as ecstatic selving that is the living energy of transcending.

Mystical agapeics and divine darkness

Beyond the analytical intellect, beyond speculative reason there is the agapeic mindfulness of the heart. This lives in a knowing of religious finesse, beyond determinate and self-determining cognition, a knowing that is a loving, engaging the whole of selving,

---

5   John of the Cross speaks of "the union of likeness": *The Collected Works of Saint John of the Cross*, trans. Kieran Kavanaugh, O.C.D. and Otilio Rodriquez, O.C.D. (Washington, DC: ICS Publications, 1991), p. 116.

idiotic, aesthetic, erotic, agapeic. Agapeic selving is the idiotic loving that reaches out beyond itself, never just hitting a univocalized end or constructing a holistic completion in which it can now finally rest. It is a limitless reaching out after the passage of the divine darkness into its own inaccessible light. Mystical knowing is a loving: not neutral objectivism, not subjectivism, not transcendental or speculative science, but agapeic mindfulness that flowers out of our divine eros for the divine agape.

If we are fixed to being as determinate and its univocal logic, or to the self-determining logic of speculative dialectic, we find it hard to follow. If one passes by way of negation, one knows one does not know univocally, nor dialectically either; and yet one discerns symbolically, analogically, metaphorically, hyperbolically. The mystical movement can be tied to this last fourfold. Metaphorical discernment takes us into, through, and beyond the fixities of univocity and the confusions of equivocity. Symbolic suggestiveness intimates the moment of togetherness, of *sunousia*, beyond the *askēsis* and *skepsis* of the way of negation. Analogical order disciplines us to search out the likenesses of an other space of transcendence. Hyperbolic exaggeration heightens transcending mindfulness of the excess of the origin – the *huperousia* is not just the *sunousia*, and this on the way of excess, not just the *via negativa*. At the end there is no resolution that returns us to the simplicities of univocity or the sublations of dialectic.

While the language must remain paradoxical it is not unintelligible. It is rendered intelligible if we attend with religious finesse to the passage of the process, and the kinds of "reality" at play in these passages, none of which, and not only origin and end, can be reduced to determinate or self-determining intelligibility. There is darkness in this light. There is darkness in being with the divine. There is the darkness of our knowing which knows nothing. There is the darkness of God. There is a blind wordless peace – wordless peace that yet words the between. At the end the re-turn to the origin is idiotic. It is a mindful idiocy, but it is not a knowing, if that means determinate or self-determining cognition. And yet it is knowing as an opening of mindfulness to the truth of transcendence that exceeds determinate categorization and self-determining knowing. The *excess of God* is not just what is turned away from us but more the turning towards us – the agape into the between, into the intimate universal. Coming as too much for us, it is like a going away – an approach that is a retreat, a giving that is a reticence, an immanence that is a transcendence, a thereness not there, a fullness empty. The intermediation from this otherness is immediate, sometimes seemingly overpowering, sometimes not overpowering at all but silent, still, unnoticeable, not descending but always already there. We are searching, but we are being searched, searched out, being found, being found out, revealed as what we are, hence the terrifying vulnerability and consummation.

The darkness of God is not turned away from us, but, as inexhaustible, it deepens in its elusiveness as we go deeper into its night. The more we discern, the more we are lost. The more we know, the more we know we do not know. The more we are satisfied, the more a deeper dissatisfaction springs up and sends us seeking again. The more our lack is fulfilled, the more this fullness sets out beyond itself in a different lack beyond all finite fullness. Our eros for the divine is met with the divine agape for us. There is the paradoxical conjunction of lack and fullness, desire and peace, immeasurable attainment and illimitable longing. God passes, God passes beyond, and we are beckoned to follow the passage. The desire for full presence is never absolutely satisfied, though it is satisfied, for one has been approached by the holy. The allowance of the holy places one closer to what always overflows, and as overflowing retreats and draws us further into the presencing of absence that is the reserve of God. There is a holy unhappiness which is unhappy just because it has been offered happiness. The holy has offered it the suffering of this blessing.

Mystical agapeics: the holy beyond moral good and evil

In the mystic way the movement is to a hyperspace beyond dualism and dialectical totality, though not beyond the re-doubling required for communion, re-doubling beyond the opposition of selving and othering. What of the doublet: good and evil? We sometimes find the movement to the beyond of good and evil. The mystic space cannot be defined by their dualistic opposition or dialectical sublation. This, again, is fraught with dangerous ambiguity. I think there are ethical practices that go with the mystical, and that at the deepest have to do with the holy and the community of agapeic service.

This is not always granted. An ascetical mysticism may take a negative attitude to things. Things are temptations, snares; we must free ourselves from them, learn detachment and indifference. This negative attitude runs the risk of nihilism fed on spiritual contempt. It can be dyed by streaks of Gnosticism. Sometimes we find the opposite: evil is illusory. Released from false attachment to things, things stand there, glorious in their thereness, perfect after their own being. To be is to be good. Why then do we not see it? We are benighted, and it is not a holy night. What of the malign will, corrupted so intimately as to be verging on being irredeemable? Is there anything that is irredeemable? What sense can the mystical make of damnation, as a turning away and turning into the darkness of evil?

We might say: Evil is nothing. Yet again we face the ambiguity of the nothing. To say "it is nothing" can mean different things: the nihilistic gesture of contempt; the forgiving sign of consent; the Amen of trust that there is an inexhaustible good that takes the malignity into its own healing heart, where it is as if it were nothing. "It is nothing" – let it be, not as turning away, but as turning towards, and saying "yes" in suffering the affliction of negation. "It is nothing" – promise of the re-creation of the good of the "to be," in its coming to be anew.

If we say that the mystic moves towards a hyperspace beyond good and evil, is this beyond the good that is beyond good and evil? Must we not say that human measures of good and evil are not ultimate? That there is a more ultimate measure? An agapeics of the mystical is not a Nietzschean ecstatics beyond good and evil offering a kind of Dionysian mysticism. Nietzsche is a dithyrhambic ecstatic, a pagan mystic turned to the rapture of nature even while excessively intoxicated with his own soul's self-apotheosis. The service of the agapeic is merely servile for him. He succumbs to the temptations of sovereignty too full of itself, not knowing enough the purged porosity and the passion of the divine communicated thereto.

The hyperspace of religious porosity is beyond moral good and evil. There is a holy good beyond moral good and evil which does not lead to a "higher" immoralism. It flows out into an ethical life of agapeic service. Touched by this holy good, one is transformed into some likeness to it, and this likeness is expressed in a transformed participation in the world, human and natural. We can be touched by the promise of a universal love for all things, not just for human things. The great monotheistic religions point in this direction. One thinks also of the compassion of the Buddha.

Of course, as with the Gnostic, the claim to be beyond good and evil is also tempted by an antinomianism in which the enlightened one cannot sin. Nietzsche suggests sinlessness: sin a mere interpretation; Raskolnikov would be sinless – favored agent of a "higher" cause. Sinless privilege has been claimed by the political terrorist, the revolutionary. Think, too, of claims of artistic genius to be beyond morality – mystic devotee of an aesthetic antinomianism, though the word "God" be never even whispered, except perhaps as a silent hiss of dismissal. There is a being beyond good and evil that is not the holy. More often than not, it is another mask of protean will to power overpowering the primal porosity, ecstatic with itself, parody of sacred transcending, corrupt in its self-divinizing. There can be a mysticism of the erotic in which license is taken to plumb the mysteries of flesh down to the thrill of excremental degradation and even death.[6]

None of these is the compassionate service of being agapeic. There is something outlaw here – beyond the law. John of the Cross drew a sketch of the ascent of Mount Carmel as an aid to seekers, but at the summit of the drawing we find these words: "Here there is no longer any way because for the just man there is no law, he is a law unto himself."[7]

---

[6] George Bataille – a Nietzschean outdoing Nietzsche in the thrill of pornographic provocation – is an example in which an erotic mysticism and an excremental mysticism seem indistinguishable.

[7] The Collected Works of Saint John of the Cross, pp. 110–11.

"Being a law unto oneself" – dangerously equivocal, in that the same is claimed for *evil* beyond moral good and evil, but this is infernal, not holy. Evil beyond moral good and evil is the counterfeit double of the holy beyond moral good and evil. How discern the difference? By considering if this "beyond" fructifies or not in a life of agapeic service. The compassion of the Buddha is released beyond *nomos*; it is beyond the law. But, becoming enlightened, he remains among the unenlightened, or those still seeking. The essence is not one's own sovereignty, not even one's own release, it is release towards the others who continue to travail beside one. This is close to the practice of agapeic service.

God as the holy good beyond the law is the agapeic source of law that is good. This holy good communicates freedom: a space of porosity in which refusal is let be. It thus allows an outlaw beyond that will stamp on the good; outlaw beyond that takes formless form in the freedom we are given; outlaw beyond running to terror and madness. This outlaw beyond dwells in the void beyond good and evil, but that void has not been let as the porosity that is opened to the divine. We fill it with the creations of our own will to power. With an action that is no action, by uncreation we "create" idols in this void, and then the idols migrate into the ordinary world and doom it to bitterness, wrath, and waste. It is we who are the wrath of the idol, mimicking the wrath of God. We are the bitterness and the waste – all the crop of an idolatrous mysticism. Holy communion has been desecrated.

For communion again to be consecrated, we must participate in the Golgotha of our false selvings and communications, participate in the shattering of the self-closures of selvings and communications, participate in the breaking through of the holy ultimate, even in the brokenness. With some the coming into the breach is more gentle and gradual – with others more abrupt. With some the fixity of false selvings and communications is like a granite hard to crack; with others the malleability to the divine is never quite so congealed or petrified. Fire and the flow have been let continue under the crust of fixity, and so a touch, or a word, rather than a blow or repeated blows, is all that is needed to release the freer flow.

Part IV
God

Chapter 14

God: Ten Metaphysical Cantos

GOD

If God is God and nothing but God is God, we are dealing with an absolute singularity about which, in a sense, we can say nothing. Its own terms alone would allow saying something of it, but its own terms are its alone, and hence only the divine singularity could speak (about) itself. It must bespeak itself for us to be able to speak of it; communicate itself for us to be able to divine any sense of it. True "naming," then, would not be our naming of God, but the utterance of God who names Godself and enters communication with what is other. True "naming" would enable communication in the most original sense: naming God as communicating Godself, and communicating the very space of communication between God and God, and between God and us. The name would offer the true word of absolute singularity but would also be the most original endowing of community.

For us to be able to say anything at all, our speech would have its truth, if it has any truth, from gleaning God's singular communications, given in its wording of the between. We ourselves might be seen as communications of it, communications that must glean from themselves, and their world, what they communicate of their source. Here again the hyperboles of being offer us some aid. In finitude they communicate of what is hyperbolic to finitude. We are not the divine singularity, and so all our speaking must carry the admission that we cannot be the measure of the difference of the divine singularity, though we may listen to what is communicated in and of this difference, and especially if it makes possible an original porosity of intermediation which gives the medium of communication in which we come to attend and hear. This work as a whole is an attempt to heed such communications – to hear, as it were, God's own metaxology.

In Part IV we ask how Godself might be, so far as we can glean this from the turning of God's manifest energies towards us in creation, a turning originating creation itself, into which and in and through which we search. This asks of us again an adventure in speculative metaxology (see Chapter 7). Speculative metaxology is not the same as speculative dialectic in Hegel's sense. Finding our indirect direction to God via the hyperboles we are engaged in hyperthetical thinking that finds itself "being placed above." One is not listing off the attributes of an object distinctly delimited. One is groping in darkness or feeling one's way in a fog or being turned in the turning, full of bafflement and episodic astonishment. We must be diffident about saying what God in self is, and yet we must dare. To re-think the "attributes" of God, in light of the fourfold sense of being, is not a matter of an uncritical natural theology but rather calls on the mindfulness that presupposes our previous passage through godlessness, ways to God, and the different understandings of God(s). What we say is not a matter of conceptual determinations we construct but a matter of metaxologically finessing what the idiotic, aesthetic, erotic, and agapeic hyperboles tell us of God, passing through and beyond univocity, equivocity, and dialectic. To say something significant here is too much in a number of senses: too much as exceeding the powers of human determination, too much as asking more from us than we can guarantee through our own self-determination, too much as bearing on the exceeding too muchness of the divine as such. The granted hyberbolic stress of what is to follow is inseparable from a consenting humility that still asks of us a considered audacity.

Reflection on God, especially in monotheistic theologies, has traditionally tried to speak of God's being in terms of a group of fundamental notions, sometimes called attributes, such as being, unity, eternity, immutability, impassibility, absoluteness, omnipotence, omniscience, infinity, goodness. With a few exceptions (such as some recent analytic approaches), philosophers since Kant have given them scant attention. Mindful of difficulties pressed from a critical angle, mindful that the relative silence reflects the ethos of post-Kantian thought, but mindful also that a metaxological philosophy offers the resources of a different understanding of the ethos of being, we are encouraged to venture some thoughts in this matter. An uncritical natural theology might without further ado assign this or that predicate to God, but clearly, such "attributes" are not exactly familiar or everyday. Moreover, they tend to be mutually implicating and defining. This is appropriate in that it appears misleading to think of the divine as having attributes in the way a finite object has attributes or predicates. To "attribute" anything to God is also problematical if the origin exceeds finite determination, and if our attributions are tied to what we can define in terms of determinate characteristics. Doctrines like analogy try to address the limits of finite attribution, or at least offer cautions about any enterprise speaking of divine attributes. It is hard to forget Aquinas: we know that God is, not what God is. Yet he spends page after page talking about God, not perhaps as if he did know, but certainly as if it were worth the trying. The task is impossible and destined to fail, and yet we must ask how in failing it is possible still to respond to the impossible. In this try, a wise agnosticism is needful.

Some "attributes" can be correlated with different senses of being. The movement of our metaxological rethinking will be from the idiotic through to the agapeic, from being to good, as consonant with a recharged sense of the primal ethos, and renewed porosity to transcendence as other (T³). The movement is also connected with a certain breakthrough of our finite fixations of the reconfigured ethos: the overdeterminacies of being in the between, communicating something of the ontological charge of the primal ethos, communicate something of the divine overdeterminacy, and the more so as we approach the overdeterminacy of agapeic goodness. God's being as overdeterminate is over-being: above being in one sense, yet in another sense intimate, as intimate as the idiotics, the aesthetics, the erotics of being. The poetics of God are dramatic, with episodes of tragic loss and hilarious comedy – the drama of an agapeic community, enabled by and enabling of a releasing generosity. Coming to goodness through the good of the "to be," the community of agapeic service offers an absolute sign of the God of the between, an absolving sign of God in the between.

Our exploration is a single unfolding, but to aid the reader I present it in ten metaphysical cantos. I worry there is too much of the God of the philosophers in the undertaking. Hence we must not forget the struggle with godlessness, the ways to God, and the different ways God has been understood – all these are taken as having been worked through. All in all they bring us back to the passion of the religious, and lessen the danger that a new idol of theory will overtake our awe at this last stage. Cantos can also be laudations. If the undertaking is a philosophy of God, God is God not philosophy. Philosophy is not God. Only God is God.

FIRST METAPHYSICAL CANTO: GOD BEING OVER-BEING

Being (over)-all
Do not say
It is
It is more
Even less say
It is not
It is even more

It is over
All being
& it is
No-thing
Above all being
It wanders
Unknown
In all things

Is this the place to start: God as being, perhaps as over-being? I would visit the philosopher Paul Weiss in his old age, and coming in the door he would ask me, almost shouting: "How do you get from being to God?" A very good question, not an easy question, not one to be directly answered, as if there were a univocal path from one to the other.

We have to think in terms of the first hyperbole: the "that it is at all." Being is not a predicate, not a form, being is not a being, but refers us to original power to be. Is this what is the most original: the agapeic power to be, or give to be? But relative to finite being, origin as original can seem to be no-thing. We find ourselves in the fore-ground of the gift of being at all. We come to ask: What is being given to be at all? What is the original of coming to be that does not itself come to be but, as giving to be, makes coming to be possible and actual?

Is God, or is God not? If God is, what is this "is"? What is it to say: God is? Nothing, it seems, more than an indeterminacy. We seem to be told (almost) nothing. What (or who) is God who is? Immediately we run into the difficulty that our sense of "what" is determinate. The origin is not a determinate being but rather gives them to be as being at all. If there is something idiotic about being there at all, does this mean a kind of hyperidiocy to the "being" of God? It seems we cannot say what God is, if "what" is a determinate characterization or essence. Can we even ask then what God is?

The question generates different responses, but two are noteworthy. On the one hand, God is said to be Being Itself. Thus Aquinas: *verum ipsum esse*. The name God is said to give in *Exodus* is seen as religiously converging with what metaphysics reasons out of God as Being. On the other hand, it will be said God is no being, we must rethink God without being. For instance, the Heideggerian ontological difference is appropriated and radicalized such that not only is Being different to beings, but God is neither Being itself nor a being (Marion?). This venerable response especially wants to take into account reverence for the excess of the origin: God will always be other, *epekeina tēs ousias*, like Plato's Good, and perhaps even further beyond, like Plotinus's One *epekeina nous kai episteme*. *Hyperessential*: beyond essence, and the "to be."

The rationale is clear with both these options. God's difference is acknowledged, but as we must avoid univocity with the first, we risk equivocation with the second. In the first case, some community of God with the beings that are is at least implied in calling God Being itself, tempting one to enclose God and beings in one ontological totality, which then might seem to be the truer name for the ultimate. The difference of God would be compromised, and God as Being domesticated in terms of God's necessary place in the one totality which is the whole of beings. Of course, this univocity of being is not the only possibility; the analogical conception is obviously relevant, for this clearly wants to keep open the space of transcendence, even while not blocking some relativity to the immanence of creation. The doctrine of analogy complexly qualifies the "is" of being with the "as" of similitude, such that the temptations to univocal reduction or assimilation are noted, guarded against, and transcended. It calls attention to the participation of finite beings in being, a participation first made possible as a gift of the origin, a participation pointing to both the intimacy of the origin and also to an *asymmetry*, since the gift is exceeded by the giver. There is something absolute in the asymmetry: if God is as unconditional in self, God also is as absolving, in letting the finite creation be as irreducibly other. God is absolute in the intimacy of its own being for self, and absolving in the releasing of creation that is the love of finitude of agapeic origination. God's agapeic giving releases the creation into being its own open whole, and hence not just a part of a more inclusive totality. In this respect, the analogical "as" points us towards a metaxological understanding.

Relative to the second option, God's very otherness tempts us to see the Being of the divine as *not* Being, but other than Being. The reasoning has its points of persuasiveness. The origin cannot be reduced to what it originates, and hence is always over and above. It is no thing, and hence a name for God might be Nothing, and perhaps God has no proper name. The point is not a merely empty nothing, but an originative nothing that is creative of the finite beings. Since we cannot think this in terms proportionate to finite beings, it is better to exceed or transcend the language of beings.

The danger of equivocation here is that we vacillate between the full and the empty nothing. Perhaps we can hardly avoid talking in terms *both* full and empty. Univocal thinking will insist that a nothing that is absolutely empty is the only possibility. (Univocal thinking cannot think the porosity.) But how dare we talk about a full nothing? Will we not be seduced by negation, even in our affirmation of God, as we say again and again: God is not this being, not that being, not any being at all – and the "not" takes over and we forget the fullness, and a space of emptiness opens between God and the world, and then once again an impenetrable veil of dualistic opposition descends. A new equivocal outcome emerges, namely, that God and world have *absolutely nothing* to do with each other. We say God is beyond being, but if so beyond, what can we say of God but nothing, and if nothing, then when we look at the world we see nothing of God there. It appears to us then as a Godless scene, and the religious reverence that would guard divine transcendence ends up atheist. God without being becomes being without God.

These equivocations turn us to pondering the nothing in less than empty ways. There must be senses of being which do not reduce God to a being, without making God a vacant nothing. I would connect such thoughts about the nothing to the *porosity of being*. Consider thus the porous space between the human and the divine in which communication passes. We are what we are in this porous between, and, in another sense, we ourselves are a porous between. We are an open space in which the divine communicates when we wake to ourselves in prayer – wake to ourselves as being woken to the divine beyond us. The porosity is *a kind of nothing*, but it is such as the en-abling milieu of communication, and indeed en-abling of the being of beings as a something created out of nothing. God is not this porosity, but primally possibilizes the porosity. God as creating is in kenotic and agapeic passage in this porosity. God is not the porosity, but the porosity is a kind of token of the kenotic agapeics of the God that creates. God, in creating from nothing, gives the porosity as the en-abling milieu of communication. And since it is through the porosity that God is communicated, we think that the God communicating is like the porosity – and it, of course, is (a kind of) nothing. If we were to talk about God as a full nothing, God would be like such an en-abling nothing, empowering all communicative being (for self and for the other), creating the porosity that allows the finite creativity of the creature.

There is a peculiar incontrovertibility about being, however we understand it. We deny it and we have to affirm it; for denying it, presupposes some sense of the "is," a point clear to philosophers since Parmenides, though its meaning remains difficult and obscure. This incontrovertibility suggests nothing outside being, but in such a wise that there seems to be no "outside." What could such an "outside" mean? Somehow being envelops all that it. Would this include God in an ontological totality, such that God is not ultimate, but the whole is, with God perhaps the highest being in the totality? We would have to give up God's radical originality, singular ultimacy and absoluteness. If we wish to preserve these latter, some sense of the nothing has to be granted by our thinking, to ground essential differences, not only relative to the "outside" or "beyond" of being but within being itself. And there must be a truth more ultimate than the whole, the truth of God beyond the whole.

I suggest the following approach. We know this incontrovertibility in the between, for in the between we cannot think being away, for every thinking reveals a bond with being that is intimate to the thinking itself. This bond is ultimately metaxological, though it also has its univocal, equivocal, and dialectical modes. We cannot think being away and yet (in the porosity of the between) we intimately know the finitude and possible nothingness of what is incontrovertible. What is incontrovertible is our bond with being, revealing a necessity that we cannot sidestep; and yet the being (and bond) so revealed is not absolutely necessary, since we also know that it once was not, that now it is ontologically frail, and that once again (to all appearances, given our mortality) it will not be anymore. The incontrovertibility is the immediacy of the "that it is," but when we mindfully meditate on the "that it is" and mediate a sense of "what" this "that it is" is, it is not absolutely necessary in itself, even if it does prove incontrovertible in relation to us. In fact, in that relation, we come to know that the incontrovertible "that it is" is passing into being and passing away. The porosity of being is the very between of passing. We come to know *ourselves* incontrovertibly, as having come to be, coming still to be, and still too passing away. Incontrovertible being in the between, as passing in the porosity, is not absolute, thus not God.

What then of God and being? Finite being, in its hyperbolic "that it is," points further than itself. Of God we might say "That it is" but "what" the "that" is, we cannot say in the same way as we can say of beings in the between, or the between as such. For the "that it is" of finite being is, but also can not be: this is where the constitutive nothing of its finite becoming shows itself, and makes it contingent, not absolutely necessary. The "That it is" of God cannot not be. It is not a being in the between, it is not the totality of beings; its being is other. Hence the importance of speaking of the God beyond the whole. How "beyond," how other? I would say as the actualizing origin that is the actual possibilizing ground of all possible being. It is not itself possible being. It is beyond possibility and actuality, so far as this doublet defines the becoming of finite happening. It is itself the possibilizing actuality that is the source of finite possibility and actuality. It is not indefinite possibility but overdetermined original possibilizing. The difference of these illuminates something of the difference of the empty and the full nothing.

But why move beyond the relative necessity of the contingent? Deep within us emerges the urgency of ultimacy, and deeper still, often more recessed than this urgency, the porosity of our middle being, overtly manifested in the openness of our questing being. As this porosity cannot be determined in terms of finite univocal limits, as this urgency articulates the open energy of our exceeding being, so they pose us as questionings calling for an answering that is radical, original, and ultimate. The answer(ing) must address the hyperbolic nature of our quest(ioning), for, short of the truly incontrovertible, there seems no proportionate response to our patience, openness, and hunger. The proportionate response must be disproportionate: it cannot be a finite response. Given our porosity, we cannot *secure* an answer through ourselves alone; our urgency of ultimacy must befriend again the *passio essendi* intimate with the porosity. This befriending returns us to ontological astonishment at being at all. What possibilizes being at all? It is the incontrovertibility of being, intimately known in our own being at all, that is in question. No univocal answer will unequivocally answer, for the true "answer" could not be that kind of answer, for this would be to assimilate the question to one of a finite problem. Being finite at all raises the question of its possibility: what makes it possible, indeed what makes its possibility actual? What possibilizes not only its actuality but its very possibility? It is not a question of moving from a possibility to the actuality, but of what possibilizes the possibility at all, and then what possibilizes the original movement from this possibility to the actuality of finite being and its "that it is at all."

This more primordial sense of possibilizing is not a determinate or finite possibility; its original actualizing cannot be a finite and determinate causing. It is not an indeterminate possibility and actualizing. This would be *less* than the finite "that it is," whereas it must be a *more*. I would speak of overdetermined origination, expressed in agapeic creation. Agapeic creation suggests the incontrovertible "that it is" of God, not absolutely in self but relative to the side of the origin turned towards the finite between, as ultimate ground(ing) of its possible being, "that it is at all."

The metaxological sense guides us towards the more intensive sense of the primal ethos of being, where the elemental porosity is more appreciated, and where the *passio essendi*, more primordial than the *conatus essendi*, is more given for mindfulness. There we are more mindful of the giving qua giving of a more original energy of being – God as absolutely original "to be" – that originates the between as a porous medium of passing, and in which porosity and passage we know something of the nothingness of finitude, and of the divine energies as also a kind of creative "no-thing" in excess of finite fixation. The dialectical sense, *at best*, can point in the same direction: the communication of being shows a source of self-surpassing transcendence in which what is other to that source is not a dualistic opposite. There is a togetherness more fundamental than opposition, and hence neither source nor other is to be univocally fixed or equivocally opposed. The dialectical way to the overdetermined, in and through the determinate, can be likened to a *via negativa*. But negation does not lead us to nothing but to the porosity of being. The porosity is not a determinate negation.[1] I am not saying God is a dialectical being but dialectical metaphors brings something to the fore that helps us think ecstatic being that remains at one with itself in being in relation to what is other. Such ecstatic being is surpassing: a transcending that is self-transcending; just so, in its being what it is, it is the ecstatic source of energy it itself is. If there is a "self" to it, its being is itself in being transcending transcendence. It is itself in its self-surpassing that is no self-surpassing, for this hyperbolic origin cannot be exceeded.

For such reasons we can justifiably speak of God as absolute being that mediates with itself, at home with itself in relation to all others, for the others are not antagonistic opposites that limit it. But we could not leave it at that, not least because of question-able erotic interpretations of what this means. It would only be *half right* to say that while dialectic as *via negativa* leads us towards the self-transcending "no-thing," the metaxological as *via eminentiae* leads us to the excess of the divine "more," finding an affirmative role for irreducible otherness. Half right, in that the meaning of the noth-ing is modified in the metaxological way in taking us towards the intimate ontological porosity of the primal ethos of being, and the intimate receptivity and opening of our being at all as *passio essendi*. These latter (porosity, primal ethos, and so on) point more robustly than dialectic to the transcendence of God's being as requiring an irreducible otherness and not just otherness comprehended within self-mediation. There is more than the "more" of the given between. This is communicated in metaxological interme-diation *between* the between and the divine origin. We might call this "more" the surplus *huperousia* of God: surplus because in excess, *huperousia* because it is not being but above being, and, if nothing, then nothing in a manner beyond the opposition of being and nothing, or even their dialectical sublation. The being of the God of the *metaxu* is beyond the between, beyond becoming, beyond the being there at all of finite being, being beyond coming to be.

This second metaxological sense points us towards God as full, overfull being, but so full as to be as nothing for us, except in so far as its fullness is turned towards us in the between. We divine the "more" in what of it is turned towards us. What is turned to us is turned out of its own irreducible otherness, which is not a moment of the self-media-tion of the immanent whole. The metaxological allows other-being to turn towards us in the between, out of its own otherness, and remaining in its otherness even in turning to us. What is more than this turning towards us is shrouded in enigma and is as nothing to us. But it is as nothing because the pluperfection of its inaccessible mystery is intimated in the fullness turned towards us. It is as nothing because it is too much for us. That it is too much for us is intimated in the way its turn is proportioned to what of it we can take in. It meets us in the measure of the hospitality of our being, but this meeting is its disproportionate hospitality, of which we cannot be the measure. We cannot take it in or be the measure of it: an excess both overfull and as nothing for us. But the overflow of the overfull passes for us agapeically in the porosity of the between, a porosity that is

---

[1] Dialectical thinkers are not always clear enough on this, sometimes wavering between the empty and full nothing. Hegel, for instance, does not understand the porosity, does not appreciate the metaphysi-cal and religious significance of the *passio essendi*, and there is too much of a self-determining *conatus essendi* – expressed in the absolute urge to be of the divine that must determinate itself to be itself (in his *Logic* Hegel even speaks of the drive, *Trieb* of the Idea).

as if it were nothing, so quietly does the divine absolve finitude – indeed not just absolve it but rather love it.

We have to say both these things, retain the doubleness at the end, as at the beginning. God is not a being and yet as origin of being is. God is thus Being itself and yet beyond Being, since Being itself is *huperousia*. God is Nothing and yet this Nothing is not nothing, in that the origin as no-thing is the inexhaustible creative source that brings to be any thing or being, abiding as more than any thing it originates. Nor is this Nothing the determinate negativity we find in the becoming of beings in the between; nor indeed the nothingness constitutive of originated beings (that have come to be), also more than determinate negation. The porosity as the enabling medium of (ontological) communication gives us a truer, more secretly agapeic sense of the Nothing. Just as one might say there is more to the being of a thing than its determinate presence, so one might say there is more to God than this "more" of the being and its determinate presence, as well as say that there is also a nothingness more (and less) than the determinate negation ingredient in defining things, and further again a divine Nothing that is more (and less) than both this nothingness and determinate negation. More and less? It is on another scale, in the dimension of the hyperbolic.

I summarize these different senses of the being of God and the nothing: *First*, God as the hyperbolic "more": exceeded by no thing, an exceeding no-thing that is absolute original power to be. *Second*, the *nihil* out of which God brings being(s) to be: this is not God's nothingness, since God is agapeic and not simply erotic, and hence can originate coming to be as a giving of being in excess of nothing, defining the character of the being that is brought to be; yet God's being is not defined by either the nothing from which beings are called into being, or by the beings so given to be. *Third*, the porosity of the given being of the between: this is the open milieu of the primal ethos of being; this enables all communicating, passing, and becoming. *Fourth*, there is something like the more derivative determinate negation that presupposes the more primal coming to be of beings, given by original creation, but that qualifies the various immanent processes of becoming as they unfold towards a more full self-becoming.

Agapeic being and the nothing might be seen together in light of how in everyday life we diversely say "It is nothing." "It is nothing": this can be a gesture of nihilistic dismissal, but also one of release, of giving, even unto forgiving. See the agapeic being of God as more than nothing, hence creative, beyond nothing, calling finite being to be out of nothing. Finite being is nothing without this calling, this being gifted to be. But think of how a generous person gives and, when thanked, might give in reply: "It is nothing" (even though it is everything). For the point is to point away from the giver to the gift and the recipient: "It is nothing" accepts and returns the gratitude to the grateful recipient. And so there is not just a give and take, but a giving and re-giving. Giving is amplified in being gratefully received. There is no limit to the "more" of agapeic amplification. (Owning nothing, the loaves and the fishes are miraculously multiplied.) "It is nothing" gives manifestation to the porosity of a love that gives generously for nothing, and returns generosity to generosity, and perhaps also to hatred and enmity. This "It is nothing" is the communication of good, of love, in the between. (Wandering with destitution, as if falling from the heavens at night, divine manna is given in the desert.)

Thus, also, there is an "It is nothing" of forgiveness. It is the willingness to set the evil "at naught": to offer again the promise of life, and so to restore primal faith and hope in being. "It is nothing": an unclogging of the porosity in which the good of the "to be" communicates itself and freely passes. "It is nothing": a relativization, an absolution of the relation from guilt and indebtedness that frees gratitude into a released modality: beyond obligation, beyond morality in that sense also, beyond the law, though it is not evil. "It is nothing": a kind of anarchic good, a mercy beyond the moral law. There is a transfiguration of the first hyperbole "It is" into "It is good": nothing but the communication of good being in and through the porosity of the between.

SECOND METAPHYSICAL CANTO: GOD BEING (OVER)ONE

Do not say
It is one
It is One
Say more
It is the One
God
& exceeds one

Alone
Above all things
Alone
Among all things
Yet it is never alone
Through it alone
Nothing else
Is ever alone

Can we, how can we speak of God as One? We say: God is God. Is this an empty tautology? It depends. The "is" might be said univocally, equivocally, dialectically, metaxologically, and more is said in each successive saying. The tautology, as a *logos* of *to auto*, is not empty, if by *to auto* we mean a unity (perhaps comm-unity) whose sameness harbors internal richness and which the *logos* articulates. This internal richness might be plenitude hyperbolic enough to give rise agapeically to finite being as other to it, and without any defection from its absolute at-oneness. We are referred to a unique sense of unity: God is God, and nothing but God, and nothing other is God; God alone coincides with God. God is absolutely singular, a unique One on a par with which none of our terms can be.[2] How speak of it in our terms, if ultimately only its own terms must bespeak it? Listening to its communications, we must try to be on some terms with its terms, some sense of which we divine from the hyperboles of being.

How think of this unique One at all, since what we know of unity is governed by the determinate integrities of being we encounter in the finite between? This is a unity, we claim, because it is not that other unity; we can stand outside it, delimiting it as this and not that. This is impossible with God. God is not the between or a being in the between but hyperbolic. Should we speak of a hyperbolic unity? If so, our guides must be the hyperboles of being. There is an elusive unity in the holding together of idiotic being in the universal impermanence of creation; there is unity more than determinate in aesthetic happening; there is energetic unity as dynamically self-defining in erotic selving and it cannot be fixed to this or that; there is a community in the agapeics of communication revealing how the exceeding One and the more than One might be thought to assume superlative form.

Bear first in mind a certain movement to unity of all beings.[3] All beings exhibit the exigence to be, the counter movement to the disintegrating possibilities ingrained in finite beings. So far as beings are, they are held together, and hold themselves together into some integrity of being (see BB, Chapter 8 on things). The power to be is concretized as a multiplicity of integrities of being, each of which is the exigence to live the affirmation of its own power to be. Each integrity is also held together by other integrities, in the network of intermediating relations that define the between, coming and going in different forms in the universal impermanence. This sustaining is not absolutely self-sustaining: the givenness of being is not absolute *causa sui*. There is the primal *passio essendi*: being given to be: being created; receiving being, received to be. We find a kind of ontological spread of being in the universal impermanence, an utterly evanescent yet entire constant holding together into unity of the beings that are. What is this unity? What could such an integrity of creation, even as universal impermanence, be? The pantheist is tempted to identify it with God's unity. The pan(en)theist has the intimation that there is something about this unity that exceeds an entirely determinate whole. One appreciates the sources of these intuitions, but there is a more hyperbolic sense of unity intimated in the idiotics

---

[2] "[I]t is plain that the One Itself and God are the same, and that is not some particular God, but God Himself (*autotheos*). Those, then, who say that the first God is Demiurge or Father are not correct; for the Demiurge and the Father is a particular god." *Proclus's Commentary on Plato's Parmenides*, trans. G. R. Morrow and J. Dillon (Princeton: Princeton University Press, 1987), p. 443.

[3] Aquinas on God's unity and on being and one as convertible: *Summa theologiae*, Ia, ques. 11, art. 1–4.

of happening. More than the whole, more than the unity of the pan(en)theist, it is reserved for itself, even when it gives signs of itself in immanence.

I pursue the thought relative to the fourfold sense of being. Our first concern is with being in the between; our second will essay to speak about what is beyond the between. First, "being one" appears as univocal in being itself and not another. Second, it appears as equivocal in being itself but also not completely itself, since the movement of its power to be is a becoming that moves to be coincident with itself in a fuller way. This is clearly evident in the contingency of finite being as a being of possibility as well as actuality. Important here is the *affirmative* equivocal as *surplus* being – more than itself as univocally determinable. Equivocal being is *saturated* in a hyperbolic sense. This plenitudinous equivocal draws us towards the plurivocity of the divine unity. Third, the non-coincidence in equivocal being is not the division of the "being one" into two unities, such that we have two beings and not one. It bears on the internal differentiation of the one. Hence the doubling is held together in itself in a unity more mediating and including than we meet on solely univocal terms. The movement of the unity is its becoming: in becoming itself, there is a gathering of self to self, or a mediated oneness with self, in the very process of self-differentiation. In short, the unity, as self-transcending, is dialectically self-mediating.

Fourth, this "being one" is not the finite being's own self-creation or *causa sui* because it is as much held together by its emplacement in the intermedium of relativity with others as through its own holding of itself together. This metaxological "being one" is one and more than one: being in comm-unity. It is as much given its unity by its intermediating relativity to other integrities as its relative shape is constituted through its self-becoming. The ontological integrity of a being is always open to the integrities of other beings. It is self-transcending from the beginning, not only as self-becoming, but as transcending self to what is other. There is an already given space of reception to the transcending of the others towards it. Thus we come to a doubly mediating, an intermediating (co)unity rather than solely a self-mediating unity. This is not just a unity open to become itself; it is an open (comm)unity, allowing the self-becoming of each, the surpassing of this and that unity into the between, the interplay of one with the other allowing each its own integral otherness, hence a (comm)unity open to both self-becoming and communication of the integral other, and all of this from the origin. This last sense of "unity" points to the richest expression of "being at one" as agapeic community. With reference to it some sense might be made of God being (Over)One. Here is a try.

The monotheistic claim means there is no ultimate rivalry of absolutes. Were there more than one, one would limit the other, and hence the limited one would not be the One. But if the ultimate God is an unlimited One, what can that be? Since our basic tendency is to identify oneness with univocity, God seems to flow away into formlessness, and absolute unity is dissipated in *to apeiron*. Here we must rather think of *God beyond the whole*: not containable within any whole, not even the supposed totality of all that is. Monotheism has not always avoided some understandable reactions here. If unity is univocally secured by a certain determination of limit, the One must be set off from, and potentially set in opposition to, all other ones. In the course of religious life, as we know, this can turn into hostility to the other gods and their devotees. No rivalry of absolutes then means nothing but rivalry of absolutes. Red war rages rather the green agapeics of communication. We must grant that there is the One and none other besides the One, but define that One with sufficient nuance as to leaven any wrath of the peremptory monism of the univocalized God.

Suppose we say God is a "center" of creative power, and we use the language of the Same to describe the center. God's (over)wholeness as absolute sameness would seem to be pure homogeneity. Thus we come on such doctrines as that of the divine *simplicity*. Is the result then homogenous wholeness without parts, reminiscent of Hegel's too tart metaphor (no argument this) relative to Schelling's absolute or *Indifferenzpunkt*: the night in which all cows are black? Should we rather think of the idiocy of God – the divine as intimately communicating in a porosity of being where fluency and passage are more noteworthy than delimitable parts? The simple idiotic unity would also be the intimate flow, the fluency of communicability, communicating without limiting boundaries.

But how avoid sheer formlessness? What is the fluency of communicability/communicating in passage? Where the unity, if fluency flows over fixed form?

Say this: In the divine unity there is inner differentiation but there are no "parts," and the different divine powers relative to us, communicated towards us, are, in God's unique self-relation, the One fluent power. The powers are communications of the flow of the origin that streams through ways that mark boundaries but that qua streaming knows no boundary. Of course, if we univocalize the divine we might think of unity as immobile identity, especially whenever we interpret becoming as change due to defect. One must question an absolutely static univocity, for it could not generate beyond itself and hence be in relation to the between where we are. There would only be block immobile unity and no energies turned towards us, for there would be no turning in any direction. This type of unity is *lower* than a becoming or self-becoming. We compare God to the rock of ages, and the rock is a symbol of unshakeable constancy, but it is also relatively inert. It is the constancy we want to stress not the inertia. We have to think of the divine unity in dynamic terms, or sing with Yeats's Crazy Jane: "Men come, men go. *All things remain in God.*"

Beyond univocal unity, divine constancy suggests the unshakable yet dynamic grounding of multiplicity and the derived unities in the between. We might pay our dues to the equivocal in this qualified respect: sometimes we do need to resort to contrary predicates to describe this giving unity. Thus, it is constant yet ever active; always resting within itself, yet in eternal movement; beyond time, yet intimate to time; fully "there" and yet not; absolute being and no-thing; and so forth. More positively, the One is internally differentiated, while always remaining one, hence simply at home with itself; the differentiation would be the self-activity (if we could talk that way) whereby it is itself as act. If there is a "becoming" in the divine (if we did talk that way), it would not be a temporal becoming; not a movement from initial lack to progressive fulfillment, or from defect to perfection through a process of overcoming defect. It would be an eternal movement (but what is that?) from (plu)perfection to (plu)perfection, a kind of (hyper)movement hard to image in the between where we are dominated by dynamism as movement from unrealized potential to energeia as realized dunamis. There is dynamism and nothing but dynamism in the divine: beyond becoming, beyond coming to be. This is less the seeking than the enjoyment: dynamism always and ever energized. The point is equivocal for us, since we know this joy episodically. But joy is not inert, and joy is at home with itself, but not in a univocity closed into its own fixity, and hence it is more than being at home with itself. Joy is at one with itself as radiance beyond self. What is the "becoming" of radiance? Radiant "at oneness" would be communicative being, which would be to be outside itself in relation to what is other, and yet still never leaving itself behind. Such a unity would be infinite openness; as such it might also look less like a unity and more like a creating porosity.

A plenitudinous sense of the equivocal can draw us towards the plurivocity of the divine unity. It can intimate a kind of compacted wholeness which is an "all in all," enfolding in one what we usually consign to opposite categories, or see in strife. Such a compacted wholeness might be said to show the joyful tenseness of equilibrium and accomplished poise. Also suggested is the outgoing of the energy of wholeness that cannot be compacted into an inert identity, for it is as passing out of itself into what is other, a passing out that is also immediately a passing back into its own "at oneness."[4]

---

[4] In *BB* (see pp. 270–8) I connect what I call a rapturous univocity, itself inseparable from the equivocal, with *elemental rapport* with being, rapport with the all-in-all, in a kind of promiscuous univocity. More might be said about the being of God from this equivocal condition, for this is the matrix of all metaphor, symbol, figuration. God comes to us in these ambiguous figures which can be closer to a richer sense of oneness than is a more literal univocity. Thus: the-all-in-all: simple yet infinitely differentiated within itself, where differences are not finite determinations but infinite self-expressions of itself that are immediately returned to the simplicity of the wholing from which they are not separated. The separated is not separate; there is no separation and return, for this is a metaphor taken from the motion of becoming in the between, a metaphor to be negated once it is affirmed, and perhaps for humans to be affirmed again once negated. Granting there is something to this all-in-all, does not mean we forget the God beyond the whole.

An ambiguity to be negotiated here concerns how some pan(en)theists identify the whole with the divine. I would say rather that the whole gives a sign of the God beyond the whole, in the way the great art work carries the secret signature of the creator. The metaxological approach, as addressing the hyperbolic, passes in the porosity of the between by way of keeping open the difference of images and original. The whole is *not* divine transcendence as other. Nor is that transcendence as other an opposite extrinsic to the whole. With proper qualifications, the process of dialectical self-mediation that returns to itself in relation to what is other can serve as a metaphysical metaphor to image the divine unity as one of absolute wholeness. Perhaps we should call this radiant energy of being whole a *wholing*, not a whole? For it does not become a whole where before it was not a whole. It does not whole what before was lack; there is no lacking; there is just wholing: over-accomplished, ever-accomplished and over-accomplishing. In finite life, we know something of self-mediating unity as a kind of wholing – but as a *becoming* whole from the mixed condition of the power to be which is also lacking full being. An absolute wholing would be absolved from lack in that sense. If we called it an eternal coming to itself, to this wholeness of itself it would always already have come, and so there would be no coming, no coming to be, hence also no wholing. It is the ever-accomplished overwhole.

The notions of unity and trinity have been important in different traditions, but any notion of a "three in one" induces severe conceptual migraine for univocal logic. The Trinitarian view is importantly suggestive of a social understanding of the divine. The divine unity is not a univocal unity but a community. I would distinguish here between an *erotic self-doubling trinity* which moves from lack to self-completion, and which follows a Hegelian logic of dialectical self-mediation in and through its own other, and *the agapeic trinity* that proceeds from fullness to fullness, from the overfull to the overfull, the thinking of which procession of love is facilitated by way of the logos of metaxological intermediation. Both views allow a self-communication of the divine. In the first case, self-communication seems finally to circle around itself. In the second case, there is a communication beyond self in the creation of the irreducible other with finite creation, whose otherness does not obviate communication but rather qualifies the meaning of the self-giving – now as for the other as other, in a surplus of generosity that is willing to give even with no anticipation of any return to itself. This giving for the other is already consummate in the superplus of the immanent divinity, allowing a free giving of the finite other "outside" the divine immanence. Thus this second agapeic trinity points to more than the self-mediation of the divine unity; it affirms the creation of the finite other as given being for itself, as good for itself. In this creation there is communication between God and the world which is enabled by a porosity through which the divine generosity continues to pour itself forth to the bringing to be, the sustaining in being, the en-abling of the good, of the finite being.

The metaxological way calls attention to a togetherness of self-communication and communication to the other as other. There is a paradox in talking about a unity that is whole and yet double: in one sense wholing, in other sense doubling. Dialectic points us *via* the *dia* to this doubling, but only to one side of it, namely the self-mediation, self-communication of the unity; and is tempted to do so in terms of an erotic self-doubling The metaxological points us better to the other side, namely, its communication to the other as other beyond itself; and it does so in terms of the agapeic community in which otherness is not just a self-doubling, but a genuine redoubling of plurality without which no community could be said to be at all. The overwholing of the agapeic God gives this redoubling.

How does this fit in with Trinitarian language? Is there some tension with a One that returns to itself in being three? The figure of the Trinity must do justice to the complexity of relations such that it does not privilege a dialectical return to self where there is too much of love disporting with itself (pace Hegel) and not enough of the love that exceeds itself infinitely in the passage of giving for the other. We need a pluralism beyond any Trinitarian self-relation that is perhaps too *mono*theistic when it too finally stresses the return to self. But we need a pluralism that is also *more* monotheistic, in that God alone is God, but as alone God the astonishing origin of the prodigious multiplicity of creation. There is a monotheism that is too monistic in stressing self-return, such that a hyperbolical predominance is conferred on thought thinking itself and the autarchic self-sufficiency, such as Stoicism elevates into the heights. The hyperboles of metaxological being rather draw us towards the thought that thinks what is other to thought, and not just to think itself again but to go forth in an ecstasis of self-exceeding, where there is more exceeding than self in the passing of pure giving that streams from the ultimate source to the finite other; streams now as if from nowhere, for the giving source has, so to say, made itself as if it were nothing, to be everything in the passing over of pure giving. And so the (comm-)unity of the One beyond the one is the inexhaustible fullness of agapeic being, and yet it is nothing, and so like an absolute lack of absolute eros, but this is not an eros that seeks itself, for it is pure passage of kenotic giving that gifts, and passes through, the porosity of the between.

THIRD METAPHYSICAL CANTO: GOD BEING ETERNAL – SURPLUS TO COMING TO BE

Eternal	Working over time
Before all	In love with time
Coming to be	Its gift
Before all	Kissing the upsurge
Becoming	Of all coming to be
Never coming to be	Reserved companion
Never becoming	Wooing the surge
	Of time's becoming

It is not easy for us, living through interim time, to envisage what eternity might be. Many modern thinkers, and not alone process philosophers, demur at the idea. In premodern thought we find a deep "feel" for the matter, in modern, awkwardness, uncertainty, often rejection. Why this second? A certain ontological privilege is afforded to time: time seems to be the "horizon" of being beyond which we cannot go – the horizon greater than which none can be conceived. Whichever way we turn we meet the fluctuating, processive power of this forming and deforming god. Do hymns sung to time as the horizon of horizons serenade a dubious deity if these songs are silences on eternity as time's other? Time is interim: a between – not nothing, but not ultimate, for becoming has come to be, and it comes to being as an intermedium of passage: arising and perishing, passing into being and passing out. The interim of time: defined neither by some dualisms, perhaps dubious, in premodern ways, nor by more modern ways, perhaps too monistically temporalizing. Does the interim of time as between nothing and coming to be put us in mind of eternity as time's other?

We are proximately drawn to the hyperbole of the erotics of selving, not only as something human but relative to the (self-)becoming of creation as universal impermanence. Drawn proximately to this, we are also pointed beyond, opened through the erotics of (self-)becoming to the agapeics of communication. Our perplexity about eternity comes up in our pondering the difference of "becoming" and "coming to be." God's eternity is more primordially related to "coming to be" as ontologically prior to "becoming." Time's other is even more primordial than "coming to be."

We have to define eternity relative to what we know of time in the between where our thinking is time-saturated. How speak at all of a "before" time if this "before" is not itself temporal? There is becoming in the between, but always with respect to given happening, given already as granted. But in every instant becoming presupposes something already having *come to be*. There is a "coming to be" that is not itself a "becoming" in the more determinate sense. "Coming to be" names the more original coming into being that grounds creation as universal impermanence, and hence gives creation as "becoming" in the more determinate sense we know from the already given between. "Coming to be" is related to *passio essendi*, just as "(self-)becoming" is related to *conatus essendi*. As the *passio* is presupposed by the *conatus*, so "coming to be" is presupposed by "becoming," just as being given to be is presupposed by giving oneself to be. *Passio essendi* evidences a patience of being not only relative to human being but to the givenness of being at all. This patience is ontological: the given happening of creation is a "being created" before being any self-creation, or (self-)becoming. It is also metaphysical: it points to the giving origin of the *passio* which manifests itself immanently as created to be, not self-created. The hyperbolic is shown in immanence in the necessarily presupposed *passio essendi* in every *conatus essendi*. To be at all is to be given to be, but the meaning of this exceeds the terms of what is given in the givenness, and hence the givenness points further than itself, in and through itself. Time as arising, as given to be, points immanently to its other which is not simply temporally immanent. Thus we find arising for us the thought of eternity.

This "coming to be" is the granting of the possibility of time itself; but this granting, and so this "coming to be" is not itself temporal. What possibilizes time is not itself time. You might object: Time is self-possibilizing; it generates itself, makes itself possible. If I were to reply, perhaps yes, this would be so only in a relative sense: time temporalizes itself, becoming possibilizes itself but only relative to the fact of its already having been given to be itself as time. Time's self-possibilizing is never absolute; rather, it is a given from a more ultimate source, itself not a temporal product, or indeed a relative source of generation within the process of time itself. "Coming to be" is a name for the original arising of finite being which comes to be from the origin, but with the mark of its own possible nothingness written on its nature as happening, namely, as contingent reality that is, but that yet might not be at all. Happening, hence, is equivocal between coming to be and nothing, an equivocity ingrained in the plurivocal character of becoming as a determinate arising into being, a determinate formation of finite being in the between, and as a perishing of that determinate formation and its dissolving again into nothing. *"Coming to be" names the junction of what is other to time and time, of eternity and the becoming of creation in the universal impermanence.*

Through becoming, in so far as it points us to a more original "coming to be," we gain a sense of the other to time that is surplus to time, and that yet is in intimate relation to it. God's eternity, as God is in self, is ever prior to this prior "coming to be." *That* other to time is even more reserved to us than the enigmatic "coming to be" of which I speak. This reserve is the plus and sur-plus of the pluperfection of the divine. Time itself arises, arises with creation and relative to becoming. Becoming has its own timing, though we tend to be more at home with human, historical time. But the universal permanence has a sweep that recedes into abysmal backwards beyond the measure of human recall, as well as impenetrable forwards surprising beyond all our anticipating. Yet time arises; becoming itself comes to be. Becoming might even be *everlasting* but it is not eternal. That it comes to be at all has no absolute necessity: it is an interim happening, contingent in its possibly not being at all, actually there in that it does, after all, just happen to be. Eternity concerns the non-temporal arising of happening in its "coming to be," a "coming to be" that is not a becoming within the happening of time. This suggests an origin in another dimension to the first beginning of time, understood as the first "moment" of the happening of the universal impermanence, if there is such a first "moment."

Philosophers have resorted to the distinction between *logical and temporal priority* to make an approach to the issue, but the logical priority of eternal possibility is not enough. Such eternal possibility is like a transcendent univocity – it is not the living originative eternity required by the thought of God. We are too tied to dianoetic determinations and fail to give cognizance to the dynamic transcendings of the hyperboles of being, especially at the erotic and agapeic levels. To say something further, and in terms more or less determinate, we must recourse to the fourfold sense of being. The following points are important: The univocal is bound to a *negative* definition of eternity in opposition to time, the first static being, the second wavering becoming. The equivocal is also implicated in this oppositional dualism, but so as to signal our need for an affirmative relation to time, although with a positive stress on becoming. Dialectic furthers the mediation of time and eternity but continues to be equivocal in this mediation, tending to be more focused on "becoming" rather than "coming to be," tending to underplay otherness, with inverse consequences regarding eternity. While dialectic furthers "upward" erotic ascent, the metaxological signals "downward" agapeic descent, being true to "coming to be," the signs of its surplus origin, and hence the intermediation which communicates between eternity and time. I now follow the path of the fourfold.

Consider univocity relative to the classical idea of eternity as the *nunc stans*. Time is the *nunc movens*, eternity the standing now, the *nunc stans* of the *totum simul* (always already full simultaneity), in Boethius's formulation: "the complete possession all at once of illimitable life" (*Aeternitas igitur est interminabilis vitae tota simul et perfecta possession* – *The Consolation of Philosophy*, book V, prosa 6).[5] Perfection in one act, but not an act time bound – what kind of act, what kind of perfection this? The *nunc stans* is not moving, if moving is understood as a becoming from defect to realization. But what if we think of a "moving" that is a "coming to be," and then again of eternity not as "coming to be" but as the origin of "coming to be"? The *nunc stans* seems to set stasis in opposition to dynamism, motionlessness to moving. Suppose we think of the *nunc* as the instant which *instans*, so to say: standing in, instanding. The instant, or the instanding, is the *Augenblick*, the blink of an eye, and we cannot pin it down at all, as Augustine in his deep exploration found (see the *Confessions*, book XI, Chapter 11; or *The City of God*, book XI, Chapter 21). We might say: *Instancy* is related to constancy: the instance in which the eternal not only stands in, but stands with (*con-stans*), time. That we cannot pin it down should make us rethink the standing nature of the *nunc*. The *nunc* does not stand, it is moving, but not always as transition from defect to realization, but moving with the arising into being as the origination of the sur-plus of the origin.

The instant instands into the *becoming* of the between. The instant is a standing in the becoming; the becoming comes to be in that instanding. The coming to be, being instanding, is a movement of creation, though not a temporal movement, but one giving rise to temporal becoming. This cannot be univocalized, though the univocalization of the *nunc stans* might want to extrude any moving from it. To univocalize the *nunc stans* is to find oneself with nowhere to stand. That there is nowhere to stand should be seen in a different light: the moving now is always being moved into being, instanding in being, not with the motion from determination to determination but from nothing to the singular "once" of the now. Eternity is not so much the instanding as the source of the instanding, and not itself a standing now, but a sending of the instanding now, and its commission to being at all. We should think the movement of time's other as sur-plus to the movement of the *nunc movens*, as an other "movement" – as the sending and commission of the instanding – and not just as the absence of motion.

Time's own resistance to univocalization suggests a return to the ambiguity of becoming with an openness to its double process as intimating something other. The presenting of the present is not a fixed univocal determination of being that falsifies the flux of becoming. "Presenting" shimmers with the showing of becoming as a double process of coming to be and passing away, and this showing intermediates an ambiguous intimation of the sur-plus source of the coming to be that gives time its eventuating and evanescent being. The "presenting" shimmers with its own hyperbolic promise. The "presenting" of being is metaxological. The *totum simul* seems to bespeak a totalization of time from the standpoint of a transcendent timelessness, but I would prefer to take it as metaxologically naming an absolute over-wholeness that originates time but that is not itself a temporal product, such that intimacy with time is embraced by it. The over-wholeness is not the whole, but acknowledging both the surplus and the dynamism, an *over-wholing*. For "coming to be," pointing to the over-wholeness of the origin, is not a movement

---

[5]   Aristotle seems critical of Plato, but his description of the Prime Mover has echoes of Plato. On Plotinus's concept of eternity see *Enneads* III 7. Like Boethius's views, Augustine's views influenced later medieval speculation. See Anselm's *Monologion* (Chapter 24) and *Proslogion* (Chapter 13); Aquinas, for example, *Summa theologiae* Ia, quest. 10.

from defect to perfection, but from the overflow of an over-fullness already perfect. The over-wholing of this movement suggests the pluperfection of the origin.

What the pluperfecting movement of such an over-wholing would be remains enigmatic, of course, in that so much of our thinking is determined temporally by a becoming from lack to more, not from more to more. Nevertheless, our own episodic rupturing by a piercing movement of excessive fulfillment is a small sign that this other movement breaks into time: the acme moment, inexhaustible with a significance we cannot univocally determine, indeed it might take us a whole life to understand, a whole life to know we have not understood. The eternity of God as acme of being is in a dimension other to time, intimated in the rupture of time by such moments of breakthrough. Breakthrough is related to the deeper meaning of a "coming to be" that is not first a becoming, though it may seed a becoming that transforms the recipient of the gift. The breakthrough is *exaiphnes*, in the instand, of a sudden. What is the sudden? The sudden intimates the primal arising of a new "coming to be" – a new "once," happening at once and as a "once." The suddenness of happening intimates a surplus origin, always once, always new and ageless, beyond time and before time and giving arising in time, hence older than age beyond age, older than death, and yet younger than the youngest baby, born and unborn.

What of the Nietzschean declaration of love for time, the inversion of the Platonic love of eternity? Is it also not captive to a dualism of time and eternity, even if it now excoriates the other side rather than this side? This is true, at least at first. For the excoriation of the other side also leads to the evanescence of this side. And then there are no sides: only now. And then (when?) there is not even the eternal return, for "now" there is now and nothing but now. Does this not mean that a hypertemporalizing philosophy conducts once again to a new eternalized, eternalizing now? If this is so, the differences between the Nietzschean and the Platonic seem to cancel each other out.

The equivocal doubleness of becoming might suggest either of these philosophies, but the truer love of time awakens in becoming to the astonishing happening of "coming to be," hence indirectly to the source of "coming to be," itself not a temporal becoming, or being in temporal becoming, or product of it. The truer love does not stifle porosity to eternity, for it is not flight from time that puts us in mind of God but the unfathomable mystery of time itself, as the becoming given out the happening of "coming to be." Eternity "names" the original other of time gleaned from the mysterious matrix of time itself.

Dialectical helps with this gleaning by directing us beyond dualism to the play of creation between eternity and time. As time is not an unreal succession of static instants, eternity is not a static transcendence closed univocally into its own unity. As an instanding ecstasis pointing beyond itself, time testifies to a transcending in becoming itself. It is in the ecstasy of life that the energy of eternity is communicated. There is dunamis on both sides, hence intermediation, and not between stasis and dunamis but between energy and energy. Dialectic opens a way to see eternity as an origin mediated in itself, yet exceeding itself into the between. Always in excess of univocal unity, eternity is intermediated in the immanence of time.

If we correlate dialectic with erotic selving through the other, we might conceive of eternity as producing time to *mediate with itself*. Eternity is an ecstasis of original energy in love with time, bringing time to be as its own other in order to *come to be itself* fully. I am not advocating this view. It overplays the erotics of selving to the concealing of the agapeics of communication, hence underplays the enabling otherness between time and eternity. Eternity must become, must become time, becoming in time in order to be itself fulfilled, or fully determinate coming to be. The surplus pluperfection of eternity as time's other vanishes from proper consideration. With some dialectical conceptions, especially Hegel's, God will be identified with complete self-determining being through the other that is no real other. "Coming to be" is viewed as dialectical "becoming" out of an initial indefiniteness, and eternity comes to be the absolute self-determination of time. Eternity makes itself redundant in this dialectical way rather than, as previously, being made redundant by the dualistic way. We find this with many of Hegel's successors, but the seeds of the redundancy are not only sown but entirely flourishing in Hegelian dialectic.

By contrast, and first, metaxological mindfulness bids its *adieu* to any idolatry of immanent time, as if that were absolutely autonomous; as if time itself did not come to be; as if becoming did not come to be or were unoriginate. Rather, what is in time becomes, but time itself "comes to be," because it is given to be. About time there is no absolute necessity; it is inseparable from the happening of becoming which, as showing the patience of happening, comes to be. In that respect, time is not autonomous but heteronomous: its origin is surplusly other.

Second, metaxological mindfulness is forged in memory of godsends: witnesses to radical heterogeneity, and each a glorious "once." The absolutization of autonomous immanent time cannot witness to these godsends. In some strands of modernity, at least, it produces, rather, its own idolatry of futurity. This it secreted (perhaps unknowingly, perhaps knowingly) from a sometimes undernourished, sometimes misdirected fervency for immanent transcendence (say in the form of T^2). I mean, among other things, a temporalizing apocalypticism in which we will a total transfiguration of our immanent being in the between, often to be ushered in with extremest violence. Whether in religious apocalypticisms or in secular, political apocalypticisms this can come from an ideological squinting at the interim of time that gives rise to a badly blurred double-vision of eternity. Eternity now seems to be just immanent in the glorious future – there, there just a little bit beyond the edge of the blur! – about to arrive, violently overthrowing and redeeming the oppressive ambivalences of the now-time. Eternity blurred to apocalyptic futurity breeds disastrous contemporaneity.

Eternity as origin of "coming to be" is in another dimension, and if it breaks into time, its break-in is and is not here-and-now, and it is not in destruction simply, but in the renewed creation of the "once" of given being, and in the passing of the "once" into the "never." Here-and-now in that the break-in recreates coming to be; not here-and-now since the break-in does not first regard becoming. The renewal of coming to be leavens becoming like yeast. How is the kingdom of God both among us, and yet coming (Jesus)? Because this being among us and this coming are neither just the becoming of time towards a future telos. Being among us and ever coming, it is now and not now, always already now, forever now, and never just now. (None of these temporal predicates is quite right.)

Third, the metaxological asks for memorial mindfulness about the signs of excess in equivocal becoming. It is struck by astonishment about the surplus otherness of "coming to be" over determinate becoming. Its passage on the way of excess is open to perplexity about the eternal origin of "coming to be" in its utter otherness and transcendence. The way of excess gives presentiment of the origin as an agapeic source of the "coming to be" that releases the coming into its own time. Since it is a mistake to see this "coming to be" as the coming to be of the origin, since the origin as eternal, as source of "coming to be," does not come to be in that sense, it is never appropriate to think eternity homogeneously with any form of finite self-becoming. Moreover, the metaxological sense of transcending eternity does not reintroduce dualistic opposition. Rather, it draws attention to an essential pluralism between the origin and creation. The pluralism arises from the incomprehensible (idiotic) *communication* of being by the origin in the primordial "coming to be." Pluralized intermediation is communicative being, is a communication of being, and a community of being. The agapeic character of eternity's love for the creatures of time is more intense than the most passionate eros, and yet so quietly un-insistent as to be hardly noticeable.

Fourth, beyond speculative dialectic's mediated sameness in otherness of eternity and time there is the hyperbolic otherness to temporal becoming of both the origin and "coming to be." This otherness participates in the possibilization of communication. Communication is the overflow of the overdeterminate origin into the creative "coming to be" that originates the between, and this "coming to be" is the giving of a creative agape, not just erotic self-transcending and self-seeking. It is giving of the other as other. The metaxological way stresses the intermediation of time and eternity, not the self-mediation either of eternity in time or time in eternity. As an intermediation it is beyond univocity and dualism; it tries to divine in the equivocal the trace of transcendence as other; beyond speculative synthesis, it affirms an other equipoise of immanence and transcendence, time and eternity. There is consent to eternity's otherness, not complaint that it surpasses our determination and self-determination. It is the surplus surpassing source of all determination; as surpassing, it is not nugatory or redundant; out of its own absolute otherness as thus sur-plus, pluperfect, we are enabled as self-determining and led freely to contemplate a downward agapeic descent.

In sum: we are led to think of God as an eternal agapeic origin: always already having given the other its being as for itself – and the giving of "coming to be" is not its own coming to be but is given for the other as finite creation that comes to be. The agapeic giving releases this "coming to be" into its own otherness; hence, from this "coming to be" arises the gift of time, as given into its own goodness and created creativity. Becoming, too, is released for itself, as an ecstasis of originated original being. The ecstasy of time is time's own ecstasy, but as given from the origin, it is also a rejoicing with the origin which leaps in its leaping: in loving itself it loves eternity, though it may not know it; it loves eternity because in its ownness it is loved by eternity. Eternity as giving source keeps its *distance*, so to say, to let the creature of time come into its own, out of the "coming into being," and the determinate becomings in the between. This distance means there are asymmetries between eternity and time, but these are not invidious, since the superiority of the superior is put in suspension by agapeic love. It is willing even to be as nothing for the sake of the coming into its own of time. We may think it nothing, but this is not to understand the meaning of agapeic being as nothing.

Eternity is as always coming, yet never coming to be, and yet never completely determinate here. It is beyond all coming, yet source of all coming to be. It is always already coming to be, never becoming, nor become, yet always already having come to be, and always already forever being.

FOURTH METAPHYSICAL CANTO: GOD BEING INCORRUPTIBLE – AGAPEIC CONSTANCY

Firm like mountains fluid like seas
Moving but not moved
Moved and moving
More than we can know
Our words butterflies
Flimsy
& blown about the skies

Fire that revives
Wind that cools
Rain that drenches
The thirst of the desert
That holds itself ready
To receive
With boundless reserve

Immutability is closely connected with eternity, and the traditional line of thought is tied to a certain interpretation of becoming. Becoming is a movement from the potential to the actual, because the potential lacks self-actualization. Just this lack, albeit not absolute lack, is not appropriately attributed to God. God has no lack. Corruptible things show forth the ontological lack; beyond all lack, God is the immutable.[6] Notice again the movement from equivocity to univocity. As mixing lack and actuality, becoming is equivocal; beyond these vagaries, God is immutable unicity.[7] But, as before, an oscillation between equivocal time and univocal eternity is not enough, so also here. We know the dynamic of life to be mutable, but this dynamic has to be properly underscored not negated. Immutability is often our image of death, but the apotheosis of death is not what we mean by God.

There is a paradox here. A major impetus to ponder on God's immutability is just our exposure to death. In the transience of becoming there is suffering and pathos, and the

---

[6] Philo of Alexandria (20 BC–AD 50) is said to be one of the first to defend divine immutability in relation to scriptural texts suggesting God's changeableness, for instance, God's repentance after the Flood. See *On the Unchangeableness of God*, trans. F. Colson and G. Whitaker, *Philo* (Cambridge: Harvard University Press, 1960), Vol. 3.

[7] Many thinkers connect immutability with perfection, but Augustine and Aquinas make a connection with simplicity, see *Summa theologiae*, Ia, quest. 9, art. 1.

quick evanescence of the temporary gift of finite life. We come fresh to this world, greedy for life and more life, and we live, or are lived. We surge on the swell of young life, we crest and settle into domestic arrangements with time, but the mystery of life cannot be tamed and it is passing as we think of ourselves as settled. And then the downward plunge of the wave shows us as sliding to a breaking over which we lack governance. Aging we are living but also dying, into light or into nothing, we are not sure. Greed for life, clinging to life, does not drown without dissent. We dream of our deathlessness. We dream of God as deathless, whether transfiguring our deaths or as beyond all dying, we are not sure. For every mutation is also a death, hence the becoming of finite beings is death, even in the novelty of each new birth. Death is woven into the fabric of life, and as we age the fabric unravels, the strand of nothingness is unloosed and its strangling power stifles, slowly or suddenly, the singular beings we are. The deeper source of our speaking of God's immutability arises from perplexity about deathlessness – life as deathless, not a mask of death shrouding life. Such deathless immutability cannot be the negation of mutable life, but incorruptible excess of life above mutability.

It is evident from this that, in the immanence of interim time, we need to think more dialectically of mutability and immutability. The dynamism of life holds them together even in their opposition. It is not that the ceasing of the mutable makes us fly life; it is that life in the mutable longs for its consonance with life as excessive to being nothing. What threads the opposites together is the original power of being, given to us in the mutable but surprising us in its exceeding surplus, with intimations of life beyond cease. We need not counterpose becoming to static being. We divine in becoming the more primordial "coming to be," and further see a figuration of the origin in the constancy of "coming to be," brought before us in the incontrovertibility of the "that it is" of being. We move from life to more primordial life to the origin: from becoming to "coming to be," to the constant origin of "coming to be." Is there change in the origin? The question makes no sense if we think in terms of the change of determinate becoming; the dynamism of the origin is not that kind of becoming. Nor need we exclude "movement" if we think of this through "coming to be."

The dialectical unity of opposites in life can incline us to seek the divine life in terms of *transition* from immutability to mutability, or perhaps, more sophisticatedly, from "coming to be" to becoming. One result can be a historicization of God: initially seemingly immutable to us, God is in the life that comes to be, giving itself over to the completion of its determination in the mutable process of becoming. One of the most influential historicizations we find in the self-becoming of the Hegelian God. The view can even suggest a kenotic interpretation of the "death of God." The immutable univocal God dies into equivocal mutability. The dialectic of historical life is the surpassing of dualistic transcendence and the progressive creation of the unity of God and time. The death of the otherworldy God is the divinization of this life of mutability itself: finitude itself the temporal process of the becoming God, of becoming God. Process thought offers a variant. God's primordial nature is the static abstract immutable principle, eternal in its own way but indeterminate apart from its determination as God's consequent nature. The latter is formed by the interplay of the primordial nature with the course of the becoming of nature and time; the interplay with becoming determines the self-becoming of God such that the consequent nature is the more concrete God, as having become involved with and prehended the vagaries of mutability.

An agapeic God makes it impossible to deny the divine involvement with time. But the question is the "how" of that involvement, and of a "how" that does justice to both a richer appreciation of the traditional sense of immutability and the equally traditional sense of divine involvement. If there is truth to the view that origin and "coming to be" ought not to be identified with the determination(s) of becoming in time, there is then space for the transcendence of God that cannot be rendered in the categories of mutability. We may need not quite categories but more attunement to the singing of the "mutability cantos" of things (with a bow to Spenser), singing not mum about the kenotic passing of creative change. We may also need a metaxological understanding of constancy.

Who would want an inconstant God, a fickle ultimate unable to stand with (*constans*) the finite creature? The finite being is relatively constant, relatively inconstant. How think a constancy that stands with the inconstant, without itself being inconstant? Instead of immutability as a denial of mutability, and hence an abrogation of dynamism, suppose we view the origin of "coming to be" in terms of such an *absolute constancy*. Constancy marks that which "stands with," *stare cum*. To "stand with" is a relation to the other in which the being and good of the other is upheld. The constancy of God would be the agapeic upholding of the otherness of becoming as creation itself. In the universal impermanence the upholding origin is constant(ly) with the creation.

"Standing with" entails a plurivocal relativity, a fidelity that offers confidence (*confides*). First, standing is a constancy within itself: God is upstanding within self, and hence absolute integrity as reliability. God's standing means always already having come to a stand, standing for something – embodiment of ultimate fidelity. Divine standing in self in an upstanding that, entirely at one with itself, is yet a standing in for the other as other. Constancy would signify something like the absolutely reliable integrity of the origin that, as also giving itself into relativity, always already stands up for the finite other.

Second, there is the *cum*, the "with," of constancy, here now as a being for the other as other: the agapeic derivation of the coming to be is not the self-becoming of the other but the arising of creation as an integral whole. Standing with and for this created other, the origin as agapeic is always with the immanent whole. Constancy as changeless reliability is always a moving with the otherness of creation and thus a relation of intimacy, an intimacy not cloyingly smothering the creation but freeing it into its own being good. This constancy of intimacy is a love that does not reduce the other to itself. It can be mistaken as a colder distance, but there is a distance nearer than a more overt intimacy seems to be. This intimacy, as much reserved as expressed, would be the secret constant involvement of the agapeic origin with the mutable itself. A confiding other is there even in death, beyond death. Constancy would refer finitude to its own most secret source of strengthening: God's own courage that takes the risk of letting finitude be for itself, including in its promise the possibility of its failure or defection.

I try this: the *nunc stans* of eternity does stand, but it stands not in lifeless stasis but with the standing reliability of absolute constancy. The divine stance (*stans*) is a constance (*con-stans*), a standing with. The *nunc* is ecstatic beyond itself, and not shrunken back into lifeless instantaneity. But this instancy is not alone an ecstasis of time; it is a more hyperbolic ecstasy. The instant as *in-stans*, as standing in, reveals the "in" in the intimacy of the constant in temporal process itself. The constant stands in the instant; however, as agapeic, its intimate instanding always sustains that distance (di-stance: *diastans* as double standing. Dia: God) which preserves both the otherness of the origin, and the created integrity of the finite being. This distance holds together eternity and time, equally in the intimacy of instancy, the "standing in" of eternity in time, as well as the otherness of constancy, the "standing with" of eternity in community with time.[8]

The dia-stans might also be seen as serving to source the porosity of the between, as well as the immanent ecstasis of time. The inner distention of this dis-tance is most secretly a love of eternity. This secret love is stirring in our temporal being. The mutable is mutable because, through itself alone, it does not have absolute constancy. In the end there is no ultimate reliance except on the reliable constancy of the ultimate. But – it is

---

8   *On divine distance*, think of the Greek word *hypostasis* as describing coming into being, a kind of creation. Something comes to stand. This is the in-stance. It stands in the instant: the instanding. Then there is the con-stant: it stands with. But we also need di-stance: this is the di-stand. *Dis* (dia) – two: names the space between the source of the hypostasis and what the hypostasis brings to be, as well as the space of difference between beings that have come to stand (together: con-stand) in the between. Hypostasis might refer to the below (*hupo-*), but beyond an immanent coming to be from below, we need also a coming to be from above: a *hyperstasis*, so to say. The hypostasis, as coming to be below, comes to be from above, the hyperstasis. This hyperstasis, open affirmatively to the instance, the constancy, and the distance, would more evidently be an *agapeic* origination. The primal porosity between the hyperstasis and the hypostasis is the between.

important to remember this – this does not at all mean a degradation of the finite. Its very mutability raises in us, and in the agape of God, a measureless love. In our case, we are raised to it with respect to one, or two, or a few beloved others. The saints are raised to show something of its unrestrictedness in readiness. With God the constant, it is with all created being.

Think of the ache beauty occasions in us. The beautiful delights us, rouses joy; it also causes the smart of an obscure suffering; the very mortality of the beautiful lacerates the opening to eternity that has appeared in the beautiful face, or flower, or open roll of the ocean. Beauty visits us with a graced instance of promised constancy. We love the beautiful, and in our suffering of it, we would that it were eternal, though we know, again as a smart in the flesh, that it will fade. Beauty is arresting, but it is fugitive, and we fly after it, as it flies from us – but the lure of eternity is in the knowing love of pain and joy. The constancy of eternity passes over the face of the beautiful, though mostly, in the in-stance, we do not note the passing, until it is too late, and in loss we are rent by the absence of what was so absolutely intimate and immanent that we failed to greet it and thank it while it passed. In happenings like this we have the metaxological doubleness of otherness and intimacy, transcendence and immanence. We are graced with an instant of standing there that in its fading draws the desiring soul into a constancy that touches us in passing, and that never passes: fades and remains, flees and comes towards us, being fugitive and full standing.

This idea of "immutability" as agapeic constancy is beyond determination in terms of the dualism of the changing and unchanging, yet without being a dialectical unity of these opposites. In the porosity of the between, one has to live the pathos of passage and passing and suffer the glorious gift of given life and the withdrawal of interim time, to be aroused from the sleep of finitude (see *ISB?* Chapter 1). Such a somnolence has not been woken to mortality, much less dreamt of deathlessness. It is the suspension of this sleep that puts us differently in mind of the dream. Like a godsend, a taste of agapeic mindfulness is offered to us, though we must sing our mutability canto. This taste nourishes a thankfulness for the gift of mortal life, mortal life loved with a strange love beyond mortality itself, as if we were gods in love with the creatures of time, down to the last insignificant detail, a greying hair on a scrofulous head. Like such an incalculable love of the singular as singular is the agapeic constancy of God.

FIFTH METAPHYSICAL CANTO: GOD BEING IMPASSABLE – ASYMMETRICAL AGAPEICS

Do not say	It does nothing
It is inconstant	It is patient to all
It does not waver	Above all passion
It bears all	It is below
Its forebears	With all
It acts in all	In constant compassion

With regard to impassability the focus falls on the form of relation or relations. Traditionally God is said to effect the world, the world not to affect God. World needs God, God does not need world. There is an asymmetry of relation: world is essentially related to God, but world has no essential relatedness to God, that is, no relatedness to God that is essential to God. World is what it is in essential relation to God, but God is what God is outside all relation to the world. One appreciates the rationale: to preserve the transtemporal pluperfection of God as God. The point at issue is also patent: If God is insuperably impassive as a circle of self-sufficient being, how be in relativity to anything other to Godself? If there is a transitive relation of creation from origin to world, there is no transitive relation from world to God, hence God as origin of creation

---

[9] See Aquinas, *Summa theologiae*, Ia, quest. 45, ad 3 on creation as a relation which changes nothing in God.

itself as "transition" to world is essentially unaffected by whatever transpires to the other term of the one-way relation. Thus Aquinas: creation is a relation between God and world which effects everything in the world but nothing in God.[9] Attention is drawn to a singular asymmetry, God alone being God – but is this affirmed by denial of a relation of more interinvolved intermediation with the world?

There is a by now traditional critique of this traditional view. The impassible God is not the God of religious traditions which tell of divine involvement with creation. Process philosophy has tried underscore the divine relativity, a relativity said to affect God, even as the world is effected by God. It is right to couple absoluteness with relativity: the more absolute a being, the more rich its relations of community with what is other. Absoluteness without relations would be the absoluteness of the solitary sovereign who retracts the passage ways of Jacob's ladder, backing up into a lonesome heaven beyond all passing below and all going up.

I would also say the following. First, the impassable God owes something to the transcendental univocity of an absolutely self-sufficient being in need of nothing outside itself to be the absolute it is. We are reminded more of the autarkic Stoic sage than the agapeic servant. One thinks too of the exalted self-circling of Aristotle's thought thinking itself. But why should being touched by the other be a compromise on absoluteness? If God is agapeic origin this question requires a response different to autarkic self-sufficiency or thought thinking itself.

Second, the agapeic God is beyond *noēsis noēsis noeseōs*, for thought thinking itself points through the space of its own self-differing to an other that is other to thinking thinking thinking. Plotinus made a somewhat similar point relative to Aristotle. We could modify the point relative to the exceeding One that is the agapeic origin. Why should thought thinking itself create other-being beyond itself? An agapeic God creates other-being beyond itself, and is in relation to other-being, and this is not just its own internal otherness. The agapeic God is the communication of the full with the full, in a love that is overfull, and there is a kind of hyperbolic otherness to this love recalcitrant to the besetting temptation of thought thinking itself, namely, of closing into itself, beyond all otherness, or perhaps reducing all otherness to itself alone. Plotinus's One is more like an idiotic One whose simplicity seems to exclude otherness; Hegel's speculative unity includes all otherness, and hence excludes the proper otherness between the One and the many, such as is named by the metaxological difference of God and creation. Higher than thought thinking itself, the agapeic One already is agapeic community, communication with the other in its primordial oneness with itself, a communication itself the ground of its going outside of itself in relation to the world it creates. This latter creative communication is also agapeic, hence requires metaxology rather than dialectic to remain faithful to the plural forms of relativity between sameness and otherness.

This agapeic community is passage, passing, passability: it is a going over that releases the other, a going over such that the other does interrelate to the being of the goer. God effects the being of the finite other, but is affected by that being in that everything is given as it is by relation to the agapeic love of the divine. The relation is an intermediation, but is this a mutual mediation? In one sense yes, since the freedom of the finite other is released into being as itself communicative, a communicative power that in humans awakens to mindful porosity to the divine communication. In this awakening, it is not God who wakes up; it is we who wake from the sleep of finitude, and find ourselves in communication. In another sense no, the intermediation is not a mutual mediation, in that there is an asymmetry between the terms, marking God as hyperbolic in an unsurpassable way to our terms. There is no term of similarity that is not more exceeded by a term of dissimilarity. But the asymmetry in an agapeic relation is peculiar: there can be a reversal of what we expect on the terms of either a univocal or speculative logic. The hyperbolic term can show its height by placing itself in service to the lower term: it can give itself over to the lower, even unto death, and, shockingly, the mode of its being given over to the inferior shows just its superiority. Its love of what is below shows its being above. Its absolute majesty is agapeic service of the other.

Does this mean God is affected by the world? In a sense yes, but in a hyperbolic mode of still being absolutely free, for the love that is affected by the other, if agapeic, is not the less at home with the joy of goodness in this, and when we think of this joy as hyperbolic, its affection is redemptive rather than diminishing. Does it mean God is changed, and hence already deficient? I think the question thus put presupposes too rigid univocal terms, and the dualistic opposition back and forth between deficiency, understood as equivocal self-lack, and perfection, understood as univocal self-sameness. These latter terms may be adequate to describe certain determinate forms of relation between determinate things and happenings in the between. They are not adequate to the being of God, nor the relation between God and world – especially if we think in the dimension of the hyperbole of the pluperfection. We need more dialectical and metaxological terms even to attempt to do this.

Third, the dialectical way, properly qualified, points beyond the above limitations. The porosity of the between, and the promise of community there, already suggest something more than such autarkic self-sufficiency. God effects the world, and the world as other is defined in relation to God – but if God originates world, and origination is a relation, why should this relation also not affect (I do not say effect) God? Is there not an intermediation from the world to God more than any merely extrinsic relation? Is the finite forever knocking on the outside door, but never given entry to the *sanctus sanctorum*? Suppose the door is permeable, suppose it opens, suppose the cry of the creature enters the heart of God. Suppose the agapeic asymmetry reserves itself in revealing itself. It seems as if we knock, but perhaps we are rather knocked on, for we have closed ourselves in, and we hardly hear this knock, so gentle as to be almost silent, yet unfathomably patient in its continuous *incognito* communication.[10]

Consider: If "coming to be" is not the same as becoming, nevertheless what becomes shapes the promise of "coming to be." Becoming can stifle the promise of "coming to be"; it can act in companionship with that promise such that the gift of "coming to be" and the determinate shaping of becoming seem to dance in a redeemed unison. Is "coming to be" the door on which we creatures knock, and the *sanctus sanctorum* the intimacy of the origin that we never enter and that remains impassable? But again, suppose we are the closed door that has shut itself in and hardened the porosity on which now the knock falls? What now answers its soundless summons? It seems nothing answers but silence, silence porous to communication beyond finite fixation. But silence communicated can also be the reserve of a tireless patience on which we can count. Suppose the constancy of the origin remains constant, and in that sense impassable, but impassability is not now a non-reactiveness. *It is the never spent reserve of being patient.* It is an inexhaustibility of availability that can take patience for everything and its good and not be shaken in its being by waywardness: take in patience the bilge of evil, and allow it passage into itself, through itself, and offer this filth in passing the sieve of purification, and yet remain in unshaken con-stance with the promise of creation, which is just the good of the creature.

Fourth, the dialectical way can illuminate the eros of God. What could this be? It will be said, God seeks the creature, loves with the eros of which the lover sings in the *Song of Songs*. There is an eros in love with the beloved, so obsessed the love would sing to it, would stroke its skin, drink up its flesh, inhale its fragrance, seek it from the pit of its longing, untiring till it comes into the company of the beloved. Such eros does not wound the aloof God of univocal impassability. The erotic God is wounded, is wet with desire as passing out of itself, on fire with transcending, tireless in wooing the beloved. We have touched on this in the mystic woo.

---

10 See *HG*, Chapter 8 on the reserves of God and divine patience. Waiting and God's patience: this looks like indifference. Think of parable of the wheat and the tares: they must be allowed to grow together till the time of the harvest lest we destroy the wheat as we try to uproot the tares. This is to respect the mixed condition of the between. There is an essential letting be: leave the mixed condition to the end of time lest in purifying the mix we also destroy what is good in it. We lack the finesse of God's patience. We must not take the last judgment into our own hands. Religious and secular apocalypticisms tend to do this; these are forms of idolatry defective in divine patience. This appears to them as our weakness not God's forbearance.

If God is erotic like that, the love is not out of lack but out of the fullness of soliciting and willingness to give. Eros is too often connected with the *conatus essendi*, the endeavor to be, and not enough with the *passio essendi*, the pathos of being. If we pay more attention to the latter, the patient porosity of the divine eros will seem more credible. Dialectic underplays this patience, privileges the drive to self-determining: God's erotic seeking is less a patience, a *com-passio essendi*, as the divine self-becoming of the origin, its endeavor is to be itself most completely, overcoming impassible identity in its self-mediating wholeness. In my view, here "coming to be" is mixed up with becoming, and the origin as other to both is not granted in its otherness. The drive from lacking indeterminacy (as indefinite) to determination to mutual determination to self-determination hides from us the *overdetermination* of the origin, and the infinite patience folded into the divine reserves of this overdetermination. This, in the end, produces a kind of dialectically totalized impassability: within the One self-mediating absolute there are changes that change the life of the whole, but within the embrace of the whole, these change are subordinated to the impassability of the whole in relation to itself. This is a return of univocity.

Fifth, corrective to this is the insight that eros is not just an expression of lack, and that the patience of love, the *com-passio essendi*, is released freely towards the other out of a saturated fullness always already available. There is an erotic seeking of the other released by fullness, not lack. This is the eros of God, with all the passion of eros but released from self-insistence, too much to the fore in many understandings of *conatus essendi*, released also from an enclosed, entirely self-referring self-relation that impassability seems to imply. It is beyond these, not because it initially lacks self-relation or a certain impassability but because the divine eros is the seeking patience of the agape that is the giving qua giving. Patience to the freedom of the other actuates the generosity that makes way for the promise of the other, that waits on its consent to generosity. The agape of God is the giving of being and coming to be. The eros of God is the seeking of the agapeic origin, a seeking that as overfull is for the creature as other. Divine eros shows forth the seeking side of agapeic fullness, a seeking that as patience might look like no seeking, though as seeking patience it is never simply a self-seeking.

Sixth, the metaxological way indicates a two-way intermediation, but not to compromise the asymmetry of the origin's otherness. It resists reduction of intermediation to a mutual determination, itself a stepping stone to the self-determination of the One. This does not preclude the asymmetry of agapeic service in which the highest places itself in uncalculated availability for the lower. The good of the creature is sought and embraced by the origin, but that seeking and embrace are not the becoming of the origin or its self-becoming. To think thus is to destroy the difference and asymmetry of the origin, not to understand its agapeic pluperfection.[11] The origin alone surpasses this difference, this its own otherness, surpasses its own asymmetry. Its giving and seeking as agapeic are the abrogation of its asymmetry and superiority. It gives itself over in its seeking, makes itself as nothing for the creature to come to be itself. This is kenotic agape, in which not only is impassability as unaffected self-relation surrendered, but the origin embraces the radical otherness of the creature in its consignment to mortality. Death knocks on the door of eternity, but the door is already open and death has been taken in. We are knocked on, not just knocking. Time is drawn (up) to the beyond of time, by that beyond itself.

[11] Because we suffer, often we want a God not passive, not suffering or undergoing, not altering, or becoming other. God's availability seems to be of no avail – it avails us not. Is suffering always an imperfection? Is there a suffering that manifests higher perfection – suffering showing pluperfection? Can we square providence with impassability? Why should providence not also mean God "suffering with" (*sum-pathēs*) or being the compassionate companion? Compassion is also a "suffering with." Is an impassive God an indifferent God – beyond difference, beyond anything other, and not making a difference to it? In the *Symposium* (203a2–5) it is said God with man does not mingle, though eros as daimonic allows converse between them. Metaxological being, as here developed, means mingling without reduction. Is such mingling needed if suffering is to be redeemed – by agapeic excess. This is not Rousseau's pity, not Schopenhauer's compassion.

Can God die because of death? If so, this would be an extreme patience in undergoing the condition of the mortal creature. The ultimate passion, divine patience, takes death within itself, and tastes intimately the bitter gall. But the sur-plus origin is surplus to death too, and hence the death of God is the being of God beyond death. Impassability here would mean the surpassing of death in patience to it, overcoming it in the hyperbolic surplus of divine pluperfection. The absolute consent, the affirming "yes," transforms the negation of becoming back into coming to be. Nevertheless, there is a difference between the renewal of being in becoming and the recreation of the promise of "coming to be" and the embrace of death in the inner life of the origin. What the latter might mean remains reserved, and not for us to know in immanent life.

Perhaps we have the barest inkling in the way we "interiorize" death as we age. "Interiorize" it, not just in becoming aware of mortality but in finding the mindfulness of death converting one's comportment towards the gift of being. Growing consent to death becomes a growing radiance of thankfulness. The affirming "yes" to the good of the "to be" is reborn again and again. In this "interiorization" the seed of something deathless, rooted in our flesh, is trying to grow, even as that flesh is being consumed. Love of the deathless consumes the host of life offered in the extremest passion – divine patience – absolute porosity. This other mindfulness of being as beyond immanent life and death is *posthumous mindfulness*. To die is to be reborn as prayer, as nakedness, as poverty, as being nothing, as porosity. Posthumous mind is impassable as beyond life and death, and beyond the self-insistent endeavor defining the first immersion in life. This release is the highest love, *com-passio essendi*, highest patient attentiveness to the worth of being and beings, the beloved others radiant with the strange aura of the beyond of deathless life. I confess this try at understanding is as straw compared to the being of God: beyond immanent life and death, radically intimate to life and death – more intimate than life and death are to themselves.

SIXTH METAPHYSICAL CANTO: GOD BEING ABSOLUTE – ABSOLVED AGAPEICS

It is not
Within itself
It is beyond
Itself in itself
Full
Overfull
Empty of itself
It passes
From overfull
To overfull to
Overfull

It absolves
It gives itself away
It gives way
It offers a pure porosity
& we fill it
With annunciations of ourselves

We congest the porosity
Block up the between

Fill the field
With flags of ourselves
We clot on ourselves
& there is nothing
Between us
Save ourselves alone

Unblock the passageways
Unclog the passageways
Save us from ourselves alone

Some religious people object that the language of the absolute reflects the God of philosophers, not the God of Abraham, Isaac, and Jacob. I understand the objection, but is it possible to avoid such language? I have reservations about what the absolute means within classical idealism, when the whole is substituted for the One God who alone is God beyond the whole? Still, the relevance of the objection is evident when we ask how a certain philosophical understanding of absoluteness can be reconciled with religious claims about God's relation to the world. Is not a certain inseparability of absoluteness and relativity also required by metaxology?

Traditionally, what is absolute is defined as *ab-solo*: from itself alone. The absolute is the ultimate integrity of being, not defined by another. Thus there is one true absolute, since, were there two, one would be limited by the other, and so either one or none would be absolute, but not two. We see this in the Spinozistic monism of substance (to be conceived through itself alone), and in the holism of the pan(en)theistic God, especially in post-Kantian idealism with its transcendental transposition of Spinozistic substance to subject. This being from itself alone makes absoluteness a variation on ultimate self-sufficiency: the absolute needs nothing other, even if all else and everything other needs it. God alone is God: nothing but God is God; in that sense, God is *ab-solo*. Primordially, the absoluteness of God is defined by God as self-defining. We have to be careful here referring this absoluteness to inclusive totality, for what then of the hyperbolic transcendence of God? Has God not been relativized to one being or moment within the inclusive totality? The philosopher will say God is the whole, but they will mean rather that the whole is God, and the God of monotheism, as personal and hyperbolic transcendence, will be relativized as a lower-level representation suitable for the many but less than absolute for the thinking few.

This is one reason I speak of the God beyond the whole: to preserve God's unique singularity and transcendence. The hyperbolic conception implies that God is beyond the whole, with an absoluteness to be defined more by agapeic overwholeness than by the whole, understood as an immanent totality. If God's absoluteness is from God as absolute whole, God is not the whole, for the whole is not the whole: God is the overwhole beyond the whole.[12] Problem: If this overwhole is only defined as what the world (even as immanent totality) is *not*, then the effect of such an overwhole seems to place in a precarious position all relativity to an other. Either, the absolute overwholeness seems too transcendent to be involved in the immanences of finitude, or, what looks like a negative definition of the absolute as not the immanent whole seems to cut relations with all finite others. Either way, it seems impossible for us to think this absoluteness: it is too absolute, too transcendent, too other to appear within the horizon of the immanent (whole).

Response: I prefer to speak of immanence in terms of the between, rather than in terms of the whole. For the between is more open and porous to what is other to itself, while with the whole we are tempted to close it in on itself, and, in face of this hyperbolic transcendence of God, either shut it out of considerations, declare its ontological redundancy, or re-configure itself as the true ultimate or last god. The between, I believe, holds us truer to our own finitude and to an honest facing of immanence, in its depths and heights, its abysses and hyperboles, none of which can be smoothed into one seamless immanent totality, even if this totality does call itself *the* whole. We pass by way of the between, attentive to the poverties and plenitudes, the deserts and oases, and with due mindfulness that relation to the other is affirmatively constituent of what is absolute. The impossible too muchness of transcendent absoluteness can be approached in a new poverty of spirit, porous in its relative nothingness to what is beyond it.

On a purely *univocal* view, the *ab-solo* must be a solo God, a divine solitude that does not even show self-reflexive difference by which it might know or recognize itself as itself. Its so-called simplicity would exclude mindfulness of itself, hence exclude self-relation as known in the absolute itself. It would be the absolute as sleeping in the bottomless abyss of its own bosom, before the emergence of any difference whatever, whether immanent to it or between it and creation as other. What kind of absolute would this be, since it would be radically impotent to give rise to its own mindful self-relation and any existence of, or community with, being other than itself? For it to be absolute would be for it to be the genuine power to effect these forms of relation. It would be an utterly autistic God: blank idiocy; incommunicable for not even in communication with itself. The world corresponding to this autistic God would be the block universe.

The deeper we explore absoluteness, the more we see it as inherently leading to relativity. We cannot have absoluteness if it does not genuinely function as a source whence

---

[12] For convenience I will speak of "overwholeness" rather than "overwholing," as I did earlier. The dynamic sense of the second is more ultimate than the substantive sense of the first. Take it that I mean this dynamic sense when I speak of overwholeness

arises relations, intimately in its own self-relation and, through its communicability beyond sheer autism, relations with what is other. Is it the less absolute by the arising of such relations? The deeper the reserves of self-relation, the more there is a plenitudinous idiocy that communicates beyond autism. The extensive range of a being's communicability is in the measure of the intensive reserves of its own most intimate self-being. Intensive immanent reserves and extensive range of communicability are inseparable. Absolutely intensive reserves are evident in the power *to bring to be*, to give being at all; evident in the most intensive extension of communicability of creation – not a communication to this or that but the communication of the very being of this or that, in the first instance. One might say: the plenitudinous idiocy of the divine, its infinite reserve, is shown in the idiotic happening of creation of the gift of being at all, and its infinite promise. The fullest range of relations to what is other shows something of the range of original power of the absolute as absolute. The absence of relations shows rather the impotence of its claim to be absolute.

In the univocalization without difference of absoluteness, the absolute vanishes in our very fixing of it, and so the univocalization turns out to be equivocal through and through. Dialectic helps us conceive of absoluteness in terms of "unity" that, while self-transcending towards the other, still remains in unity with itself. Relation to the other, it is held, in no way detrimental to its absoluteness. Being for the other is an absolving from the fixity of univocal sameness, and a going from itself into difference, even opposition; its relation to otherness is a constituent of its absoluteness. I concur with the importance of such insights, but I demur concerning an unmistakable insinuation of a higher univocity in the *return* of unity with self as somehow more absolute than relatedness to the other. The unity of absoluteness as self-relating is more absolute than relatedness to the other. The doubleness of intermediation is dialectically turned into two moments of a singular inclusive mediation of the one absolute with itself. God's absoluteness is the inclusive self-mediation of the one total whole with itself. Relatedness to other is subsumed into relation to self. The difference of God as the whole and God beyond the whole is, to say the least, blurred. God becomes the whole, rather than the overwhole beyond the immanent whole. We need a different language of infinity to do justice to the overwhole.

With dialectic we find the *erotic absolute*: a self-becoming within which can be distinguished the undeveloped beginning, the process of determination in finite becoming, and the self-determination of the absolute becoming properly absolute only in the end. Or: the indefinite origin, God's self-becoming in the world, the properly concrete absolute God inclusive of the finite world. Absoluteness is the sublation of the relative within itself, for the finitely relative is a mediated form of the relation of the absolute to itself. The relative is finally the absolute's self-relation. Once again, this means that finally a self-sublating self-relation itself is the absolute relation, and the "relative" relation is the relation to the other.

The hyperbole of the erotic selving of God is not entirely beside the point, nevertheless, this divine self-becoming is questionable. What kind of absoluteness is it that initially, even if eternally, is "lacking" indeterminacy, and that has to become the relative world to become itself? Surely, if the absolute is only at the end, we cannot have any absolute at all? If there is not absoluteness in properly affirmative form in the origin, not only would we lack the absolute's self-relation apart from creation, but there would be nothing of the latter, and then nothing of the supposedly more inclusive self-relation of God. The issue is not only, as it were, God's self-love but God's love of the world: whether we need more than the hyperbole of erotic selving in both instances to do justice to either loves. Both are different, but in each instance a different deployment of the hyperbole of the agapeics of community is more appropriate – one qualified by the difference of "coming to be" and "becoming," even granting that these are not up to the excess of the divine, and "becoming" less so than "coming to be."

Divine eros points to the agapeics of God. I connect the doubleness of the indeterminate – either the indefinite or the overdeterminate – with the doubleness of the origin of eros itself, as parented by both plenty (*poros*) and poverty (*penia*). The plenty is the overde-termined that also en-ables porosity. The poverty seems to be the indefinite, but there is a plenitudinous poverty: a richness in nakedness, in porosity, in the *passio essendi* itself as more intimate with the divine communication of surplus being. I take the "plenty" as referring us to the agapeic origin prior to "coming to be" and to becoming. This plenty might be said to be absolute, in being from itself alone; it gives the porosity; it is not con-stituted as absolute by relation to the "coming to be" and then becoming in the between; the latter would be nothing were the plenty not eternally absolute. It is out of this abso-luteness as for itself, on the other side of porosity, of "coming to be" and of becoming, that there arises absoluteness as relatedness to the all of finite others.

While the metaxological way draws attention to the (re-)doubled relativity of interme-diation, the hyperbole of the agapeics of community points to an absoluteness, not out of relation to what is other, but communicative of absolving relativity to the other. This again implies the "coming to be" and becoming of the finite from an overdetermined origin that does not become itself but gives from its sur-plus to being other than itself, remains absolute in itself while entering into communication with what is genuinely other. The metaxological defines a relativity to the other, but in such an absolving way that the terms in relation are genuinely for themselves, yet self-transcending and communica-tive. There is no dualistic "either/or" between, or dialectical sublation of, self-relation and relation to the other. God's absoluteness is best conceived by way of the absolving agapeics of community. Here we can grant a unity for self that is self-transcending and communicative in a radically relative sense, radically for the other in a love that reckons on no return to self. The unconditionality of relation to the other is a measure of the com-municative absoluteness of the origin so related. The inexhaustible reserves of Godself are affirmed, while the relatedness to the other is seen to be more absolute than uncom-municative self-relation: God as absolutely more in self and for itself, and God as more absolved in the release towards the other as other.

The absolving is not an absorbing relation but a freeing of the creation into its own otherness and goodness. The absolving thus grounds a community with the free creation that is en-abled by unconditional love for free difference.[13] Agapeically there is no indi-gence in the origin, though one might see the hyperbole of the erotics of God as indicating a kind of absolving indigence, if we remember that the agapeic relation reveals richness to be a kind of "being nothing" that the other may be everything, a poverty that wants nothing for itself to want the good for the other, a richness that is an emptying of the absolute even of its absoluteness, to be there at the disposal of the free other, should the other seek aid and succor. This agapeic relation to the finite other absolves by dissolving absoluteness as standing over against, or even standing above, this freed other. Absolving is a descent into the abjectness of finiteness itself, an assumption of the nothingness to which the creature can come but beyond which it cannot go through itself alone. This is not the logically necessitated self-becoming of the absolute. It is an agapeic abdication by the absolute God of determinative force, an abdication that does not wash its hands of finitude but that will sit in the dirt of the ash heap in love for the creature that dies.

The measure of God's absoluteness must be such as to be in relation not only to the living but also to the dead, and to the living as under the threat of death. Divine absoluteness must be porous even to death, in an embrace that redeems relations to the other; for the willingness to die for the other is the greatest love, hence greatest relation to the other. This absoluteness is a being given over to nothing. Agapeic absoluteness is a relativization of itself by entry into the heart of finite otherness, and by that

---

[13] I explain in *Being and the Between* (see especially Chapter 11 on "Communities") why "inclusion" in community is not the dialectical subsumption of otherness into a more absorbing unity. The absolv-ing of the absolute is not this subsumption into the absorbing god. It implies agapeic relation to the singular as singular and other. Community comes to be in that agapeic relation which initially, as from God, is simply the gift of otherness as such to the finite other (this is "coming to be"), and which is the supporting of otherness in the self-becoming of finite beings in the metaxological community which is the between. See *EB*, Chapter 16 on the community of agapeic service.

relativizing raising finiteness out of its travail, touching the wound of the most reviled relative thing and offering uncoerced healing. And this, not because God must become absolute but rather that an absolved and absolving community may come to be in the between, a community also between the origin and the finite middle itself. This is the community of agapeic service.

In sum: beyond the univocalization of absoluteness, beyond the equivocal divorce of being for self and being in relation, beyond their dialectical homogenization, we must keep these two relations together metaxologically in thinking agapeic absoluteness. Overfull in itself, this is as transcending relative to the other, and not as becoming absolute in this transcending, but being already absolute. Absolving itself from self-enclosure, it is communicatively being in relation to creation. Hence, also, it is a relativizing of itself in a creative abdication of any "absoluteness" that only stands over against, or only above.

SEVENTH METAPHYSICAL CANTO: GOD BEING INFINITE

Do not say	It is above all measure	More than the whole
There is a line	It releases free measure	Less than every whole
Enclosing it	It draws all measure to itself	Its excess opens all ways
A boundary	Knowing no measure	Its reserve always gives way
Encircling it	The things it lets	
	They draw themselves	
	Yet these things are drawn	

In metaxological agapeics God is beyond the whole, a "beyond" at issue in the question of God being infinite. How make sense of this? Relative to God beyond the whole, I would connect the infinite with overwholeness, and the overwhole. The overdeterminate beyond the indeterminate, the determinate, and the self-determining also comes in here.

God's infinity as overdeterminate cannot be merely privative.[14] I find it helpful to distinguish four conceptions of infinity: the numerical (or quantitative) infinite, the infinite of succession, the intentional infinitude, and actual infinitude. These correlate with the indeterminate, the determinate, the self-determining, and the overdeterminate. The first two infinitudes correlate with determinacy and indeterminacy (in the sense of the indefinite) and their interplay; the third correlates with self-determination; the fourth with the overdeterminate. There is also a correlation with respective dominances in each of the univocal, equivocal, dialectical, and metaxological senses of being. In truth, the fourth sense of infinitude is the first, and hence is to be correlated with origin, while the other three can be differently correlated with coming to be, becoming, and self-becoming. In the discussion to follow, we move towards this fourth. This is appropriate, given that the relevant sense of divine infinity is hyperbolic: beyond the indeterminate, the determinate, and the self-determining. If we were to correlate this hyperbolic infinity with third transcendence (T³), it is the superior relative to the coming to be of beings, to any projective sum total of beings in becoming (T¹), and to every putatively self-determining

---

14 On the infinite as potential, see Aristotle, *Physics*, Book III, Parts 4–8; recall the Greek ambiguity about *to apeiron*: the intelligible is determinate, not indeterminate; see Plato's *Philebus* on the mixing of limit and unlimit. The unlimited, infinite is negative, till perhaps Plotinus who associates infinity with the divine, and henceforth and in medieval thought onwards, it is associated with God, and is something positive. Aquinas: infinity qua magnitude of quantity cannot be ascribed to God; yet: with respect to power, and to goodness or perfection. See *Summa Contra Gentiles*, I, 43; Aquinas cites Augustine: "in things that are great not by quantity, to be great is to be good"(*De Trinitate*, VI, 9).

15 Some philosophers speak of a categorematic and syncategorematic use of infinitude. The hyperbolic use is beyond categories, and not either categorematic or syncategorematic – though there are categorematic aspects in the referring of the hyperbole to what is, and syncategorematic aspects in that there is a more or less self-conscious concern with difficulties about the how of our speaking about the (divine) infinitude.

whole (T^2). It is sublime relative to first transcendence (T^1), and holy relative to second transcendence (T^2), for it comes from the heights relative to immanence, and disrupts the false wholeness of our idolized autonomy.[15]

The *first form* of infinity is based on the unit of numbering and the possibility of infinitely redoubling this unit. The unit 1 epitomizes the nature of univocal thinking: 1 is 1, and nothing either more or less than that; neither .99999 nor 1.00000000009, or whatever: 1 is itself and nothing but itself. But we can add 1 to 1 indefinitely, hence thus unity of univocity can be redoubled, and redoubled indefinitely. So we get the indefinite infinity of 1, 2, 3, 4 . . . and so on [a,b,c,d . . . n+1]. Clearly this notion of infinity is not much help as to God, just as the One is not the numerical unit. This is not to deny that God is Godself and nothing but Godself (as 1 is 1 and not an other). With infinity defined as thus numbered, we also can always add 1 more. Moreover, there is the indefiniteness of further quantitative additions. We may approach infinity as a limit, but since we can always add another 1, we never quite reach it. If we say we have the form of infinity in n+1, still God's infinity cannot be mathematical form, for mathematical form as form is not originative. Perhaps it may supply the form of possibility but is not itself creatively originative of the actualized reality of the possibility.

Transfinite numbers generate fascinating perplexities, but whichever way we turn, there is something inappropriate to think of divine infinitude as mathematical. The latter, of course, has suggested something about possibility as transtemporal, but possibility itself is not ultimate if we ask about what makes transtemporal possibility itself possible. It is possibilized by a source that itself is more than possibility, and more than actuality in finite form if it is creative of possibility itself, creative of the "coming to be" of finite actuality, and its promise, and enabling of (without absolutely determining) the transition from possibility to determinate reality in the finite becoming in the between. The attempt to mathematicize God is not entirely devoid of a point, but if this other sense of originative power is not only beyond determinate beings but also beyond form and possibility, we risk putting a kind of dead mathematical intelligibility in place of the living and mindful God. Cusanus makes very ingenious and helpful use of mathematical images to symbolize the hyperbolic God beyond all images. Even if God writes the book of nature in the language of geometry, he is not only a geometer, and there is the more ultimate matter of the God of finesse who gives the point of all the geometry, the purpose hyperbolic to mathematical form.[16] The fullness of finesse would not be geometric mind but agapeic mindfulness.

The need for reference to mindfulness (mathematical yes, but also more) is most evident in the operation "and so on . . ." even if we forget this reference in the mindfulness that determines the 1 to be 1 and not 2, and so on. The "and so on . . ." reminds us of the living intelligence that has seen the intelligible connection between 1 and 2 and 3, and so on. It has grasped the truth of transition, and indeed of this transition as both quite determinate (the next number is 1 more than the previous), and yet as indeterminate in being indefinite (this addition can go on without a limit). The point of the "and so on . . ." is seen *now* about what has *not yet* been counted, and though one has not definitely gone beyond this definite series of number. There is mindfulness of the ongoing order in the numbers and the process of passing from one to the other. In a word, something more is involved than mathematical order: living mindfulness of order, indefinitely extended. There is a dynamism that transcends the unit in order for there to be the counting of units, and the insight that the dynamic pattern just can go on and on. There is no absolute univocal objectivity which simply fixes the "and so on . . ." – which is not to deny univocal objectivity.

---

[16] See *AOO* (pp. 29, 49–50, 220) on this with regard to the Demiurge in *Timaeus*; also in *BB* (pp. 95–7) on Kepler. See also Leibniz on the orders of efficient causality and final (providence), though this transposes into a modern dualistic frame something that in the pre-moderns was not dualistic, say, in either Aristotle or Aquinas. When Leibniz's two orders re-appears in Kant's dualism (mechanism and morality) it is as a garbled text of/on an older palimpsest.

The *second form* of infinity explicitly implicates the mindfulness of process as dynamic. It might be called temporal infinity rather than mathematical or quantitative. It might be called also infinity as *successiveness*. If the first sense is more tied to univocity, this one brings us to the equivocations of infinity. We see that one time is preceded by a prior time, even as it is succeeded by another time, itself in turn both prior to and succeeded by another time, and so on indefinitely: t1 is followed by t2, which is followed by t3, and so on and on and on, tn+1. This is part of our experience of becoming: one thing comes from another, as that first thing becomes other to its present state. The process of succession shows a greater inherence of the prior and the following, since, in becoming, the prior one is an earlier form of the later one, which is itself the more fully realized, or perhaps decaying form of a yet earlier one. Every phase or moment of a becoming is both a beginning, an end, and a medium of transition. A beginning that ceases in proceeding to something other than itself, an end in that it is the moment to which precedent becoming(s) lead, and a medium of transition in that both this beginning and end can never be statically univocalized.

Moreover, there is the reference to mindfulness again, in so far as to grasp this endless succession as infinite, we must consent to the intelligibility of the "and so on and on." There is the play of determination and indefiniteness. There are quite determinate successors to the predecessors, but the process of succeeding, or of being an inheritor, has a necessary indefiniteness and unfinished character ingrained in it. This last point is important in that the unfinished character of the endless succession makes it less than apt as an image of God. What looks like openness is or may be, in fact, a kind of emptiness. The void space of future expanse is nothing until it is determined in the present; this unfinished infinity goes on and on, *ad indefinitum, ad infinitum*. We cannot hide the specter of emptiness in the ease with which we add the uneasy characterization: *ad nauseam*. One damn thing after another, short of further specification, after all, is just one damn thing after another, not some glorious generation of fulfillment.[17]

Change, as now offering something new, is not necessarily any betterment; for there are changes for the worse, and the infinite succession can offer us examples in plenty. It is one damn thing after another, but this damn thing can turn out to be more damned than that and we long for what we lose. This is why Hegel is not wrong to speak of the bad infinite, *die schlecte Unendlichkeit*, even if his reason for doing so is contestable. Here we encounter some of the equivocities of time: for the succession of time brings death, as much as renewed life; brings evil more intractable than ever imagined, as much as refreshing innocence and the penitence of the surprising good; brings the withering of finite energies, as much as the untired trying of virgin life. The endless succession again is a privative infinite marked by equivocal doubleness: it may open to the more full, it may be the futile endlessness that disgusts desire, wounding hope into pleading for release from Samsara. It offers novelty and boredom, expectancy of renewal and the despair that nothing ever changes – with time no more redeemed now than as at time's own dawn.

Admittedly, our dismay at time's endless flux might serve to mirror the unlimited power over life and death we think of as God's: time gives birth to all, time devours all; God is origin of all, and unmastered master of death. And though we think we know nothing of time's mother/father, this unmastered power can make us go quiet, and in the calming, the idea of God can shape itself for quieter mindfulness, like soundless music arranging itself in our soul. The created and creative infinity can throw us up and throw us down, elevate us and demoralize us. We sink to nothing, but in being nothing, we might become more disposed to what transcends us, infinitely. There can be a seductive equivocation with this infinity. (Seduction is the guile of loveless love, but there is love

---

[17] For Kant the infinite (understood in a metaphysical–transcendental rather than mathematical sense) is ideally regulative, not actually constitutive. We can proceed under the regulative ideal, *as if* the world were infinite, we cannot say simply *it is*. Given the antinomy between limited and unlimited, we are equally justified in using both, as we are equally unjustified in using either. If Kantianism is a philosophy of finitude, it evinces an equivocal relation to our transcendence (T²) and the transcendent (T³ as God).

that loves.) This is evident in the temporality of *Macbeth*: promising and then betraying us, fair and foul, leading us on and leaving us in the lurch. This is not all, of course, for the equivocity returns on itself, and the evil deed carves out a karma of interiority in which the corrupt heart will crown its kingdom of desolation with the outcry: "Out, out, brief candle! Life's but a walking shadow; a poor player that struts and frets his hour upon the stage, and then is heard no longer. It is a tale told by an idiot, full of sound and fury signifying nothing." And there is no divine idiocy. Time succeeds time, and succeeds in showing that it comes to nothing.

It is not culturally correct to say such things in our (post-)Nietzschean times that glorify time, but there it is. We must face a futility to temporal life which no amount of singing about something like eternal recurrence will finally hide. Time carries us swiftly into the dark, and when we say it is finished, there is nothing finished at all. We have been struck down, taken back, taken aback that in this the end, there is no end. Hurried into the thick oblivion, the heart cries out again for more, cries out when still alive. When it has not consented to the death of despair, the heart cries for release. We want to save time. We want time to be saved. But it is not we who save time. It is not time that saves time.

A *third form* of infinity I call *intentional infinitude*.[18] I do not mean a process that is just master of itself; I mean more a mindful transcending that is as much an undergoing as self-directing, as much a suffering as an acting. This is the kind of infinitude we might ascribe to human being. The becoming of the human being is always exceeding its present limit, and knows itself in the return of desire in every desire fulfilled. Desire goes on and on, and in satisfaction it tastes the nausea of futile endlessness. It knows the doubleness of fulfillment and futility, but its desire is not extinguished; it is spurred to renewed restlessness and search. In knowing itself as double in its becoming, it shows itself as mindful self-becoming. While carried along in the stream of succession, human desire also recurs to itself in that stream, is brought to know itself as more than merely successive, and as desiring more than the infinite endlessness of one thing after another.

This intentional form of infinitude might be correlated with the dialectical sense of being, as the previous two might be correlated with the univocal and equivocal. It helps us make more explicit sense of the "and so on and on," relative to the understanding that there is a recurrent pattern in the succession, a definite pattern that recurs indefinitely. The source of the recognition is not either a determinate occurrence or a recurrent pattern. It is the very mindfulness that holds these together, and that is itself in its becoming other to itself, which becoming other is just again its self-becoming. We thus have a dialectical form of infinitude in which there is a mediated interplay with its own finitude. We have an indeterminacy that plays with its own determination, and becomes itself in the definition of its original open power, an indeterminacy that in a sense becomes its own whole in this interplay and self-mediation, and yet in another sense never becomes completely its own whole, since there are reserves to the original openness that cannot be completely (self-)determined. This is why this dialectical infinitude in another sense always remains intentional, in that the intention of the infinite is never completely fulfilled by it. Its restlessness for the infinite remains restless. This is not all, but it is something not to be denied.

This intentional infinitude is not the same as the divine infinite, though there is something divine about it in the human being. It is not the actual infinite. There is a doubleness: lack mingles with open original power, but the original power cannot completely

---

[18] A term I use in *DDO*, a work that, taken as a whole, plots the convergence of intentional and successive infinitudes in the between, convergence that metaxologically intermediates a sense of the hyperbolic infinity. This is comparable to T^1, T^2, T^3 as external transcendence, internal transcendence, and eternal/superior transcendence. The exterior, the interior, the superior: the metaxological intermediation of the first two mediates a sense of the third (in the present discussion the fourth form), as the superior infinite. Suggestions of the actual infinite are intermediated both via the sensuous being there of creation, as achingly fugitive beauty and toweringly sublime, and via the passing of human self-transcendence in erotic self-surpassing and the surpassing of eros in agapeic communication.

conquer its own lack; indeed, this is why it must be self-transcending, for it needs the other to be itself fully. That is why it needs God as the infinite to fill its own infinite lack. Though we are full of ourselves, we are also infinitely lacking and cannot fill ourselves.

The doubleness generates equivocities in the dialectical infinite, for we can overstate one side of the matter. We might think then of an *erotic infinity* determining its immanent wholeness by passing into relation to the other, and through the other giving itself back to itself, beyond its lack. As I pointed out before (Chapter 11, note 9), Hegel describes the true infinite as a "self-sublating infinite." "The infinite is . . . the self-sublation of [the one-sided] infinite and finite, as a *single* process – this is the *true or genuine infinite*." Note the singleness of the process: if there is otherness it is immanent otherness. As he puts it in the *Encylopedia* (§94, *Zus*), speaking against the "bad infinite" as an "ought-to-be": "But such a progression to infinity is not the real infinite. This consists in being at home with itself, or, if enunciated as a process, in coming to itself in its other." And again, in *Encylopedia* §95: "something in its passage into other only joins with itself. To be thus self-related in the passage, and in the other, is the genuine infinity." Hegel's infinite is nothing apart from its own self-becoming in finitude; equally the finite is nothing apart from the infinite, and is said to be, so to say, the sleeping infinitude that wakes up to its own self-determining power in the human being. The play of infinite and finite is self-sublating in the true infinite, which as a *single process* means that the self-becoming of the Hegelian God is dialectically-speculatively identical with the self-becoming of *Geist* in human history. The true self-sublating infinite is identical with the absolute self-mediating whole. There is no divine overdeterminacy. This amounts to a dialectical-speculative reconfiguration of the infinite in terms of an absolutely immanent whole. Since there is no God beyond the immanent whole, Hegel's true infinite is truly a counterfeit of God's being infinite.

Is there a further, and *fourth* sense of the actual infinite other than the self-actualization of the erotic infinity? Affirming the doubleness of human and divine as itself affirmative, and not a dualism to be sublated, we must acknowledge metaxologically the excess of divine infinity to our or any erotic self-infinitizing.[19] Exactly to the point in this acknowledgement is, paradoxically, our standing at the *extreme* of human self-becoming, finite at the extreme of our self-mediation, where we are recalled to the *passio* essendi, resurrecting the porosity of being such that it is opened to what may come into the between from beyond immanence. Our own erotic infinity remains open, both in its lack and immanent power, to what exceeds us. There is in us what exceeds the lack of eros, but this is given to us, not self-produced. We may intermediate with it, but not bring it into being. The sense of excess found in our own metaxological dwelling in the between, the doubleness understood otherwise, points to another sense of infinite excess. This sense of the actual infinite has no mathematical, temporal, intentional, or holistic analogues entirely adequate to it. It is not a becoming or self-becoming, not a self-completing, not even a "coming to be." As inexhaustibly actual, the fourth infinite is hyperbolic.

In the metaxological space between finitude and infinity we have to attend to the hyperboles of being as pointing to the overdeterminate excess of divine infinity.

[19] Perhaps the self-infinitizing subject in modernity reaches its height in Nietzsche, but there are kitschy versions that surround us since then. They seem to smash the idol of autonomy but do not open to transcendence (T³) again; thanks to a postulatory finitism they make finitude the horizon greater than which none can be conceived. Levinas saw the point about totality and infinity, and powerfully in relation to the ethical other. Bruno gives an interesting argument about the *the infinite that creates infinitely*: especially interesting if we interpret it relative to the astonishing arising of affirmative manyness. Cusanus is more true to the matter than Hegel to the degree that the beyond of the infinite remains beyond, without necessitating a dualism of finite and infinite.

[20] The symbol as a *sumballein*, a "throwing together" or a "being thrown together" is related to the conjectural. We find a sense of "conjecture" in Nietzsche and Kant (see *IST*? Chapter 1) that is more postulatory or projective than genuinely con-jectural, in the meaning of "being thrown together or with (*jacere-con*)." The sense of conjecture in Cusanus as symbolic (*sumballein*) of the infinite stresses more this sense of "*con*" – opening it more to the "*huper*," the "above" of "*huperballein*." The religious significance of imagination as not just projective is also here at stake (see *IST*? Chapter 4).

The hyperbolic stresses something other to Hegel's self-sublating infinitism or the postulatory finitism of post-Nietzschean thought. The Greek meaning of *hyperballein* suggest a "throwing above," or a "being thrown above."[20] "Being thrown above" takes us beyond postulatory finitism, for we do not postulate simply but are carried above ourselves in a surpassing of self-exceeding. Nor is it self-sublating infinitism, for the infinite restlessness of our being caught up in self-exceeding is not the determining measure of its own movement above itself. Neither is the "*hyperballein*" a postulatory infinitism (suggested, for instance, by Kant's regulative ideal), for this fourth infinitude is not at all our project or projection, as if it were we who threw ourselves above. This entails a kind of reversal of the directionality of the self-transcending of our intentional infinitude. Between finitude and this fourth infinitude there is a movement of being carried beyond every whole which comes home to us when we attend to the signs of the overdeterminate in immanence. The hyperboles are happenings in immanence that are not determined by immanence alone: neither determinate, nor indeterminate, nor yet self-determining, something about them communicates of the overdeterminate.

The best way I can think to make some sense of this other inexhaustible, actual infinite is by way of excess, not primarily relative to erotic infinity but relative to communications of the surpluses of agapeic being in finitude itself. But there are signs of this fourth infinitude in the idiotic overdeterminate givenness of being. There are signs in aesthetic happening, especially as shown in the sublime as the overdeterminate appearing in sensuous determinacy. There are signs in erotic selving as carried in its self-surpassing by an energy of being overdeterminate to all our self-determinings. There are signs in agapeic communications, where the overdeterminacy of divine goodness passes between finitude and infinity in a released metaxological community of surplus generosity.

Agapeic being in the between is the hyperbolic image of this actual infinite. I say image in a strong hyperbolic sense, in that we deal with a showing in immanence of what exceeds immanence, in finitude of the inexhaustible infinite. Agapeic being reveals a self-transcending, but out of surplus, not lack; a self-transcending that is not a self-becoming but a donation of itself to the other, for the other. With God it is indeed the giving of the other, the gift of its coming to be. Moreover, this giving of being from sur-plus does not diminish the infinite reserve of the giver. Its infinite reserve is not spent in (ex)spending itself, nor does it lose its infinitude in giving over to the other. In a way, it is augmented, but this is not quite meaningful when already there is an exceeding fullness that cannot be augmented. Only the finite can be augmented. The giving augments the being of the finite, in the sense of making it more than nothing, making it to be, with an otherness that is its own. This is not an infinity that is limited by another, for the notion of limitation as diminishing one while augmenting another is defined in the network of relativities that condition beings immanent in the between.

Consider *generosity* as we know it from our lives. In giving I am more than myself and yet just myself; and you, in being generous, are more than yourself, even in just being your own generous self. But in your being generously more, I am not any the less, or lessened, even though I receive; indeed, for me to receive your generosity, I too must partake of the spirit of generosity, for a generous giver calls for generosity in the receiver, calls for the generous receiver. And so the promise of an agapeic "more" is called into being on all sides – for this is an economy of plenty, not scarcity; there is no economy; there is the generosity of being as giving and as gift. Does generosity thus give us a hyperbolic image of something like the actual infinite that is not diminished in spending itself, for it is never spent in spending itself? The images that strike us here are not images of a solitary self, or a sovereign: they are incarnations of community, of being for the other, of release beyond all autonomy, beyond all autisms of immanent being. And yet, in the expending of generosity there is also something reserved: there is giving out of a reserve of re-source that gives out of its exceeding, exceeds itself in spending, and yet that is as exceeding still what it spends. This is not a *quid pro quo*; it is giving (given) for nothing – beyond the goodness of giving. The restless serenity of generosity: absolutely at rest and without rest.

The images needed here bring us back to elemental communities of love. Think of the intimacy of family relations: when the parent gives to the child, one is not diminished as the other is augmented; the giving of one diminishes not the giver as it augments the receiver. Consider the relation of teacher and learner: the one who knows is not diminished by passing on knowledge to one who does not know; knowing is a reserve of richness that is not diminished or spent in being given over to another; the generous sharing of knowing is intimate to the brimming actuality of knowing itself. Consider the radiant reserve, suggesting something inexhaustible, that we divine about an exceptionally good or holy person. The holy person is especially porous to the divine, and intimate with the *passio essendi* wherein is born in us our communicative being with the other beyond ourselves. In a different register, the hyperbole of inexhaustibility is communicated sensuously in great beauty and in the stunning over-wholeness of a great work of art.

Consider this hyperbolic image from the moral space between the domestic and the extreme: the person considered as end in self, of unconditional, infinite worth. What could this unconditional worth, this infinity, be? It cannot be rendered mathematically. If one were to take a check for an infinite number of dollars into a bank, it could not be paid out; there would never be enough dollars to cover it. This infinite worth cannot be counted, that is, calculated or spent or indeed "possessed"; it has no cash value. Nor can it be constituted by a temporal process, no matter how infinitely successive. This infinite worth is incarnated already in one's being from the origin; there is no temporal approach or augmentation to its infinity. Nor, finally, can it be constituted by a self-becoming, even an infinitely intensive self-determination, since it is a worth we are given to be *before* we are given to ourselves, and can give ourselves to ourselves, as ethical beings. It is in excess of counting, of becoming, of self-becoming, the first three forms of infinity. It is given in a "coming to be" which is the primal ontological gift of being given to be at all as an ethical being. It is the good person, and more truly, the holy person, who serves to remind us of this fourth infinity. Their lives have not tarnished the shine of this infinite worth, and so they have the least retarded the show of the hyperbolic infinite in its unsurpassable excess and its undiminished reserve.

All these hyperbolic images, offering presentiment of actual infinity, direct us to the limits of erotic self-determination. They also return us to the idiocy of the intimacy of being, and point us beyond to what exceeds the terms of immanence, be these terms domestic or extreme. A mustard seed may make the point, or a servant who is no worldly sovereign, or the criminal innocence of the holy one.

EIGHTH METAPHYSICAL CANTO: GOD BEING (OVER)ALL-POWER

Empowering
It does not overpower
It is over all power
The enabling origin

It enables nothing for itself
It enables everything for itself
It has no need to insist
Its reticence gives to exist

We speak of the "God of power and might," but today we also find a widespread distaste for speaking of God in any connection with power at all. In the past, absolute power has been understood in terms of unlimited self-expression, infinite fullness of being, the absence of potential, the completion of acting actuality. Can we make any of this intelligible? The notion of absolute power itself seems hyperbolic, for we only find conditional power whichever way we turn in the network of finite being. Trying to find some way to express the hyperbolic, I use the phrase "God being (over)all-power." By (over)all-power I mean over power in the sense of being potentially overpowering; over power in the sense of being over all finite forms of power; over power in the sense of being above power, beyond power; over power, also, in the sense of an empowering letting that releases and allows the other to go free. Relating to empowering letting, the over of (over)power is put in parenthesis to indicate the agapeic suspension of being overpowering.

Agapeic (over)power is not nothing but an agapeic being as nothing. This will become more clear.

Generally, power is inseparable from some kind of originality: it brings to be, enables being, or allows a becoming. But there are different kinds of power. One kind is determinate and determinative: a determinate power determines A to be B, or to become B. We detect a strain of coercive force in this: in the event of A, B *must* be, or become. Another kind of power might be self-determining: A determines *itself* to be B, or to become B. Such power has a certain freedom from coercive determinacy, in that A manifests the free power to determine itself thus and not otherwise. Another kind of power is the power to free: not determining or self-determining, but releasing power – power that lets, or allows. You say, "Let me do this please . . ." I respond, "Very well, I stand aside, I let you do it." There is letting on both sides here, but what is this power of letting? I think this question has much to do with divine (over)power. Letting suggests an empowering and creative possibilizing: not only power to be, and power to bring to be, but power to allow to be. I would say agapeic (em)powering – as release of the power to be. In what now follows, we will move from determinate and determining power, to self-determining power, to overdeterminate power that is before and beyond the determinate, the determining, and the self-determining. The overdeterminate will bring us best to God being (over)all-power, suggesting also the hyperbole of good letting power, of agapeic empowering.

First consideration: The most obvious form of power seems shown to us in the presence of given actuality that brooks no resistance, or that overcomes all otherness standing in its way. Power, in this regard, seems to be pure self-expressing presence, pure self-affirming force. A mighty wind blows over us, and blows away, or down, all that stands against it, in its way. The big wind: we cannot resist its self-manifestation; we cannot stand in opposition to it. The surge of the sea overwhelms all it passes over, effortlessly lifts up or casts aside whatever happens to be before it. What is power in all this? We humans find it hard to locate any *center* of power in the wind or the sea. The eye of the storm is quiet. Can we then conceive of a source of power as itself nothing but self-manifestation in its overcoming of all opposition that stands against it? But there is no "it" that we could pin down, for it is what it is just in its self-manifestation. We might think of God's (over)all-power as such a non-centered "center" of pure self-affirming power that asks nothing from what is other; power that, should it so express itself, will overcome or cast down what is other. One is here tempted to consider the *idiotics* of divine power – immeasurably beyond us, transobjective, transsubjective. (Over)all-power overpowers what as other to it has no say in determining how the pure self-affirmation of this idiotic non-centered "center" of power expresses itself.

One might correlate this with the *univocal*, in so far as we conceive power as the pure expression of determination: the power is itself and nothing but itself, and, in relation to what is other, it reduces differences to its own immediate unity with itself. It is not univocal as a *definite* "center," but as the incontrovertible capacity to determine the life and death of all other definite centers of being. It is univocal because it is the immediacy of power, in its seeming carelessness with difference, its recklessness in bringing to be and bringing to death too.

We are offered some access to this, for instance, in encounter with the sublime irresistibility of power in nature. This power is not of this thing or that, but the power that determines this thing or that, and it is not this or that determinate thing. This seeming absolute univocity of power to determine is not a univocal thing, though it is imaged in terms of the exceeding power of great things or events that, as within nature, have their own relative determinacy: the greatness of the hurricane or the flood or the driving storm, the desert expanse, the thunder of the waterfall, the leviathan breaking the surface of remote seas. I think these tell us something of God, not exhaustively what the (over)all-power of God is, but something of what the power of God is like. The origin is like the creation and hence the greatness of power in creation has some likeness to the power of the origin. The becoming of the great tells of the greatness of coming to be, and hints at the exceeding greatness of the even more radical source of both the becoming and coming to be. God is not the power of the wind, but something in excess of this. "Absolute power" means unconstrained by anything, since anything that is, is already an originated determination of this more original (over)all-power. Would we not have to say: The very being there of the powers of nature are themselves given to be by this absolute original (over)all-power to be which is itself and nothing but itself, and which does not need resources of power from another to express itself, to be the self-affirming (over)all-power of being that it is? It redoubles itself effortlessly, and hence is absolute (over)all-power, for prior to it there is nothing?

Since such images of great power in nature are already determinations of the power of being, nevertheless, we must be circumspect. We must not identify such sources of power in the between with divine (over)all-power, for the unlikeness is as important as the likeness. It is especially important not to become fixated on overpowering univocity, so that absolute power does not become power as dominating force. God then becomes something like the *ens realissimum* who is also the supreme *efficient cause*, and in such a wise that our use of these notions does not distinguish between coming to be and becoming and the original of these that yet is more. If God is power to effect, it all depends what you mean by "effect," and certainly in modernity effective force has been too long identified with deterministic mechanical causation, with God turned into the deistic machine-maker. Efficient power becomes hard to distinguish from a kind of blind necessity. Perhaps a blind watch-maker will be ventured, one in an astonishing collusion with chance. Of course, a blind maker can collude in nothing, for collusion calls for minding.[21]

All of this is not to think in the dimension of the hyperbolic, properly speaking. Rather, the hyperbolic is treated only as an extension of finite determinacies, finite determining power blown up without determinate limit: the hyperbolic as the "biggest" of "big" powers, not the hyperbolic as bearing on transcendence as other (T³). We have a God we cannot love, a God we fear perhaps, and hate because we only fear, for our own effective power is dwarfed by this finally overwhelming power. In hatred we hatch our plot to make ourselves masters of power. One must say that our non-mechanical exultation in nature's power, as elemental and qualitatively present, outside of the mechanistic world-picture, offers a truer presentiment of God as living (over)all-power. The restless sea is a better image of God's power than the dead metallic constancy of the clock, or the blind watch-maker tapping his unknowing way through the empty halls of endless possibility.

Second consideration: In the sublimity of nature we might get a hint of the *poetic* power of the divine, and also the *equivocity*. The hyperbole of the *aesthetics of happening* communicates something of the power of the word as creating: bringing to be. The forms of incarnated life are formings – formings as opened, open, and opening. These intimate giving sources are beyond mechanism and the geometric mind. There is poetry of overdetermined power in aesthetic happening that requires the minding of finesse. We get the insinuation of an inspiration at work in the equivocities of nature's power. The hyperbole of aesthetic happening makes us porous to, if perplexed before, the poetics of the divine.

Of course, in earlier times it was often the dominating force of the emperor or the irresistible patriarch who defined the meaning of power – power over all. The tyranny of things is mirrored in the mortal god. There too the effort to univocalize absolute power leads to decidedly ambiguous consequences. Certainly the needed difference of the erotic sovereign and the agapeic servant is seriously compromised – and within erotic sovereignty, the difference of the tyrant and the king.

---

[21] If we relate absolute power to dianoetic intelligibility some thinkers will say that God's power is limited by what contravenes the law of contradiction: God cannot make a square circle. The law of contradiction is to be understood in terms of the logic of univocal determination. The deeper consideration of God's power is beyond this univocal level of consideration. The logic of God is beyond contradiction. This is not to say that God is self-contradictory, but that the unity of God is not a univocal unity subject to the determinacy of the law of contradiction. Our logic is *our* logic.

Such absolute univocalizing power, while seeming absolute, will strike us as less than divine. We become more disinclined to conceive of God as dominating power the more we see power's double face: power may create, power may destroy. This equivocity of great power is evident in the power of water: it may nourish and form all that is and make things full of growing; it may overwhelm all formed things with wanton reckless-ness, as in the great flood that restores things to their original chaos, if not nothingness. This equivocity of power buoys us up and drowns us, carries us up and casts us down. Should we be frightened by God? Yes, in that absolute (over)all-power has a side not proportioned to human power, indeed to all powers in creation itself. This the earlier peoples spoke of as the wrath of God. Wrath is fiery self-manifestation, self-expression that is potentially destroying, and outside the predictability of human rationality: it expresses itself beyond the human measure, and seems to have no measure at all, given what appears as its formlessness, unless perhaps it is itself its own measure. What is in excess of us and its own measure must terrify us, since we are in its power, and its power seems to show an ambiguous face to us. The power to give being is the power to take being away. Commanding life is commandeering death.

The terror of the double face of equivocal power is not such that we can put to one side the so-called bad power, and to the other side, the good power. Going by what nature itself reveals, there are powers which show no respect for the measure of human morality and its restraint: amoral power, power that seems senseless cruelty to us, power of death itself as absolutely intimate to the very powers of life. Think again, with Blake, of the tiger: not a tame, domesticated power; ordered yes, and relatively predictable, but predicable in its mindless energy to kill in an instant what distant mortals in their breezy safety sing as life's loveliness. If what looks to us as the equivocal power of the absolute is beyond the meas-ure of our sense of good and evil, the question it raises is whether this beyond of absolute (over)all-power is indifferent, even hostile to good and evil. Or is there another sense of (over)all-power as good, above all destruction, and beyond our measure of good and evil?

These equivocities in nature's powers make us think of power beyond the amoral force of self-affirming, self-expression. Must we not turn to the human being for other hyperboles that take us beyond dominating effective force, by taking us more deeply into the equivocities? Remember this turn is in the face of immeasurable power that, as univocally determining, is equivocal between good and evil for us. Is there (over)all-power other than finite power, but not finite power infinitely extended or expanded: (over)all-power manifesting a *qualitative difference* with finite power, however infinitely extended? How think this qualitative difference? Again we must rely on manifestations in immanence that communicate of what is hyperbolic to immanence. We get more a sense of the qualitative difference of transcendence as other (T^3) the more we proceed from univocal mechanism through organic to human powers, both in the erotics of selv-ing and the agapeics of community. Dialectic and metaxology help us by taking us into, and beyond, the immediacy of univocal powers and the equivocities of amoral power seeming indifferent between life and death, good and evil.

Third Consideration: Dialectic suggests that power's equivocity is more than a mere opposition between life and death, between the mindless and mindful, between sheer external power and inward impotency. Power is mediated. It is not just immediate self-expression but expression that mediates with what is other to itself. There are forms of powers that are mediated by mindfulness. If the power of God is the absolute original (over)all-power to be, then the image of irresistible overcoming cannot be enough. The qualification of the hyperbolic is again needed, for one should not just say that God's (over)all-power "mediates": rather it "creates": brings to be the "coming to be" and the determinate becoming of beings, though there is more reserved to it than even these hyperbolic happenings. Supposing even that we were to think of the givenness of being as mindless, we would have to say that the power that originally mediates them, creates them, is not thus mindless, and just its power to mediate, to create, draws us into the space of its deeper mindfulness. The character of that minding is another issue, and we will take it up next when discussing God's being true and (over)all-knowing.

A major question: Are images of power taken from the human more fundamental than images taken from the other than human? Both have their place. We need non-human images to guard against a questionable anthropomorphism, as well as to acknowledge the transhuman. Yet the excess of God to both the non-human and the human, means we must also image the divine in terms of the richest forms of power we find in the between: power that most richly enables beings to be, and to be as themselves, and not just as mere instruments or playthings of effective force.

In the last two hundred years we have tended to reverse this way of thinking, even as the human being elevates itself into the supreme power. We come upon a strange collusion between the reduction of beings to what is "below" and the elevation of the human to what is "above." *Reduction:* All being is reduced to dark power, like Schopenhauer's will, or Nietzsche's will to power. The darkness of this power is its absurdity, and perhaps hostility to humans, particularly in our will to cultivate and civilize. Instead of the mindful origin, perhaps like *Geist*, there is privileged the other of thought thinking itself, but now imaged on power that is not mindful but indifferent, even hostile. Man seems the plaything of this dark source. *Elevation:* This is the other face of the first face of reduction. Like everything else we are will to power and, like the dark source, beyond good and evil, but we are said to be the supreme will to power. Reducible to the lowest, we can become elevated to the highest. There is no God in the dark source, but we will become the god that most expresses the fullness of the self-affirming power. (Foulness becomes fullness; for fair is foul, and foul is fair.) Elevation may range from poetized dominion of the earth to its technological mastery. The second in Descartes becomes the first in Nietzsche, but both are brothers along the same continuum. After all, the willful God of Descartes is not so far from the amoral will to power of Nietzsche. This paradox of reduction (even debasement) and elevation (even deification) seems to me to reduplicate, with reference to the human god, the same equivocity of power it was intended to measure. One fears it is more deeply mired in the equivocity because its power is its impotency, its impotency its power. Neither is true to being in the between, for God becomes as nothing when God's power is as everything indifferently.

Dialectic passes more deeply into the equivocity, but since we have a gross tendency to think of power as external forcing or coercive superimposition, it requires some discipline to see the power of being as self-mediating and intermediating, and to see this being of power as inseparable from being in act, from the being of being. The power of being mediates selving and communication. If we think of God as such power, we think of a power that extends to the intimacy of finite singularity, in so far as we can say all things selve and communicate. If you like, God will be absolute selving in communication, in so far as the absolute form of being takes the form of communicative selving. Selving here does not refer to univocal determinacy, but to the *energeia* of mindful being, or being mindful. Since this is communicative, selving does not mean anything solipsistic, or introvertedly monadic. The absolute selving of God need not be understood to refer us to power as potential but to power as fully self-mediating, and to more again, since full self-mediating communicates agapeic surplus, and so is more than self. Hence divine (over)all-power would be the superlative in communicative power, given that all selving is inseparable from communicative being. So we are led to venture that the power of God is that of community, that is, of absolute love. One might even say that absolute power is in love with itself in a non-invidious sense, is absolute self-affirming. As self-affirming it is mindful of selving to the ultimate that in no way precludes the superlative self-exceeding of agapeic communication.

Contrast this line of thought with the way ultimate power is conceived by thinkers like Schopenhauer and Nietzsche. For both, ultimate power is self-affirming but this, originally at least, is more like a blind, mindless energy. These thinkers are instructive points of reference, since they epitomize an attitude pervasive in our time, namely, a sense of the darkness of the original power. Both are sworn atheists who deal with the ultimacy of power, and in a way that mimics some of the features of the God they reject, but without reference to any goodness of the ultimate power. They impel us to ask if the ultimate power in any sense is good? Their atheism is tied up with rejection of the moralized God and its moral good. Schopenhauer expressed a somewhat more complex view that the "traditional" God had a dark side that the moralization of the divine tended to make anodyne. In Nietzsche, too, there is the striking equivocity that the original will to power, utterly amoral, seems to strive to become, in the great human being, the apotheosis of self-affirming, beyond all moralization, in a self-divinizing that looks like mimicking divinity. One is tempted to say Hegel is superior in this respect at least: in thinking of *Geist* we cannot glorify blind coercive force or stifle the suggestion of a subtle mindfulness to the ultimate power. Dialectically we see the point that, though the blind energy of will or will to power performs many of God's "functions," the form of being of these gods is ontologically inferior to the richer forms of selving we find in creation. One would rather say that a truer sense of God reverses this inversion of above and below. If we think of the divine as a kind of selving (we know there are limitations to this way of thinking), it would exceed the measure of the human self.

The hyperbole of the erotic sovereign may be of service to think of God seeking the singular as singular, even in the agapeic constancy of absolved power. If this sovereign has a "will," it is not like our wayward will, nor like a blind striving, not like any will to power that is essentially self-glorifying. Of course, variations on the power of the erotic sovereign can be found all throughout different religious traditions that resort to metaphors of God as master, as warrior, as king, or lord or ruler. These metaphors have their own equivocities since the glory of the sovereign can assume a majestic monadism, even selfishness, with all the world there simply for the sovereign's glorification. Self-glorifying will to power infiltrates our image of divine power, as we look to the princes of the world to shore up, in the universal impermanence, our own self-securing. Not far off is the idolatry that replaces the (over)all-power of God with the power over all of Caesar.

There may be benevolent despots, there may be evil rulers, but we must always guard against an idolatry of power which seeks and enforces its own self-glorification. To worship this is to impoverish the fullness of communicative selving, divine and human. The releasing power of the good that frees selving into agapeic communication has been subjected to coercive power. One might say that the true sovereign is not a tyrant but a king who – over power as "above and beyond" power – broadcasts power differently, that is, as the power of justice which enables the releasing order of good community. The Lord may be glorified in his creation yet is not jealous for glory but glories in the splendor of what he makes so magnificently.

Fourth Consideration: This is more evident with power correlative with metaxology. There may be power in selving, but this is because selving is empowered: not enabled through itself alone but more originally in receipt of the empowerment of a generous community. The God of erotic sovereignty can be counterfeited by many false lords, the gods of a people, the people itself as divinely sovereign, and so on. All such sovereigns are tempted to configure themselves as closed wholes that relate to what is other to them, by being over all them, either winning sovereignty by topping the struggle of external opposition or subduing their foreignness to its internal appropriation. Power thus expressed either expunges the foreign or assimilates it (which is also to expunge the different). The power of the absolute (over)whole that is God is not thus closed. It is not a closed circle of power empowering itself – as if it were thought thinking itself but now manifested as power empowering itself. It is (over)all-power that allows a pass over to the other, empowering that other to be and become itself – analogous to thought thinking what is other, this is willingness willing what is other to itself. It releases the power of being, the good power of power to be, from itself towards the other. This is what its creation is: gift of the power of being to make come to be the finite other, itself a definite concretion of the original power of being, invested with its own integrity. The sovereign power of the divine, one might say, abdicates its own self-possession and gives the gift of being: gives it away, so to say, gives it from itself.

Absolved (over)all-power, understood in light of the hyperbole of the agapeics of communication, consents to a kind of powerlessness in so far as it gives finite being away from its own self in order to let finite being just be itself in its otherness. The power that empowers being other than itself is an agapeic possibilizing of creation as other. It makes possible in an ultimate sense the created finite senses of possibility and actuality. This absolving possibilizing points to (over)all-power more than any possibility, since it is originative and creative. Power is always original, in the sense of originative. The question concerns the how and form of originality. Metaxology points to an agapeic communication which radically possibilizes both the primal good of selving and of being together with others. Beyond the closed circle of power powering itself, agapeic possibilizing points to an intermediating powering that empowers the being of the other, the other to the original source itself.

The point is not the opposite of full sovereignty, since there is an original (over)fullness here that is even more accentuated than the erotic sovereign. But there is a strange reversal, and the scandal of the paradox in the consent of absolute power to its own powerlessness. Agapeic power makes a way for the other, makes way for the other, such that it seems to be nothing at all, seems even not to be there. The porosity of being in the between, enabling it to be a milieu of communication, is possibilized. Our own being is such a porous between, allowed to be actual as the promising power of communication and communicability. This is why in our own *passio essendi* we divine something of the intimate attendance of the divine (over)all-power in this very porosity. Instead of shouting its own self-glorification, this power, as over, as above, stands still with transhuman constancy, and with a silence that does not insist on itself, nor wills to be recognized or justified. Its silence, or forbearance, can seem to be horrifying to those of us who worship all-too-present sovereignty, for this forbearance seems to be an empty face indistinguishable from that of an idiot or a dead man or an innocent child or a smile whose permeable serenity we cannot construe. The scandal of absolute power is that it communicates itself in an enabling *letting*: it lets the finite being be as other, it lets it be power – and the letting forces nothing, constrains nothing, coerces nothing; it simply releases into the goodness of free power itself. The scandal of divine (over)all-power is that it is the ultimate patience: it is manifest in giving, in giving away from itself, not giving such that the recipient is forced to recognize the good of the giver, for the pure giving is for the good of the receiver, who may not comprehend he, she, or it is recipient. The giver of power even may seem to have vanished into anonymity, seeking no reward, no fanfare, no flattery, no recognition, nothing at all. Seeking nothing at all: an idiotic seeking, an absolutely opening willing of the good of the other. Its patience is the reserved hope of all (given) freedom.

This idiocy of "being nothing" is the paradoxical reversal in which absolving power opens the truth of transcendence, of transcendence as pure giving, pure en-abling letting, pure allowing as empowering. Of course, we recoil from "being nothing" and feel more comfortable with the secure(d) power of the sovereign, or the irresistible power of an elemental energy or indomitable necessity. Or we would impose the measure of our power on the intermedium of the ethos and insist that there is absoluteness only in self-determining power. We cannot or will not see that "being nothing" opens a way to overdetermining power that releases from coercive determination and that is beyond self-determination. The witness of genuinely good persons, or, more truly, the holy one, can show us, humans of the squinting eyes, something about the overdetermining power of "being nothing." Remarkably, it is often the horror of evil that makes us ponder, or protest, the unbearable allowance of the divine (over)all-power. The divine release is the release of free being, and this allowance lets be even the refusal that execrates the goodness of being, the good of God, refusal that hates the divine for the power of its consent to powerlessness. It will spit in the face of God with the assurance that many a sovereign of the world will stand by and not be bothered. There will be no revenge from the violated face. And yet the power that takes glee in debasement will be uneasy that its own superiority is vile.

The ultimate power over us does not overpower us. The absolving power of the divine is revealed in the power of agapeic service that consents to its community with the powerless. God as absolute is agapeic service, his creation the origination of the between as the promise of agapeic community, his passion for humans a compassion that we too will mindfully participate in the community of agapeic service. Of course, we fail, or hold back, and in large part because our sense of being makes idols of less ultimate forms of power, more proportioned to the measure of our own self-assertive finitude, and its intoxication with determinate, determining, and self-determining power. We fail to be the overdetermining power of agapeic freeing. We take power for ourselves by closures of being that we secure according to our measure. This means that our power is always necessarily an impotence – impotence masquerading as power, hating every hint that its majesty is wretched.

We kill the hint of the holy that reminds us that our sovereign power is, in the sight of God, as nothing. And not because God overpowers us but because another power over us is shown that does not overpower. Of course, this showing is no show for those who will yield only to the threat of being overpowered. When the lord does not make them quake they have no wisdom. But there is a wisdom beyond overpowering might and terror. It is the wisdom of playing children, or of the lilies of the field, or in the flight of chasing swallows, or of sparrows singing in the thorns, or of old people in love strolling in the evening sun along the bank and shoal of time. There is a wisdom that, having known mercy, has assumed compassion. As power beyond will to power, as willingness beyond will to power, God's (over)all-power is also the Good beyond the good and evil measured by our moral righteousness. In "being nothing" our crude righteousness is chastened, as is the pride of our coarse justice. But we have also been cleansed of terror.

NINTH METAPHYSICAL CANTO: GOD BEING TRUE – AGAPEIC (OVER)ALL-MINDING

Being true
It keeps in mind what is
Sleeplessly
It minds what is
Minding what it gives
It gives way
& passes out of mind
Letting, it watches over
The sleep of finitude

Being true
Its passing calls to mind
That we too must mind
Our vocation –
To come out from sleep
Calling all to mind
Called to minding
All

To approach God through the hyperboles of selving and community is to think in terms of mindfulness: knowing of self and other. Knowings are ways of being true. Divine minding cannot be divorced from God's being true. The ways of being true are plural, but all are informed by the constancy of fidelity. Ways of being true are ways of loving. Being true is being faithful – minding that guards the being and good of what it minds. Being true is a loving. Minding as being true points power in the direction of the absolving love of agapeic generosity. Divine being true does not suggest absentee transcendence but agapeic love of immanence.

Traditionally, "omniscience" indicates a knowing of all, but what could this be? What we know of knowing seems to bear on the determinate knowing of a this or a that, of a somewhat that can be finitely delimited. How unify "knowing" and "all"? Is this the most helpful way to put it? Must all-knowing be an (over)all-minding? A hyperbolic minding over all our determinate and self-determining knowings? Can we speak of an *overdeterminate minding*? An overdeterminate being true, intimately mindful of this and that determinate being and of self-determining beings, but more than them, over and above them? How proceed? By interpreting knowing in terms of univocity, equivocity, dialectic, and metaxology we move from the determinate to the overdeterminate and the agapeic being true that might be said to mark the divine minding.

If we proceed univocally, we will conceive of knowing in terms of determination: determinate cognition of a determinate state of affairs, correlated with a determinate correspondence theory of truth. Divine "all-knowing" would be the complete sum of all determinate cognitions of all determinate states of affairs. Thus we indefinitely expand the embrace of determinate cognition of determinate things. God's omnipotence and omniscience would imply, for instance, no future contingents since all determinations are already determined if they are known, and something like predestination follows – and this without saying anything about the difference of time and eternity. Moreover, the nature of being will itself seem completely determined and becoming as manifesting indeterminacy deemed illusory. The static determinate eternity of univocal omniscience will freeze all being in its own image. For we do not think of God as determined but as determining the being of the determinate – but this means that "all-knowing" being must completely determine the being of all determinate beings. There can be no openness in the nature of things, or in our being, or indeed in God's own being.

The limitless expansion of univocal knowing of everything determinate about everything cannot be quite what the divine (over)all-knowing is. For such a totality of univocal knowing could not be identified with *wisdom*. To be wise is not to possess an unsurpassable quantity of information, such as an absolute computer might store in an absolute "data-bank."[22] There would be nothing in all this of being true as a loving, or of being true as fidelity to being good. That said, the alternative is not a formless indefiniteness. There must be a different knowing: a knowing of *divine finesse* beyond the knowing of univocalizing geometry. One might venture that God's (over)all-knowing as hyperbolic is transfinite finesse for the finite, and hence must be creative and responsive, and hence while responsive to the equivocities of the between cannot be only responsive. We run into this paradox: a knowing that is originative, that yet is responsive; a knowing that in originating the finite other does not univocally determine that other; a knowing that frees that other, allowing it as free to go its own way, to which way then the originating knowing responds, and respond creatively; a knowing that in creating the other, not only frees that other, but dwells with that other, even as it is genuinely other. Such a knowing of finesse, beyond the determinacies of universal geometry, will point us finally towards the being true of agapeic mindfulness.[23]

There are senses of "being true" corresponding to equivocity, dialectic, and metaxology, all pointing beyond the determinate truth of univocal correspondence (see *BB*, Chapter 12). Equivocity might seem to subvert all ultimate determinacy, but one might argue that it puts questions to the *spirit of truthfulness*, which cannot be pinned down to, or exhausted by this determinate truth or that. Determinate truths presuppose a more primordial opening or porosity to the true. The promise of this openness is inherent in human knowing, even when we do not know this or that truth for certain. The spirit of truthfulness, rather than being merely indeterminate, is overdeterminate: the openness shows a receptivity to the true that in principle is unconditional, thus transfinite in finitude itself. The spirit of truthfulness shows an engaged and enacting promise of being true that companions all determinate seekings after this truth or that. This promise is

[22] If God's foreknowledge is understood by analogy with the artist or artisan (as it sometimes is by Anselm and Aquinas, for instance), this art cannot be only geometrical. Divine knowing as art would be the only truly divinatory one. Not the art that rests on technical knowing, this art is a bringing to be springing from the knowing of finesse. We have to consider the finesse of the true poetic word as creating. Poetic art expresses an overdetermined minding of finesse. Inspired and prophetic, it gives spirit, inspires – it gives the porosity that lets communication. Only by being opened in this do humans participate more intimately in divine inspiration. The aesthetic hyperbole is connected with the divine poetics – or divine music: we are as sung into being, and can freely sing back our longing and our praise. Alone, geometrical mind does not sing, or hear this music – though it is not necessarily deaf to it, as the ancient Pythagoreans, and moderns like Kepler, remind us, in attunement to the spheres.

[23] See my study of agapeic mind in *PU* Chapter 4. If one thinks of knowing in terms of determination and self-determination, one ends up with intractable aporiai of fore-knowledge and freedom.

itself overdeterminate since its full redemption points towards an overdeterminate being true. The overdeterminate spirit of truthfulness calls for finessed minding.

Univocal determination cannot explain knowing as a *relation between*: the "relation between" in the *self-relation* of the knower; the "relation between" that is the *relating of and to the other known*. "Relation between" asks for a being true that enacts a fidelity to the fullness of both self and other in relation. Being true asks deepest fidelity to the agapeics of selving and community. For us, knowing as a "relating between" is enabled by the onto-logical porosity of the between. The between is the space of creation, first given to be, first come to be, but as such creating the space of all subsequent becomings: not this determi-nation or that, not any self-determination, but an overdeterminate ethos of being wherein beings or happenings are determined and relations between them. The ontological porosity of the between allows determining becomings and self-becomings, including our coming to knowing. Thus our knowing is not a determination only, even when we know determinate things. It is a relating which, albeit determinate, also has a certain reference to indeterminacy or overdeterminacy, relative to the very patience and activity of relating. Relation reveals a relating that reveals a dunamis which itself shows us the energy of transcending at work, and passing in the given porosity, and this beyond static univocal determination.

We might think of God's knowing thus as relating and transcending and hence never to be confined to univocal determination, not even a complete aggregate of all determi-nations, for there is no such complete aggregate, since the dunamis of determining will always be more, and generate more determinations. Moreover, if God's transcending is originative, the primal relating would here be itself creative. Thus we have a more than determinate knowing that itself transcends to the other and does so by creating this other. Recalling the aesthetics of happening, we might think of the God's minding as the original divine poetics that gives coming to be, and brings being to be. The created poetry has all the moving power of utterance and the saturated density of mystery we find in great art. We need something of divine finesse to hear or see or decipher this art.

Divine art utters to us now ambiguous poems, sings songs whose surplus equivocity is the fertile seedbed of beings, like humans, who are the created poets of the finite middle. Creating is itself more than determining; it is, so to say, an originative determining, for it determines its creation as originative itself in becoming. And so what is created is, in its finite determinate kind, also dynamic, hence open or overdeterminate in some measure. Could one say that the creative relating of the origin is a "desire" for the being of the creature that "wills" that being into being, and "wills" it so because it is good for it to be? If so, could one not also say that the origin as agapeic source of creation knows by creative love? To speak of love as creative brings to mind agapeic finesse, beyond univo-cal geometry, equivocal indefiniteness, and dialectical-speculative logic.[24]

Dialectic helps us with knowing as self-relating, but we need agapeic finesse here too. Dialectic suggests the following: to know is to be in mindful relation to the other, but in that mindful relation the self knowing is mediated to itself, and so is offered more articu-lated self-knowledge through the other; alternatively, the other as known is inseparable from the knower knowing self. Apply this to God: there is a knowing that is creatively self-transcending, and that brings the finite other to being, but the knowing of this finite other is inseparable from God's self-knowing. Then we might say: *God knows the crea-ture in knowing himself*, as in classical theisms like Aquinas's: divine knowing of crea-tion is included in the self-knowing of the divine. Perhaps here, because of the influence

---

[24] We must free ourselves from thinking of creation as determination, confining ourselves to a kind of efficient causality. The more primordial "coming to be" is prior to any form of efficient causality, which itself does not describe the fullness of becoming. This throws light on the problem of freedom and predestination. Does not foreknowledge predetermine the future? How can something like free choice be foreknown, if it is not yet? The issues that arise from the homogenization of eternity and temporal becoming do not arise in such form if knowing is not confined to determining, if agapeic mindfulness is a knowing that is more than a determining or self-determining but is a freeing of the other in an overdeterminate manner.

of the correspondence view of truth, the inclusive self-knowing of the divine will tempt us to think of an all embracing determination of the divine which is not easily reconciled with the temporal openness and indeterminacy of the creature. That aside, such divine determinism could not work, as we saw, if we remember relation as relating between, and in excess of fixed univocal determination.

We find here an influence of the idea of God as thought thinking itself: divine self-relation is absolute knowing, and knowing the finite is included in the absolute thought that thinks itself. There is here the risk of a dialectical equivocity that while claiming to reconcile divine and human knowing confuses them, and hence hides the equivocity in its claim to higher speculative totality. Hence we might be tempted to say: instead of God knowing the creature in knowing himself, *God knows himself in knowing the creature.* Thus God's creative power is determined to be the creature as other, but this creature as other is the self-transcending of this God, and hence is this God in otherness. The self as othered in transcending must be brought back to itself: God recognizes himself again in the creature. Resulting claim: the self-relation of knowing is dialectically more inclusive than the relation to the other. This is the Hegelian route, but in a strange way it ends up in something like Aquinas. The finite other is taken up into the self-knowing of divine dialectical self-relation: God knows all others within self. That is not to deny differences, of course.

Beyond (over)all-knowing as a univocal sum of determinations, does the self-relation of divine knowing enjoy such a primacy that it is unclear if and how God can know the other as truly other? But if God cannot know the other as truly other, how then do justice to the creative transcending that genuinely gives the other its being for itself? Does a certain stress on self-relating knowing actually undercut the releasing knowing involved in a creative coming to be? Are we then led to a totalizing minding of the sum total of all determinations; indeed, to a totalizing *minding of itself* in the sum total of all determinations, for these now immanent determinations are its own self-determination(s)? This last view is Hegel's, but it is not the agapeic mindfulness that creatively releases the finite other into its being for itself and loves it in being true to it without instrumentalization and without necessitated return in its unique singularity. There is a different being true to the finite other, entailed by a different being true to Godself, if the selving of the God is broadcast in the agapeics of communication.

The primary emphasis in idealistic epistemologies on the constituting knower leads to an equivocal blurring of the doubleness of human knowing, as mixing receptivity and activity, *passio* and *conatus*, porosity and transcending. There is too much of the second and not enough of the first, and all this in line with a project to overcome givenness in absolutely autonomous, or self-determining knowing. The gift of creation as the primal givenness, I hold, asks a different stress on the *porosity*, the *passio*, the receiving. Generally, idealistic epistemologies are also similarly equivocal on divine knowing, modeled on this conception of the constitutive self-activity of knowing. This might seem justified by the creative power of divine knowing, but, I would argue, because constitutive idealism does not understand the agapeic character of that creative origination it is blind to the implication that in creating the finite other God is not creating himself. The difference is upheld, indeed is granted by the meaning of agapeic creation itself. This agapeic character means both a preservation of the reserve of divine transcendence in its superplus love, and the irreducible marvel of creation in its finite givenness. The first love is itself a being true to this second givenness and remains in fidelity with it.

Thus too constitutive idealisms tend to collapse the doubleness of divine knowing, in its immanent self-relation and in its creative knowing of the finite other. (Theologically, this might be put as collapsing the difference of the immanent and the economic Trinity.) They also tend to collapse the difference between the divine and human self-knowing. In the extreme case of Hegel, we can finally make no difference between God's absolute self-knowledge and the absolute knowing claimed by the Hegelian philosopher: both are absolute here, both are the same in no longer having to go beyond themselves. Eckhart: "The eye by which I see God is the same eye by which God sees me: my eye and God's eye are one eye, one seeing, one knowing and one love" (German Sermon, no. 12).

Hegel liked to cite this – the same Hegel who claimed that man's self-knowledge in God is God's self-knowledge in man. Ultimately there is no difference of human self-transcending (T²) and divine transcendence as other (T³). Transcending has come into, by self-producing, its absolute self-fulfilling immanence: transcending from self to other to self again. The holistic circle is self-circling. Beyond the sum total of determinations, we have the absolute whole of total self-determination. But where is the hyperbolic God beyond the whole? Only with a knowing hyperbolic to knowing knowing itself, only with a love hyperbolic to a love that loves only itself do we get a glimpse of agapeic mindfulness.

Metaxology helps us better with the true pluralism. To speak of *our* knowing: The relation of knowing is always a communicative one, though never just a self-communication, but one in which the other is also allowed to communicate itself to the relation as between self and other. Being in communication with and from the other, self-communication presupposes the enabling opening of the porosity of metaxological being. On this view, even the self-relation of knowing is not within itself but within the intermedium of the ethos and hence in ecstatic communication with what is other – as the other is also in the intermedium, and communicating on its own terms to that intermedium, and out of the integrity of its own self-relating being. Ecstatic porosity places self and other in a middle that could never be defined by the self-relation of either, or indeed their reciprocal self-mediation. There is a more released intermediation which allows the communicative "being beyond itself" of both self-knowing and knowing of the other. This communicative "being beyond" is plurivocal. It is always companioned by the spirit of truthfulness – we ourselves do no create this but rather find ourselves endowed with its promise. A knowing that could understand this communicative plurivocity would have to actualize the promise of a kind of infinite mindfulness which we, obviously, do not have.

How relate this to *God*? With diffidence, also obviously. For when we think of God, there are not first two distinct finite terms, even if these terms have infinite promise, as one might say about the above. For one of the "terms" brings the other to be: God creates the finite other, and this is a knowing as originative transcending; there is no second term without God as this unsurpassable First. Finite beings are seconds: given to be with an integrity of being; integral seconds, but given to be, nevertheless. This does not mean that these finite seconds are just the media of the self-expression, self-knowing of the transfinite First. *The First is not cloning itself: not producing in the seconds just doubles of itself, for then these seconds would not be truly integral and God's being true to them would not really be a being true, for the other so brought to be would not be truly for itself.* If this were so, we would end up with an autism of the whole: an autism of God, an autism of creation and humanity; and even every claim to autonomy or self-determination, whether of God or of creation or of humanity, would be meaningless. For if there were this autism of the whole, there would be no meaning to genuine freedom. The "all" as this autistic autonomy would be indistinguishable from an absolutely tyrannical "heteronomy" (if we could even say this).

But if the First is agapeic origin, the creative relation to the other brought to be, the second, will also be an agapeic being true to that other: the creature as an integral second will be released into its own otherness, not as a medium for the self-knowledge of the First, but as a mediating integrity of being, truly being on its own behalf. The intermedium, the between, is creation as other to the origin; God's creative knowing releases beings out of excess of generosity; the porosity of being is communicated to be by this origin, and it is also the ontological space wherein this generosity is communicated. If we could talk of God's mindful origination as a kind of metaxological self-transcending, God would know the other as other because the other is created, but created out of agapeic generosity, and hence given an otherness other than the divine self-relation. If this creative knowing releases the other into its own ontological freedom, the finite other is not a univocal determinacy merely, but "more." If God knows creation, there is always "more" to creation than the sum of determinations, for to be is more than to be a determination. Being true to creation entails fidelity to the full ontological dimensions of determinate beings, but also a generous allowance of irreducible freedom.

In sum: The immeasurable knowing of the divine would be hyperbolic to any totalizing minding of the sum total of all determinations. It would be hyperbolic to a totalizing minding of itself, in the sum total of all determinations, even if these determinations were its own self-determinations. In itself it would be the hyperbolic knowing of agapeic love, eternally self-communicative being, for one can love oneself agapeically. In relation to the finite other, it would be the agapeic giving that creatively releases that finite other into its being for itself, in its full ontological voluminosity, and mindfully loves it, both beyond and keeping determinacy and self-determination, in the infinite promise of the finite being's own unique singularity.

This is agapeic minding: (over)full in itself, yet capable of being nothing, such that the other becomes everything for it – a minding abdicating the power to determine through univocalizing power, because original freedom is more than such determination. Creative freedom is a love that cannot be determined, for it is surplus – surplus even to self-determination because overdetermined, a truly original good. This agapeic minding can be called "realistic" – in creating the real, and in knowing the created real as real and as created. God, one might say, is not an idealistic (inter)subjectivity but an ecstatic communist realist whose transcending exceeds the former, while giving a glimpse of creative originality beyond the dreams of every constitutive idealism. Others are not sets of univocal determinations but singular integrities of being, truly for themselves yet in communicative relativity. They are known in a love: agapeic knowing is a communicative love of the singular, existing as itself in communicative relativity. To be minded is to be *bemind* ("beloved" in Dutch). As a "relating between," knowing incarnates as a love in relation. Its incarnation is the vocation of the community of agapeic service. The divine spirit of truthfulness calls to our being true in the intimate universal.

Why at all couple the agapeic and the knowing? To acknowledge porosity, *passio essendi*, relating between, transcending, creating, the integrity of beings, their singularity, the otherness of the other, the community of being. In regard to God, it helps make some sense of the "outward" transcending of creation; of the integrity of what is there; of the free transcending of creatures; of the possibility that God is responsive to the creature, as other and as determinate and self-determining integrities for themselves. This is the double requirement above mentioned: a knowing that even in creating the other not only does not determine that other but frees that other beyond even the divine's own self-determination – and yet a beminding that abides with, even dwells with(in) that other, responding to the integrity of that other, even as it is and remains genuinely other, an other whose absolute allowance is revealed in its letting the finite other choose evil, if it so will. Agapeic allowance extends even unto the hyperbolic refusal of the good that is evil.

There is something mysterious and idiotic about such beminding love from an objectivist point of view, but it is not merely subjective (this is true even of self-love). There is also something in agapeic love not entirely comfortable for moderns who insist on their own autonomy: an *asymmetry* that is more than symmetrical mutual recognition – a surprising *releasing* asymmetry. There can be an excess of generosity that gives love asymmetrically, in that it does not insist on a reciprocation but gives for the goodness of giving. This does not mean that no return is possible, but if there is to be a reciprocation it too must be offered in the surprising freedom of the agapeic relation. We humans are more at home with a giving and receiving that is symmetrically reciprocal, where surprise has ceded to justified expectation, or even sameness on demand.

For lack of agapeic beminding, the classic problem is often put as to how to reconcile the sum total of determinacies with the openness of self-determining freedom: If God is absolutely determining, there is no human self-determination – and we end up with predestination. If humans are self-determining, there is no absolute determination, hence no God. You might say Calvin and Sartre are relatives: theological determinism and atheistic self-determination are cousins. But agapeic mindfulness as overdeterminate love is beyond determination and self-determination. There is openness beyond the first, there is promise not exhausted by the second, and the agapeic beminding of the hyperbolic God lets the openness and the promise be as other, offering in the porosity of the between the invitation that calls them beyond the closures of finite determination or infinitizing self-determination.

Can God ever be surprised? Any ventured answer must be diffident. We experience surprise in temporal arising – minor surprise with the unanticipated determinations, major surprise with unforeseen events that rupture the homogeneity of the series of determinations, or with ruptures qualitatively beyond our self-determination. The surprising is beyond us, and issues in a new surge of overdeterminate minding of the "too much." The more deeply surprising is less occasioned by a new event in a process of becoming as by the coming to be of the radically new. If there were divine surprise it would bear more on the overdeterminacy of the second than on the determinacies or self-determinations of the first. And yet if the nature of divine minding is hyperbolic, there is something to it in excess to the surprises of both (self-) becoming and coming to be. But perhaps, in another sense, agapeic beminding is "always" in a condition of surprise: joy in the giving to be, in the arising of the new, for all finite being is refreshed and freshly created, again and again.

Could we talk of a "transtemporal surprise"? The truly surprising lifts us up in the blink of an eye. Could one say the truly surprising shows something of the instancy of the eternal? If we could talk of "transtemporal surprise," I would connect it with what we know as agapeic astonishment (*BB*, Chapter 1): wonder at the mystery of being, admiration that is love, startlement before the "that it is at all," joy at the splendor of simply being and good as being. Would God be as absolute astonishment, affirming mindfulness, never dull, always joy, and enjoyment of the good of being, eternal uplift of surprise, a draft that carries inspired mind into ever fresh ecstasis? What kind of wonder would this be? Not a prosaic determination, not an earnest self-determination, but something more like a poetic laughter, a kind of "self-forgetting" singing, an idiocy so absolutely conscious of itself it is not conscious of itself, an unconditional serenity. Our image of God as absolute self-sufficiency makes our understanding falter before such excess of enjoyment, as always spilling over limits, as anarchic and wild pleasure. Pure being pleased: yes, yes, and yes again. The idiocy of God – mad joy, reckless, and not reckoning the cost. Abandon: this would be agapeic beminding too; not always demure, since it is down in the dirt, rolling around on the ground in an undignified pleasure; nothing alien to its yes, save evil, in which there is no yes. Divine surprise would be enjoyment of the divine yes, enacted not only to itself but to what is other to it, as joy in the creation, sung in the hyperbolic "It is very good."

TENTH METAPHYSICAL CANTO: GOD BEING (TOO) GOOD

Being good
It dies beside the mortal
It comes to life again
It never dies alone
We do not realize
The love reserved for mortals

Being good
It is not the unborn child
Its promise is more
Without its promise
The unborn child
Is not sent out
From darkness
To darkness

Without its promise
The wandering born
Are lost
In wayless wastes

Being good
You alone
Keep your promise
The bird in the dark
Sings three times
& its song is not the rooster's
Announcing triple treason
To the dawn

The killers know
The secret streak of
God's quietness
& are not shamed
The living forget its radiance
The holy feel its flame
& are branded with its blaze

By the flaring of this fire
We behold Your face
In the criminal innocence
Of the saving one

Are you are getting carried away? Perhaps. Is this too good to be true? How one answers is all important. A generous person gives us a gift and we reply: "You are too good!" We cannot quite credit it, and yet, there it is, the gift given. Given our inability to credit goodness, to credit gifts given as too good, what I now want to say expresses not certainties but directions for mindfulness opened up by metaxological philosophy.

These directions are ways to religious astonishment, perhaps praise, opening up in and through philosophical perplexity.

With the hyperbole God being good, in a sense, *everything* is at stake. It effects how we relate to everything, as good or not. Is there a goodness to creation – in the first instance, and in the end? What is at stake is the *ultimate love* and what we are to love as ultimate. Love is at issue with the good, for the truly good is the lovable. If the absolutely good would be the absolutely lovable, is the issue not alone we loving, but we being loved – ultimately? We might love the good but does the good love us?

To speak of God as the good seems to be both the easiest and the hardest. Easiest: this is the "highest" name, goodness itself. Hardest: here we are most challenged to avoid mere "speculation" – we are brought back to earth in terms of honesty. We must be true to what we know of goodness from the between – and what we know of evil. We might hope that God in being true keeps faith with the goodness of being. Being true is not living a lie, and this is something ontological. Must the ultimately good also be true to tragic loss? Either tragic loss is the ultimate truth, or ultimate truth passes beyond tragedy, transfigures death. Either death is the truth, or being true is beyond death (*BB*, 479). God being good faces us into the knowing of suffering, the *pathei mathos*. The question of ultimate evil is hyperbolic even to tragic loss.

Thus also, God being good seems the most necessary and most challenging. Necessary: a neutral God unthinkable; an evil God impossible; an immoral God hateful; and amoral God contemptible. Challenging: how think the hyperbolic in terms of immanent good; in terms of immanent evil; in terms of what is beyond the measure of our justice; in terms of what is senseless and cruel in finite life? Everything is a stake: the goodness or the pointlessness of the whole; God or nothing at all.

Our being in the between is exposed to a mingling of good and evil, and very often we define the good relative to ourselves. In that respect to think of *the* good would be to ponder something hyperbolic to the between and its mixed condition. How at all conceive of such a hyperbolic good, if our familiar engagement is with the mixed? Or does the hyperbolic good, so to say, mix with the mixture? If so, would it not then be itself mixed, and if so, how then still *the* good?

We are directed to a togetherness of transcendence and immanence, mystery and intimacy in the good of being agapeic. There is something hyperbolic about being agapeic, in exceeding the determinate and self-determining measure; yet there is something intimate, since it goes to the heart of being at all, in terms of its love of the "to be" as good. We are dealing with what is "over above," "beyond," and always "more," and yet is radically immanent; with what is serenely universal yet ardently engaged with the singular as such. Being agapeic is the communication of good in the intimate universal. The agapeic good is the way – making a way by not getting in the way. Following thinkers like Dionysius and Bonaventure, there is a fitting sense in which the good is the hyperbolic name *par excellence* for God. Once again in the following, we seek help from the fourfold sense of being good, shaped by the differences and relations between the determinate, the indeterminate, the self-determining, and the overdeterminate.

Good more than determinate goods

The univocal sense suggests the oneness, the complete self-coincidence of the good with itself. Thus the traditional convertibility of one and good, and of each with being. Is the unity of the good God, then, the same as the good of a determinate being? Univocity might pull us in this direction, but the hyperbolic suggests otherwise. God's goodness is in excess of the good of determinate beings. Plato is right to speak of the Good beyond being – a philosophical analogy to the God beyond the whole. What exactly can a good be that is beyond being? For if so beyond, is it then no being, and rather a nothing? How then can it still *be* beyond being? Being must not be exhausted by the being of beings, or the whole, there being a beyond to the whole that transcends beings.

If there is a good beyond being, beyond determinate goods, is it then nothing but an indeterminate good? Often we think of good as perfection, meaning here the complete realization of a being's power to be. As the good of being, perfection overcomes the indeterminacy of potency and is the enactment of the full determination of being. Were this all, we would contract good to this good or that good, goods delimited thus and thus, and God would be the absolutely determinate good. If so, would we then have no place for good that is not this good or that good? Does the assertion of a good beyond determinate goods founder on an equivocation of indefiniteness? For if this good beyond is indefinite, is it not imperfect? Does this suggest a God of possibility, perhaps of the maybe (Kearney)? Perhaps it may become perfected, but if so, how can it then be the absolute good?

This argument, however, depends on the presumption that being and being good are (to be) determinate, and the more completely univocal the better. But clearly the ultimacy of the good exceeds this, for even in determinate goods being good is not this or that determination, but the fullest being of the being, and this integrity is not another determination, but just the whole of the being that gathers the determinations into a fullness or perfection. Even in finite goods there is what exceeds objectification as this determination or that. An analysis of finite goods will lead to the dissolution of any fixed univocity and the emergence of equivocities suggestive of the promise of a more than determinate good. This, I think, communicates to us of the overdeterminate good, not the dissolving of good in the indefinite.

Dialectic often sees the above equivocity of perfection and imperfection thus: the good is in the end; passing beyond equivocity, there is a mediation of the indefinite that effects its determination, its consummate self-determination. There are serious shortcomings in thus understanding God as the good. God is not only good in the end but in the origin, without which there is no good in the end. The origin is not the indefinition of the good to be completed in the perfection of the end. The good is already good in excess of all determinate goods, and thus so not in a negatively indeterminate sense, but positively overdetermined beyond beings. We need as much an archeology of the surplus good as a consummate teleology. Indeed if there is to be an "eschatology," it is hard to see its promise without remembrance of such a hyperbolic good beyond the immanence of finite goods. *Eschaton* can mean "edge" as well as "end": "edge" refers us back to origin as well as forward to end. If we think the good of God as *archē*, as origin of the immanent whole, this good is not "to be completed" within the immanent whole. To make it thus immanent would be to construct a counterfeit double of the absolute good.

If the prior good is agapeic, as excessive it is not perfect, it is pluperfect – beyond perfection. If there is dynamism immanent to it, this is not movement from the imperfect to the more perfect but communication from pluperfection to pluperfection that is not any diminishment of the prime pluperfection. The energy of being of the prime pluperfect is just in its giving of the good from the overfull to the overfull. As always already overdetermined pluperfection, this good can release the being of creatures as gifted with being itself good. Creation is gifted with the promise of the good. Were we to say the good is self-diffusing, we would have to qualify self-diffusion in a metaxologically agapeic direction. Good communicates itself, yes, but agapeic good communicates the good of the "to be" of the other, in giving being to the other, and not ceasing to give once the being of the finite other has come to be. Its giving is inexhaustibly renewed in being given, and its reserve not spent or diminished. This giving is clearly hyperbolic to our more usual sense of giving: I give you everything, and now depleted, I have nothing more to give. Agapeic good: I give you everything, and I have kept nothing back, but I have everything more, and yet, to give. With God, there is no meaning to the assertion, I have nothing more to give. Unless one were to say, God has nothing more to give, for everything has been given, and yet everything is still to be given.

If we grant the agapeic nature of the original good, it is not only that existence cannot be rendered neutral or indifferent, but its good is its own good. Even if God is the One, a certain monistic language of unity, coupled with dualistic languages of fall, is not appropriate. Creation is divine poetics but it is not for the good of God's own self-poiesis that the world is. Because God is agapeically poetic, the world as art is for the sake of its own good. And what is its own good? That, being good, it realizes the promise of agapeic being. This means that it be like God. This is most fully manifested in the between in the community of agapeic service.

This view is at odds with the nihilisms of recent times as well as the Gnosticisms of earlier. True, these Gnosticisms testify to an attunement, these nihilisms pose a perplexity, we cannot simply sweep aside. Beyond any "neutrality" of being, they claim to come into the worthlessness of being, at bottom even its disgusting and revolting character. The prince of darkness spreads his shadow over ontology; the philosopher suspects that the origin is not good but beyond good and evil, with a duplicitous character more like to our evil than our good. An archaic recoil from being is resurrected: "better not to be at all, and if in being, better to be quit of it as quickly as possible" This ancient "wisdom" attributed to Silenus, companion of Dionysus, reappears in the metaphysics of Schopenhauer and Nietzsche. We are exposed to being sucked into the nihilism of a degraded erotic absolute – degraded, in that the erotics of becoming loses contact with its more primordial agapeic reserve, while a lacking negativity overtakes the whole process of immanent (self-)becoming: nothingness in the beginning, the middle masking nothing, and in the end nothing more, just nothing. If this nothing is the last word, we must choke on saying: "It is good." This appears as a monstrous saying. Does the mystery of evil render incredible the hyperbole of God as agapeic good?

Good beyond equivocal indeterminacy

Evil sometimes seems unloosed with a life of its own, outside our best good will and power. It seems to have a power disproportionate to anything attributable to the evil we undoubtedly originate. Anguish torments us, not despite but *because* of the promise of hyperbolic good: Why evil at all, if the origin is good as giving "coming to be," and if "coming to be" as issuing in creation is good? I try a reply. Creation comes to be over nothing, it is the arising of being as something and not nothing, Coming to be is double – mixing the giving of being and the possibility of (being) nothing. Out of this doubleness, beings in creation are given over to becoming: becoming what they are not yet, becoming what they are to be: exigent to be yet marked by the vulnerability of ontological fragility. The mixing of the power to be with the nothing means that the power to be, affirmative as it is for itself, is also expressed ambiguously as the power of negation. Thus any process of becoming, as open to novelty, is always the alteration of the mixing of the power to be and negation, with the possibility of disturbing either their equilibrium or the proper excess of the power to be. How does the unruliness arise if creation is a good? The very openness of creation to novelty and freedom means that its processes of becoming are inseparable from the power of negation, which itself shows the ontological mixture of the power to be and the nothing. The possibility of not being is constitutive of the being of creation. A being's affirmation of the power to be may refuse to consent to its own *passio essendi*, for this tells it of its own being given to be as something rather than nothing, and it is against this possibility of being nothing that its self-affirming power to be strives – for the most part remorselessly.

Whence disequilibrium, disorder, unruliness? Through a certain inordinate hypertrophy of the power of self-mediation in the double being. Beings that are seconds want to be the primal First. I mean: beings are given for themselves, and as the promise of self-mediation; but this co-exists always with relation to the other and intermediation, first from the gift of the origin, second in relation to other finite beings. Within itself the power of self-mediation can be drawn to its own fulfillment, though never severed from its own *passio essendi*, and the possibility of its not being. Self-mediation can so affirm itself so that it seeks to recess or overcome the *passio* and the possibility of being nothing. The latter is finally impossible for a finite being, both on its own terms, and in relation to others. The double relativity is disordered in reduction to single self-mediation through an endeavor to be that is inordinately affirming of itself as the good. This is absolutizing what cannot be absolute, in the sense of *ab-solo*. The relation to the other is deformed, and so then also is the relation to self. Seconds given for themselves want to be First absolutely through themselves. Metaxological community is blocked, and the promise of creation betrayed. The creature's freedom to be other turns into the dualism of opposition rather than the solidarity of community. Our porosity to the divine becomes clogged: at odds with the given character of our created being as *passio essendi*, we absolutize our own *conatus essendi*, as now circling around itself and nothing but itself. By means of this self-(en)circling *conatus*, impatient and self-clogged, we figure ourselves as gods. In truth, we have re-figured ourselves as counterfeit doubles of God.

In us the reduction of intermediation to self-mediation can be intensified in innerness to the point of infinity, hence can extend beyond itself infinitely in destructiveness. There is no limit to the possibility of human destruction, whereas animal destruction is finite. The lamb devoured, the lion will rest in peace, till hunger disturbs anew its satisfied self-mediation with new lack. As we human beings seek infinitely, we come to express lack infinitely, and this turns to unlimited violence when its lack is nothing but lack, turned against the surplus promise of agape still in reserve in itself, even when it is turned towards evil. There arises the infinite project of the reduction of other-being to the medium, or means of our own self-mediation. As given to be for ourselves, we make other-being be for us – for our good. One might say: We make ourselves the whole. This is being evil: being (the) whole in a non-agapeic way: being (the) whole closed to agapeic porosity. True goodness is beyond the self-enclosing whole – as the agapeic God is. We claim life. We grab. We have no claim. Life is gift.

Finite life, such as we know it, is impossible without some striving for sovereignty. We *are*, and *are to be*, self-affirming. Evil comes with a defection from the plural promise of metaxological community, when self-mediating beings, in one sense rightly affirming themselves, strive to seize sovereignty over all forms of intermediation with otherness. Making ourselves gods we rise up as sovereigns of a kingdom of death. We overlay the goodness of creation with our defection, and our kingdom comes.

And yet without the promise of being itself as good no power of evil would emerges. Evil power is parasitical, growing on the forgiving enabling of the host on which it battens. Gorging itself on the good, evil curdles the honeyed milk into poison. The honey of the good may yet arrest our taste for mischief, stop us with a new savor for the truly worthy. Satan in Milton's *Paradise Lost* (Bk. 9, 459–66) was *disarmed* by his first sight of the beauty of Eve; overtaken, arrested, he stood for a while enchanted, and as Milton marvelously puts it, "stupidly good." Stupid: idiot: return to the elemental: rocked back on himself totally, taken out of himself totally: sacred stupor as involuntary amazement, and admiration. The good stuns us when, unguarded, the primal porosity of our being is briefly unclogged. The porosity decomposes the idol of self-mediation. We clot on ourselves again and close the porosity. The blood stream of life is made the carrier of death, and unless the clot is dissolved it may move and strike the heart. How does Satan clot? By returning to himself again. Satan *collects himself; clots himself, makes himself* impervious to beauty. He resumes his unswerving will to self-mediation, and the fire of his hate returns more fierce (470–1).

A double movement between self and other is reduced to one. It is *first* the self-affirmation of self-affirming power that becomes the unruliness, because it becomes *only* self-affirming. Recoiling from its possible nothingness, its song of itself becomes haunted by the presentiment of threat to its own being, a presentiment crystallized as threat in the other as beyond me. This crystallization is more like an infinitesimal turn (twitch, almost) of the self-affirming of self-affirming power that turns from the other to itself as absolute. Here is the disequilibrium: the turn in (twitch, almost) choice of oneself. Paradoxically, this self-affirming is the truth of the self, but it is not the whole truth, and it is the "choice" of self as the whole truth that begins the distortion of the whole truth which must maintain the equilibrium of "choice" of self with good openness to the good of the other. For if to be is to be agapeic, this "choice" of self is already a turn from being, and hence one's first kiss with death. This first kiss will seem so sweet, as seeming to release exultation in self as self. This freedom is the first simulacrum of true release.

The simulacrum will be exacerbated by further refusals, all the way to violence and malice and death. The death that was in the kiss may take a life to take off its mask of life. Evil: this is it – the mask of life but nothing lives in it.

Evil comes in the inversion of agapeic self-transcendence that to all the world might well look quite unclosed: a turn of self that returns to self – a defecting return in being a turn in refusal of the other, and revolt (a turning around) against self-transcendence as agapeic. Could the infinitesimal turn, twitch almost, be called a *primal* evil? I refer to something that does not seem to be any kind of *temporal arising*. Can one find a time when evil had not already arisen? Is there already an evil that is before determinate *becoming*? Better put: an evil on the border between coming to be and determinate becoming? Not an absolute blocking of *coming to be* (this is impossible for one has already come to be), but a "refusal" of coming to be as beyond us, and hence, implicitly, a will to block the origin as agapeic creator? We clog the porosity of the between, though we are what we are as given to be by the agapeic origin within that porosity and its own agapeic promise. Is this not why evil it bound up with death, this blocking on "coming to be" which carries into the corruption of the process of becoming? The seed is sown in the soil of the first, the equivocal flowers grow in the element of the second. Nevertheless, within becoming, there can be new beginning at all points, hence the element of the second can be re-sown with a different willing, or consent. The promise of agapeic porosity continues always to be given. The new beginning may be very hard since the brambles of evil have twisted themselves into almost immovable tares. They can be uprooted. At any moment we can go to the root. The gift of being able to begin again reveals the promise of agapeic freedom.

If the primal evil is a blocking of coming to be, of creation itself, it happens as more than a determinate negation. The primal blocking is a nihilation more primordial than negation in becoming which itself is determinate negation. The blocking is idiotic: it happens with, so to say, the "unborn infant" that is to be born to time. This is not to deny evils that can be correlated with determinate negations, not at all, but the root, the radix, is in an indeterminate nihilation prior to determinate negation in becoming. This indeterminate nihilation of evil is the reversed negative of the overdeterminate affirmation of goodness. It shows a rancor towards being as such, that does not hate this or that simply, but that *is* hatred, and that thus can hate this or that or anything at all: a rancor extraordinarily devious in hiding itself even in the guises of ethical nobility, but when it surfaces, it can batten onto anything. This refusal seems to be nothing or paradoxically to reject nothing but it is the inversion and perversion and block on being as agapeic. Idiotic as indeterminate, it is yet capable of insinuating itself into anything determinate. It is like the evil eye. There is a look the opposite of the divine beholding that sees "it is good." This look of the evil eye is bent on the corruption of life. The bale of its glare longs for death on life and the extinction of its good. It lays a blight on being. What it beholds it fouls.

There are evils which are due to failures of knowing, but there is a more radical evil in "will" as refusing or consenting. The primal affirming is a radical willingness (of goodness) that is not a matter of this or that act of free will. Mindfulness and willing put their roots deepest into the inward otherness of selving. It is "there" in the idiotic "nowhere," prior to becoming determinate, that the seed of the evil is planted. Since it is prior to becoming determinate, it is also prior to determinate becoming in the more normal sense of temporal unfolding. In that regard, the "fall" is prior to time and becoming; it is in the idiocy of being, in what I called metaphorically the "unborn infant," that a primordial "yes" or "no" takes place. Determinate becoming is already caught up in the equivocity of the original "fall." Hence there is no time when we are not caught up in the equivocity of evil/good. We carry the unborn into time, even after we have been born to time. To be born into self-becoming is to be given over to the equivocity of good and evil. This is why in the between there are deaths that are also amazing rebirths. The "unborn infant" is reborn anew to time. Life is stressed by sorrow and much of it is fitful, grieving and struggling, but there are deaths or births that bring us back to what is yet unborn in us. What it means to be unborn is not clear; what it means to be born is clouded; what it is to die is dark; what it is to be reborn to the unborn is mysterious.

Much of our torment about evil arises in the equivocity of (self-)becoming which tests our trust in the hyperbolic good of God. Why the ultimate allowance of evil? Does the unborn that allows being reborn suggests something like the *reserve of an infinite patience*? But is not the forbearance of the good God horrifying? Creation is saturated with the cries of horror, and the sky smiles serenely. One looks up at the battered face of the crucified man. Is the crushing weight of limp death taken into the heart of the divine? Must the aga-peic God taste evil, not taste but become subjected to death – death the outcome in nothing of the free refusal let be by the first agape? Free being has been given, but finite free being gives itself to itself and comes to be lord of death not life. The horror of the inversion can-not be turned around, or turned over by that free finite being, for now its freedom is unfree, for there seems to be no release of agapeic being intimate to it any longer.

The divine agape of the good has to (re-)enter intimately in this extinction of freedom, give itself over to the monstrous idiocy of evil: die into the blocked promise of the unborn child and allow its rebirth. This abandon is the redeemed release of agapeic being at the furthest limit of the evil. God is given over to desecration: not an insulted warlord requir-ing blood ransom; an agapeic servant revealing God as there in the instance of death itself, and not outside, but within this instance with the most intimate immanence. This intimate immanence is nothing other than generosity transcending for the other as other, for its good as the gift of life itself. Creative coming to be recreates the promise of becoming.

Good beyond self-determining

Does the primal assent or dissent prior to our determinate self-becoming also tell against the *dialectical* emphasis on the good as *self-determining*? Within time we insist on our own self-determination in the face of equivocity, and rightly, yet there is something more, and this has significance for God as overdetermined good. As the determinate distinction of good and evil is not always as univocal as we would like, our self-determination is not devoid of its own equivocity.

Think of self-determining good with respect to Kantian autonomy. Kant stresses our self-legislation, and yet the law is given. Our being given the law suggests a good more than our self-determination. Kant points to a God of moral law, but there is still more than this, if the good is agapeic. We do sometimes hold, perhaps not as univocally cat-egorical, as Kant, that something is simply good (being truthful, for instance) and its opposite wrong (lying). A sign of the unconditional is communicated in the distinction of moral good and evil. God as agapeic suggests not that this distinction is obliterated but relativized by the hyperbolic good beyond moral good and evil. I do not mean relativized as justifying something less than moral but as calling us to a good in excess of the measure of our moralities, freeing in us of a forgiving agape, of mercy beyond justice, of service for the other beyond autonomy. The revelation of this good is not the perfect sovereign power but the agapeic servant who consents to the good by being willing to be as noth-ing. The hyperbolic good holds together what we often deem opposites: serene sovereign power and community with destitution; absolute majesty and love of the refused. Often we recess one side when we foreground the other. God's face of infinite forbearance is equally the radiance of ultimate compassion and the reserve of unfailing patience.

What of God as the absolute judge? We tend today to be uncomfortable with judgment: we think it smacks too much of revenge. Can we evade judgment, finally? Justice is God's, it is said. But true judgment is not vengeance, it is doing justice.[25] We would ourselves be done justice; we would do justice to ourselves. Doing justice has to do with redeeming the promise of what we are to be: being agapeic. There is a sign of the unconditional in judgment: this is; this is good. The "is" and "is good" make an ultimate claim on us. Not to acknowledge it would be a betrayal, a treason. God as (doing) justice concerns the ultimate in bring true, and with redeeming the unconditional promise of

---

[25] On this, see "Doing Justice and the Practice of Philosophy," *Proceedings of the ACPA*, 79 (2005), pp. 41–59.

being agapeic. The hyperbolic good suggests more than justice on the measure of human retribution. Doing justice in the hyperbolic dimension is immeasurable.

The last judgment is thought to determine the ultimate difference of heaven and hell. We might wonder about God's justice by asking: What is damnation? Do we have to deny damnation if there is a hyperbolic God, good beyond a univocal retributive justice and beyond counteracting vengeance? Do the damned damn themselves? We incarnate a certain absoluteness. We enjoy the given absoluteness of being for self. We can forget or neglect the givenness. We can hate it. Then the absoluteness becomes evil: I am God – I am the whole, the whole that is untrue, the counterfeit double of God. Hell is when we make ourselves our own heaven. Damnation is the self-closure that bars the door from within, devouring the key it has turned, the key which turns itself into itself. The damned turned themselves into themselves and become what they endeavor to be – themselves only. They are given what they will – themselves as entirely themselves and nothing but themselves. Themselves as circling in the singularized self-mediation which has cut off, and cut itself off from, the other side of its given nature, namely, its intermediation with the other. Damnation is absolute autonomy. We excommunicate ourselves.

Hell is the counterfeit double of heaven – the deconsecrated parody of being agapeic. Hell is being God – by a being who is not God. Hell is not the other but a kind of selving, frozen in the fire of its own envy of God. It is so stuffed with itself, there is no porosity. Its mouth is so full of itself it cannot speak to another. It cannot pray, it is so full with itself. Refusing repenting, it also damns the source of its own vulnerability – unbecoming for self, hell becomes the other. The self for whom hell is the other is *already* in hell, for it is already hell. It is a living lie. Hell is a detestation of the metaxological truth of finite being, the execration of a selving that loathes its own porosity, its own *passio*, as it turns the key on its own closure, irrevocably from the inside. Does the God of agapeic good-ness leave it at that? Is what is left be also awaited? The key can be turned again but only freedom can unlock what is here shut in, become porous again to the pluralism of the metaxological relation. Autonomy realized as hell is beyond self-determination. Heaven gifted freedom is also beyond self-determination.

Does God wait at the gates of hell? More, is there a harrowing of hell, a descent of the divine into the infernal? Is a music of release sung there, melting the frozen fire, allowing the damned to turn again and go, to be let go? I do not know. Does the fig tree once cursed come back to life again? I do not know. Is there a limit in our self-becoming beyond which the self we have made ourselves to be is irrevocable? I do not know for sure. Heaven is beyond self-determination, but is there any entry into heaven, except for those who will it heart and mind and spirit? Are those who refuse it with heart and mind and spirit damned, not just continuing to be in a place/noplace of absolute closure, but consigning themselves to nothingness by insisting and persisting in being everything? I do not know. For one cannot *be at all* outside of metaxological relation to the origin, and this relation is what is radically declined here. Is this turning down not an undoing that repudiates being, and the good of "to be"? Ontologically, it is impossible to sustain the "to be" out-side the affirmation of its goodness, but is this "outside" not where the damned would place themselves? Is not the conclusion, then, that there is no possible place for such beings to be, and they are given their will, and become nothing? Does God give us what we exact? My will be done, on earth, as it is in heaven – except the result is hell. My will be done – in hell – as it is in heaven.

Nietzsche hated the God of hell, seeing therein the apotheosis of hateful vengeance. The moral God will not do, and he refers us to a condition beyond good and evil. Nietzsche's "beyond" is not the hyperbolic goodness of agapeic love but self-affirming will to power. One might agree that any moral interpretation tailored to the measure of our self-media-tion risks being an idol. But we do not want to erect new *amoral idols* beyond good and evil. There is an ethical–religious freedom beyond moral autonomy. God is more than the law; the free human is more than law. Law is a name for constancies of integrity that must be respected if the good of being is to be loved. But being good exceeds the law, even as the law articulates the necessary more or less determinate constancies of integrity.

Agapeic freedom is not an autonomy that hates law, as constraining its putative liberty as self-law, and that bucks under anything superior to itself.

There is an idiocy to the divine beyond moral good and evil that would present difficulties for both Kant and Nietzsche, so far as each wants to secure his own will, be it moral or amoral. Is not this divine idiocy an agapeic mindfulness beyond our principle of sufficient reason? Beyond object and subject? Beyond determinate being and self-determining? A willingness beyond willfulness, beyond this or that will, beyond self-determining will? Is it not imaged for us in those elemental ones with a taste for the elemental beauty of creation, like the lilies of the field? The mad love of ethical–religious heroes? The Buddha: compassion and smiling serenity? Francis: joy the sign of God? Jesus – becoming as little children – dead man or divine child? Resurrection in death of the unborn infant? Is this the idiot wisdom of excessive goodness such as we find in the madness of the beatitudes: blessed are the poor; blessed are those who weep . . .? We must ask for everything, for everything is asked of us. We must ask for nothing, for already we have been given everything.

If we *take* everything, we cease to be divine children and make of our excess something monstrous. There is a "becoming nothing" that is other to the nihilation of the damned. There is a "being nothing" that is the hyperbole of "being good." It is agapeic consent that, in making way, makes a way. The opening of the God beyond good and evil to the good of beings is an outpouring of agapeic letting. The letting to be at all of finite beings is agapeic generosity. The letting of this being good would be like a "being nothing" or "becoming as nothing," such that the opening for the other is created. God becomes nothing, in giving the good of being over to those who seem as if nothing. We too are asked to be such a giving. In truth, we are all as nothing, and are at all because God consents to be as nothing. Kenotic goodness places us at the opposite extreme to the nihilation of the damned. It is a liberation, a consent, a "yes" that frees. The finite being that is freed is also free to refuse the agapeic promise given to it, and can turn to evil. But beyond evil, there is yet a "being as nothing" with the forgiving "yes" that offers release again, beyond the "no" that blights being. The forgiving "yes" is one which sets at naught. It says, "It is nothing." Such a setting at naught is the release of new life and joy. The uplift of life is given in forgiving, and the downthrown are recreated as if from nothing. It is the agapeic letting of the good which allows one to begin again. "Being as nothing" allows again the communication of goodness in the erstwhile clogged porosity of the between, uncongealing a defective self-becoming, allowing "coming to be" to regenerate the promise of life, beyond the partially redeemed or betrayed promise we have become. The flagging "once" of our "coming to be" is marvelously refreshed.

No moral understanding can completely comprehend this kenotic nothing. It visits us with a mercy beyond justice. This is a transmoral good, but it is no joyless mercy. The good of being is for nothing, nothing but goodness itself. We want that good to be for us. The release of "becoming as nothing" releases us beyond the good that we would make for ourselves. This is for us to learn how to look on life as God looks: with agapeic love. This becoming as nothing calls to mind again our exposure to nihilism and its return to zero (see Chapters 1 and 2). The good beyond good and evil makes its call in this return to zero. This return is the possibility of re-creation, of beginning again. There are breakdowns, but there are different nothings. There is the empty nothing of nihilism; the howling nothing of the damned; the forgiving nothing that consents to the good, even of the evil; there is the kenotic nothing which sings in the porosity of the between the release of generosity that redeems by accepting.

Overdeterminate goodness

The metaxological way most helps us remain true to the porosity of being, keep faith with the mingling of *passio* and *conatus essendi*, and redeem the promise in the incarnate equivocity of our being – between being given to be and given as good for ourselves. It remains true in a released freedom beyond autonomy that fulfills erotic sovereignty through an agapeic service that gives rebirth to the idiotic love of God that is the very intermediated communication of goodness itself in the intimate universal. Understood thus, the metaxological way most points to the overdeterminate good. Of course, we have been talking about this all along, in talking about the indeterminate, determinate and self-determining goods. Is there not again something incredible about such a hyperbolic good in this time of nihilism? Nihilistic return to zero more hollows out the ethos of being than unclogs our porosity to the divine, and in this evacuation we struggle to shake the suspicion that, in the last analysis, there is no ultimate good at all. God or nothing: the extreme alternative still haunts us. Breakdown of our sense of the ultimate, but no breakthrough of the ultimate? Or is it that we are not truly beholding what is there – the good given, the goodness giving?

Sometimes the equivocity of our dwelling in the ethos in this time of nihilism so overwhelms us that it seems impossible to contemplate a providential ovderdeterminacy. Does it make any sense to speak of the between as communicating something of the agapeics of providence? I am tempted to speak of four forms of "theodicy." First, the theodicy of the *divine idiotics*: the good is the most radically intimate to being – this is the good of the "to be" as intimately universal; it is not nothing. Evil is not a passive privation, but an energetic nihilation of this primal good of the "to be" – a defection from the intimate universal. Good is primal, evil parasitical, and there is asymmetry of the two. Second, the theodicy of the *divine aesthetics*: the creation of aesthetic happening reveals the poetics of the good – goodness shown to us in the saturated ambiguity of the ontological art work. Though good in an ontological sense is primal, there is a chiaroscuro in the play of evil and good, and finesse is required by us: the ontological work of art is the creation of divine poetics, moved by the ultimate in divine finesse. Third, the theodicy of the *divine erotics*: in the chiaroscuro there is the drama of an open wholeness, hinting at a process of perfecting at work, despite the hindrances and betrayals of evil. This is especially so in ethical life; this is an open wholeness rather than an absolute immanent whole beyond which there is nothing. God is beyond every immanent whole as the hyperbolic good, yet seeking, desirous for the good of the finite wholes. Fourth, the theodicy of the *agapeics of God*: this is the beyond of wholeness, and more expressly bears on the transmoral good, the superlative life of the holy; more than every immanent whole, it is that to which every open whole is allowed passage. The life of the holy – it is the *nec plus ultra* in ethical–religious transcendence. Its finesse for the chiaroscuro of good and evil points to redemption as unclogging the primal porosity between the divine and the human, issuing in a new life of agapeic service, gifted with the agapeic mindfulness of the mystical life of the intimate universal. What has agapeic theodicy to say to the slaughtered innocents? An idiotic trust that coming to nothing will be coming to be again? Not so much that they will be revenged but that the good of their singular "to be" is safe, saved in divine love? The innocent will live.

If there is providential overdeterminacy, it cannot be identical with univocal necessity. Sometimes we do find consolation in necessity, when the burden of perplexity seems lifted because things cannot be other than they are, and whatever will be will be. We can do nothing: *Que sera sera*; henceforth cease from care. If there is a necessity to providence, however, it must be more than necessity thus understood to the exclusion of surprising otherness. This exclusion reflects an undue dominance of univocal determination in how we think dramatic necessity in the course of things. Providence then becomes a univocal determination of this course in which the heartaches of ambiguity are to be denied. Of course, they cannot be denied. Providence itself provides for this ambiguity. Its goodness is manifest more in the finesses of time than the geometries.

We must face ambiguity. If so, we might be tempted to say that providence is nothing, for instead of univocal necessity, we seem in the sway of chance, indefinitely equivocal. Instead of necessity as unable to be otherwise, the opposite seems to hold: a contingency with no reason for it being thus and not otherwise; it just happens, with no reason beyond that, no reason at all. Ironically, such chance and contingency are not opposite to univocal necessity. If they might seem to liberate our liberty, this liberation itself is contingent and so without reason, hence is as equally justified as unjustified. In this indifference, the celebration of chance seems hardly distinguishable from indifferent submission to the indifference of univocal necessity. Meaningless contingency is as equally a tyrant of things as is block necessity.

Beyond univocal necessity and equivocal chance, the good is communicated, intermediated in the between. This communication is not tyranny in either of the above senses. There is a constancy even in radical contingency; there are necessities that are the friends of freedom. Contingency: and yet as agapeic gift that is so and not otherwise, it is something which arouses joy in the good of its being at all, and indeed thanks for the origin that gives. "It happens" does not mean "it is indifferent." Rather: this coming to be at all has something of marvel to it. One of the blessings of life: finding that the accidental turns out to be the gracious. The circumstantial, like the constant, stands around us, stands with us. The godsends that arrive tease us into thought, coax us unto praise, in receipt of, turned towards, an *incognito* generosity. Constancy in necessity: beings are what they are not in virtue of any self-creation but in terms of being enabled to be through source(s) more original than themselves. The ontological patience of things reveals their being as in the gift of an enigmatic source other to their own construction. The question of providence concerns the overdeterminate goodness of this other giving origin.

Under the sign of equivocity, time is a becoming of glorious opportunity and a vast expanse of waste. The gleam of God breaking through transfigures the equivocity. The breakthrough is not always for us a gentle opening. It is often suffered in breakdown. We would erect time into its own law, its *auto nomos*, curve it from its transcendence to time's other, curve it back on itself. But there is no circle to complete this curve. Surprise is the law of time, even in the most reliable of its constancies. Every "once" is once only in time and hence new – and every "once," though coming to be, will come not to be. In its temporary being it reveals the ontological dissimulation of autonomy. "Never" is the Siamese twin of the "once," and these are twins no human surgery can separate. Breakdown in the guise of "never" breaks through the self-closing of every "once," the surging for itself of time's transcendence. The breakthrough uncongeals a more ultimate porosity on the boundary of time's endeavors at self-determination. Providence is divined in suffering: what has to die is the idol of selving curved back on itself, or time recurring only to itself, or autonomy circling around itself in its own curvature into itself. The self-encircling of finite becoming is the false whole that defects from its own porosity and its between-being: between nothing and God. Being broken can mean being broken open – exposing again, exposing us again to, this between-being. Between nothing and God, there are deaths that let the "unborn infant" be reborn.

The gleam re-doubles our human being: in life now and yet not; in love with the mortal yet caught in an impossible longing for eternity. This longing returns us to life now, as if posthumous to the first time, in a minding love on the look out for the signs of God in the ambiguity of time. One has passed through a dead sleep, or an epilepsy of spirit, or seizure of otherness, or somersault of transcendence, and instead of autonomy, there is a hyperbolic vulnerability: an abashment, not evident to the outside, a humility confessed deep in the heart that the gulf between oneself and the good is infinite, even as the intimate call of the good becomes more nuanced and stressed. One has passed into an insomnia, sleepless even as one sleeps, for one's dreams are disquieted. Everything is shaken. It is hard to keep balance. It tries one to stand in the storm and keep to one's feet. One tries to turn one's face upwards to the sky and the rain pelts down. The wind blows one over and strips off all one's covering. One is as naked as a baby. Undergoing an ultimate exposure, one suffers the loss of the last protection against God – the protection we call our selves. That intimate shelter is blown down. One has no self to protect oneself. Being nothing one subsides into darkness, as if entering an underground peace, a grave over which still all the shadows of self-willing continue to stamp. The storm is over; one is as nothing; a seed takes root in the ground and germinates. Strangely the simple things never before shone with such enchantment. The halo of the good is on them. A bird breaks through the dead of night and sings. One is not dead, one was being born to the hyperbolic good in the grief of the storm. The "unborn child" is reborn in the death of the idol self, and released transcending is freed with its interring.

This will seem senseless to most of us, most of the time, but it suggests a posthumous life beyond life and death, as it does a hyperbolic good beyond moral good and evil. The call of this life is to live the holy in the good of being, vigilant to the hyperboles of the agapeic that in immanent life communicate of divine transcendence. Most often these communications are godsends that come quietly. The agapeics of the divine arrive unobtrusively in the most hidden of elemental things: a mustard seed, a smile, a song, a glint of sun, a drink of pure water, a child holding one's hand, the comfort of fire on a bitter day, the uninsistent aid of an agapeic servant. The agapeics of the good communicate almost nothing and yet without them life loses its charge of worthiness, becoming loveless and unloved. Like the simplicity of the broken bread in which the risen Christ was recognized, there is no world-historical fanfare that prepares for us an overpowering spectacle. There is just the elemental and unfathomable mystery of the sweetness of the "to be" as gift of God. Overdeterminate providence provides the bread and wine of consecrated time.

If we are shaken to the elements, the presentiment of the good of God issues a call to a different life. Life becomes permeable to prayer, the ultimate porosity in communication with the divine. For most of us, most of the time, the prayer may be intermittent. The intermittences are perhaps the silences needful for all communication to be properly minded. Intermittence and silence are themselves communications of the necessary otherness between those in communication. In our middle condition, sojourn in the light of God cannot be uncoupled from being shaken by the darkness of time, and from being unsettled in the darkness of God.

What credentials have I to speak of these things? I have no credentials. No philosopher has unimpeachable credentials – beyond creditworthy thought that is strained in fidelity to metaxological being. But though univocal certainty is not granted, the uncertainty is not absolutely equivocal. The equivocal itself precipitates an interplay of trust and distrust. While we are brought to a kind of absolute uncertainty about ones every claim to be absolute, uncertainty is not absolute. One cannot forsake trust, even while being truthful about the straining distrust. Can the trust be entirely destroyed that being is at bottom good, though we cannot pin it down to this good or that? Try to pin it down, and providence reserves itself in elusive recesses of ongoingness. The reserve may make it seem that God is nothing. We may have to undergo the ordeal of the vanishing of God as if into nothing. God's finesse calls forth finesse from us. Brought to the pass of this moment of truth, God as nothing can reveal, *in extremis*, a certain doubleness.

First, it can precipitate a turning *from* God: we give ourselves over to an unbelief that relishes the refusal of every soliciting trust, even to an extreme of active nihilism. This night of nihilism, of course, also nihilates our idols, that is, all formations of selving we have falsely absolutized, and hence its vastation can be, despite itself, a restoration to the idiot self (we saw something analogous with the negation of the mystic). As such, it can be a re-opening of communication with what is beyond us. It can be a regress to the overdeterminate source in selving, the "unborn infant" we are, and always are, as if we are just always being born again and again. Like a reversal of time, this looks like an "unbecoming" of what we have become. To the extent that our self-becoming has closed itself into an idol, it is as if "layers" of selving are unpeeled and slowly the false selvings dwindle and there is nothing, no self, just the "unborn infant." Suffering the vanishing of God we find ourselves in the reversion to what we are without God, which is nothing. The limit of this reversion to nothing is the "unborn infant." The "unbecoming" leads to the most radical point of "being unborn" where we face a fork in the way: consummate the impulsion to nothing, or assent to the offer given of being born again.

One must not think of this as taking place in "public" time. It occurs in the intimacy of the idiotic selving: coming to the point of death is reversion to being born, to the point of where we are like the "unborn infant." That is now the promise of the good we were from the origin, and always remained, even when we betrayed the promise. The betrayals are being stripped off, but the offer of birth is not withdrawn. Only if we irrevocably refuse this offer is the "unborn infant" given its will and the nothingness to which it consigns itself. This then is hell, where the "unborn infant" turns absolutely into itself, as if still it would be the absolute, at the most extreme point of "being nothing" where its birth is offered to it again. This turn into itself as its own heaven is the creation of hell. This self-creation as hell is just to consign itself to absolute nihilation: the "unborn infant" "lives" and "dies" in the heaven of its self-willed absoluteness, that is, in the hell of its own nothingness, which is just its negation of the promise of being reborn to the good.

Second, the vanishing of God as if nothing can be our *purification* by the ordeal of nihilation. Skepticism turns us back to ourselves, but one can be purged in truthful mindfulness, come to hate all the idols one has created of oneself and for oneself. There is a shattering: being abandoned, being forsaken, as the Psalmist has it (Psalm 22), God-forsakenness. This too is the return to the "unborn infant," to the elemental idiocy of being in extreme suffering, the radical undergoing of death itself which is the opposite of the extreme patience of being created, being born. The latter patience we undergo without mindfulness; the former undergoing we come to know, and hence know the anguish of forsakenness.

Here the most extreme willing of God is asked: the born and lived self faces a "being unborn" in death, but does it, will being born, being reborn? Does it, can it will pure trust? Does it, can it abandon itself to the good of God in being radically abandoned? This is the question of ultimate trust in face of the absolute nothing. This is the freedom to give oneself up to consummate trust in the intimate companionship of the hidden God. In the undergoing of ultimate forsakenness, absolved trust is the opposite extreme to the nihilism which would back into its own selving as self-willing absoluteness. With death this is finally ontologically impossible. It is either hell, or trust in the goodness of God, and perhaps the promise of rebirth. (In prayer, our porosity participates in this death and rebirth, and we are prepared for the ultimate death, and perhaps rebirth.)

If the "fall" primally relates to the "unborn infant," relates first to coming to be and not to becoming, then being reborn cannot be effected by becoming or self-becoming. The re-creation has to be effected at the level of coming to be, otherwise all becoming, self-becoming will only break against itself, even as it strives for complete(d) self-becoming. Every striving for complete(d) self-becoming will be marked by the primal defection, if the more primal coming to be is not redeemed. Indeed this striving will itself be a consummate form of the defection, to the degree that it refuses to grant that the recreation has to take place in terms that exceed its own self-determination. It must come to know and confess the latter before the granting of re-creation can come to flood again the empty spaces of autonomous self-becoming, self-exceeding. The flood flows into the reopened porosity.

Evil disables the porosity of the intimate universal, good en-ables it. Heaven, like hell, is a place that is no place. Heaven is the porous intermedium of trust, for trust releases life, creates it. (Jesus said one might move mountains if one had faith; but we have not faith, hence the mountains are unmoved; only God has, rather is this absolute trust, this creative power – the absolving "yes," the agapeic originating "yes.") Would resurrection follow ultimate trust? We do not have this trust. We sometimes manage to stammer "It is good" in poor echo of the divine agape. The equivocity of our trust remains, hence the gleam, the opaque presentiment of providence in the darkness of God. Purified by the nothing, we cannot absolutely distrust trust – and as long as we would still say "yes" to life, we show we have not given ourselves over to absolute distrust.[26]

---

[26] Must we will life beyond death to be given it? Could this willing be a willing of ourselves simply? If it were, would not willing ourselves also deny life beyond death? Must not this question be the least unselfish, if we selfishly will immortality, we actually will the opposite? Must we agapeically will the good of life itself, of the other as other, give ourselves over to the good of being as other, to be released into this life as other, this other life, this other life as also given to me? Would not this view repudiate the objection that the significance of death is just my death? Does it not concern the release of love beyond death, beyond my death? Is this love not more evident in my love of the other, and the willing that absolute good be the lot of that other? How could this be a concern to have the absolute good for oneself alone? And yet does it not also concern one, concern oneself – absolutely?

In truth, if there is life beyond life and death, and the holy beyond moral good and evil, there is a *hyperbolic trust beyond the first trust and distrust*. The dialectic of providence points us metaxologically through the between, where the suffering of otherness opens onto this second trust beyond all determinate trust and distrust and the interplay between them. This second overdeterminate trust is perhaps what has been called faith. In coming before the absolute nothing, the second trust will let selving go, will let go of selving but not of God, and will give itself over to God, and may just say "God is," or just will to say "God is, God is God," and that may enough. "God is God" may release for us a rebirth of God.

Purgatory purges all determinations of being that stand in the way of "God is" – absolute being and nothing else but absolving being – hyperbolic goodness itself. As return to the "unborn infant," purgatory offers the promise of overdeterminate trust in God.

In an elemental sense, the idiocy of our own being *is* this overdeterminate trust. It can go astray or be betrayed in the equivocity of time and of good and evil; be distorted in the idols of dialectical self-mediation; be expiated in the shatterings of loss in metaxological being; and be heartened by generous others that help free us from the idols of our being. Our determinations and self-determinations can dim for us this overdeterminate trust. Nevertheless, our determinate being and self-determinings can newly be relived in light of the gleam of overdeterminate trust in them. They can come to incarnate the second trust, the posthumous life of faith. This is an overdeterminate willingness: an idiotic trust in God. It is the unborn and always reborn infant of the agapeic promise of being good in us. This idiotic trust does not fit into the usual opposites of the rational and the irrational; other to the determinate, it is not indefinite; other to determinate and self-determining reason, it is not absurd; it is the mustard seed of agapeic minding in us. The overdetermined willing finds it impossible to shake off trust in the goodness of God, even though it be shaken to its roots. This trust is not immune from bafflement, from suffering, from grief at bewildering evil, from the oppressive opaqueness in the course of things. This overdetermined trust faces the moment of truth in the never comprehended mystery of death, mystery here only surpassed by the incomprehensible mystery of life. Agapeic providence is an answer that deepens mystery, deepens faith in the midst of mystery itself. The darkness of God is the first light but also the last.

Our end is in that dark light. And in that dark light we end. There is a "being nothing" that purges our clogged porosity, letting us differently sojourn in the between. In an ultimate patience, I am nothing, the other is more than enough to fill the heart, there is nothing between us, nothing but the enabling between, and I too am more than enough for myself and I am nearer home. There is nothing empty about the nothing we have become. We are released to what is passing. The overdeterminate between is saturated. The child, delicate skin, intricate ear, gentle breath, soft murmur, sleeping peace, mystery of golden presence – over such thereness God looks, being nothing but the look of love always outside itself, peace, there in the midst of the singulars loved singularly and without reserve: passage of love, passing from the nowhere of love almost nothing, sojourning among beings, love not locked in, released, and releasing, and the passing of release, coming and going, going towards, peace there awake, abiding in between, reserved luminescence, dark radiance.

Index

Wooing, 1, 3, 38, 39n.4, 143, 178, 233, 241; and mystical, 259–61, 268, 270, 292, 302

Xenophanes, 199n.8

Yeats, William Butler, 79, 222n.26, 231, 265n.1, 270n.3; and Crazy Jane, 290

Zen, 212, 264, 267
Zero, return to 19, 28–32, 34–5, 41, 58, 87, 121, 130, 132n.10, 133, 168, 177, 179, 186–7, 269, 335
Zoroastrianism, 80